AN OUTLINE-HISTORY OF
ENGLISH LITERATURE

Volume II: SINCE MILTON

ABOUT THE AUTHORS

William Bradley Otis is Professor Emeritus of English Literature of the College of the City of New York. He received the B.A. degree from Grinnell College, Iowa, the M.A. degree from Columbia University, and the Ph.D. degree from New York University. Dr. Otis joined the faculty of the College of the City of New York in 1904 and taught there until his retirement in 1948. He is the co-author of another College Outline, *An Outline-History of English Literature, Volume I.*

Morriss H. Needleman has had many years of teaching experience. He has received the B.A. degree and the M.S. degree in Education. He is the co-author of *An Outline-History of English Literature, Volume I* and *American Literature,* both in the College Outline Series.

COLLEGE OUTLINE SERIES

AN OUTLINE-HISTORY OF

ENGLISH

LITERATURE

Volume II: Since Milton

MORRISS H. NEEDLEMAN

WILLIAM BRADLEY OTIS

Second Edition

BARNES & NOBLE, Inc. NEW YORK

PUBLISHERS • BOOKSELLERS • SINCE 1873

PREFACE

It is hoped that the OUTLINE-HISTORY will not be regarded as merely another summary of English literature. The OUTLINE-HISTORY covers the field, we believe, with an eclectic adequacy not attempted by any other manual. In matters of selection and interpretation the authors always have remembered the probable and the practical needs of both the undergraduate college student making his first long excursion into English literature and the majoring or even the graduate college student desiring a comprehensive handbook in compact form.

To make the volume primarily usable it has been found necessary to deviate from the conventional plan of most textbooks. The following are some of the departures:

1. The OUTLINE-HISTORY brings the treatment of the subject abreast of modern research and criticism. Where opinion contrary to that of the traditional is prevalent, the authors call attention to the fact by notes usually so specific in reference that the teacher or the student can check the statements made and correct any errors of judgment. While indicating where counsels are divided, an endeavor is made to avoid both antiquated opinions and crotchety modern preferences.

It is a cause for regret that we can not discharge completely our indebtedness to earlier source-studies. Were one able to ferret out the borrowed ideas and to assign to each scholar his particular contribution to the field, such citation of authorities would still be prohibitive because of a number of considerations, chiefly the limitation of space. On the one hand, our general plan of stating matters of common knowledge without recording our indebtedness has meant that in not a few cases outstanding sources of information are mentioned only scantily, or not at all. But it is that very restriction that has made possible a fuller acknowledgment of our obligations in the more specialized instances.

2. The OUTLINE-HISTORY gives representation to all aspects of the field. For example, the diversified scope of the content provides for the allotment of considerable space to significant minor writers who too frequently have been neglected. A knowledge of these lesser contemporaries is essential to any real understanding of the temper and spirit of an age. In addition, more than cursory attention is accorded the earlier periods of our literature. The conviction that such material should be more generally accessible accounts not only for putting as much emphasis upon Chaucer and Spenser, for example, as upon Shakespeare and Milton, but also for devoting more space to Sir Walter Scott than to Charles Dickens. In its discussion of the fifteenth century in English literature, one usually dealt with fragmentarily or skipped altogether, the OUTLINE-HISTORY's fuller re-statement gives that period its long due; while, on the other hand, in its approach to the Victorian age and our

own, the biographical sketches are reduced and the critical comments
finally eliminated. If the OUTLINE-HISTORY should be considered over-
minute in its analysis, it will at least have avoided in the main the mere
tabulation of the names of authors, and the titles of their works, and
also the general barrenness of scrimped accounts and one-sided inter-
pretations. College students might well be expected to approach the field
of English literature from a mature point of view much in that spirit
with which for many years they have been expected to approach the
field of mathematics or physics or biology or chemistry.

3. The OUTLINE-HISTORY lends itself to immediate use for further
study. Cross-references, footnotes, and other editorial aids have been
utilized at strategic points so as to reduce to a minimum the necessity
of directing students to other books. The footnotes themselves while
stimulating the student's interest in specific literary problems are a
concise, up-to-date bibliography. It should be apparent that the OUTLINE-
HISTORY has been made, so far as space limitations would permit, a single
unit, yet also a point of departure for supplementary readings and
explorations.

4. The OUTLINE-HISTORY indicates foreign as well as native influences upon English literature. Occasionally, it is true, a textbook or
two will indicate by a chart that, for example, Machiavelli wrote his
Prince and Castiglione his *Cortegiano* at approximately the time More
wrote his *Utopia*. But the OUTLINE-HISTORY makes the point of contact
more immediate and more specific: thus, for example, it records the
influence of Machiavelli's *Prince* upon Elyot's *The Boke named the
Governour* and upon Spenser's *Veue of the Present State of Ireland*, and
that of Castiglione's *Il Cortegiano* upon Spenser's *Fowre Hymnes* and
Marlowe's *Hero and Leander*. As for Sir Thomas More's *Utopia*, the
OUTLINE-HISTORY indicates the obligation to Amerigo Vespucci's account
of his voyages, to Plato's *Republic*, St. Augustine's *De Civitate Dei*
(upon which More once lectured), and Erasmus's *Institutio Principis
Christiani*.

5. The OUTLINE-HISTORY has further departures from the usual textbook. A case in point is its attempt at correlation. Thus, in evaluating
the most original portion of Anglo-Saxon poetry (*Deor, The Wife's
Lament, The Husband's Message, The Ruin, The Wanderer*, and the
like), the OUTLINE-HISTORY points out that those lyrical or elegiac poems
anticipate the dramatic monologue, a form of which the ultimate master
is Robert Browning; in outlining Chaucer's *Pardoner's Tale*, the OUTLINE-
HISTORY states that one of the most recent analogues occurs in Kipling's
Second Jungle Book. When examining William Godwin's *Enquiry
concerning the Principles of Political Justice*, the OUTLINE-HISTORY refers
the student to various ideal commonwealths previously encountered, such
as Bacon's *New Atlantis*, Hobbes's *Leviathan*, Bernard de Mandeville's
Fable of the Bees, and also looks forward to Bulwer-Lytton's *The Coming Race*, Butler's *Erewhon*, Morris's *News from Nowhere*, H. G.
Wells's *A Modern Utopia*, and Aldous Huxley's *Brave New World*.

While designed, therefore, primarily for the college undergraduate and the majoring or even the graduate student, it is felt that the OUT-LINE-HISTORY is useful as well for all who do not have access to adequately equipped libraries or who may find it convenient to have in succinct form a representative discussion of English literature.

The OUTLINE-HISTORY doubtless will call for revision. All criticisms will be welcome. Suggestions that may improve the volume's usefulness will be incorporated, if possible, in succeeding editions. Kindly address the authors in care of Barnes and Noble, Inc., New York City.

M. H. N. — W. B. O.

Acknowledgments

In the preparation of *An Outline-History of English Literature Since Milton* we have been assisted by many scholars, both friends and strangers, who have volunteered valuable suggestions for improving the manuscript. Our obligations to all of these can not, for lack of space, be specifically acknowledged here; but for generous aid we must express our special gratitude to Professor A. C. Baugh of the University of Pennsylvania; Dr. Alexander Boecker of Brooklyn, New York; Professor Haldeen Braddy of Sul Ross State Teachers College; Professor Carleton Brown of New York University; Professor Joseph George Cohen of Brooklyn College; Professor Emeritus Morris Raphael Cohen of The College of the City of New York; Professor R. D. Havens of The Johns Hopkins University; Professor Florence Hilbish of Cedar Crest College; Professor Karl J. Holzknecht of New York University; Professor T. H. Johnson of the Hackley School; Dr. Paul Klapper, President of Queens College; Professor Dawn Logan of Waynesburg College; Professor T. O. Mabbott of Hunter College; Professor Emeritus Lewis Freeman Mott of The College of the City of New York; Professor Vincent H. Ogburn of Leland Stanford University; Professor Charles G. Osgood of Princeton University; Professor J. J. Parry of the University of Illinois; Professor A. W. Secord of the University of Illinois; Dr. Samuel A. Tannenbaum, Editor of *The Shakespeare Association Bulletin;* Professor Homer A. Watt of New York University; and Professor Donald G. Whiteside of Brooklyn College. To Professors Charles F. Horne, Alfred D. Compton, Bird Stair, Arthur Dickson, and Ralph Gordon we must also acknowledge our indebtedness, as well as to Messrs. Donald A. Roberts, Maximilian G. Walten, Arthur K. Burt, Warren B. Austin, and John C. Thirlwall, Jr., all of the English department; also to Professors Samuel B. Heckman and J. Salwyn Shapiro, of The College of the City of New York. We owe a special debt of gratitude to the Honorable Francis J. Sinnott, Postmaster of Brooklyn, New York, and to Claire and Lee Howard, of Brooklyn, New York, without whose assistance the book would have been delayed considerably. For general guidance and detailed help in the preparation of the work we are deeply obligated to the editors of the COLLEGE OUTLINE SERIES.

M. H. N. — W. B. O.

AN APPROACH TO THE COLLEGE SURVEY COURSE

English literature is a required study for all college students, yet there is a dearth of investigation as to the proper materials for teaching the subject at college levels. Even in the secondary school, where much emphasis has been placed upon subject-matter and educational procedures, the authorities are not agreed as to aims in the study of literature. Accordingly, the usual survey course in the college is narrow; it seems to lack the omnibus material that might lend itself to various points of view and methods.

A condition contributing much to the difficulty of determining the scope and methods of teaching the subject at the college level, is the ineffective articulation between the secondary school and the college. Frequently a more or less helter-skelter and shallow survey course of English literature has been required before students entered college and another such course often fails to stimulate a new enthusiasm. The partly known territory traversed may hold out no hope of discoveries because the instruction often falls below the level of college standards. In other courses, such as history and mathematics, the method is frequently imposed by the content, but this is less true, if true at all, of English literature. Whereas in the secondary school the recognized criterion in selecting reading material is the interests of the students, here in the college the cultivation of a taste for reading too commonly yields in importance to a more intensive study (usually through the over-worked lecture method) of literature as a "knowledge subject." This may not in itself be a discouraging approach, but tends to be made so by formalization. Moreover, what are social and political values to the student are lost when textbooks of literary history and consorting anthologies are dependent upon conventional and traditional ideas.

What, therefore, should be the educational procedures in the teaching of English literature to college students? If there is a consensus it is, first, that the main aim should be to relate the literature to life, vitalizing ideas and ideals, and integrating broad intellectual and philosophical connections. It is not good for literature, any more than it is for man, to be alone; and a periphery course, or preferably, an orientation course, can perform an important service. Second, a first college course should be designed in a fashion permitting adjustment to the needs of *all* students, both those who purpose to go no further than the first course and those who plan to go beyond. Third, the method in each case should grow out of both the problems of the subject and the problems of the student. The textbook itself should avoid undue stress on material apparently intended to yield entertainment suitable for adolescents rather than to provoke thinking on an adult level. If a choice is offered it should favor intellectually stimulating ideas rather than factual matter barren of ideas.

These main procedures have energized the growth of the Outline-History until it has assumed the present proportions. Our convictions are that abstract account and dogmatic presentation deserve at the collegiate level a smaller place than they usually receive, and that divergent ideas are to be included for the purpose of putting before the students material that stimulates reflection and calls for solution of problems. To the suggestion that difficulties could be diminished by consigning the notes to an appendix, we would say that their neglect might thereby be encouraged. Moreover, it is not difficult, when advisable, to disregard the footnotes. If we have erred, we have preferred to do so on the side of fullness, for the reasons stated and also in the expectation that the instructor or the instructor and students will select the material to be studied.

Selective choice by the users of this handbook—that is the basis of the approach. It is obvious that the instructor or the instructor and students should have a large measure of freedom in planning and carrying on the course. The ideal approach would be to test the entering students and then group them according to their abilities and needs, as revealed by the placement tests, into first courses at differing levels of achievement. However, most classes include students of varying abilities. Containing more material than any specific survey course may require, the Outline-History can be adapted to any class. It is expected that more or less of the material will be omitted. Specific minimal requirements should, however, be prescribed for each class. Some units will merit further consideration and some will be skimmed or even skipped in preparation for class. Specific study-guides with organizing questions might well include not alone the general assignment but also the supplementary work for successive levels. Some classes might even follow the procedure of the Outline-History in basing apportionment of space, not upon conventional treatment elsewhere but upon the omnibus needs of a course planned to inform, interest, and stimulate varied groups of intellectually mature students. However, those who wish some minimal signposts may give heed to the works marked by an obelisk (†); those who wish to enrich the minimal requirements may make the reference notes the basis of additional work; and, finally, those who plan to do graduate work may follow up for themselves the various problems raised throughout the Outline-History.

Selection, therefore, is imperative for the instructor, or the instructor and students together. This manual is not a substitute for thinking.

It must not supplant personal contact with the literature itself. Indiscriminate mastery of the material in the OUTLINE-HISTORY is not the
desideratum. The student is not to work for the memorization of biographical facts, dates of literary works, or even critical judgments, except
in a naturally subordinate degree. Were the OUTLINE-HISTORY not meant
for heterogeneous classes of college students, its array of reference notes
might be construed as exemplifying vivisection or over-annotation of
literature, but in view of the specific purpose of the book the footnotes
can be developed into a body of stimulating aids to the proper interpretation of the literature from which the OUTLINE-HISTORY itself has developed. Especial emphasis is to be placed upon the study of historical,
intellectual, and aesthetic backgrounds of the literature, and upon the
study of masterpieces rather than of literary types. By planning larger
units designed for a more intensive study of individual authors and of
specific works most representative of a particular period, the connections of literature with that period's social, political, and intellectual
movements can be established effectively.

Whether in a first-year class where only two or three of
Chaucer's Canterbury Tales or of Shakespeare's plays may be assigned,
or in a majoring class where possibly all the tales or plays may be prescribed, the OUTLINE-HISTORY in each case provides a graduated editorial
apparatus that can be utilized as an energizing guide to ideas and
ideals according to the varying abilities and selective needs of a particular class or student. As a final caution may we again urge that in
no case should the purpose of the college survey course be merely to
supply aesthetic occupation or a like kind of relief after the work in
other subjects in the curriculum; in all cases the instructor should keep
in mind the needs, interests, purposes, capacities, or experience of the
students either as individuals, distinctive groups, or varied classes.

TABLE OF CONTENTS

ON THE USE OF THIS HANDBOOK

I

It is essential to read both the *Preface* (pages v-vii) and the *Preliminary* (pages viii-x) in order to comprehend the plan and scope of the OUTLINE-HISTORY OF ENGLISH LITERATURE, and to make full and proper use of it. The *Table of Contents* and the *Index* have their obvious uses, although it should be remembered that the latter does not include the *Supplementary List of Writers* (pages 601—613), nor the works listed in the final chapter (pages 581—600).

II

The main text of this manual is set in ten-point type. The original intention of utilizing a reduced type to indicate the works of minor writers, the lesser works of major writers, and like matters, had to be abandoned when it was found that the contemplated frequent use of a smaller font would be a definite strain on the eyes. Unwilling, however, to forego entirely the plan of indicating subordination, it was decided not only to restrict the use of a reduced type but also to mark the more important works as indicated below.

KEY TO SYMBOLS

† The dagger-mark or obelisk denotes the more important works.

* The asterisk indicates additional information alphabetically arranged in *Appendix B* (pages 615 to 623).

1 The raised number refers to the note at the bottom of the page.

Volume II: SINCE MILTON

Chapter XV

THE RESTORATION PERIOD: THE BEGINNINGS OF NEO-CLASSICISM

(1660—1700)

Historical Background

General View. (1) General increase in parliamentary power. (2) Rise of the great political parties. (3) Advance of colonization and trade in India, America, and the East Indies. (4) England's sea power increases. (5) Further colonization of America; the founding of Pennsylvania and Carolina. (6) Rebuilding of London, after the Great Plague of 1665 and the Great Fire of 1666. (7) The Bloodless Revolution of 1688. (8) The development of a general foreign policy.

The Reign of Charles II (1660—1685). (1) Declaration of Breda (1660). (2) Prosecution of Regicides (1660—1662). (3) Insurrection of the Fifth-Monarchy Men (1661). (4) Royal Society of London chartered (1662). (5) Act of Uniformity (1662). (6) Outbreak of Dutch War (1664). (7) Great Plague of London (1665). (8) Second Dutch War (1665—1667). (9) Great Fire of London (1666). (10) Newton's theory of fluxions (1666). (11) Rise of the Cabal ministry (1667—1673). (12) Treaty of Dover (1670). (13) Newton's theory of light (1671). (14) Third Dutch War (1672—1674). (15) Test Act (1673). (16) End of Cabal (1673). (17) Rise of Whigs and Tories (1674—1679). (18) Invention of Popish Plot (1678). (19) Disabling Act (1678). (20) Habeas Corpus Act passed (1679). (21) Rye House Plot (1683). (22) Death of Charles (1685). (23) Accession of James II.

The Reign of James II (1685—1688). (1) Persecution of Covenanters (1685). (2) Chief Justice Jeffreys and the Bloody Assizes (1685). (3) Insurrection of Monmouth (1685). (4) Violation of the Test Act (1685). (5) Revocation of Edict of Nantes (1685). (6) Court of Ecclesiastical Commission (1686). (7) Declaration of Indulgence (1687). (8) Newton's Second Declaration of Indulgence (1688). (9) The Glorious Revolution (1688).

The Reign of William III and Mary II (1689—1702). (1) Act of Toleration (1689). (2) Bill of Rights (1689). (3) Rise of Cabinet Government (1689—1714). (4) Abjuration Bill and Act of Grace (1690). (5) Treaty of Limerick (1692). (6) Origination of the national debt (1693). (7) Triennial Act (1694). (8) Bank of England chartered (1694). (9) Navigation Act (1696). (10) Treaty of Ryswick (1697). (11) Dampier explores the shores of Australia (1699). (12) Act of Settlement (1701). (13) Death of William (1702).

General View of the Literature

Poetry. The poetry is dominated by neo-classic traits. (1) The lyrical spirit, whatever there is of it, is marked by Caroline charm and skill. It is, however, often artificial in thought and deficient in originality. Except for Dryden, only the court poets (p. 296) merit much consideration. (2) The ode is a favorite form; and again Dryden is pre-eminent. (3) The most spectacular type is the satire: see Butler (p. 297) and Dryden (p. 325). (4) Outstanding is the development of the heroic couplet.

Prose. The period of the Restoration is primarily a prosaic age in which scientific curiosity and philosophical reflection take the place of emotional release and high imagination. Its very poetry becomes prosaic, while its prose shows marked preferences for the avoidance of ostentatious decoration. In the essays, journals, and histories, in the critical, scientific, and philosophical treatises are seen tendencies that culminated in the Augustan age: emphasis upon form, smoothness and clearness, sobriety and elegance, restraint and familiar ease. The Restoration writers, when they strait-jacketed prose, began the development of modern prose style.

Drama. In 1642 the theaters were officially closed (see Vol. 1, p. 251), and were not officially opened until 1660. Four years earlier, however, Sir William D'Avenant presented *The Siege of Rhodes* (1656), which is notable in innovating movable scenery, women actors, and the English opera. The chief foreign influence on the drama of the period came from Spain and, especially, from France. (1) *The Heroic Play*. Its chief features are a blameless heroic figure for the central personage, a succession of conflicting loves or of stage incidents of exalted character, and an abundance of pompous declamation in rimed couplets full of bombastic sentiment. This short-lived, exotic form made great use not only of overstrained rhetoric and violent action but also of songs, dances, elaborate scenery, and extravagant stage movement. Worthy of special note is *The Rehearsal* (1671; 1672), an amusing burlesque of the heroic play. (2) *The Comedy of Manners*. The most important single fact is that the spirit of the anti-Puritan reaction pervades almost the whole body of polite literature of the reign of Charles II. The quintessence of this spirited war between wit and morality—for that is what the war had become—is found in the comic drama. The new comedy, while developing partly from the work of Jonson and Middleton, and Beaumont and Fletcher, owes much to contemporary comedy in France. It presents a surface picture of the life of courtiers and their class in an atmosphere that is more artificial than real; it treats amorous intrigue with cool licentiousness; the style is sparkling and artificial, the dialogue rapier-like. Notable is the increasing naturalness of action. (3) *Tragedy*. Restoration tragedy is presented in a poetry that is usually inadequate; it often has a dullness, a flatness; and has often been called a species of historical oratorio. Dryden's *All for Love* (p. 331) is the best example of Restoration tragedy.

POETRY[1]

Lyric Poets

Edmund Waller, 1606—1687, poet. Educated at Eton and King's College, Cambridge. Married the much-sought-for heiress, Anne Bankes (1629), who died in 1632. When "Waller's Plot" (1643) to seize London for Charles II was discovered, Waller saved his life in some obscure way, probably by bribing, by confessing, and by implicating his colleagues[2]; he was imprisoned, fined ten thousand pounds and banished. Married Mary Bracey (1644). **Pardoned** (1651). Commissioner of Trade (*c.* 1655). Served in Parliament from a short time after the Restoration until his death.

Ease, perfection of form, polished sugary simplicity; but ardorless. Note the lack of obscenity. If he did not introduce the closed couplet, he at the very least helped popularize a form later carried to perfection by Dryden and Pope.[3] Well-known are: *A Panegyric to My Lord Protector* (1655), *Instructions to a Painter* (1666), *Of Divine Love* (1685); less known are *The Triple Combat* (*c.* 1675), *The Night-Piece; or, A Picture Drawn in the Dark,* and *On St. James's Park as Lately Improved by His Majesty* (1661).

Of the danger His Majesty (Being Prince) escaped in the road at St. Andere (1645). Sometimes asserted to be the poem that introduced the closed couplet of precision and neatness—the classical meter that prevailed in English poetry until almost the twentieth century.

Go, Lovely Rose! (1640) and *On a Girdle* (1645). Two gallant poems, simple in their directness and Elizabethan in their singing quality.

---

1 It is customary to discuss only two important non-dramatic poets of the "Restoration period—John Dryden and Samuel Butler. Such a picture is somewhat incomplete, for there are others who should be included, as they are in the *Outline-History*. All the poetic versifiers of the period could well be regarded as the later Cavalier writers. For example, Charles Cotton is always associated with the name of Walton; Waller, with the transitional poets such as Cowley and Marvell; and Thomas Traherne, with the religious school of Herbert, Crashaw, and Vaughan. See Volume One of the *Outline-History*, pp. 259-268, and the "General View of the Literature," p. 251.

2 Fox, A. W., *Men and Marvels in the Seventeenth Century* (1936), "Waller's Plot," pp. 149-186.

3 Poets of his day credited Waller with first using in English the heroic couplet. While that verse form may be traced back to Chaucer, it does seem that Waller refined the heroic couplet by completing and closing up the sense within the couplet, and that he did prepare the way for the school of Dryden and Pope by popularizing the antithetic distich. See, however, Wood, Henry, "Beginnings of the 'Classical' Heroic Couplet in England," *The American Journal of Philology*, XI (1890), pp. 55-79.

Addressed to Sacharissa[1] (Lady Dorothy Sidney, daughter of Robert, Earl of Leicester, and later the Countess of Sunderland).

Of the Last Verses in the Book (1686). Composed when he was more than eighty years old, the lines are a good example of Waller's mastery of the closed couplet.

Charles Cotton, 1630—1687, author, poet. While chiefly remembered for his contribution to Walton's *Compleat Angler* (Vol. 1, p. 276), he also wrote *Scarronides* (1664—1665), a gross burlesque of the first and fourth books of the *Aeneid,* and edited the essays of Montaigne (1685—1686), a closer translation than Florio's. Directness and sincerity are the main characteristics of his *Poems on Several Occasions* (1689), which includes songs, epigrams, burlesque epistles, Pindaric odes of the Cowleyan variety, and, especially, lyrics descriptive of nature. Examples of his poetry: *Old Tityrus to Eugenia, Resolution in Four Sonnets,* and *The New Year,* which was praised by Charles Lamb.

Thomas Traherne. *c.* 1637—1674, poet, prose writer.[2] Son of a shoemaker of Hereford. Entered as a commoner of Brasenose College, Oxford (1652). B.A. (1656). Country rector of Credinhill or Crednell near Hereford 1657—1667). M.A. (1661). Private Chaplain to Sir Orlando Bridgman, Lord Keeper of the Seals (1667). B.D. (1669). "Minister" of Teddington (1667—1674).

Until the beginning of the twentieth century Traherne was known only as the author of such ecclesiastical tracts as *Roman Forgeries* (1673), *Christian Ethicks* (1675),[3] and *A Serious and Patheticall Contemplation of the Mercies of God* (1699). He was rediscovered, identified, and published by Bertram Dobell in *Poems* (1903) and *Centuries of Meditations* (1908). About his verse, which draws a philosophy from the recollection of childhood, there is a glowing tenderness. The love of nature is his central theme, and he reveals the mystic wonder of childhood and the beauty of the natural world. Traherne is a belated metaphysical or religious poet, belonging with Herbert, Crashaw, and particularly with Vaughan,[4] whose central theme in "The Retreate"—childhood and the wisdom of innocence—is in essence Traherne's theme, and may have inspired the poems on childhood (for the Metaphysical School, see Vol. 1, pp. 259—262); yet Traherne is primarily a poet of his own generation: his verse, not infrequently failing in workmanship, compactness, and lyricism, is often prosaic, while his prose, rich in enthusiasm and musical quality, is prettily poetic. Quiller-Couch is not

---

1 G. Thorn Drury knew of no definite authority for connecting the name of Sacharissa with Waller's famous poems. See his introduction to *The Poems of Edmund Waller* (1893), p. xxv *f.* (pp. xiii-lxxiv).

2 Iredale, Q., *Thomas Traherne* (1935).

3 The assertion has been made that *Christian Ethicks* is indebted to the *Summa Theologiae* of St. Thomas Aquinas: Wade, G. I., "St. Thomas Aquinas and Thomas Traherne," *Blackfriars,* xii (1931), pp. 666-673.

4 Leishman. J. B., *The Metaphysical Poets* (1934).

alone in believing that in time to come Traherne's *Centuries of Medita-tions*, which are short prose reflections on religion and morals, may have an importance equal to his verse. Examples of his poetry: *Wonder, Innocence, On News, The Salutation, Silence, The Rapture, Christendom, On Christmas Day, Shadows in the Water, Desire, The Person, The Recovery, The Circulation.*

Court Poets

John Wilmot, Second Earl of Rochester,[1] *c.* 1647—1680, poet, courtier, libertine, wit. In many of his writings obscenity substitutes for wit and foulness for licentiousness. The most notorious rake of the court of Charles II is also its supreme court poet, for he goes far beyond elegant and indecent triflings into a poetry remarkable for scepticism and irony, intense sincerity and intellectual energy. For intense bitter-ness read *History of Insipida;* for the spirit of heroic irony, the *Maim'd Debauchee;* for probing, vigorous characterizations of his contemporaries, *An Allusion to the Tenth Satire of the First Book of Horace. Love and Life* represents perhaps his supreme lyricism; *Satire against Mankind,* his superior satirical talent and concentrated cleverness., Rochester is the only serious court poet, but has left love lyrics of grace and songs of distinction.[2] Examples: "While on those lovely looks I gaze"; "An age in her Embraces past"; "I cannot change, as others do"; "All my past Life is mine no more"; "Give me leave to rail at you"; "Vulcan contrive me such a cup"; "Nothing adds to your fond Fire"; "Absent from thee I languish still"; "My dear Mistress has a heart"; and *Epitaph on Charles II.*

Charles Sackville, Lord Buckhurst, and later **Sixth Earl of Dorset,**[3] 1638—1706, poet and courtier to whom Dryden dedicated his *Of Dramatick Poesie* (p. 333). He wrote epigrams, mordant satires, and such prettily-turned songs as "Phyllis, for shame! let us improve," "At noon, in a sunshiny day," and "Methinks the poor town has been troubled too long." "Corydon beneath a willow" is an example of light satiric verse; and *On a Lady Who Fancy'd Herself a Beauty* ("Dorinda's sparkling wit and eyes") is a satire on Katherine Sedley, mistress of James II. Most famous is the ballad of eleven stanzas called *Song Written at Sea* ("To all you ladies now at land"), which Gosse declared as inaugurating "the epoch of *vers de société* as it has

1 Many poems attributed to Rochester are not by him; the text of *Poems on Several Occasions* (1780) is hopelessly corrupt (*e.g.*, the pornographic *Sodom, Bath Intriques, The Perfect Enjoyment, Lord Rochester on His Whore-Pipe*). See *Collected Works of John Wilmot, Earl of Rochester,* edited by Hayward, John (1926); Prinz, Johannes, *John Wilmot Earl of Rochester* (1927).

2 Pinto, V. de S., (1) "The Poetry of Rochester," *The New Oxford Outlook,* I (1933-1934), pp. 339-347; (2) *Rochester* (1935).

3 Pinto, V. de S., *Restoration Carnival* (1954), pp. 109-148.

flourished from Prior[1] down to Austin Dobson." But Sackville is nevertheless only a charming minor poet while Rochester is possibly a great one.

John Sheffield, Third Earl of Mulgrave, and afterwards **First Duke of Buckingham and Normanby,** 1648—1721, poet, statesman.[2] Of the court wits Sheffield was the most respectable. His *Essay upon Satire,* published anonymously, provoked Rochester to hire bullies to cudgel Dryden (p. 325); while the rimed criticism, *An Essay on Poetry* (1682) provoked Robert Wolseley's excellent critical preface to Rochester's *Valentinian* (1685).[3] Among his fluent verses are *Love's Slavery, Inconstancy Excused, Despair, The Reconcilement, To a Coquet Beauty,* and *The Relapse.*

Wentworth Dillon, Fourth Earl of Roscommon, of Ireland, c. 1633—1685, poet; first critic to praise Milton's *Paradise Lost.* Translated Horace's *Ars Poetica* (1680) into blank verse. Wrote the *Essay on Translated Verse* (1684), a rimed criticism first definitely enunciating the principles of "poetic diction" destined for fuller development. He was quite free of the low code of morals of his contemporaries.

Satiric Poets

John Oldham, 1653—1683, ode-writer to whose memory Dryden wrote a noble ode (p. 326), and satirist designated by Scott as "the English Juvenal."[4] His rimes are rugged and often defective. *"The Careless Good Fellow"* is a good toper's song. Important to the historian and the *littérateur* is the *Satyrs upon the Jesuits* (1681), a fulminatory declamation influenced possibly by Phineas Fletcher's *Locustae* or *Apollyonists* (Vol. 1, p. 252), and Jonson's *Catiline* (I, 230-231).

Samuel Butler, 1612—1680, satiric poet. Son of a Worcestershire farmer. Educated at the King's School, Worcester. Gentleman servant to Elizabeth, Countess of Kent at Wrest Park (c. 1619). Served the Earl of Carbery (c. 1661—1662). Money obtained by marriage to Mrs. Herbert soon lost. Secretary, during lifetime, to several country squires, including Sir Samuel Luke, a rigid Presbyterian who may have been

---

1 Speaking of Sackville, Matthew Prior stated that "the Manner in which he wrote will hardly be equalled: Every one of his Pieces is an Ingot of Gold intrinsically and solidly Valuable." That is recognizably an exaggeration. But the literary world may be indebted to Sackville, for in the words of Prior: ". . . *Dryden* determines by him, under the character of *Eugenius,* as to the laws of Dramatic Poetry; *Butler* ow'd it to him that the Court tasted his *Hudibras; Wicherly,* that the Town liked his *Plain Dealer;* and the late Duke of *Buckingham* deferr'd to publish his *Rehearsal,* 'till he was sure (as he expressed it) that my Lord *Dorset* would not Rehearse upon him again." Prior, Matthew, *Poem on Several Occasions* (1709), p. VI, p. V (pp. I-XXI).

2 "A Short Life of the Duke of Buckingham" is available in *Miscellanea* (The Haworth Press, 1933), pp. 11-23; Pinto, V.deS., *Restoration Carnival* (1954), pp. 213-245.

3 *Critical Essays of the Seventeenth Century,* edited by Spingarn, J. E. (Three volumes, 1908) Vol. II, pp. 286-296; III, p. 9 *ff.* (pp. 1-31).

4 Brooks, H. F., "A Bibliography of John Oldham," *Oxford Bibliographical Society, Proceedings and Papers,* V, Part I, 1936, pp. 5-38.

the prototype of the hero in *Hudibras*,[1] and to George Villiers, Duke of Buckingham (1673), who is probably the butt in "A Duke of Bucks" in *Characters*. Although granted an annual pension of one hundred pounds (1678), yet is said to have died in obscure penury, and to have been buried at the expense of William Longueville.

Hudibras†* (Part I, 1663[2]; II, 1664; III, 1678). Unfinished mock-heroic epic poem of more than ten thousand lines, popular because topical. Satirizes the Roundheads by exploiting the "humours" of the long-faced Hudibras accompanied by his Squire Ralpho. Not the somewhat tedious adventures involved in a loose plot hard to follow through the complex dialogue and unrecognized allusions, but the anti-Puritan pictures of the poem are important.[3] Withering surface-portraiture, broadly comic adventures, cutting buffoonery, irreverent wit; brilliant apothegms, many of which are still current; mock-solemn parade of erudition. Jolting doggerel verse in biting octosyllabic couplets (iambic tetrameter meter) abounds in outlandish rimes and concise, droll verbal pranks sprung with impudent ease. While Pepys (p. 323) was consistently "against that which the whole world cries up to be the example of wit,"[4] yet the Aldine edition lists twenty-seven direct imitations.

Name of *Hudibras* probably borrowed from *The Faerie Queene* (II, ii, 17; see Vol. 1, pp. 131—135); that of Ralpho derived from *The Knight of the Burning Pestle* (Vol. 1, p. 243). Influenced by *Don Quixote,* by the work of Paul Scarron (1610—1660), and by the conventions of chivalric romance (Vol. 1, p. 23, p. 39 *ff.*) As Butler's monument puts it, he "pluck'd the mask from pious hypocrisy."

The General Remains in Prose and Verse of Mr. Samuel Butler (1759). Includes:

(1) *Characters.* Excellent imitations in the tradition carried on by Overbury and Earle (Vol. 1, p. 248). Among more than ninescore sketches—drawn up, according to Thyer, between 1667 and 1669—are "A Modern Politician," "The Henpect Man" who lets his wife wear the spurs and govern the reins, "A Ranter," "A Lawyer" who retails justice by using false weights and measures, and "A Quaker."

(2) *The Elephant in the Moon.** Nimble-fingered satire on natural scientists and their experiments: levelled at Sir Paul Neale, a conceited member of the Royal Society.[5]

---

1 It is still uncertain whether Hudibras represents the portrait of a particular Puritan, such as Sir Samuel Luke or Sir Henry Rosewell, or whether the titular hero is a personified picture of a type.

2 The title page of the first edition is dated 1663. The book, however, was available at least in the latter part of 1662, for on December 26, 1662, Pepys is already commenting upon it.

3 Veldkamp, Jan, *Samuel Butler* (1923), pp. 99-167.

4 Pepys's *Diary*: December 26, 1662; February 6, 1662-1663; November 28, 1663; December 10, 1663.

5 Sidrophel, one of the most interesting types in Butler's gallery in *Hudibras*, may be meant for Sir Paul Neale. For a discussion of the fraudulent astrologer, consult Curtiss, J. T., "Butler's Sidrophel," *Publications of the Modern Language Association of America*, XLIV (1929), pp. 1066-1078.

† * Explanation of symbols immediately precedes Chapter XV.

DRAMA

Tragedy

Thomas Otway, 1652—1685, dramatist. Son of a clerygman. Educated at Winchester (1665—1668). Christ Church, Oxford (1669—1671). London (*c.* 1672—1675). Failed as an actor. Unrequited passion for the tragedienne Mrs. Barry, mistress of Lord Rochester, drove him to Flanders on military service (1678). Returned (1679). M.A. degree at Cambridge (1680). Died in destitution at the Bull on Tower Hill.

Lines contain much rant and bombast, plot construction often weak; poor wit, lachrymose tendencies, definite coarseness. But searching pathos, abundant humor, interest of situation and character, power of dramatic intensity in portraying the height of passion or the depth of despair. Of historical value are his political poems, prologues, and epilogues; *e.g.,* the prologue and epilogue of *Venice Preserv'd* are indirect attacks on Lord Shaftesbury, while *The Poet's Complaint of his Muse* contains much satire on the Whigs.

Comedies: (1) *The Cheats of Scapin* (1677), successful farce from Molière's *Les Fourberies de Scapin.* (2) *Friendship in Fashion* (1678), prose comedy of the indecent Restoration type, enfeebled by the lusterless quality of the characters, the wit, and the intrigue. (3) *The Souldiers Fortune* (1681), farce-comedy, influenced by Shackerley Marmion, Fletcher, and Molière, and spiced by personal reminiscence, is more vivacious than *Friendship in Fashion* in conversation, movement, and plot. (4) *The Atheist*: or, *The Second Part of the Souldiers Fortune* (1684), a cynical comedy. Tragedies: (1) *Alcibiades* (1675), in which Alcibiades is a typical Otwavian character in an undistinguished rimed tragedy based on Plutarch, and influenced by *Macbeth* in the best scene, the murder of the King. (2) *Don Carlos, Prince of Spain* (1676), rimed tragedy, with distinctive characters and striking passages, and based upon an historical romance of the Abbé Saint-Réal, was rated the best of Otway's day. (3) *Titus and Berenice* (1677), dull riming translation from Racine's *Bérénice* (1670). (4) *The History and Fall of Caius Marius* (1680). Despite the sameness of its blank verse and the ineptness of its characterization, the cento was for fifty years considered superior to Shakespeare's *Romeo and Juliet,* the version of which Otway patches on to the history of Marius as found in Plutarch.

The Orphan: or, The Unhappy Marriage†* (1680). Domestic tragedy in blank verse much less indebted to Shakespeare's *Cymbeline* and Racine's *Mithridate* than to "The History of Brandon" in *English Adventures. By a Person of Honour* (1675), possibly by Roger Boyle, Earl of Orrery. Several characters are added. Simple language, directness, pervasive pathos, psychological insight; overpadding, weak characterization, poor in thought, somewhat protracted pathetic scenes.

---

† * Explanation of symbols immediately precedes Chapter XV.

Venice Preserv'd or A Plot Discover'd†* (1682). Gloomy
tragedy in blank verse does not scruple to subordinate story to underlying political promptings.[1] Romantic beauties of verse are buttressed
by such romantic accessories as the madness of Belvidera (his most
triumphant creation), ghostly apparitions, and horrible stage deaths.
Poetic passion (weakened by leanings toward conventional sentimentality), genuine theme (even if grandiose). Varied movement of plot,
emotional intensity, naturalness of expression, and aptness of imagery;
but crippled by diffuse verse, absence of genuine humor in lighter parts,
and indecent comic scenes. Source is *La Conjuration des Espagnols contre
la Rèpublique de Venice, en l'année MDCXVIII* by César Vischard,
l'abbé de Saint-Réal. Also indebted to Shakespeare's *Othello* and *Julius
Caesar.*

Often designated as the greatest of all Restoration tragedies, or even
the greatest tragedy since Shakespeare; others admit its masterly dramatic
scenes, but deny it great distinction as drama.[2]

Nathaniel Lee, *c.* 1649—1692, playwright.[3] Son of a Presbyterian
divine of Hertfordshire. Educated at Westminster School. Entered
Trinity College, Cambridge (1665). Took his B.A. degree (1668).
Collaborated twice with Dryden in writing tragedy (1679, 1683). He
went mad, and was confined in Bethlehem Hospital or Bedlam (1684—
1689). Some time after 1690 his mental balance again became completely upset. Is said to have died in a drinking fit, being killed or
stifled in a fall.

Works include (1) *The Princess of Cleve* (acted 1681; published
1689), a coarse adaptation of Madame de La Fayette's novel of sentiment, *La Princesse de Clèves;* (2) *The Tragedy of Nero, Emperour of
Rome* (1675), a successful heroic tragedy of his day; (3) *Sophonisba:
or Hannibal's Overthrow* (1676), a tragedy founded on Orrery's
Parthenissa, and one for which Purcell wrote the music; (4) *Caesar
Borgia, Son of Pope Alexander the Sixth* (1680), an energetic, bombastic,
historically-absurd political tragedy concocted from an Elizabethan blood-
and-thunder formulary mixed with Lee's own ingredients gathered
from Francesco Guicciardini and from Dacres's translation of Machiavelli; (5) *Lucius Junius Brutus; Father of his Country* (1681), a
tragedy, indebted somewhat to Madeleine de Scudéry's *Clélie,* was
banned by the Lord Chamberlain because of its political propaganda.
It may be the basis of Lessing's *Das befreite Rom.* Additional historical

---

1 The sub-plot is a deliberate satire upon Anthony Ashley Cooper, Earl of Shaftesbury.
Its decadent scenes have been defended only by Taine on the ground that they give
relief to the serious action; they are also a contrast to the noble love of Belvidera
and Jaffeir.   The general opinion is that the Nicky-Nacky scenes are revolting, cloacal,
and masochistic; and that the underplot in which Antonio represents Lord Shaftesbury
is not entirely unjust caricature.

2 It has, according to Allardyce Nicoll, a stupendous power and a hitting-the-mark
psychology; but, according to William Archer, *Venice Preserved* is a "clumsy, blunder-
ing, coarsely bombastic work."

3 Stroup, T. B., and A. L. Cooke, eds., *The Works of Nathaniel Lee* (Two vols., 1954-
1955).

† * Explanation of symbols immediately precedes Chapter XV.

or quasi-historical tragedies are (6) *Gloriana, or the Court of Augustus Caesar* (1676); (7) *Mithridates, King of Pontus* (1678); (8) *Oedipus* (in collaboration with Dryden, 1678); (9) *Theodosius: or, The Force of Love* (1680); (10) *Constantine the Great* (1684); and (11) *The Massacre of Paris* (1690), one of his better plays part of which had been incorporated into the Tory tragedy, *The Duke of Guise* (acted 1682; published 1683), written in conjunction with Dryden, and prohibited at first because of its political allusions. (12) The more effective scenes in the first and fourth acts of *The Duke of Guise* are probably by Dryden, while the love-scenes between Guise and Marmontier are probably by Lee. See page 332.

The Rival Queens, or The Death of Alexander the Great†* (1677). Tragedy mainly in blank verse. Its passionate interpretation of love shivered the conventions of Platonic love found in the heroic play. Note that the hero has both good and bad qualities. Splendid rhetoric often becomes extravagant and bombastic. Based on La Calprenède's *Cassandre,* and on such classical historians as Quintus Curtius Rufus, Arrian, and Plutarch.

Comment. Were it not for Dryden (p. 325), Nathaniel Lee would be recognized as the most typical heroic dramatist. He modelled his plays after the French, and from classical antiquity he drew most of his material for historical or quasi-historical tragedies. Most of his earlier plays are in rimed couplets, and his later in blank verse; but all are exploded by blazing rant and unreasonable extravagance of metaphor. Nor is he lacking in felicity of phrase, even if marked by bombast, nor in a command of pathos, nor in lines of pregnant poetic quality. His show and rhetoric make him very effective on the stage, although not under a reading lamp in the study. As a matter of fact, he anticipated Dryden by experimenting with blank verse, by throwing overboard the gallantry of the heroic play and by substituting in its place passionate love-scenes, and by employing spectacular devices.

Nicholas Rowe, 1674—1718, dramatist, poet, first modern editor of Shakespeare. Won a King's Scholarship at Westminster School. Entered the Middle Temple (1691). Upon inheriting three hundred pounds a year when his father died in 1692, he forsook the legal profession for that of playwright. Married Antonia Parsons (1698). Under-Secretary to the Duke of Queensbury, Secretary of State for Scotland (1709—1711). Succeeded Nahum Tate as poet laureate (1715). Buried three years later in Westminster Abbey.

Dramas include (1) *The Ambitious Stepmother* (1700), a negligible blank verse tragedy; (2) *Tamerlane* (1701), propagandistic tragedy presented annually for more than a hundred years on November 5th, the date of William III's landing at Torbay: William figures as the conqueror and Louis XIV as Bajazet; (3) *The Biter* (1704), an unsuccessful

---

† * **Explanation of symbols immediately precedes Chapter XV.**

attempt at comedy; (4) *Ulysses* (1705), a negligible attempt to combine classical tragedy and Elizabethan; (5) *The Royal Convert* (1707), a poor heroic play based on early British history; and (6) *The Tragedy of Lady Jane Grey* (1715), a "she-tragedy" modelled, like *Jane Shore*, on the historical tragedies of Shakespeare, and treating the story in a pseudo-classical, domestic-sentimental manner.

The Fair Penitent (1703). Domestic "she-tragedy" in blank verse is an eighteenth-century version of Massinger and Field's *The Fatal Dowry* (Vol. 1, p. 245). Reduced the number of characters, regularized the plot, simplified the action, and shortened the end. However, note the refined diction of the well-born characters, the conveying of Massinger's sprightly action by means of exposition, and the anti-climax of the fifth act. Characters: the gay Lothario, who for two centuries has been a current figure of speech, and perhaps suggested Richardson's Lovelace (p. 390); and Calista, who may have suggested Richardson's Clarissa (p. 99).

The Tragedy of Jane Shore† (1714). Historical characters are lowered in importance in order to enhance the pathetic fall of the altogether too-perfect Lady Jane. Narration too often substitutes for action. Best character: Pembroke. Main source of his second "she-tragedy" is More's *Richard the Third* (Vol. 1, p. 115) and the ballad called *The Woefull Lamentation of Jane Shore, A Goldsmith's Wife in London, Sometime King Edward IV, his Concubine.*

The Works of Mr. William Shakespeare† (Six volumes, 1709). First critical and first illustrated edition of Shakespeare.[1] Based on text of corrupt fourth folio of 1685. Many errors in text because of not collating the folio with the quartos, but Rowe prefixed a list of the *dramatis personae* to each play, divided the plays into acts and scenes, noted the exits and entrances of the players, modernized the spelling, punctuation, and grammar—in short, made the text more intelligible.

Comment. To the world Rowe is known today primarily as the editor of the first octavo issue of Shakespeare's plays. By reason of his patriotic tone, moral dignity, pure purpose, and lofty conception he also merits some attention as a playwright. The latest of the Restoration writers of tragedy and the last of the tragic poets of the age, he links the drama of his period to that of the Augustan Age: his moral tone is in strong contrast to the licentiousness of Restoration drama (*e.g.*, in his advocacy of lawful wedlock in *The Fair Penitent* and *Jane Shore*). True, Johnson may have exaggerated in describing Rowe's translation of Lucan's *Pharsalia* as "one of the greatest productions of English poetry"—it does preserve the spirit of the original—but he came closer to critical consensus when stating that Rowe's plays have not "any deep

---

[1] Jackson, Alfred, "Rowe's Edition of Shakespeare," *The Library*, x (Fourth Series, 1929-1930), pp. 455-473.
† * Explanation of symbols immediately precedes Chapter XV.

search into nature, any accurate discriminations of kindred qualities, or
a nice display of passion in its progress. All is general and refined. But
his reputation comes from the reasonableness of some of his scenes, the
elegance of his diction, and the suavity of his verse." But, in the words
of Saintsbury, this elegance and suavity have long palled.

Comedy

Sir George Etherege or **Etheredge,** *c.* 1634—*c.* 1692, dramatist,
poet. Dates of birth, marriage, and death uncertain. Born either in
Bermuda or in England. Not until 1664, when his play appeared, is
there any certain knowledge of "Easy George" or "Gentle Etherege."
Secretary to Sir Daniel Harvey, English Ambassador to Constantinople
(1668—1671). Married wealthy Mary Arnold, and at about the same
time was knighted (*c.* 1680). Became the lover of Mrs. Barry, who is
said to have borne him a daughter.[1] Envoy to the Diet of Ratisbon
(1685—1689), a period of his life recorded in his both involved and
succinct *Letterbook.* Probably died in Paris (*c.* 1691).

His comedies, in each case dominated by the figure of an attractive
heroine, are sprightly and licentious, frivolous and immoral. Contain
excellent touches of dress and scene, and vivid pictures of the fine airs
of London society. Renouncing traditional "humour" types, Etherege
limns real persons. He is credited with the first real dramatic use of the
heroic couplet. Crowning all, he invented the comedy of intrigue.

*The Comical Revenge; or, Love in a Tub** (1664). First full-
fledged example of the Restoration comedy of manners. Is a *mélange*
of comic scenes usually in prose and of serious portions usually in rimed
heroics. Novel characters, broad farce. Shows familiarity with Molière.
Comic underplot, with its play of wit,[2] realism of prose scenes, and
"war-of-the-sexes" theme, is recognized as having introduced the comedy
of Congreve, Goldsmith, and Sheridan.

She wou'd if she could (1668). Comedy. Discarded the incompatible elements of sentimental heroics, prodigal farce, and traditional
roguery. Some scenes are reminiscent of the Jonsonian comedy of
humours. Described by Pepys as a silly play.

The Man of Mode, or, Sir Fopling Flutter† (1676). Urbane
picture of the artifice and foppery of the day. Excellent wit-combats
between lovers, brilliant character-drawing, pleasing songs, barbed satire;
negligent plot, easy morality. Chief figures probably represent originals
in society: Medley may be Sir Charles Sedley; Dorimant may be Lord
Rochester. Creation of Sir Fopling Flutter, the prince of fops, possibly
influenced by Mascarille in Molière's *Les Précieuses Ridicules.*

---

1 Chancellor, E. B., *The Lives of the Rakes* (The Restoration Rakes: Vol. II, 1924),
   Chaps. VI and VII, pp. 119-196.
2 To John Evelyn it was a "facetious comedy" (*Diary*, April 27, 1664), and to Pepys
   it was "very merry, but only so by gesture, not wit at all" (January 4, 1664-1665).

† • **Explanation of symbols immediately precedes Chapter XV.**

Letterbook.[1] Through the mixture of awkward and lucid, urbane and felicitous phrasing shine the tolerance and personality of Etherege.

Sir Charles Sedley, *c.* 1639—1701, dramatist, poet.[2] Son of Sir John Sedley. Educated at Wadham College, Oxford (1656). Was the "Lisideius" of Dryden's *Of Dramatick Poesie, An Essay* (p. 333). Fined for an indecent occurrence in Bow Street.[3] Member of Parliament. Father of Catherine who became the mistress of James II and was created Countess of Dorchester.[4]

As a court poet Sedley helped found *vers de société* by such light and fluent songs as "Love still has something of the sea," and "Hears not my *Phillis,* how the Birds." Of special merit are *"Phillis* is my only Joy," which for its day shows an unusual metrical ingenuity and lyrical -sincerity; *"Chloris* I cannot say your Eyes," catching by its easy rhythm and clear thought; and "Not *Celia* that I juster am," noteworthy for its pointed conclusion.

Tragedies: (1) *Antony and Cleopatra* (1667), colorless in meter and diction, and occasionally echoing Shakespeare, this feeble heroic tragedy is based chiefly on Plutarch; and (2) *The Tyrant King of Crete* (1702), an unmeritorious adaptation in blank verse of Henry Killigrew's *Pallantus and Eudora.*

Comedies: (1) *The Mulberry-Garden* (1668) is partly based on Molière's *L'Ecole des Maris,* especially in its opening. Very much like Etherege's *Comical Revenge,* mixes romantic scenes in riming couplets with realistic scenes in conventional prose. Granting that the comic and realistic scenes have some value, the play is on the whole loose, incoherent, and, in A. W. Ward's opinion, "worthless" drama. Lyric: *"Ah,* Chloris! *that I now could sit."* (2) *The Grumbler* (1702; first public performance, 1754), doubtfully ascribed to Sedley, is a translation of *Le Grondeur,* a comedy (1691) written by the Abbé David Augustin de Brueys and Jean de Palaprat. Sedley keeps close to the original, notably in the first act. (See page 377.)

Bellamira, or the Mistress† (1687). Based upon the *Eunuchus* of Terence, the comedy dexterously reflects Restoration life. Unified, vigorous, lucid. Schelling has described it as "a lively, if coarsely realistic, picture." Well-known: "Thyrsis, *unjustly you Complain."*

---

1 *The Letterbook of Sir George Etherege,* edited by Rosenfeld, Sybil (1928).

2 Pinto, V. de S., *Sir Charles Sedley* (1927).

3 He stripped naked on at least two occasions. See Chancellor, E. B., *The Restoration Rakes* (1924), Chap. VIII (pp. 159-187); Pinto, V. de S., *Sir Charles Sedley* (1927), pp. 61-67.

4 His *bon mot* at the expense of James II: Sedley stated that he hated ingratitude, and, since James II had made Catherine a Countess, he would endeavor to make the King's daughter a Queen.

† * Explanation of symbols immediately precedes Chapter XV.

William Wycherley, *c.* 1640[1]—1715, possibly the founder of Restoration comedy and the father of modern English comedy. Abroad in France at the age of fifteen. Returned to England (1660). Gentleman commoner at Queen's College, Oxford (1660), which he probably left without taking a degree. Took to sea for a short time. Secretly married the Countess of Drogheda (*c.* 1680), who was morbidly jealous. Wife died (1681). Unable to pay his debts he was thrown into prison for several years. At the age of seventy-five, less than a dozen days before his death, he married Elizabeth Jackson, a young woman upon whom he settled a widow's jointure.[2]

Vigorous, straightforward style; Molière-like animation of dialogue; genuine wit. Lively, cynical, well-constructed comedies, permeated by savage but truthful satire and animal strength. "Manly" or "Brawny" Wycherley yields to "Easy" Etherege in polished speech and to Congreve in technique; but is more audacious and earnest than the latter and more direct and terse than the former. In a coarse age Wycherley was—at least in dialogue—probably the most brutally coarse of all.[3]

Love in a Wood; or, St. James's Park (published 1671; dated 1672). Indecent, somewhat biting satire on contemporary life. Allegedly indebted to Sedley's *Mulberry-Garden:* but Sedley has puppets while Wycherley has real characters. Vagrant structure, ripe dramatic scenes.

*The Gentleman Dancing-Master** (acted about 1672; published 1672 with 1673 on title-page). Most pleasant work is a more unified and more diverting farce than *Love in a Wood*. Slightly indebted to Calderon's *El Maestro de Danzar*, from which he adapted a rather hackneyed situation.

The Country Wife†* (performed *c.* 1672—1674; published 1675). Sardonic comedy. Bears but a superficial resemblance to Molière's *L'Ecole des Femmes* and *L'Ecole des Maris;* real basis of plot is Terence's *Eunuchus*—but even Terence's device he makes his own. Marjorie Pinchwife has been declared the original of Congreve's Miss Prue and Vanbrugh's Miss Hoyden. Vigorous, daringly witty, pornographic farce; rapid action; conventional humor braced by animal spirits. Implicit, not explicit, in its satirical element and moral standard; compare with *The Plain Dealer*.

The Plain Dealer†* (acted *c.* 1674; published 1677). Disillusioned, indecent comedy of "humours," stuffed, according to George Meredith,

---

1 His date of birth may be 1641. Thus asserts Vincent, H. P., "The date of Wycherley's Birth," *The London Times Literary Supplement*, March 3, 1932; p. 155, col. 2.

2 It now seems that Wycherley did not marry Elizabeth Jackson for her money, but was rather victimized by Captain Thomas Shrimpton, a cousin, whose mistress Elizabeth was. Consult Vincent, H. P., "The Death of William Wycherley," *Harvard Studies and Notes in Philology and Literature*, xv (1933), pp. 219-242.

3 Famous is the attack on Wycherley made by Macaulay in his essay on the *Comic Dramatists of the Restoration*, and even more of a classic is Lamb's defense of Wycherley's licentiousness in his essay *On the Artificial Comedy of the Last Century*.

† * Explanation of symbols immediately precedes Chapter XV.

"with lumps of realism."[1] Good characterization and dialogue, clear pictures of manners; loosely-knit scenes, yet a graceless strength and heartiness. Explicit in its satirical element; openly recognizes the existence of moral values.[2] Possibly his greatest comic creation: Widow Blackacre. Possibly influenced by Molière's *Le Misanthrope* in its main plot, and by Shakespeare's *Twelfth Night* in the characterization of Fidelia; in turn, gave a basis to Voltaire's *La Prude.*

William Congreve, 1670—1729,[3] greatest master of the English comedy of repartee, and possibly of manners, yet his influence was neither wide nor lasting. Son of an army officer. Kilkenny School (*c.* 1681—1685). Trinity College, Dublin (1685). London (1691), where he entered the Inner Temple. Commission for licensing hackney and stagecoaches (1694). A Commissioner of Wine Licenses (1705—1714). Government Secretary for Jamaica (1714). An undersearcher of the customs in the port of London (1714—1729).[4]

Consummately dazzling dialogue, unceasingly smart impudence, cynically powerful drama, nervous beauty of language, and a coarseness more connotative than that of Wycherley. Not only are his comedies an incomplete picture of England as a whole, but even of the small section of English society taken for his subject-matter. Congreve is unable, furthermore, to express passion directly; and, too, a diagrammatic summary is needed as a guide through the complexity of plot. He possesses more energy and insight than Etherege. In poetry, his best work is the ode[5] "On Mrs. Arabella Hunt Singing" (1692). Other poems are "Doris," "The Decay," and "Song: False though she be to me and love."

Incognita, or Love and Duty Reconciled (1692). Immature prose novelette.[6] Conventional theme treated with some delicate banter and somewhat effortless urbanity.

*The Old Bachelor** (1693). Comedy of intrigue with a minimum of five definite actions in plot. Frequent soliloquies, bright and immodest dialogue, deftly-handled situations, bustling play of wit; marred by conventional paradigms, poor plot, scurrilous language. Imitative: Bluffe, Sir

---

1 Meredith, George, *An Essay on Comedy*, edited by Cooper, Lane (1918), p. 94.

2 "But, not until we reach *The Plain Dealer,* Wycherley's last and best comedy, do we recognize that this savage blasphemer in the halls of beauty and of art is, after all, at heart a moralist, indignantly flagellating vice as well as gloating over her deformities." Schelling, F. E., in *The Cambridge History of English Literature* (1920), VIII, p. 145 (Chap. V, pp. 115-177). See, however, Palmer, John, *The Comedy of Manners* (1913), p. 134 *ff.* (Chap. IV, pp. 92-140).

3 Taylor, D. C., *William Congreve* (1931); Hodges, J. C., "On the Date of Congreve's Birth," *Modern Philology*, XXXIII (1935), pp. 83-85.

4 Hodges, J. C., "William Congreve in the Government Service," *Modern Philology*, XXVII (1929-1930), pp. 183-192.

5 Possibly overpraised by critics, for only the first four lines seem to be poetic. His occasional verse, says Dobrée, "is as good as anything printed between the death of Dryden in 1700 and the appearance of *The Rape of the Lock* in 1712, and it is often more scholarly." Dobrée, Bonamy, *Variety of Ways* (1932), p. 51 (pp. 44-65, 66-86).

6 To Macaulay it was a novel of no great value, while to Morley it would not make a bad little play.

† * **Explanation of symbols** immediately precedes Chapter XV.

Joseph Wittol, and Fondlewife resemble Jonson's Bobadil, Master Stephen, and Kitely; Heartwell, Sharper, and Bellmour are modelled on Wycherley's Manly, Freeman, and Horner. Songs: "Thus to a Ripe Consenting Maid"; "As Amoret and Thyrsis Lay." Bellmour's speech is supposed to reflect Congreve's own philosophy: "Come, come, leave business to idlers and wisdom to fools; they have need of them; Wit be my faculty and pleasure my occupation, let Father Time shake his glass."

The Double-Dealer†* (1694). Possibly the only good English comedy built upon a single idea. Implacable irony, subtle dialogue, realistic characterization, preservation of the unities of time and place, careful construction; but also over-elaborate intrigue. As an acting play, inferior to *Love for Love*. Character: Maskwell. Influenced by Molière.

Love for Love†* (1695). His masterpiece in plot, human interest, and pure stagecraft has been termed the best artificial comedy or comedy of manners in English. Avowedly a satire upon the vices and follies of the time.[1] Deft wit. More lively than *The Way of the World* and better-constructed (if improbable) plot. Angelica's honest emotions almost inhibited by her worldly wit. Original characterization: Foresight; Sir Sampson; Miss Prue, a complete portrait of a country hoyden; Ben Legend, the earliest full-length specimen of a long line of salty stage-sailors.

The Mourning Bride* (1697). His only tragedy. Blank verse. Has passages of deep feeling. Improbable plot. Overpraised by Johnson as containing in its second act the finest poetical passage he had ever read. Memorable among its fustian for its first line, "Musick has Charms to soothe a savage Breast," and for "Nor Hell a Fury like a Woman scorn'd."

The Way of the World†* (1700). True comedy of manners, independent of Molière though indebted to him. Ablaze with sustained repartee and voluble, yet scintillating and economical, dialogue. Consummate stage-master of a complicated, almost static, action concentrated around one intrigue, at times so teasing and purposelessly confusing that its plot-structure obviously lacks cohesion. Clear-cut characterization: Mirabell has been compared with Shakespeare's Benedick, while Millamant has been compared with Shakespeare's Beatrice, Dryden's Melanthea, and Meredith's Diana. Yet the play received a lukewarm

---

1 Yet Collier, in *A Defense of the Short View of the Profaneness and Immorality of the English Stage*, a reply to Congreve's *Amendments*, describes *Love for Love* as a play in which Congreve makes "a Martyr of a Whoremaster." See p. 313.

† * Explanation of symbols immediately precedes Chapter XV.

reception, attributable, in some measure, to Collier's *Short View* (p. 22) arraigning the lubricity of contemporary drama.[1]

Sir John Vanbrugh, *c.* 1664—1726, dramatist, architect. Probably in France (1683—1685). Returned to England (1686). Imprisoned in France, on the charge of espionage (1690—1692). Captaincy in Lord Berkeley's Marine Regiment of Foot (1696). Captaincy in the Earl of Huntingdon's Regiment (1702). Comptroller of the Royal Works (1702). Built Castle Howard for the Earl of Carlisle (1702—1714). Clarenceux King-of-Arms (1704—1726). Began to build Blenheim Castle for the Duke of Marlborough (1705). Designer and manager of Haymarket Theatre (opened 1705). Knighted (1714). Surveyor of Greenwich Hospital (1716). Married Henrietta Maria Yarborough (1719)—a happy union.

Writings include (1) *Aesop* (1697), a somewhat biting adaptation of Boursault's *Les Fables d'Esope;* (2) *The Country House* (*c.* 1698), a ridiculously-concluded and somewhat funny farce freely translated from Dancourt's *La Maison de Campagne;* (3) *The Pilgrim* (1700), a fairly good prose alteration of Fletcher's romantic comedy, *The Pilgrim;* (4) *The False Friend* (1702), a poor comedy of intrigue adapted from Francesco de Rojas-Zorilla's *La Traición busca el Castigo* and Le Sage's French version called *Le Traître puni* (1700); (5) *Squire Trelooby* (1704), in which he may have collaborated with Congreve and Walsh[2]; (6) *The Mistake* (1705), a free translation of Molière's *Le Dépit Amoureux;* and (7) *The Cuckold in Conceit* (1707; but not printed), attributed to Vanbrugh, and translated from Molière's *Sganarelle; ou, Le Cocu Imaginaire.* (8) The characters of *The Confederacy* (1705), an adaptation of Dancourt's *Les Bourgeoises à la Mode,* are middleclass people; well-contrived and rather amusing in plot. Character: Corinna. (9) As in *The Relapse* and *The Provok'd Wife,* so in *A Journey to London* (1728) Vanbrugh raises important questions of character and conduct. Unfinished play completed and produced by Cibber as *The Provoked Husband,* has two loosely-joined plots, good-humored satire, broad characterization. Characters: John Moody, Miss Betty.

The Relapse, or Virtue in Danger†* (1697). Racy farce is a professed continuation of Cibber's *Love's Last Shift* and a protest against the false presentation of human nature in Cibber's work. Medley of

---

1 Neither his famous remark to Voltaire in 1726 nor his lean legacy to Mrs. Bracegirdle are obviously as important as the question: Why did Congreve abandon the stage after 1700? For twenty-nine years he wrote almost nothing, unless one includes *The Judgment of Paris* (1701), a masque, *Squire Trelooby* (1704), which he helped translate from Molière's *Monsieur de Pourceaugnac,* and *Semele* (1707), an opera. Probably several reasons contributed to his silence: the ill state of his health, Collier's philippic, the comparative lack of success of *The Way of the World,* and the security resulting from a government income. See Hodges, J. C., "The Authorship of *Squire Trelooby,*" *The Review of English Studies,* IV (1928), pp. 404-413.

2 It is still doubtful whether Vanbrugh had a hand in *Squire Trelooby.* See Hodges, J. C., "The Authorship of *Squire Trelooby,*" *The Review of English Studies,* IV (1928), pp. 404-413.

† * Explanation of symbols immediately precedes Chapter XV.

romantic and comic threads. Noteworthy for its vivacious dialogue and for its character-creations: *e.g.*, Lord Foppington has been pronounced the best fop on the English stage, although Etherege's Sir Fopling Flutter is the first and possibly the greatest fop.[1] Criticized for its bedroom scene.

The Provok'd Wife†* (1697). Spontaneous dialogue; broad, uproarious, possibly gross, merriment; better plotting than usual although action occasionally squeaks; well-drawn characters. In technique, a better play than *The Relapse*. Memorable: Sir John Brute.

Comment. While his letters reveal his genial, hearty character, and why he was called "Brother Van," it is his dramas that have the greater importance. Management of plot is often loose, portrayal of characters not subtle; easy morality, coarse realism. His decadence from the pure Restoration comedy is evidenced in his farcical action and coarse characterization.[2] But usually displayed architectural construction of plot, bold and alive delineation of character (even in the character of the servants), unerring sense of fun and animal spirits. Has been called a lesser Congreve; while Vanbrugh's dialogue is less brilliant and polished, it is also less artificial; while his characters are less witty, they are more human; while his plots frequently show a disregard for probability, they are simpler and less confusing; and, above all, Vanbrugh raises problems calling for serious consideration.[3]

George Farquhar, *c.* 1677—1707, dramatist. Born at Londonderry, Ireland. Sizar at Trinity College, Dublin (1694). Actor at the Smock Alley Theatre in Dublin (1696). After accidentally wounding a fellow-actor, vowed never to tread the boards again. Reached London (*c.* 1697). Procured an army commission; served in Holland (1700). Married Mrs. Margaret Pemell of Yorkshire (1703), who bore him two daughters. Was appointed Second Lieutenant in Lord Orrery's Regiment on Foot (1704).

Among his plays are (1) *The Adventures of Covent Gardens* (1699), an imitation of Scarron's *City Romance* doubtfully ascribed to Farquhar; (2) *Barcellona* (*c.* 1702—*c.* 1707), a halting epic in a half-dozen cantos narrating Peterborough's successes in Spain; and (3) *The Stage-Coach* (1704), a one-act farce adapted from Jean de la Chapelle's *Les Carrosses d'Orleans,* but with an original *dénouement.* (4) *Love*

1 Ward, A. W. *A History of English Dramatic Literature* (1889), III, p. 479.

2 Vanbrugh accelerated the decay of the comedy of manners not only by introducing luscious passion into his love scenes but also because, first, the characters, according to Dobrée, "are not in the grip of destiny," and, second, his presentation, according to Mueschke and Fleisher, "is sympathetic, rational, and sustained, rather than indifferent, impersonal, and incidental."

3 Mueschke, Paul and Fleisher, Jeannette, "A Re-Evaluation of Vanbrugh," *Publications of the Modern Language Association of America,* XLIX (1934), pp. 848-889

† * **Explanation of symbols immediately precedes Chapter XV.**

and a Bottle (1698), influenced by Molière's *Le Bourgeois Gentilhomme,* is a hackneyed, if occasionally bustling, comedy that ends in many improbable tangles. (5) *The Constant Couple or A Trip to the Jubilee* (1699),[1] of negligible plot, coarse and farcical, is possibly his feeblest play, even if it is better in dramatic art than *Love and a Bottle,* and surer, if still weak, in dialogue. Its "worst fault," says Strauss, "is a tendency to break into bastard blank verse disguised as prose." Characters: Sir Harry; Lady Lurewell, whose character was partly derived from D'Urfrey's *Madame Fickle.* (6) *Sir Harry Wildair* (1701), an inferior and improbable sequel to *The Constant Couple,* with labored salacious scenes between Sir Harry and Lady Lurewell, who degenerates from a realistic coquette into a petty strumpet. (7) *The Inconstant, or The Way to Win Him* (1702), a revision that somewhat emasculates the gaiety of Fletcher's *The Wild-Goose Chase* (Vol. 1, p. 241). Farquhar himself points to the factual if melodramatic adventure of the Chevalier de Chastillon of Paris introduced in the last act—a semi-tragic situation that departs from the light comedy of manners. (8) An original melodrama in which his moral sense dominates is *The Twin-Rivals* (1702), where, avowedly because of Jeremy Collier's blast (p. 313), he strains his theory of poetic justice; yet the plot is uglier than usual.

The Recruiting Officer†* (1706). Satire. No play of his is heartier and fresher, or contains more of his personal experiences acquired during the early years of the War of the Spanish Succession. Slender plot. Scenes often slovenly written, but natural. Characters more attractive than those in *The Beaux Stratagem*: Sylvia is possibly his most delightful heroine; also memorable are Captain Plume and Sergeant Kite.

The Beaux Stratagem†* (1707). Quiet, straight-to-the-point, alive masterpiece. Simple, cleverly-engineered, but conventional, the plot, though less plausible and more ingenuous than *The Recruiting Officer,* is unfolded with genial humor, forceful and lively dialogue, and a flowingly dramatic style. Character: Lady Bountiful. Widens the scope of the comedy of manners to include many bourgeois characters. Last comedy of the Restoration is one of the first comedies of sensibility. Prototype of Goldsmith's *She Stoops to Conquer* (p. 376).

Comment. *Love and Business* (dated 1702; probably published 1701) is a small miscellany of stray verses, readable love-letters, and letters from Holland; and, most important, includes *A Discourse upon Comedy, in reference to the English Stage,* a sensitive, witty, and incisive piece which attacks the three unities and rejects Aristotelian authority.[2] Of his other works, note that his comedies of the early period (*Love and a*

---

1 Yet, with *The Recruiting Officer,* inspired German plays by Gottlieb, Stephanie, Lessing, and others.
2 *A Discourse Upon Comedy, The Recruiting Officer and The Beaux Stratagem,* edited by Strauss, L. A. (1914), pp. XLIII-XLV (pp. V-LVI).
† * Explanation of symbols immediately precedes Chapter XV.

Bottle, The Constant Couple, and *Sir Harry Wildair*) continue in the tradition of the comedy of manners; that his works of the middle period (*The Inconstant* and *The Twin-Rivals*) are avowedly experimental dramatic sermons designed to rescue comedy from the moral censure of Jeremy Collier; and, finally, that the works of the last period (*The Recruiting Officer* and *The Beaux Stratagem*) break new ground in plot and characters, and are as unlike his preceding works as they are unlike those of the Restoration comedy.

In his *Discourse upon Comedy* Farquhar states that he tests a play largely by the receipts of the box-office: "To make the moral instructive, you must make the story diverting" for all classes of people; "and he that can do this best, and with most applause, writes the best comedy, let him do it by what rules he pleases, so they be not offensive to religion and good manners." Possibly this independent attitude is a clue to Farquhar's transitional place between the comedy of the Restoration and that of the mid-eighteenth century. The easy morality of his time, its impudent wit and sophisticated creations, are still evident in his works, but also a return to the romantic treatment of love, a different kind of genial merriment, a more asserting conscience and a healthier humanity underlying the flock of new characters he introduces, and a more abiding morality. His best effects are dependent less upon intricacy than upon variety of plot and structure, less upon the wit of the dialogue than upon the humor of the situation, less upon quasi-aristocratic characters in a drawing-room than upon middle-class people in an eighteenth-century market-place or country inn, and, finally, less upon unfragrant intrigue than upon romantic passion and rattling, theatrically-effective adventures. Not only do his works look forward to the complete triumph of Sentimentalism upon the stage—for he is the connecting link between the comic dramatists of the Restoration and the Cibbers and Steeles, the Goldsmiths and Sheridans—but he is, moreover, the one in whose works the step was finally taken between the play and the novel— a step carrying us toward the realistic fiction of Fielding and Smollett.

THE BEGINNINGS OF MODERN PROSE

Woman Writers

Lucy Hutchinson, 1620—1675, biographer, letter-writer. *The Memoirs of the Life of Colonel Hutchinson,* a biography of her husband, is interesting for the comparatively lighter touch of its prose and is important for its picture, from the Puritan point of view, of the state of the country and of the outbreak of the Civil War.

Margaret Cavendish, Duchess of Newcastle, *c.* 1624—1673, prolific writer. She wrote verses, plays, essays, philosophical opinions— so much, in fact, that she filled a dozen printed volumes. Her best work is her poetry; but she is known primarily as a letter-writer and the biographer of her husband. *Sociable Letters* (1664) has permanent worth in its entertaining picture of the period extending from the accession of Charles I to that of Charles II. Unlike Lucy Hutchinson, she writes from the standpoint of a woman whose husband was a Royalist. *The Life of William Cavendish, Duke of Newcastle* (1667) was criticized by Pepys as a "ridiculous history" revealing the Duchess as "a mad, conceited, ridiculous woman" and the Duke as "an ass to suffer her to write what she writes to him and of him," but Lamb spoke of the work as one for which "no casket is rich enough, no case sufficiently durable to honour and keep soft such a jewel."

Mrs. Aphra Behn, *née* Amis or Amies, 1640—1689, poet, playwright, novelist; the first Englishwoman who earned a livelihood by her pen.[1] As a child probably lived in Surinam, Guiana. Returned to England (1658). Married Behn, a London merchant of Dutch extraction. After his death (*c.* 1665), she was employed by Charles II as a political spy in the Netherlands (1666—1667). Probably about this time she assumed the name "Astraea." On her return to London she was clapped into a debtor's prison. Released, she began to write for a living. She is buried in the east cloisters of Westminster Abbey.

"The Incomparable Astraea" wrote a dozen novels, a larger number of plays, and many poems. Her verses are defaced by bawdiness, but are in the main pretty, pointed, spicy, and superficial. "The grove was gloomy all around" and "A thousand martyrs I have made" are less well-known than "Love in fantastic triumph sate." Her dramatic works, totaling at least seventeen, are clever, genial, witty, well-contrived, and indecent. These include (1) *The Amorous Prince, or, The Curious Husband* (1671), a coarse comedy of intrigue; (2) *The Rover, or, The Banished Cavaliers†* (I, 1677; II, 1681), her best-known comedy, founded on Killigrew, noted for bustle and wit, and thematic with sexual intrigue; (3) *Abdelazar, or, The Moor's Revenge* (1677), noted for its "Love in fantastic triumph sate"; (4) *Sir Patient Fancy* (1678), founded on Molière; (5) *The Feigned Courtezans, or, A Night's Intrigue* (1679), a lively, entertaining, witty, indelicate comedy; (6) *The Roundheads; or, The Good Old Cause* (*c.* 1682), a pasquinade directed at the Puritans; *The City Heiress, or, Sir Timothy Treat-all* (1682), indebted to Massinger's *The Guardians* and Middleton's *A Mad World, My Masters,* lampoons Shaftesbury as Sir Timothy; and (7) *The Lucky Chance, or, An Alderman's Bargain* (1686), another comedy excellent in its wit and humor but also indecent in its scenes. Her *Love-Letters to a Gentleman* (1696) are simple, romantic, sentimental, prettily-expressed, agonizingly passionate, and without any marked trace of obscenity. Finally, her novels, like her plays, were obviously influenced by French and Spanish intrigue, and cloak-and-sword romances; her romantic stor-

---

1 *The Works of Aphra Behn,* edited by Summers, Montague (Six volumes, 1915); Sackville-West, V., *Aphra Behn* (1927); Jerrold, Walter and Clare, *Five Queer Women* (1929), Chap. I, pp. 1-82; Platt, H. G., Jr., "Astrea and Celadon: An Untouched Portrait of Aphra Behn," *Publications of the Modern Language Association of America,* XLIX (1934), pp. 544-559.

ies colored by realistic detail and showing a command of character-study undoubtedly influenced the development of the novel. Among them are *The Adventure of the Black Lady* (written *c.* 1684; published 1696), an episodic transcript from life energized by colloquial speech; *The Unfortunate Bride, or, The Blind Lady a Beauty* (1687); *The Dumb Virgin, or, The Force of Imagination* (1687); *The Fair Jilt, or, The Amours of Prince Tarquin and Miranda* (1688), and, most significant,—

Oroonoko, or, The Royal Slave* (1688). First novel in English literature to express vehement sympathy for the oppressed Negroes and a rage at cruelties of the slave drivers. Vivid, realistic, energetic, her most original contribution is influenced by her professed experiences at Surinam and colored by her acquaintance with heroic romances.[1] Like her *Letters to a Nobleman,* can not be charged with impropriety. Excited a distinct influence on the fiction of Chauteaubriand and Fielding, and foreshadowed the romanticism of Rousseau's "natural man."

Criticism

Thomas Rymer, 1641—1713, author, archaeologist. Most valuable is his *Foedera, Conventiones, Litterae, et cujuscumque generis Acta Publica* (1704—1735), a collection of public records in twenty volumes, modelled on Leibnitz' *Codex juris gentium diplomaticus* (1693), and providing for the first time a scientific groundwork for the writing of history. To the literary critic he is known for *Tragedies of the Last Age Consider'd* (1678), memorable for careful criticism of Beaumont and Fletcher, and for *A Short View of Tragedy* (1693), condemning Shakespeare's Othello as "a bloody farce without salt or savour." Rymer's criticism is a vigorous application of Aristotelian principles, with an emphasis upon general common sense. Despite the dogmatic assertions of Macaulay and Saintsbury, there have been worse critics than Thomas Rymer.

Jeremy Collier, 1650—1726, nonjuring clergyman whose chief work eventually precipitated, it is said, the closing of the theatre. Educated at Ipswich and Caius College, Cambridge. Rector of Ampton, Suffolk (1679—1685). Ordained a nonjuring bishop (1713).

A Short View of the Immorality and Profaneness of the English Stage (1698).[2] Muscular, if occasionally ungrammatical, ill-proportioned, and pedantic, Puritan attack upon the stage of Congreve, Vanbrugh, Wycherley, and even Dryden. Collier's own raw epithets accuse the plays of complete "bawdry and profaneness," and the "Short

---

1 Ernest Bernbaum considers *Oroonoko* a pure romance with the fiction masquerading as fact. He has been opposed by Montague Summers and Sackville-West. Bernbaum, Ernest, "Mrs. Behn's Biography a Fiction," *Publications of the Modern Language Association of America,* XXVIII; New Series, XXI (1913), pp. 432-453.
2 Taylor, D. C., *William Congreve* (1931), Chap. VIII, pp. 106-120; Chap. IX, pp. 121-144.

† * Explanation of symbols immediately precedes Chapter XV.

View" terminates with the belief that the end of art is morality. Influenced by Thomas Rymer's *Tragedies of the Last Age Consider'd* (p. 313). Unhappy answers made by Wycherley, Congreve,[1] and others. Collier had no immediate effect: without him the Restoration plays would have passed inevitably into the dull incompetence of the succeeding period; with him the declination was accelerated.[2]

Political and Historical Writers

Edward Hyde, First Earl of Clarendon, 1609—1674, statesman, historian. Tediously overloaded with state papers, *The History of the Rebellion and Civil Wars in England* (published 1702—1704; first true text 1888) is redeemed by fairly direct narrative and is distinguished by a series of well-known portraits influenced somewhat by the character-writers (Vol. 1, p. 248).

Sir William Temple, 1628—1699, statesman, scholar.[3] By espousing the spurious epistles of Phalaris, Sir William Temple's essay *On Ancient and Modern Learning* drew the censure of Bentley's *Dissertation on the Epistles of Phalaris*. Jonathan Swift's *Battle of the Books* (p. 351) gave permanent fame to the controversy. Temple's references to old foreign literature—in his essays *Of Poetry* and *Of Heroic Virtue*—may have influenced medievalists like Gray, Percy, and Macpherson. Not for depth of thought is he to be treasured, but for a clear and simple, balanced and glossed, prose style that holds an importance only a little below that of Halifax and Dryden.

George Savile, Marquis of Halifax, 1633—1695, statesman, writer. *The Lady's New-Years Gift or Advice to a Daughter* (1688) is an aphoristic, gay letter, as brilliant as the discerning portrait of *The Character of Charles the Second* (1750). While his *Lady's Gift* written to his own daughter is the most endearing of his excellent works, the best remembered is the brilliant and humorous *The Character of a Trimmer* (written *c.* 1685; published 1688). In it is best seen his qualities of moderation and detachment; he was known as the "Trimmer" because he advocated the middle or moderate course 'in politics. His

---

1 Congreve's answer, *Amendments of Mr. Collier's False and Imperfect Citations* (1698), while containing some excellent reasoning, was a lame defense. The reply (as Bonamy Dobrée has Swift say in an imaginary conversation) was no more than a feather tickling a pachyderm: for twenty-five years, J. W. Krutch states, Collier continued as "the acknowledged inspiration of a movement against the stage." ("Governmental Attempts to Regulate the Stage After the Jeremy Collier Controversy," *Publications of the Modern Language Association of America,* XXXVIII [1923], pp 153-174.) Nor was Vanbrugh any more successful in *A Short Vindication of the Relapse and the Provok'd Wife from Immorality and Profaneness* (1698). Much better replies to Collier's homily were made by John Dennis in *The Advancement and Reformation of Poetry* (1701), and *The Grounds of Criticism in Poetry* (1704).

2 Krutch, J. W., *Comedy and Conscience after the Restoration* (1924).

3 Marburg, Clara, *Sir William Temple* (1932).
    For the side of his life too little known, refer to *The Letters of Dorothy Osborne to William Temple,* edited by Smith, G. C. M. (1928); *The Early Essays and Romances of Sir William Temple Bt.,* edited by Smith, G. C. M. (1930); and a review of both by Falconer, J. A., "Dorothy Osborne and William Temple," *English Studies,* XIII (1931), pp. 97-105.

opinions, undistorted by personal satire, are moderate, tolerant, and sensible; his style is akin to the French in its neat finality and epigrammatic mannerliness.[1]

Religious Writers

Isaac Barrow, 1630—1677, mathematician, theologian. His long sermons rank among the best in English for weighty earnestness, clear if elaborate organization, and fairly lucid style.

John Tillotson, 1630—1694, Archbishop of Canterbury. The lucidity and the orderliness of style distinguishing his sermons make him, with Dryden, Halifax, and Temple, one of the four chief introducers of modern prose.

Thomas Sprat, 1635—1713, Bishop of Rochester, Dean of Westminster. His refutation (1665) of Samuel Sorbières's observations in England (1664) has been crowded from memory by *The History of the Royal Society* (1667).[2] It is a popular, patriotic, even chauvinistic account, important for demanding that the members of the Royal Society should strive for a more positive and natural way of expression, for a style approaching mathematical plainness. Sprat's own style has a certain hardness, clearness, and ease.

Robert South, 1634—1716, clergyman, preacher. His bitter onslaught upon William Sherlock in 1693 has been forgotten, but not his sermons, of which many editions have been issued. South, if partisan and intemperate, is clear and picturesque, masculine and vigorous.

John Bunyan,[3] 1628—1688, great religious prose writer and great preacher. Son of a tinker[4] or "brasier" of Elstow, near Bedford. Learned reading and writing at the village school. Followed his father's trade. At sixteen, served in the Civil War, and was stationed at Newport Pagnel under the Sir Samuel Luke satirized in Butler's *Hudibras* (1644—1647). Married (*c.* 1649). Among his wife's books were Arthur Dent's *The Plain Man's Pathway to Heaven* and Bishop Bayley's *The Practice of Piety,* and the reading of these made him undergo the amazing emotional experience of sin, despair, and repentance that he described in *Grace Abounding.* Joined John Gifford's non-conformist church in Bedford (1653), where he soon began to preach. Coming into conflict with the Quakers, he wrote *Some Gospel-truths Opened* (1656), a provocative attack upon the teachings of George Fox and his followers. Wife died (*c.* 1656), leaving him with four children. Married Elizabeth (*c.* 1659). At the Restoration Bunyan was arrested under the Con-

1 Foxcroft, H. C., *A Character of a Trimmer* (1946).
2 Edited by Cope, J. I., and H. W. Jones (1958).
3 Brown, John, *John Bunyan* (revised by Harrison, F. M., 1928); Talon, Henri, *John Bunyan* (1951) (Paperbound).
4 More properly, a whitesmith, or worker in the softer metals.

venticle Act, and, upon his refusal to give up preaching, was thrown into the Bedford jail where he remained, except for one short period of freedom, for twelve years (1660—1672). While in prison he wrote nine books, including not only *Grace Abounding,* but also *The Holy City: Or the New Jerusalem* (1665), inspired by a passage in the book of *Revelation* and including an anticipatory picture of the celestial city in *The Pilgrim's Progress: The Holy City* is a commentary upon the symbolism of St. John and may prove Bunyan's familiarity with the Fifth-Monarchy tradition.[1] During his confinement he also wrote *A Confession of My Faith, And A Reason of my Practice* (1672), a statement of his theology that is essentially an explanation of his prejudices. Freed in 1672 by the Declaration of Indulgence, he was appointed pastor to the same church in Bedford, and preached under a license (1672—1675). When the Declaration of Indulgence was revoked, Bunyan was again clapped into jail for a period of several months, during which time he probably wrote the first part of *The Pilgrim's Progress.* Thereafter to the end of his life he was allowed to preach without much hindrance.

Grace Abounding to the chief of Sinners: Or, A Brief and Faithful Relation Of the Exceeding Mercy of God in Christ, to his poor Servant John Bunyan†* (1666). Spiritual autobiography not unworthy of a place beside the *Confessions* of St. Augustine and the *Apologia pro Vita Sua* of Cardinal Newman (p. 533). So concrete and intense is the Puritan conception of the conviction of sin, the sense of damnation and salvation through grace, that it yields not even to *Pilgrim's Progress* in depth of spiritual analysis. Occasionally morbid, sometimes overdone, and frequently overloaded with didactic explanations, but on the whole is intensely absorbing in its plot development, vividly dramatic in its situation, life-like in its homely diction, and passionate in its simplicity of message. Is an excellent preface to *Pilgrim's Progress* and a fine comment upon it.[2]

The Pilgrim's Progress From This World To That which is to come†* (1678—1684).[3] Dream allegory (like *Piers the Plowman,* Vol. 1, p. 56) remarkable for dramatic rather than allegorical values, for romantic aspects,[4] intense presentation of human character and incident,

---

1 Tindall, W. Y., *John Bunyan, Mechanick Preacher* (1934), p. 128 *f.*

2 Grace—abounding grace—is Bunyan's legacy. *The Pilgrim's Progress,* for example, may be described "as the allegorized story of Grace Abounding for all sinners." See Fullerton, W. Y., *The Legacy of Bunyan* (1928); Baillie, J. B., "The Mind of John Bunyan," *The Hibbert Journal,* XXVII (1928-1929), pp. 385-405.

3 There are two parts to *The Pilgrim's Progress* (I, 1678; II, 1684). In naturalness and vividness the first part is superior.

4 *The Pilgrim's Progress* was undoubtedly influenced by romance literature. See Golder, Harold, (1) "John Bunyan's Hypocrisy," *The North American Review,* CCXXXIII (1926-1927), pp. 323-332; (2) "Bunyan's Valley of the Shadow," *Modern Philology,* XXVII (1928-1930), pp. 55-72.

† * Explanation of symbols immediately precedes Chapter XV.

and imaginative projection of actual life[1]—all charged with spiritual meaning. Its homely Saxon English of simplicity and concreteness has a Biblical inevitability and raciness of expression. Inconsistencies do creep in, the allegory may at times break down, the theology may be outworn, and tbe intellectual aspect of the contemplative life may be neglected; but this prose epic of Puritanism lives in more than one hundred languages and dialects into which it has been translated.[2]

The Life and Death of Mr. Badman (1680). In *Pilgrim's Progress* the godfearing travel the road to salvation; in *Mr. Badman* an incorrigible scamp follows the easy way from this world to perdition. Allegorical discourse between Mr. Wiseman and Mr. Attentive approaches the novel in its analytical characterization and anticipates Defoe in its realistic portrayal of vulgar provincial life and contemporary manners. It has, however, moralizing comments and tedious discussions of Mr. Badman's sins, and is also marred by somewhat coarse parts.[3] Inspired by Arthur Dent's *Plain Man's Pathway to Heaven;* indebted to Samuel Clarke's *Mirrour or Looking-Glass Both for Saints and Sinners.*

The Holy War, Made By Shaddai Upon Diabolus, For the Regaining of the Metropolis of the World. Or, The Losing and Taking Again Of The Town of Mansoul* (1682). Flat, long, complicated prose allegory of how Shaddai, the builder of the tcwn of Mansoul, and his son Emmanuel, recapture the metropolis from Diabolus (*i.e.,* the devil). Some dramatic passages in this, his longest work, the central theme of which is the fall and redemption of mankind; compare it with Milton's *Paradise Lost* (Vol. 1, p. 286). Spiritual insight, but lusterless characters. Draws upon his knowledge of soldiering. P. E. More has declared its strong affinity, with *Pilgrim's Progress,* to the old Morality plays (Vol. 1, p. 106); Macaulay has asserted that, after *Pilgrim's Progress,* it is our best allegory. Indebted to Bernard's *Isle of Man.*

The Heavenly Foot-Man: Or, A Description of "The Man that gets to Heaven" (1698). Tract which in plan and detail is suggestive of *Pilgrim's Progress.*[4]

---

1 "The characters whom we recall in *Pilgrim's Progress* are portraits of Bunyan's sectarian ehemies and friends, and the episodes of their pilgrimage were determined by the social and religious preoccupations of the literary mechanick." Tindall, W. Y., *John Bunyan, Mechanick Preacher* (1934), p. VIII.

2 Many works have been said to contain the germ of *The Pilgrim's Progress* or resemblances to it. Some of these putative sources are Jean de Carthenay's *The Voyage of the Wandering Knight,* St. Augustine's *City of God,* some version of Guileville's *Le Pelerinage de L'Homme,* and Bernard's *Isle of Man.* But probably true is Firth's statement that if Bunyan took the hint from any book, it was the Bible.

3 No one can read *Mr. Badman* without recognizing "the absolute honesty of the man who wrote it." The style, too, has Bunyan's voice, "with its Biblical intonation, its love of the plain phrase, its sparing use of the long word." But being more polemical than *The Pilgrim's Progress,* "the long words creep in more often." Dobrée, Bonamy, *Variety of Ways* (1932), "Bunyan's Mr. Badman," pp. 36-45.

4 Gibson, Daniel, Jr., "On the Genesis of *Pilgrim's Progress,*" *Modern Philology,* XXXI: (1935), pp. 365-382.

† * Explanation of symbols immediately precedes Chapter XV.

Comment. In poetry[1] John Milton is the supreme spokesman of seventeenth-century Puritanism; in prose, John Bunyan. Milton the scholar is classical and erudite; Bunyan the self-educated tinker is everyday and earthy. *Paradise Lost* is indebted to several sources; but *Pilgrim's Progress* in any significant sense may have had no other source than the Bible and Bunyan's own imagination.

It would be difficult to say whether Dryden or Bunyan writes the better prose of their period; they share the palm between them. Bunyan's style has an unrehearsed sureness of touch[2]; it is an English shaped out of the rich vernacular of the homely congregations for whom he wrote and to whom he preached, an English enriched and chastened by the reading of the Bible so that possibly no prose is more Biblical in its cadences.[3]

Finally, *The Pilgrim's Progress* occupies an important place in the history of prose fiction. As Raleigh asserts, it is not a novel, but in form and outline it bears the same relation to the novel proper as the Morality bears to the drama proper.[4] Its romantic furniture of giants and dragons and exciting adventures is reminiscent of the romances of chivalry; its humorously natural scenes forecast the realistic novel of manners that flourished in the eighteenth century. Bunyan influenced the novel by his direct narrative method, by writing for the middle classes rather than for fine gentlemen and ladies, and by making his symbolical characters perfectly real and not frigidly artificial.[5]

Philosophy and Science

Thomas Hobbes, 1588—1679, political philosopher. Educated at Magdalen Hall, Oxford. Travelled thrice to the continent, where he made the acquaintance of Descartes, Galileo, Gassendi, and Mersenne (1610, 1629—1631, 1634—1637). Political writings forced him to flee the Continent (1640—1651); unorthodox views, particularly in *Leviathan,* read him out of the exiled court, and he returned to England, submitted to the Council of State, received a pension after the Restoration, and finally retired to Hardwick.

1 Bunyan has left us two deathless songs, both appearing in *Pilgrim's Progress*: "He that is down, needs fear no fall" and "Who would true Valour see." On the whole, however, his poetry is doggerel. It may be fairer to describe his poems as didactic rather than poetic in motive and accomplishment: see Benson, L. F., "The Hymns of John Bunyan," *The Papers of the Hymn Society*, No. 1 (1930).

2 The inspired tinker's style was influenced by Foxe's *Actes and Monuments,* by devotional tracts and books of piety, and, primarily, by the Bible.

3 "As a matter of fact, Bunyan's language was often highly artificial." His dialectical mental habits influenced his language. Moreover, his style was casuistic. Thus contends Haraszti, Zoltán, "The Biography of John Bunyan," *More Books* (The Bulletin of the Boston Public Library), III (1928), p. 380 *f.* (pp. 373-385).

4 Raleigh, Walter, *The English Novel* (1929), p. 116.

5 Mackail has pointed to Bunyan's "extraordinary power of characterization" (p. 21), power "in the relation of incidents and even description of scenes and landscapes" (p. 23), "power as a landscapist" (p. 23), "the largeness of his dramatic sympathy" (p. 25), "strokes of malicious humor" (p. 29), "the sense of romance, and even of romantic beauty" (p. 30), and "mixture of satire with high idealism" (p. 36). Mackail, J. W., *The Pilgrim's Progress* (1924).

Wrote many works, in English and in Latin, including a translation of Homer and a self-satisfied autobiography in Latin verse. Philosophical writings include: *De Cive* (Latin, 1642; English, 1651); *Human Nature* (1650) and *De Corpore Politico* (1650), both of which are really his *Elements of Law, Natural and Politique* published in 1640; *De Corpore* (Latin, 1655; English, 1656), which defended the psychological doctrine of determinism; and *De Homine* (1658), a short sketch of elementary psychology with some chapters on optics.

Hobbism emphasized that the most perfect form of civil government is an absolute monarchy with despotic control over all sanctions whether supernatural or natural, and that man is under obligation to submit unquestionably to such government. This doctrine is consistent with his strict materialism. Hobbes gave a naturalistic basis to ethics and politics. Associational psychology owes him a debt for his teachings as a strict sensationalist. Finally, Hobbes had not only a tremendous influence upon mechanical philosophy but also upon other philosophies.[1]

Behemoth, or an Epitome of the Civil Wars of England (1679). In *Leviathan* he attacked the university system as existing chiefly to support papal against the civil authority; in *Behemoth* he is led by the theory of State Absolutism to oppose education, on the ground, for example, that "the Core of Rebellion . . . are (*sic*) the Universities, which nevertheless are not to be cast away, but to be better disciplin'd."[2] Wished to root out this stimulus to the love of political liberty.

The Leviathan, or the Matter, Forme and Power of a Commonwealth, ecclesiasticall and civill† (1651). Full statement of his doctrine of sovereignty puts its main emphasis upon the thesis that the fundamental characteristic of human nature is egoism,[3] and that man by surrendering his selfish rights in order to create a state of civilized order out of a state of primitive anarchy, owes supreme allegiance to the limitless scope of the sovereign power. Advocates, as he did in *The Elements of Law, Natural and Politique*, the necessity for an arbitrary power, but an absolutism stemming from the divine right of the people as opposed to the divine right of kings. Cogent imagination revealed in hard, economical, clear prose.

---

1 Excellent works on Hobbes are Robertson, G. C., *Hobbes* (1886); Stephen, Leslie, *Hobbes* (1904); Catlin, G. E. G., *Thomas Hobbes* (1922); Brandt, Frithiof, *Thomas Hobbes' Mechanical Conception of Nature* (1928); and Laird, John, *Hobbes* (1934)

2 Hobbes, Thomas, *Behemoth, or an Epitome of the Civil Wars of England, From 1640, to 1660* (1679), p. 56.

3 Hobbes's ethical teaching is based on a mistaken conception of the social order. Consult Nicolson, M. H., "Milton and Hobbes," *Studies in Philology*, XXIII (1926), pp. 406-408, p. 415 (pp. 405-433); Kyle, W. M., "British Ethical Theories: The Intuitionist Reaction Against Hobbes," *The Australasian Journal of Psychology and Philosophy*, V (1927), pp. 113-123.

† * Explanation of symbols immediately precedes Chapter XV.

John Locke, 1632—1704, most influential philosopher of his day and political writer.[1] Son of a Somersetshire attorney. Educated at Westminster School (1646) and Christ College (1652). B.A., 1655; M.A., 1658. Tutor at Christ College (1660). Held the censorship of moral philosophy in Christ College (1661—1664). He secured the degree of Bachelor of Medicine. Physician to his patron, Anthony Ashley Cooper, first Earl of Shaftesbury, to whose Exeter House he moved in 1667. Helped draw up a constitution for the proprietary colony of what later became North Carolina and South Carolina.[2] Expelled from Oxford studentship because of supposed complicity in Shaftesbury's plots. Lived in exile abroad, chiefly in Holland (1683 – 1688). Returned to England after the Revolution of 1688. Became Commissioner of Appeals (1689) and Commissioner of Trade and Plantations under William and Mary (1696). From 1691 until his death Locke lived with Sir Francis and Lady Masham at Oates Manor in Essex.

Truth and Usefulness were his criterion; Reason was his method. Usually called the founder of empirical psychology.[3] Influenced Hume, Berkeley, Voltaire, and Rousseau. Gave a basis to deism and latitudinarian doctrines in religion. Has been regarded as the forerunner of experimental psychology and child study.

His style, while pedestrian and of reasonable clarity, is not infrequently wordy and tedious.

Letters on Toleration (I, 1689; II, 1690; III, 1692). Advocates religious toleration of practically all sects;[4] rejects the idea of absolute monarchy, whether from divine right or from the consent of the people. Second letter ridicules Jonas Proast's scheme; third is a verbose restatement of the tersely-expressed theories in first letter.

Two Treatises of Government (1690). Written upon return to England. An exposition of democracy based on natural law and stemming from the social contract theory: first treatise confutes the doctrine of absolute monarchy founded on divine right—an answer to Sir Robert Filmer's *Patriarcha, or the Natural Power of Kings;* second, professedly written to justify the Revolution of 1688, vindicates the right of a people

---

1 Possibly the best short biographical study of John Locke is Benjamin Rand's introduction to *The Correspondence of John Locke* (1927), pp. 1-73; while an excellent bibliographical introduction to Locke's work is available in Christophersen, H. O., "A Bibliographical Introduction to the Study of John Locke," *Skrifter utgitt av Det Norske Videnskaps—Akademi I Oslo (II. Historisk—Filosofisk Klasse),* 1930, No. 8.

2 Broad, C. D., "John Locke," *The Hibbert Journal,* XXXI (1923-1933), p. 257 (pp. 249-267).

3 His is a half-hearted empiricism, according to Lamprecht, S. P., "John Locke and his *Essay,*" (Tercentenary Lecture Delivered at Columbia University, 1933). A. E. Taylor has reiterated that Hobbes is the founder of empirical psychology: Taylor, A. E., *Thomas Hobbes* (1908), Chap. III, pp. 55-75.

4 According to Locke, both a Catholic, by reason of allegiance to a foreign power, and an atheist, by absence of respect for a moral standard on which social intercourse depends, forfeit the right to toleration.

to depose a monarch. Second treatise, declares Sir Frederick Pollock, is "probably the most important contribution ever made to English constitutional law by an author who was not a lawyer by profession." Proponents of the American War of Independence and the French Revolution found constitutional justification in Locke's politics.

Essay concerning Human Understanding† (1690).[1] Sensible philosophical masterpiece is possibly the earliest extensive critical inquiry into the bases of thought. Rejects the scholastic Aristotelian theory of knowledge; denies the existence of innate ideas; maintains that all knowledge arises ultimately from sense perception or experience.[2] While Locke stated that all knowledge is of empiric origin, yet he believed that knowledge based on experience or demonstration must be supplemented by opinion or faith. May have influenced Pope's *Essay on Man* (p. 362).[3]

Some Thoughts concerning Education† (1693). Experience as a tutor and college teacher taught him that the process of learning, rather than the thing learned, is the desideratum: therefore stressed the information of useful character rather than the inculcation of rote knowledge. Discipline the body through diet and exercise, form good character habits and manners through training, apply reason to all acts. For example, advocates that all children be permitted to run hatless in the wind and sun, fixes the exact time for paying "court to Madam *Cloacina*," and urges that a whipping, when given "upon very urgent Necessity, and as the last Remedy," should be administered by the tutor in the presence of the father.[4]

The Reasonableness of Christianity (1695). Natural religion, he maintained, is founded on reason. While insisting that the interpretation, by man or institution, of difficult passages in the Bible could not be accepted as infallible, emphasized, as he did in his famous essay, that knowledge must be supplemented by faith.

Sir Isaac Newton,1642—1727, mathematician, natural philosopher. To his *Optics* (1704) he appended his *Method of Fluxions,* a great

---

1 The manuscript, originally drafted in 1671, was recently found. It has been edited by Benjamin Rand (1931).

2 Despite the statement of many educators, it may be an error to hold John Locke responsible for a formulation of the doctrine of formal discipline. He may not even belong with the formal disciplinarians. Consult Cuff, Mary Louise (*Sister*), *The Limitations of the Educational Theory of John Locke Especially for the Christian Teacher* (A Dissertation, 1920), and Thayer, V. T., "The Misinterpretation of Locke as a Formalist in Educational Philosophy," *University of Wisconsin Studies in the Social Sciences and History,* Number 3, 1921.

3 McColley, Grant, "Locke's Essay Concerning Human Understanding as a Partial Source of Pope's Essay on Man," *The Open Court,* XLVI (1932), pp. 581-584.

4 Locke, John, *Some Thoughts concerning Education* (1699), pp. 13, 37, 132. See also Jones, D. I., "John Locke, as a Contributor toward Education," *Education,* XLV (1924-1925) pp. 284-295; Schlesinger, E. B., "A Forgotten Champion of Children's Rights," *The Harvard Graduates' Magazine,* XL(1931-1932), pp. 363-371; Broad, C. D., "John Locke," *The Hibbert Journal* XXXI (1932-1933), p. 263 *f.* (pp. 249-267).

† * Explanation of symbols immediately precedes Chapter XV.

mathematical discovery (the elements of differential calculus). He published his epoch-making *Philosophiae Naturalis Principia Mathematica*† (1687), which embodied the law of gravitation and the laws of motion. He is one of the world's greatest scientists.[1]

Diarists

Samuel Pepys (pronounced "Peeps" or "Peps" or, sometimes, "Peppis"), 1633—1703, prince of diarists, outstanding bibliophile, and the father of the British Admiralty.[2] Son of a London tailor. Educated at Huntingdon Grammar School and at St. Paul's School, London. Entered into residence at Magdalene College, Cambridge (1650—1651). B.A., 1653. M.A., 1660. Married fifteen-year-old Elizabeth St. Michel (1655). Entered the service of Sir Edward Montague (1656). Clerk to Sir George Downing, Teller of the Exchequer (1659). Diary begun (January 1, 1660). A clerk of the Privy Seal (1660—1662); Treasurer (1664—1665). Surveyor-General of the Victually Office (1665). Spoke in defense of the Naval Administration at the bar of the House of Commons (1668). Because of failing eyesight,[3] discontinued the *Diary* (May 31, 1669). Death of wife (1669). Secretary of the Admiralty (1673—1679). Master of the Trinity House (1676) and of the Clothworkers' Company (1677). M.P. (1679). Resigned Secretaryship, May 21, 1679; committed to the Tower in connection with the Popish Plot, May 22; released on bail, July 9; discharged, February 12, 1680. Accompanied Lord Dartmouth to Tangier; wrote Tangier Diary (1683). President of the Royal Society (1684—1686), in which capacity he authorized the publication of Newton's *Principia*. Reappointed Secretary of the Admiralty (1684), and not deprived of post until the Revolution of 1688. Retired (*c.* 1690). Died (1703) .

Memoires relating to the State of the Royal Navy(1679—1688; published 1690). His only acknowledged publication.

Correspondence of Samuel Pepys.[4]   While shrewd and human, his letters are not on the whole a literary gold mine.[5] The "Admiralty Letters" comprise fourteen volumes.

---

1 Andrade, E. N. da C., *Isaac Newton* (1954); Cohen, I. B. and R. E. Schofield, eds., *Isaac Newton's Papers & Letters on Natural Philosophy* (1958); Turnbull, H. W., ed., *The Correspondence of Isaac Newton* (1959 – -).

2 "This day died Mr. Sam. Pepys," writes John Evelyn in his *Diary* (May 26, 1703), "a very worthy, industrious and curious person, none in England exceeding him in knowledge of the navy." Consult Tanner, J. R., *Samuel Pepys and The Royal Navy* (1920); Abbott, W. C., *Conflicts with Oblivion* (1924), "The Serious Pepys," pp. 21-25 (pp. 3-33); Chapell, Edwin, (1) *Samuel Pepys as a Naval Administrator* (1933) and (2) *The Tangier Papers of Samuel Pepys* (1935).

3 There are differing views concerning the trouble with his eyesight. See Power, D'Arcy, "Why Samuel Pepys Discontinued His Diary," *The Lancet*, CLXXX (1911), pp. 1687-1690.

4 Edited by Smith, John (1841); Tanner, J. R. (1926, 1929); Heath, H. T. (1955).

5 For a comparison of the letter style of Evelyn and Pepys, who exchanged more than six-score letters, see *Letters and the Second Diary of Samuel Pepys* edited by Howarth, R. G. (1932), p. xv (pp. v-xviii); Marburg, Clara, *Mr. Pepys and Mr. Evelyn* (1935); Ponsonby, Arthur, *Samuel Pepys* (1928), pp. 19-37.

† *   Explanation of symbols immediately precedes Chapter XV.

Diary† (1825). Extends from January 1, 1660, to May 31, 1669. The Plague, the Fire, and the Dutch War, the theatres, operas, and other London amusements, events in the political world and at court, Pepys's flirtations and amours,[1] reflections and repentances—all the minutiae of public and private life are mirrored in the *Diary*. Repetitious, indifferent to grammar, but withal a lovable book of unsparing self-revelation and an invaluable picture of social history told in racy, intimate, egotistic, expressive style, and in gossipy, artless, extremely frank human tone.[2] Written in a kind of shorthand, the *Diary* was first transcribed by John Smith and edited by Lord Braybrooke in 1825.[3] Classic peroration: "And so to bed."[4] Memorable passages: the incident at the funeral of Sir Christopher Mings; the life of the shepherd on Epsom Downes.

John Evelyn, 1620—1706, memoir-writer rather than diarist, a man of means, and an embodiment of cultivated tastes and scholarly interests. He was a Royalist, but took little active part in the Civil War. Twice Secretary of the Royal Society. Wrote more than a score of discourses, tracts, essays, and translations, most of which are interesting and erudite. His works include (1) *The Golden Book of St. John Chrysostom concerning the Education of Children* (dated 1659), a pathetic tribute to the memory of his eldest son Richard; (2) *Fumifugium: or the Inconveniencie of the Aer and Smoak of London Dissipated* (1661), a slim work pointing out many evils; (3) *The History, and Art of Chalcography and Engraving in Copper* (1662); (4) *Kalendarium Hortense* (1664); (5) *Navigation and Commerce* (1674); (6) *Terra, a Philosophical Discourse of Earth* (1676), asserted to be possibly the earliest English scientific study of agriculture; (7) *Numismata. A Discourse of Medals* (1697); and (8) *Acetaria. A Discourse of Sallets* (1699).

---

1 Gamaliel Bradford states that the *Diary* "reeks with love affairs, innumerable, indiscriminate, and infinitely disreputable." Bradford, Gamaliel, *The Soul of Samuel Pepys* (1924), p. 203; see Wilson, John H., *The Private Life of Mr. Pepys* (1959).

2 "The *Diary*," Dr. Wheatley has stated, "is a microcosm, worthy of all elucidations." Yet the *Diary's* one million three hundred thousand words have never been completely transcribed; *e.g.*, Lord Braybrooke's edition contained less than thirty per cent of the whole. Moreover, all printed editions are somewhat unreliable, either because of the transcriber or because of the editors. Even H. B. Wheatley's version seems to be textually corrupt. See the letters to *The London Times Literary Supplement* concerning "The Text of Pepys"; Edwin Chapell, August 11, 1932, p. 569, col. 2; F. McD. C. Turner, August 18, 1932, p. 581, col. 1; W. Matthews, August 25, 1932, p. 593, cols. 1 and 2; W. Matthews, February 2, 1933, p. 76, col. 1. According to H. L. Stewart's "The Pepys Tercentenary," *The Dalhousie Review*, XIII (1933-1934), p. 291 (pp. 273-292), "those who have seen the original, in the *Bibliotheca Pepysiana* at Cambridge, know why a quite unexpurgated copy can never be issued, at least in England." See Bright, Mynors, ed., *The Diary of Samuel Pepys* (Three vols., 1953 edition); O. F. Morshead, ed., *The Diary of Samuel Pepys* (1960) (Also paperbound).

3 The system of shorthand that Pepys used was Thomas Shelton's *Tachy graphy* (1639), which to some degree may have limited Pepys's choice of words, sentence structure, and homely manner of statement. Matthews, W., "Samuel Pepys, Tachygraphist," *The Modern Language Review*, XXIX (1934), p. 404 (pp. 397-404).

4 Franklin P. Adams, a journalist and humorist known widely as F. P. A., has popularized Pepys by a diaristic Saturday column. His work is available in *The Diary of Our Own Samuel Pepys* (Two volumes, 1935).

† * Explanation of symbols immediately precedes Chapter XV.

Sylva, or a Discourse on Forest-Trees and the Propagation of Timber in his Majesties Dominions (1664). Encyclopedic in scope and overrun by classical allusions, this plea for afforestation is one of the earliest authoritative treatises on arboriculture written in English.

Memoirs comprising his Diary and a Selection of his Letters† (1818). More comprehensive but less intimate than Pepys's *Diary,* Evelyn's covers almost seven decades (1640—1706).[1] Includes his travels on the Continent, good portraits of contemporaries, and theatre-goings; but is most valuable as a chronicle of public affairs, especially under the last Stuart rulers and William III. Passage on Pepys's death may be the only contemporary estimate of the great diarist. His most readable work, for there is less of his stylistic tendency to be heavy and involved. Placid, impersonal, keen observation; subdued tones are a slow distillation of his leisurely process of accretion and refinement. Memorable: the description of Whitehall on the eve of the death of Charles II.

The Life of Mrs. Godolphin (1847). Affecting account of extraordinary and delightful friendship begun when Evelyn was past fifty, with Margaret Blagge, who at the age of twenty-four died shortly after the birth of her son.[2] Extant letters and meditations, however, help penetrate "the falsities" of this "equivocal biography."[3] (Written 1678).

---

1 First printed in full by Beer, E. S. De, ed. *The Diary of John Evelyn* (Six vols., 1955). It has been observed that neither Pepys nor Evelyn records any conversation with the other. Note, also, that "Pepys and Evelyn exchanged at least 127 letters in the course of their long friendship": Marburg, Clara, *Mr. Pepys and Mr. Evelyn* (1935).

2 Roscoe, E. S., "A Seventeenth-Century Friendship: John Evelyn and Margaret Godolphin," *The Contemporary Review,* CXXXIX (1931), pp. 78-84.

3 Cropper, Margaret, *Flame Touches Flame* (1949), pp. 155-181; Hiscock, W. G., *John Evelyn and Mrs. Godolphin* (1951), p. 198; *ibid., John Evelyn and his Family Circle* (1955), pp. 119-139.

CHAPTER XVI

THE RESTORATION PERIOD: JOHN DRYDEN

John Dryden, 1631—1700, poet, dramatist, satirist, critic, translator, and miscellaneous writer: one of the chief founders of modern English prose, the first great English critic,[1] the most representative writer of the Restoration,[2] and the greatest literary man of his time. Born at Aldwinkle All Saints in Northamptonshire, of a family with Puritan and anti-monarchical bent. At Westminster School, under Dr. Busby (*c.* 1644—1650). At Trinity College, Cambridge (1650—1654). B.A. (1654). Death of father left him a small estate worth about sixty pounds a year. Probably attached himself as secretary to his wealthy cousin, Sir Gilbert Pickering, Cromwell's Chamberlain. Shifted from Parliamentarian to Royalist (1660). Elected a fellow of the Royal Society (1662).[3] Married Lady Elizabeth Howard (1663), eldest daughter of the Earl of Berkshire and sister of Sir Robert Howard, who bore him three sons and who survived him until 1710. At Charlton, Wiltshire (1666). Granted the M.A. degree from Cambridge (1668). Designated Poet Laureate (*c.* 1668), in succession to William D'Avenant; appointment confirmed when Dryden received a patent as both Poet Laureate and Historiographer Royal (1670). Probably at instigation of John Wilmot, second Earl of Rochester, who attributed to Dryden a passage in Lord Mulgrave's anonymous *Essay upon Satire* probably circulated in manuscript in 1679, Dryden was thrashed by bravos in Rose Alley, Covent Garden (1679). Joined the Roman Catholic Church (1685).[4] With the Revolution of 1688 Dryden, neither abjuring

---

1 His prefaces "are the first serious literary criticism in English by an English poet"—that is, "the first poet to theorize, on any large scale, about his own craft." Eliot, T. S., *John Dryden: The Poet, The Dramatist, The Critic* (1932), p. 54 *f*.

2 "Above all, he has a representative character. This is a peculiar character not always belonging to the greatest men. Milton, for example, though the highest name in his age, does not represent that age; and many other lofty intellects, though *in* one epoch, are of another. But Dryden has this character to a degree not equalled by his successor Pope himself." Kellett, E. E., *Suggestions* (1923), "John Dryden," p. 188 (pp. 185-204).

3 Emerson, O. F., "John Dryden and a British Academy," *Proceedings of the British Academy*, X (1921-1923), pp. 45-58; Bredvold, L. I., "Dryden Hobbes, and the Royal Society," *Modern Philology*, XXV (1927-1928), pp. 417-438; Lloyd, Claude, "John Dryden and the Royal Society," *Publications of the Modern Language Association of America*, XLV (1930), pp. 967-976.

4 It has been customary to criticize Dryden on the ground that he joined the Roman Church in order to curry favor with James II. As T. J. Treadaway states: "Dryden professed allegiance to three established religions in succession: he was a Puritan under Cromwell, an Anglican under Charles II, and a Catholic under James II." But see Root, R. K., "Dryden's Conversion to the Roman Catholic Faith," *Publications of the Modern Language Association of America*, XXII; New Series, XV (1907), pp. 298-308; MacDonald, W. L., "John Dryden: 1631-1931." *The Bookman*, LXXII (1930-1931), pp. 484-488 (pp. 481-488); Jordan, Arnold, "The Conversion of John Dryden," *The Month*, CLVIII (1931), pp. 18-25; Treadaway, T. J., "The Religious Sincerity of John Dryden," *The Ecclesiastical Review*, LXXXV (1931), pp. 277-290.

Catholicism nor pledging allegiance to William III, lost his office and pension[1] as Laureate and Historiographer Royal (1688). Dryden died of gangrene and was buried in the yard of the College of Physicians; but a few days afterwards was disinterred and buried in Westminster Abbey, in Chaucer's grave. A few years later a monument to him was erected there by Lord Mulgrave (John Sheffield, first Duke of Buckingham and Normanby).

POETRY [2]

Political and Personal

Heroick Stanzas (1659). Decasyllabic (iambic pentameter) quatrains in praise of Cromwell. Moves somewhat stiffly and shows discipleship of John Donne; occasionally marred by extravagant fancy. The thirty-fifth stanza may faintly echo Milton's ode, *On the Morning of Christ's Nativity* (Vol. I, p. 278).

Astraea Redux (1660). Panegyrical poem ushers in Charles II and the Restoration, its leitmotif being possibly the political instability of England for almost twenty years. Sound, smooth heroic rimed couplets foreshadow his mastery; but still reminiscent of tortured conceits.

To the Lady Castlemaine (written *c.* 1663; printed 1693). It "runs straight on, swiftly and sweetly," says Mark Van Doren, "quickened into life by the sun of gallantry which shines upon it."

Annus Mirabilis (1667). Iambic pentameter quatrains treat primarily of two events of the "Wonderful Year" of 1666: the first two-thirds describe the engagement with the Dutch fleet culminating in the naval victory over the Dutch on July 25th; the last third treats of the Great Fire in London, September 2 to 7. Like *Heroick Stanzas* and *Astraea Redux,* has an eloquent tone. A certain masculine firmness and musical quality compensate for the strained figures, and the artificially formal, somewhat cloyingly rhetorical, and often dull heroic quatrains. Possibly the victory over the Dutch was too slight to bear the weight of epic grandeur. Examine the interesting preface.

To the Memory of Mr. Oldham† (1684). Mark Van Doren considers these lines to be Dryden's Lydian stone.

Threnodia Augustalis (1685). Pindaric ode is a panegyric of Charles II.

Britannia Rediviva (1688). Poem in honor of the birth of James II's heir.

---

1 Bredvold, L. I., "Notes on Dryden's Pension," *Modern Philology*, xxx (1932-1933), pp. 267-274.

2 Kinsley, James, ed., *The Poems of John Dryden* (Four vols., 1958).

Satiric

Absalom and Achitophel† (I, 1681; II, written chiefly by Nahum Tate, 1682). Allegorical satire in heroic couplets on the Whig attempt of the Earl of Shaftesbury to set up James, Duke of Monmouth, a Protestant, in place of James, Duke of York, a Roman Catholic, as the successor of Charles II. Called the greatest political verse satire in the language; energetic presentation of the political principles of both sides, dignified but damaging characterization, deadly wit, blazing diction, devastating invective. Adapts the Biblical narrative (2 Samuel XIII-XVIII) of Absalom's rebellion against King David to the political situation. *Key*: Absalom (Monmouth), Achitophel (Shaftesbury), King David (Charles II), Zimri (Buckingham), Bethel (Shimei), Corah (Dr. Titus Oates), Doeg (Settle), Ogg (Shadwell), Barzillai (Duke of Ormond), Jotham (Halifax), Abdael (Monk).

The Medall. A Satyre against Sedition (1682). Satire attacks the policy of demagogic appeal to the people. Written when the Whigs (anti-court party) commissioned George Bower to strike a medal (bearing the inscription *Laetamur,* or "Let us rejoice") in commemoration of Shaftesbury's acquittal in November, 1681.

Mac Flecknoe, or a Satyr upon the True-Blew-Protestant Poet, T.S.† (1682). Personal verse-lampoon savagely and blisteringly trounces Thomas Shadwell for his answer, in *The Medal of John Bayes,* to Dryden's *Medall.*[1] Flecknoe is represented (not quite fairly) as the symbol of the mediocre versifier—the holder of first place in the realm of Stupidity who abandons his crown of Dullness to Shadwell. May be the first example of an epic episode employed in a mock epic composed of heroic couplets.[2] Provided the hint for Pope's *Dunciad* (p. 363).

Religious

Religio Laici (1682). Didactic verse-thesis in closely-laced couplets gives a "Layman's Faith"—an eloquently clear and sustained, if not too cogent, argument against Deism, and, crowning that, a spirited support of the Protestant Church of England especially against the Catholics and the Presbyterians. Not entirely without a political purpose. Avowed imitation of Horace's *Epistles* suggested by Henry Dickinson's translation of Richard Simon's *Histoire critique du Vieux Testament.*

---

1 It is doubtful whether or not *The Medall* was intended as an answer to *The Medal of John Bayes,* or whether Shadwell even wrote the latter work. Consult: Babington, P. L., "Dryden Not the Author of 'MacFlecknoe,'" *The Modern Language Review,* XIII (1918), pp. 25-34; Thorn-Drury, G., "Dryden's 'Mac Flecknoe.' A Vindication," (same volume), pp. 276-281; Belden, H. M., "The Authorship of *Mac Flecknoe,*" *Modern Language Notes,* XXXIII (1918), pp. 449-456; and Van Doren, Mark, *The Poetry of John Dryden* (1920), "Appendix: The Authorship of *Mac Flecknoe,*" pp. 339-350.

2 Diffenbaugh, G. L., *The Rise and Development of the Mock Heroic Poem in England from 1660 to 1714* (Thesis, 1925).

† * Explanation of symbols immediately precedes Chapter XV.

The Hind and the Panther† (1687). Allegorical beast-fable defends the Roman Catholic Church as against the Church of England (which he had espoused in *Religio Laici*). "A milk-white hind, immortal and unchang'd" is a symbol of the Roman Church, pursued by the panther, "fairest creature of the spotted kind" (Church of England), the *"Quaking Hare,"* the *"Baptist Boar,"* and other animals representing such sects as the Quakers, the Anabaptists, the Calvinists, and the like. Dryden's most famous religious manifesto is as lucid, logical, and sincere as *Religio Laici;* also intolerant. Sprightly occasional passages. Effective expression not crippled by the tedious argument and the machinery of inappropriate allegory.

Odes

To the Pious Memory of Mrs. Anne Killigrew (1686). Ode or elegy of some musical lines is almost strangled by metaphysical conceits. Johnson considered it the best ode in the language, forgetting, for example, its inferiority in structure to the two St. Cecilia odes. Condemns the licentiousness of Restoration literature: its "lubric and adulterate age" and "the steaming ordures of the stage."

A Song for St. Cecilia's Day† (1687). Ode, a little marred by bombast at end. Prevailingly iambic in measure. Forceful example of onomatopoeia: original score by Giovanni Baptista Draghi still preserved.[1] Both poems in celebration of St. Cecilia's Day have little depth of feeling.

Alexander's Feast; or the Power of Musique† (1697). Second ode written for a London musical society in honor of St. Cecilia, patron saint of music and alleged inventor of the pipe-organ. Like the first, it is mainly iambic in measure, and irregular in meter and stanza. Spirited variety of measure, elaborateness of expression, swing of refrain. Dryden rated it his best poetic piece; Pope praised it highly (*Essay on Criticism, ll.* 374); more than one critic has called it the noblest lyric in the English language but is, according to J. C. Collins,[2] "merely a rhetorically-imposing masterpiece," and, according to Van Doren, perhaps "only immortal ragtime."

DRAMA

Heroic Plays

The Indian-Queen (1663—1664; 1665). Tragedy in heroic verse in which Dryden assisted Sir Robert Howard. Despite good passages, most of the verse seems inapposite to the plot of intrigue, derived from Gomberville's *Polexandre* (1629).[3] Great success attributable in large measure to the melodramatic scenic accessories.

---

1 Brennecke, Ernest, Jr., "Dryden's Odes and Draghi's Music," *Publications of the Modern Language Association of America*, XLIX (1934), pp. 1-36.
2 Collins, J. C., *Essays and Studies* (1895), "John Dryden," p. 89 (pp. 1-90).
3 Clark, W. S., "The Sources of the Restoration Heroic Play," *The Review of English Studies*, IV (1928), p. 55 *ff.* (pp. 49-63).
† * Explanation of symbols immediately precedes Chapter XV.

The Indian Emperour, or, The Conquest of Mexico by the Spaniards (1665; 1667). Popular heroic play deficient in dramatic development of character and artificial in diction; passages of beauty overbalanced by passages of bombast. Song: "Ah fading joy, how quickly art thou past?" has a haunting, reflective beauty. Indebted to such historians as Gómara, Cortez, and Mariana.

*Tyrannick Love, or the Royal Martyr†** (1669; 1670). Heroic play in rimed couplets. Beautiful passages are not entirely lacking, but most of the play is blotched by extravagant language and absurdities which were lampooned in *The Rehearsal*. Stage sacrifices, singing spirits, and "the god of dreams ascending through a trap" were scenic accessories of *The Indian-Queen;* "the magic incantations, the singing angels, and the view of Paradise" are the accessories here. Song: "Ah how sweet it is to love."

The Conquest of Granada by the Spaniards (I, 1670; 1672) and *Almanzor and Almahide, or The Conquest of Granada†** (II, 1670—1671; 1672). Heroic tragedy in rimed couplets outstanding because of its embroiled action: duels and dances, murder, suicide, and trial by combat, three love plots and ten acts. Two parts. Song: "Beneath a Myrtle shade." T. S. Eliot says that Dryden never wrote a better play in rimed couplets. Elaborate scenic effects, sonorous declamation. It is the heroic play *par excellence,* with all the virtues and absurdities, rant and bombast of character, action, and dialogue. Part-influence possibly Madeleine de Scudery's *Almahide.* One of the principal targets of *The Rehearsal* (p. 293).

*Aureng-Zebe†** (1675; 1676). Dryden's last and possibly best heroic tragedy in rimed couplets. In prologue declared himself grown "weary of his long-lov'd Mistris, Rhyme": thereafter he adopted blank verse. Source is Francois Bernier's *Histoire de la dernière révolution des États du Grand Mogol.*

Comedies

The Wild Gallant (1662—1663; 1669). Commonplace prose comedy of "humours." Preposterous plot, artificial characters, very little wit, evident licentiousness. Pepys (February 23, 1662—1663): "so poor a thing as I never saw in my life almost." Conjecture is that plot is possibly borrowed from a Spanish source *via* a French adaptation.[1]

Sr. Martin Mar-all, or the Feignd Innocence (1667; 1668). Sprightly, coarse comedy is an adaptation in prose of the Duke of Newcastle's version (now lost) of Molière's *L'Étourdi.* One scene seems drawn from Quinault's *L'Amant Indiscret ou Le Maitre Étourdi.*

---

1 Allen, N. B., *The Sources of Dryden's Comedies* (1935), Chap. I, " 'The Wild Gallant,' " pp. 1-49.

† * Explanation of symbols immediately precedes Chapter XV.

An Evening's Love, or the Mock-Astrologer (1668; 1671). Best scene of prose comedy is derived from Molière, yet Jacinta and Wildblood seem to be Dryden's creations. Founded on *Le Feint Astrologue* by Thomas Corneille, who had taken it from Calderón's *El Astrologo Fingado;* and also definitely influenced by Molière's *Le Dépit Amoureux.* Four charming songs.

Marriage A-la-Mode†* (1672; 1673). Sprightly comedy, the theme of which is expressed in the first lines of its opening lyric: "Why should a foolish Marriage Vow." Admixture of rime, prose, and blank verse. Two-in-one plot: one is amusing in its comedy, the other ridiculous in its heroics. Somewhat indebted to Molière's *Les Précieuses Ridicules.* Melantha may be the prototype of Congreve's Millamant.

The Assignation; or, Love in a Nunnery (1672; 1673). Entertaining play, borrowed from Scarron's *Le Roman Comique* and perhaps Calderon's *Con·Quien Vengo Vengo,* was driven off the boards by the nature of its theme. Irreverent jokes.

The Kind Keeper; or, Mr. Limberham (1677—1678; 1680). His most original comic drama was prohibited after three performances because, as Dryden explained, it suffered from the crime of expressing too much of the vice it described. Realistic depiction. One group of critics (Langbaine, Saintsbury) praises its dramatic qualities; another (Scott, Nicoll) deplores its indecencies. Influenced by *Tartuffe* and *Les Fâcheux,* but, as in the case of *The Wild Gallant,* no definite source proven.

Amphitryon; or, The Two Socia's† (1690; 1690). Enthusiasm of style distinguishes the early part of this immoral comedy of prose and blank verse. Has added felicitous characters to Plautus's *Amphitruo.* Song: "Fair *Iris* I love, and hourly I dye."

Tragi-comedies

The Rival Ladies (1664; 1664). Drama usually criticized for its plot and characters. Humorless, despite Pepys's assertion (August 4—6, 1664) that it is a "most pretty witty play." Improbable intrigue—derived partly from Scarron's *Le Roman Comique,* Samuel Tuke's *Adventures of Five Hours,* and Petronius Arbiter's *Satyricon*—is more intricate and interesting than *The Wild Gallant.* Introduces some scenes in rime. Significant as a *tour-de-force*: its use of the rimed couplet in blank verse marks it an incipient heroic play.

Secret-Love or the Maiden-Queen† (1666—1667; 1668). Tragicomedy based on Madeleine de Scudéry's *Artamène ou Ɔe Grand Cyrus* and *Ibrahim ou L'Illustre Bassa,* is a compound of heroic couplets, blank verse, and pleasant prose. Memorable for its witty prologue and comic sub-plot.

---

† * Explanation of symbols immediately precedes Chapter XV.

*The Spanish Fryar or The Double Discovery** (1679—1680; 1681). Tragi-comedy mocks at the Roman Catholic priesthood: the only play which James II prohibited after his accession. Well-managed, vigorous plot; the comic parts are in prose. Song: "Farewell ungratefull Traytor." Traces of Fletcher, Molière, Quinault's *L'Astrate,* and, especially, of Gabriel de Bremond's *Le Pelerin.*

Love Triumphant; or, Nature will Prevail (1694; 1694). His last play is a tragi-comedy the farce of which is suggestive of the *commedia dell'arte.* Probably not indebted to *Monsieur de Pourceaugnac.*

Tragedies

Amboyna (1673; 1673). Negligible tragedy in bitter prose and blank verse traditionally interpreted as designed at the request of Lord Clifford in order to stir up war sentiment against the Dutch.[1]

All for Love: or, the World well Lost† (1677; 1678). His first play in blank verse is possibly his best play. While deficient in the exuberant poetry, sweeping and human scope of characterization, and subtle analysis of Shakespeare, it is more than a mere retelling of the story of Antony and Cleopatra: it is actually a better piece of dramaturgy than Shakespeare's play, and in Dobrée's words, "has a more tragic effect." Good re-creation of North's characters, artificial preservation of the unities; energetic, noble blank verse, though full of sentiment, is, as Dobrée says, never sentimental.[2] Something of his old stiff rhetoric still in evidence. In 1695 Dryden himself said, "I never writ anything for myself but *Antony and Cleopatra."*

Don Sebastian, King of Portugal†* (1689; 1690). Dignified tragi-comedy in blank verse shares the palm with *All for Love,* as Dryden's best play. Both possess tragic power, but *Don Sebastian* has a more intricate plot. Comic plot derived from Bremond's *Le Pelerin.* Sinewy verse, extravagant sentiment.

Cleomenes, The Spartan Heroe (1692; 1692). Last heroic play, based on Plutarch's account of the Spartan, was banned at first because its chief character was thought to remind people of the fate of James II.

Adaptations and Collaborations

The Tempest or the Enchanted Island (1667; 1670), a poor new version of Shakespeare in collaboration with D'Avenant; *Troilus and Cressida, or, Truth Found too Late* (1679; 1679), its ineffectively

---

1 *Amboyna* and *The Spanish Fryar* are often utilized in an attempt to prove that Dryden was a trimmer and time-server. This is not so, says Bredvold, L. I., "Political Aspects of Dryden's *Amboyna* and *The Spanish Fryar," Essays and Studies in English and Comparative Literature,* by Members of the English Department of the University of Michigan, VIII (1932), pp. 119-132.

2 But see Spencer, Hazelton, *Shakespeare Improved* (1927), pp. 210-221.

† * Explanation of symbols immediately precedes Chapter XV.

rewritten dialogue making the adaptation verge upon a travesty of Shakespeare's drama, but containing "Can life be a blessing"; *Oedipus* (1678, 1679), written in collaboration with Lee (p. 300) and showing, in Dryden's contribution of the first and third acts, traces of Dryden's recent study of Shakespeare; and *The Duke of Guise* (1682, 1683), political venture with Lee, to which Dryden probably contributed the opening scene, the fourth act, and part of the fifth. See page 301.

Operas

The State of Innocence, and Fall of Man (entered at Stationers' Hall, 1674; printed 1677; never acted[1]), an adaptation of part of Milton's *Paradise Lost* in rimed couplets, the purpose being to demonstrate the inferiority of blank verse to rime; *Albion and Albanius* (1685; 1685); and *King Arthur: or, The British Worthy* (1691; 1691), for which Purcell wrote the music, and including "How happy the Lover," "Your Hay it is Mow'd, and your Corn is Reap'd," and "Fairest Isle, all Isles Excelling."

Translations and Paraphrases

Despite the note of independence struck for modern writers in *Of Dramatick Poesie,* Dryden was a frequent translator and paraphraser of classical and other literature. By these translations, "almost as much as by his original poems,"[2] Dryden "helped to form our English tongue."

His translations appeared in: *Ovid's Epistles, Translated by Several Hands* (1680—the Preface and two epistles by Dryden); *The Satires of Juvenal and Persius* (begun 1690; prefatory "Discourse Concerning Original and Progress of Writing," dated 1692; published 1693); *The Works of Virgil* (begun 1693; published 1697); and in six volumes of *Miscellany Poems—Miscellany Poems by the most Eminent Hands* (1684—translations from Ovid, Virgil, and Horace); *Sylvae, or, the Second Part of Poetical Miscellanies* (1685—besides Preface, contains translations from Virgil, Lucretius, Theocritus, and Horace); *Examen Poeticum: Being The Third Part of Miscellany Poems* (1693—comprised of Preface, translations from Ovid and Horace, and, notably, the paraphrase of the Latin hymn, "Veni Creator Spiritus"[3]); *The Annual Miscellany* (1694—containing a translation of Virgil's Third Georgic); *Poetical Miscellanies: The Fifth Part* (1704); and *Poetical Miscellanies: The Sixth Part* (1709).

Other translations include such works as Bouhour's *Vie de Saint Ignace de Loyola* ("The Life of St. Ignatius," 1686), Maimbourg's *The*

---

1 Thaler, Alwin, *Shakspere's Silences* (1929), Chap. V, "Milton in the Theatre," p. 222 ff. (pp. 209-256).

2 Eliot, T. S., *John Dryden: The Poet, The Dramatist, The Critic* (1932), p. 20.

3 *Hymns attributed to John Dryden,* edited by Noyes, G. R., and Potter, G. R. (1937).

History of the League (1684), St. Euremont's *Miscellaneous Essays* (1692), and Du Fresnoy's *De Arte Graphica* (1695). But most important were:

The Works of Virgil (1697). Vigorous but reckless translation in which the poetry of the original is dwindled into the rhetoric of Dryden. Absence of the Virgilian spirit; nervous couplets.

Fables Ancient and Modern† (1700). Successful verse-paraphrases of tales by Homer, Ovid, Boccaccio, and Chaucer. Admirable narrative verse, the best being Boccaccio's *Cymon and Iphigenia* and *Theodore and Honoria,* and Chaucer's *Palamon and Arcite* and *The Cock and the Fox.* Preface is a delightful apologia for his life and works.

Literary Criticism[1]

DEDICATION to *The Rival Ladies* (1663; 1664). Defended the propriety of rime in serious poetry, stating that rime curbs the very imagination it stimulates and that rime is as natural as blank verse. Praises the romantic plays of Shakespeare while defending neo-classical rime.

DEDICATION to *Annus Mirabilis* (1667). Already much beyond the embryonic stage is his mastery of a prose style fit for everyday use.

Of Dramatick Poesie, An Essay† (1668). Dialogue in Socratic form among four persons: Eugenius (Charles Lord Buckhurst, afterward Earl of Dorset); Lisideius (Sir Charles Sedley); Crites (Dryden's brother-in-law, Sir Robert Howard); and Neander (Dryden himself). The interlocutors discuss whether the Ancients were superior to the Moderns and whether Elizabethan taste in the drama should yield to that of the French; the main purposes, however, are to vindicate the use of rime in drama and to vindicate the English stage over the French: but the result is chiefly a vindication of the Restoration dramatists and, beyond that, of the *modern* writer.

Probably the finest example of the precision and range of his prose style and his critical powers. Long speeches; imaginative, rhythmical, direct prose; critical soundness. Indebted to Corneille's prefaces and discourses. Only Bernard Shaw, according to Bredvold, is a greater preface maker.

PREFACE to *The Indian Emperour* (Second Edition, 1668). Sir Robert Howard, in the "preface" to *Foure New Plays* (1665), questioned the propriety of using the rimed couplet in dramatic verse, there-

---

1 Bohn, W. E., "The Development of John Dryden's Literary Criticism," *Publications of the Modern Language Association of America,* XXII; *New Series,* XV (1907), pp. 56-139; Frye, P. H., *Literary Reviews and Criticisms* (1908), "Dryden and the Critical Canons of the Eighteenth Century," pp. 130-189. Saintsbury, George, *A History of English Criticism* (1925), pp. 111-131 (Chap. III, pp. 105-157); Gardner, W. B., *The Prologues and Epilogues of John Dryden* (1951); Wimsatt, W. K., Jr., and Cleanth Brooks, *Literary Criticism* (1959), pp. 182-220.

† * Explanation of symbols immediately precedes Chapter XV.

by opposing Dryden's statement in the dedicatory epistle to *The Rival Ladies*. Dryden took issue with Sir Robert by characterizing him as Crites in *Of Dramatick Poesie*. Howard retorted in a preface to *The Great Favorite, or the Duke of Lerma* (1668). "A Defence of an Essay of Dramatique Poesie," prefixed to the second edition of *The Indian Emperour* and not reprinted with later editions of the play, is Dryden's sarcastic and reasoned rejoinder.[1] Nowhere else is there a more complete statement of Dryden's theories about the use of rimed couplets in tragedy.[2]

PREFACE to *The Conquest of Granada by the Spaniards* (I, 1670; 1672). "Of Heroique Playes," prefixed to this tragedy, defends the use of heroic verse as being naturally suited to the elevated and artificial diction of the heroic play. Also states that the dullness of French plays has its source in the French decorum in character.

EPILOGUE to *Almanzor and Almahide, or The Conquest of Granada* (See page 329). "The Defence of the Epilogue" criticizes Fletcher and certain aspects of Shakespeare, and maintains the superiority of Restoration comedy over that of Elizabethan.

PREFACE to *The State of Innocence* (1674). Possibly receiving its impulse from Boileau's commentary upon Longinus, "The Author's Apology for Heroique Poetry, and Poetique Licence" denounces the merely correct writer and hymns Milton's *Paradise Lost* as one of the noblest poems in English. Milton, Dryden has said, has both the Virgilian majesty and the Homeric loftiness of mind.

PROLOGUE to *Aureng-Zebe* (1675, 1676). Confesses himself to be tired of rime, re-affirms his genuine admiration for Shakespeare,[3] and retracts his belittling contrast of the Elizabethan with his own age. (In *Of Dramatick Poesie* he had criticized even Shakespeare for his irregularities.)

PREFACE to *Troilus and Cressida* (1679). Prefixes to his adaptation almost a textbook of dramatic technique. Urges contemporary dramatists to excel the Elizabethans in greater compression and unity of plot: successfully exemplified in *All for Love* (p. 331). This preface, called "The Grounds of Criticism in Tragedy," applies Aristotle's theory of tragedy to the practice of Shakespeare and Fletcher.

---

1 Dryden's personality, however, must have been · a very likeable one. Despite this literary quarrel, in which he worsted Sir Robert, Dryden seems to have remained on good terms with his opponent.

2 "On three other important points the two authors were in fact in full agreement. Both admit that verse is attractive when used in the right way, that on the whole English plays are to be preferred above all others, and that the old rule of the Unities is absurd. But Dryden unfairly makes Howard stoutly maintain the opposite views on the last two questions when metamorphosed into Crites in the *Essay*." *Dryden and Howard, 1664-1668*, edited by Arundell, D. D. (1929), p. XIV (pp. V-XIV).

3 Of Dryden's criticism of Shakespeare, particulary in *Of Dramatick Poesie*, Johnson has written: "It is a perpetual model of encomiastic criticism, exact without minuteness, and lofty without exaggeration."

Preface to *Sylvae, or the Second Part of Poetical Miscellanies* (1685). Of significance because its main subject is the matter of translation, to which Dryden devoted some years.

Dedication to *Examen Poeticum* (1693). Important piece of critical writing. Protests against unfounded critical abuse (probably having Rymer in mind); defends the English drama against those who would belittle it by comparison with Aeschylus, Euripides, and Sophocles; and discusses all too briefly his own principles of prosody.

Preface to *Fables Ancient and Modern*† (1700). Not only famous for its re-discovery of Chaucer but also for being, except for *Of Dramatick Poesie,* his best prose work. Also contains an incidental answer to Jeremy Collier (p. 313), who had plainly described the songs in Dryden's plays as "smutty"; but it should also be recalled that Dryden, in *To the Pious Memory of Mrs. Anne Killigrew,* anticipated Collier's criticism of the licentiousness of Restoration literature by thirteen years.

Comment. Primarily because of his very competent and remarkable versatility Dryden is one of our greatest men of letters. Tales and satires, prologues and epilogues, odes and songs, religious poems and translations; comedies and tragedies, heroic dramas and operas; literary questions of the day—Dryden excels his contemporaries in every field except that of comedy.[1]

POETRY — His poems have the qualities of his plays — some middling songs and unspontaneous lyrics, careful and melodic versification, and lack of poetic expression of the different emotions. Despite touches of false ornament and operatic banality, his odes are splendid. As a verse-satirist and character-writer he is unequalled, for he is consummately compact of thought and even musical, devastating in portraiture, and so superb in handling the heroic couplet that it became established as the fashion for satiric poetry. Taine describes his poetic genius as "pre-eminently robust and unromantic"; Gosse describes him as "the strongest poet of the age of prose."

PLAYS—Dryden reveals skill in devising the kind of situations and type of performance demanded by his frivolous and somewhat debauched audience, which anticipated not human action or genuine passion but rhetorical discussion of love and indecency of expression. His comedies pandered deliberately to the corrupt taste of the Merry Monarch's court[2]; and, in later years, Dryden himself regretted their

---

1 Dryden himself admitted that he was not cut out for writing comedy, that he lacked "that gaiety of humour which is required," and that "some of my contemporaries, even in my own partial judgment, have outdone me in comedy."

2 His coarseness is deliberate. At one time he avowed: "Nothing but madness can please madmen, and a poet must be of a piece with the spectators to gain a reputation with them." At another moment: "I confess my chief endeavors are to delight the age in which I live. If the humour of this be for low comedy, small accidents and raillery, I will force my genius to obey it . . . ." Recall, however, his manliness in apologizing for his attitude.

catchpenny character. The comedies are often interspersed with songs, frequently excellent, but, like his Prologues and Epilogues, just as frequently disfigured by the *double-entendre* and coarseness of sentiment. Its prose-parts, according to T. S. Eliot, are couched in a transition prose rather than in the perfected style of his best prefaces. Although condemned by Horace Walpole as being compounded of bombast and heroic obscenity, his tragedies contain lines still current and speeches still rhetorically powerful. His dramas are immoderate in humor and extravagant in action, and are possessed of a comic imagination impoverished to depletion by the conventional machinery of low jokes and intrigue. Yet throughout there are evidences of clear thinking, sure touch, excellent versification, copious power to carve out uninspired thoughts, powerful declamatory dialogue, and charming prefaces.

PROSE—Dryden wrote such prose works as a "Life of Plutarch" prefixed to *Plutarch's Lives, Translated by Several Hands* (1683), "A Character of Polybius and His Writings," prefacing a translation of Polybius by Sir Henry Sheers (1693), "A Parallel betwixt Painting and Poetry," which preceded the translation of Du Fresnoy's *De Arte Graphica* (1695), and a "Life of Lucian" written in 1696 for a projected translation of Lucian's *Dialogues* by several hands (1711)[1]; but his most important prose writings consist in the main of "occasional" essays and critical prefaces to poems and plays. While somewhat hastily written and not too well organized, his prose represents a convenient, an informal and everyday intimacy at variance with the style known to England for two centuries. Dryden's style anticipated the great prose writers of the succeeding age in more concise sentences and natural word-order, idiomatic energy and unmannered, clear, fluent style, and in sound sense, a sane viewpoint, and an enthusiasm for literature. That Dryden's chief glory is his prose is a frequent statement[2]; but a more accurate one may be that it is largely to his work as literary critic that he owes his pre-eminent position as a man of letters.

---

1 Craig, Hardin, "Dryden's Lucian," *Classical Philology*, XVI (1921), pp. 150-163 (pp. 141-163).

2 "The main point, which I wish to drive home about Dryden is this: that it was Dryden who for the first time, and so far as we are concerned, for all time, established a *normal* English speech, a speech valid for both verse and prose, and imposing its laws which greater poetry than Dryden's might violate, but which no poetry since has overthrown." Eliot, T S., *John Dryden: The Poet, The Dramatist, The Critic* (1932), p. 21 *f.*

Chapter XVII

THE AUGUSTAN AGE: THE TRIUMPH OF NEO-CLASSICISM
(1700—1744)

Historical Background

The Reign of Queen Anne (1702—1714). (1) War of the Spanish Succession (1701—1713); called, in the United States, Queen Anne's War. (2) Battle of Blenheim (1704). (3) Whigs obtain a majority in Parliament (1705). (4) Battle of Ramillies (1706). (5) Last royal veto of a Parliament act (1707). (6) England and Scotland are united under the name of Great Britain (1707). (7) Battle of Oudenarde (1708). (8) Battle of Malplaquet (1709). (9) Property Qualification Act (1711). (10) Occasional Conformity Act (1711). (11) Peace of Utrecht (1714). (12) Schism Act (1714). (13) Death of Anne (1714); the crown passes to the Hanoverians, George I, George II, and George III.

The Reign of George I (1714—1727). (1) The Riot Act passed (1715). (2) Jacobite demonstrations (1715). (3) Septennial Act (1716). (4) Repeal of the Occasional Conformity and Schism Acts (1717). (5) The Triple Alliance (1717). (6) The "South Sea Bubble" (1720). (6) The leadership of Walpole (1721—1742). (7) Death of George I (1727).

The Reign of George II (1727—1760). (1) The First Annual Bill of Indemnity (1728). (2) The Rise of Methodism (1729—1791). (3) Use of Latin in law courts abolished (1731). (4) War of the Polish Succession (1733). (5) Porteous demonstrations (1736). (6) War with Spain, or War of Jenkins's Ear (1739—1741); War of the Austrian Succession (1740—1748). (7) Fall of Walpole (1742). (8) War declared between England and France (1744), bringing the latter into the War of the Austrian Succession. (For a continuation of the important events in the reign of George II, see page 366.)

Social Conditions

a) **Coffee-Houses.** Coffee had been introduced into England in 1652, and the coffee-houses had become fashionable *foci* for gambling, gossip, and literary-political discussion. Coffee-houses are especially important during the Augustan period. Among the most famous were Will's, White's, Button's, Child's, the Cocoa-Tree, Jonathan's, St. James s, Dolly's Chop House, Lloyd's, and the Grecian.

b) **The New Morality.** This period saw in general a reaction against the extreme licentiousness of the Restoration, just as the latter had seen one against that of extreme Puritanism. Order, measure, and propriety became the cardinal neo-classic qualities in literature; gentler manners, cleaner morals, and true gentility became fashionable in society. (See *The Spectator* and *The Tatler,* pp. 341, 344.)

Economic Conditions

In rainy weather the gutters still became torrents carrying animal and vegetable filth. At night it was hazardous to walk about the streets, for not only were they infested by thieves and robbers but also by swaggering, dissolute young gentlemen who broke windows and beat peaceful citizens. If such was true of the city of London, how much truer, then, was it of the highways of England, where the ruts were deep and the descents precipitous, and where the traveller always ran considerable risk of being knocked down and robbed. The criminal law was cruel; the death penalty was often enforced for petty offences.

GENERAL VIEW OF THE LITERATURE

The Augustan age in English literature marks the triumph of neo-classicism. The writers endeavored to imitate the characteristics of Virgil, Horace, Cicero, and Lucretius, and others of the age of Augustus Caesar in Rome, who in their day had sought to emulate the methods of the classical Greek writers of a few centuries earlier; they flattered themselves that with them English life and literature had reached the culminating stage of human perfection in social manners and in letters, a period of civilization and elegance corresponding to that which had existed at Rome under the Emperor Augustus. For almost a century, reason and the critical habit continued to prevail over emotions and the creative spirit. Rationalism and formalism were supreme in this self-styled Augustan period, one that took its primary cue from Descartes's statement: *Cogito ergo sum* ("I think, therefore I exist"). The Queen Anne period, as it is sometimes called, was essentially a second-hand Augustanism or a third-hand classicism. Despite its superficial, pseudo-classical imitation and a relatively uninspired spirit, this age of prose and reason set up rules of writing and principles of good form, and established worthy standards of restraint, decorum, and common sense.

The Beginnings of the Essay

The essay originated in France with Montaigne, who explained in his *Essais* (1580—1588) that by the word he meant an *attempt.* In English literature the essay begins with Bacon (Vol. 1, pp. 269—271); and with Cowley's *Several Discourses* (Vol. 1, p. 266) the form is brought close to perfection by an easy vivacity, colloquial frankness, and perfect lucidity. Another contributory influence in the seventeenth century was the character-writers (Vol. 1, p. 248).[1]

The Beginnings of Journalism

a) **The Newspaper.** The *Acta diurna,* posted daily in a public place by order of Julius Caesar, is probably the earliest recorded effort to inform citizens of current events. In Venice, in 1562, began the posting of the *Notizie scritte,* often called the *Gazetta* because that was the small fee charged readers by the government. News-sheets written by professional letter-writers were published irregularly during the reign of Elizabeth. The first regular English paper was Nathaniel Butler's *The Weekly Newes* (1622 — 1641). During the Civil War many courants, diurnals, and news-sheets were issued. Prominent were Roger L'Estrange's *The Intelligencer* (1663); *The London Gazette* (1666), the only serious attempt at journalism during the seventeenth century, one controlled by the Under-Secretary of State; John Dunton's *Athenian Gazette* (1690); *The Daily Courant* (1702—1735), the first daily paper in England; Steele's *Guardian* (1713), a daily, and his *Englishman* (1713—1715), thrice weekly; and John Wilkes's *North Briton* (1762). See also Defoe (p. 352).

b) **The Periodical.** Probably the first periodical in Europe was the French *Journal des savants* (1665). The first English literary periodical was *Mercurius Librarius* (1680). Others were *Weekly Memorials for the Ingenious* (1682—1683), and Peter Motteaux's *Gentleman's Journal* (1691—1694). It was chiefly through the weekly review that the essayists reached their readers. Not until the publication of the *Gentleman's Magazine*[2] (1731—1866) was the word *magazine* used in the sense of a periodical designed primarily for entertainment. For other eighteenth-century periodicals, see the work of Addison, Steele, Swift, Defoe, Pope (this chapter), and of Johnson (p. 367), Goldsmith (p. 374), and Fielding (p. 391).

Prose and Poetry

In prose the most important feature is the emergence of the middle style, as represented by the school of Addison, and of the plain style, as represented by the work of Swift and Defoe; in poetry the most outstanding feature is the domination of the heroic couplet. Of importance as a forecast of the revival of the freer forms of poetry is the blank verse of Thomson's *Liberty* and Young's so-called *Night Thoughts* (pp. 411, 415). The triumph of neo-classicism is complete: while the lyric and the ode survive feebly, the pastoral and the satire are most popular.

---

1 The English essay has its roots in the Elizabethan period, in the pamphleteering work of Nash, Greene, and Lodge, and even in the essay-pamphlet of Sidney's *Defence.* See Vol. 1, pp. 139, 143, 153.
2 Carlson, C. L., *The First Magazine* (1939).

MAJOR PROSE WRITERS

Joseph Addison, 1672—1719, essayist, playwright, poet, states-man.[1] Son of a Wiltshire clergyman. Educated at Queen's College (1687) and at Magdalen College, Oxford (1689). M.A. (1693). Fellow-ship (1697—1711). Travelled four years (1699—1703) in France, Germany, Italy, and elsewhere on government pension granted through the influence of Charles Montagu, later Lord Halifax; but withdrawn on the fall of the Whigs at the death of William III. While abroad, wrote the poor *Dialogues on the Usefulness of Ancient Medals* and the equally poor *Remarks on several parts of Italy* (1705). Under-Secretary of State (1706—1708). Member of Kit-Kat Club. Parliament (1708—1719). Secretary to Lord Halifax (1708). Chief Secretary in Ireland to Lord Wharton, the Lord Lieutenant (1709). Founded the *Whig Examiner*. Contributed to *The Tatler* (1709—1711), *The Spectator* (1711—1712), *The Guardian* (1713), and *The Freeholder* (1715—1716). A commissioner for Trade and Colonies (1716). Married Charlotte, Countess dowager of Warwick (1716), which aided him in obtaining the appointment as Secretary of State (1717—1718). Buried in Westminster Abbey.

Poems

Letter from Italy. Best poem. Stereotyped rhapsody and British cant about Liberty can not destroy the basic poetic warmth and imagination. Epistle in verse written by Addison during his residence abroad (1699—1703), and sent to Lord Halifax.

Account of the Greatest English Poets (1694). Shakespeare is unmentioned, while Cowley is described as "a mighty genius."

The Campaign (1704). Poem in elegant heroic couplets exults over the victory at Blenheim (August, 1704). Uninspiring catalogue of places and persons; smoothly-wrought but middling couplets. Best known for its angel-simile. Commissioned by the Chancellor of the Exchequer, upon Halifax's recommendation, to write the poem that brought him the post of Under-Secretary of State.

The Spacious Firmament on High (1712). Generally considered unlyrical in his poetry, Addison is best remembered for his "Divine Ode" or hymn. (*The Spectator,* No. 465.)

---

1 While Addison's life was so ordered that it has never become the prey of the biographer, yet it is only too likely that his character is less flawless than that described by Macaulay, and that Steele's has more shrewdness than that with which it is usually credited. Addison's unpublished letters "disclose his extreme eagerness for fees and his great fondness for the bottle." Addison is usually regarded as a paragon, and Steele, in Colley Cibber's words, as "the most innocent rake that ever trode the rounds of indulgence"; and, furthermore, the estimate of the merits of both Addison and Steele as men has affected the estimate of their merits as writers. Murray, R. H., "Addison in Ireland," *The Nineteenth Century and After*, LXXV (1914), p. 1274 (pp. 1067-1084, pp. 1257-1274); Walker, Hugh, "Wise Men Who Have Passed for Fools," *The Yale Review*, V (1916), pp. 590-595 (pp. 587-604); and Strahan, J. A., "Swift, Steele, and Addison," *Blackwood's Magazine*, CCVIII (1920), pp. 499-504 (pp. 493-510); Smithers, Peter, *The Life of Joseph Addison* (1954).

Plays

Rosamond (1705). Written "after the Italian manner" in order to oust the influential Italian opera from the English stage. Only time when he manifests an almost unbecoming gaiety. Bits of song represent his warmest and most imaginatively-expressed poetry. Unsuccessful until T. A. Arne re-wrote the libretto some years after Addison's death.

Cato* (1713). Wooden blank-verse tragedy on Greek classical lines as interpreted by the French school of Racine and Boileau; prologue by Pope, a notorious Tory, and epilogue by Dr. Samuel Garth, a notorious Whig. Frigid plot, lifeless characterization, devitalized speech, anemic love-scenes, unpoetic poetry, absurd observance of the unity of place. Motivated by rationalized rant, stilted declamation, and moral philosophy rather than by tragic conflict and dramatic imagination.[1] Dazzling triumph attributable to political *reclamé*: Whig and Tory each dared not but see in the banished Cato's devotion to liberty the glorification of the principle that his party represented.[2]

The Drummer (1715). Moral prose comedy of little consequence.

Major Periodical[3]

The Spectator† (March 1, 1711—December 6, 1712[4]; revived June 18, 1714—December 20, 1714). Periodical, appearing daily except Sunday, succeeded the thrice-weekly *Tatler* (p. 344); imitated both in England and on the Continent. Among the contributors, who included Pope and Thomas Tickell, Addison became the dominating figure. Out of 555 essays of the original publication, Addison wrote 274, all signed by one of the four letters, C.L.I.O.; and Steele wrote 236. Prominent members of the mythical club included Sir Roger de Coverley (the country gentry), Will Honeycomb (the men of fashion), Sir Andrew Freeport (the men of commerce), and Captain Sentry (the men of

---

1 In *Remarks upon Cato, a Tragedy,* John Dennis acutely and witheringly pointed out the defects and absurdities of this excellent example of pseudo-classical tragedy.
   At this point of contact between Addison and Dennis, it may not be entirely inopportune to reaffirm that Addison had no antipathy to mountains and that Gray was not the first literary gentleman of the eighteenth century to find beauty in them. As a matter of fact, both Dennis and Addison had an emotional appreciation of mountain scenery. Havens, R. D., "Romantic Aspects of the Age of Pope," *Publications of the Modern Language Association of America,* XXVII; New Series, XX (1912), p. 313 *ff.* (pp. 297-324): Thorpe, C. DeW., "Two Augustans Cross the Alps: Dennis and Addison on Mountain Scenery," *Studies in Philology,* XXXII (1935), pp. 463-482.

2 Samuel Johnson: "The Whigs applauded every line in which Liberty was mentioned, as a satire on the Tories; and the Tories echoed every clap, to show that the satire was unfelt."

3 Marr, G. S., *The Periodical Essayists of the Eighteenth Century* (1924), Chap. II, "The *Tatler* and *Spectator*—and Other Periodical Work of Addison and Steele," pp. 21-63.

4 The Stamp Act of 1712 is generally believed to have been the cause of suspension of *The Spectator.* Many have charged that Swift was the first to suggest such an act, but this is not true, according to Thomas, J. M., "Swift and the Stamp Act of 1712," *Publications of the Modern Language Association of America,* XXXI; New Series, XXIV (1916), pp. 247-263.

† * · Explanation of symbols immediately precedes Chapter XV.

soldiery), each representing a different class of society, with the Spectator himself representing the observing gentleman who had settled in London.

Expressed purpose was "to enliven morality with wit, and to temper wit with morality," and to bring "philosophy out of closets and libraries, schools and colleges, to dwell in clubs and assemblies, at tea-tables and in coffee-houses" (No. 10, March 12, 1711). Banteringly but effectively holds up to ridicule prevailing manners and morals of the day; cases in point are men who import French military terms into their letter-writing, women who collect books for show, theatregoers who indulge in catcalling, upper-class gentlemen who parade their drunkenness. Sometimes adopted other kinds of essays; witness the allegorical type (*The Vision of Mirza, Public Credit*), literary-critical (*Chevy Chase,* and a Saturday series on *Paradise Lost*). With Steele, was the pioneer of the Woman's Page in the daily newspaper, catering to her as a group and revealing her weaknesses; for example, by instancing the barren itinerary of a Fine Lady, he revealed how empty her life is: one ageless item being, "Ten o'clock. Staid within all day not at home."

Urbane humor, punctilious but cat-like and gentle persuasion, venomless but rapier-like irony (achieved by lumping together numerous examples to attack some prevailing absurdity), and notable character sketches anticipatory of excellent characterization in the approaching modern novel (the famous Roger de Coverley papers need but a love-plot to be resolved into a novel). Charm, simplicity, rhetorical punctuation, logical development of ideas and structure. Polish of style and harmony of diction, representing the neo-classical ideal, evoked Johnson's encomium: "Whoever wishes to attain an English style, familiar but not coarse, and elegant but not ostentatious, must give his days and nights to the volumes of Addison."[1] While he was the typical exponent of the period's new upper-middle class morality and culture, Addison definitely elevated the tone of English thought and life.

ADDISON	STEELE
1. Greater meditative appeal; little sentiment and pathos.	1. Greater emotional appeal; more sympathy and humaneness.
2. Suave ironic insight; but, except for his Essays, a deficiency of humor.	2. Incapable of irony; but keen in wit and spontaneous in humor.
3. More erudite than Steele, and less original.	3. Keener knowledge of the world and of character; fertile invention.[2]
4. Consistently polished, classically dignified.	4. Frequently careless, more colloquial.

5. "I prefer open-hearted Steele with all his faults," so Leigh Hunt puts it, "to Addison with all his essays."

6. Compared with Defoe's periodical writing, they neither expose current evils as thoroughly, nor have the practical vision of suggesting general schemes of improvement in the social organization. (For Defoe, see page 352.)

---

1 But to imitate Addison to-day might well result in archaism.

2 It was Steele who conceived *The Tatler,* just as it was he who suggested Sir Roger de Coverley.

Sir Richard Steele, 1672—1729, essayist, playwright, Whig pamphleteer, politician.[1] Irresponsible but fundamentally honest Dubliner, born in the same year as Addison. Educated at Charterhouse School (1684), where was formed an intimate friendship with Addison, and at Christ's Church College, Oxford (1689). Without waiting for a degree, he enlisted in the Duke of Ormond's guards (1694), and was forthwith disinherited by his uncle. Captain in Lord Lucas's Regiment of Foot (now First Battalion, The Border Regiment). Gentleman Waiter to Prince George of Denmark (1706). Appointed Gazetteer (1707). Married the widow Margaret Stretch (1705); and then Mistress Mary Scurlock (1707), the "dear Prue" of his letters. Lost Court appointment. Parliamentarian (1713); was impeached for alleged seditious utterances in his political pamphlet, *The Crisis,* which sided with the Hanoverian succession, and was expelled by the Tory majority from the House (1714). Re-elected to Parliament. Appointed patentee of Drury Lane Theatre (1715). Knighted by George I (1715). Launched *The Guardian* (1713), its successor *The Englishman* (1714), *Town Talk* (1715), *The Plebeian* (1718), *The Theatre* (1720), and lesser periodicals. Retired to Wales (1724). (For his contributions to *The Spectator,* see page 341.)

His comedies, feeble, morally innocuous, occasionally lively with their flair for the comic spirit, and with the recurring theme of sentimentalism, are important both for a conscious attempt to purify the tone of the theatre and for the introduction (practically) of the Sentimental Comedy. The value of his essays lies in their tactfulness and warm sincerity, their inventiveness and humanity, their spontaneous humor and rich pathos, and their recognition of women as an important part of the reading[2] public. Both Steele and Addison reflected and moulded English middle class opinion. (For his style as contrasted with Addison's, see page 342.)

Early Work

The Procession (1695). Conventional, reflective poem on the death of Queen Mary. Grandiose imagery. Dedicated to Lord Cutts; obtained for him an ensigncy in the Coldstream Guards.

The Christian Hero (1701). Manual of ethics, written to steady himself on the path of virtue, primarily concerned with demonstrating that human motives are improved and best utilized when joined with Religion, that decency is a requisite of a gentleman, and that the preceptors of proper conscience are not the classical philosophers but Christ

---

1 Connely, Willard, *Sir Richard Steele* (1934).

2 Steele, too, suggested that six women should be on a jury of twelve. However, he should not be hailed as an unqualified proponent of feminism ahead of his time. Consult Blanchard, Rae, "Richard Steele and the Status of Women," *Studies in Philology,* XXVI (1929), pp. 325-355; Dobrée, Bonamy, *Variety of Ways* (1932), "Richard Steele," p. 95 ff. (pp. 86-99).

and St. Paul. Personal value of devotional work is its expression of ideas (*e.g.*, the mawkishly sentimental Eve) later developed in his plays and periodicals; historical value, its presentation of ideas that became prominent during the eighteenth century; general value, its new tone of Puritan idealism, a change from the licentiousness of the Restoration period.[1]

Comedies

The Funeral, or Grief à-la-Mode† (1701). Satirical comedy aimed primarily at lawyers and undertakers is an embryonic sentimental comedy. Sense of humor, varied action, and virtuous purpose uppermost. Often considered his best-constructed play. Written to make amends in the eyes of his soldier-friends for his religious *Christian Hero*. Steele said that it was "dam'd for its piety."

The Lying Lover or The Ladies' Friendship (1703). Serio-comic comedy based on Corneille's *Le Menteur*. Some lively scenes. Pious: exhibited the folly of duelling[2] and intemperance. Insertion of an original scene marks the first appearance of the new sentimental comedy in Steele, if not in the English drama.

The Tender Husband (1705). Comedy, with prologue by Addison, is based on Moliere's *Sicilien; ou, l'Amour Peintre*. Main story makes a mock of genuine morality; dramatic propriety of the comic scenes better than rest of play. Characters somewhat anticipate Fielding's Squire Western, Goldsmith's Tony Lumpkin, and Sheridan's Lydia Languish.

The Conscious Lovers†* (1722). Best sentimental comedy. Based upon the sentimental misinterpretation of Terence's *Andria*, but is livelier in action and original in its protest against duelling. Fielding's Parson Adams declares that it is one of two plays "fit for a Christian to read": avowedly it has a moral purpose. Specifically, it seeks to attack duelling (see the Preface), and, more generally, "To chasten wit, and moralize the stage." So chastened is the wit that its wit is doubtful; so moralized is the drama that its struggles leave us cold.

Major Periodical

The Tatler† (April 12, 1709—January 2, 1711). Suggested by Defoe's periodical (p. 354), and named in honor of women by the pseudonymous author, Isaac Bickerstaff, a nom-de-plume previously em-

---

1 Blanchard, Rae, "The *Christian Hero* by Richard Steele: A Bibliography," *The Library, Fourth Series*, x (1930), p. 60 (pp. 60-72).

2 The didacticism of *The Christian Hero* had aroused the ire of Captain Kelly, a soldier-comrade, and in the duel that followed Steele dangerously wounded his antagonist. Thereafter Steele always disliked duelling: in this connection, see also *The Tatler*, No. 25, June 7, 1709.

† * Explanation of symbols immediately precedes Chapter XV.

ployed by Swift in *Predictions for the Ensuing Year 1708* (p. 351). Tri-
weekly, possibly the first in which the literary element outdid the element of news, supplied the public with information in five sections.
"All Accounts of Gallantry, Pleasure, *and* Entertainment, *shall be under
the Article of* White's Chocolate-house; Poetry; *under that of* Will's
Coffee-house; Learning, *under the Title of* Graecian; Foreign *and*
Domestick News, *you will have from St.* James's Coffee-house; *and
what else I shall on any other Subject offer, shall be dated from my
own* Apartment."

The general editorial policy was "to recommend truth, honour,
and virtue as the chief ornaments of life." Other main contributor was
Addison (p. 340),[1] who entered in the eighteenth number.[2] Whereas
Addison's style is cool-headed and finished, Steele's is impetuous and
often careless, but more kindly and sympathetic in the evolution from
destructive criticism and satirical portraits of society pests (bores, fops,
swindlers, chatterboxes, and women who stormed the Old Bailey to
hear cases of rape) to a deeper criticism of intimate domestic problems.
Eventually the news articles were excluded, and each number became
confined, as in *The Spectator,* to a single essay on one theme, dated
chiefly "from my own apartment."

Posthumous Publication

Letters (1787).[3] Over four hundred letters to his second wife are
extant. Delightful love epistles to "dear little, peevish, beautiful wife
governess," sweet Prue, make him one of the five great writers of love-
letters in English literature, the others being Swift, Keats, and the
Brownings. Somewhat lachrymose, but buoyant, frank, graceful, and
impulsive.

Jonathan Swift, 1667—1745, greatest English prose satirist; political pamphleteer, verse-writer.[4] Posthumously born in Dublin of
English parents. Educated at Kilkenny Grammar School and at Trinity

---

1 Out of two hundred and seventy-one *Tatlers*, one hundred and eighty-eight are by
Steele, forty-two by Addision, and thirty-six are by both of them; out of five hundred
and fifty-five *Spectators*, two hundred and seventy-four are by Addision and two hundred
and thirty-six by Steele: the total seems to indicate that Addision was less active
than Steele.

2 We are inclined to agree with Steele when he himself states "that *Steele* has been
so candid and upright, that he owes nothing to Mr. *Addision*, as a Writer; but whether
he does, or does not, whatever *Steele* owes to Mr. *Addision*, the Publick owes *Addision*
to *Steele*." (Sir Richard Steele's "To Mr. Congreve, Occasion'd by Mr. *Tickell's*
Preface to the Four Volumes of Mr. *Addison's* Works," prefixed to *The Drummer*
(1722—tenth page, unnumbered).

3 *The Letters of Richard Steele*, edited by Johnson, R. B. (1927); Blanchard, Rae,
ed., *The Correspondence of Richard Steele* (1941).

4 Craik, Henry, *The Life of Jonathan Swift* (1882); Taylor, W. D., *Jonathan Swift* (1933);
Davis, H. and Ehrenpreis, I., eds., *The Prose Works of Jonathan Swift* (12 vols., 1939-1959);
Van Doren, Carl, ed., *The Portable Swift* (1948) (Paperbound); Murray, J. M., *Jonathan
Swift: A Critical Biography* (1954); Williams, Kathleen, *Jonathan Swift and the Age of Com-
promise* (1958).

College, Dublin, the latter being an Anglican institution. Confidential secretary to Sir William Temple, a distant kinsman, at Moor Park, Surrey (1688—1694; 1696—1699), where he met Esther Johnson, natural daughter and protégée of Sir William Temple; she is often asserted to be Swift's secret wife.[1] Took holy orders (1695). Held the Prebend of Kilroot on the shores of Belfast Lough (1694—1696). Chaplain and Secretary to Lord-Deputy Berkeley in Ireland (1699). In England (1701—1704). Transferred his allegiance from the Whig to the Tory party (1710),[2] editing its periodical *The Examiner* (1710—1711). Appointed to the Deanery of St. Patrick's Cathedral, Dublin (1713). Joined the Scriblerus Club (1714), other members being Pope, Gay, and Congreve. Henceforth resided mainly in Ireland.[3] Brain disease began to cloud intellect about 1736; made him violently insane, 1741; caused his death, 1745. Bequeathed most of his fortune to found a hospital for the insane in Dublin (opened 1757). Buried in St. Patrick's Cathedral, by the side of Stella,[4] his own chosen words being inscribed on his tablet:[5]

An absence of pathos, not infrequent obscurities of detail, inexcusable coarseness and masculine indecency, and brutal cynicism were his obvious defects. But with this "determined vindicator of human free-

---

1 Woffersdorf-Leslie, A. von, "Was Swift Married to Stella," *Anglia*, XVIII (1896), pp. 1-55, Lane-Poole, Stanley, "The Alleged Marriage of Swift and Stella," *The Fortnightly Review*, XCIII; New Series, LXXXVII (1910), pp. 319-322; Hearsey, Marguerite, "New Light on the Evidence of Swift's Marriage," *Publications of the Modern Language Association of America*, XLII (1927), pp. 157-161. M. B. Gold believes that the marshalled but scant evidence indicates that Swift and Stella were married by the Bishop of Clogher some time in 1716 (p. 116). It is also his opinion that the marriage was never consummated; and M. B. Gold leans upon Krafft-Ebing's statement that Swift's case was one of sexual anaesthesia, which eliminates sexual love but does not exclude tender emotion (p. 127 *ff.*). Gold, M. B., *Swift's Marriage to Stella* (1937). However, although Swift did refer to himself as lacking the archidiaconal "faculty of increasing the Queen's subjects," it is unlikely that he was impotent.

2 Babcock, R. W., "Swift's Conversion to the Tory Party," *Essays and Studies in English and Comparative Literature*, By Members of The English Department of the University of Michigan (1932), pp. 133-149.

3 "It is not generally known that Swift paid a last flying visit to England in 1730; it has, indeed, been universally ignored by his biographers, and is here made public for the first time." Dobrée, Bonamy, *As Their Friend's Saw Them* (1933).

4 Contradictory statements have been made. But see Lawlor, H. J., "The Graves of Swift and Stella," *The English Historical Review*, XXXIII (1918), pp. 89-93.

5 Too frequently only one-third of his epitaph is quoted: *Ubi saeva indignatio Ulterius cor Lacerare nequit* ("Where savage indignation can no longer lacerate the heart"). This part-quotation is supposed to put emphasis upon his morbidity and hatred of mankind—an interpretation wide of its mark, for Swift had in mind a local and special interpretation, as can be seen from the last third of his epitaph: *Abi viator, Et imitare, sipoteris, Strenuum pro virili Libertatis vindicatorem* ("Turn aside, traveller, and imitate, if you can, the resolute vindicator of human freedom"). Undoubtedly he wished to stress his vigorous championship of freedom.

    Jeffrey, Macaulay, Thackerary, and others have left unsympathetic and possibly erroneous statements concerning Swift's character and personality. Consult Whibley, Charles, *Jonathan Swift* (The Leslie Stephen Lecture, 1917); Strahan, J. A., "Swift, Steele, and Addison," *Blackwood's Magazine*, CCVIII (1920), pp. 494-497 (pp. 493-510); Walters, J. C., "Jonathan Swift: Man and Idealist," *The Manchester Quarterly*, XL (1921); and Stockley, W. F. P., "Swift as an Irish Writer," *The Irish Ecclesiastical Review*, XXVII (1926), p. 129 *f.* (pp. 127-147). Moreover, as John Wesley perceived, Swift's view of men—as found, for example, in *Gulliver's Travels*—is essentially the view of the classical and Christian tradition: see Wedel, T. O., "On the Philosophical Background of *Gulliver's Travels*," *Studies in Philology*, XXIII (1926), p. 441 (pp. 434-450); see also Ehrenpreis, I., *The Personaltiy of Jonathan Swift* (1958).

dom" (as he called himself in part of his own epitaph) went cold, penetrating, corrosive intellectual power; muscular perfection of idiomatic strength—studied simplicity, biting economy of phrase, clarity of exposition and argument; savage ironic dignity, couched in the classical style of the day and rising clear of rhetoric; and a fundamental sincerity and common sense in his sardonic hatred of sham and oppression. His work helped standardize the language.

Major Prose Works

Journal to Stella† (Written 1710—1713). Least typical and most human work.[1] Collection of letters distinguished by baby tenderness, unexpected playfulness, and free confidences, although disfigured by infrequent vulgarities. Also important for its pictures of London, Swift's daily doings and comments on life. Has not appealed much to the general reader. (Improperly converts "Esther" into the Greek *aster,* and then understands *aster* in Latin to mean, like *stella,* "a star.")

Travels into Several Remote Nations of the World. By Lemuel Gulliver†*[2] (1726). Popularly known as *Gulliver's Travels.* Universal satire[3] on the pettiness and vices of man and human institutions, especially the English. What is frequently considered merely a wonder-story and a nursery classic is actually a diabolical indictment of man's folly, oppression, and animalism, of man's education, politics, wars, and commerce.[4] Unflinching expression, unbroken development of the narrative, magnificence of malignant irony. Chief source of ironic masterpiece is Swift's originality. Other sources levied upon are Philostratus's *Imagines,* Lucian's *Icaromenippus, or A Voyage to Heaven* and *Dialogues of the Dead,* Rabelais, Dampier, Tom Brown, Berkeley, Samuel Sturmy's *Mariner's Magazine,* and Pope's concluding

---

1 While Irvine states that Swift is a masculine writer, yet his letters surpass those of Mrs. Carlyle in domesticity, and those of every letter-writer in familiarity of language. Meanwhile Rossi and Hone insist that the *Journal* merely chronicles the day's work and that therefore it is an error to state that the *Journal* enables us to follow Swift *intimately.* Irvine, L. LL., *Ten Letters Writers* (1932), pp. 181-201; Rossi, M. M., and Hone, J. M., *Swift or The Egoist* (1934) p. 179 ff., p. 394, Note 2.

2 It is not true that *Gulliver's Travels* was completed by 1720. See *The Letters of Jonathan Swift,* edited by Smith, D. N. (1935), Introduction, p. XL (pp. VII-XLVII).

3 Taylor, W. D., *Jonathan Swift* (1933), pp. 217-233 (Chap. VIII, pp. 209-233). Leslie Shane has said that Gulliver must be read as Swift's own autobiography. But Gulliver is not Swift in disguise; he is a "credible, probable, recognizable, and trustworthy" figure: such is the opinion of Moore, J. B., "The Rôle of Gulliver," *Modern Philology,* XXV (1927-1928), pp. 469-480.

4 *Gulliver's Travels* abounds in veiled personal and political allusions; for example, the hostilities between Lilliput and Blefuscu probably refer to Bolingbroke's part in terminating the War of the Spanish Succession; the quarrel between the Big-Endians and the Small-Endians represents that between the Roman Catholics and the Protestants. Again, in the fourth voyage, "he assails the foundations of the social system, capital, trade, and private property, exalting the natural life at the expense of civilization, and horses at the expense of men." Firth, C. H., "The Political Significance of Gulliver's Travels," *Proceedings of The British Academy,* IX (1919-1920), pp. 237-259.

† * Explanation of symbols immediately precedes Chapter XV.

chapter of *Memoirs of Martinus Scriblerus.*[1] It has been asserted that "*Gulliver's Travels* could not have been written before the period of microscopic observation."[2]

Church Questions

A Tale of a Tub†* (1704). Most original prose satire in allegorical form. Object is to demonstrate the superiority of the Church of England while twitting the Roman Catholic and the Presbyterian churches; but criticism[3] of church quarrels over matters of almost nugatory importance somehow succeeds in ridiculing the Church of England, thereby prejudicing Queen Anne against Swift, costing him a bishopric.[4] Of the three brothers symbolizing the different religious bodies, Peter (St. Peter) represents the elaborate ritual and hierarchy of Roman Catholicism; Martin (Martin Luther), the reform tendencies of Lutherism and Anglicanism; Jack (John Calvin), the iconoclasm of Calvinism, Presbyterianism, and Non-Conformism. Title probably takes name from the sailor's tradition of throwing out an empty tub to divert a whale about to attack a ship. Energetic pressure and violently cruel sweep of sustained irony and satire. Marvelous constructive skill, despite inconclusiveness, irrelevant digressions, and not infrequent incoherent narrative.[5]

An Argument to Prove that the Abolishing of Christianity in England May, As Things Now Stand, Be Attended with Some Inconveniences† (1708). Prose satire ironically castigates the Deists. First considers "the most important objections against Christianity, and the chief advantages proposed by the abolishing thereof," some of the deliberately absurd arguments being that such abolition would make it possible for men not to be obliged "to the belief of things too difficult

---

1 Many commentators have collected plagiary; it seems that *Gulliver's Travels* lends itself to elusive traces or parallels in other works. We have followed H. H. Williams in his decisions concerning the possible sources of *Gulliver's Travels;* those who wish to continue with this aspect are referred to Poll, Max, "The Sources of *Gulliver's Travels,*" University of Cincinnati, Bulletin No. 24, Series II, Volume III; Eddy, W. A., *Gulliver's Travels: A Critical Study* (1923); Hubbard, L. L., *Notes on the Adventures and Surprising Deliverances of James Dubourdieu and His Wife* (Privately printed, 1927); Frantz, R. W., "Swift's Yahoos and the Voyages," *Modern Philology,* XXIX (1931-1932), pp. 49-57; and Williams, H. H., *Dean Swift's Library* (1932), pp. 89-93.

2 Nicolson, Marjorie, "The Microscope and English Imagination," *Smith College Studies in Modern Languages,* XVI, No. 4 (1935), p. 50 *ff*. While the statement has in it some truth, it is probably hyperbolic.

3 "It may be peremptorily asserted," said George Saintsbury of *The Tale of a Tub,* "that irreligion is neither intended nor involved in it." He thereby anticipated the excellent approach of Darnall, F. M., "Swift's Religion," *The Journal of English and Germanic Philology,* XXX (1931), pp. 379-382. Unwarranted is the interpretation that the *Tale* is a sweeping satire against all religion; it is, in reality, a serious and constructive criticism, and, fundamentally, a plea for unity of Christians destroyed by trivial controversies and man-made doctrines and ceremonials.

4 Firth, C. H., "Dean Swift and Ecclesiastical Preferment," *The Review of English Studies,* (1926), pp. 1-17.

5 It is possibly reminiscent of the German romance, *Der Eislebische Christliche Ritter, Ein Reformationsspiel* (1613): see Webster, C. M., "A Possible Source for *A Tale of a Tub,*" *Modern Language Notes,* XLVIII (1933), pp. 251-253.

† * Explanation of symbols immediately precedes Chapter XV.

for free thinkers"; that in England there are "above ten thousand persons, whose revenues, added to those of my lords the bishops, would suffice to maintain at least two hundred young gentlemen of wit and pleasure ....."; that one additional day in seven could be obtained for purposes of trade, business, or pleasure; and the like. Among the inconveniences, however, Swift points out that "these wise reformers do not consider what an advantage and felicity it is for great wits to be provided with objects of scorn and contempt, in order to exercise and improve their talents, and divert their spleen from falling on each other, or on themselves; especially when all this may be done without the least imaginable danger to their persons." Again, with Christianity abolished, "how could the free-thinkers, the strong reasoners, and the men of profound learning, be able to find another subject, so calculated in all points, whereon to display their abilities." Note the whimsical style, the ironical humor.

The Sentiments of a Church of England Man with respect to Religion and Government (1708). An Erastian discussion.

A Project for the Advancement of Religion and the Reformation of Manners (1709). Suggests that government proctors should supervise the morals of the people.

Pamphlets Relating to Ireland

A Proposal for the Universal Use of Irish Manufacture (1720). Advocates, energetically and ironically, the boycotting of English clothes and furniture: burn everything that comes from England except its people and its coal.

A Short View of the State of Ireland (1727). Answers without his usual irony the assertion that Ireland was prosperous. Enumerates fourteen points of prosperity in a nation, not one of which, he said, was enjoyed by the Irish.

The Drapier's Letters† (1724). A Dublin draper professedly issues a series of letters,[1] of which the fifth is possibly the best-written but the fourth probably the greatest, which united all Ireland in a national boycott and forced the Whig government to abandon the unprincipled[2] project of William Wood's debased copper coinage in

---

[1] *The Drapier's Letters to the People of Ireland against receiving Wood's Halfpence,* edited by Davis, Herbert (1935), Introduction, pp. IX-LXVII (pp. IX-XCV).

[2] "Regarded as an isolated incident, Swift's attack on Wood's halfpence in the first three of the *Drapier's Letters* appears a somewhat discreditable business. The copper coins were genuinely needed, and Wood fulfilled his contract honestly. There is much in these letters which savours of deliberate misrepresentation, if not hard lying. But Swift was not so utterly unscrupulous as his enemies pretended; he fomented the agitation deliberately to draw attention to the scandalous way in which English politicians regarded Ireland as a mere Tom Tiddler's ground for their friends." Harrison, G. B., "Jonathan Swift," p. 204 (pp. 189-209), in Hearnshaw, F. J. C., *The Social & Political Ideas of Some English Thinkers of the Augustan Age* (1928). As a matter of fact, what was a considerabe factor in stirring up indignation in Ireland was Wood's payment of ten thousand pounds to the Duchess of Kendal, the royal mistress by whose influence he obtained the patent.

† * Explanation of symbols immediately precedes Chapter XV.

Ireland. Swift, who disliked Ireland, which to him was "a place good enough to die in" and the best country to live out of, through his protest paradoxically became an Irish idol. Quotation: "For in reason, all Government without the Consent of the Governed is the very Definition of Slavery."

Modest Proposal for Preventing the Children of Poor People in Ireland from Being a Burden to their Parents or Country, and for Making Them Beneficial to the Public† (1729). Most famous of his tracts on Irish affairs is also the best example of Swift's ferocious mockery. Simple analysis points out that the Irish are dying of famine, that there are too many people in Ireland, and therefore proposes revoltingly that the Irish should fatten and eat their children for food. Parallels the proposal for the extinction of the Yahoos in the fourth book of *Gulliver's Travels*. He has been assured "that a young healthy child, well nursed, is, at a year old, a most delicious, nourishing, and wholesome food, whether stewed, roasted, baked, or boiled, and I make no doubt that it will equally serve in a fricassee or a ragout . . . ." He then points out six major advantages of his cannibalistic scheme, some of them being that "it would greatly lessen the number of Papists"; that the "poorer tenants will have something valuable of their own" with which to help pay their landlord's rent; that the "constant breeders, beside the gain of eight shillings sterling per annum by the sale of their children, will be rid of the charge of maintaining them after the first year"; and that it would be a great inducement to marriage, would introduce a new dish, and the like.

Political Papers

A Discourse of the Contests and Dissensions between the Nobles and the Commons in Athens and Rome (1701). Defends the Whig lords (Somers, Orford, Halifax, Portland) against threatened impeachment. Athletic clearness of diction. General sameness of vehement tone verges upon monotony.

A Short Character of His Excellency Thomas Earl of Wharton† (1711). No other piece of Swift's is so fiercely and malevolently insulting.

The Conduct of the Allies (1711). Trenchant Tory pamphlet that, like *Some Remarks on the Barrier Treaty* published the same year, favors peace with France. Contends that the continuance of the war against France was, while piling up a national debt, benefitting only the moneyed Marlborough-Godolphin family, the Whigs, and the Dutch. Consistent clarity; occasional slovenly grammar. Leslie Shane has declared it worthy of a Nobel Prize.

The Public Spirit of the Whigs (1714). Rejoinder to Steele's *The Crisis* (p. 343) severely worsts his provoker.

---

† * Explanation of symbols immediately precedes Chapter XV.

Some Free Thoughts upon the Present State of Affairs (1714; 1741). Prose tract coolly and Bolingbroke-like urges the discharge of all Whigs and Dissenters from public office—a comparatively moderate suggestion on the part of Swift.

Other Papers and Essays

The Battle of the Books† (written 1697—1699; published 1704). Prose satire stages an imaginary battle between the Ancient and Modern books in St. James Library, a controversy known in France as *La Querelle entre Les Anciens et Les Modernes*. Swift apparently throws his weight in the direction of the ancients, but neither side is accorded definite victory.[1] Mock epic written ostensibly in defense of Sir William Temple (p. 314), who had aroused criticism, particularly from Richard Bentley, by an urbane defense of the spurious *Epistles* of Phalaris in an essay on the comparative value of Ancient and Modern Learning—a discussion that was part of a literary squabble raging in France, in which Charles Perrault and Nicolas Boileau, as well as Fontanelle and La Fontaine, were participating.[2]

Predictions for the Ensuing Year 1708 (1708). First of a short series of pamphlets issued by Swift under the pseudonym of Isaac Bickerstaff, who competes with the quack almanac writer and plot-prophet John Partridge by predicting the latter's death on March 29, 1708. Partridge's reply that he was still very much alive evoked from Bickerstaff his circumstantial *Account of Partridge's Death* and his *Vindication of Isaac Bickerstaff, Esq.* (1709). Burlesque paper war made the name of Bickerstaff so popular that subsequently Steele, in *The Tatler*, adopted the pen-name of Isaac Bickerstaff, Esq., Astrologer.

A Meditation upon a Broom-Stick (1710). Parody of Robert Boyle's *Occasional Reflections* (1665) is delicious in its irony against sermonizing. Is a "bite" upon Swift's friend Lady Berkeley.

Verse[3]

"Cousin Swift," Dryden is reported by Dr. Johnson to have said bluntly, "you will never be a poet." Certainly his early *Pindaric Odes* were flat and labored; and just as certainly Swift will never hold a high

---

1 The Ancients are represented by such men as Homer, Virgil, Pindar, Aristotle, and Plato; the Moderns, by Milton, Hobbes, and Descartes. The most satirically humorous in the encounters is that between Virgil and his translator Dryden.
   Famous is the epilogue of the Bee entangled in the Spider's web; the Moderns, like the Spider, spin their knowledge wholly out of themselves, producing only dirt and poison, while the Ancients, like the Bee, go to nature for their scholastic lore, choosing to fill their "hives with honey and wax; thus furnishing mankind with the two noblest things, which are sweetness and light." (The phrase, "sweetness and light," is used frequently by Matthew Arnold, p. 567.)

2 Burlingame, A. E., *The Battle of the Books in its Historical Setting* (1920), pp. 103-195. It is unlikely that the *Battle* was influenced by François de Callierès' *Histoire* (1688): see Williams, H. H., *Dean Swift's Library* (1932), p. 84 f.

3 Davis, Herbert, "Swift's View of Poetry," *Studies in English*, By Members of University College, Toronto, collected by Wallace, M. W. (1931), pp. 1-58; Williams, Harold, *The Poems of Jonathan Swift* (Three volumes, 1937).

† • Explanation of symbols immediately precedes Chapter XV.

position as a poet. But his unwinged, anti-heroic, and anti-romantic verse merits some attention. *Baucis and Philemon,* a pleasant translation of Ovid, is possibly his best narrative poem; *On Poetry: A Rhapsody,* properly regarded by Swift himself as one of his best attempts; *The Legion Club* (Irish Parliament, 1736), verse-satire concentrated into mad fury; *The Day of Judgement,*† possibly his best short poem. Swift is generally charged with inherent nastiness; he seems to be obsessed with the excremental functions of the body, and with the intimate unpleasantries of some aspects of the marriage chamber: this charge is supported by such verse as *The Journal of a Modern Lady* (1728), *Cassinus and Peter* (1731), *The Lady's Dressing Room* (1732), *Strephon and Chloe* (1734), and *A Beautiful Young Nymph going to Bed* (1731). Most of his poems may have a satirical purpose; and, to quote Aldous Huxley, "if you happen to be delicately stomached," you had better read his ferocious poems about women "with a bottle of smelling-salts handy."

Cadenus and Vanessa† (1726). Longest and, except for *The Day of Judgement* possibly his masterpiece in poetry. Ease and piquancy, urbanity and delicacy, pathos and humor, considerateness and sincerity. Only Taine has refused it praise. Swift apologizes for his conduct with 'Vanessa," his pet name for Esther Vanhomrigh, who is said to have died of a broken heart over the Dean.[1] ("Vanessa" is formed from *Van* in Vanhomrigh and *Essa,* diminutive of Esther; "Cadenus" is an anagram of *Decanus,* Latin for "Dean.")

Verses on the Death of Dr. Swift† (1731). His own political obituary is delightful and ironic. Contains an apology for drawing ugly pictures by stating that the fault is in mankind.

Daniel Defoe or **De Foe,** *c.* 1659[2]—1731, pioneering novelist, pamphleteer, opportunistic journalist, historian, secret agent. Son of James Foe, tallow-chandler, to whose name he prefixed *De* (*c.* 1703). Educated at the non-conformist Academy of Newington Green (1674—1679). Intended for the Presbyterian ministry. Married Mary Tuffley, a girl of twenty, by whom he had several children (1684). Joined Monmouth's rebellion (1688). Probably travelled in Spain and on the Continent as a commission merchant. Bankrupt (1692), with a deficit of about £17,000, most of which he succeeded in repaying. Accountant to the Commissioners of the Glass Duty (1695—1699). Eventually became chief owner of a tile establishment at Tilbury, in Essex, but this business, too, failed in 1703 for £3,000. Befriended by Robert Harley (*c.* 1704), for whom he worked in the capacity of political agent (1705).

---

1 For Swift's relationships with women, see Freeman, A. M., ed., *Vanessa and Her Correspondence* . . (1921); Williams, H., ed., *Journal to Stella* (Two vols., 1948); Johnston, Denis, *In Search of Swift* (1959), Barnes & Noble.

2 Aitken, G. A., "Defoe's Birth and Marriage," *The Athenaeum,* XCVI (1890), p. 257; Sutherland, James, *Defoe* (1938), p. 1 *f.* Watson, F., *Daniel Defoe* (1952), p. 231.

† * Explanation of symbols immediately precedes Chapter XV.

Employed by Godolphin as a secret agent of the Government, and carried on activities chiefly in Scotland, in favor of the Union (1706—1707), but the evidence seems to indicate that he was a political trimmer. Convicted for libelling Lord Annesley, but released later by the favor of Lord Townshend, the Whig Secretary of State, on condition of becoming a secret government agent (1715). Died at Ropemaker's Alley, Moorfields.[1]

Versatile nature matched by voluminous output; over two hundred books and pamphlets attributed to him. First great realistic writer; spans the interval between the old picaresque novel of adventure and the modern realistic novel of character; fixed the form of the historical novel, making permissive the entrance of actual historical characters.

Prose Pamphlets

An Essay upon Projects† (1697). Suggestive pamphlet on social and political questions; advocates the income tax, the establishment of a chain of county banks, the creation of an English Academy (along lines similar to the French Academy), the endowment of an asylum for lunatics, the abolition of press-gangs, a commission of inquiry into bankruptcy, a system of national poor relief, and higher education for women[2]: teach the latter French and Italian, Defoe venturing, as he puts it, "the injury of giving a woman more tongues than one." Wide range, patient detail, argumentative force, and modernity of thought.

The Shortest Way with Dissenters† (1702). Masterpiece of sustained irony, surpassed only by Swift's *Modest Proposal* (p. 350), shows the absurdity of ecclesiastical intolerance by rigoristically advocating that all Non-Conformist preachers be hanged and their congregations extirpated. Defoe, a Dissenter, puts proposal into mouth of a high-church Tory: both Whig and Tory London misunderstood this literary hoax. Sentenced to pay a fine, to be pilloried for three days (during which he was pelted with flowers by the populace, who regarded him as a martyr), and to be imprisoned (1703). Ears were not lopped off for offense, despite Pope's line in *The Dunciad* (p. 363): "Earless on high, stood unabash'd De Foe."

The Family Instructor (1715). Semi-fictitious treatise representative of his common sense and practical morality.

The Compleat English Tradesman (I, 1725; II, 1727). Practical manual of apprenticeships, overtrading, credit, bookkeeping, and the like. Second part deals with graduate material for the experienced tradesman. Even gives two business letters, exemplifying the satisfactory and unsatisfactory kind. Classic on business principles also illustrates transitional conditions of trade and capitalism of the time.

---

1 Sutherland, James, *Defoe* (1938).
2 Burch, C. E., "Daniel Defoe's Views on Education," *The London Quarterly Review*, CLIV (1930), pp. 220-229.
† * Explanation of symbols immediately precedes Chapter XV.

The Compleat English Gentleman (*c.* 1729; published 1890). Underlying purpose to induce people to afford their children a better education. Disquisitions enlivened by homely dialogue and sprightly anecdotes.

Verse Pamphlets

The True-Born Englishman† (1701). Animated doggerel satire shivers the myth of racial superiority. Neatly turned against one John Tutchin and those who sympathized with the latter's scurrilous, satirical poem, *The Foreigners,* which had branded William III by declaring it intolerable for a true-born Englishman to be governed by a Dutch king. Not only a Williamite but also himself of Flemish extraction, Defoe hits the mark with this ruggedly humorous skit by pointing out that there is no true-born Englishman—the English are a mongrel race.

Hymn to the Pillory (1703). Mock-Pindaric ode, written while imprisoned (see *The Shortest Way with Dissenters*), points out how honorable it was to stand where Prynne and Bastwick had stood. Excellent piece of satire.

Periodical Writing

His work on periodicals and newspapers included the *Mercurius Politicus* (1716—1720), which he founded; *Mist's Weekly Journal* (1717—1725), a Jacobite organ in which he carried on his political spying; *The Whitehall Evening Post* (1718—1720); *The Daily Post*(1719—1725); *Applebee's Original Weekly Journal* (1720—1726); *Universal Spectator; Fog's Journal;* and the *London Post,* in which *Robinson Crusoe* first appeared. The most important, however, was:

The Review of the Affairs of France and of all Europe as Influenced by that Nation† (February 19, 1704—June 11, 1713. With intermissions).[1] Pugnacious political sheet—originally of eight pages, but reduced, after the first two numbers, to four—with a two-fold purpose, that of instruction and of amusement. Latter department entitled "Mercure Scandale; or Advice from the Scandalous Club, being a Weekly History of Nonsense, Impertinence, Vice, and Debauchery" suggested *The Tatler* to Steele. *The Review,* which antedates *The Spectator* as well, was conducted, probably single-handed, by Defoe as a Whig; published for the most part tri-weekly. Great variety of papers; forthright common sense. One general method was to arrest attention by a surprising statement which, apparently supported at the beginning, is toppled over at the end of the article. *The Review* is said to have ushered in the Queen Anne essay periodical; possibly for the first time in our language treats public and domestic topics of general interest.

---

1 Not reprinted until recently by the Facsimile Text Society. Consult E. L. Tinker's "New Editions, Fine & Otherwise," *The New York Times Book Review,* August 27, 1939, p. 23, cols. 1-3.

† * Explanation of symbols immediately precedes Chapter XV.

May be of less importance to literature than to history and economics,[1] advocating as it did many schemes of social improvement and being a source of information for international politics.

Narrative and Historical Writing

A Journal of the Plague Year† (1722). Graphic pseudo-historical narrative concerning London in the year of the Great Plague (1664—1665), presumably by "H. F.," an eyewitness who signs the account: another example of Defoe's minuteness in creating verisimilitude. Not even the repetitious details, moral bias, and sentimental tendency, can obscure the vividness of the account, which sets down the minutest documented-synthesized items in a simple, homely style. Indebted to Nathaniel Hodges's *Loimologia* (1720), Thomas Vincent's *God's Terrible Voice in the City* (1667), and Dekker's *Wonderfull Yeare* (Vol. I, p. 236).

A True Relation of the Apparition of one Mrs. Veal† (1705). Accurately vivid circumstantial report of a current ghost story, among the first of its kind in the age: proves by the evidence of a scoured silk gown that the spirit of Mrs. Veal did appear. Accumulation of details creates the realism. Its style, to quote Walter de la Mare, is "a kind of copious breathless gossiping."

A Tour thro' the whole Island of Great Britain (Three volumes, 1724—1727). Vivid details of guide-book have been used by historians (Trevelyan, for example) as reliable source for the social and economic conditions of England during the first quarter of the eighteenth century.

Stories of Adventure

The Life and Strange Surprizing Adventures of Robinson Crusoe, of York, Mariner†* (I, 1719, the best part; II, 1719; III,

---

1 Defoe's work "was educating a nation into political sense and morality. It was Defoe who applied and popularized Locke, and drove home the philosopher's principles." (*The Cambridge Modern History*, 1918, Volume VI, p. 817.) His main contribution to political thought may have been, as asserted, the power to interpret Locke to the layman. But, above all, he was a great pioneer in economics, as is pointed out most excellently by J. R. Moore. Defoe anticipated Adam Smith's famous phrase, "The Wealth of Nations"; Defoe favored legislation to protect the consumer from exorbitant charges; attacked the coal barons who drove coal up to an artificially high price; objected to the use of pauper labor on the ground that it was in effect a reduction of wages in general and would undermine the prosperity of the whole country; advocated high wages, distinguishing clearly between real wages and nominal wages, recognizing that the cost of living was as important as the wage rate; and opposed the long working day. Consult Moore, J. R., "Daniel Defoe and Modern Economic Theory," *Indiana University Studies*, XXI, No. 104 (1934, published 1935), pp. 1-28.

† * Explanation of symbols immediately precedes Chapter XV.

1720).¹ Supposedly based upon the adventures of Alexander Selkirk,² a Scottish sailor who was marooned by his own request on the desolate island of Juan Fernandez³ in 1704, and lived there until rescued by Captain Woodes Rogers in 1709. Astounding success of book attributed to its universal appeal—the courageous struggle of a solitary human being against the apparently insuperable forces of Nature—and to its lively narrative, clear visualization, and Biblical brevity and strength of style, to its business-like approach to the problems (involving prudence, foresight, and thrift), poverty of imaginative details (the latter two representing eighteenth-century ideals), and the emphasis on concrete suggestions for everyday life. Defects include repetitions and inconsistencies, retrospective asides and frequent moralizings, weakness in character-portrayal as well as in plot, shapelessness (not utter formlessness of structure), and lack of emotional and imaginative force. Sources, other than the adventures of Selkirk, include Dampier's *A New Voyage Round the World,* Knox's *Ceylon,* Le Comte's *China,*⁴ Hakluyt, and Purchas (see Vol. I, p. 148). To Rousseau, who thought not too highly of books, *Robinson Crusoe* was "the finest of treatises on education according to nature"⁵; to Gorki, it was "the Bible of the unconquerable."

The Life, Adventures, and Piracies of the Famous Captain Singleton (1720). Professedly an autobiographical romance of a pirate who raided the African coast. Homely realism, dry (somewhat satiric) touches. Indebted to *The Voyages and Travels of J. Albert Mandelslo* (1662), Maximilien Misson's *The New Voyage of François Leguat* (1707), Exquemelin's *Bucaniers of America* (English, 1684), Dampier, Hakluyt, Purchas, and others.

---

1 Book II, *The Farther Adventures of Robinson Crusoe* is an anti-climax, and so inferior that many readers do not know of its existence. The character of the hero has degenerated and many incidents are but weak repetition of Book I.
   Book III, *The Serious Reflections . . . . of Robinson Crusoe* is not a narrative but a series of essays on various topics.
   Defoe declared *Robinson Crusoe* to be no romance but an allegory of his own life; it is to some extent autobiographical. George Parker has gone much further: "The whole of Defoe's life is given us in the Crusoe story. *He merely antedates every event in his own life 29 years, and represents it by some adventure of Crusoe's at that time.* Thus Defoe was born in 1661, Crusoe in 1632." Parker, George, "The Allegory of Robinson Crusoe," *History,* New Series, ix-x (April, 1925), pp.17-25 (pp. 11-25).
   A. W. Secord, in a very helpful letter, states that Parker's theory is old and discredited. In a footnote Parker himself writes: "Various biographers have touched on the Allegory: Lee for instance. Most of them disbelieve in its existence, and few have given more than a guess or two towards the solution of the problem."
2 The experiences of Alexander Selkirk "may not have furnished the motif for 'Robinson' nor anything more than some 'meagre outlines' for it, if they did even that." Consult *The Narrative of the El-Ho 'Sjouke Gabbes' (1708),* translated from the Dutch of Hendrik Smeeks by Hibbard, L.L. (1921), p. xix f.
3 In describing Crusoe's island, did Defoe have Tobago, in the West Indies, specifically in mind? Such is the affirmative claim of Howard, Clifford, "Crusoe's Real Island," *The Bookman,* xxxix (1914), pp. 505-511.
4 While Le Comte's work, "with some suggestions from Dampier, supplied Defoe with all the information he needed for Crusoe's brief remarks on China," Ch'en Shou-yi questions A. W. Secord's implication that Le Comte "is plainly the source" for Defoe's attacks on the culture of China. See Shou-yi, Ch'en, "Daniel Defoe, China's Severe Critic," *Nankai Social & Economic Quarterly,* (1935), pp. 511-550.
5 Not only a great philosopher but also an important economist has done it signal honor. Frédéric Bastiat has studied *Robinson Crusoe* as showing the simplest type of human society: see his *Harmonies Économiques* (Second edition, 1851).

The History and Remarkable Life of Colonel Jacque, Commonly call'd Colonel Jack (1722). Autobiographical romance of a convicted pickpocket. Achieved remarkable success in France.

The Fortunes and Misfortunes of the Famous Moll Flanders*[1] (1722). Autobiographical romance of a disreputable pickpocket and sentimental harlot deported to the Virginian colony. As in *Colonel Jacque,* so here the central figure ultimately becomes rich, lives honestly, and dies a penitent. Moral, if immodest, incidents; vivid pictures of England; resolute realism; little analysis of character; conclusion an anti-climax. Superior to *Roxana.*

Roxana, or the Fortunate Mistress (1724). Purports to be an autobiographical romance of a courtesan flourishing, unlike Moll Flanders, among the aristocracy.[2] Verisimilitude (despite blunders and anachronisms); some scenes of dramatic intensity; vigorous English never becomes touched with emotion or imagination. Declares Willa Cather: "Lewd situations are dispatched without lewdness. The book is as safe as sterilized gauze."

Memoirs of a Cavalier. Semi-historical romance probably by Defoe. First half, which concerns the Cavalier's service under Gustavus Adolphus, King of Sweden, is better than the second half, which concerns the hero's adventures under Charles I of England. Photographic and circumstantial character of details; splendid passages, especially those dealing with battles and skirmishes. Not purely a work of fiction: was accepted by Lord Chatham as genuine history.

Comment.[3] Throughout his life Defoe remained a tradesman in his outlook and morality, and his plebeian origin, religious training, activity and views of life influenced immeasurably the humanized fictions that he wrote in later years. Undoubtedly the dominant quality in his works is Verisimilitude, built up by rhetorical use of suspense, concrete statements, elaborate explanations of sources of his stories, use of first person (the *Outline-History* calls his adventure stories "autobiographical"), unadorned language, scheming forecasts, sly humor, and cautions against possible inaccuracies of his work. In *Robinson Crusoe* he gave us the earliest novel of incident—a narrative invested with a sense of reality and carrying the middle-class message of patience, honesty, and industry as the formula for success.

---

1 W. P. Trent declared in 1916 that the full title is unquotable. But today our stomachs can endure it: "The Fortunes and Misfortunes of the Famous Moll Flanders Who was Born in Newgate, and during a Life of continu'd Variety for Threescore Years, besides her Childhood, was Twelve Year a *Whore,* five times a *Wife* (whereof once to her own Brother), Twelve Year a *Thief,* Eight Year a Transported *Felon* in Virginia, at last grew *Rich,* liv'd *Honest,* and died a *Penitent.*"

2 Williams, Orlo, *Some Great English Novels* (1926), Chap. v, pp. 120-148.

3 Secord, A. W., *Studies in the Narrative Method of Defoe* (1924); Harlan, Virginia, "Defoe's Narrative Style," *The Journal of English and Germanic Philology,* xxx (1931), pp. 55-73; Burch, C. E., "British Criticism of Defoe as a Novelist, 1719-1860," *Englische Studien,* LXVII (1932-1933), pp. 178-198.

† * Explanation of symbols immediately precedes Chapter XV

SUGGESTED MERITS	SUGGESTED DEFECTS
1. Sense of fact or detailed realism. Achieved by inimitable power of reproducing, even inventing, circumstantial minutiae.	1. Poverty of ideality and passion. Absence of creative imagination. Lack of sustained dramatic conflict. Frequent inadequacy of character-portrayal.
2. Narrative mastery. Unsurpassed novelist of low life.	2. Amorphousness of form. In the most rigid sense, lack of plot.
3. Moralistic attitude.[1] All characters, except Roxana, repent; even Moll Flanders serves as a warning against evil.	3. Over-moralistic attitude. Characters repent, and spend their declining years in prosperity.
4. Homely, robust, idiomatic style.	4. Frequently, an unpolished, slipshod style.
5. Practically everything he writes is social in import.	5. No probing of the soul. Essentially an editorial commentator.

MAJOR POETS

John Gay, 1685—1732, playwright, poet, and inventor of ballad opera. Born of humble parents in Devonshire. Educated at Barnstaple Grammar School. Apprenticed to a silkmercer of London. Friend of Pope, Swift, and Arbuthnot. Secretary to the Duchess of Monmouth (1712—1714). Secretary to the Earl of Clarendon (1714). Published his two-volume collection called *Poems on Several Occasions* (1720), realized at least one thousand pounds, invested it in South Sea stock, and lost it all. Lottery Commissioner (1722). Because of his *Fables* (1727), he was offered the sinecure post of Gentleman-Usher to the Princess Louisa, who was about three years old, with a salary of two hundred pounds a year; but Gay refused it. Joined the household of the Duke of Queensbury, where the Duchess continued patronizing him. Buried in Westminster Abbey, and on his tomb (following Pope's epitaph) is Gay's own couplet:

> "Life is a jest, and all things show it;
> I thought so once, and now I know it."

As a poet Gay is best remembered for his sprightly songs and *vers de société;* his best-known ballad is *Sweet William's Farewell to Black-Ey'd Susan* (*c.* 1720), as charming as " 'Twas when the seas were roaring," despite the artifice of both.

Poems

Wine (1708). Negligible blank-verse poem written in the mock-heroic style: water-drinkers can not be successful authors. Possibly suggested by John Philips's *Cyder* (1708).

The Fan (1713). A poem in three books declared by Austin Dobson to be unreadable.

---

1 A. W. Secord has discussed the four theories prominently given to account for Defoe's fundamental methods of narration. His conclusion is that Defoe's narratives are not a continuation of the picaresque tradition of *Lazarillo de Tormes,* and that they grew chiefly out of such moral treatises as *The Family Instructor* and *The Continuation of the Letters of The Turkish Spy.*

Rural Sports: A Georgic (1713). Poem written in workmanlike heroic couplet on the model of Pope's *Pastorals* and *Windsor Forest*. Not its conventional expression but a slight feeling for natural scenery makes it Gay's first significant poem.

The Shepherd's Week (1714). Series of six pastorals drawn, like *Rural Sports,* from English rustic life. Instigated by Pope, its purpose was to pour ridicule upon the artificial pastorals of Ambrose Philips; like Fielding's *Joseph Andrews,* however, Gay's collection grows away from its parody of weak imitators of Virgil and Spenser; it develops into the best bucolic poem of the period and the first notable attempt at realistic pastoral. Witty pictures of the country, although marred by instances of poor taste.

Trivia, or the Art of Walking the Streets† (1716).[1] Has been declared the greatest poem on London life. Its three books, disfigured by discursiveness and an inept use of the mock-heroic style, are saved from neglect by a sustained framework of burlesque classicism in conventional if well-turned rimed couplets and by its realistic details of eighteenth-century manners, especially of London in the time of George I: describes twoscore separate localities; threescore ways of earning a livelihood; the proper boots to wear and canes to carry; the methods of detecting and avoiding such characters as pickpockets, bullies, rascally boys who pull off wigs, immoral women, rakes, and the like.

Alexander Pope his safe return from Troy, or Mr. Pope's Welcome from Greece (*c.* 1720; 1776). A delightful and poetical epistle celebrating Pope's completion of the translation of the *Iliad*.

Fables† (First Series, 1727; Second, 1738). One of his main achievements is also among the best examples of fables in English verse. Each didactic, witty, original little story is neatly moralized at the end. Sprightly spirit in keeping with the easy iambic tetrameter couplet. First series written for six-year-old Prince William, later the Duke of Cumberland; second series meant for adults.

Plays and Operas

His plays and operas include *The Wife of Bath* (1713), in which the Franklin, Dame Alison, and Chaucer are characters; *Three Hours after Marriage* (1717), written in collaboration with Pope and Arbuthnot, is a sorry piece of farce condemned by the public; *The Captives* (1724), a partly successful tragedy; *Acis and Galatea* (1732), an English pastoral opera with music by Handel and famous for such songs as "O the pleasure of the plains," "Love in her eyes sits playing," and "O ruddier than the cherry"; and *Achilles* (1733), a posthumous opera slight in its music but witty in dialogue and entertaining in plot.

---

1 Irving, W. H., *John Gay's London* (1929), Chap. III, "*Trivia* and the Life of the Streets," pp. 150-222.

† • Explanation of symbols immediately precedes Chapter XV.

The What D'Ye Call It (1715). Satirical "Tragi-Comi-Pastoral Farce" on contemporary tragedy, ridiculing, for example, Addison's *Cato*. Absurd plot, lively dialogue; but failed because the public did not grasp its features as a dramatic skit.

The Beggar's Opera†* (1728). Under cover of a ballad-opera, first suggested by Swift in a letter to Pope, Gay caricatured Sir Robert Walpole and satirized the corruptions of the governing classes. Like most comic opera or musical comedy, its "book" is somewhat thin; but what made the production a tremendous success was some brilliant prose-dialogue, pretty and lively lyrics,[1] genuine though boisterous humor, sustained irony, and ruthless political allusions to Walpole and Molly Skerrett. For a time drove from the stage the Italian opera, which Gay ridiculed just as Addison had burlesqued it in *Rosamund*. First comic opera unequalled until the arrival of Gilbert and Sullivan. Probably inspired Burns's *Jolly Beggars* (p. 433).

Polly* (1729). Sequel to *The Beggar's Opera* banned by the Lord Chamberlain, no doubt through the influence of Walpole, who feared its political lampooning. Published by subscription, bringing Gay more than one thousand pounds. Like his *Beggar's Opera,* is distinguished by satirical quips political in import.

Alexander Pope,1688—1744, the consummate exemplar of Augustan poetry.[2] Son of a well-to-do Roman Catholic linen-draper of London. At about twelve years of age, a severe illness, possibly infantile paralysis, left him dwarfish and in perpetual ill-health. Partly because of his poor constitution and partly because governmental restrictions made formal education for Catholics somewhat difficult, Pope was largely self-educated. Friend of Wycherley, who introduced him to London life. Friend of Addison, who published Pope's *Messiah* in *The Spectator* (No. 378, May 1712) and who got Pope to write a prologue to *Cato* (p. 341). Drifted away from Addison and Addison's circle, one cause being *The Spectator's* praise of Ambrose Philips's *Pastorals* and another being a disagreement with Addison's politics. An allusion to the Treaty of Utrecht in *Windsor Forest* gained him an acquaintance with Swift (1713). Member of the Scriblerus Club, a literary group numbering among its members Swift, Gay, Arbuthnot, Parnell, Congreve, Lord Oxford, and Atterbury. Quarrelled with Addison (1715—1716).[3] Correspondence with Martha Blount, begun

---

1 For the sources of the tunes, refer to W. H. G. Flood's notes in Melville, Lewis, *Life and Letters of John Gay* (1921), pp. 150-155. See, also, Swaen, A. E. H., (1) "The Airs and Tunes of John Gay's Beggar's Opera," *Anglia,* XLIII; N. F., XXXI (1919), pp. 152-190; (2) "The Airs and Tunes of John Gay's *Polly,*" *Anglia,* LX; N. F., XLVIII (1936), pp. 403-422.

2 Griffith, R. H., *Alexander Pope: A Bibliography* (Two parts, 1922 and 1927); Sherburn, George, *The Early Career of Alexander Pope* (1934).

3 But remember that the two were never really intimate and never openly quarreled. Sherburn, George, *The Early Career of Alexander Pope* (1934), Chap. v, "Addison, The Little Senate, *Et Al.,*" pp. 114-148.

† * Explanation of symbols immediately precedes Chapter XV.

in 1712, developed after 1717 into an intimate friendship lasting throughout his life. Assisted Gay and Arbuthnot in writing *Three Hours after Marriage* (1717). Tremendous financial as well as literary success of his translation of the *Iliad* made possible his retirement to Twickenham (1719), where he spent his remaining years in affluence. Left income of his property to Martha Blount till her death. Pope was admired as a poet; but apparently disliked for his vanity, petty vindictiveness, and snobbishness.

Pastoral Poems

Pastorals (1709). Four artificial poems on the seasons, following the muse of Virgil. Best eclogue is "Autumn." Smooth texture, precocious over-delicacy, middling melody, tepid feeling for nature. Supposedly written at the age of sixteen. Led to the famous quarrel with "Namby-Pamby" Ambrose Philips.

Messiah (1712). Sacred verse eclogue on the Messianic prophecies of Isaiah. Excellent technique, steely sublimity. It "seeks," says Courthope, "to Hellenize ideas that are in spirit Hebraic."

Windsor Forest (1713). Descriptive poem, continuing the design of Denham's *Cooper's Hill* (1642), synthesizes pastoral descriptions and rococo mythology with historical and political passages. More dignified yet less artificial than the *Pastorals*. Contains at least one poetic passage. Opportune praise of the Peace of Utrecht appealed to Tories, caused a break with the Addison coterie, and brought an introduction to Swift.

Didactic Poems

Essay on Criticism† (1711). Preceptive poem in antithetic heroic couplets on the canons of literary taste and style, according to the classical rules of Aristotle and Quintilian, and the classical models of Homer and Virgil. Possibly influenced by Horace's *Ars Poetica,* Vida's *De Arte Poetica,* and Boileau's *L'Art Poétique.* One body of opinion depreciates its goaded antitheses and aphoristic platitudes; the other, exalts its declamatory power and gnomic wit: both groups agree upon its economical condensation, structural excellence, and its inclusiveness in summary and interpretation of essential neo-classical tastes and standards.

Moral Essays (1731—1735). Four ethical poems in the form of epistles, part of a contemplated larger work to consist of ten moral epistles. Like the *Imitations of Horace,* not infrequently political in purpose; as a matter of fact, the *Moral Essays* prepare the way to his Horatian satire. Epistle I, addressed to Sir Richard Temple, Lord Cobham, "Of the Knowledge and Characters of Men" (1733), emphasizes that the clue to character is found in the ruling passion. In Epistle II, addressed to a Lady (Martha Blount), "Of the Characters of Women"

---

† • **Explanation of symbols immediately precedes Chapter XV.**

(1735), we do not find that Pope's affection for Martha has changed his low opinion of women; more satirical than moral, this epistle contains the picture of Chloe (Lady Suffolk), and especially that of Atossa (Sarah Jennings, Duchess of Marlborough? Katherine, Duchess of Buckingham, natural daughter of James II?). Epistle III, addressed to Lord Bathurst, "Of the Use of Riches" (1733), besides containing a frontal attack on Walpole's methods of corruption and general financial policy, satirizes the newly-rich, presents a pungent portrait of Sir Balaam, and praises John Kyrle, "The Man of Ross." Epistle IV, addressed to Richard Boyle, Earl of Burlington, called originally "Of Taste," and finally "Of the Use of Riches" (1731), was the first written. Its alleged unwarranted attack on James Brydges, first Duke of Chandos, one of Pope's supposed patrons, yields in importance to its examples of the tasteless use of wealth, particularly in building and gardening, and to its esthetic principles in favor of Palladian architecture. Central idea possibly derived from the Italian preface to *Fabbriche antiche disegnate da Andrea Palladio Vincentino* (1730).[1]

Essay on Man† (1733—1734). Episodic and incompatible philosophies pieced together in heroic verse into four didactic epistles dealing with man's relation to the universe, to himself, to society, and to happiness. Addressed to Lord Bolingbroke, whose shallow deism[2] influences Pope's theodicean purpose[3]: to "vindicate the ways of God to man," for *"Whatever is, is right."* Presents the complacent philosophy of the eighteenth century. Not a conceptual poem; erudition only superficial and half digested; argument dogmatic and unsustained. Metrical dexterity and borrowed comfortable precepts, however, are catalyzed into such brilliant epigram that, outside the work of Shakespeare, no other is so fertile a source for memorable quotations.

Satiric Poems

The Rape of the Lock†* (Two cantos, 1712; enlarged to five cantos, 1714). Mock-heroic epic, perhaps the finest in the language. Based upon an actual incident in which Lord Petre stealthily snipped off a lock of Miss Arabella Fermor's hair, thereby rupturing the friendship between the two families. Partly achieved the purpose for which written—the allaying of the quarrel. Social satire of the frills of the day modelled after Boileau's *Le Lutrin*, Vida's *The Game of Chess,* and

---

1 Sherburn, George, " 'Timon's Villa' and Cannons," *The Huntington Library Bulletin*, Number 8: October, 1935, pp. 131-152.
2 It is not likely that Leibnitz's *Essais de Théodicée* did not influence Pope's philosophical ideas. See Moore, C. A., "Did Leibniz Influence Pope's Essay?" *The Journal of English and Germanic Philology*, xvi (1917), pp. 84-102. It is generally agreed that the *Essay* is a statement of the Deist philosophy, and is therefore inconsistent with Pope's practice of the Catholic faith. That Pope was a Catholic only in name is disputed by Segar, Mary, "Some Notes on Pope's Religion," *The Dublin Review*, cxc (1932), pp. 237-253.
3 Thornton, F. B., *Alexander Pope: Catholic Poet* (1952), pp. 180-184, 189-201, 206-221, 258-262.
† * Explanation of symbols immediately precedes Chapter XV.

Tassoni's *Sacchia Rapita*. Unity of structure better than that of *The Dunciad*. Humorous bathos, airy fancy, good-natured raillery, razor-edged versification; but also rhetorical devices. Introduced machinery of the Rosicrucian[1] sylphs and gnomes; this proved delightfully effective despite Addison's fear that it might mar the work. To Addison, Pope's most imaginative work was "a delicious little thing; *merum sal"*; to Hazlitt, "the triumph of insignificance"; to De Quincey, the "most exquisite monument of playful fancy that universal literature offers."

The Dunciad† (1728, 1729, 1742; complete edition, 1743). Personal lampoon and, especially, general satire on literary hacks and people who had provoked Pope's anger. Schematic epic of dunces in four books annihilates Lewis Theobald, who had ventured (1726) to show the Bard of Twickenham's incapacity as a Shakespearean editor, by elevating him to the throne of Dulness now made vacant by the demise of Dryden's MacFlecknoe (p. 327). Fourth book of the Iliad of the Dunces, issued in 1742 as the *New Dunciad,* dethrones Theobald in favor of Colley Cibber, who had incurred Pope's displeasure. Also pilloried are Richard Bentley, Sir Richard Blackmore, and Ambrose Philips; while among those praised are Dryden, Congreve, and Newton. Brilliant versification and diction, clever irony, spicy satire, appropriately-hewn grotesque images; broad burlesque, indecent abuse, mean-spirited invective. Cf. *Peri Bathous* (1727/8), chiefly Pope's.

Imitations of Horace (1733—c. 1739). Group of pungent satires portraying contemporary characters and manners, in imitation of Horace. Reveals Pope's brilliant, concise style and conveys his satirical, moral, and political sentiments. Excellent example is his "Imitation of the Second Epistle of the Second Book of Horace" (between the poet and William Fortescue). Supreme is the *Epistle to Dr. Arbuthnot*.

Epistle to Dr. Arbuthnot† (1735). Brilliant, venomous, auto-biographical prologue to *Imitations of Horace*. Dialogue between Pope and his friend-physician superbly castigates some of Pope's enemies, including Addison (in the guise of Atticus) and Lord Hervey (Sporus).

Lyrical Poems

Ode for Music on St. Cecilia's Day (written *c.* 1713; published 1717). Lyrically inferior. Treats of the passion of love. (*Cf.* with Dryden's odes, p. 328.)

---

1 It is alleged that the Rosicrucian romance-poem, *The Salamanderine,* influenced Pope's epic. See Clymer, R. S., *The Sacred College of the Ancient Mysteries* (1917).

† • Explanation of symbols immediately precedes Chapter XV.

Eloisa to Abelard (1717). Heroic epistle.[1] Heatless passion, rhetorical imagery; melancholy touches; yet quietly stirring and dramatic. Eloisa renounces love for the service of God: its distinctly romantic subject helped "swell the growing tide of romanticism."[2]

Elegy to the Memory of an Unfortunate Lady (1717). Rhetorical, melodramatic emotion. She finds in suicide an escape from a hopeless love; refused Christian burial, her ghost haunts the glade. Like *Eloisa to Abelard,* contains a little more real feeling than is usual in Pope; like it, too, is a tragic monologue.

Translations

The Iliad of Homer (Six books, 1715—1720). Translation in the hampering regularity of the heroic couplet. Not Homer, as Richard Bentley pointed out; but it is Pope: impeccable couplet, economical terseness, level technical excellence, and vitreous lucidity. It has every merit, to repeat Gibbon, except that of fidelity to the Homeric spirit.

The Odyssey of Homer (1725—1726). Larger part of translation by William Broome and Elijah Fenton. Some effective passages are the opening of Book III and Calypso's speech to Ulysses in Book V. Less successful than the translation of the *Iliad*.

Editing and Correspondence

The Works of Shakespear (1725). Preface is an excellent piece of critical appreciation. But the text is as slipshod and unsatisfactory as Lewis Theobald's *Shakespeare Restored* (1726) made it out to be.

The Grub-street Journal (1730—1737).[3] Weekly satirical review, founded by John Martyn. First issue opened with a quotation from *The Dunciad.* Almost with certainty it was undertaken as an organ of Pope, its chief purpose being to lampoon those who answered his *Dunciad* and to proclaim Pope's greatness.

Correspondence. Edited, amended, and doctored his letters before publication, and employed somewhat discreditable maneuvers to make it appear that they were published against his will. Addressed chiefly to notable persons, such as Swift, Gay, and Bolingbroke, they

---

1 Pope based his amatory epistle upon a French version of six letters of Heloise and Abelard, translated by John Hughes (1713). But the French version had little connection with the genuine Latin letters that had passed between the two lovers. See Audra, E., *L'Influence Francaise dans L'Oeuvre De Pope*, Chap. III, "Les Sources Françaises De L'Éloise," pp. 399-443 (available in *Bibliothèque de la Revue De Littérature Comparée*, Tome 72, 1931).

2 Wright, L. S., "Eighteenth-Century Replies to Pope's Eloisa," *Studies in Philology*, XXXI (1934), p. 533 (pp. 519-533).

3 Hillhouse, J. T., *The Grub-Street Journal* (1928).

are frequently nothing but pompous essays upon abstract subjects; but occasionally they show dignity and terseness, genuine affection and feeling.[1]

SUGGESTED MERITS	SUGGESTED DEFECTS
1. Unsurpassed perfection of the neo-classical couplet.	1. Lack of warm emotion, sensuous beauty, and continuous inspiration.
2. Heatless, faultless lucidity. Polished and brilliant diction. Unerring choice of right word, incisive clarity.	2. Poor in largeness of imagination. Rhetoric, not poetry. Periphrastic constructions and pretentious expressions.
3. Supreme satire and artifice. Cool wit, keen epigram, and mordant irony.	3. Falls short in large constructive power, great thinking, or any achievement in original narrative, lyric and dramatic poetry.
4. Outranks Dryden in keenness and polish of satiric verse.	4. Less versatile, vigorous, and possibly less coherent than Dryden.

5. Whereas Pope, in his satire, chiefly attacks immediate persons, Dryden attacks parties and sects, and Swift fulminates against all mankind.

---

1 Sherburn, George, ed., *The Correspondence of Alexander Pope* (Five Vols., 1956).

CHAPTER XVIII

THE AGE OF JOHNSON: THE DECLINE OF NEO-CLASSICISM
(1744—1784)

Historical Background

The Reign of George II (continued from page 337). (1) Peace of Aix-la-Chapelle (1748). (2) Adoption of Gregorian calendar (1752). (3) Beginning of the French and Indian War in America (1754). (4) Seven Years' War (1756—1763). (5) Clive wins his second great victory at Plassey (1757). (6) Opening of the British Museum (1759). (7) Accession of George III upon the death of his grandfather (1760).

The Reign of George III (1760—1820). (1) War declared on Spain (1762). (2) Declaration of a new policy (1763) marks the beginning of friction between Great Britain and the American colonies, which culminated in the American Revolution. The Peace of Paris (1783) marks the end of the conflict. (3) Arrest of John Wilkes (1763). (4) Letters of Junius (1769—1772). (5) France declares war on Great Britain (1778). (6) Defeat of Edmund Burke's bill advocating mild economic reform of government (1780). (7) Gordon demonstrations (1780). (8) Rodney's naval victory (1782). (9) Peace of Versailles and Paris (1783). (10) Pitt's India Act (1784). (11) Sinking Fund Act (1786). (12) Commercial treaty with France (1786). (13) French Republic declares war (1793). (14) Treasonable Correspondence Act (1793). (15) Spain declares war on Great Britain (1796). (16) Bank of England suspends specie payments (1797). (17) Rebellion in Ireland (1798). (18) Nelson defeats the French (1798). (See, also, page 440.)

Industrial Movement

The period was primarily transitional. It saw the beginnings of the phenomenal changes in social and economic structure that continued to the middle of the nineteenth century. Among the new methods and new machines introduced were Kay's flying shuttle (1733), Hargreave's spinning jenny (1764), Arkwright's water frame (1769), Crompton's "mule" (1779), Cartwright's power loom (1785), Watt's double-action steam engine (1785), Cort's method for rolling iron (1775—1785), and Davy's safety-lamp for miners (1815). Among the ultimate results of the industrial and agrarian revolutions (1730—1830) were the birth of the factory system, the decay of yeomanry, the doctrine of *laissez faire;* and, primarily, the division of society into the opposing classes of capital and labor. See, also, Chapter XXI, p. 440 *ff.*

General View of the Literature

a) **Classicism.** To a large extent classicism prevailed to the end of the period. Samuel Johnson, the literary czar, was a mighty defender of Augustan standards. Many of the poets who are classed as romanticists show traces of neo-classicism. (See Chapter XX, pp. 409—439.)

b) **Return To Nature.** In literature there were many evidences of transition. Most marked was the search for greater naturalness and freedom of expression. Many writers cast aside conventional literary technique, deserted the artificial pastoral, and revealed a sympathy for the poor and oppressed. (See Chapter XX, pp. 409—439.)

c) **Prose and Poetry.** Like the first half of the eighteenth century, the latter half is pre-eminently an age of prose, one becoming increasingly metropolitan. It continued the emphasis on classical learning and the ancient standards of literature, and the negation of enthusiasm and uncontrolled emotion. Essayists, historians, and philosophers were conspicuous; but the most important single development was the novel (see Chapter XIX, pp. 387—408). Finally, the prosaic spirit found expression in didactic and satiric verse.

Samuel Johnson, 1709—1784, poet, lexicographer, essayist, critic, romancer, dramatist, bibliographer; the greatest literary personality (not necessarily the greatest writer) of his age. First child of a fifty-two-year-old Lichfield bookseller of pronounced Tory views. Educated at Lichfield Grammar School (1717). Entered Pembroke College, Oxford (1728).[1] Left the University without a degree (1731).[2] Usher at Market Bosworth (1732). Married Mrs. Elizabeth Porter, a widow, his senior by twenty years (1735). With her seven hundred pounds he established an unsuccessful private school at Edial, near Lichfield. Accompanied by David Garrick, one of his few pupils (who later became the leading actor of the day), Johnson tramped to London to seek his fortune (1737). Accepted a life-pension of three hundred pounds a year from George III (1762). Gave shelter to Levett, a pauper's doctor, Miss Williams, blind daughter of a deceased physician, Mrs. Desmoulins, a penniless daughter of Johnson's godfather, and to a Miss Carmichael—his "seraglio," as he called it. Met Boswell (1763). Seconded Sir Joshua Reynolds in founding *The Club* (*c.* 1764), among whose nine original members were Burke, Goldsmith, and Sir John Hawkins. Intimate with the Thrales, to whom he frequently paid long visits, with whom he travelled to France (1775), and with whom he remained on terms of intimacy until after the death of Thrale (1781)

---

1 Pembroke College was the most Jacobitical in England, and it is still debatable whether Johnson, who sympathized with the Stuart cause and who disliked the House of Hanover, was a Jacobite. See Russell, Charles, "Johnson the Jacobite," *The Fortnightly Review*, New Series, CXI (1922), pp. 229-240; Ward, J. L., "Dr. Johnson the Jacobite," *Chamber's Journal*, I, Eighth Series (1932), pp. 372-374.

2 Whibley, Leonard, "Dr Johnson and the Universities," *Blackwood's Magazine*, CCXXVI (1929), pp. 369-383.

and the re-marriage of Mrs. Thrale (1784).[1] Received the LL.D. from Trinity College, Dublin (1765), and the D.C.L. from Oxford (1775). Buried in Westminster Abbey by the side of Garrick.

Satiric Poems

London: A Poem, in Imitation of the Third Satire of Juvenal (1738). Sharply expresses in the heroic couplet the disillusioning experience of Thales over the vanities and sins of London—its French fashions, dangerous criminals, oppression of the poor. "Reasoning-in-verse" adaptation of the Latin original betrays some political bias in its denunciation of the pension system, and some bitterness in its abuse of the town. Has been labeled somewhat insincere; his praise of the country is commonplace and his love of London undoubted.[2]

The Vanity of Human Wishes. The Tenth Satire of Juvenal (1749). Like *London,* is an expression of pessimism—an exhortation to be under no illusions concerning the futility of human endeavor. Serenely Christian conclusion of moralistic dissertation on the nothingness of life is the noblest poetry he ever wrote; and Oliver Elton has declared that "No stronger lines have ever been written in the heroic couplet than the conclusion." Admired by Scott.

Play and Novel

Irene (1749). Blank-verse pseudo-classical tragedy, suggested by Richard Knowles's *The Generall Historie of the Turkes* (1603).[3] Approaches unreadable dullness by the abounding artificial dialogues on moral truths. In Johnson's own words, "declamation war'd whilst passion slept"—passion that seldom awakened because it was benumbed by concepts, not exhilarated by intuitions. Racine's *Bajazet* (1672) is similar in theme.

The Prince of Abissinia. A Tale* (1759).[4] Romance of Rasselas, said to have been written in the evenings of one week to defray the expenses of the funeral of Johnson's mother, is a thinly-jointed moralistic work lacking in plot and incident, and honeyed primarily by a series of didactic, pensive disquisitions on life and man's normally disillusioning search after happiness. While sometimes conceding its occasional humor and kindly irony, detractors designate it as an expanded essay Johnsonese in its style and pompous in its melancholy.

---

1 It is asserted that our knowledge of Johnson will be considerably increased by our knowledge of his relation with the Thrales, and also their daughter Hester Maria or "Queeney." Consult *The Queeney Letters* edited by The Marquis of Lansdowne (1934), [H. W. E. Petty-Fitzmaurice]; and Vulliamy, C. E., *Mrs. Thrale of Streatham* (1936).

2 Its bitterness may be attributable in part to the tone of Juvenal from whom it is imitated, in part, perhaps, to the temper of Savage to whom it is addressed. Parrott, T. M., *The Personality of Johnson* (1909), p. 155 (pp. 132-172).

3 Smith, D. U., "Johnson's *Irene,*" *Essays and Studies by Members of The English Association* (1929), pp. 35-53.

4 *The History of Rasselas,* edited by Chapman, R. W. (1927).

† * Explanation of symbols immediately precedes Chapter XV.

His curious philosophy on the art of flying foresees the potentialities of destructive aircraft. Contemporary with Voltaire's *Candide*, a superficially parallel work differentiated by a pervasive satirical purpose.

Periodicals

Johnson contributed to *The Birmingham Journal, The Gentleman's Magazine, The Adventurer,*[1] *The Student, The Universal Visiter, The Literary Magazine, or Universal Review.* More important periodicals, imitative of *The Spectator* (p. 50), are:

The Rambler† (March 20, 1750—March 14, 1752). Of two-hundred-and-eight *Ramblers,* all except five are by Johnson. Purpose of two-penny paper, appearing Tuesdays and Saturdays, was to "inculcate wisdom and piety." Moral truths, enforced by precept and example, are their chief staple; but the ponderous essays, following *The Spectator,* in Lady Montagu's words, "as a packhorse would do a hunter," range from an essay on "Bashfulness" to one on "The Narrowness of Human Fame," from character-studies to allegories. His solemn generalizations on the vanity of human wishes have truth and beauty, and in many cases are written in excellent prose.[2] A record of Johnson's moral earnestness and penetrating insight into human character.

The Idler† (April 15, 1758—April 5, 1760). More than one hundred papers contributed to *The Universal Chronicle,* all save a dozen being his own. Variety of character-sketches includes Dick Minim the Critic, Betty Broom, Jack Whirler, and Mr. Sober (Johnson himself). Appeared once a week—perhaps one reason for a lightness and freshness greater than found in *The Rambler*. Linked the somewhat Latinized style of *The Rambler* to the more familiar style of *The Lives of the English Poets.*

Biographies and Critiques

An Account of the Life of Mr. Richard Savage (1744). First popular work, subsequently included with few changes in *The Lives of the English Poets.* Interesting, while not seldom inaccurate, account of a bohemian friend reputed to be the illegitimate son of the Countess of Macclesfield. Perhaps best account extant of Grub Street existence.

The Plays of William Shakespeare (Eight volumes, 1765). Strange judgments and errors of detail, yet this variorum edition is valuable for its notes, its clear prose renderings of some difficult passages in Shakespeare, and its meditative approach to the Avon poet as a student of man. Concentrated wisdom and sound sense make the *Preface*

---

1 Powell, L. F., "Johnson's Part in *The Adventurer,*" *The Review of English Studies,* III (1927), pp. 420-429.

2 *The Rambler* has popularized Macaulay's view that Johnson wrote in Johnsonese. In a limited sense this is true; but in the main it is excellent prose despite Macaulay and despite Archibald Campbell's witty burlesque in *Lexiphanes* (1767).

† • Explanation of symbols immediately precedes Chapter XV.

(despite Saintsbury's assertion of its worthlessness) possibly the finest essay of the day on Shakespeare. Somewhat declamatory style. Deficient, too, in a full understanding of the melodic and imaginative qualities of the plays.

The Lives of the English Poets† (Four volumes, 1779; Last six volumes, 1781). Selection of poets to be discussed made chiefly by the sponsors, two-score London booksellers. Considers the life and place in literature of fifty-two poets, from Cowley and Waller to Collins and Gray. Unequal critical estimates, colored by his prejudices; yet, outside Boswell's *Life*, no single work brings closer Johnson's opinions upon life and neo-classical principles. Sense of fact so dominates or excludes the imaginative qualities that he is unappreciative of lyric poetry; undersympathetic towards Gray and Milton, possibly oversympathetic towards Pope and Dryden. However, while political bias invalidated his attitude toward the great Puritan, it could not vitiate his liking for *L'Allegro* and *Il Penseroso*. Style lighter and more sagaciously conversational than usual.

Lexicography

The Plan of a Dictionary of the English Language (1747). Addressed to Lord Chesterfield.

A Dictionary of the English Language† (Two volumes, 1755). Foundation of all subsequent dictionaries. First to introduce illustrative quotations from standard authors to support definitions, citations being drawn from as far back as Sidney[1] to Johnson's *Vanity of Human Wishes*. Weak, however, in etymology. Indebted to three predecessors: Edward Phillips (1658), Robert Ainsworth (1735), and Nathan Bailey (1721, and especially 1730); in his revisions, to Benjamin Martin (1749).[2] Numerous definitions given with such precision and clarity that they are standard today; but occasionally colored by a personal and prejudiced approach. Not only did his lexicographic labors affect his style; they affected his conversational powers, without which his place as a man of letters would be much less secure.

Miscellaneous Works

Letter to Lord Chesterfield† (1755). Chesterfield's overtures in *The World* provoked this dignified, ironical letter containing little of the so-called "Johnsonese" style. Often regarded as having dealt the death blow to parasitic literary patronage in England. (See Johnson's definition of "patron," which seems to hold Chesterfield up to lasting obloquy.)

---

1 Johnson, however, despite his intention, made excursions beyond Sidney. For his sources consult Watkins, W. B. C., *Johnson and English Poetry Before 1660* (1936). For the contention that Johnson did not have as wide a knowledge of Elizabethan and pre-Elizabethan literature as is generally attributed to him, although his interest was undeniable, see Watkins, W. B. C., *idem*, p. 4 *ff.*

2 Only by comparing Johnson's work with preceding histories of lexicography can one realize how far he is ahead of his predecessors.

† * Explanation of symbols immediately precedes Chapter XV.

A Journal to the Western Islands of Scotland (1775).[1] Concerns the tour of Scotland and the Hebrides undertaken two years before by Johnson and Boswell. Stately prose, sometimes untactful in its comments; aside from some asperities that must have stung the Scottish people, is sympathetic and kind. (Boswell's account is better— see p. 374).

Taxation no Tyranny (1775). "An Answer to the Resolutions and Addresses of the American Congress" is a vain, sophistic defense of England's policy toward the American colonists.[2]

Prayers and Meditations (1785). Anguished confessional of his resolutions, few of which he carried out. A key to his personality.

Letters to and from the late Samuel Johnson (1788). Correspondence with Mrs. Thrale adds to our understanding of his versatile character.[3]

Johnson The Writer

SUGGESTED MERITS

1. Frequently racy, tonic sentences; apt, concentrated expressions. Complex but readily understood sentences.

2. Effective, orderly thinking and exposition.[4]

3. Teacher of moral wisdom.[5] Commonsense attitude toward problems.

4. Sonorous words.

SUGGESTED DEFECTS

1. Over-nicely balanced sentences; abstract rather than concrete; monotony (e.g., a continual use of the direct declarative sentence).

2. Cumbersome manner of expression and awkward inversions.

3. A moralist in everything he wrote. Opinions frequently colored by prejudice.

4. Copious use of Latinized vocabulary.

---

1 Knox, D. H., "Dr. Johnson in Scotland," *Proceedings of the Royal Philosophical Society of Glasgow*, LII-LIII (1922-1925), pp. 46-57.

2 Dr. Johnson abhorred war—and the Americans were stirring it up. He hated rebellion or insubordination—and the Americans were guilty of it: Harvey, C. W., "Johnson's Hatred of America," *The Cornhill Magazine*, LXVII (1929), pp. 656-668. In several ways he was archaic—notably in his opposition to women and their social rights: Vulliamy, C. E., *Mrs. Thrale of Streatham* (1936), pp. 245-251.

He believed not only that free discussion tended to promote a breach of peace, but that physical force becomes the measure of liberty. In his opinion, "every man has a right to utter what he thinks is truth, and every other man has the right to knock him down for it. Martyrdom is the test." He clung to old doctrines and established institutions; and in Literature he usually upheld established principles. Yet in his *Thoughts on the Late Transactions respecting Falkland Islands* (1771) he demonstrated keen eyesight into how war is utilized to befog and divert the minds of the common people from the struggles of liberty: for war "withdraws the attention of the publick from domestick grievances, and affords opportunities of dismissing the turbulent and restless to distant employments."

3 Edited by Chapman, R. W. (Three vols., 1952).

4 To-day not a few poets are turning back to the Augustan ideals, to Johnsonian "Reason." One recent example is Robert Bridges's *The Testament of Beauty*. Johnson "is commonly pictured as the last sturdy defender of a dying neo-classical faith. . . . In the first place, we find that Johnson was not sympathetic with the bulk of the literary output of his age . . . . Johnson also attacked with vigour many—perhaps most —of the prevailing fashions of the old established school of poetry." *The Critical Opinions of Samuel Johnson*, arranged and compiled by Brown, J. E. (1926), p. XVIII f. (pp. XV-LIV).

5 Everywhere, even in *The Lives of the English Poets*, Johnson wants to be a moralist. In his private book of prayers and meditations, he states that he wrote his *Lives* in such a manner, he hopes, as may tend to the promotion of piety.

"Johnsonese Style"

The defects of his sesquipedalian style—intensified by a lack of genuine appreciation of external Nature, and an earnest morality which contributes much to his present-day dullness—have given the name "Johnsonese" to the language. His early works, especially, are ponderously rich in Latin locutions.[1] Characterized by this style is Johnson's definition of *network* as "Any thing reticulated or decussated, at equal distances, with interstices between the intersections." As Goldsmith once commented, were Johnson to write a fable, he would make all the little fishes talk like whales; or, in Dr. John Wolcot's words, Johnson

> "Uplifts the club of Hercules—for what?
> To crush a butterfly or brain a gnat;
> Creates a whirlwind from the earth, to draw
> A goose's feather or exalt a straw."

Johnson The Man

In physical appearance Johnson loomed large and uncouth: Lord Auchinleck, Boswell's father, dubbed him *Ursa Major,* a "Great Bear" whose face was disfigured by scrofula.[2] His recorded talk by Boswell (p. 372) is his best monument[3]—talk which is foolish in its superstitions, gruff in its good will, benevolent in its bearishness, serious in its piety, dogmatic in its Toryism, unsleeping in its huge commonsense intellect. Of greater significance than Johnson the writer is Johnson the man: he was slovenly in dress and person, and dilatory in action: but in his idleness he found his true vocation.

James Boswell, 1740—1795, the prince of English biographers. Son of Alexander Boswell, a Scottish judge whose honorary title was Lord Auchinleck. Educated at Edinburgh University, Glasgow (1759). Made the acquaintance of Samuel Johnson on May 16, 1763. Studied law at Utrecht (1763), where he formed a friendship with Isabella de

---

1 It is a mistake, however, to believe that Johnson's style was primarily one of amplification depending upon the utilization of a Latin word in preference to an English one—briefly, it is a mistake to believe that his style was mainly Johnsonese.

2 Rolleston, Sir Humphrey, "Samuel Johnson's Medical Experiences," *Annals of Medical History,* New Series, I, (1929), pp. 540-552.

3 The assertion is now being made (with apparently good reason) that Boswell is not to be trusted for his pictures of Johnson's circle or of Johnson himself. For example, the scurrilous, ribald *Ode by Dr. Samuel Johnson to Mrs. Thrale, upon their supposed approaching Nuptials,* formerly attributed to Johnson, is much more likely by Boswell. However, the ode helps disprove the charge that Boswell's attitude toward Johnson was one of idolatry. Consult Howard, Geoffrey, "The Early Rising of Dr. Johnson," *The Cornhill Magazine,* Third New Series, LII (1922), p. 735 (pp. 729-735); Pottle, F. A., The Literary Career of James Boswell (1929), p. XXII *f.;* Kingsmill, Hugh, *Samuel Johnson* (1933), p. 198 *ff.;* Vulliamy, C. E., *Mrs. Thrale of Streatham.*

Zuylen ("Zélide").[1] Toured Europe, meeting Voltaire and Rousseau, and concluding with an interview with General Pasquale Paoli[2] (1765—1766). Admitted to the Scottish bar (1766).[3] Published *Dorando, a Spanish Tale,* a thin allegory of a *cause célèbre* openly discussed in his more ambitious *Essence of the Douglas Cause* (1767).[4] Married the dowerless Margaret Montgomerie (1769), who left him a widower with several children in 1789. Visited Johnson (1772), who brought him in as member of *The Club* (1773). Called to the English bar (1786). Recorder of Carlisle (1788—1790). Frequently visited Johnson in London; finally made his residence there (1789). Defeated for Parliament (1790). Published his *Life of Samuel Johnson* (1791).

Boswell is neither the miserable wine-bibber and witless parasite described by Macaulay and concurred in by Lytton Strachey, nor the genial figure others think him.[5] Women thought him despicable, yet admittedly droll-humored; his own father regarded him as a kind of Sancho Panza. He produced a masterpiece of biography, but not by accident; he was an industrious writer.[6]

An Account of Corsica, The Journal of a Tour to That Island: and Memoirs of Pascal Paoli (1768). Journal of travel and adventure[7] has easy, vivid touches and causeries that foreshadow the popularity of the Boswellian literary method.

British Essays in Favour of the Brave Corsicans (1769). Indicates his interest in the Island's struggle for liberty. (Supervised this publication written by several hands.)

The Hypochondriack (1777—1783).[8] Seventy informal essays, one appearing each month (see No. LXX) in the *London Magazine,*

---

1 Filon, Augustin, "Boswell's Love Story," *The Fortnightly Review,* LXXXVI; New Series, LXXX (1906), pp. 487-495; Gribble, Francis, "Boswell's Dutch Flirtation," *The Nineteenth Century and After,* LXXII (1912), pp. 942-952; Brown, J. T. T., "James Boswell: An Episode of His Grand Tour (1763-1766)," *Transactions of the Glasgow Archaeological Society,* New Series, VII, Part II, (1920) pp. 197-215.

2 It was Rousseau who gave Boswell an introduction to the Corsican patriot.

3 His fee book seems to indicate that he was an advocate in considerable practice. But see Henderson, J. S., "James Boswell and His Practice at the Bar," *The Juridical Review,* XVII (1905), pp. 105-115; Simpson, T. B., "Boswell as an Advocate," *Juridical Review,* XXXIV (1922), pp. 201-225.; Duke, Winifred, "Boswell Among the Lawyers," *The Juridical Review,* XXXVIII (1926), pp. 341-370.

4 Duke, Winifred, "Boswell Among the Lawyers," *The Juridical Review,* XXXVIII (1926), pp. 345-350 (pp. 341-370); Bailey, Margaret, "James Boswell: Lawyer or Press-Agent," *The Dalhousie Review,* X (1930-1931), p. 481-494; Esdaile, Arundell, "Boswell in his Diaries," *The Library Association Record,* I (1934), p. 37 (pp. 34-40).

5 Vulliamy, C. E., *James Boswell* (1932), Chap. XVI, "Macaulay's Boswell," pp. 227-243; Kirwan, H. N., "The Boswell Supplement," *The London Mercury,* XXVII (1933), pp. 335-340 (pp. 331-340).

6 Pottle, F. A., *The Literary Career of James Boswell* (1929); *The Private Papers from Malahide Castle,* edited by Scott, Geoffrey, and Pottle, F. A. (Sixteen volumes by Boswell, 1928-1932); *Boswell on the Grand Tour: Germany and Switzerland* (1953).

7 Boyle, Edward, *Biographical Essays* (1936), "Pasquale Paoli," pp. 115-134.

8 Brown, J. T. T., "James Boswell as Essayist," *The Scotch Historical Review,* XVII (1921), pp. 102-116; *The Hypochondriack,* edited by Bailey, Margaret (Two volumes, 1928).

dealing frequently with hackneyed subjects and weighted down with Latin, Greek, and other quotations. Important for his prejudices, political tenets, and social standards: *e.g.*, No. III wonders at the short-sightedness of human beings who soberly prepare "the instruments of destruction of their own species."

Journal of a Tour to the Hebrides with Samuel Johnson, LL.D.† (written 1773; published 1785; first completely published 1936).[1] Important travel-journal inimitable for its picture of Scottish conditions in 1773. Trevelyan has described it as the sprightliest travel-book in the language: it assuredly is more intimate than Johnson's account (p. 371), and, above all, is a standard of indiscretion.

The Life of Samuel Johnson LL.D.† (Two volumes, 1791).[2] Perhaps the greatest English biography. Draws Johnson "warts and all"[3]—his short temper and violent prejudices, his careless but independent and cogent table-talk (see p. 372). Includes the whole Johnsonian circle—Burke, Dr. Charles Burney, the Earl of Chesterfield, Garrick, Goldsmith, Mrs. Samuel Johnson, Sir Joshua Reynolds, Hester Lynch Thrale (later Mrs. Piozzi), and many others. Felicity of diction, vivid imagination, clearness of style, acuteness of perception, three-dimensional life-likeness of portraiture; its deadwood, some say, lies in its poor gossip, vexing footnotes, and list of variant readings. In immortalizing Samuel Johnson, Boswell immortalized himself.

Oliver Goldsmith, *c.* 1730[4]—1774, novelist, dramatist, poet, essayist.[5] Born in Ireland of a poor English Protestant family. Son of a vicar. Sizar at Trinity College, Dublin (1744). B.A. (1749). Rejected for ordination (1751). Went to the University of Edinburgh to study medicine (1753), but soon left for Leyden[6] (*c.* 1754), whence he set out on foot "disputing his passage through Europe" (1755—1756). May have taken a medical degree at either Louvain or Padua. Returned to England (1756). Abandoned two-year-old plan to go as a doctor to

---

1 Edited in full by Pottle, F. A., and Bennett, C. H. (1936).

2 The best edition is *Boswell's Life of Johnson,* edited by Hill, G. B.; revised and enlarged by Powell, L. F. (Four volumes, 1934).

3 Johnson is being de-Boswellized on the ground that his biographer may have distorted facts by selecting his materials. Pearson, Hasketh, "Boswell as Artist," *The Cornhill Magazine* LXXIII (1932), pp. 704-711. See also footnote 3, page 372.

4 K. C. Balderston casts doubt upon the conventionally accepted date of his birth, stating that it may possibly be 1730 or 1731. See Balderston, K. C., (1) *The History & Sources of Percy's Memoir of Goldsmith* (1926); (2) "The Birth of Goldsmith," *The London Times Literary Supplement,* March 7, 1929, p. 185 *f.* Consult, also, the anonymous article, "Oliver Goldsmith, 1728(?)-1774," *The London Times Literary Supplement,* November 8, 1928, p. 813 *f.*

5 Prior, James, *The Life of Oliver Goldsmith* (1837); *The Works of Oliver Goldsmith,* edited by Gibbs, J. W. M. (Four volumes, 1884); Moore, F. F., *The Life of Oliver Goldsmith* (1911); Balderston, K. C., *The History & Sources of Percy's Memoir of Goldsmith* (1926).

6 Swaen, A. E. G., "Fielding and Goldsmith at Leyden," *The Modern Language Review,* I (1905-1906), p. 327 *f.* Proves that Goldsmith was not a regular student at Leyden in 1754, or at any other time.

† *   Explanation of symbols immediately precedes Chapter XV.

the coast of Coromandel (1759).[1] One of the nine original members of *The Club.* After successively attempting to become a clergyman, lawyer, doctor,[2] teacher, and actor, he finally became a writer. Goldy's quill poured out works that made him the prince of literary hacks, yet he wrote masterpieces in at least four forms of literature—prose fiction, drama, poetry, essay. General characteristics are their easy optimism, sweet purity, rollicking perceptions, genial sympathy and common-sense, delicate irony, finished but fluent lines, idealizing felicity of touch, and natural simplicity and sincerity.[3]

As a poet, his two principal works are in the loose heroic couplet measure; on the whole he is Augustan in frame and spirit. As an essay-ist, he is also neo-classical, and many of his essays are in the tradition of Steele and Addison. As a dramatist, he blends the comedy of the Restoration, without its *double-entendres* and indecent situations, with the Comedy of Sentiment, without its mawkishness. But in the traces of sentimentality the Doctor Minor is an embryonic precursor of the romantic movement.

Poetry

The Traveller, or a Prospect of Society† (1764; dated 1765). Ethical poem, in rimed couplets, dedicated to his brother, a country clergyman. Despite stock phrases and thoughts, is notable for sweet versification, simplicity and elegance of diction, arresting descriptive passages, and philosophic thought not to be described as scholiastic. Mood of pensive melancholy anticipates the Romantic poets. (Nine lines have been ascribed to Johnson.)

The Deserted Village† (1769; dated 1770). Compact, homesick poem-with-a-purpose gives, in artless but consummate way, romanti-cally simple pictures of a happy, rural community from which the pea-sants are emigrating because of the encroachments of the new industrial order, and also sweet pictures of the chief characters. Rimed couplets. Both its economics and sociology are questionable. Some factual blem-ishes and incongruous parts, but yet a classic. Of greater depth and emotion than *The Traveller,* although less carefully elaborated: both are characterized by a sympathetic social outlook preluding the romantic

---

1 An explanation of his change of mind is available in Balderston, K. C., *The Col-lected Letters of Oliver Goldsmith* (1928), pp. xxx-xxxiii.
2 Clarke, Ernest, "Oliver Goldsmith as a Medical Man," *The Nineteenth Century,* LXXV (1914), pp. 821-831.
3 The following is considered an excellent criticism of Goldsmith's style: "Goldsmith, then, was not inventive, nor fertile, nor varied, nor astonishing. Though he may sometimes be called a painter of *genre,* his work is essentially not *genre;* that is, it does not exhibit common life as common life. His greatest gift is one of transforma-tion. The earthly he renders unearthly, the commonplace strange. . . . The counterfeit presentment of real life which others furnished him he has touched with a kind of magic that fills it with delicate half-visionary charm, causing it to recede into an untraveled world . . . ." Osgood, C. G., Jr., "Notes on Goldsmith," *Modern Philology,* V (1907-1908), p. 252 (pp. 241-252).

† * Explanation of symbols immediately precedes Chapter XV.

age. Inscribed to Sir Joshua Reynolds in an exquisitely-couched dedication: "The only dedication I ever made was to my brother, because I loved him better than most men. He is since dead. Permit me to inscribe this poem to you."

Retaliation (1774). Kindly, witty, unfinished series of mock-epitaphs good-naturedly sharp in their portraits of Burke, Reynolds, and others. Goldsmith, previously characterized quite falsely by Garrick as "Noll,"
"Who wrote like an angel, but talked like poor Poll,"
hits off this answering epitaph:
"On the stage he was natural, simple, affecting;
'Twas only that when he was off he was acting."

The Haunch of Venison, a Poetical Epistle to Lord Clare (1776). Excellent light-verse satire, in acknowledgment of the venison sent Goldsmith by Lord Clare, contains a personal attack upon the parson Scott, author of *Anti-Sejanus.*

Novel and Dramas

The Vicar of Wakefield†* (1766). Novel[1] concerns the immortal family of Wakefield, with its inimitable types, naive simplicity of narrative, pungent but venomless ridicule, restrained expression, homely sentiment, sparkling wit, Arcadian pathos. Neither the inconsistencies and improbabilities of the plot nor the almost farcical *dénouement* can cripple the wholesome charm of this domestic epic. Happy mingling of idyllic life and practical wisdom, of nature and humanity. Lacks the ribaldry of contemporary novels like *Pamela* and *Tom Jones.* Famous creations include the Reverend Dr. Primrose, his son Moses, his daughters Olivia and Sophia, and Miss Carolina Wilhelmina Amelia Skeggs. Contains also two poems, "Elegy on the Death of a Mad Dog," and "When lovely woman stoops to folly"; also the famous sentimental ballad, "The Hermit" (originally called "Edwin and Angelina" about a year prior to appearance of the novel).

The Good-Natur'd Man* (1768). Prose comedy not wholly free from sentimentalism. Confused in plot, but interesting for its irresistible humor and the comic creations of Croker and Lofty.

She Stoops to Conquer: Or, The Mistakes of a Night†* (written 1771; produced 1773). Full-blooded farce-comedy of incident, unlike the anemic imitations of the *comédie larmoyante* of the day.[2]

---

1 Why did Goldsmith call his novel *The Vicar of Wakefield* when the place itself plays but a small part in the story? See *The Plays of Oliver Goldsmith, together with The Vicar of Wakefield,* edited by Doble, C. E., and Ostler, G. (1928), p. 484 *f.,* p. 508.

2 More than once this play has been declared as dealing a death blow to the sentimental type of drama. While antagonistic to the sentimental comedy because the latter was lachrymatory rather than mirth-provoking, it is important to note that Goldsmith merely attacked the extreme form of humorless sentimentality of the *comédie larmoyante.*

† * **Explanation of symbols immediately precedes Chapter XV.**

Ridiculous incidents, sketchy characterization, plot and technique still faulty. Pronounced comic humor, brisk action, naturally spirited dialogue, mellow sentimentality, dramatic irony. Memorable creation: Tony Lumpkin. Title possibly derived from Dryden; sources in Numbers 289 and 427 of *The Spectator*. Obvious resemblance to Farquhar's *Beaux Stratagem*.[1]

The Grumbler (1773). One-act farce[2] in which Sourby the Grumbler is eventually persuaded to renounce Clarissa to his son Octavio. Compressed adaptation of Sir Charles Sedley's translation of *Le Groundeur* (1691) by D. A. Brueys and Jean Palaprat. (See p. 304.)

Periodical and Essay Writing

The Bee (1759). Short-lived (October 3 to November 24, 1759). Edited by Goldsmith.[3]

Weekly magazine: or, Gentleman and lady's polite Companion (1759—1760). Contributed several pieces.[4]

The Citizen of the World; or Letters from a Chinese Philosopher, Residing in London, to his Friends in the East† (1760—1761). Series of one hundred and twenty-three mellow pot-boiling essays, originally contributed twice a week to Newbury's *Public Ledger* under the title of "The Chinese Letters," represents "the classic example of the pseudo-letter in the English language," and gives a fairly complete picture of the middle and lower classes in the England of 1760. Purpose of pseudo-letter device was to discuss and expose the political intrigues and moral opinions of the English; advocating, for example, the reform of the laws of marriage and divorce, and foreseeing both the successful secession of the American colonies and the rise of Russia. In this graceful, delicately-humored, common-sense work, in which Lien Chi Altangi the Chinaman is the central figure, appear the two memorable characters, Beau Tibbs and the Man in Black. Forerunners of these letters professedly written by a Chinese visitor, are

---

1 Both *The Vicar of Wakefield* and *She Stoops to Conquer* are generally regarded as original works. But see Ingalls, G. Van A., "Some Sources of Goldsmith's *She Stoops to Conquer*," *Publications of the Modern Language Association of America*, XLIV (1929), pp. 565-568. Even Goldsmith's *Life of Christ* (1774) and *Lives of the Fathers* (1774) may not be translations but taken from *Apostolici* and *Ecclesiastici*, two works by William Cave: see Seitz, R. W., "Goldsmith's *Lives of the Fathers*," *Modern Philology*, XXVI (1928-1929), pp. 295-305.

2 *The Grumbler*, edited by Wood, A. I. P. (1931).

3 Some essays have been declared under the influence of a Dutch essayist. Consult Barnouw, A. J., "Goldsmith's Indebtedness to Justus van Effen," *Modern Language Review*, VIII (1913), pp. 314-323.

4 Possibly Goldsmith contributed more essays to the *Weekly Magazine* than is generally believed. Consult Friedman, Arthur, "Goldsmith and the *Weekly Magazine*," *Modern Philology*, XXXII (1934-1935), pp. 281-299.

† * Explanation of symbols immediately precedes Chapter XV.

Montesquieu and Addison. Sources are pseudo-letters and reference books, mainly Oriental: Voltaire, Lyttleton, Walpole,[1] Le Comte, Du Halde, Byrom, Johnson, and others.[2]

Essays. By Mr. Goldsmith (1765). His masterpieces are the "Reverie at the Boar's-Head Tavern" and "Asem, an Eastern Tale," which has been declared as anticipating the theory of Nathaniel Hawthorne's *The Marble Faun*. Most apparent defect of his essay-writing is repetition, an outgrowth in part of his fundamental poverty of ideas.

Miscellaneous Works

An Enquiry into the Present State of Polite Learning in Europe (1759). Fairly sensible and lively analysis of the decline of polite learning in France, Italy, Holland, Germany, and England, attributing the decline in England to the artificialities of poets, the restrictions upon them, and the shortcomings of the universities. Pleads for humor in comedy, just as the preface of *The Good-Natur'd Man* tilts at the false delicacy of genteel comedy, which excluded humor and "low" characters. Clear style, musical quality.

An History of the Earth, and Animated Nature (Eight volumes, 1774). Account, based on such men as Linnaeus, Gesner, Boyle, Buffon, and Aristotle,[3] reveals the picturesque English and delightful personality of Goldsmith while simultaneously betraying his deficient critical spirit and shallow "transplanted knowledge": he describes giants nine feet high, tigers in Canada, monkeys that preach sermons.

Richard Brinsley Butler Sheridan, 1751—1816: "at once the heir to the best traditions of Restoration comedy and the most notable English dramatist of the eighteenth century."[4] Dubliner educated at the English school of Harrow (1762). Ran off with Elizabeth Ann Linley, daughter of the famous composer (1772); married her (1773). Became part owner and director of the Drury Lane Theatre (1776). M.P. for Stafford (1780—1812), during which he made his great six-hour speech against Warren Hastings in 1787. Under-Secretary of State for Foreign Affairs in Rockingham's Administration (1782). Secretary to the Treasury in Coalition Government (1783). Opposed Burke's at-

---

1 While it is likely that Horace Walpole's *Letter from XoHo, a Chinese Philosopher at London, to his Friend Lien Chi, at Peking* may have influenced Goldsmith, it should not be assumed that Walpole's letter from a Chinese philosopher furnished Goldsmith with the plan for *The Citizen of the World*. Such is the contention of Davidson, L. J., "Forerunners of Goldsmith's *The Citizen of the World*," *Modern Language Notes*, xxxvi (1921), pp. 215-220. See, also, Stuart, D. M., *Horace Walpole* (1927), p. 139.

2 Smith, H. J., *Oliver Goldsmith's The Citizen of the World* (1926), Chaps. v-vi, pp. 39-85, pp. 85-114; Crane, R. S., and Smith, H. J., "A French Influence on Goldsmith's *Citizen of the World*," *Modern Philology*, xix (1921-1922), pp. 83-92.

3 For the sources see Pitman, J. H., *Goldsmith's Animated Nature* (1924), pp. 137-152.

4 Nettleton, G. H., *English Drama of the Restoration and Eighteenth Century* (1932), p. 313.

tack on the French Revolution. Married Esther Jane Ogle (1795), three years after death of Ann. Arrested for debt (c. 1813). Buried in Westminster Abbey.[1]

In Sheridan the artificial comedy reaches its climax, and the anti-sentimental movement its culmination. Amusing scenes, clever situations, epigrammatic wit, satiric character-drawing; displays Congreve's brilliance of dialogue without the cynicism and the salaciousness. Deeper insight, more sophisticated dramatic irony and satire, surer mastery of stage technique than Goldsmith; but less sympathetic. In the oft-quoted words of Sir Henry Irving, "Sheridan brought the comedy of manners to the highest perfection."

The Duenna (1775). Successful comic opera (music by Thomas Linley) interspersed with proverbial sayings and lilting lyrics. On the whole, uses familiar stage machinery. Songs: "O what a plague is an obstinate daughter"; "Had I a heart for falsehood framed"; "Oh, the days when I was young."

St. Patrick's Day; or, The Scheming Lieutenant (1775). Slight piece, sometimes considered possibly an over-long farce, as amusing but less polished than his other works. Some sprightly dialogue. Somewhat reminiscent of Molière.

The Rivals† (1775). Prose comedy reveals the carefree wit and accomplished sophistication of Sheridan in his early twenties.[2] Extravagantly sentimental creations of Faulkland and Julia, of the sub-plot, contradict the traditional assertion that this comedy is an attack upon the school of sentimentalism. Stock caricatures more than counterbalanced by their varied and distinguished characterization, the skillfully-managed plot, and farcically boisterous scenes (between son and father, and the duellers, for example). Note the "referential" swearing of Bob Acres and the "malapropisms" of Mrs. Malaprop. Resemblances have been found in Shakespeare, Congreve, and Steele, but the play is Sheridan's own.

The School for Scandal†* (1777). His masterpiece is the best English drama of the eighteenth century. Prose comedy, originally composed of two plays called *The Slanderers* and *The Teazles,* satirizes the canting tittle-tattles of fashionable society, their vices and foibles. Sparkling wit, epigrammatic conversation, brilliant raillery, happily-managed plot, kindly sentimentalism, incisive insight into human character. Most famous is the screen episode. Resemblances have been located in Wycherley, Congreve, and Fielding's *Tom Jones*.

---

1 Darlington, W. A., *Sheridan* (1933); Rhodes, R. C., *Harlequin Sheridan* (1933).

2 The first presentation was a failure, and eleven days after, when presented for the second time, it was a success. To discover what had been done in the interval consult *The Rivals*, edited from the Larpent MS. by Purdy, R. L. (1935).

† * **Explanation of symbols immediately precedes Chapter XV.**

A Trip to Scarborough (1777). Prose comedy, which modifies competently the plot of Vanbrugh's *The Relapse* (page 308).

The Critic, or A Tragedy Rehearsed* (1779). Prose comedy, deficient in dramatic symmetry, satirizes the contemporary sentimental drama and burlesques its literary criticism. Has mock-heroic, learned footnotes parodying the erudite commentaries of scholars. Sir Fretful Plagiary is identical with the dramatist, Richard Cumberland. Forerunners of idea were Beaumont and Fletcher's *The Knight of the Burning Pestle* (Vol. I, p. 243), Villiers's *The Rehearsal* (p. 293), and Fielding's *Tragedy of Tragedies* (p. 394).

Philip Dormer Stanhope, Fourth Earl of Chesterfield, 1694—1773, author, orator, statesman, man of fashion.[1] Entered Trinity Hall, Cambridge (1712). Appointed Gentleman of the Bed-Chamber to the Prince of Wales (1715). Whig member of House of Commons (1715). Captain of the Gentleman-Pensioners (1723). Upon death of father, succeeds to the Earldom (1726). Ambassador at The Hague (1728—1732), where Mlle. du Bouchet became mother of his natural son (1732) to whom the famous letters are addressed. Elected Knight of the Garter (1730). Resigns from The Hague (1732). Dismissed from office by the King in consequence of his opposition to Walpole's Excise Bill (1733). Married Petronilla Melusina von der Sculenberg (Countess of Walsingham), bastard daughter of the King by the Duchess of Kendal (1733).[2] Led an unsuccessful attack on Walpole's bill for restricting the liberty of the theatre (1737). Begins to write *Letters to his Son* (1739). Travelled on the Continent (1741). Fall of Walpole (1742): fall of Carteret (1744); Chesterfield appointed Envoy to The Hague (1744). Lord Lieutenant of Ireland (1745—1746). Secretary of State (1746). Resigns (1748). Proposes and secures the adoption by England of the Gregorian calendar (1751). Owing to deafness, retires from public life (1755). Birth of his godson and successor, Philip Stanhope (1755). Elected member of the Academy of Inscriptions at Paris (1755). Evokes Johnson's famous letter (1755—see p. 370).[3] Begins series of *Letters to His Godson* (1761). Death of his natural son (1768). Complete breakdown of health (1772). A Charles Grandison to the end: as someone came into the room, he roused himself to say: "Give Dayrolles a chair"—and said no more (1773).

---

1 Shellabarger, Samuel, *Lord Chesterfield* (1935).

2 Quoting Lytton Strachey: Melusina "is described as *amiable* and *accomplished*, adjectives commonly applied in the eighteenth century to ladies about whom there is not much to say!" His marriage seemed to be entirely a matter of convenience, and in his letters he advises his son to polish off his education by forming an attachment to a lady of quality.

3 Whibley, Charles, "Lord Chesterfield," *The Criterion*, II (1923-1924), pp. 236-239 (pp. 236-257); Baker, H. A., "Chesterfield and Johnson," *The Contemporary Review*, CXXXVII (1930), pp. 352-360.

† * Explanation of symbols immediately precedes Chapter XV.

Letters†[1] (to his natural son, 1774; to his godson, 1761—1763, first published 1890). Good-tempered worldly instruction[2] designed to make recipient a complete gentleman and courtier.[3] Not written for publication. Denounced by Johnson as teaching "the morals of a whore, and the manners of a dancing master"[4]; unjustly so denounced, for Chesterfield's intellectual honesty urges neither one nor the other, but rather a practical morality whose defects were those of the society to which he belonged, one that aimed at stability, balance, and self-possession. One of his repeated rules "suaviter in modo, fortiter in re." In advocating proportion in conduct, admonished his son against frequent and loud laughter because it is vulgar and unaesthetic.[5] Occasionally witty, yet humorless. Tedious and repetitious, the monotony often arising from a sameness or theme. Unadorned English with few metaphors and no similes; well-turned phrases, unfaltering style, scrupulous finish.[6] Chesterfield improved not only the standard of English manners but also advanced that of English prose.

Edward Gibbon, 1737—1794, the best eighteenth-century historiographer.[7] Scion of a well-to-do Protestant family. Educated at Westminster (1748) and Magdalen College, Oxford (1753). Converted to Roman Catholicism (1753)[8]; sent immediately by his father to Lausanne, where he was reconverted to Protestantism (*c.* 1755)—but finally became an agnostic. Falling in love with Mlle. Suzanne Curchod, afterwards Madame Necker, Gibbon, when threatened with disinheritance,

---

1 The best edition of his *Letters* is edited by Dobrée, Bonamy (Six volumes, 1932).

2 The same wordly advice appears in *Letters of Lord Chesterfield to Lord Huntingdon*, edited by Steuart, A. F. (1923).

3 Sherman, Stuart, *Shaping Men and Women*, "Lord Chesterfield's Ideas on Education," pp. 144-157, edited by Zeitlin, Jacob (1932).

4 That was Johnson's remark at a time when he still smarted over Chesterfield's lukewarm attitude toward the Dictionary (p. 370). Both had no high opinion of women, but Chesterfield disregarded the virtue of chastity. The latter Cowper described in *The Progress of Error* as the "polished and high-finished foe to truth" and the "Graybeard corrupter of our lasting youth."

Johnson's true opinion came out later when he described the *Letters* as the work of a statesman and a wit: with the immorality taken out, the *Letters* "should be put into the hands of every young gentleman."

5 Allen, E. S., "Chesterfield's Objection to Laughter," *Modern Language Notes*, XXXVIII (1923), pp. 279-287; Heltzel, V. B., "Chesterfield and the Anti-Laughter Tradition," *Modern Philology*, XXVI (1928), pp. 73-90.

6 The French quality of Chesterfield's mind and style has often been pointed out. As a matter of fact, it was Sainte-Beuve who re-discovered the richness and value of the *Letters.*

7 Low, D. M., *Edward Gibbon* (1937); Norton, J. E., *A Bibliography* (1940); Norton, J. E., *Letters* (Three vols., 1956).

8 Hutton, Edward, "The Conversion of Edward Gibbon," *The Nineteenth Century and After*, XCI (1932), pp. 362-375.

† * Explanation of symbols immediately precedes Chapter XV.

"sighed as a lover," but "obeyed as a son."[1] Captain in the South Battalion of the Hants Militia Regiment (1759); Major (1763); resigns his Commission as Lieutenant-Colonel Commanding (1770). Member of Parliament (1774—1780).

L'Essai sur l'Étude de la Littérature(French version 1761; English, 1764). Reflective, if unoriginal, poorly ordered, and somewhat incoherent "Essay on the Study of Literature" in eighty-three chapters purposes a vindication of classical studies. Succeeds in indicating the value of knowledge and the importance of history in scientific criticism. As Gibbon put it, "written in two months and forgotten in four," his style, he continued, "degenerated into a verbose and turgid declamation."

Mémoires littéraires de la Grande Bretagne (1767—1768). About a score of good, comprehensive reviews of English books of his day. Written in conjunction with Georges Deyverdum.[2]

Ephemerides or Journal of My Actions, Studies and Opinions† (1761—1764).[3] Of greater personal value than his *Memoirs,* meant for publication. "My Life" carries Gibbon to the end of his militia experience.

The History of the Decline and Fall of the Roman Empire† (I, 1776; II, III, 1781; IV, V, VI, 1788). When regarded as pure literature, is a supreme work of prose. Historical masterwork covers about thirteen centuries, from the age of Trajan (A.D. 98) to the taking of Constantinople (1453). Guiding idea or "moral," says J. B. Bury, is Gibbon's statement: "I have described the triumph of barbarism and religion"—thus epitomizing his belief in an inextricable connection "between the decline of the Empire and the growth and triumph of the Church." His *History* has been described as a monumental landmark in the historic vistas of rationalism.[4]

---

1 Their supposed engagement did not last four years but a few months. An unexcelled brief account of the affair is presented in *Gibbon's Journal,* edited by Low, D. M. (1929), pp. LXIV-LXXXII (§ 4, pp. LIV-LXXXII) in the Introduction, pp. XIII-CXVII. For Gibbon's own account, see *Memoirs of the Life and Writings of Edward Gibbon,* edited by Emerson, O. F. (1898), p. 87.

2 Helming, V. P., "Edward Gibbon and Georges Deyverdun, Collaborators in the *Memoires Litteraires De La Grande Bretagne.*" *Publications of the Modern Language Association of America,* XLVII (1932), pp. 1028-1049.

3 *Gibbon's Journal,* edited by Low, D. M. (1929).

4 Gibbon was the first to give a comprehensive treatment of the rise of Christianity as a natural phenomenon, thereby attacking the teaching that Christianity appeared in the world as a divine revelation and that its triumph was wondrous and providential, and emphasizing that the rise of Christianity and the fall of the Empire were "parallel effects of a general collapse of the intellect under the pressure of a world-tyranny" (the Church). As early as 1783, he was placed on the *Index Librorum Prohibitorum.* To-day we recognize that the Roman Empire fell because of a process of sociological decay.

† • Explanation of symbols immediately precedes Chapter XV.

SUGGESTED MERITS
(Gibbon's *History*)

SUGGESTED DEFECTS
(Gibbon's *History*)

1. Unobtrusive antithesis, descriptive brilliance, and luminous architectonic structure of his unit, the paragraph.[1]

2. Nervous flow of narrative. Diction stately and ornate.

3. Dryly cultivated and mordant irony. Vast erudition. Picturesque, dramatic, allusive, laconic. Original power and ordered judgment. Epic gravity of utterance.

4. First great history to be based on scientific research, still substantial in its general accuracy. Marvellous condensation of details. Proportional and organized sequence of cause and effect. Solidity of structure. Sustained logic.

1. Tendency toward stiffness, monotony, repetition of expressions, and Johnson's sesquipedalianism.

2. Occasional ornateness where plainness of diction might be more appropriate.

3. Deficiency of philosophic insight and historic imagination. Absence of emotional response. Want of sympathy with the spiritual nature of man, while stressing the historic side of human problems.

4. Descriptive rather than analytical. Some want of proportion. Somewhat sneering in its ironical deference toward Christianity.[2] Not only may his anti-Christian arguments be antiquated but his method of historical research may be defective or obsolete.

Memoirs of My Life and Writings† (1795).[3] Fascinating glimpses of his intellectual life. Compact structure, unvarying elegance, fine edge of sardonic humor.

Edmund Burke, *c.* 1729—1797, statesman, orator, writer. Born in Dublin of a Protestant father and a Catholic mother. Educated at Trinity College, Dublin (1744—1748). Founded *The Club,* the first student debating society that history records (1747). Entered the Middle Temple in London (1750). Married Jane Nugent (1756). Private secretary to "Single-speech" Hamilton, Secretary for Ireland (1761—1763). Member of the famous literary group known as *The Club* (*c.* 1764). Private Secretary to the Marquis of Rockingham (1765—1782). Member of Parliament (1766). Entered the ministry as Paymaster of the Forces (1782). Opened the case for the impeachment of Warren Hastings, Governor-General of India (1788). Spoke against the French Government (1790). Broke with his Whig friends on account of his opposition to the French Revolution. Was pensioned upon his retirement in 1794. Dominant tone of his mind was conservative; dominant objective of this philosophical realist was—so runs the opinion—the championing of justice for Britain and her colonies, including not only

---

1 Black, J. B., *The Art of History* (1926), "Gibbon," pp. 143-183.

2 His fifteenth and sixteenth chapters dealing with the origins of Christianity provoked a storm of controversy. Gibbon's *Vindication* (1779) of his chapters in which he explained the rise of Christianity in terms of natural social causation practically routed his opponents. Consult McCloy, S. T., *Gibbon's Antagonism to Christianity* (1933).

3 These memoirs were put together out of six autobiographical fragments extant.

† * Explanation of symbols immediately precedes Chapter XV.

America but also Ireland and India.[1] Was nicknamed the "Dinner
Bell" because usually he emptied the House when he rose to speak.

Lucid, eloquent prose vies with occasional bombast; Celtic luxuriance of expression, with exaggerated coloring; and echoing prose, with
rhetorical tricks. Throughout, however, is sustained a classical idiom,
a withering scorn, and an introspective poise. He perfected an exposition and argument characterized by starting with topic sentences and
ending with summaries. According to J. R. Green, his characteristics
are passionate ardor, poetic fancy, amazing prodigality of resources; "the
dazzling succession in which irony, pathos, invective, tenderness, the
most brilliant word-pictures, the coolest argument followed each other."

The Reformer (1747—1748).[2] Thirteen numbers of a weekly miscellany written and edited almost exclusively by Burke. Its design was
to examine "our Theatrical Amusements" as well as works of literature
—and in its second number Burke denounces the immorality of
Sheridan's plays.

A Vindication of Natural Science (1756). Ironical treatise refutes clearly, but superficially, and with sobriety Bolingbroke's indictment of natural or revealed religion by showing that the same specious
reasoning might be employed in a similar fashion to subvert all forms
of organized and civilized society. (See the preface added to the 1765
edition.) Able parody of style made people mistake the tract for a
posthumous work by Bolingbroke. "Artificial theology has inflicted injury," says Burke, "but has not artificial law done the same?"

*A Philosophical Enquiry into the Origins of our Ideas of
the Sublime and the Beautiful* (1765). Treatise attempts to formu-
late a theory of aesthetics. Conceives that from the two principles of
self and of society are derived our ideas on the subject, that of the sublime being founded on the emotion of terror (pain and danger), and

---

1 "The most conspicuous features of his political outpourings are, first, his avoidance
of abstract political speculation and his denunciation of the metaphysical treatment
of practical affairs; secondly, his insistence on the empirical nature of the art of
government; thirdly, his appeal to history and experience as the only satisfactory
guides in administrative matters; fourthly, his emphasis on considerations of expediency,
rather than on arguments based on rights, in all debatable problems of policy; and,
finally, the essential moderation of all his opinions, even when he expressed these
opinions with extreme immoderation of language." Hearnshaw, F. J. C., "Edmund
Burke," in *The Social & Political Ideas of Some Representative Thinkers of the
Revolutionary Era*, edited by Hearnshaw, F. J. C. (1931), p. 89 (pp. 72-99). Consult,
also, Pillans, T. D., *Edmund Burke: Apostle of Justice and Liberty* (1905); Butler,
G. G., *The Tory Tradition* (1914), "Edmund Burke," pp. 30-59; B(aumann), A. A.,
The Founder of Conservatism (1929); Whitney, Lois, *Primitivism and the Idea of
Progress* (1934), pp. 193-205 (Chap. vi, pp. 168-205); Einaudi, Mario, "The British
Background of Burke's Political Philosophy," *Political Science Quarterly*, XLIX,
No. 4 (1934)

2 Samuels, A. P. I., and Samuels, A. W., *The Early Life Correspondence and Writings of The Rt. Hon. Edmund Burke LL.D.* (1923), Chap. iv, *"The Reformer,"*
pp. 160-179.

that of beauty having its source in the passion of love (pleasure).[1] Rather imperfect formation of theory was a forerunner of Lessing's *Laocoön*.[2] A monumentally dull book.

Observations on the Present State of a Nation (1769). Refutes George Grenville's charge that Rockingham's administration had ruined the country by repealing the Stamp Act.

Thoughts on the Cause of the Present Discontents (1770). Conclusion is that the right of free election be restored, and, through that, open party government. An ordered, limited liberty—that was his answer to Bolingbroke's *Idea of a Patriot King*, which would sacrifice independent principles to attain monarchic supremacy. Solid force, reasoned gravity.

On American Taxation† (1774). Closely reasoned and impassioned exhortation to the Government to abandon the American Tea Duty. First part discusses the expediency of repealing it; the second gives a survey of the whole subject of American taxation from the time of the Navigation Act. Vivacious sketches of Townshend, Grenville, and others.

On Conciliation with America† (1775). Speech was designed to find a peaceful solution of the difference with the American colonies. Conclusion is that the only expedience is to comply with the demands of the colonists. Sustained passages of figurative illustration. Famous passage is that which starts with "The proposition is peace."[3]

A Letter to the Sheriffs of Bristol† (1777). General purpose was to discuss further his views on American matters as a kind of reply to the several charges made by enemies since his speech on Conciliation; immediate purpose was to explain his secession from Parliament whenever discussion arose about such legislation as the issuance of letters of marque and the suspension of the habeas corpus as punitive measures levelled against the American colonists. "This great letter," Hearnshaw declares, "is a passionate plea for pacification, a masterly argument for the reconciliation and harmonisation of *imperium* and *libertas*."

Reflections on the Revolution in France† (1790). Passionate but undiagnostic denunciation of the violent change from the established order and a defense of the French Bourbons. Detected, however, the

---

1 Wichelns, H. A., "Burke's Essay on the Sublime and Its Reviewers," *The Journal of English and Germanic Philology*, XXI (1922), pp. 645-661.

2 Howard, W. G., "Burke Among the Forerunners of Lessing." *Publications of the Modern Language Association of America*, XXII; New Series, XV (1907), pp. 608-632.

3 G. R. S. Taylor has pointed out that Burke was not quite the knight-errant of Liberty we have thought him. When he was delivering speeches in favor of the American Colonies, he was receiving seven hundred pounds a year as the official agent of New York. Recall, however, that Burke, in his *On Conciliation*, asked, "Is a politic act the worse for being a just one?"

† * Explanation of symbols immediately precedes Chapter XV.

world-wide significance of what seemed so petty to other statesmen.[1] Turned the current of English opinion against the Revolution; in fact, says Etienne Dumont, the pamphlet was probably the salvation of all Europe.

Letters on a Regicide Peace (I, II, 1796; III, 1797; IV, posthumously). Acutely sarcastic, violent attack upon Jacobinism, after the French government had with contempt rejected England's overtures for peace.

Letter to a Noble Lord (1796). When the Duke of Bedford, and other peers, opposed the granting of a pension to Burke upon his retirement from Parliament, the "Dinner Bell" rang out in elaborately wrought and gorgeous tones a contrast between his own services rendered to the state with those rendered by the Duke—irrelevant to the main question, but a masterpiece of withering if not delicate irony.[2]

The Idea of a Wife (*c.* 1769). Beautiful, appreciative essay presented to his wife Jane on the thirteenth anniversary of their wedding day. "Her gravity is a gentle thoughtfulness . . . . her smiles are inexpressible . . . . her voice is a low soft music."

---

1 Why was Edmund Burke friendly to one revolution (the American uprising) and extremely hostile to another? But he based his pleas for the Americans chiefly on the ground of expediency or political wisdom, while he reacted with bitter antipathy to the revolutionary proceedings in France, where it was, not a movement for political rights with which Burke could sympathize, but a great mass attack upon the privileges of a ruling class. Out of the two-score replies made to Burke, the most detailed was probably Godwin's *Enquiry* (p. 406). Consult *Burke: Select Works*, edited by Payne E. J. (Vol. II, 1898), p. XII ff. (pp. V-LXX); Taylor, G. R. S., *Modern English Statesmen* (1921), Chap. v, "Edmund Burke," pp. 165-209; Cobban, A. B. C., "Edmund Burke and the Origins of the Theory of Nationality," *The Cambridge Historical Journal*, II (1926-1928), pp. 36-47; Osborne, A. M., *Rousseau and Burke* (1940); Carver, P. L., "Burke and the Totalitarian System," *University of Toronto Quarterly*, XII (1942-1943), pp. 32-47; Barker, Ernest, *Essays on Government* (1945), pp. 207-235.

2 To Somerset Maugham, this letter is the greatest piece of invective in the language. In the *Letter's* brief compass are displayed all Burke's dazzling gifts for epigram and for pathos, for indignation and for nobility.

CHAPTER XIX

THE EIGHTEENTH CENTURY: THE NOVEL

The Rise of the Modern Novel

The beginnings of the novel are found in the tales of ancient Egypt, in the *Panchatantra,* a collection of Sanskrit beast-fables, in the *Arabian Nights,* a series of Eastern stories related by Scheherezade; in the *Milesiaka* (no longer extant) by Aristides, in *Lucius or the Ass* and *True History,* both by Lucius; in Homer, in Xenophon's *Cyropaedeia,* Heliodorus's *Aethiopica,* Apuleius's *Golden Ass,* Longus's *Daphnis and Chloe,* Petronius's *Satyricon.*

Italy. (1) *Il Novellino* or *Cento novelle antiche* (thirteenth century). (2) Francesco da Barberino's *Documenti d'Amor* (fourteenth century). (3) Boccaccio's *Filocopo* (*c.* 1339), *Fiammetta* (*c.* 1345), and *Decameron* (*c.* 1348). (4) Sacchetti's *Trecente novelle* (*c.* 1380). (5) Fiorentino's *Il Pecorone* (*c.* 1738). (6) Tomaso Guardato's, or Massuchio's, *Novellino* (1476). (7) Cornazzano's *Proverbii* (*c.* 1490). (8) Bandello's *Novelle* (1554). (9) Firenzuola's *Ragionamenti d'Amor* (1548).

France. (1) *Quinze joyes de mariage* (*c.* 1450). (See *The Bachelor's Banquet,* Vol. 1, p. 236.) (2) Des Périers's *Cymbalum mundi* (1537) and *Nouvelles récréations et joyeux devis* (1558). (3) *Le Moyen de Parvenir,* possibly by Béroalde de Verville. (4) Rabelais's *Gargantua* (1533) and *Pantagruel* (1535). (5) Honoré d'Urfé's *L'Astrée* (1607), a famous romantic pastoral. (6) Gombauld's *Endymion* (1624). (7) Gomberville's *Polexandre* (1629). (8) Mlle. de Scudery's *Ibrahim, Artamène ou le Grand Cyrus* (1649—1653), *and Clélie* (1654—1660). (9) Sorel's *Histoire comique de Francion* (1622) and *Le Berger extravagant* (*c.* 1627). (10) Scarron's *Roman comique* (1651). (11) Furetière's *Le Roman bourgeois* (1666). (12) Marguerite de la Vergne's (Comtesse de La Fayette's) *Princesse de Montpensier* (1662) and *Princesse de Clèves* (1678). (13) La Fontaine's *Amours de Psyche et de Cupidon* (1669). (14) Fénelon's *Télémaque* (1699). (15) Le Sage's *Gil Blas.* (16) Marivaux's *Marianne* (1731) and *Le Paysan parvenu* (1735). (17) Prévost's *Manon Lescaut* (1731).

Spain. (1) *Amadis de Gaula.* (2) *Palmerin of England.* (3) *Lazarillo de Tormes* (*c.* 1550). (4) Jorge de Montemayor's *Diana* (*c.* 1555). (5) Cervantes's *La Galatea* (1584), *Don Quixote* (1604), and

Exemplary Novels (1613). (6) *Historia de la vida del Buscòn* (1626), by Quevido y Villegas. (7) J. F. de Isla's *Historia del famoso predicador fray Gerundio de Campazas* (1758).

Germany. (1) Grimmelshausen's *Der Abenteuerliche Simplicissimus* (1669). (2) A series of *Robinsonaden,* or imitations of Defoe's *Robinson Crusoe.* (3) Goethe's *Die Leiden des jungen Werther* (1774) and *Wilhelm Meisters Lehrjahre* (1795—1796). (4) Richter's *Quintus Fixlein* and *Sibenkas.*

England. (1) Translations of Latin stories, such as the *Gesta Romanorum* (Vol. 1, p. 37). (2) Malory's *Morte d'Arthur* (Vol. 1, p. 92 *f.*). (3) Berners's *Boke of Huon de Bordeaux* (Vol. 1, p. 96). (4) Lodge's *Rosalynde* (Vol. 1, p. 139). (5) Sidney's *Arcadia* (Vol. 1, p. 141). (6) Nash's *Unfortunate Traveller* (Vol. 1, p. 144). (7) Lyly's *Euphues* (Vol. 1, p. 150). (8) *Greene's Pandosto* (Vol. 1, p. 153.) (9) Boyle's *Parthenissa* (1664), a long, tedious romance. (10) Congreve's *Incognita* (p. 306). (11) Mrs. Aphra Behn's *Oroonoko* and other novels (p. 312 *f.*). (12) Bunyan's *Pilgrim's Progress* and other works (p. 315 *ff.*). (13) Addison's Roger de Coverley papers (p. 341). (14) Swift's *Gulliver's Travels* (p. 347). (15) Defoe's works (p. 352 *f.*). (16) Johnson's *Prince of Abissinia* (p. 368). (17) Other prose forms that contributed to the development of the novel were the character-sketches of Overbury and Earle (Vol. 1, p. 248), Walton's *Lives* (Vol. 1, p. 276), Butler's *Characters* (p. 298), and Margaret Cavendish's *Life* (p. 312).

Samuel Richardson, 1689—1761, first of the great English novelists, and first psychological-analytical-sentimental novelist[1]; letter-writer. Son of a Derbyshire joiner. Apprenticed at seventeen to John Wilde, an Aldersgate printer whose daughter Martha he married in 1721, and who died in giving birth to his sixth child (1731). Married Elizabeth Leake, another printer's daughter who also bore him five daughters and one son. Second wife survived him by twelve years. Eventually became master-printer, Printer of the Journals of the House of Commons, Master of the Stationer's Company, and King's Printer.[2] Did not write first book until past fifty.

To him the world owes four literary types—the polished rake, the pure gentleman, the chaste woman, and the Protestant martyr. To him the world is indebted for the epistolary novel. Richardson influenced Sterne, Mackenzie, Jane Austen; Diderot, Rousseau, Balzac, George Sand, Alfred de Musset, Goldoni. Defoe had discovered the novel of incident; Richardson discovered the novel of character.

.1 Analyses of Richardson's novels are available in Hudson, W. H., *A Quiet Corner in a Library* (1915), "Samuel Richardson: The Father of The English Novel," pp. 163-238; Krutch, J. W., *Five Masters* (1930), "Samuel Richardson," pp. 109-173.

2 Thorne, W. B., "A Famous Printer: Samuel Richardson," *The Library,* N. S. II (1901), pp. 396-404.

Letter-Writer

Letters written to and for Particular Friends, on the most Important Occasions (1741). Commissioned by two publishers to compose a letter-writer, the work suggested to Richardson a method developed by him into *Pamela;* when the latter was completed, he turned to finish his *Familiar Letters.* Preface explains the chief objects to be "Nature, propriety of character, plain sense, and general use," addressed "to the judgment, rather than to the imagination." Endeavors "to in culcate the principles of virtue and benevolence; to describe properly, and recommend strongly, the social and relative duties; and to place them in such practical lights, that the letters may serve for rules to think and act by, as well as forms to write after."

Surprising range of subject-matter: general rules for agreeable conversation in a young man (Letter VIII); recommending a wet-nurse (XXXII); to a friend on his recovery from a dangerous illness (L); a warning against a merry French lover, revelatory of Richardson's insularity (LXX); an excuse to a person who wants to borrow money (CXVI). Moral, temperate, dignified, serious in style and purpose. Important predecessors in form include William Fulwood's *The Enimie of Idlenesse* (1568), Abraham Fleming's *A Panoplie of Epistles* (1576), Angel Day's more original *The English Secretorie* (1586), and Nicholas Breton's *Poste with a Packet of Mad Letters* (c. 1603).[1]

Letter-Novels

Pamela: or, Virtue Rewarded†* (I, II, 1740; III, IV, 1741—1742). Epistolary novel generally accepted as the first modern English novel of character and sentiment, and the first to profess a moral purpose. Pamela is neither delicate in feeling nor pure-minded, but rather vulgar in her view of honor and dishonor; her business-like, adventurous view of morality is warped.[2] In the first part, Pamela is *Aggressive Chastity;* in the second, *Provocative Prudence.* Faithful, dramatically-realized portrait of a complacently-vulgar and calculating type of character. Pamela's letter-style is clear and vivid; her occasional versification is bad; throughout are mirrored her emotional susceptibility and self-conscious piety. Occasional coarseness; pruriency. Realistic in form, but idealistic in conception and intention: Pamela is an ideal servant girl. Originality of plan and subject matter, but with the author's characteristic defects. (Title of *Pamela* obtained from Sidney's *Arcadia:* Vol. I, p. 140.)

---

1 *Familiar Letters on Important Occasions by Samuel Richardson,* edited by Downs, B. W. (1928), pp. IX-XXVI.

2 The hothouse morality, sanctimonious propriety, and prurient imagination of *Pamela* were recognized by more than one of Richardson's contemporaries, notably by Fielding (p. 391).

† * Explanation of symbols immediately precedes Chapter XV.

Clarissa, or, the History of a Young Lady†* (I, II, **1747; III—VII, 1748**). Only by virtue of a moral aim is this epistolary novel similar to *Pamela.* Central idea of tragic theme over-complicated by the machinations of Lovelace, the prototype of the eighteenth-century roué, by long-winded letters, redundant detail, improbabilities of plot, irrelevantly interminable gossip, and obtruding judgments. Unlike *Pamela,* herein are letters written by others, as well as by the heroine. Rich in pathos. Shows his amoral conception of love. On the whole, his masterpiece: Clarissa Harlowe is a maiden spiritually virtuous, not materialistically virtuous like Pamela; the style of *Clarissa* is less forced, the theme and treatment more refined and sustained. This eighteenth-century book of etiquette, probably the longest novel in English (the average modern novel is less than 100,000 words long, but *Clarissa* totals about a million[1]), has been declared the first complete biography of a woman in modern fiction. Rousseau's *La Nouvelle Héloise*[2] is generally recognized as the successor of *Clarissa.*

History of Sir Charles Grandison†* (1754). Novel-in-letters in which the hero is a male counterpart of Clarissa. The character of Clementina, the heavy disquisitions, the protracted conversations, and a lack of strong dramatic interest are its defects. Technically better than his two preceding novels, being more skillfully constructed and more varied in interest despite fewer events. A distinct failure, even in its own day.

SUGGESTED MERITS

1. Strength of sentiment.
2. Creation of complex characters, especially as an anatomist of the female heart. Some perfectly drawn if not completely alive.
3. Realism and Verisimilitude. Minute profusion of outward details (often termed "tediousness" by detractors); frequent vivid, economical description.
4. High moral aim exemplified by his trilogy of virtue-novels. Repudiates the degenerate so-called code of honor of the upper classes.
5. Advantages of Letter-Method: (a) revealing and intimate form of natural expression; (b) creation of suspense; (c) introduction of many persons; (d) tendency towards racy language.

SUGGESTED DEFECTS

1. Weakness of passion.
2. Woodenness in the portraiture of men; only Lovelace is unwittingly made human.
3. Inordinate profuseness and prolixity. His laborious accumulation of details often becomes tedious.[3]
4. Lack of detachment overloads work with obtrusive moralizings and mawkish platitudes. Moral standard not high; see discussion under **Pamela.**
5. Disadvantages of Letter-Method: (a) tendency toward unsymmetrical plot; (b) wastefulness in its procedure; (c) spinelessness in its sentence-style: frequently at least in Richardson; (d) all characters seem to have a like facility with the pen.

---

1 Long novels today are again coming into fashion: *teste* James Joyce's *Ulysses,* Galsworthy's *Forsyte Saga,* Proust's super novel-cycle in fifteen volumes, under the title of *À la recherche du temps perdu* ("The Remembrance of Things Past"), and, recently, Hervey Allen's *Anthony Adverse.*

2 Richardson's influence on Rousseau is evaluated by Texte, Joseph, *Jean-Jacques Rousseau et les origines du Cosmopolitisme Littéraire* (Paris, 1895), Chapitre III, pp. 193-197 (pp. 171-197); IV, pp. 198-253; and V, pp. 254-309.

3 But see Utter, R. P., "On the Alleged Tediousness of Defoe and Richardson," *University of California Chronicle,* XXV (1923), pp. 185-193 (pp. 175-193).

† * Explanation of symbols immediately precedes Chapter XV.

For Further Discussion of Richardson's Style, See Under Fielding, p. 395 f.

Henry Fielding 1707—1754, founder of the English prose epic and of the modern novel of incident; burlesquing dramatist, miscellaneous writer[1]. As a Justice, is said to have established the first detective force in England.[2] Cadet of a moderately well-born family. Educated at Eton. Entered the University of Leyden (1728). Married Charlotte Cradock (1734). Manager of the Haymarket Theatre (1736). Entered the Middle Temple (1737). Wife died (1743). Ordered by court to pay the sum of £400 for which he had been surety (1747). Married Mary Daniel, his servant girl, on November 27, 1747, to whom a son was born on February 25, 1748. Appointed Justice of the Peace for Middlesex and Westminster (1748). Chairman of Quarter Sessions at Westminster (1749). Died soon after he reached Lisbon, where he went for his health in 1754.

Praised by Boswell, Gibbon, Coleridge, Hazlitt, Lamb, Byron, and Meredith; disparaged by Johnson, Smollett, Walpole, De Quincey, Carlyle, and Browning.

Novels

An Apology for the Life of Mrs. Shamela Andrews (1741). Satirizes Richardson's *Pamela* by presenting Shamela as a designing woman who tricks her master into marrying her. Witty, mercilessly cutting. Issued under the name of Conny Keyber, but generally assumed to be by Fielding.

The History of the Adventures of Joseph Andrews, and of his Friend Mr. Abraham Adams†* (1742). Forgetting original intention to burlesque Richardson's *Pamela* and its hot-house morality, Fielding (after his ninth chapter) writes a real polemical novel of contemporary characters and domestic manners. Virtuous serving-man Joseph is represented as Pamela's brother, and as one who can not be seduced by his mistress; while Squire B—of *Pamela* is filled out to become Squire Booby. The central figure becomes Parson Abraham Adams, a lovable comic-heroic creation, the English Don Quixote.[3] Not artificial or insipid as the narratives then being written, but fresh, original, truthful, exuberant. Clear expression, much burlesque diction, unmoral (not immoral) approach to life, vital episodes, dramatic characterization. Plot not always well constructed. Defines his book as the "comic Epic-Poem in Prose," distinguishing it from comedy by its more extended action, its much wider sphere of incidents, and characters

---

1 Cross, W. L., *The History of Henry Fielding* (Three volumes, 1918); Banerji, H. K., *Henry Fielding: His Life and Works* (1929).

2 Jones, B. M., *Henry Fielding: Novelist and Magistrate* (1933), Chap. IV, "The Establishment of the First Detective Force in England," pp. 143-154.

3 Priestley, J. B., *The English Comic Characters* (1925), "Parson Adams," pp. 106-127.

† * Explanation of symbols immediately precedes Chapter XV.

selected from society at large.[1] Mock-heroic introductions to the different "books" have their prototype in Cervantes and Scarron. Indebted to Marivaux's *Le Paysan Parvenu* (1735).

The Life of Mr. Jonathan Wild the Great†* (1743). Satirical romance-with-a-purpose.[2] Grimly humorous masterpiece of sustained naked irony and logical workmanship veils an attack upon the political schemes, pretended virtues, and real vices of mankind. Living characters. Skillful plot construction burlesques the adoration—or, as Jonathan Wild says, "adwhoration"—of the thief—an exaltation common today. "Roguery, and not a rogue, is the subject"; and Fielding reveals first-hand knowledge of the criminal class, including even their jargon. Several have said that Fielding has written no greater book.

The History of Tom Jones, a Foundling†* (1749). Possibly the first great novel in the English language, and possibly the greatest.[3] Delightful vestibule essays ("prolegomenous" chapters) on art and his philosophy, more or less allied to his story, precede and delay each of the eighteen "books"; a method later adopted by Thackeray. Hackneyed central theme, huddled at the end; digressions; only improbabilities are the two characters, the almost jet-black Blifil and the almost morally-white Allworthy; Tom's reformation at the end not altogether convincing. Crowded with twoscore characters and abounding life; Squire Western is a most vital, if coarse, portrait of a country squire. Coherent, if artificial, plot; rounded characters; inexhaustible merriment; profound insight; comic tone, easy morality, screened but merciless irony, fearless portrayal of human passion.

Amelia (1751). Realistic, humanitarian-sentimental novel, occasionally heavy with moral or religious or social propaganda. Half autobiographic: Mrs. Amelia Booth, plain and long-suffering, is modelled, as was Sophia Western, on Fielding's devoted first wife; iniquities of prisons, petty tyrannies of bailiffs, and corruption of magistrates derived from personal experience. Less satirical and less vivacious, but more moral, than *Tom Jones*. Anticipates the slum-novel of Dickens (p. 535). (For Fielding's purpose, see the Dedication.)

Dramas

(1) *The Temple Beau* (1730), somewhat amusing, and, in its prologue, clever; (2) *The Author's Farce; and the Pleasures of the Town* (1730), two separate pieces which laughed at Colley Cibber, Bohemian

---

1 Bissell, F. O., Jr., *Fielding's Theory of the Novel* (1933); Thornsbury, E. M. "Henry Fielding's Theory of the Comic Prose Epic," *University of Wisconsin Studies in Language and Literature*, Number 30 (1931), especially pp. 97-167.

2 Wells, J. E., "Fielding's Political Purpose in *Jonathan Wild*," *Publications of the Modern Language Association of America*, xxviii; New Series, xxi (1913), pp. 1-55.

3 One of the best attacks on Tom-Mania is the article by Loomis, R. S., "*Tom Jones* and Tom-Mania," *The Sewanee Review*, xxvii (1919), pp. 478-495.

† * Explanation of symbols immediately precedes Chapter XV.

authors, and daily absurdities; (3) *Rape upon Rape; or, The Justice Caught in his own Trap* (1730), later called *The Coffee-House Politician*, a part-satire on contemporary manners, generally weak in character-painting, much humor, sordid in plot; (4) *The Letter-Writers: Or, a New Way to Keep a Wife at Home* (1731), a tenuous subject typical in its features of Restoration comedy; (5) *The Welsh Opera: or, The Grey Mare the better Horse* (1731), subsequently titled *The Genuine Grub-Street Opera*, modelled on *The Beggar's Opera*, not only is interesting for its satire on Walpole but for its famous song, "The Roast Beef of Old England"; (6) *The Lottery* (1732), an indulgent satiric piece against state lotteries; (7) *The Modern Husband* (1732), in which the attempt to indict fashionable corruption contains unsparing realistic material poorly adapted to comic ends. Anticipates the plot of *Amelia*. (8) *The Debauchees: or, The Jesuit Caught* (1732), a coarse anti-papist play not without wit; (9) *The Covent-Garden Tragedy* (1732), while occasionally amusing in its burlesque is coarse in theme[1]; (10) *The Mock-Doctor, or The Dumb Lady Cur'd* (1732), genial-humored ballad-opera translated from Molière's *Le Médicin malgré lui;* (11) *The Miser* (1733), among his best plays, for this translation of Molière's *L'Avare* has real humor and nervous, albeit long, dialogue; (12) *The Intriguing Chambermaid* (1734), two-act comedy based on Regnard's *Le Retour Imprévu;* (13) *Don Quixote in England* (1734), an extravaganza notable for its "A-Hunting We Will Go" song ("The dusky night rides down the sky") and for Squire Badger, who is the earliest sketch of Squire Western in *Tom Jones;* (14) *An Old Man taught Wisdom; or, The Virgin Unmask'd* (1735), a simple one-act play with humor; (15) *The Universal Gallant: or, The Different Husband* (1735), a dull comedy hissed in its own day; (16) *Tumble-Down Dick: or, Phaeton in the Suds* (1736), although supposedly a continuation of *Pasquin*, is a parody on Rich's presentation of the *Fall of Phaeton;* (17) *Eurydice, a Farce* (1737), one-act based on the classical story; (18) *The Historical Register for the Year 1736* (1737), a three-act satire renewing attack on Walpole *via* the character of Quiddam; and (19) *The Wedding-Day* (1743), although based on the Restoration model, is a discordant medley of sentiment and humor.

Love in Several Masques (1728). Indelicate comedy, influenced by Congreve and Wycherley. Stilted dialogue, wooden characters, improbable plot, passionless lovers, faded speech, undeveloping construction. Only fair portrait is that of Sir Positive Trap.

---

1 Fielding himself recognized this by his ironical analysis of his play; he defined a tragedy as "a Thing of five Acts, written Dialogue-wise, consisting of several fine Similies, Metaphors, and Moral Phrases, with here and there a Speech upon Liberty. That it must contain an Action, Characters, Sentiments, Diction, and a Moral." He goes on to demonstrate that his play has none of these necessary qualities.

The Tragedy of Tragedies; or The Life and Death of Tom Thumb (1731).[1] Spirited, often ludicrous, sometimes playfully ferocious burlesque in mock-heroic style. Bombastic conventions and inflated extravagances characteristic of heroic and pseudo-classic drama, especially of Dryden's age. Pokes fun at Addison's *Cato* (p. 341), Thomson's *Sophonisha* (p. 411), and several plays by Dryden. Long, ironical, mirth-provoking preface and annotations by "H. Scriblerus Secundus." Original version, called *Tom Thumb, A Tragedy* (1730), containing a scene in which Lord Grizzle kills Tom Thumb's ghost, is historic for having made Swift (p. 345) laugh. Basic idea used previously in Villiers's *Rehearsal*.[2]

Pasquin. A Dramatick Satire of the Times† (1736). Modelled on *The Rehearsal* (p. 2), Fielding's ripest drama is actually a rehearsal of *The Election,* a comedy, and *The Life and Death of Common Sense,* a burlesque tragedy. Satirized theatrical, political, and social conditions; *e.g.,* the electoral corruptions.[3]

Periodicals

The Champion, or, British Mercury (1739 — 1741). Tri-weekly modelled on *The Tatler* and edited by Fielding under the pseudonym of Captain Hercules Vinegar.[4] Fought Walpole. Occasional flashes of humor.

The True Patriot: and The History of Our Own Times (1745—1746). Anti-Stuart weekly attempted to influence public opinion against the Pretender—to discredit the Jacobite cause.

The Jacobite's Journal, by John Trottplaid, Esq. (1747—1748). Ironically-named periodical heaped ridicule upon the Jacobites.

The Covent-Garden Journal† (1752).[5] Issued under the pseudonym of Sir Alexander Drawcansir, it contained essays on literature and manners. Famous for its attack on Smollett's *Peregrine Pickle* and *Roderick Random.* Purpose seems to be that of reform: even his modern glossary (Number IV) shows his realistic attitude: "BEAUTY: The Qualification with which Women generally go into Keeping"; "ROGUE [and] RASCAL. A Man of a different Party from yourself."

---

1 *The Tragedy of Tragedies or The Life and Death of Tom Thumb the Great,* edited by Hillhouse, J. T. (1918).

2 Possibly influenced by James Ralph, assistant-editor of *The Champion.* See Hughes, H. S., "Fielding's Indebtedness to James Ralph," *Modern Philology,* xx (1922-1923), pp. 23-30 (pp. 19-34).

3 It is often stated that the Licensing Act of 1737 was aimed directly at Fielding.

4 Captain Hercules was not a fictitious personage, however, but the pseudonym of an actual prize-ring champion. See Wells, J. E., "Fielding's 'Champion' and Captain Hercules Vinegar," *The Modern Language Review,* viii (1913), pp. 165-172.

5 *The Covent-Garden Journal, by Sir Alexander Drawcansir,* edited by Jensen, G. E. (Two volumes, 1915).

† * Explanation of symbols immediately precedes Chapter XV.

Social Pamphlets

A Charge Delivered to the Grand Jury (1749). Clear exposition of the history and functions of grand juries. Sound legal learning, vigorous diction.

An Enquiry Into the Causes of the late Increase of Robbers, &c. (1751). Attributes the increase of crime to the increasing number of gaming houses, gin-drinkers, and many prevalent vices. Discusses the ineffective administration of the poor laws, the inadequacy of the police force, and the demoralizing conditions of prison life.

A Proposal for Making an Effectual Provision for the Poor (1753). Bill of three-score clauses planned to provide work for the poor, for the purpose of "amending their morals and for rendering them useful members to society." Fielding recognized that the main cause of crime may be pauperism.

Journeys

A Journey from this World to the Next (1749). Unfinished and unequal Lucianic satire. First ten chapters are the happiest and most humorous. Self-revealing.

The Journal of a Voyage to Lisbon (1755).[1] Candid, charming, pathetic, valedictory account of a voyage to Portugal, made to recover his health. Last product of his pen is an intimate key to Fielding's urbane stoicism.

Comment. The writings of Fielding show a tendency toward irrelevant elements, wordy digressions, and a broadness to the point of vulgar, but not prurient, wit. They are distinguished, however, by fresh, lifelike dialogue; exuberant romantic faculty and frank gaiety of approach; masculine and athletic vigor of language in a bustling narrative, with mock-heroic turns of a droll style; broad psychological realism, and fundamental human sympathy and insight into human nature; and a keen, satiric, ironic perception of the laughable and ridiculous in character and action that searches out social abuses. If Defoe is credited with the novel of incident, and Richardson with the novel of analysis of sentiment, then Fielding should be credited with the first complete novel of contemporary manners.

---

1 It is important to note the differences in the two versions appearing in 1755. Consult Dickson, F. S., "The Early Editions of Fielding's 'Voyage to Lisbon,'" *The Library*, Third Series, VIII (1917), pp. 24-35; and two articles in the same volume: Pollard, A. W., "The Two 1755 Editions of Fielding's 'Journal of a Voyage to Lisbon,'" pp. 75-77; De Castro, J. P., "Henry Fielding's Last Voyage," pp. 145-159.

FIELDING	—	RICHARDSON
1. Characters alive with super-abundant life. Superior in characterizing the robustness of men.		1. Great genius in portraying female character. Hence he is called the "Apostle of Feminism."
2. Healthful morality.		2. Smug sentimentality.
3. Truth-probing content.		3. Falsely-commonplace content.
4. Rambling, picaresque-structured stories, effective in their very plotlessness; yet possibly surpasses Richardson in ability to construct a plot.		4. Novels in letter-form often charged with clumsiness in handling of construction and technique, while, possibly, stricter in the selection of incidents.
5. Excellent sense of humor.		5. Almost total absence of humor.
6. Virile satire and coarse fun—the objective method.		6. Sentimentality and analysis—the subjective method.
7. To take Fielding up after Richardson, Coleridge has said, "is like emerging from a sick-room heated by stoves, into an open lawn, on a breezy day in May."		

Tobias George Smollett, 1721—1771, originator of the nautical novel; historian, translator, surgeon. Of Scottish descent. Born in Dalquhurn, Dumbartonshire, the grandson of Sir James Smollett. Educated at Dumbarton School, and at Glasgow University, which he attended while serving an apprenticeship to Dr. John Gordon (1736). Proceeded to London (1739). Served as surgeon's mate on H.M.S. *Chichester* (1740), and the disastrous siege of Cartagena (1741) is recounted in *Roderick Random.* The fleet returned to Jamaica, where he met Anne Lascelles, whom he married (1747).[1] Probably failed in medical practice on Downing Street (1744—1745). Took his M.D. degree at Marischal College, Aberdeen (1750).[2] Edited the *Critical Review* (1756—1763), during which, in 1759, he was fined and imprisoned for libelling Admiral Knowles. Death of Elizabeth, his only child, greatly affected him (1763). Went abroad (1763—1765). London (1768). Poor in health, he left England (1769) to die about two years later at Monte Nero near Leghorn.[3]

Miscellaneous works include *The Reprisal, or The Tars of Old England* (1757), a successful play directed against the French navy and made sprightly by four songs; the compilation of *A Compendium of Authentic and Entertaining Voyages,* including his own to Cartagena (1756), and *The Present State of All Nations* (1764); an *Essay on the External Use of Water* (1752),[4] an attempt to enhance his medical

---

1 Knapp, L. M., "Ann Smollett, Wife of Tobias Smollett," *Publications of the Modern Language Association of America,* XLV (1930), pp. 1035-1049.

2 His years in London from about 1743 to 1750 are of importance. Consult Knapp, L. M., "Smollett's Early Years in London," *The Journal of English and Germanic Philology,* XXXI (1932), pp. 220-227.

3 His health, however, a month before his death, was much better than usually described.

4 Drinker, C. K., "Doctor Smollett," *Annals of Medical History,* VII (1925), pp. 31-47; Jones, C. E., "An Essay on the External Use of Water, by Tobias Smollett," *Bulletin of the Institute of the History of Medicine* (The Johns Hopkins University), III (1935), pp. 31-82.

standing by endeavoring to prove that the mineral water of Bath is not superior to ordinary water; the frequently reprinted and readable *Complete History of England, from the descent of Julius Caesar to the Treaty of Aix-la-Chapelle 1748* (1757; continuations 1760—1765); translations of *Gil Blas* (1749), *Don Quixote* (1755), and the works of Voltaire in many volumes (1761); and editorship of *The Critical Review* (1756), *The British Magazine* (1760), and *The Briton* (1762).

Novels

The Adventures of Roderick Random* (1748). Unsymmetrical, coarsely-brutal, rapid rogue-novel avowedly modelled on Le Sage's *Gil Blas*. Distinction resides in personal experiences[1] as a surgeon's mate, the development of the unprincipled Roderick, the realistic scenes on shipboard,[2] and the super-scamp's broad-winking and ironical attitude in narrating the story. Cynical approach, noisy rowdiness; weak in unity of plot structure. Characters: Strap, Tom Bowling; Morgan recalls Shakespeare's Fluellen. Also important to the student of medical history.

The Adventures of Peregrine Pickle† (1751).[3] His longest picaresque novel is sometimes considered his best. *Merits*—brilliant descriptive passages, amusing and fine characterizations(Gamaliel, Grizzle, the choleric Trunnion), the pathos of the deathbed scene of Commodore Hawser Trunnion; satire on literary, social, and political conditions. *Defects*—grotesque humor, brutal heartiness of Peregrine, repellent license of expression, cynical personal asperities[4]; the seamy excrescence of "Memoirs of a Fine Lady" (Chap. LXXXI), contributed most likely by the notorious Lady Vane.[5] Influenced Sterne, Scott, and Dickens.[6]

The Adventures of Ferdinand Count Fathon (1753). Romance is a permanent contribution to the literature of roguery and to that of criminology. Merits lie in the Dedication, Ferdinand's mother, who is a shameless harridan, the robber scene, and the Count's address upon landing in England. Some episodes foreshadow the Gothic or Terror Tale. Plot superior to all his other novels. Strained dialogue; crude gusto often becomes indecent; much of the story is labeled repulsive. (Compare its sardonic irony with the superior type in Fielding's *Jonathan Wild*, p. 429).

---

1 Knapp, L. M., "The Naval Scenes in *Roderick Random*," *Publications of the Modern Language Association of America*, XLIX (1934), p. 598 (pp. 593-598).

2 *Idem*, pp. 593-598.

3 See Buck, H. S., *A Study in Smollett* (1925).

4 Smollett attacks many contemporaries; Fielding, for example. Consult Buck, H. S., *A Study in Smollett* (1925), Chap. II, "Smollett's Quarrels," pp. 53-121.

5 It is charged that Lady Vane paid Smollett handsomely for interpolating her *Memoirs* in his book.

6 Huse, W. W., "Pickle and Pickwick," *Washington University Studies*, x (1922), pp. 143-154.

† * Explanation of symbols immediately precedes Chapter XV.

The Adventures of Sir Launcelot Greaves (1760).   Bungling satiric novel, very obviously influenced by *Don Quixote*.

*The Expedition of Humphrey Clinker†** (1771). Rambling epistolary novel. Mellowest and most mature work, with vitalized characters and penetrating understanding of life but still maliciously ill-humored. Includes his two greatest creations, Matthew Bramble and Lieutenant Lismahago; and also Winifred Jenkins, whose letters are about as humorous as any in the language. Less important for the story than for the variety of telling characterization and the brilliant portrayal of manners; the same events discussed from different points of view. Has been termed the greatest of the letter-novels. Anticipates philosophical comedy and the Gothic romance.

Other Works

Travels through France and Italy (1766).[1] Caustic account, notable for its fresh portraits of the road. Humor, good sense. Has brought Smollett the designation of the discoverer of the Riviera. Splenetic point of view provoked the name *Smellfungus* from Sterne (p. 399). Important key to his personality.

The History and Adventures of an Atom (1769). Virulent allegorical satire on contemporary political events. Extreme license of expression makes it his most unpleasant work.

Letters.[2]   Many are appeals for financial assistance—for others as well as for himself. Business-like; sincere.

Poetry[3]

Smollett is not a great poet, but occasionally shows poetic insight. Four of his poems are in *Roderick Random* and one in *Humphrey Clinker*. In addition he wrote *Advice: A Satire* (1746), which, in heroic couplets, has some repellent qualities, said to be a protest against sexual perversion; *Reproof: A Satire* (1747), a sequel to the first; *The Tears of Scotland* (written *c.* 1746), his most famous poem, an emotional outburst provoked by the Highlanders's defeat at Culloden Moor in 1746; and *Ode to Independence* (written *c.* 1767), which may be of biographical significance.

---

1 *Travels through France and Italy,* edited by Seccombe, Thomas (1907), Introduction. pp. V-LX; Chancellor, E. B., "Smollett as a Traveller," *The Fortnightly Review,* CXV; New Series, CVIII (1921), pp. 478-488.

2 *The Letters of Tobias Smollett, M.D.,* edited by Noyes, E. S. (1926).

3 Buck, H. S., *Smollett as a Poet* (1927).

† *   Explanation of symbols immediately precedes Chapter XV.

SUGGESTED MERITS	SUGGESTED DEFECTS
1. Master of fertile incident.	1. Absence of imaginative sympathy.
2. Photographic power of external details; reportorial realism; wakeful common sense.	2. Distortion of realism.
3. Astringent painter of contemporary manners.	3. Indecent coarseness of language.
4. First introduction to the true-to-the-life British tar.	4. "Humour" characters.[1] (Comic types suggest Sterne and anticipate Dickens.)
5. Prodigality of wit and ironic perception of life.	5. Brutality of humor.
6. Economical pointedness of style.	6. Obtrusive didacticism.

7. Smollett inclines to the romantic and pictorial, and Fielding, to the classical and epic; the latter is better in plot construction and meditative study of people, the former is richer in variety of character creations; Smollett is unexcelled in his descriptive power, but his humor is coarse, while Fielding is less harsh in his criticism of humanity and has an exhilarating humor.

Laurence Sterne, 1713—1768, humorist.[2] Born at Clonmel, Ireland, the son of an impecunious subaltern. Spent several years at Halifax Grammar School. Sizar at Jesus College, Cambridge. B.A., 1736; M.A., 1740. Ordained deacon (1736). Vicar of Sutton-in-the-Forest, near York (1738—1759). Married Elizabeth Lumley (1741), who became insane in 1758; notorious for his philandering with other women. Birth of daughter Lydia (1747), who afterwards, as Madame Medalle, edited his *Letters* (1775). Presented by Lord Fauconberg to the perpetual curacy of Coxwold (1790). Wrote *A Political Romance* (1759; published 1769), a humorous skit.[3] Because of illness, went to Toulouse (1762—1764). Began his seven months' tour of France and Italy (1765). Died of pleurisy in his lodgings at Old Bond Street, London, in a state of insolvency.

Sermons of Mr. Yorick (Seven volumes, 1760—1769). Helps round out an understanding of Sterne's approach to life. Between his *Sermons* and his humorous works there is a unity of style.[4]

The Life and Opinions of Tristram Shandy, Gent.† (Nine volumes: I, II, 1759; III—VI, 1761—1762; VII, VIII, 1765; X, the ninth volume, 1767). Like Fielding's *Joseph Andrews,* it outgrows original conception as a lampoon. Important neither for the inconsequential details of the life of the nominal hero nor for Tristram's opinions, of which there are few; but for its galaxy of humorous creations, described with dramatic vigor and subtle discrimination, and for its reflection of

---

1 Ellison, L. M., "Elizabethan Drama and the Works of Smollett," *Publications of the Modern Language Association of America,* XLIV (1929), pp. 854-856 (pp. 842-862).

2 Cross, W. L., *The Life and Times of Laurence Sterne* (1929).

3 Sterne did not keep out of politics. He contributed to *The York Gazeteer* and to the *York Courant.* His political activities revealed him in several ways. Consult Curtis, L. P., *The Politicks of Laurence Sterne* (1929).

4 Like his *Sermons,* Sterne's two chief works have a moral purpose. Thus asserts Read, Herbert, *The Sense of Glory* (1929), p. 133 *f.* (pp. 124-151).

† * Explanation of symbols immediately precedes Chapter XV.

Sterne's whimsical personality. Inimitable characters include the hero's father, Walter Shandy (whose parade of learning shows the influence of Burton—Vol. 1, p. 271), Uncle Toby, Corporal Trim, Yorick the parson, the Widow Wadman, Dr. Slop, and Mrs. Shandy, the ideal of nonentity of character. Despite long-winded and philosophic disquisitions—in which is seen the influence of Rabelais—some notable parts are those concerned with the curse of Bishop Ernulphus, the discourse of Corporal Trim on morality, the incident of Le Fevre, and the dialogue between the Shandys on the breeching of Tristram, who when born, in the third volume, is named "Tristram" instead of the contemplated "Trismegistus."

Jenny is Miss Catherine de Fourmantelle, with whom Sterne corresponded; Eugenius is his Cambridge friend, John Hall-Stevenson, witty epicurean, owner of "Crazy Castle," and one whose writings resemble Sterne's in spirit. Other aspects show the influence, in addition to that of Burton and Rabelais, of Bouchet, Scarron, Montaigne, and Swift.[1]

A Sentimental Journey through France and Italy, by Mr. Yorick† (1768). Memoirs of Sterne's pleasure tour, 1765—1766. Elusive humor. Over-exuberant sentimentality[2] and incessant moralizings predominate. Most famous quotation: "God tempers the wind to the shorn lamb." Only two of four volumes completed.

Letters of Yorick to Eliza (1775). To the twenty-two-year-old Mrs. Eliza Draper, a woman of some intellectual attainments with whom he flirted. Reveal his personality.[3]

Comment. While many overlook Sterne's typographical tricks and mannered punctuation (sprinkling of dots, dashes, asterisks, and index hands; uncapitalized sentences, unfinished sentences, one-sentence chapters, blank pages, shuffled chapters), they find it difficult to condone his pruriency of taste and morals. In spite of an apparent plotlessness of narrative, Sterne is clear, for his chaotic formlessness is a plan ordered by an eccentric imagination. His merits are not few: vivid creations or

---

1 W. A. Eddy has suggested that it is not unlikely that Sterne was also influenced by Tom Brown's *Description of a Country Life:* see Eddy, W. A., "Tom Brown and *Tristram Shandy,*" *Modern Language Notes,* XLIV (1929), pp. 379-381.

2 "Sentimentality," in Sterne's day, meant an emphasis on delicate feelings. For a fuller explanation of the degeneration of the word's meaning, see Read, Herbert, *The Sense of Glory* (1929), p. 139 *ff.* (pp. 124-151).

3 Undoubtedly it is to Sterne's letters that critics will go for illumination of his character. But still debatable is the important question as to which of the letters attributed to Sterne are his. Several volumes have been issued since 1775; some of these seem to be spurious. For example, while one critic asserts that the *Second Journal to Eliza,* hitherto known as *Letters supposed to have been written by Yorick and Eliza* (1779), is a later version by Sterne of the *Journal to Eliza,* another critic states that the letters are a forgery by William Combe. Consult (1) *The Letters of Laurence Sterne,* selected by Johnson, R. B. (1927); (2) *Second Journal to Eliza,* introduction by Shaw, M. R. B., pp. V-VII; foreword by Whibley, Charles, pp. V-VII (1929); (3) Curtis, L. P., "Forged Letters of Laurence Sterne," *Publications of the Modern Language Association of America,* L (1935), pp. 1076-1106; (4) *Letters of Laurence Sterne,* edited by Curtis, L. P. (1935).

† * Explanation of symbols immediately precedes Chapter XV.

character; gift of delicate pathos or pervasive sentimentality; charm of digressions; sense of raillery and fantastic humor (no writer is more droll); simplicity of description concerning elemental facts of life; limpid phraseology, rhythmic and nervous prose, colorful and vitalized language: his is conversational writing of the highest rank.

Henry Mackenzie 1745—1831, Scotch disciple of Sterne, literary critic, and a link between the "graveyard poets" and the Romanticists.[1] Son of Dr. Joshua Mackenzie. Educated at Edinburgh High School (1753—1757) and Edinburgh University (1758—1761). Married Penuel, daughter of Sir Ludovick Grant (1776). Edited the Tory periodicals, *The Mirror* (1779—1780), and *The Lounger* (1785—1789), both modelled on *The Spectator*. *The Lounger's* most famous essay is No. 97, December 9, 1786: the first review by an important man of letters publicly welcoming the Kilmarnock Edition of the *Poems* of Robert Burns[2] (p. 429). Founded the Royal Society of Edinburgh (1783) and the Highland and Agricultural Society (1784). Comptroller of taxes for Scotland (1804—1831). Known as the "Man of Feeling" (although he was a hard-headed person) and as the "Addison of the North." As a playwright, *The Shipwreck* (1784), an adaptation of Lillo's *Fatal Curiosity*, and *False Shame, or The White Hypocrite* (1789), a comedy, were both failures; only *The Prince of Tunis* (1773), a romantic tragedy, was successful.

The Man of Feeling (1771). Novel is a series of lachrymose sketches loosely woven around the sentimental hero, Harley, who is dominated by the moral sense. Loosely constructed, virtually plotless, strainedly didactic; indebted to Sterne for its sentiment, but Mackenzie's is a false, second-hand pathos. Done in somewhat the manner of Addison's Roger de Coverley papers. Character: Sindall.

The Man of the World (1773). Is in spirit a second part to *The Man of Feeling*. The hero, Annesley, braves his moral sense, lapsing blindly into a villain and a seducer. Plot somewhat involved, style smoother. In the main, Mackenzie uses the stock conventions of the eighteenth-century novel.

Julia de Roubigné (1777). Tragic epistolary novel is his best work. The episode of Yambu is an important plea against the institution of slavery. Nowhere else does he come closer to a Richardsonian sentimentality.

---

1 Thompson, H. W., *A Scottish Man of Feeling* (1931).

2 The review is available in *Early Critical Reviews on Robert Burns*, edited by Ross, J. D. (1900), pp. 1-7. Henry Mackenzie also started the literary career of Scott and first encouraged Byron. It is necessary, however, to emphasize that Mackenzie's review appeared five weeks after the first published review by James Sibbald. See page 429, footnote 5.

The Anecdotes and Egotisms of Henry Mackenzie   (1927).[1]
Important for its pleasant picture of Scotland of the eighteenth century
and for the charm of Mackenzie himself.

Frances Burney (or **Fanny Burney**, later **Mme. D'Arblay**),
1752—1840, inaugurator of the novel of home life. Shy[2] daughter of
Charles Burney, a music master and writer on music, whose rhetorically-
languaged *Memoirs of Dr. Burney* she edited in 1832, which may
gain some worth from its pleasant vignettes of David Garrick. Hob-
nobbed with Dr. Johnson's circle. Served Queen Charlotte for five years
as Second Keeper of the Robes or Dresser to Her Majesty (1786—
1791)[3]; upon her resignation, was pensioned (1791). Married General
Alexandre D'Arblay, a French *emigré* (1793).[4] Lived at Passy in
France (1802—1812). Husband died (1818). Spent remaining years in
complete retirement in England.

Novels

Evelina, or a Young Lady's Entrance into the World†* (1778).
First novel of family life. Epistolary: Evelina writes most of the letters.
Good farce, admirable caricature. Sprightliness of conversation, spontaneity of realistic comedy, and a zestful, mischievous insight into the
foibles of human beings revealed in this swiftly-moving, lucidly-told
(quoting Fanny) "pleasant broad comedy of manners" that inimitably
verges upon vulgarity. To Johnson she was a "character-mongerer."
Possibly the chief interest is its picture of life and manners, especially
the atmosphere of social London.

*Cecilia, or Memoirs of an Heiress** (1782). Less spontaneous,
more complicated novel; but better constructed than its predecessor.

Camilla, or a Picture of Youth (1796). Early chapters show
her skill in quiet-farcical comedy, and in absurd characterizations such
as those of Sir Hugh Tyrold and Dr. Orkbourne. Subsequent pages become labored with sententiousness and wet with exaggerated sentimentality. Dates her waning as a novelist; but, it is asserted, pictures literally
the eighteenth-century ways and manners of Sensibility.

The Wanderer, or Female Difficulties (1814). Indifferent last
novel bares the influence, for the worst, of Johnson's elaborate style; but
her magniloquence is also part of her changed outlook with the passing
years. Artificial conversations, emaciated humor, boring disquisitions

---

1 *The Anecdotes and Egotisms of Henry Mackenzie*, edited by Thompson, H. W.
  (1927).
2 Fanny was always a girl of marked timidity, an important point about her person.
  See Overman, A. A., *An Investigation into the Character of Fanny Burney* (1933).
3 Hill, Constance, *Fanny Burney at the Court of Queen Charlotte* (1912).
4 In the same year she published *Brief Reflections relative to the Emigrant French
  Clergy* (1793), the object of which was to raise funds for the needy emigrants from
  the Reign of Terror in France.

† * Explanation of symbols immediately precedes Chapter XV.

on the soul's immortality. W. D. Howells did not err in describing *The Wanderer* as representing, with *Camilla,* a conscious and an academic pose of a once spontaneous talent.

Autobiographic Works

Early Diary† (written 1768—1778; published 1889) and *Diary and Letters*† (written 1778—1840; published 1842—1846).[1] Primarily photographic, she is always sound in depicting the circles in which she mingled, and the life and manners of which she was a part; yet, paradoxically, unlike a woman she seldom gives details upon dress. Nor does she give pictures of industrial conditions or poverty. At her best is probably unrivaled. In her very strength of picturing external details and small personal peculiarities, and of forming a gallery of almost all the great men and typical characters of her day, lies her weakness: no probing beneath the surface.

Comment. Her first three novels epitomize the life, thought, and feelings of young women in the last quarter of the eighteenth century. To-day her works seem to suffer from horseplay characterization and false emotion, thin plots, and, primarily, from skimmed pictures of contemporary manners. As time went on, her pen became increasingly prolix and sententious. Yet as our first society or domestic novelist she presents caricature excellent in its strength, lively character-mongering in dialogue, and scenes graphic in their close observation of her small tea-table world and its manners. Her domestic realism blazed the way for Maria Edgeworth and Jane Austen.[2]

Horatio or **Horace Walpole, Fourth Earl of Orford, 1717—** 1797, possibly the greatest English letter-writer, founder of the novel of mystery and terror, varied miscellaneous writer, virtuoso. Educated at Eton and King's College, Cambridge (1735—1739). Travelled with Gray on the Continent (1739—1741); quarrelled with Gray at Reggio (1741); resumed friendly relations (*c.* 1745). Member of Parliament for three successive constituencies (1741—1754, 1754—1757, 1757—1768). Made his residence at Strawberry Hill, Twickenham (1747), which he transformed into a Gothic castle equipped with secret passages and dark staircases, and where he set up his own printing-press. Visited Paris (1765), where began his famous Platonic love-affair with Madame du Deffand, an old blind woman of seventy with whom he corresponded until her death in 1780.[3] Made other visits to Paris (1767, 1775). Succeeded to the Earldom of Orford (1791).

---

1 *Fanny Burney and the Burneys,* edited by Johnson, R. B. (1926); *The Diary and Letters of Madame D'Arblay,* edited by Masefield, Muriel (1931).

2 Morley, E. J., *Fanny Burney* (The English Association, Pamphlet No. 60, 1925).

3 Bradford, Gamaliel, *Bare Souls* (1924), Chap. IV, "Horace Walpole," p. 122 ff. (pp. 97-132); De Koven, Anne, *Horace Walpole and Madame Du Deffand* (1929); Gwynn, Stephen, *The Life of Horace Walpole* (1932), Chap. x, "Madame Du Deffand," pp. 211-238; Irvine, L.LL., *Ten Letter-Writers* (1932), pp. 49-78 (pp. 31-78).

† * **Explanation of symbols immediately precedes Chapter XV.**

Other works[1] include: *A Letter from XoHo, a Chinese Philosopher at London, to his Friend Lien Chı, at Peking* (1757), an essay which influenced Goldsmith's *Citizen of the World* (p. 377); *A Catalogue of the Royal and Noble Authors* (1758); *The Parish Register at Twickenham* (*c.* 1759). *Historic Doubts on the Life and Reign of King Richard the Third* (1760), an excellent piece despite an assertion that Shakespeare's *Winter's Tale* is a sequel to *Henry VIII; Anecdotes of Painting in England* (1762—1771); *Catalogue of Engravers who have been born or resided in England* (1763); *Reminiscences* (written 1788; published 1819); and his series of *Memoirs of the Last Ten Years of the Reign of George II* (1846); *Memoirs of the Reign of George III* (1845, 1849); and *Journal of the Reign of George III from 1771 to 1783* (1859).

The Castle of Otranto†* (1764). Pseudo-medieval tale represents first attempt to make use of a Gothic setting, and inaugurates a new era of supernatural and terroristic romance, henceforth called "Gothic."[2] First edition was masked as a translation from the Italian. Pseudo-history of Italy in the twelfth or thirteenth century thinly threaded by incorrect descriptions and sentimental phrases, and overloaded with the ghostly machinery of the somber villain, the distressed heroine, the praying cowled skeleton, the nose-bleeding statue. Constructed on dramatic principles of technique. Ancestor of the modern detective novel.

The Mysterious Mother† (1768).[3] Blank-verse "Gothic" tragedy of incest. Edmund marries Adeliza, unknowingly the daughter both to him and to his own mother, the tragic Countess of Narbonne. Powerful theme of involuntary incest blends racy dialogue and rapid action, emotional phrases and nervous verse, wild construction and romantic gloom with a fine dramatic restraint. Occasionally prolix and bombastic. Details very much like the thirtieth novel of Margaret of Navarre's *Heptameron.* Play withheld from stage by Walpole himself.

Letters† (Written 1732—1797). More than 3,000 letters,[4] notable not for originality of thought but for their vivid, brilliant panorama[5] of autobiographical, social, and political life. Generally considered the

---

1 Stuart, D. M., *Horace Walpole* (1927).

2 A study of the influence of *The Castle of Otranto* from 1764 to 1820 is made by Mehrotra, K. K., *Horace Walpole and the English Novel* (1934). For a comprehensive bibliography of Walpole and the Gothic movement, consult *The Castle of Otranto,* edited by Doughty, Oswald (1929).

3 Dobson, Austin, *Horace Walpole* (Fourth Edition, 1927, revised and enlarged by Toynbee, Paget), pp. 216-219; Holzknecht, K. J., "Horace Walpole as Dramatist," *The South Atlantic Quarterly,* xxvIII (1929), pp. 174-189; Melville, Lewis (pseudonym of Benjamin, L. S.), *Horace Walpole* (1930), pp. 186-189.

4 Mrs. Paget Toynbee has edited his letters in sixteen volumes (1918 1925), but an excellent choice of his best one hundred and fifty letters is made by Lewis, W. S., *A Selection of the Letters of Horace Walpole* (Two volumes, 1926).

5 *Horace Walpole's England,* as his letters picture it, edited by Mason, A. B. (1930).

† * Explanation of symbols immediately precedes Chapter XV.

best English letter-writer. Clever persiflage, sparkling irony, caustic wit; telling characterization, illustrative memory, fertile fancy; naked style generally correct and always graceful in expression, turns of thought frequently happy. Restraint and decorum representative of the eighteenth-century's avoidance of enthusiasm. Among the more than one hundred and fifty correspondents, the principal one is his relative, Sir Horace Mann (1701—1786), British envoy to the court of Tuscany. Two notable letters: (1) Apology to Lord Nuneham, and (2) Description of Lady Caroline Petersham's party at Vauxhall. Horace Walpole has been called "London's Walter Winchell of his time."

Mrs. Ann Radcliffe, *née* Ward, 1764—1823, novelist. Married William Radcliffe (1787), editor-proprietor (1787) of the *English Chronicle.* Lived an unsocial life. Walpole had introduced the Gothic romance, but Mrs. Radcliffe established its vogue. Influenced Byron, Scott, the Brontë sisters, and possibly Coleridge and Keats. Posthumous publications included *Gaston de Blondeville* (1826) and *Poems* (1834).

The group of romances by which she is best remembered are (1) *The Castles of Athlin and Dunbayne* (1789), a negligible work that makes use of her characteristic element of suspense by its somewhat apparent use of secret passages and sliding panels; (2) *A Sicilian Romance* (1790), influenced by Baculard d'Arnaud's *Euphémie,* represents her best plot, although it barely misses overcomplication; (3) *The Romance of the Forest* (1790), an intricate plot that is somehow simpler than the others, and probably indebted to Charlotte Smith's *Romance of Real Life;* and—

The Mysteries of Udolpho†* (1794). Her most popular Gothic novel. Customary fixtures of distant and unexplainable cries, sliding panels, secret chambers, weird groans, labyrinthine passages, moonlit casements, hooded figures, clanking chains, and abductions. Characterized by a warm delight in natural beauty, by a romantic sentiment toward the Middle Ages, and by a vivid depiction of both concrete and emotional experience.

The Italian, or the Confessional of the Black Penitents† (1797). Best novel. Her most dramatic plot is woven from a commonplace theme. Best portrayed character of all her romances is the implacable, villainous monk—Schedoni, the ancestral Byronic hero.

Comment. Her obvious defects are poorness of motivation, artificiality of dialogue, over-sentimentalism, improbability of plot. There is a deficiency of characterization—she describes types, not individuals—and a general inaccuracy of local color, for she aims to reproduce the manners of her own time. But the scale is easily balanced by her merits—the suggestive use of the unknown and the supernatural, the creation and maintenance of suspense, the distinct romanticism, the imaginative power of describing the landscape, of which the natural scenery is har-

---

† * Explanation of symbols immediately precedes Chapter XV.

monized with the feelings evoked. According to Hazlitt, she is unrivalled among English writers for harrowing up the soul with imaginary terrors, and making the flesh creep, and the nerves thrill with hopes and fears. What is most significant is that the apparent element of the supernatural is later explained by natural causes.[1]

William Godwin, 1756—1836, social revolutionary writer.[2] Son of a dissenting minister, a strict Calvinist. Was, possibly, even a Sandemanian or Glassite when he entered Hoxton Presbyterian Academy to study for the ministry (1773). Non-conformist minister at Ware, Stowmarket, and Beaconsfield. Went to London (1782), a philosophic radical determined to regenerate society by advocating complete revolution to be attained by calm discussion and non-resistance, not by violence nor, possibly, by group communism. Became an atheist by 1787. Married Mary Wollstonecraft (1797), who died in giving birth to a daughter, Mary, the future second wife of Shelley. Married Mrs. Mary Jane Clairmont (1801), a widow with two children, one of whom, Clara Mary Jane Clairmont, became the mistress of Byron. Established a small publishing business (1805). Bankrupt (1822). Received the small sinecure office of Yeoman Usher of the Exchequer (1833). In his later years he grew conservative.

Miscellaneous writings include: *Sketches of History* (1784), a series of six sermons that declared even God without the right to be a tyrant; *Memoirs of the Author of A Vindication of the Rights of Woman* (1798), a simple account of Mary Wollstonecraft that merits high praise; *Antonio* (1800) and *Faulkener* (1807), two tragedies; *The Life of Lord Chatham* (1783) and *The Life of Chaucer* (1803); *The Enquirer* (1797), a series of essays on morals and politics, livelier and simpler than *An Enquiry concerning Political Justice,* and demonstrative of his changed points of view; *Essay On Sepulchres* (1809), a pleasant small volume; *Of Population* (1820), a rebuttal to Malthus; *History of the Commonwealth* (1824—1828); *Thoughts on Man* (1831), another volume of essays that repeats the main ideas of *Political Justice;* and such novels as *Fleetwood* (1805), *Cloudesly* (1830), *Deloraine* (1833), and *Mandeville* (1817), which shows the influence of C. B. Brown's *Wieland* and especially Joanna Baillie's *De Monfort*. Godwin also put out tales for children under the name of Edward Baldwin.[3]

An Enquiry concerning the Principles of Political Justice, and its influence on General Virtue and Happiness† (1793). For the first time formulates (no matter what the sources) a full philosophy of

1 Sypher, Wylie, "Social Ambiguity in a Gothic Novel," *Partisan Review,* XII (1945), pp. 50-60. Ellis, S. M., "Ann Radcliffe and Her Literary Influence," *The Contemporary Review,* CXXIII (1923), pp. 188-197.

2 Brown, F. K., *The Life of William Godwin* (1926).

3 He assumed the pen-name because he felt that his own name would predispose readers to avoid the publications, just as he had led people to believe that *Antonio* was a play by his friend, Mr. Tobin.

† * **Explanation of symbols immediately precedes Chapter XV.**

anarchism, anticipating Proudhon and Mikhail Bakunin, and affecting Shelley,[1] Wordsworth,[2] Coleridge, and Southey. Influenced in one way or another by Locke, Helvetius, Hartley, Holbach, Priestley, and Price. Rhetoric somewhat weighted down by a Latinized vocabulary, but prevailingly clear in its anarchic social philosophy on morals and government.[3]

The doctrine of anarchism advanced by Godwin is based on certain propositions[4] (*e.g.,* the propositions that all men are equal, that man is perfectible even if incapable of perfection, that Reason has unlimited power over the emotions), and assumes that character is mainly the product of education (meaning the sum total of all environmental influences from birth to death) and that man is ultimately guided by reason. The greatest force for the perpetuation of injustice is man-made institutions, and therefore such institutions as centralized government and social distinctions would be abolished in his ideal society. (In 1799 he retracted his views hostile to marriage.) His anarchistic treatise conceives of a new kingless state where custom imposes no restrictions upon the individual, where man works a mere hour or two every day, where punishment is abolished, and where property is owned in common. Compare with Bacon's *New Atlantis* (Vol. 1, p. 269), and with Hobbes's *Leviathan* (p. 319), Mandeville's *Fable of the Bees,* Bulwer-Lytton's *The Coming Race* (p. 545), Butler's *Erewhon* (p. 552), Morris's *News from Nowhere* (p. 577), H. G. Wells's *A Modern Utopia,* and Aldous Huxley's *Brave New World.*

Things as they Are, or the Adventures of Caleb Williams†* (1794). Possibly the first detective novel in the language, and probably the first propagandist novel devoted to the study of a criminal mind. Fictional interpretation of some of the doctrines in his *Political Justice; e.g.,* criticizes penal conditions, denounces oppression exercised by propertied members of the community against those less powerful and hence less privileged, and emphasizes the powerful influence of environment upon character. Style for the most part involved, infrequently direct, blending adventure, mystery, and suspense; content generally reasoned in its emotion (for there are sentimental strains in

---

1 Sen, Amiyakumar. "Godwin and Shelley," *Journal of the Department of Letters (University of Calcutta),* xx (1930), Article I, pp. 32-36 (pp. 1-123).

2 Wordsworth may have outgrown the Godwinian influence, as is indicated by his *The Borderers* (p. 446), an attempt to expose the ethical fallacies of *Political Justice.* But this is not true, for example, of all the men Godwin influences; see, as a case in point, Allen, B. S., "William Godwin's Influence upon John Thelwall," *Publications of the Modern Language Association of America,* xxxvii; New Series, xxx (1922), pp. 662-682.

3 His doctrines especially in the *Anti-Jacobin* were attacked. Anti-Godwinian novels sprung up: see Allen, B. S., "The Reaction against William Godwin," *Modern Philology,* xvi (1918), pp. 63-75 (pp. 57-75).

4 *An Enquiry Concerning Political Justice and Its Influence on General Virtue and Happiness,* edited by Preston, R. A. (Two volumes, 1926), pp. xx-xxxiii (pp. xi-xxxiii).

† * Explanation of symbols immediately precedes Chapter XV.

Godwin the rationalist[1]) and real in its depiction of a spiritual conflict. Memorable creation: Falkland. Forerunner of the novel of purpose. (Third volume was written first, and the first was written third.)

St. Leon (1799). Occult tale, pompous in its presentation of the ideal of brotherhood and the simple life, sentimental in its endeavor to be rational, and protracted in its idea that not even the elixir of life and the philosopher's stone are able to bring happiness. Better than *Caleb Williams* in its portraiture of real life. Preface recants his attitude concerning affection and every form of sentiment.

---

1 Allen, B. S., "William Godwin as a Sentimentalist," *Publications of the Modern Language Association of America*, XXXIII; New Series, XXVI (1918), pp. 1-29.

Chapter XX

THE EIGHTEENTH CENTURY: THE APPROACH
TO ROMANTICISM

General View of the Literature

During the later eighteenth century, many poets, revolting against the set and formal rules of the classical tradition, turned to nature and the simple life (a movement encouraged by the doctrines of J. J. Rousseau) and to the past, particularly medieval tales and ballads. Instead of confining themselves to the Town, the anti-Popeans turned away from the metropolitan outlook and spirit toward nature and rural life. Their subject-matter became the remote and unfamiliar, or the out-of-door aspects of the world, or human nature in terms of the brotherhood of man. They renewed the sensuous elements of love and adventure characteristic of the old *romans;* English romanticism, for example, was foreshadowed in the horror tales of Mrs. Radcliffe (p. 405). In place of the precision, symmetry, and regularity of the Augustan school, the poets of the new school substituted a deepening sense of the wonder and mystery of life; in place of a poetry of the intellect, they emphasized passion and imagination; in place of the conventional diction and the classic couplet, they revived earlier verse forms, such as the Spenserian stanza and the ode, and endeavored to attain a simplification of diction. While it is true that the prevailing standards of the neo-classical forms often cropped up in one way or another in the work of these poets of revolt, the subject-matter manifested a more direct break with rigid traditions. The essential ideas were a belief in the intuitive powers of the imagination, in the value of the individual as opposed to group conformity and external authority, in the exaltation of rural life and external nature over urban life, of content over form, of the subjective over the objective, of the emotion and imagination over the intellect and judgment. Briefly, it was the victory of mysticism over clarity, of color over symmetry, of sympathy over law, of feeling over intellect, of romantic atmosphere of matter over classical precision of form. Among the precursors of romantic poetry were the rediscoverers of nature such as Allan Ramsay (1686—1758), John Dyer (*c.* 1700—1758), and James Thomson (p. 410); the revivers of the past including (a) such imitators of Milton as Thomas Parnell (1679—1718), Robert Blair (1699—1746), and Edward Young (p. 414); (b) such imitators of Spenser as William Shenstone (1714—1763), Mark Akenside (1721—1770), and James Beattie (1735—1803); and (c) such antiquarians as Richard Hurd (1720—1808), Thomas Percy (p. 421), Thomas Warton (1728—1790), Joseph Warton (1722—1800), Horace Walpole (p. 403), James Macpherson (p. 419), Thomas Chatterton (p. 422), William Collins (p. 412), and Thomas Gray (p. 416); the humanitarians and naturalists such as William Cowper (p. 424), George Crabbe (p. 427), Robert Burns (p. 429), and William Blake (p. 435).

James Thomson, 1700—1748, earliest important precursor of the Romantic movement. Born at Ednam, in Roxburghshire, Scotland. Son of a Presbyterian minister. Entered Edinburgh University (1715). Went to London (1725), where he met such literary celebrities as Pope and Gay. Travelled on Continent as companion-tutor to C. R. Talbot, son of the Solicitor-General (1730—1731). Granted the sinecure office of Secretary of the Briefs (1733). Pensioned (1737). Granted another sinecure as Surveyor-General of the Leeward Islands (1744). Pension ceased (1748).

Accurate observation, delicate sensitiveness, and selective compositional skill, all coupled to a sincere love of Nature, brought back from exile the romantic treatment of Nature banished by the Popean school. Yet his treatment of Man, too, was sentimental. Thus in both ways James Thomson, although shackled by many neo-classical conventions of style and vocabulary, foreran the Romantic movement. Famous tribute of William Collins: *Ode Occasion'd by the Death of Mr. Thomson* (p. 414).

Lesser works: *Poem to the Memory of Sir Isaac Newton* (1727), significant in showing Thomson's interest in the scientific movement of his day; *To the Memory of Mr. Congreve* (1729), usually attributed to him; and, finally, some tragedies—*Agamemnon* (1738), modelled upon Aeschylus and political in implication; *Edward and Eleanora* (1739), banned by censors who feared its political intent, and the plot of which resembles parts of *The Talisman* by Scott (p. 416); *Tancred and Sigismunda* (1745; produced 1752), its plot derived from *Gil Blas;* and *Coriolanus* (1749), the only interest residing in the prologue.

Principal Works

The Seasons (1726—1730).[1] Significant by virtue of being the earliest important eighteenth-century blank-verse poem and by virtue of challenging the classical ideal of eighteenth-century poetry through truthful and romantic treatment of rural beauties. Extended descrip-

---

1 McKillop, A. D., *The Background of Thomson's Seasons* (1942); Grant, Douglas, *James Thomson: Poet of 'The Seasons'* (1951); McKillop, A. D., ed., *James Thomson (1700-1748): Letters and Documents* (1958).

tive passages relieved by emotional outbursts on such matters as liberty, scientific facts, and writers, and by three major sentimental tales (one of which, that of Damon and Musidora, is frowned upon for its suggestiveness).

Descriptive and humanitarian poem in four books, later arranged in logical order: (1) *Winter* (1726), which ends in a religious vein, is of note, among other things, for its picture of the red-breast, and for its natural description of a snowdrift. (2) *Summer* (1727), which terminates in a scientific vein, includes the well-known episode of Celadon and Amelia, two innocent lovers, the latter of whom is struck lifeless by a lightning-bolt in a summer thunderstorm. (3) *Spring* (1728), made fragrant by its blossoming violets, and distinguished for its panegyric on nuptial love. (4) *Autumn* (1730), containing some of his best idyllic scenes, notable for its denunciation of the sport of hunting, and dignified by the Ruth- and Boaz-like episode of Palemon and Lavinia. The Four Seasons are completed by "The Hymn to Nature" (1730). Wide influence both in England and on the Continent.[1]

SUGGESTED MERITS *(The Seasons)*	SUGGESTED DEFECTS *(The Seasons)*
1. Discards the fashionable closed couplet for Miltonic blank verse, which it popularized.	1. Traces of neo-classicism: **e.g.,** end-stopped lines and artificial classical allusions. Stiff movement. Does not capture Milton's music.
2. Felicitous touches of natural scenery. Objective description influenced somewhat by the scientific interest of the day.[2]	2. Padded descriptions. Treatment of landscape somewhat inhibited by his scientific rationalism. While notable for objective description, is deficient in emotional treatment.
3. Some freshness of expression. Frequently happy in his compound epithets.	3. Ornate style. Neo-classical clichés, mechanical epithets, Latinized vocabulary, frigid diction, colorless personifications.
4. Humanitarian ideas. Interesting philosophical digressions.	4. Conforms with pastoral traditions with regard to love. Boring didacticism.

Hymn on Solitude (1729). Cadenced lyric poem.

The Tragedy of Sophonisba (1730). Imitation of Otway. Famous for one line: "O Sophonisba! Sophonisba O!"—parodied by Fielding s *Tragedy of Tragedies* (p. 394).

Liberty (1734—1736). Whig panegyric dedicated to Frederick, Prince of Wales. Only its blank-verse form gives it significance, for its approximately four thousand lines, abounding in platitudes and mag-

---

1 Thomson has had British, German, French, Dutch, and Norwegian imitators; he, for example, exerted a major influence on Sweden during his own century. Consult Johnson, W. G., "James Thomson's Influence on Swedish Literature in the Eighteenth Century," *Illinois Studies in Language and Literature*, XIX (1936).

2 Drennon, Herbert, (1) "James Thomson's Contact with Newtonianism and His Interest in Natural Philosophy," *Publications of the Modern Language Association of America*, XLIX (1934), pp. 71-80; (2) "Scientific Rationalism and James Thomson's Poetic Art," *Studies in Philology*, XXXI (1934), pp. 453-471.

niloquence, and barren save for some traces of moderate description and sentiment, tell lifelessly of British Liberty's ageless vicissitudes in different countries. Second book has strains of Romantic Hellenism.

The Masque of Alfred (1740). Written jointly with David Mallet. Famous for its spirited national song, "Rule Britannia," generally attributed to Thomson. As long as England maintains her political powers, Southey has said, it will be the political hymn of England.

The Castle of Indolence (1748). Romantic allegory of about fifteen hundred lines in the Spenserian stanza, has something of *The Faerie Queene's* magic, a subtle melody and mystic seriousness. For the first time in the eighteenth century, the first canto, languid in its melody and dreamy in its vision, anticipates fully the Romantic Period. In an age of heroic couplets, Thomson re-introduced the Spenserian stanza; despite still-born and burlesque areas, the poem is the best eighteenth-century imitation of Spenser.

Canto I describes how the Enchanter Indolence lures jaded pilgrims into his castles in the lotus-land of Drowsy-Head, and there victimizes them out of their energy and free will into an enervating state of indulgence and disease. Canto II describes how the Knight of Arts and Industry conquers Idleness and razes his castle.

William Collins, 1721–1759, poet. Son of a wealthy Chichester hatter. Entered Winchester College (1733), and Queen's College, Oxford (1741), where he was a commoner. Obtained a demyship at Magdalen College, Oxford (1741). B.A. (1743). Renouncing church leanings, sought a literary career in London (1744). Probably made two visits to Colonel Martin, in Flanders (1745, 1746).[1] Generally in financial difficulties; but relieved, in 1749, by Colonel Martin's legacy of about two thousand pounds. "Poor Collins": for the last nine years of a short life he was intermittently deranged. Was for a time in a Chelsea madhouse. Died at the home of his married sister Anne (Mrs. Hugh Sempill). William Collins, a lyrist of aerial music and romantic love of nature, is an early and influential harbinger of English romanticism.[2]

Miscellaneous poems include his four *Persian Eclogues* (1742), Augustan in rimed couplets, limpidity, and sentiment, and in its second edition renamed *Oriental Eclogues* (1759); "When Phoebe form'd a wanton smile" (1739), his earliest extant piece, an excellent sonnet signed "Delicatulus"; "Young Damon of the Vale is Dead" (written *c.* 1739; published 1788), a Wordsworthian song; *Verses Humbly*

1 White, H. O., "The Letters of William Collins," *The Review of English Studies,* III (1927), p. 12 f. (pp. 12-21).

2 Woodhouse, A. S. P., "Collins and the Creative Imagination: A Study in the Critical Background of His Odes (1746)," *Studies in English,* collected by Wallace, M. W. (1931), pp. 60-66.

Address'd to Sir Thomas Hanmer (1743), a negligible review of poetry in heroic couplets, culminating in commendatory verses to Shakespeare, all occasioned by Hanmer's Shakespeare of 1743; *An Epistle: Address to Sir Thomas Hanmer* (1744), a revised second edition of his *Verses Humbly Address'd,* interesting for its skillful handling of the heroic couplet, and important for including the first edition of the "Dirge in *Cymbeline,*" inspired by Shakespeare's *Cymbeline* (IV, ii, *ll,* 215—259), and, if expressed somewhat weakly, sweetly phrasing a genuine feeling. No major poet has left behind a smaller bulk of work.[1]

Odes on Several Descriptive and Allegoric Subjects (1746; but dated 1747). Slim volume of fifty-two pages contains twelve odes. Genuine fervor and exquisite imagery are part of his essentially lyric voice. Brevity, selective power, delicate restraint, compressed intensity. Includes the odes to *Simplicity* (possibly over-rated, although to be noted as a protest against artificial and ornate poetry), *On the Poetical Character* (possibly under-rated, even though faulty), *Liberty,* and—

a) *Ode to Evening.* Unrimed lyric is probably his highest achievement in the ode. Dreamy, but pellucid, style; fragile music, magically felicitous in its allusions to nature, enhanced by expert use of assonance and onomatopoeia, and haloed by its perfect form. Based on Milton's translation of Horace's fifth ode of the First Book (stanza invented by Milton), it reveals a Miltonic purity of diction and versification, and notable alliteration and color.

b) *Ode, Written in the Year 1746.* Commonly known as "How Sleep the Brave." Elegy nobly and touchingly laments the English soldiers who died in battle in 1745 (*e.g.,* as part of War of the Austrian Succession). His most fluent poem is possibly "more perfect" than the *Ode to Evening,* but less great. Note its classic spirit of restrained passion.

c) *The Passions, an Ode to Music.* Most popular ode is of high excellence. Venturesome and swiftly-moving personification of such passions as Anger and Pity, Fear and Hope, Melancholy and Cheerfulness—in measures as varied in kind and in sound effect as the distinguishable emotions. Pindaric form.

Ode on the Popular Superstitions of the Highlands of Scotland (Written *c.* 1749; printed 1788). Longest poem, incompletely sustained and somewhat labored, is instinct with some passages of delicate sweetness, sober beauty, and elevated verse. Generally over-valued; but of historical importance by reason of the rich melancholy and the medieval supernaturalism that herald romanticism.

---

1 Garrod, H. W., *Collins* (1928); Ainsworth, E. G., Jr., *Poor Collins* (1937).

Ode Occasion'd by the Death of Mr. Thomson (1749). Commemorative elegy exemplifying his "skill to complain," a gift also illustrated by his "Dirge to *Cymbeline*" and "How Sleep the Brave." Reveals personal feeling (although phrases could be more appropriate), delicate melancholy, and exquisite form.

SUGGESTED MERITS	SUGGESTED DEFECTS
1. Uniting of human emotion to natural beauty.	1. Want of sentiment and mystery. No human being in any poem.
2. Wide range of his few poems. (Note, however, the absence of love-poetry.)	2. Weak in the faculty of direct perception.
3. Possesses the "skill to complain."	3. Lacks lyrical rapture and verges on emptiness.
4. Classic and sculpturesque in its clarity. Generally is Hellenic rather than Augustan. Personifications reminiscent of Milton, and anticipatory of Wordsworth	4. Artificial in its conventional phrasing, pseudo-classic in its abstract personifications. Stock epithets (primarily in Eclogues), pieces of falsetto (even in Evening), and neo-classical echoes (even in The Passions) tag him as an eighteenth-century poetaster.

Edward Young, 1683—1765, poet of the graveyard tradition.[1] Son of a cleric. Educated at Winchester College and New College and Corpus Christi College, Oxford. Obtained a Law Fellowship at All Souls College, Oxford (1708). B.C.L. (1714). D.C.L. (1719). Took holy orders (1727). Rector of Welwyn, Herts (1730). Married Lady Elizabeth Lee, granddaughter of Charles II (1731). Many thought him deserving of a bishopric. Influenced French, Italian, and German, as well as English, literature.[2]

The Last Day (1713), in heroic couplets, is a mingling of gloom and querulous rhetoric foreshadowing *The Complaint, or Night Thoughts; The Force of Religion: or Vanquished Love* (1713) is a flat didactic poem in somewhat better heroic couplets on the beheading of Lady Jane Grey and Lord Guilford Dudley, her husband; and *Resignation* (1762) is a protracted but dignified poem. Dramas include *Busiris* (1719), a pseudo-heroic tragedy in which anachronisms are apparent and bombastic passages prevail; *The Revenge* (1721), a poorly-motivated tragedy of violence and passion, as unbridled in its declamation and fustian as *Busiris,* and both gibed at by Fielding's *Tragedy of Tragedies;* and *The Brothers* (c. 1728; published 1753), his best-constructed play, one indebted to Corneille and classical biography. Finally, his letters, while Johnsonese in diction, are human and humorous.

---

1 Shelley, H. C., *The Life and Letters of Edward Young* (1914).

Love of Fame, or the Universal Passion (1725—1728). Series of seven wittily shrewd and rather venomless satires. Character sketches in heroic couplets unimportant as poetry, but significant as vividly-stroked sketches of exaggeratedly self-important, ridiculous types (rake, slut, miser, hypocrite). Follows Pope in the same field. Famous for its quotations.

The Complaint, or Night Thoughts on Life, Death, and Immortality (Nine parts, 1742—1745). Reflective poem in ten thousand lines of plodding, dignified blank verse, to some extent personal and autobiographical. Professedly attempts to repudiate atheism and to vindicate Christianity; prominent is its interest in Christian apologetics.[1] Pretentious didacticism and empty philosophy ruin particularly the last five books; but neither the opera-mannered style nor ornamented platitudes and absurdities can hobble some beautiful lines, magnificent in their dreamily aesthetic melancholy, and some passages of somber eloquence. Sublime: *"Death* loves a shining mark, a signal blow."* Proverbial: *"Procrastination* is the thief of time"; "Man wants but little; nor that little long." (The latter was used by Goldsmith a score of years later in *The Hermit.*)

Conjectures on Original Composition (1759)[2]. Remarkable prose essay addressed to Richardson (p. 388). Deficient in clear expression and orderly arrangement, but brief, picturesque, and vigorous. Revere the ancients, says Young, but reject them as models; be independent, rely upon inspiration, and be creative rather than imitative: he demands greater freedom for the writer and asserts that native genius is greater than rules. Influenced German thought.[3]

SUGGESTED MERITS

1. Romantic melancholy, personal and singular.
2. Abandons the classic couplet for Miltonic blank verse.
3. H. H. Clark, refuting those who believe that Young is scarcely a romanticist, points out Young's
   a) Scorn for the commonplace,
   b) Recognition of nature "as the felt presence of the Deity," and
   c) Idiosyncratic subjectivity.[4]

SUGGESTED DEFECTS

1. Sermonizing attitude, and bathos.
2. Miltonic in purpose but neo-classical in method: end-pauses, excessive ornaments, and the like.
3. Prolixity. Strained sententiousness. Poor arrangement of material. Frequent anti-climax. Builds upon sepulchral rhetoric, not upon imagination. Taine, although acknowledging his merits, says that Young "makes the most of his grief, and strikes attitudes. He exaggerates and declaims, studies effect and style, confuses Greek and Christian ideas."

1 Bliss, I. St.J., "Young's *Night Thoughts* in Relation to Contemporary Christian Apologetics," *Publications of the Modern Language Association of America,* XLIX (1934), pp. 37-70.

2 *Edward Young's Conjectures on Original Composition,* edited by Morley, E. J. (1918).

3 Kind, J. L., "Edward Young in Germany," *Columbia University Germanic Studies,* II (1906), pp. 11-58.

4 Clark, H. H., "The Romanticism of Edward Young," *Transactions of the Wisconsin Academy of Sciences, Arts and Letters,* XXIV (1929), pp. 1-45.

Thomas Gray, 1716—1771, poet, letter-writer, classical scholar.[1] Son of a selfish and harsh money-scrivener. Through the efforts of his mother, he entered Eton (*c.* 1725),[2] where he formed "The Quadruple Alliance" with Thomas Ashton, Richard West, son of the Lord Chancellor of Ireland (whom he fruitlessly mourned in the *Sonnet on the Death of Richard West*,[3] 1742), and Horace Walpole, with whom was formed (except for a lapse of a few years) a remarkable friendship. Entered as pensioner at Peterhouse (1734), which he left without taking a degree. Accompanied Horace Walpole on a Continental tour (1739—1741); but, after a quarrel with Walpole at Reggio (1741), travelled alone. He had visited the Grande Chartreuse (1741), and in the Visitors' Book wrote his *Alcaic Ode*, "O Tu severa Religio loci," and thenceforth attempted unsuccessfully to bring about the fulfilment of his invocation. Reached London (September, 1741). Began his first English poem, *Agrippina*, a fragmentary two-scened "classical" tragedy (1741). Returned to Peterhouse as a fellow-commoner (1742). Took the degree of B. C. L. (1744). Reconciled with Horace Walpole (*c.* 1745). House in Cornhill burned down, and for a time he was in straitened circumstances (1748). Meets Miss Speed (1750),[4] protégée of Lady Cobham. Declined the offered post of poet laureate (1757). Toured places of interest in the north (1761). Toured Scotland (1764, 1765). Travelled in Kent (1766). Appointed Professor of Modern History and Languages at Cambridge (1768), an honorary position requiring no lectures. Composed the *Ode for Music* to be performed at the Installation of the Duke of Grafton as Chancellor of the University of Cambridge (1769), a piece of flattering bombast with few virtues. Visited the Lake District (1769). Made an excursion through the Western Counties (1770). By his wish Gray was buried by his mother's side in the churchyard at Stoke Poges, conjectured to be the scene (if any is) of the *Elegy*.

Thomas Gray illustrates in his narrow limits the progression of poetry from the neo-classical style of Dryden and Pope (first period, 1742—1750) to the second period (1750—1755) of Thomson and the nature poets, and the graveyard school, and to the final period of the romantic Pindaric odes, Norse and Celtic themes, including *The Triumphs of Owen* (1761; published 1768), and *The Death of Hoel*

---

1 Northup, C. S., *A Bibliography of Thomas Gray* (1917); Martin, Roger, *Essai sur Thomas Gray* (1935); Ketton-Cremer, R. W., *Thomas Gray* (1935).

2 Whibley, Leonard, "Thomas Gray at Eton," *Blackwood's Magazine*, ccxv (1929), pp. 611-623.

3 Richard West may be the "youth to Fortune and to Fame unknown" in the *Elegy*. Read Shepard, Odell, "A Youth to Fortune and to Fame Unknown," *Modern Philology*, xx (1922-1923), pp. 347-373.

4 Gray had a deep affection for his mother. The only other woman to whom this bachelor seemed to be even slightly attached was the beautiful and witty Henrietta Speed, who married the Baron de la Peyrière, son of the Sardinian Minister, the Comte de Viry, and who became a political intrigante.

(1761; published 1768). While reflecting some characteristics of the classical school, Gray is also an important precursor of the Romantic movement.

Augustan Period

Ode on the Spring (1742). Less a poem of lyrical impulse than a semi-humorous meditation: pseudo-classicism attained by the matching of ruthless allegory and everyday moralizing. Melancholy; appreciation of nature.

Hymn to Adversity (1742). Human life is its theme and pensive melancholy its shroud. More impressive and better designed than the *Eton College* ode. Tovey has declared it "perhaps the most faultless of his poems."

Hymn to Ignorance (1742). Didactic. Heroic couplets.

Ode on a Distant Prospect of Eton College (1747). Ostensibly a tribute to Eton, but more likely an expression of sorrow at the death of his friend, Richard West, in 1742, and possibly reminiscent of his quarrel with Walpole. Conventional in its theme, Augustan in its tone and spirit, and platitudinous in its moral conclusion. Despite its neo-classical tags of stilted phrasing and overloaded personifications, there are critics who see evidence of romantic leanings in the responses to nature and in the gloomy moralizings.

Essay on the Alliance of Education and Government (1748). Like his *Hymn to Ignorance*, is an unfinished didactic work in heroic couplets, giving promise of Augustan stateliness.

Transitional Period

Ode on the Death of a Favorite Cat Drowned in a Tub of Gold Fishes (1748). Playful light verse, celebrating an occurrence in Walpole's household, furnishes a pleasant contrast to his graveyard moralizing and complacent twilight. Dr. Johnson pointed to the concluding lines as a *non-sequitur*.

A Long Story (1750). Delightful piece of mock-heroic, suggested possibly by Prior's *The Dove* but treated with originality.

An Elegy Wrote in a Country Church Yard (1751). Reflective, melancholy poem in quatrains of ten-syllabled lines is supreme example of the "graveyard" school, and possibly the most widely known single poem in the English language. Occasional vagueness of phrase; personifications and conventional diction. Least successful are the concluding stanzas, redeemed by the noble epitaph. Three reasons for success: (1) its new sympathy for lowly folk ("the short and simple annals of the poor"), (2) its mosaic of suggestive phrases and ideas synthesized from several literatures, and (3) its wondrous coalescence of meter and disciplined rhapsody with pensive melancholy and romantic nature.[1] In the poem, Melancholy is made human. Gosse, representing one body of opinion, declares it to possess the "charm of incomparable felicity, of a melody not too subtle to charm every ear, of a moral persuasiveness that appeals to every generation, and of a metrical skill that in each line portrays the master."[2] Another group sums up its attitude about Gray by pointing out, in Saintsbury's words, "the other fact that he is, after all, but a second-rate poet." The truth, probably, lies between the two: while his ideas are derivative and platitudinous, his expression is chiselled and harmonized; while not so great a poet as he seemed to his generation, he is a far better one than he appears to this. (Practically every utterance is quotable: note how his lines have both pictorial and imaginative qualities. No other poem of its length has given us so many phrases as part of our everyday speech.[3])

Romantic Period

Pindaric Odes (1757). His contemporaries[4] criticized the work for its obscurity; Coleridge thought the odes frigid and artificial; Wordsworth described the phraseology of all Gray's poetry as gaudy and inane.[5] Has been considered over-ornamented by metaphor and invocation, and by constant cloudy allusions to classical and medieval learning. Gray's notes to the 1768 edition cleared away difficulties, and also revealed his frequent imitations and borrowings from other writers. Uses a remarkable variety of measures, an elaborate metrical scheme. Important for three reasons: (1) a romantic interest in older literatures, (2) a romantic love of wild scenery, and (3) spirited declamation, romantic fervor, and exalted imagination.

a) *The Progress of Poesy* (written 1754). Like *The Bard*, a splendid example of a genuine Pindaric ode, in rimed iambics; and like it, too, attacked by Johnson. Into its dignified poetic matrix is poured a vigorous and romantic, a warm and spontaneous utterance glorifying such older poets as Shakespeare, Milton, and Dryden. To Tennyson the lines toward the end were among the most liquid in any language.

---

1 Beresford, John, "The Author of the 'Elegy,'" [a review], *The Edinburgh Review*, CCXXIV (1926), pp. 121-134.

2 Paget Toynbee and Leonard Whibley have stated that Edmund Gosse's *Life of Gray* (1882), unhappily accepted as reliable, has many errors of fact and unwarranted assumptions.

3 Famous is the anecdote of Wolfe's reciting the *Elegy* to his officers that night on the St. Lawrence river as he drifted down to his heroic death, and declaring, "Gentlemen, I would rather be the author of that poem than take Quebec." Such historians as Carlyle, Bancroft, and Green repeat the tale—possibly a true one, for Wolfe's annotated and underlined copy of the *Elegy* given to him by Katharine Lowther, whom he had hoped to wed, still exists.

4 Jones, W. P., "The Contemporary Reception of Gray's Odes," *Modern Philology*, XXVIII (1930-1931), pp. 61-82.

5 Wordsworth tried to show that even the *Elegy* was unintelligible. Hazlitt has dryly remarked, "It has been understood."

b) *The Bard* (1757). Ode on Welsh theme, in rimed iambics, written in imitation of Pindar's structure, is an attempt to translate the background of his romantic interest in the Middle Ages into the language of his day. Romantic qualities are evident in its medieval theme, based on a tradition that Edward I had decreed that all Welsh bards be put to death, and in its nature imagery, provided chiefly by mountain scenery. Dramatic quality, imaginative intensity; brilliant historical scenes, crowded allusions.

The Fatal Sisters (1761). Based upon a Latin translation (available in *Corpus Poeticum Boreale,* Volume I) of an Icelandic poem of the eleventh century celebrating an invasion of Ireland by Sigtrygg or Sitric, King of the Dublin Norse. Like The Descent of Odin, has neoclassical *clichés;* and, like it, is romantic in content, form, and spirit.

The Descent of Odin (1761). Lay, drawn from northern folklore, illustrates his penchant for the remote.

Letters and Journal

Letters[1] and *Journal* (1775). His letters are a brilliant revelation of his companionable humor, charm, sense of loyalty, scholarship, and character. Love of nature, particularly an appreciation of mountain scenery. Unlike Walpole, he notices the simple or ordinary things, clothing them with the apt epithet. Fluent, vigorous style. "Gray never spoke out" does not apply here.[2] His most finished prose work is the *Journal,* which commemorates his journey among the English lakes, and where his sharp eye for nature invests Gray with importance in any study of the growth of the romantic spirit.

SUGGESTED MERITS	SUGGESTED DEFECTS
1. Thorough scholarship explored the origins of romance in Norse and Celtic legend.	1. Acquired knowledge loads down his work with inversions, personifications, and obscurities. Phrases and thought are derivative.
2. Condensed diction. Highly finished style.	2. Attained perfection inhibits his writings.
3. Romantic qualities include sincere feeling, tender and pensive moods, love for the past, delicate treatment of nature, sense of grandeur, democratic sympathy for the poor.	3. Is, in the main, a commonplace moralist: utterances a little too well-rounded and cautious; overpensive melancholy, or, to quote Gray's own word, leuchocholy.

James Macpherson, 1736—1796, "poet-translator" of the so-called Ossianic works,[3] antiquary, historian. Educated at King's and Marischal Colleges, Aberdeen, removing later to the University of Edin-

---

1 *Correspondence of Thomas Gray,* edited by Toynbee, Paget, and Whibley, Leonard (Three volumes, 1935).
2 "He [Gray] never spoke out," a chance phrase used by his friend and executor, has been made famous by Matthew Arnold. The emphasis seems to have been misplaced. See Ketton-Cremer, R. W., *Thomas Gray* (1935), Chap. IX, pp. 128-133.
3 Black, G. F., "Macpherson's Ossian and the Ossianic Controversy," *Bulletin of the New York Public Library,* xxx (1926), pp. 424-439, pp. 508-524.

burgh. Took no degree. Schoolmaster in his native village of Ruthven, in the shire of Inverness, Scotland. Travelled as private tutor to Thomas Graham of Balgowan (1759). Secretary to Governor Johnstone of Pensacola, West Florida (1764—1766), and, despite his continual quarreling with the Governor, when Macpherson returned to Scotland he was allowed to retain his salary of two hundred pounds as a pension for life (1766). London agent to Mohammed Ali, nabob of Arcot (1779). Member of Parliament for Camelford (1780—1786). In failing health he retired to his mansion in Inverness-shire (1795). Was buried in Westminster Abbey, not far from Poet's Corner.

History: *An Introduction to the History of Great Britain and Ireland* (Second edition, 1772), one of two works avowedly used by Gibbon (p. 381); *The History of Great Britain from the Restoration to the Accession of the House of Hanover* (1775), a Jacobite work, which brought him a few thousand pounds; and *Original Papers, containing the Secret History of Great Britain from the Restoration to the Accession of the House of Hanover* (1775), his most important historical work. He wrote also liberal pamphlets on the American Revolution.

Poetry: *Death*, a blank-verse imitation of Robert Blair's *The Grave*, is probably his earliest work; *The Arrival of the Lord Mareschal in Scotland*, an ode in imitation of Pindar; *The Highlander* (1758), six cantos in classic couplets on an eleventh-century invasion of Scotland, a poem he later tried to suppress; and the *Iliad* (1773), an unsuccessful translation in Ossianic prose.

Fragments of ancient poetry, collected in the Highlands of Scotland, and translated from the Galic or Erse language (1760). The fragments aroused the Faculty of Advocates in Edinburgh to finance Macpherson on a trip through the Highlands and Western Isles for the purpose of collecting like material. Critical dissertation by Hugh Blair, Regius Professor of Rhetoric and Belles-Lettres at Edinburgh, pronounced the verses to be genuine remains of ancient Gaelic poetry.

Fingal, an Ancient Epic Poem, in Six Books (1762). Measured prose concerning a Norse invasion of Ireland represents the first fruits of his financed trip. Includes "several other Poems, composed by Ossian, the Son of Fingal."

Temora, an Epic Poem in Eight Books (1763). Continuation of the story begun in *Fingal* includes more than a dozen smaller pieces.

The Works of Ossian (1765). Collected edition. Some of the miscellaneous poems of Ossian are *Cath-loda, Comala, Lathmon, The Battle of Lora, Carthon, Oina-Morul, The Songs of Selma.*

The Ossianic Poems[1]

Macpherson published poems in a loose, rhythmical prose imbued with supernaturalism and steeped in deep melancholy; these poems professed to be translations from a legendary third-century Gaelic bard, called Ossian, son of Fingal (Oisin, putative son of Fionn mac Cumhail), traditional Highland hero. While Hugh Blair, Gregory, Lord Kames, and Sir John Sinclair considered the translations genuine, Johnson, Gray, Hume, and Malcolm Laing impugned their authenticity, regarding them as forgeries by Macpherson.[2] Consensus is that, while based in part on authentic fragments (whether oral or written), yet the translation is not a genuine transcription from ancient originals. Neither the fact of the forgery nor its exposure is important, but the great sensation created by the poems in Europe—poems which were translated into French by Turgot and into Italian by Cesarotte, which gave impetus particularly to the romantic movement in Germany, where it made its greatest capture in Goethe. While remote from the Gaelic classics, the Ossianic poems are informed with a Gaelic atmosphere and spirit unlike any previous English writings. Imitations of Ossian by writers of Gaelic gave body to the Macpherson tradition. As a result of the European romantic movement, which was considerably influenced by the Ossianic world of heroic simplicity set in a landscape of "mountains and mist," Anglo-Ireland discovered in the nineteenth century an interest in Gaelic literature that left its stamp on the Celtic Renaissance.[3] (See pp. 598—600.)

SUGGESTED MERITS	SUGGESTED DEFECTS
1. Romantic description of wild scenery. Fidelity to Nature.	1. Minute descriptions of landscape are foreign to early Scottish Gaelic poetry. Bombastic, grandiloquent.
2. Celtic love intuition.	2. "Graveyard" gloom.
3. Melancholy tenderness, lofty sentiment.	3. Absence of Gaelic firmness. Sentimentalized attitude toward life.
4. Abandons Augustan rigidity of versification for a free-moving rhythmical prose. Impressionistic in its imagery. Short, balanced clauses.	4. Sameness of style, vagueness of narrative. Reminiscent of Homer, Milton, and the Hebrew. Confuses the Ulster and the Fenian cycles. Strains at idiom and language.

Thomas Percy, 1729—1811, antiquary, editor, poet, commentator on the Bible, translator.[4] Educated at Christ Church, Oxford. Married Anne Gutteridge (1759). Chaplain to George III (1769). Protestant

---

1 Fraser, G. M., "The Truth About Macpherson's 'Ossian,'" *The Quarterly Review*, CCLXV (1925), pp. 331-345; *The Poems of Ossian*, with an Introduction by Shairp, William (1926); Hanson, W. G., "James Macpherson (1736-1796)," *The London Quarterly and Holborn Review*, CLXI, Sixth Series, v (1936), pp. 510-515.

2 Wordsworth not only denounced *Ossian* as a worthless forgery but asserted that the poems are false in nature-representations of mountain scenery. But Wordsworth himself was not above the influence of Macpherson: Moore, J. P., "Wordsworth's Unacknowledged Debt to Macpherson's *Ossian*," *Publications of the Modern Language Association of America*, XL; New Series, XXXIII (1925), pp. 362-378.

3 De Blácam, Aodh, *Gaelic Literature Surveyed* (1929), pp. 363-365.

4 Gaussen, A. C. C., *Percy: Prelate and Poet* (1908); Smith, D. N. & Cleanth Brooks, eds., *The Percy Letters* (Six vols., 1944-1946).

Bishop of Dromore, in Ireland (1782—1811). "O Nanny wilt thou gang with me?" is his best poem, indebted to several sources, and inspired by his wife. His *Northern Antiquities* (1770), a translation of Paul Henry Mallet's *Introduction á l'histoire du Dannemarc,* aroused interest in the Scandinavian mythology and the Eddas.

Reliques of Ancient English Poetry (1765). Collection of about 180 old English and Scots ballads, historical songs, metrical romances, and sonnets; also some modern poems as well as some spurious pieces. Edited, for most part, from an old folio manuscript. Anthology, with the works dating from the fourteenth century to Percy's day, ranges from the ballads of Robin Hood to those of Douglas, from the sonnets of Lovelace to those of Johnson. Percy's adaptations often indifferently sentimental; often his editing is invigorating, notably in *Heir of Linne.* Book contains, among others, *Sir Patrick Spens* and *Chevy Chase* (see Vol. 1, p. 100 *ff.*).

Percy's *Reliques* is a landmark, not only of English balladry, but also of the Romantic Revolt. It swept away the lifeless artificiality of contemporaneous poetry, and ushered in a naturalness of approach which fertilized the ground of a new literary epoch.

Thomas Chatterton, 1752—1770, precocious poet with intense medieval sympathies.[1] Posthumous son of a poor writing-master of Bristol. At the Colston Free School (1760—*c.* 1767). Spent large part of his time delving among the dusty parchments in the muniment room of St. Mary Redcliffe, where for many generations his paternal ancestors had served as sextons. Apprenticed to John Lambert (1767), an attorney who later dismissed him. Travelled to London (1770). Discouraged, penniless, and facing starvation,[2] when not yet eighteen he poisoned himself, probably with arsenic.

His prose writings are unoriginal and imitative; his political letters are reminiscent of Junius; *Maria Friendless* is a story paraphrased from "Misella" in Johnson's *The Rambler* (p. 369). His minor poems, essentially non-lyrical, range from love verses (written for another) to comic elegies. Among his verse satires are *Resignation,* a diatribe against Lord Bute and the London Tories; *The Consuliad,* a scurrilous political piece; *Kew Gardens* (called, in original form, *The Whore of Babylon*), a cacophonous philippic that does not glove its malevolent treatment of personalities; and *The Exhibition,*[3] a bitter, splenetic attack upon Alexander Catcott, the Bristol clergy, and doctors. To his best friend, who died in 1769, he wrote one of his best lyric poems, *Elegy to the Memory of Mr. Thomas Phillips, of Fairford:* "Now rest, my muse,

---

1 Meyerstein, E. H. W., *A Life of Thomas Chatterton* (1930); Ellinger, E. P., *Thomas Chatterton* (1930); Nevill, John C., *Thomas Chatterton* (1948).
2 That is the traditional interpretation. But see Meyerstein, E. H. W., *A Life of Thomas Chatterton* (1930), pp. 435-442.
3 Ingram, J. H., *The True Chatterton* (1910), Appendix B, p. 295 *f.;* Ellinger, E. P., *Thomas Chatterton* (1930), pp. 55-60.

but only rest to sleep." *The Revenge* (1770), is a vigorous burletta in which Cupid revenges himself upon Jupiter by revealing Thor's assignation with Maia. Walpole, after consulting with Gray and Mason, pronounced spurious *The Ryse of Peyncteyne yn Englande wroten by T. Rowleie, 1469, for Mastre Canynge,* which Chatterton had sent. There remains, finally, *The Last Will and Testament of Me, Thomas Chatterton, of the city of Bristol* (1770), in which he ironically directs the disposal, at his death, of his character-possessions — bequests of his humility, religion, abstinence, and generosity; *e.g.,* "Item. I give and bequeath to Mr. W—— M—— a mourning Ring with this Motto, 'Alas, poor Chatterton' provided he pays for it himself."[1]

But Chatterton lives because of his inseparable connection with the Romantic Movement.[2] His medieval forgeries echo Chaucer, Spenser, Shakespeare, Milton, and Ossian; these same works influenced Coleridge's *Christabel,* and Keats's *Eve of St. Agnes,* as well as the poetry of Blake, Rossetti, and Morris. To Chatterton, "the most English of Poets except Shakespeare," Keats dedicated his *Endymion;* among others Shelley honored Chatterton as one of the "inheritors of unfulfilled renown"; because of him Coleridge penned *A Monody on the Death of Chatterton.* It remained for Wordsworth's *Resolution and Independence,* however, to stamp him permanently as

". . . . the marvellous Boy,
The sleepless Soul that perished in his pride."

Poems, supposed to have been written at Bristol, By Thomas Rowley, And Others, in the Fifteenth Century (Written 1765—1770; First collected edition, 1777). Black-letter poems ascribed by Chatterton to Thomas Rowley, a fictitious priest of the fifteenth century, and to others; but really by Chatterton himself. Thin forgeries in counterfeit Middle English deceived many until exposed partly by Thomas Tyrwhitt, their first editor (1777)[3]; final blow dealt by Skeat's *Essay on the Rowley Poems* (1871). Despite an imposture often worked out immaturely, at their best the poems invent meters, reveal a joy in natural beauty, demonstrate a rare and intense imagination—all energized by a fertile invention often original, deeply capable of delicate feeling, and anachronistically beautiful.

Includes the *Battle of Hastings,* a dignified and inspired ballad sometimes over-realistic in description; *Balade of Charitie,* a finished

---

1 Dixon, W. M., "Chatterton" (Warton Lecture on English Poetry), *Proceedings of The British Academy,* XVI (1930), p. 196f. (pp. 183-202).

2 It is not the actual value of his poems that obtains for Chatterton such considerable space in the *Outline-History.* What makes him important is less the fact that no youth of Chatterton's age ever wrote such remarkable poetry than the fact that the Rowley poems were praised by the neoclassicists, were venerated by the Romantic poets, and were worshipped by the Pre-Raphaelites. Alfred de Vigny, a leader of the Romanticists in France, included a study of Chatterton among the unlucky youthful poets in his *Stello* (1832), and wrote a tragedy, *Chatterton* (1835), based remotely on the life of the Engish poet.

3 Powell, L. F., "Thomas Tyrwhitt and the Rowley Poems," *The Review of English Studies,* VII (1931), pp. 314-326.

and noble poem in archaic language; *Bristowe Tragedie: or the dethe of Syr Charles Bawdin,* distinguished by a jogtrot tune, pathos, and climax; *Aella: a Tragycal Enterlude,* sustained in its strong portrayal of character and in its dramatic treatment; *Goddwyn; A Tragedie,* notable for the martial lyricism of the "Ode to Liberty"; and *On Happienesse,* a calm poem, one of the few not showing his ruffled soul. The only Rowley poem published before Chatterton's death was *Elinoure and Juga,* a romantic eclogue-duologue written when he was about twelve years old, and describing the sorrows of two maidens whose sweethearts had been killed in the Wars of the Roses.

William Cowper, 1731—1800, poet. Son of John Cowper, an Anglican rector, and Ann Donne, who belonged to the same family as John Donne (Vol. 1, p. 254). Educated at Dr. Pitman's school at Market Street, Hertfordshire, where he was bullied (1738), and at Westminster School (1741—1748). In later years he wrote *Tirocinium* (1785), a vigorous poetical attack on public schools. Entered at Middle Temple (1748). Is articled to Mr. Chapman, solicitor (1749). Falls in love with his cousin, Theodora Cowper, daughter of his uncle, Ashley Cowper (1749). First attack of melancholy (1752). Called to the bar (1754). Relinquishes idea of marrying Theodora, the "Delia" of about a score of poems. A Commissioner of Bankrupts at sixty pounds a year (1759). In straitened circumstances (1760—1762). Has a nervous breakdown upon facing an examination for Clerk of the Journals of the House of Lords, an office for which he had been nominated (1763). His mental unbalance causes three attempts at suicide, and he is removed to Dr. Cotton's private asylum at St. Albans (1763—1765). Resigns his Commissionership (1765). Boards at Huntingdon with the Reverend and Mrs. Morley Unwin, the "Mary" of his poems (1765—1767). Upon Mr. Unwin's death (1767), Cowper moved with Mrs. Mary Unwin and her two children to Olney in Buckinghamshire, where he met John Newton, an evangelical preacher whose influence aggravated his depressive fits. Engagement to Mrs. Unwin is broken off by another attack of madness (1772). Again is treated by Dr. Cotton, and again attempts suicide (1773). Begins to keep hares as pets (1774). Publishes *Anti-Thelyphthora* anonymously (1781), as an answer (in a kind of Spenserian allegory in which the victims of the enchantress Hypothesis are ridiculed) to his cousin Martin Madan's *Thelyphthora* which advocated polygamy on Scriptural grounds. Meets Lady Austen, destined to inspire his greatest work; she also stirred up in Mrs. Unwin an extravagant jealousy. Beginning of friendship with the Throckmortons (1784). Moves with Mrs Unwin to Weston in Norfolk (1786). Fourth attack of madness (1787). Publishes *Homer* (1791), a blank-verse translation duller than Pope's but more faithful and more poetic. Mrs. Unwin stricken with paralysis several times from 1791 to her death in 1796. Fifth attack of melancholy (1794). Granted a pension of three hundred pounds year (1794). Dies at East Dereham, Norfolk. Throughout his life Cowper was subject to intermittent fits of melancholia and insanity. In his own words (*The Task,* Book III):

> "I was a stricken deer that left the herd."

Olney Hymns (1779). Most famous of his hymns, distinguished by sincerity rather than literary merit, are *Walking with God* ("Oh for a closer walk with God!"), *Praise for the Fountain Opened* ("There is a fountain filled with blood"), *Lovest Thou Me?* ("Hark, my soul! it is the Lord"), *On Opening a Place for Social Prayer* ("Jesus! where'er thy people meet"), *Light Shining Out of Darkness* ("God moves in a mysterious way"), and *Joy and Peace in Believing* ("Sometimes a light surprises"). Of the three hundred and forty-eight in the collection written jointly with Newton, Cowper wrote about sixty-eight, which are signed with the letter "C." "From this volume of hymns the Church has drawn a larger proportionate number than from almost any other volume."[1]

Poems (1782). Includes the spirited *Boadicea,* an ode, and *Verses supposed to be written by Alexander Selkirk* ("I am monarch of all I survey"). Volume mainly composed of eight mild Horatian satirical poems in uninspired heroic couplets somewhat more freely handled than by Pope. Not only the poetic form but also the abstract titles reveal the current taste of the period. Less satiric than moral and didactic, yet the sermonizing content shows already Cowper's political liberalism and social humanitarianism.

Expostulation exhorts Englishmen to avoid the downfall that has overtaken the Chosen People; *Hope* emphasizes that surcease of weariness lies in the religious vision of an after-life; and *Charity* contrasts what Man has made out of God's creation of Man. Possibly the best three didactic ones are *Table Talk,* in all appearance a dialogue on the need of character in public servants; *The Progress of Error,* that sees in the cult of pleasure only eventual ruin; and *Truth,* a sermon on "grace." *Conversation* is a lighter piece, showing some old-quality humor; and, finally, *Retirement,* his best piece, including a somewhat humorous character-sketch of the politician.

The Task and Other Poems (1785). Cowper's "Advertisement" gives the source: "A lady, fond of blank verse, demanded a poem of that kind from the author, and gave him the *Sofa* for a subject." Accepting the task imposed by Lady Austen, Cowper, in writing on that comparatively new piece of furniture, "having much leisure, connected another subject with it; . . . ." Spineless poem became six books of Miltonic blank verse on subjects related to Cowper himself, on the sights and sounds of nature, on simple country life, on domestic, social, and moral topics. Within the statement of *The Task's* conception is discernible the reason for discursive and interspersed didactic passages;

---

1 Marks, H. B., *The Rise and Growth of English Hymnody* (1937), p. 112 (pp. 109-114).

yet, deficient in an artistic unity, is made cohesive by the revelatory nature of Cowper himself. Soon departs from its mock-epic beginning to close observation of rural scenes, including famous descriptions of hay-carting, the postman, the waggoner breasting the storm, and the snowfall. Its six subdivisions, with a few of the famous lines, are: I. *The Sofa.* "God made the country, and man made the town." II. *The Time-piece.* "Oh for a lodge in some vast wilderness"; "England, with all thy faults, I love thee still." III. *The Garden.* "Great contest follows, and much learned dust." IV. *The Winter Evening.* "The cups that cheer but not inebriate." V. *The Winter Morning Walk.* "He is the freeman whom the truth makes free." VI. *The Winter Walk at Noon.* Refuses to consider as friend the man "Who needlessly sets foot upon a worm."

The Diverting History of John Gilpin (written 1782; published anonymously 1783; in same volume with *The Task,* 1785). Ballad, based on Lady Austen's account of an adventure of a Mr. Beyer of Paternoster Row (died 1791), relates how John Gilpin and his wife celebrated their china wedding-day. Generally considered rollicking.

Letters. Of equal interest with, if not greater interest than, his poems. His small world is described smilingly, playfully, lovably, chitchatingly, sensibly, and imaginatively. Charm and whimsicality of a pure, lucid English wedded harmoniously to his moods—now playful with Lady Hesketh, now grave with the curate John Newton, or droll or ironical. Unlike Walpole's letters (p. 404), Cowper's are almost barren of current events. Southey (p. 462) has called Cowper the best of English letter-writers.

Other Poems

On the Receipt of My Mother's Picture out of Norfolk, a tender tribute in conventional heroic couplets; *Epitaph on a Hare,* with its peculiar pathos; *On the Loss of the Royal George,* that tolls for the eight hundred (of the eleven hundred souls aboard) who lost their lives when Admiral Richard Kempenfelt's flagship capsized at Spithead on August 29, 1782—a poem of sonorous opening, quiet gravity, noble simplicity and restraint. Of importance is *To Mary,* a poem of almost intolerable sadness, and *To Mrs. Unwin,* a sonnet eulogizing faithful Mary's "chronicle of actions just and bright!" *The Poplar Field* is frequently listed among his best poems, and *Yardley Oak* (1791), a fragment, is considered his greatest imaginative achievement. In lighter vein is *The Colubriad,* a mock-heroic, and *On the Death of Mrs. Throckmorton's Bullfinch,* a mock-elegy, an admirable trifle. Finally, *The Castaway* (1799), inspired by an incident in Lord Anson's *Voyage Round the World* (1748), and Cowper's last poem, is religiously self-revealing. Believing his soul to be damned eternally, Cowper likens his spiritual doom to that of a sailor swept overboard in a storm, and concludes:

> "But I beneath a rougher sea,
> And whelmed in deeper gulfs than he."

SUGGESTED MERITS	SUGGESTED DEFECTS
1. Generous, almost Wordsworthian, appreciation of Nature. Links the school of Pope to that of Wordsworth.	1. More of an essayist than a poet expressing great ideas in a notable manner. As a poet of the landscape, may be inferior to Crabbe.
2. Quiet humanitarianism, opposing the oppression of animals as well as of men.	2. On the whole is largely pseudo-classical in his manner of thought. Moralizing, and morbidly theological.
3. Diction partly resistant to eighteenth-century mannerisms. Popean couplet somewhat more simple.	3. Uses the verbal furniture of the age. Lapses into "poetic diction." Retains the Augustan couplet.
4. Subjective note and self-revealing intimacy in language unadorned. Emotional hymns. Heroic couplet is married to power of natural emotion.	4. Lack of eloquence, deficiency of deep feeling, and absence of passion. On the whole, reminiscent of the older age rather than indicative of the new.
5. Direct, realistic observation—delight in rustic life, detestation of large towns.	5. Lack of sustained imagination. Bulk of work prosy, often trivial. Provincial approach to life.
6. Best in shorter pieces—excellent singing, careful lyricism.	6. Poorer in the artistry of and less elegiac in the longer poems.

George Crabbe, 1754—1832, humanitarian-realistic poet.[1] Son of a collector of salt-dues whose avocation was mathematics. George Crabbe was largely self-schooled. Apprenticed to a village doctor, near Bury St. Edmund (1768). Assistant to a surgeon in Woodbridge (*c.* 1771). Unsuccessful physician (1774—1780). Went to London (1780). Seconded by Burke (1781), at whose suggestion he took orders. Curate of his native Aldeburgh, Suffolk (*c.* 1782), and successively of other places. Chaplain to the Duke of Rutland at Belvoir, Leicestershire (1782—1785). Married Sarah Elmy, the "Mira" or "Myra" of his poems, for whom he had waited for more than ten years (1784). Rector of Muston and Allington (1787). Probably started to take opium (*c.* 1790). Sarah inherited a small fortune (1792). Vicar of Trowbridge (1814—1832).

Poetic Works: *Inebriety* (1775), an immature satiric poem; *The Candidate* (1780), a literary "epistle"; and *The Library* (1781), matter-of-fact reflections on books—all three Popean in manner. *The Newspaper* (1785); *The Parish Register* (1807), a work in three parts (which includes the famous tale of Phoebe Dawson), each telling of the memories conjured up within the mind of the country parson as he thumbs the entries in the register of (1) Baptism, (2) Marriages, and (3) Deaths; *Belvoir Castle* (1812); *Tales in Verse* (1812), a collection of twenty-one stories, including "The Patron," a narrative of what a poet of sensibility suffers in the home of his host, and "The Frank Courtship," in which the spiritually minded Josiah courts the earthly-minded Sybil; *Tales of The Hall* (1819), declared at least by one critic

---

1 Whitby, Charles, "A Student of Humanity," *The Poetry Review*, XII (1921), pp. 251-259; Scott, Temple, "George Crabbe and The Collector," *The American Book Collector*, 1 (1932), pp. 332-336; Evans, J. H., *The Poems of George Crabbe* (1933); Henderson, P., ed., *George Crabbe: Poems* (1946).

to be his best work, includes the story of the husband who realizes too late how witless is the girl he has married, and the narrative of Ruth who, although seduced, drowns herself rather than prostitute herself in a loveless marriage,[1] and, finally, his *Posthumous Tales* (1934).

The Village† (1783). Realistic poem in two books of rusty heroic couplets. Memorable for some sordid pictures of naked squalor of eighteenth-century rustic life. (Compare with Goldsmith's *Deserted Village*, p. 375.) Crabbe promises to paint Life

"As Truth will paint it, and as Bards will not."

Sir Eustace Grey† (1804). Opium-stimulated dramatic lyric in fifty-five eight-lined (octosyllabic) stanzas. A dement in a madhouse tells how he is haunted since the murder of his wife's paramour. (In same volume with *The Parish Register*.)

The Borough† (1810). "Spoon-River Anthology" of twenty-four poetized letters describes the life in his native town of Aldeburgh in Suffolk—its church and prisons, its doctors and hospital, its lawyers and almshouse. Among the illustrative case-histories are those of Blaney, Squire Asgill, and of three in particular: of Clelia, the coquette who winds up in the poorhouse; of the iniquitous Peter Grimes, whose conscience plunges him into raving horrors of insanity[2]; and of Ellen Orford, the "trouble-woman," who despite the many tragedies of her life finds comfort in God.

SUGGESTED MERITS	SUGGESTED DEFECTS
1. Acute intuition and unromantic characterization of human nature. Uncompromising portrayal of every-day life of the common people—a paragon who falls from virtue, a schoolmaster whose principles are subverted, a parson who is worldly, a woman who wantons. Unflinching realism, minute in its truthfulness to life. Influenced Thomas Hardy.	1. Lack of imaginative sympathy. Wearisome emphasis upon seamy naturalism, unqualified and unrelieved. Reveals a tendency to describe village types, to lean upon melodrama, and to break out into parsonical reflections. Possibly it is true that the work is bleached and corroded by the author's sense of the miseries of the world.
2. Generally sincere and direct. In feeling, Crabbe is in advance of his age.	2. Not infrequently prosaic, dull, even bathetic.
3. Quiet and delicate humor.	3. Grim and sardonic humor.
4. Natural and charming story teller.	4. Plots undistinguished. Just reach adequacy.
5. Dramatic power of dialogue.	5. General fidelity to the complacent Augustan couplet.[3]
6. Objectifying, analytical interpretation of natural aspects of earth and sky that repel most poets.	6. Absence of sensitive beauty or poetic sympathy.

---

1 "The Poems of Crabbe," an anonymous review in *The Quarterly Review*, CXCIII (1901), p. 37 f. (pp. 21-43).

2 It is rapidly becoming a serio-comic poem, according to the statement in *George Crabbe* (The Augustan Books of Poetry, 1932).

3 Horace and James Smith's statement in *Rejected Addresses* that Crabbe is "a Pope in worsted stockings" is frequently quoted as a pat criticism. The opinion is hazarded that it is less a critical statement than a witticism. Much closer to the truth is Byron in his *English Bards and Scotch Reviewers*: "Though nature's sternest painter, yet the best."

† * Explanation of symbols immediately precedes Chapter XV.

Robert Burns, 1759—1796, greatest of Scottish poets, and perhaps the best song writer of the world.[1] Born in the parish of Alloway in Ayrshire. William Burness or Burnes, his father, was a small farmer, hard-working and God-fearing. Robert, the oldest of seven children, was brought up in poverty. Frequently entertained by Betty Davidson, a widowed relative, whose tales of devils, ghosts, fairies, "and other trumpery," brought him into close contact with Scottish folk-lore. Education fragmentary and informal; but Burns did read the King James Bible (Vol. 1, p. 149), Mrs. Rowe's *Moral Letters,* Masson's *Collection of Prose and Verse,* the popular Scotch poets Wallace, Lyndsay, Fergusson, and Ramsay, and many English writers. Unsuccessful in the business of flax-dressing at Irvine (1781), where he met Richard Brown, where he joined the St. David Masonic Lodge of Tarbolton,[2] and where he probably became addicted to excessive conviviality.[3] After his father's death in 1784, Burns, with his brother Gilbert, settled in the Spring on a farm at Mossgiel, in Mauchline parish (1784—1788), where within a year Robert's liaison with Jean Armour had borne fruit, making discovery inevitable.[4] To defray expenses of a contemplated emigration to Jamaica, he published a volume of forty-four poems at Kilmarnock (1786; Kilmarnock Edition), which brought him so much attention that he relinquished the idea of emigrating.[5] Accepted invitation to Edinburgh's circle of Scotch writers, where for two winters he was the literary and social lion. Published second (first Edinburgh) edition of his poems (1787), which attracted more attention than the Kilmarnock edition, although it did not reveal any additional evidence of Burns's poetic development; most of the best pieces in this edition had been written earlier than 1786 but had not been included in the volume of that year. Took a farm at Ellisland (1788), in which year

---

1 Snyder, F. B., *The Life of Robert Burns* (1932); Hecht, Hans, *Robert Burns* (1936); Ferguson, John De Lancey, *Pride and Passion* (1939).

2 Wright, Dudley, *Robert Burns and His Masonic Circle* (1929).

3 It is quite likely that the tradition of the "low company" with whom Burns is said to have associated meant merely people whose opinions were objectionable, possibly pro-America, pro-French, and pro-revolutionary. Moreover, Burns had a Jekyll-and-Hyde character: see Fitzhugh, R. T., 'The Paradox of Burns' Character," *Studies in Philology,* XXXII (1935), pp. 110-119.

4 The fact remains that Burns did have many loves. These included Nelly Kilpatrick, who may have occasioned the song called *Handsome Nell;* Peggie Thompson, who does not seem to have evoked any definitely tagged poetry from Burns; and Alison Begbie, who received some decorous letters. May Cameron, Jennie Clow, and Anne Park each bore him a child. To his and Elizabeth Paton's "Dear-bought Bess" he long afterward wrote the wistful *A Poet's Welcome to his Love-begotten Daughter.* Finally, *My Highland Lassie, Will Ye Go to the Indies, My Mary,* and *To Mary in Heaven* probably were all inspired by his love for Mary Campbell, an ideal maiden, even if recent evidence indicates that she also may have given birth to his child. For his love-life, consult Carswell, Catherine, (1) *The Life of Robert Burns* (1930), and (2) *Robert Burns* (1933). As a corrective to her somewhat over-exaggerated point of view, read Watt, L. MacL., "Burns Biography," *Burns Chronicle and Club Directory,* Second Series: VII (1932), p. 38, p. 40 f. (pp. 35-54). Consult, also Fitzhugh, R. T., "Burns' Highland Mary," *Publications of the Modern Language Association of America,* LII (1937), pp. 829-834.

5 The first published review of the Kilmarnock Edition was by James Sibbald. Five weeks later Henry Mackenzie welcomed Burns in *The Lounger.* It was these two reviews, asserts F. B. Snyder, that originated the "Heaven-taught ploughman" and "unlettered plowboy" tradition. See, also, page 401, footnote 2.

he belatedly married Jean Armour, who in 1786 and again in 1788 had given birth to twins. Exciseman (1789). Settled in Dumfries as exciseman (1791). Died at the age of thirty-seven,[1] probably from a rheumatic endocarditis,[2] or from angina pectoris.

A third edition of his poems was published in 1793 under the title of *Poems, Chiefly in the Scottish Dialect*. The first great poet of the common people also contributed more than two hundred songs (adaptations and original creations) to James Johnson's *Scots Musical Museum* (Six volumes, 1787—1803),[3] which is still the standard collection of Scottish songs and music; and Burns also contributed about sixty songs to James Thomson's *Select Scottish Airs* (Five volumes, 1793 —1818).

Throughout his short life Burns mocked at local politicians, satirized rigid religionists, lampooned the national government, espoused the cause of the Stuarts during an Hanoverian administration, and openly sympathized with the American Cause and the French Revolution. His simple philosophy of humanism stood for a passionate love of liberty, a hatred of injustice, a feeling of tender kinship with not only human life but that of the beasts and flowers, a scorn for the bigotry and cant of churches and creeds.[4] As the national poet of Scotland, he translated the spirit of a nation into his poetry; as a world poet, he voiced the brotherhood of man. To Emerson, "the Declaration of Independence and the Marseillaise are not more mighty documents of freedom than the songs of Burns"; To William Stewart, "He was born in poverty, and he died in poverty. But he enriched the world." In the words of John Drinkwater: "I ask you, gentlemen, to fill your glasses and rise to drink in silence to his immortal memory."

Epistles

His verse-letters shed light on his attitude and philosophy. These include two epistles to Davie (David Sillar, friend, neighbor, and fellow-poet, whose *Poems, Chiefly in the Scottish Dialect*, 1789, attempted to imitate not only Burns's poems but the very printing-type of Burns's first edition); *A Dedication to Gavin Hamilton*, a somewhat conventional eulogy of Burns's landlord, patron, and friend; *Epistle to John*

---

1 Catherine Carswell's last sentence (in *Robert Burns*, 1933) is: "At the same time as his body was lowered into the grave Jean gave birth to yet another boy." Consult Foster, Sir William, "The Children of Robert Burns," *Chamber's Journal*, III (1934), pp. 21-25.

2 Anderson, H. B., "Robert Burns, His Medical Friends, Attendants and Biographer, *Annals of Medical History*, x (1928), pp. 47-58; Snyder, F. B., (1) "Burns and His Biographers," *Studies in Philology*, xxv (1928), pp. 401-415; (2) "Burns's Last Years," *Studies in Philology*, xxvi (1929), pp. 457-469.

3 Dick, J. C., *The Songs of Robert Burns* (1903); Palmgren, Carl, "On the Music of Robert Burns' Songs," *Minnesskrift Af Forna Lärjungar Tillägnad* (1913), pp. 224-230.

4 This is not to call him the Enemy of the Aristocracy, or the Vanquisher of Calvinism. See Jamieson, A. B., *Burns & Religion* (1931).

Kennedy; Epistle to John Goldie, a Kilmarnock friend; and the *Epistle to the Rev. John M'Math,* Assistant Minister at Tarbolton. More important are the epistles to James Smith, J. Lapraik, and William Simpson, which reveal his methods of composition and his joy in verse writing, his thoughts and his class-consciousness. His *Epistle to John Rankin* is possibly the one most familiar by name to general readers, for it has a clever and ruffianly vivacity. In the *Epistle to a Young Friend,* Burns points out, among other things, that after the first offense against society, the feelings are petrified, and other offenses come easier, and that one can still take a neighbor's part, "Yet hae nae cash to spare him." His greatest epistle is his *Address to the Deil* (see under SATIRES).

Lyrics and Love-Songs[1]

(1) *Green Grow the Rashes, O,* which first gave definite body to his lyric genius; (2) *Poor Mailie's Elegy,* a good blend of sympathy and humor; (3) *Duncan Gray,* a great song noted for whimsicality; (4) *Tam Glen,* bantering and pensive; (5) *John Anderson, my Jo,* once an unprintable song, but now beautiful in its pathos; and (6) *I Hae a Wife o' My Ain,* impudently ribald. Personal love-songs include (7) *Mary Morison,* possibly inspired by Alison Begbie, who spurned his offer of marriage; it ends as conventionally as it begins, but is redeemed by its second stanza; (8) *Highland Mary,* a tender if rhetorical piece connected with Mary Campbell, a sweetheart who died suddenly, and to whom Burns addressed the noble ballad called (9) *To Mary in Heaven;* (10) *Of a' the Airts the Wind Can Blaw,* written during the early months of his marriage with Jean Armour; (11) *Ae Fond Kiss,* written in honor of Mrs. James M'Lehose, whom Burns would have married if she had been free, is a love-song in which there is a turgid blend of English and Scottish[2]; and (12) *O Wert Thou in the Cauld Blast,* his last lyric of distinction, created out of a shred of an old tune, and written, as was "Altho' thou maun never be mine," in honor of Jessy Lewars, his nurse and companion during his last illness at Dumfries.

Satires[3]

(1) *The Kirk's Alarm,* in which several parts are brilliantly executed; (2) *Address of Beelzebub,* a vigorous, bitter piece of social-

---

1 It has been pointed out that most of his best songs were written between his twenty-third and twenty-sixth years. The period of his chastity (ending after his twenty-second year) appears to have been unproductive of permanent poetry. All this may have a meaning, says Andrew Dakers. Possibly the birth of his power of song and his love of women were simultaneous. Possibly "the zenith of his poetic genius was contemporaneous with the nadir of his moral life." Dakers, Andrew, *Robert Burns, His Life and Genius* (1923), p. 7.

2 The love-letters that passed between Robert Burns and Agnes M'Lehose were signed Sylvander and Clarinda. See *Sylvander and Clarinda,* edited by Burr, A. J. (1917); *Letters to Clarinda,* with introduction by Bankart, M. Y. (1928).

3 The satires by Burns are reminiscent of Dunbar and the old Scots "makars." *Tam o'Shanter* particularly has a gusto and unabashed frankness. For Dunbar, see p. 89.

political satire lashing out in stinging couplets; (3) *The Twa Herds,* a satire of the dispute over parish boundaries between Russell of Kilmarnock and Moodie of Riccarton; (4) *The Ordination,* an ironical satire on the choice of a deep-dyed conservative for a parish; (5) *Death and Dr. Hornbook,* a vigorous, personal, somewhat uncongenial satire that unaccountably did not seem to offend its hero, John Wilson; (6) *Address to the Unco Guid,* the germ of which appears in a prose paragraph following his *Penitential Thought,* is an eloquent and pleading apologetic for human frailty; and (7) *Address to the Deil,* in which Satan is treated with a jesting good-fellowship and humanizing intimacy in a rapid, compressed, witty stanza frequently used by Fergusson.

The Holy Fair.† Masterpiece of personal and social satire, genial and fast-paced. Faithful characterization, natural diction, keen observation. Influenced by Fergusson's *Leith Races,* and by *A Letter from a Blacksmith to the Ministers and Elders of the Church of Scotland.* As in *The Ordination,* so here Burns uses the Christis Kirk stave (an octave meter with an added bob-wheel).

Holy Willie's Prayer.† Caustic, trenchant, ironical satire levelled with Swiftian *saeva indignatio* against the religious hypocrites whom Calvinism had narrowed down to a self-righteous belief in hell. Skilful versification and flawless rhythm, brilliant phrase and deadly humor, probably occasioned and inspired by source of pasquinade—the pilloried Pharisee-like elder, William Fisher, and the ecclesiastical-dissenter Gavin Hamilton, who appealed to the Presbytery of Ayr against the Mauchline Kirk Session. Like the *Address to the Deil* and *The Auld Former's Salutation to his Mare,* uses the six-line stanza in *rime couée.*

Humanitarian and Nature Poems

(1) *To a Louse,* a short clever masterpiece with its famous moral concerning social inequalities; (2) *Willie Brew'd a Peck o'Maut,* a carefree outburst that conjures up a picture of "Sweet-Adeline" topers; (3) *To a Mouse,* despite its flaw of riming "dominion" with "union," and its typical Augustan attempt to moralize, is a perfect blend of observation and imagination, and a rich example of sentiment without sentimentality; (4) *The Auld Farmer's Salutation to his Mare,* flavored by Scottish dialect but universal in the emotional chord struck and maintained—the sympathy existing between man and beast; (5) *It Was A' for our Richtfu,* which commemorates a lost cause; and (6) *Does Haughty Gaul Invasion Threat,* a spirited song rallying to the defense of King and Country, and one that became the song of the Royal Dumfries Volunteers, which Burns had helped organize and for which he wrote the poem; (7) *The Twa Dogs,* which, with *Man Was Made to Mourn,* has been said to express Burns's whole social philosophy; it

---

† * Explanation of symbols immediately precedes Chapter XV.

has humor, excellent characterization of men, and insight into dog psychology. (8) *Auld Lang Syne* is an old drinking-song to which Burns added two stanzas, inspired the whole piece with a new wistfulness, and metamorphosed the words avowedly transfigured "from an old man's singing" into an immortal fellowship lyric. The original version is ascribed to Sir Robert Aytoun.

The Cotter's Saturday Night.† While possibly his most popular poem, yet certainly not among his masterpieces in unity and simplicity. Neo-classical diction and simple speech; academic English and Scotch dialect are incongruously combined. Yet has virtues. While the primary appeal is local, its central theme—the simple dignity and felicity of an honest worker's home life—is enduring in its picture of earthy peasantry and Christian manhood, and idealistic in its domestic setting. Presents a faithful portrait of William Burness, his father. Spenserian stanza imitated from Shenstone's *The Schoolmistress;* idea derived from Fergusson's *The Farmer's Ingle.*

Tam o' Shanter.† Main appeal of this excellent ghost story, Burns's only attempt at a tale in verse, is local. Prototype of Tam is Douglas Graham. Avowed by Burns to be his best poem, it is as perfect and sustained in humor and humanity as the flight of Tam. Is a more studied performance than *The Jolly Beggars.* Carlyle described *Tam o'Shanter* as "a piece of sparkling rhetoric." The great attraction is the abounding humor and the *morale.*

A Man's a Man for A' That.† Its rhetorical and somewhat bombastic machinery runs with a lyrical smoothness flawlessly metered, humming forth with almost monosyllabic simplicity an eternal song of the dignity of the individual, one proclaiming a democratic and triumphant revolutionism. This may well be the touchstone of the social and political philosophy of Burns: it has been called the World's Anthem and the World's Most Democratic Poem; it is the Revolutionary cry for "Liberty, Equality, Fraternity."

Scots Wha Hae.† War-song, often described as Scotland's anthem, sings of the Battle of Bannockburn, at which Robert Bruce defeated the English under Edward II on June 24, 1314. Apparently denounces the English tyrant of 1314; in reality, denounces the reactionary spirit of the English government and of all Europe for their attitude toward the French Revolution of 1789.

The Jolly Beggars.† Amoral serio-comic cantata is probably his most satirical, most dramatic, and most imaginative work. Directness of speech, humor of description, Teniers'-like fidelity of characterization, swift precision of narrative, richness of metrical form, earthy state of mankind. This ditty on robust vagrants is the equal of anything in Gay's *Beggar's Opera,* by which it was not impossibly inspired. Note

---

† • Explanation of symbols immediately precedes Chapter XV.

the revolutionary challenge of the concluding lyric, the only place in the cantata in which Burns seems to stay in character. Consists of 16 parts, 8 of which are songs and 8 "recitativos." Except for the first and last of the "recitativos," which are in an intricate bob-wheel stanza, the poem (that is to say, the other 14 stanzas) is cast in 14 different moulds.

Prose

Letters.[1] Usually described as affected and stilted, in accord with the pompous diction of his time. That criticism, however, seems to be true mainly of Sylvander's (Burns's) pseudo-Arcadian letters to Clarinda (Mrs. M'Lehose). But for the most part Burns writes crisply and forcefully, and is now recognized not as an untaught peasant but as a deliberate artist, even if his letter-writing owed much to the early eighteenth-century English tradition. As Byron said of them, however, Burns's letters reveal a mind at war with itself: "dirt and dirty—a compound of inspired clay."

SUGGESTED MERITS

1. Supreme in lyricism. Gift of music—direct and lilting, sweet and intense, spontaneous and warm.

2. Supreme and original in the Scotch dialect poems.[2] One of the most original of the eighteenth-century poets of Great Britain.

3. Primarily emotional. Possibly unexcelled in the depth and range of his sympathetic humanity. "Democratic" love of nature.

4. Great power of satire. Reminiscent of Dunbar.

5. Prodigal ease of his verse. Masculine adequacy of expression. Sunny, lively humor.

SUGGESTED DEFECTS

1. General absence of dramatic and narrative writing and of ecstatic vision. Sentiment, even diction, not remarkable. Much of his poetry is local.

2. With few exceptions, prosy and uninspired in the literary English poems. Sometimes imitative —of Allan Ramsay and Robert Fergusson, for example.

3. Seldom intellectual. When he is, his thought is usually shallow or derivative. Emotion often sentimental and weak.

4. Satire is neo-classical in tradition.

5. Often dependent for effects upon use of dialect. Lapses into neoclassical didacticism. Suppressed poems are Fescennine—e.g., The Patriarch, The Court of Equity, The Fornicator.[3]

---

1 Burns wrote his autobiography by writing many letters; for example, no better account of Burns's life until 1787 is available than his own letter to Dr. John Moore, August 4, 1787. Consult the definitive edition by Ferguson, J. De L., *The Letters of Robert Burns* (Two volumes, 1931). See, also, Fraser-Harris, D. F., "Burns as a Writer of Prose," *The Dalhousie Review,* XIV (1934-1935), pp. 203-213. Another prose account that merits consideration in any study of Burns's life and interests is his so-called *First Commonplace Book.*

2 Heller, Otto, "Robert Burns: A Revaluation," *Washington University Studies,* II (1923-1924), pp. 171-199; Peddie, J. R., "Burns as a Craftsman of Letters," *Burns Chronicle and Club Directory,* V, Second Series (1930), pp. 80-86.

3 Many of his "Cloacinaids" are available in *The Merry Muses of Caledonia.* Consult Hecht, Hans, "Die '*Merry Muses of Caledonia*' and Burns' '*Court of Equity,*'" *Archiv für das Studium Der Neueren Sprachen Und Literaturen,* CXXIX (1912), pp. 363-374; and CXXX (1912), pp. 57-72. See also, Ferguson, J. De L., "The Suppressed Poems of Burns," *Modern Philology,* XXX (1932-1933), pp. 53-60.

William Blake, 1757—1827, mystic, poet, artist, philosophical anarchist.[1] Son of a London hosier. Studied at Pars's Drawing School (1767). Apprenticed to the engraver James Basire (1771). Studied under Moser (1778). Married Catherine Sophia Boucher or Bouchier (1782), who, though illiterate, has been described as almost the perfect (if barren) wife.[2] Removed to Lambeth (1792). At Feipham with Hayley (1800—*c*. 1804). Returned to London (*c*. 1804). Moved to Fountain Court (1821). No discussion of his poetry can be complete without an understanding of his achievement as a painter. Blake, moreover, developed a new method of printing from etched copper-plates. Among the works that he illustrated and sometimes engraved, besides his own, were Young's so-called *Night-Thoughts* (1796—1797), Gray's *Poems* (1800), Blair's *The Grave* (1804—1805), Chaucer's *Canterbury Pilgrims* (1809), the *Book of Job* (*c*. 1825), and Dante's *Divine Comedy* (1826—1827).

Poetical Sketches (1783). Verse, written between his twelfth and twentieth years, imitative of the Elizabethan lyrics; rhythmical, formless prose imitative of the Ossianic poems. Marked, however, by a departure from the poetic modes of the day, and by a distinct personality, more original than any in his age. Examples: (1) *My Silks and Fine Array,* a maiden's lament in artless Elizabethan cadences for a vanished love; (2) *Love and Harmony,* only at first reminiscent of Shakespeare's *Phoenix and the Turtle,* and marked by a sheer verbal beauty; (3) *Mad Song,* the unconventional phrasing and diction of which, despite an imitative manner, mark a new departure in prosody, and touched by a visionary mood subsequently of marked prominence in his writings; and (4) *To the Muses,* perhaps the last great neo-classical poem. Its beauty is as effortless as that in *To the Evening Star.*

An Island in the Moon (*c*. 1787). Unproportioned, somewhat coarse extravaganza satirizing Society, Science, and the Universe. Medley of lyrics. Farcical invention of hysterical names—"Inflammable Gass the Wind-Finder," "Sipsop the Pythagorean." Memorable for three songs (later included almost intact in *Songs of Innocence*) flowering in the mouths of Mrs. Nannicantipot's mother, Quid the Cynic, and Obtuse Angle the Mathematician: "The Nurse's Song," "Holy Thursday," "The Little Boy Lost." Some songs scatalogical.

---

1 Symons, Arthur, *William Blake* (1907) Berger, P., *William Blake, Poet and Mystic* (1915); Damon, S. F., *William Blake: His Philosophy and Symbols* (1924); *The Writings of William Blake,* edited by Keynes, Geoffrey (Three volumes, 1925); *The Prophetic Writings of William Blake,* edited by Slosc, D. J., and Wallis, J. P. R. (1926); Plowman, Max, *An Introduction to the Study of Blake* (1927); Wilson, Mona, *The Life of William Blake* (limited edition, 1927; general edition, 1932); Wicksteed, J. H., *Blake's Innocence and Experience* (1928); Wright, Thomas, *The Life of William Blake* (Two volumes, 1929); Keynes, Geoffrey, ed., *The Letters of William Blake* (1956).

2 Jenkins, Herbert, *William Blake* (1926), Chap. II, "The Most Perfect Wife on Record," pp. 33-50; Wright, Thomas, *Life of William Blake* (1929), Vol. 1, p. 58 *f.*; Wilson, Mona, *The Life of William Blake* (1927), p. 303; (1932), p. 297.

Songs of Innocence† (1789). Much of the poetry, if not the thought, is made timeless by reason of its apparent *naïveté* yet actual subtlety of phrase, often strained into an over-romantic mold. Not a few poems protest against social tyranny. Note that frequently a song has its complement in *Songs of Experience*. Examples: (1) *Piping Down the Valleys Wild*, a lyrical introduction full of joyous harmony; is, in its brief scope, an essay on poetry: first comes the Muse's intention and command, next the revelation and the accompanying melody, and finally the visible recording.[1] (2) *The Lamb*, the antitype of which is *The Tyger*, is a lyrical gem finished in its artistry of phrasing; its note, while solemn, is happy. (3) *Infant Joy*, telling of the feeling of a mother for a new-born babe (the contrary experience is found in *Infant Sorrow*); surface simplicity and pure-hearted bliss enfold a profundity of art in a lyricism as perfect as its technique is daring. It is without the bitter terror of *Infant Sorrow* in the *Songs of Experience*. (4) *The Little Black Boy*, inspired by anti-slavery agitation and by Isaac Watts's *Grace Shining and Nature Fainting*, is a moralistic poem that might be interpreted (in the face of the last stanza) as indicating the equality of the negro and the white. (5) *A Cradle Song*, one of his simplest, tells of a mother's crooning and watching over the Eternal Child; possibly inspired by Watts's *Hush! my dear, lie still and slumber*. (6) *The Chimney Sweeper*, a homespun voice supporting the contemplated legislation against the use of children in that vocation; (7) *Holy Thursday*, where for once, according to Damon, Blake speaks in his own person; (8) *The Divine Image*, composed in the Church of the New Jerusalem in London, and valued by Coleridge; and (9) *A Dream*, so full of woe that it might be transferred to the *Experience* volume. Is possibly a part answer to *Night*.

Songs of Experience† (1794). Mood shows, according to title-page, a state of the human soul contrary to that in *Songs of Innocence;* this is his authentic voice, which, compared to its predecessor, distills vitriol. Simplicity evokes connotative feelings which breathe mystery into the elaborate yet compressed phrases. Examples: (1) *The Fly*, where Blake, with a lyrical gift suggestive of W. H. Davies, sees humanity in a fly—a Swedenborgian doctrine—and every living thing a work of God. (2) *The Tyger*, where a perfect beauty of form and an unearthly quality of anvil-music enclose the difficult and profound symbolism of the theme, the reconciliation of the Lamb and the Tiger (of the Forgiveness and Punishment of Evil). (3) *The Clod and the Pebble*, a dramatic description of the two contrary states of love; the

---

1 Thomas Wright puts the utmost emphasis on Blake's theory of Inspiration: "Holding that Intercourse produces Inspiration, the greatest boon that can come to any mortal, Blake insisted that even the man who is feebly endowed intellectually becomes in the moments expanded by Intercourse greater than himself, while the mind of the artist and poet reaches in such moments the highest state of inspiration possible to humanity." Wright, Thomas, *The Life of William Blake* (Two volumes, 1929), I, p. 62. See also p. 56 *f.*

† * Explanation of symbols immediately precedes Chapter XV.

Clod forgets itself in ministering to others, while the Pebble devours all to increase its own delight. (4) *Holy Thursday*, which ironically denies that England is a rich and fruitful land; if that were so, would children be starving? Its counterpart in the earlier volume sings of optimism; here it is a hymn of pessimism—of reproach and despair, of indignation at a Society that soullessly underfeeds or starves children. (5) *A Poison Tree*, which teaches the error of repression, the error of cloaking wrath with an apparent friendliness that secretes a passive venom. (6) *Ah! Sun-Flower*, with its unforgettable music, symbolically picturing Aspiring Man: fettered to the Flesh, as the sunflower is to the Earth, man's face like the flower's is turned up to the Sun. (7) *The Garden of Love*, where the priests and their shalt-nots have turned Paradise into a graveyard filled with prohibitive briars stifling the joys of divine impulse. (8) *The Little Boy Lost*, where the priest sacrifices the boy to prevent the spread of the heresy that the Mind or Reason must first comprehend or judge Divinity; (9) *London*, an indictment of a Society that tolerates such abnormalities as chimney-sweeps and harlots, and of the corrupting influence of Reason and its power upon Life; and (10) *The Chimney Sweeper*, filled with a bitterness lacking in the companion piece in *Songs of Innocence*, and openly attacking the complacent attitude of father and mother, of "God and His priest and king."

The Everlasting Gospel† (*c.* 1818) Probably his greatest poem. Fragmentary, yet has been called his "Confession of Faith." In compact couplets repudiates the meek official Christianity in favor of his "eternal Christ" who overthrows all laws and who can not humble himself. Its leading revolutionary antinomian paradoxes are in *The Marriage of Heaven and Hell*.

Auguries of Innocence (1801—1803; 1863). Gnomic couplets. Stresses the unity and continuity of being. Most famous is its opening quatrain; as Damon says, a perfect description of the first act of Contemplation. The first line: "To see a World in a grain of sand."

The Prophetic Books and Other Works

These include *The Gates of Paradise* (1793); the four books called *America* (1793); *Europe* (1794); *The Song of Los*, divided into two parts, *Africa* and *Asia* (1793—1795); and *The Book of Ahania* (1789). *The French Revolution* (1791) is a diffuse, repetitious, visionary, and pseudo-historical treatment of a revolutionary attitude towards authority, a theme also treated in *Visions of the Daughters of Albion* (1793), in its teaching that every natural act is holy, an attack on conventional morality, and in *America* (1793), a phantasmal treatment throwing emphasis on complete liberty so that man can embody his impulses in act

---

† • Explanation of symbols immediately precedes Chapter XV.

The Book of Thel (1789). Simplest of his longer poems, in fairly limpid measures, is a pantheistic presentation of youth and virginity. Song of the Ante-World, elegiac in the beauty of its sixscore-and-five unrimed, fourteen-syllabled lines. Memorable is Thel's four-line motto beginning, "Does the Eagle know what is in the pit."

Tiriel (*c.* 1789; published 1874). Theme of a tyrant and his defiant children presents age and disillusionment—the bitterest expression of his mind, according to Hambell. Unlike its companion-piece, *Thel*, is dim in its symbolism and prosaic and incomplete in its poetry.

The Marriage of Heaven and Hell† (*c.* 1790—*c.* 1793). Most important prose work acquires its great popularity through its fresh and independent outlook, and its comparative freedom from symbolism. Save for a poem as prologue and a song as epilogue, it is a series of prose passages energized by torrential cogency of thought, poetic fire, and imaginative experience; but does not achieve final unity. His gospel of revolution is in disagreement with Swedenborg: the wedding of Body and Soul exemplifies the conditioning of Good and Evil, the identification of God and Man. Satiric attack on the dichotomous features of religion, revolutionary in its refutation of authority and eternal punishment. Is occupied with the dilemma of sex.

The Book of Urizen (1794). Cosmogenic myth, one of the most difficult of the minor prophecies. Urizen is reminiscent of the creation of man in Plato's *Timaeus.* Poetic, but confused in its symbolism. According to Mona Wilson, it is Blake's version of the Jehovah of the Bible.

The Four Zoas (*c.* 1797). The triumph of Orc (Anarchy) over Urizen (Reason or Authority); and the redemption and regeneration of mankind through Christ. Symbols premonitory of later books: a step, says Laurence Binyon, in his evolution from "anarchic revolutionary doctrine . . . to a not less revolutionary Christianity." The Zoas are Urizen (Reason), Urthona (Spirit), Luvah (Passion), and Tharmas (the Body), "whose harmony," to quote Binyon once more, "makes up the Perfect Humanity." On the whole, *Vala* (its original title) is an obscure work composed of an amorphous congeries of myths.

Milton (*c.* 1797—*c.* 1815). Two books consisting of two distinct episodes: the baffling obscurity of the Satan-Palambron myth, and the more important thesis of Milton's descent as the Awakener into the world in order to retract what are to Blake errors of theology in *Paradise Lost* (such as, for example, the fallacy of viewing Satan as having been punished by Providence for his sins). Autobiographical details record his rebellion against life at Felpham. Style comparatively direct. Preface is an inspired lyric: "And did those feet in ancient time."

---

† • Explanation of symbols immediately precedes Chapter XV.

Jerusalem, The Emanation of the Giant Albion (1800—1820). Theme is that of Albion's (man's) victory over Error on earth and his return to Eternity: the conflict between the Everlasting Gospel and Natural Religion, and the exaltation of the law of Forgiveness of Sins. Noblest, although chaotic, prophecy. Filled with gloom and terror. Yields memorable passages. Probably influenced by Blake's trial for high treason.[1]

The Ghost of Abel (1822). Short dramatic dialogue in simple style attributes the curse of Cain not to Jehovah but to Satan. Probably suggested by Byron's *Cain* (p. 471).

Comment. While showing the influences of the Elizabethans, Milton, Chatterton, the Ossianic poems, and Gothic art, Blake's main sources are the Bible, the Kabbala, Boehme, and Swedenborg. He anticipates Wordsworth and Coleridge in their simplicity of diction, romanticism, and communion with the earthly spirit; Byron, in his escape from conventional restraints and in his dream of democratic freedom; and Shelley, in his urge toward social unconventionality and in his mystic glimpse of an era of brotherhood and love. He is the forerunner of Nietzsche in his subversion of traditional moral values; of Freud, in the modern controversy over sex and the interchangeability of such terms as God and the Devil; and of Proust, in a dislike of surface realism, a feeling of the impotence of material pleasures and action, and a faith in an artistry that follows intuitive, spontaneous instinct and that permits the stream of consciousness to flow freely.[2]

SUGGESTED MERITS	SUGGESTED DEFECTS
1. Sings of the human soul. Intense vision, prophetic imagination, experiential mysticism.	Rhapsodical mysticism too elaborate, too chaotic, and almost unravelable in its symbolism.
2. Luminous simplicity of meaning and magic childlikeness of thought—particularly in the short lyrics.	2. Pressure of confused and confusing ideas — especially in longer works. Dogmatism.
3. Intense, ecstatic sensitiveness to impressions.	3. Unable to depict his sensibilities.
4. Pure lyric note unique in the English literature of his day Fairy-bell rimes make a complete rupture with neo-classical tradition.	4. General imperfection in a set technique of verse. Unable to weave a narrative or plot to sustain his imaginative perceptions.

1 Ives, Herbert, "The Trial of William Blake for High Treason," *The Nineteenth Century and After*, LXVII (1910), pp. 849-861; Povey, Kenneth, "The Case of Rex *v.* Blake," *The Nation and Athenaeum*, XLIII (1928), p. 562 *f.;* Wright, Thomas, *The Life of William Blake* (Two volumes, 1929), Vol. I, p. 132 *ff.*

2 Birnbaum, M., *Jacovleff and Other Artists* (1946); Kazin, A., ed., *The Portable Blake* (1946); Keynes, G., ed., *The Faber Gallery: Blake: 1757-1827* (1946); Wilson, M., *The Life of William Blake* (1948); Davies, J. G., *The Theology of Blake* (1948); Blackstone, B., *English Blake* (1949).

CHAPTER XXI

THE TRIUMPH OF ROMANTICISM: THE POETS
(1798—1832)

Historical Background

The Reign of George III (continued from page 366). (1) **Act** of Union with Ireland (1800). (2) First British census (1801). (3) Peace of Amiens (1802). (4) Rupture of the Peace of Amiens (1803). (4) Battle of Trafalgar: Death of Nelson (1805). (5) Abolition of the slave trade (1807). (6) Peninsular War begins (1808). (7) George III goes insane (1810); Prince of Wales becomes Regent (1811). (8) United States declares war (1812). (9) Peace of Paris (1814). (10) Battle of Waterloo (1815). (11) "Peterloo" or Manchester Massacre (1819). (12) Six Acts (1819). (13) Death of George III (1820); the Regent becomes George IV.

The Reign of George IV (1820—1830). (1) Bank of England resumes specie payments (1821). (2) Reform of penal code (1823). (3) Repeal of act making trade-unions illegal (1824). (4) Combination Law (1825). (5) Removal of Catholic disabilities by the repeal of the Corporation Act of 1661 and the Test Act of 1673 (1828). (6) Catholic Emancipation Act (1829). (7) Death of George IV (1830).

The Reign of William IV (1830—1837). (1) Opening of the Manchester and Liverpool railway (1830). (2) Rejection of Lord John Russell's parliamentary reform bill causes public demonstrations (1831). (3) Reform Bill (1832). See page 524.

Social and Economic Conditions

The eighteenth century had seen a bloodless revolution in England (see Chapter XVIII, p. 366). The invention of the spinning jenny, the "mule," the power loom, the steam engine, the smelting of iron ore by pit coal—all hastened the growth of industrial towns and of a powerful banking system. New centers of population arose. Industrial England, aided materially by the system of *laissez faire*, grew wealthy. The factory system was established. Against the unspeakable misery and degradation that developed was raised a potent cry for better conditions in factory, poorhouse, and prison, for more humane treatment of children, for improved educational facilities.

While industrial England presented its problems, agricultural England had its own. Large farms took the place of small holdings; wages were inadequate; housing conditions were bad; pauperism increased. Particularly in the period following 1815 there was great distress: unemployment, bad harvests, heavy war debt, and disregard of the rights of labor. From 1784 to 1830 the Tory party was supreme. Not until 1832, when the Reform Bill was passed, were the middle classes enfranchised. Finally, the transition from an agricultural and commercial society to modern industrialism brought in its wake the evil of slums, the exploitation of the masses, and the economic fluctuations between boom and depression. Not yet have these vast economic problems been decisively settled: perhaps the most influential interpretation is Karl Marx's *Das Kapital* (1867—1894), the two principal ideas of which are the existence of surplus value and the materialistic interpretation of history. It is important to fix in mind that in theory and method Marxian socialism is neither utopian nor idealistic, but scientific and logical.

General View of the Literature

By the beginning of the nineteenth century a marked change had taken place in intellectual life. It influenced not only literature but also art, music, philosophy; it manifested itself not only in England but also in Germany and France. For the simplicity, harmony, and purity of the Augustan age were substituted the mystic and passionate, the free-spirited and capricious standards of the Middle Ages. The leading advocates of the spirit of idealism as opposed to realism were Rousseau in France, and Schelling, Schlegel, and Lessing in Germany. In England the rise of Methodism, from the teaching of John Wesley, made religion a vital personal experience, revealed its social responsibilities, and became a recognized social and political factor. The literary aims and ideals of the eighteenth century were swept aside. Great was the development in all fields of literature—in poetry, in fiction, in the essay, and in literary criticism. English letters were characterized by an emotional and imaginative quality and by individuality in style. The pendulum swung from idealism to disillusionment, from revolt to reaction. The so-called Lake School of poets expressed new theories as to the subject-matter and language of poetry; the novelists succeeded in making their works rival the popularity of poetry; the romantic essayists developed a new prose type; and the later romanticists were poets of revolt who, unlike the Lake School, never recanted their revolutionary principles. It was an era of individualism. It was an age in which not only the watchwords of the French Revolution—Liberty, Equality, and Fraternity—but also Democracy and Humanitarianism became the cry of the major English romanticists. (See, also, Chapter XVIII, p. 367.)

William Wordsworth. 1770 — 1850, poet.[1] Son of an attorney of Cockermouth in Cumberland. Hawkshead Grammar School (1778). Obtained a B.A. at St. John's College, Cambridge (1787—1791), where he did not show over-much interest in his studies, interrupting them by a walking tour with Robert Jones through France and Switzerland (1790).[2] Returned to France (November, 1791), where during his stay of a year (until December, 1792) he became indoctrinated with the principles of the Revolution; he also fell in love with the daughter of a surgeon at Blois, Marie-Anne Vallon, fami'·arly known as Annette,[3]

---

1 Myers, F. W. H., *Wordsworth* (1881); Legouis, E. H., *La Jeunesse de William Wordsworth* (1896); Magnus, Laurie, *A Primer of Wordsworth* (1897); Rice, R. A., "Wordsworth Since 1916," *Smith College Studies in Modern Languages*, v (1923), pp. 31-36; Garrod, H. W., *Wordsworth* (1923); Gingerich, S. F., *Essays in the Romantic Poets* (1924), "Wordsworth," pp. 91-191; Harper, G. McL., *William Wordsworth* (1929); Herford, C. H., *Wordsworth* (1930); Read, Herbert, *Wordsworth* (1930); Burra, Peter, *Wordsworth* (1936). Consult also the letters of William and Dorothy Wordsworth, edited by Ernest de Selincourt (1935, 1937, 1939). For his philosophy, consult Brooke, S. A., *Theology in the English Poets* (1874); Shairp, J. C., *Studies in Poetry and Philosophy* (1872) and *On Poetic Interpretation of Nature* (1877); Rader, M. M., "Presiding Ideas in Wordsworth's Poetry," *University of Washington Publications in Language and Literature*, VIII (1931), pp. 121-215; Beatty, Arthur, "William Wordsworth: His Doctrine and Art in Their Historical Relations," (Second Edition), *University of Wisconsin Studies in Language and Literature*, Number 24 (1927); Inge, W. R., *The Platonic Tradition in English Religious Thought* (1926); Spurgeon, C. F. E., *Mysticism in English Thought* (1927); Stalknecht, N. P., "Wordsworth and Philosophy: Suggestions Concerning the Source of the Poet's Doctrines and the Nature of His Mystical Experience," *Publications of the Modern Language Association of America*, XLIV (1929), pp. 1116-1143; Fausset, H. I'A., *The Lost Leader* (1933).

2 Wordsworth has frequently been criticized for his supposed apostasy from his earlier faith both in politics and in religion. In the *Sonnet to Wordsworth* (1816), Shelley lamented Wordsworth's desertion of the liberal cause; in *The Lost Leader* (1845) Browning was influenced by Wordsworth's change of politics from Liberalism to Conservatism—yet Shelley admired Wordsworth's poetry, and Browning later expressed regret, denying that Wordsworth had any selfish motive and attributing to him a moral as well as an intellectual superiority. There is no denying, however, that Wordsworth's attitude on certain questions seems to be in accord with a growing conservatism; for example, with Southey he presents a reasoned case against the complete emancipation of slaves without compensation to the owners, pointing out that the existence of the slave-trade is attributable to the attitude of the public as well as of the slave-owners: see Lewis, N. B., "The Abolitionist Movement in Sheffield, 1823-1833: With Letters from Southey, Wordsworth and Others," *Bulletin of The John Rylands Library*, XVIII (1934), pp. 377-392. But Ernest de Selincourt has shown that Wordsworth renounced France as early as 1795: "The Hitherto Unpublished Preface to Wordsworth's 'Borderers,' " *The Nineteenth Century and After*, c (1926), pp. 723-741. Furthermore, his *variorum* edition of *The Prelude* (1926) indicates that the case made out against Wordsworth is not as strong as one has been led to believe, while E. C. Batho in the second chapter of *The Later Wordsworth* (1933) insists that Wordsworth's political development was not a swing to the left followed by a swing to the right, but a consistent development. In brief, Wordsworth may have been temperamentally a conservative. See, also, White, W. H., *An Examination of the Charge of Apostasy Against Wordsworth* (1898).

3 This fact was not discovered until 1916. Over-emphasis has been put upon his seduction of Annette, who was his senior by four years, upon the fact that he did not marry her, and that he had a child by her. But, as Laurie Magnus has observed, he was not doing it all the time; and Irving Babbitt has challenged the value of emphasizing the autobiographical elements in Wordsworth's poetry. Moreover, there is ample evidence to indicate his honorable intentions; for example, it is not entirely impossible that Wordsworth was in France during 1793, and it is known that Caroline Wordsworth, who in 1816 married Jean Baptiste Martin Baudouin, was well treated by her English father. See Harper, G. McL., *Wordsworth's French Daughter: The Story of her Birth, with the Certificates of her Baptism and Marriage* (1921); Legouis, Émile, *William Wordsworth and Annette Vallon* (1922); Batho, E. C., *The Later Wordsworth* (1933), "Appendix C: The Settlement on Caroline Baudouin," pp. 390-395; Patton, C. H., *The Rediscovery of Wordsworth* (1935), Chap. x, " 'Oh, Let My Weakness Have an End,' " pp. 202-216; Sperry, W. L., *Wordsworth's Anti-Climax* (1935), Chap. VI, "Annette," pp. 79-99.

who, on December 15th, just before his return to England, bore him an illegitimate daughter, Anne-Caroline.[1] Probably in France (October, 1793). Received a legacy of £900 from Raisley Calvert (1795), a friend for whom he had cared during a last illness, and who left with the legacy a request that Wordsworth devote himself wholly to poetry. Settled with Dorothy at Racedown, in Dorsetshire (1795). In the same year he met Coleridge. After the publication of their *Lyrical Ballads* (September, 1798), Wordsworth and his sister Dorothy accompanied Coleridge to Germany (1798—1799). By this time Wordsworth's republicanism had been wholly dissipated by the French invasion of Switzerland. Returning to the Lake District, Wordsworth and his sister Dorothy settled in Dove Cottage, Grasmere (1799), Allan Bank (1808), Grasmere Parsonage (1811), and finally at the well-known house at Rydal Mount, Grasmere (1813), where, except for occasional tours in Switzerland, Scotland, Holland, Belgium, and Italy, he lived for the rest of his life.[2] Married his cousin Mary Hutchinson (October 4, 1802), probably portrayed in "She Was a Phantom of Delight." Received the sinecure of Distributor of Stamps for Westmorland (1813). Last continental tour (1837). Received the D.C.L. from Oxford University (1839). Awarded government pension of £300 a year (1842). At the death of Southey, succeeded him in the laureateship (1843). Died at Rydal Mount (April 23, 1850).

Principal Publications

His chief publications include *Poems, in Two Volumes* (1807), *The Poetical Works of William Wordsworth* (I, II, dated 1836; III—VI, dated 1837), *The Sonnets of William Wordsworth* (1838), *Poems, Chiefly of Early and Late Years* (1842), *The Prose Works of William Wordsworth* (1876),[3] *The Recluse* (1888), and those that follow below.

An Evening Walk (1793). First published poem, in heroic couplets with occasional Alexandrines, avowedly influenced by the phraseology of such poets as Spenser, Milton, Thomson, and Burns, and by the heroic couplets of Pope and Goldsmith. Like the *Descriptive Sketches* that followed, is an example of his early treatment of nature; both, too, have an arbitrary and confused sentence-structure, and both lack tech-

---

1 Maclean, C. M., *Dorothy and William Wordsworth* (1927) and *Dorothy Wordsworth* (1932); De Selincourt, Ernest, *Dorothy Wordsworth* (1933).

2 Many a critic repeats Garrod's statement that the last forty years of Wordsworth's life are "the most dismal anti-climax of which the history of literature holds record." Possibly it was trouble with his eyes that contributed to the lack of creativeness in his older years: Batho, E. C., *The Later Wordsworth* (1933). More likely, it was the two-faceted personality of a poet-artist and prose-parson: Clutton-Brock, A., "The Problem of Wordsworth," *The London Mercury*, II (1920), pp. 700-710; Harper, G. McL., "The Crisis in Wordsworth's Life and Art," *Queen's Quarterly*, XL (1933), pp. 1-13.

3 The prose works are important in any approach to his philosophy; see, for example, Beatty, Arthur, *William Wordsworth: His Doctrine and Art in Their Historical Relations* (Second edition, 1927).

nique and inner formative power. Defective in a general unity. Yet has striking scenes and minute observations of nature. Harper points to its distinct confession of religious unbelief.

Descriptive Sketches (1793). Account in heroic couplets with occasional Alexandrines of his continental trip made with Robert Jones, is not merely a poem on Nature, but one revelatory of his early revolutionary principles; moreover, it does not depict a holiday tour, but, according to Garrod, the objectless wandering of a soul in despair.[1] Only *An Evening Walk* is more characterless; the heroic couplets in *Descriptive Sketches* betray the influence of Pope while the artificial manner and bold figures are derived from Erasmus Darwin; the language is occasionally distorted, the descriptions are loosely connected, and the images and epithets are drawn from such poets as Spenser, Shakespeare, Milton, Thomson, Young, Collins, and Gray. Furthermore, Wordsworth draws extensively upon the picturesque accounts of Ramond de Carbonnieres. While derivative in diction, style, and technique, and lacking in originality and a settled philosophy, this youthful, immature poem retains interest by virtue of its gleams of Wordsworth's love of liberty and by its detailed observation of natural scenery. The text of *Descriptive Sketches* was materially altered or falsified in later editions, frequently for the purpose of greater clearness and finish, and occasionally for the moderation of some enthusiastic description of liberty or strong political feeling.

Lyrical Ballads (1798). In collaboration with Coleridge (p. 163). Its publication may for convenience be said to inaugurate the renaissance of modern English poetry: it is its Magna Charta, officially ushering in the Romantic Period. Such works as varied in merit as *Goody Blake* and *Tintern Abbey* are included.

Lyrical Ballads (1800). The Preface, written by Wordsworth, made the second edition momentous: it is a critical essay outlining his poetical principles:[2]

1. SUBJECT. "The principal object .... was to choose incidents and situations from common life, and to relate or describe them, throughout, as far as was possible in a selection of language really used by men ...." To obtain such situations, "Humble and rustic life was generally chosen, because, in that condition, the essential passions of the heart find a better soil in which they can attain their maturity, are less under restraint, and speak a plainer and more emphatic language; because in that condition of life our elementary feelings coexist

---

1 Garrod, H. W., *Wordsworth: Lectures and Essays* (1923), Chap. II, " 'Descriptive Sketches,' " pp. 40-56.

2 Banerjee, Srikumar, *Critical Theories and Poetic Practice in the "Lyrical Ballads"* (1931).

in a state of greater simplicity, and, consequently, may be more accurately contemplated, and more forcibly communicated; because the manners of rural life germinate from those elementary feelings, and, from the necessary character of rural occupations, are more easily comprehended, and are more durable; and, lastly, because in that condition the passions of men are incorporated with the beautiful and permanent forms of nature."

(Note: As regards the *subject* of his poetry, Wordsworth followed quite consistently his declared opinions; a large number of his poems deal with humble and rustic life.)

2. STYLE. "My purpose was to imitate, and, as far as possible, to adopt the very language of men"; and therefore Wordsworth believed in avoiding "personifications of abstract ideas" and "what is usually called poetic diction." To him "poetry is the spontaneous overflow of powerful feelings" and "takes its origin from emotion recollected in tranquillity."[1]

(Note: As regards the *style* of his poetry,[2] Wordsworth often violated that part of his poetic theory. In his greatest poems he not infrequently uses language somewhat stiff and ornate.)

3. WORDSWORTH AND COLERIDGE. Wordsworth was to present in simple language observations of humble life, throwing over such life "a certain coloring of the imagination, whereby ordinary things should be presented to the mind in an unusual aspect." It was agreed, on the one hand, that Coleridge's "endeavors should be directed to persons and characters supernatural, or at least romantic; yet so as to transfer from our inward nature a human interest and a semblance of truth sufficient to procure for these shadows of imagination that willing suspension of disbelief for the moment which constitutes poetic faith. Mr. Wordsworth, on the other hand, was to propose to himself as his object, to give the charm of novelty to things of every day, and to excite a feeling analogous to the supernatural by awakening the mind's attention from the lethargy of custom and directing it to the loveliness and the wonders of the world before us." (The last quotation is not from

---

1 His was an emotional nature, but one that expressed itself in odes and sonnets rather than in lyrics; predominating in Wordsworth were the lack of the love-motive, a didactic spirit, and the theory of poetry as "emotion recollected in tranquillity." Reed, E. B., *English Lyrical Poetry from Its Origins to the Present Times* (1912).

2 According to Wordsworth, there is no essential difference between the language of poetry and that of prose; according to Coleridge, the language of poetry must necessarily differ from that of prose. In the past, critics have laid emphasis upon Wordsworth's revolutionary ideas of diction, upon the obliteration of the traditional distinctions between prose and poetry, and upon the renunciation of eighteenth-century formalism. Wordsworth's plea for simplicity in poetic diction, however, yields in importance to the soundness of the aesthetic and metaphysical affirmations that the Preface makes: thus asserts Campbell, O. J., and Mueschke, Paul, "Wordsworth's Aesthetic Development, 1795-1802," *Essays and Studies in English and Comparative Literature* (By Members of The English Department of the University of Michigan), 1933, pp. 40-57 (pp. 1-57).

the Preface to *Lyrical Ballads* but from Coleridge's *Biographia Literaria,* Chap. XIV.)

The Borderers (written *c.* 1795—1797[1]; 1842). His one drama, notable also as his first long attempt at blank verse, has been frequently regarded, like *Guilt and Sorrow,* as an example of Wordsworth's continued subjection to Godwinism; but it is less an exposition of Godwinian motives than a revolt against them, and it is essentially a clash between Godwinism and personal experience: the main purpose is to exhibit the dangers of trusting to reason when one has committed a crime.[2] It is not impossible that the initial aesthetic impulse was the remorse at his abandonment of Annette Vallon (Campbell and Mueschke); certainly it seems to be a clash resulting between Godwin's philosophy and his own personal experience (De Selincourt); it may be both the product of mental disease and a confession of spiritual disease (Fausset).[3] Ingenious, improbable story does not succeed in making clear the central idea. Some features are its striking verses and vivacious idiom; more prominent, however, is its Gothicism of atmosphere and scene, its probable insincerity of mood, and its indebtedness to Shakespeare's *Othello* and *King Lear* (Vol. 1, pp. 209, 211), and to such works as Mr. Radcliffe's *Romance of the Forest* (p. 405) and Godwin's *Things as they Are, or the Adventures of Caleb Williams* (p. 407).

The White Doe of Rylstone; or The Fate of the Nortons (1807—1808; 1815). Autobiographical poem, based upon a ballad in Percy's collection, "The Rising of the North," is his most romantic work. Teaches that human obstinacy results in tragedy, that active life is vanity, and that salvation is obtainable through suffering.[4] It is by no means completely unsatisfactory, for its story has variety of action. Elizabethan atmosphere: in keeping with the source-ballad.

The Waggoner (*c.* 1805; 1819). In Wordsworth's statement, "an excursion into light verse" in imitation of *Tam O'Shanter.* By virtue of its landscape and its human interest this poem merits some attention.

Peter Bell (*c.* 1796—*c.* 1798; 1819). Weird but explicable tale of the religious conversion of a lawless sinner. Illustrates Wordsworth's

---

1 If *The Borderers* was written in the autumn of 1796 and completed in the spring of 1797, a difference results in its autobiographical interpretation. See MacGillivray, J. R., "The Date of Composition of *The Borderers,*" *Modern Language Notes,* XLIX (1934), pp. 104-111.

2 Wordsworth's intention did not become clear until the preface was discovered. Consult De Selincourt, E., "The Hitherto Unpublished Preface to Wordsworth's 'Borderers,'" *The Nineteenth Century and After,* c (1926), pp. 723-741.

3 Campbell, O. J., and Mueschke, Paul, "*The Borderers* as a Document in the History of Wordsworth's Aesthetic Development," *Modern Philology,* XXIII (1925-1926), pp. 465-482.

4 For an important criticism, refer to Shairp, J. C., *Aspects of Poetry* (1882), "The White Doe of Rylstone," pp. 295-322.

belief that Nature has the power to subdue the human heart and to mould the moral life of man,[1] thereby emphasizing the influence of natural objects upon a superstitious soul and the susceptibilities to good latent in every one. Some deft touches and beautiful stanzas. As a whole, lacks congruity. Grotesque simplicity, labored playfulness, and certain ludicrous parts.[2] Observe that the motif is the same as that of Coleridge's *Ancient Mariner,* to which Wordsworth's tale is probably a counterpart, one that combines the aesthetics of terror and sentimental morality,[3] and a composition undoubtedly influenced by personal remorse. Whereas Coleridge treats a tale involving supernatural agency with naturalness of details in order to achieve an effect of reality, Wordsworth, reversing the principle, endeavors to produce the effect of supernatural awe entirely by natural means. For the total effect, read the Prologue, even if it seems flawed by attempts at humor. More than even his *Idiot Boy,* this tale, its stark and aggressive naturalism modified a score of years later by the insertion of Christian elements, is still possibly his most misunderstood work.[4] (See Shelley's *Peter Bell the Third,* p. 478.)

The Excursion, Being a Portion of The Recluse (1814). Because it is contemplative rather than dramatic, his discursive philosophical poem in nine books of blank verse that endeavors to reconcile extreme transcendentalism and purer Naturalism is generally regarded as long, parsonical, and dull; it is in large part artificial prose discourses in metrical form—thoughtful but pedestrian discourses by imaginary characters. Its sentiments are flat, moralizing, and ratiocinative, not poetic. His longest poem, one built on epic scale; but as devoid of epic structure as it is of verbal felicity and allegorical unity. Its philosophical doctrines, according to Harper, are that the universe is ruled by a spiritual Person, that human life on the whole is morally admirable, and that correspondences exist between the human soul and external nature. It seems to have no intrinsic greatness; but to those who regard poetry primarily as the expression of truth, it is a memorable and important poem. (*The Excursion* is the second member of the projected work to be called *The Recluse*: see under *The Prelude.* The first book of the first part, called *The Fragment of The Recluse,* written in 1800, was not published until 1888; Part II, *The Excursion,* was published in his lifetime; the third part was only planned. The philosophy of

---

1 For evidence of this principle, read *Expostulation and Reply, The Tables Turned, Three Years She Grew in Sun and Shower, The White Doe of Rylstone, Tintern Abbey,* and parts of *The Prelude;* for its qualified attitude, the *Ode to Duty* and *Elegiac Stanzas.*

2 For a discussion of the poem, consult Swaen, A. E. F., "Peter Bell," *Anglia,* Bd. 47; N. F. 35 (1923), pp. 136-184.

3 Campbell, O. J., "Sentimental Morality in Wordsworth's Narrative Poetry," *University of Wisconsin Studies in Language and Literature,* Studies by Members of the Department of English (1920), pp. 21-57.

4 Gosse, Edmund, *Gossip in a Library* (1891), "Peter Bell and his Tormenters," pp. 253-267.

The Excursion should be compared with the *Intimations of Immortality* and the *Ode to Duty*. See, also, *The Ruined Cottage*, p. 452.)

The River Duddon (1820). Volume famous for the thirty-four "River Duddon" sonnets which give a poetical history of a beautiful stream, and for *Vaudracour and Julia* (dated 1804), a poorly-constructed, prolix, and labored tale of thwarted love, but valued for its auto-biographical importance, since the main feelings involved are reminiscent of the relations between Wordsworth and Annette. Only two passages totaling about twenty lines rise above the inferior poetical quality of the poem.

Memorials of a Tour on the Continent (1820). Series of sonnets and poems commemorating his travels. Some interesting descriptions; but in general does not add to Wordsworth's reputation.

Ecclesiastical Sonnets (1822). Cycle of one hundred and two sonnets, later increased to one hundred and thirty-two, constitute a narrative poem written on the outstanding points in the history of the Church of England and dealing with them from an historical and an institutional point of view.[1] This series of sonnets on great personalities and crucial events reveal Wordsworth at his learned best; with an objectivity of technical mastery he presents almost an intuitive understanding of the collective growth and the indissoluble relationship of both church and state. Famous for the sonnets "Mutability" and "King's College Chapel."

The Prelude (1799—1805; 1850). Long narrative autobiographical poem in fourteen books of blank verse is, to quote De Selincourt, "the essential living document for the interpretation of Wordsworth's life and manner," and, now Garrod is speaking, the "ponderable handbook of the imaginative life." In reviewing the growth and development of his powers from childhood until 1795, the poem may be divided into three parts: his boyhood and youth, his experiences in France during the Revolution, and his reactions to these experiences that in turn evoke a theory concerned with the mystical relations of the mind and of nature. Undeniably contains pedantic psychological terms and prolix passages, but in this poem, the subject of which is nominally the growth of a poet's mind and actually the spiritual development of Wordsworth, there are beauty of blank verse, fresh power of observation, alert sensibility, and rare poetic beauty. Read has called it an epic of the man of feeling; its unity is epical rather than philosophical, and its design has something of epic structure. Shows the influence of Shakespeare and even of Milton. As Wordsworth aged, he altered into softness its original expressions of political and religious radicalism.[2] (*The Pre-*

---

1 Potts, A. F., *The Ecclesiastical Sonnets of William Wordsworth* (Thesis, 1922).
2 *The Prelude or Growth of a Poet's Mind*, edited by De Selincourt, Ernest (1926).

lude was intended as introductory to *The Recluse,* which was to be a philosophical poem on man, on nature, and on human life, and which was to have as its principal subject the sensations and opinions of a poet living in retirement. See, also, *The Excursion,* which is the middle part of the incomplete *The Recluse.* Both completed portions should be compared with the analagous *Task* by Cowper, p. 425.)

Individual Poems

We Are Seven (1798). Whether it proves that a young child can not realize the fact of death, or that a child has a simple instinct of immortality, this seventeen-stanzaed poem was influenced by the associational psychology of Hartley. (In the *Intimations* ode, Wordsworth argues for a childhood instinct of immortality reaching backward to a pre-existent state.)

The Idiot Boy (1798). Motive was to illustrate the deeps of a mother's love, but failed because of garrulous repetitions and inanities, an abortive sense of humor, and a tactless levity of style.[1]

The Old Cumberland Beggar (1798). Noteworthy for concrete detail, and important as illustrating Wordsworth's broad humanitarianism. Like *The Last of the Flock* and *Alice Fell, or Poverty,* it reveals Wordsworth's understanding of the poor.

Lines Composed a Few Miles above Tintern Abbey (1798). Poem best expresses the central creed of his faith: the never-mentioned Abbey conjures up an ivy-clad ruin "that is a Gothic symbol for the triumph of Nature over the works of man"; the various attitudes towards Nature later culminates in transcendentalism, thereby giving a mystical sanction to natural morality. It is, undoubtedly, a partly psychological sketch, in Hartleian terms, of the growth of the mind under the guidance of nature or experience, in which sensations are transformed into higher mental states either by the machinery of association (Beatty) or the alchemy of memory (Campbell and Mueschke). One group believes *Tintern Abbey* to be Pantheism; another sees in it nothing inharmonious with Christian belief. Despite a descriptive beauty, a power in managing blank verse, and a splendor and dynamic energy, it seems too unqualified in its generalizations and only intermittently grand.

Michael (1800). True pastoral[2] in blank verse relates a tragedy of an old shepherd's shattered hopes. The narrative[3] may advance

1 Mead, Marion, *Four Studies in Wordsworth* (1929), "The 'Idiot Boy,'" pp. 185-202.
2 Wordsworth departed from two conspicuous conventions of the type, dropping the convention of love and of amoebean contest, and dealing with a real English shepherd. Knowlton, E. C., "The Novelty of Wordsworth's *Michael* as a Pastoral," *Publications of the Modern Language Association of America,* xxx; New Series, xxviii (1920), pp. 432-446. Moreover, the contention has been made that Wordsworth is an excellent pastoral poet: Broughton, L. N., *The Theocritan Element in the Works of William Wordsworth* (1920).
3 For an analysis of the story, see Shackford, M. H., "Wordsworth's *Michael,*" *The Sewanee Review Quarterly,* xxxi (1923), pp. 275-280.

slowly, but the conclusion falls with tragic swiftness; it is a pastoral, but original in the absence of a love episode. Truly Wordsworthian in its avoidance of literary devices and melodramatic straining after effect, yet the pathos is maintained by a nameless grace, the sincerity of the style, the patriarchal directness of manner, and the restraint and dignity with which the deep emotions involved are treated.

"Lucy" Poems. The five so-called "Lucy" poems were written in Germany in 1799: (1) *Strange Fits of Passion Have I Known* (1799; 1800); (2) *She Dwelt Among the Untrodden Ways* (1799; 1800); (3) *I Travelled Among Unknown Men* (1799; 1807); (4) *Three Years She Grew in Sun and Shower* (1799; 1800); and (5) *A Slumber Did My Spirit Seal* (1799; 1800). Wordsworth, in this group intense with strength of emotion, achieves a rare tenderness and an exquisite simplicity of expression. No one knows who Lucy was—whether a gypsy (Legouis), or Mary Hutchinson, or Annette Vallon (Read), or an imagined composite of Dorothy and Annette (Fausset); she may have been an idealization of a real person or a figment of the imagination.[1]

Lucy Gray (1799; 1800). Pathetic ballad based on an incident recounted by Dorothy is told with matchless bareness of diction, creative naturalness, and pure imagination. (It is not a *Lucy* poem.)

To the Cuckoo (1804; 1807). Reveals the idealistic character of Wordsworth and his tendency to spiritualize the Bird into "A voice, a mystery"; and "a hope, a love; Still longed for, never seen."

Character of the Happy Warrior (*c.* 1805—1806; 1807). Portrait of a hero, in peace or in war, who centers prime care upon his moral being, was probably suggested by the character of Nelson but modelled upon that of Wordsworth's brother John. Manner more impersonal than customary; in spirit, closely allied to the *Ode to Duty* and *Elegiac Stanzas.*

The Solitary Reaper (1803—1805; 1807). One of the best of the short lyrics. Note the effective use of proper names, and the simplicity, delicate understanding, and imaginative reach.

Ode to Duty (1805; 1807). His most explicit statement of belief in a universal law of good presents the quintessence of Wordsworth's message in the realm of morals and the moral sense. Like the *Elegiac Stanzas,* it followed soon after the death of his brother John; like *Tintern Abbey,* its theme is the same, but resumed from an altered outlook; like the *Intimations of Immortality,* it shows a struggle to reconcile contradictory views, but proceeds less by intuition than by logic. Wordsworth's mental conflict and his belief in the physical world as

---

1 No one knows whether Lucy was an idealization of a real person or a figment of the imagination. Garrod, H. W., *The Profession of Poetry* (1929), "Wordsworth's Lucy," pp. 78-92; Hartman, Herbert, "Wordsworth's 'Lucy' Poems: *Notes and Marginalia,*" *Publications of the Modern Language Association of America,* XLIX (1934), pp. 134-142.

governed by moral law are expressed with restraint and dignity in this ethical work of eight flawless stanzas, modelled on Gray's ode to *Adversity* (p. 417) and pulpy with spiritual and philosophic suggestion. Freedom is to be sought by obedience to duty, and by bringing the individual will into conformity with the divine will, manifest in the human soul.

Elegiac Stanzas as Suggested by a Picture of Peele Castle in a Storm (1805; 1807). His greatest elegy, in the same meter as Gray's, is of extreme biographical importance, marking as it does the crisis of his spiritual life. Ennobled by felicity of language, spontaneity of expression, and depth of feeling.

Ode on the Intimations of Immortality from Recollections of Early Childhood (1802—1806; 1807). Masterpiece, consisting of eleven stanzas varying in length from nine to thirty-eight lines and prevailingly in the iambic meter, is premised on the Platonic[1] teaching respecting the preëxistence of the human soul, and records his convictions on immanence and transcendence. The seven tail-end stanzas, written after the crisis of 1805, endeavor to answer the questions propounded in the first four stanzas written in 1802: a reconciliation between the two contradictory views is attempted in the tenth and eleventh stanzas; while the theme is epitomized in the last three lines of *The Rainbow* (*c*. 1803—1806; 1807) prefixed to the 1815 edition:

> "The Child is father of the Man;
> And I could wish my days to be
> Bound each to each by natural piety."

Its final two stanzas are memorable for sustained religious sublimity. Criticisms sometimes made are that the poem occasionally is abrupt in its transitions, or verges on the sentimental, or is out of harmony with the spirit of a true Nature poem, or dwells protractedly on the idea of pre-existence. If not his philosophical masterpiece,[2] it is his supreme lyrical achievement.

Resolution and Independence (1802; 1807). Companion masterpiece to *Michael* finds poetic inspiration in a slight incident concerned with a humble and an obscure leech-gatherer, after whom the poem is often called *The Leech-Gatherer*. The story is almost trivial and the diction is prosaic; the value lies in the application of the story, the mysticism of the sixteenth stanza, and the imaginative power of deal-

---

1 Wordsworth's Neo-Platonism may have stemmed from the works of Plato published by Thomas Taylor in 1804. See Pierce, F. E., "Wordsworth and Thomas Taylor," *Philological Quarterly*, VII (1928), pp. 60-64.

2 Between Vaughan's *The Retreate* (Vol. 1, p. 261) and Wordsworth's ode there are similarities of ideas and expressions. Whether Vaughan was a conscious influence is discussed by Merrill, LeRoy, "Vaughan's Influence upon Wordsworth's Poetry," *Modern Language Notes*, XXXVII (1922), pp. 91-96; McMaster, H. N., "Vaughan and Wordsworth," *The Review of English Studies*, XI (1935), pp. 313-325.

ing with humble matters and of interpreting the old man with whom
Wordsworth has a casual meeting. First to reveal fully Wordsworth's
faith "that the divinity in one man may have a vital transforming effect
on another." (The sentimentalism of the poem provoked Edward Lear's
parodic *Incidents in the Life of My Uncle Arly* and Lewis Carroll's *The
White Knight's Ballad.*)

The Ruined Cottage (1814). Originally written as a separate
poem, "The Story of Margaret" or "The Ruined Cottage" was included
in Book I of *The Excursion.* Important in the history of Wordsworth's
poetic growth, showing an advance in simplicity, realism, and aesthetic
technique. Coleridge praised it highly.

Laodamia (1814; 1815). Classical source is the sixth book of the
Aeneid. Treatment is of such polish and elaboration that it may well
be the most mature of his poems. Possibly influenced by Euripides's
character study, *Iphigenia at Aulis.*

Guilt and Sorrow. (In part, under the title of *The Female
Vagrant,* 1798; published in complete form, 1842). Like *The Borderers,*
this poem in seventy-four Spenserian stanzas illustrates in a measure both
a Godwinian idea and Wordsworth's emotional personality as upset by
remorse over his treatment of Annette. Unromantic story dealing in
simple diction with humble life is essentially a protest against social
injustice and a plea for social reform: as Harper states, "The ravages
of war among the poor, raising prices, unsettling employment, causing
the horrors of forced conscription, with the breaking up of families
and impelling of innocent people towards legalized murder, are portrayed in a startling light." Observe the popular appeals of sentimental
morality and Gothic detail[1]; notably, the dignity of poor, uneducated
persons.

Sonnets

Wordsworth is one of the three or four greatest sonneteers in English literature. Of his approximately five hundred sonnets, some examples are: (1) *It Is a Beauteous Evening, Calm and Free* (1802;
1807), probably meant not for his sister Dorothy but for his natural
daughter Anne-Caroline: in it, states Gingerich, "the principle of the
indwelling of Deity in children and its regenerative influence became
fully articulate." (2) *The World Is Too Much With Us; Late and Soon*
(c. 1806; 1807), a protest against materialistic industrialism and a plea
for more intimate communion with nature. Other sonnets include:

---

1 Campbell, O. J., and Mueschke, Paul, " 'Guilt and Sorrow': A Study in the Genesis
of Wordsworth's Aesthetic," *Modern Philology,* XXIII (1926), pp. 293-306.

(3) *Thought of a Briton on the Subjugation of Switzerland* (*c.* 1807), (4) *Composed upon Westminster Bridge* (1802; 1807); (5) *London, 1802* (1802; 1807), also known as the sonnet to Milton; (6) *To Toussaint L'Ouverture* (*c.* 1802; 1803); (7) *Composed by the Seaside, Near Calais* (1802; 1807) and (8) *On the Extinction of the Venetian Republic* (*c.* 1802; 1807), two of his approximately seventy political sonnets; (9) *Nuns Fret Not at Their Convent's Narrow Room* (*c.* 1806; 1807), (10) *Scorn Not the Sonnet* (1827); (11) *Most Sweet It Is with Uplifted Eyes* (1833; 1835).

Prose Works

Wordsworth's prose writings include *Apology for the French Revolution, in a Letter to the Bishop of Llandaff* (1793; 1876), which urged the equality of income, the abolition of inheritance laws, the confiscation of church possessions, and the use of violence to overthrow despotism[1]; *Two Addresses to the Freeholders of Westmorland* (1818), which, Tory-like, argued that the surviving feudal power in England could help counteract the popular tendency to reform; and, most important, the tract on the Convention of Cintra: *Concerning the Relations of Great Britain, Spain, and Portugal, to each other and to the Common Enemy, at this Crisis; and specifically as Affected by the Convention of Cintra;* . . . . (1809). Prose tract[2] is his most important political expression, appealing for a united attack upon Napoleon, pioneering the gospel of "Nationhood" or the doctrine of Nationalism[3] (it was in opposition to Napoleon that nationalism first appeared as a vital force in European politics, having first emerged in the French Revolution), and foreshadowing aspects of the philosophy of Mazzini and Garibaldi. Occasional passages of sincerity outbalanced by rhetorical excesses that impair the lucidity and concision, if not the force, of the style. (Compare with Milton's *Areopagitica*, Vol. 1, p. 232, and with Burke's *Reflections*, p. 385.)

---

1 The *Letter* was undoubtedly influenced by both Thomas Paine and Godwin. See Hooker, E. N., "Wordsworth's Letter to the Bishop of Llandaff," *Studies in Philology*, xxviii (1931), pp. 522-531; Roberts, C. W., "The Influence of Godwin on Wordsworth's Letter to the Bishop of Llandaff," *Studies in Philology*, xxix (1932), pp. 588-606.

2 Wells, J. E., "The Story of Wordsworth's 'Cintra,'" *Studies in Philology*, xviii (1921), pp. 15-76; Brinton, Crane, *The Political Ideas of the English Romanticists* (1926), pp. 49-65 (pp. 48-107).

3 Dicey, A. V., *The Statesmanship of Wordsworth* (1917).

GENERAL CHARACTERISTICS

SUGGESTED MERITS	SUGGESTED DEFECTS
1. Spiritual love of nature; cosmic sympathy for peaceful things.	1. In a strict sense, is not always a descriptive poet nor a great nature poet.
2. Found God in nature—pantheistic philosophy.[1]	2. Philosophy unorthodox, or materialistic, or pantheistic, or mystical.
3. Moral elevation, sublime tenderness, serene spirit.	3. Disposition to be pronouncedly didactic and heavily moralistic.
4. Pardonable egoism glorified instincts and pleasures of childhood.[2]	4. Over-parading egoism.
5. Narrative poems have heroes of humble position and lowly occupation. Love poetry, while small in quantity, is important for its personal quality, intensity, and significance. Not only a poet of nature but also a poet of love.	5. Meager narrative gift, scanty dramatic power. Deficient in constructive power, in the purely lyrical gift, and in the faculty of imaginative speech. Lack of intensity and passion; note the mention but not the expression of sexual passion.
6. Seeming spontaneity of his best poems. Diction often unaffected. Variety and richness of poetic forms. Not completely devoid of the comic sense; see his letters, for example.	6. Mass of poetry is inferior.[3] Often banal in style and content. Best verse not infrequently contradicts his theory of Poetic Diction. Defective in verse technique. Lack of humor.[4]

Samuel Taylor Coleridge, 1772—1834, poet, critic, philosopher, dramatist. Born at Ottery St. Mary, in Devonshire. Son of an Anglican clergyman. Educated at Christ's Hospital, London (1781).[5] Matriculated at Jesus College, Cambridge (1791), where he may have first indulged in opium. Incurring some debts and falling into a mood of despondency, he suddenly ran away, and under the assumed name of Silas Tomkyn Comberbacke (note the initials, S.T.C.), he enlisted in the Fifteenth (Elliot's Light) Dragoons (1793—1794).[6] After his brothers had with some difficulty bought his discharge, he returned for a short time to Cambridge, but quitted the university without a degree (1794). Met Robert Southey (1794), whom he joined in a scheme, which quickly collapsed, for the establishment of an ideal society or

---

1 Herford, Irving Babbitt, and Elton charge Wordsworth with a pantheistic view of the world, but they are overwhelmed, at least in number, by such critics as Shairp, Brooke, Inge, Sneath, and Sherwood. See Brooke, S. A., *Theology in the English Poets* (1875), "Wordsworth," pp. 93-286; Shairp, J. C., *Studies in Poetry and Philosophy* (1884), "Wordsworth," pp. 1-89; Strong, A. H., *The Great Poets and Their Theology* (1897), "Wordsworth," pp. 335-372; Inge, W. R., *Studies of English Mystics* (1906), "The Mysticism of Wordsworth," pp. 173-206; Sneath, E. H., *Wordsworth, Poet of Nature and Poet of Man* (1912); Richards, I. A., *Principles of Literary Criticism* (1924), p. 252 f.; Babbitt, Irving, "The Primitivism of Wordsworth," *The Bookman,* LXXIV (1931), pp. 1-10; Sherwood, Margaret, *Undercurrents of Influence in English Romantic Poetry* (1934), "Wordsworth: 'The Unity of All,'" pp. 148-180; "Wordsworth: 'The Imaginative Will,'" pp. 181-202.

2 He has been designated as the poet of childhood: Babenroth, A. C., *English Childhood* (1922), Chap. VII, "William Wordsworth," pp. 299-396.

3 Despite his power and imagination, Wordsworth is not a great poet: his eyes are fixed on Virtue, and his verse has neither the high pitch of intensity nor the fire of passion nor the glow of beauty nor the splendor of form. Thus asserts Madariaga, Salvador de, *Shelley & Calderon* (1920), "The Case of Wordsworth," pp. 126-190.

4 L. N. Broughton endeavors to refute the charge that Wordsworth lacked humor.

5 Lamb's essay on *Christ's Hospital Five and Thirty Years Ago* gives us a picture of Coleridge as a schoolboy.

6 Hawkes, C. P., "Coleridge as a Cavalryman," *The Nineteenth Century and After,* CIX (1931), pp. 735-744.

"Pantisocracy" on the banks of the Susquehanna River in Pennsylvania. Married Sara (or Sarah) Fricker (1795), whose sister Edith in the same year secretly became Southey's wife. Coleridge never appeared too interested in taking care of his family.[1] Made the acquaintance of Wordsworth, with whom he planned the *Lyrical Ballads* (1797), published the following year. Granted annuities of seventy-five pounds each by Josiah and Thomas Wedgwood (1798). Went to Germany with the Wordsworths (1798—1799), where Coleridge attended the University of Göttingen, studied philosophy, and within six weeks had so mastered the German language that he was able to translate Schiller's *Wallenstein* (p. 460). Period of greatest poetical activity (1797—1803). At Greta Hall, Keswick (1800—*c.* 1804). Scotland (1803). Failed to repair his broken health by a stay in Malta (1804—1805), where he was for ten months secretary to the Governor, Sir Alexander Ball. Stayed at Naples and Rome (1805—1806). Meets De Quincey (1807). Lectured rather unsuccessfully at the Royal Institution (1808). Lived with the Wordsworths at Grasmere (1808—1810). Gave a successful lecture series on Shakespeare and Milton (1811—1812). Josiah Wedgwood withdraws his share of the gift (1812).[2] Laudanum in the ascendant (1806—1816). Found harborage in the home of the kindly Dr. Gillman, of Highgate (1816—1834).[3]

Coleridge is essentially a medievalist, differing from Wordsworth in a fondness for the weird and unusual romantic themes; he is the purest of romantics, powerful in his creation of hallucinatory reality and in his communication of moral truth. In his *Lectures on Poetry* he adopts Milton's prescription that poetry should be simple, appealing to the primary laws of our nature; that poetry should be sensuous, "and by its imagery elicit truth at a flash"; and that poetry should be impassioned, in order "to move our feelings and awaken our affections"— and Coleridge's verse on the whole conforms to this conception. He is a master of exquisite verbal melody and witchery of language. His imaginative power is intense. Possibly his main contribution to poetry is his subtle appeal to the Romantic sense for the supernatural. His shortcomings are an absence of concentration, and an incapability of sustained effort or continuity of purpose. Others also believe that, except for possibly a half dozen poems, he is essentially an effusionist rather than a lyricist. But, to quote Stopford Brooke, "All that he did excellently might be bound up in twenty pages, but it should be bound up in pure gold."

---

1 But see Griggs, E. L., "Coleridge and His Son," *Studies in Philology*, xxvii (1930), pp. 635-647. For important light upon the instability of Coleridge's character, consult Maclean, C. M., *Dorothy Wordsworth* (1932).

2 Josiah Wedgwood, despite the traditional opinion, did nothing unethical in withdrawing his annuity. See Griggs, E. L., "Coleridge and the Wedgwood Annuity," *The Review of English Studies*, vi (1930), pp. 63-72.

3 Watson, L. E., *Coleridge at Highgate* (1925).

His prose is as discursive and incomplete as his poetry; most marked in his planless prose are the length of his sentences and the frequency of his parentheses. Yet his prose represents the most critical work of the period. As a literary critic, for example, he is stimulating and suggestive.[1] His lectures on Shakespeare, despite their honey-combed errors and distorted judgments, proved him a redintegrator of the great dramatist. For example, Coleridge, in treating *All's Well That Ends Well*, assumes the existence of an earlier version, and appears to be the first to point out the two divergent styles in the same play (Vol. 1, p. 200). His lectures, marked by rich ethical reflectiveness, introspective analytical power, and profound insight into human nature, initiated and established the great tradition of English criticism of Shakespeare.[2] Finally, as a philosopher,[3] theologian, and conversation-alist, he was a major influence in repudiating eighteenth-century rational-ism and scepticism,[4] and in spreading German transcendentalism.

Romantic Poems

Kubla Khan, a Vision (c. 1797; 1816). On awakening from an opium dream into which he had fallen after reading a passage in Purchas's *Hakluytus Posthumus* (Vol. 1, p. 148), Coleridge began the poem, interrupted by a tailor who came to collect a bill; on his re-turn an hour later to his room, Coleridge found that he could recapture no more than eight or ten scattered lines and images, all the rest having faded from memory. Mystical fragment, haunting in its sound effects,

---

1 Lessing and other German writers blazed the way for Schlegel, to whom Coleridge is indebted for most of his principles of criticism, and in other ways. For the influence of Kant, Schelling, and Schlegel on Coleridge as a critic and philosopher, see Brandl, Alois, *Samuel Taylor Coleridge und die englische Romantik* (1886); Haney, J. L., *The German Influence on Samuel Taylor Coleridge* (Thesis, 1902); Helmholtz, A. A., "The Indebtedness of Samuel Taylor Coleridge to August Wilhelm Von Schlegel," *Bulletin of the University of Wisconsin, Philology and Literature Series*, III, No. 4 (1907); Richter, Helene, "Die Philosophische Weltanshauung von S. T. Coleridge und ihr Verhältnis zur deutschen Philosophie," *Anglia*, Bd. XLIV; N. F. B. XXXII (1920), pp. 261-290, 297-324.

2 *Coleridge's Shakespearean Criticism*, edited by Raysor, T. M. (Two volumes, 1930); Eliot, T. S., "Shakespearian Criticism: From Dryden to Coleridge," in *A Companion to Shakespeare Studies*, edited by Granville-Barker, Harley, and Harrison, G. B. (1934), pp. 287-299.

3 The problem of Coleridge as a philosopher is not without its difficulties. One critic states Coleridge's early transference from the Harleian to the Platonic tradition; another says Coleridge was a reconciler of Platonism and Transcendentalism; a third emphasizes that his philosophy is in a true sense metaphysical rather than mystical; still one more believes that in temper and training Coleridge belongs not to the German transcendental schools of his day, but to the traditional Platonism of the seventeenth century; and a fifth shows the influence of the early English Platonists on Coleridge, who employed the Kantian phraseology but relied mainly upon the Platonic thought. Recently, a writer stated that, while Coleridge occupies an important position in poetry, he can no longer enjoy the vogue as a political philosopher. He seems to have pro-ceeded from a Unitarian preaching Harleian and Spinozan doctrines around Nether Stowey as early as 1796 or 1797, to an exponent of the Tri-Unitarian Doctrine and of Kantianism. See, for example, Muirhead, J. H., *Coleridge as Philosopher* (1930), and Murray, R. H., "Samuel Taylor Coleridge," *The Contemporary Review*, CXLV (1934), pp. 49-57.

4 Shafer, Robert, *Christianity and Naturalism* (1926), "Coleridge," pp. 34-69.

perhaps the most airy and elusively lovely description in our literature, is generally considered unrivalled for pure music and power of poetic diction, for imagery and imaginative suggestiveness.

Christabel (I, *c.* 1797; II, 1800: published 1816). Unfinished ballad, the third of the famous "Mystery Poems." Medieval tale of witchcraft steeped in haunting, supernatural atmosphere represents the eternal conflict between the forces of good and evil as personified in the innocent Christabel and in the snake-woman Geraldine. Terse phrasing, well-chosen images; story delayed by long descriptions and digressions. Second part not as effective as first. The meter,[1] founded on the principle of counting in each line the accents and not the syllables, seems to be a revival of the four-stress line, divided into two half-lines of two stresses each: see "Structure of Ango-Saxon Versification," Vol. 1, p. 10 *f.*

The Rime of the Ancient Mariner (1797—1798; in *Lyrical Ballads*, 1798; in *Sibylline Leaves*, 1817). Literary ballad in seven parts in iambic measure varied by anapestic effects deals with the supernatural punishment and penance of a seaman who wantonly killed an albatross. Dramatic climax is the falling off of the albatross when the mariner blessed the water snakes: the moral is that of all-embracing love. Essence of poem is its picture of Coleridge's spiritual isolation: Irving Babbitt has declared that perhaps no work embodies more successfully the main romantic *motif* of solitude: the poem's unifying element is feeling, and in its incidents, scenic settings, and psychology, it marks "the extreme sacrifice of the verisimilar to the marvelous."[2] Only flaw seems to be its retributive moral,[3] an excrescence suggested by Wordsworth who at the time was suffering remorse from his abandonment of Annette Vallon and their child. Aside from the one weakness in form, it is a

---

1 The famous note at the close of the Preface to *Christabel* is as follows: "I have only to add that the metre of *Christabel* is not, properly speaking, irregular, though it may seem so from its being founded on a new principle: namely, that of counting in each line the accents, not the syllables. Though the latter may vary from seven to twelve, yet in each line the accents will be found to be only four. Nevertheless, this occasional variation in number of syllables is not introduced wantonly, or for the mere ends of convenience, but in correspondence with some transition in the nature of the imagery or passion."

This note the critics have quite unanimously denounced, or at least found puzzling, on the score that the meter of *Christabel* is not always what it is declared to be, that it is not new, that there is little or no connection between the metrical variations and changes in the content.

For "considering its meter as defined by Coleridge, the amount and nature of the syllabic variations, the connection of this with the thought, and the newness of the principle announced," see Snell, A. L. F., "The Meter of 'Christabel,'" in *The Fred Newton Scott Anniversary Papers* (The University of Chicago Press, 1929), pp. 93-115.

2 His point, of course, is that Coleridge is not sufficiently concerned, as a highly serious poet should be, "with moral choices in their bearing on men's happiness or misery." Babbitt, Irving, "Coleridge and Imagination," *The Nineteenth Century and After*, CVI (1929), pp. 383-398.

3 Nitchie, Elizabeth, "The Moral of the *Ancient Mariner* Reconsidered," *Publications of the Modern Language Association of America*, XLVIII (1933), pp. 867-876.

superb work[1] wherein the ballad convention prevented the appearance of Coleridge's characteristic weaknesses of substance, purpose, and lack of virility, and stimulated the terse descriptive phrase, narrative speed, minute actuality, live self-restraint, and medieval glamour and remoteness tending toward the supernatural.[2] Although Wordsworth's idea of shooting the albatross was derived from Shelvocke's *Voyage* (1726), the inspiration of the poem probably came from two voyage-narratives, the *Letters of Saint Paulinus to Macarius* (1618) and T. James's *Strange and Dangerous Voyage* (1633).[3] (Poem greatly altered in second edition, 1800.)

Personal Poems

The Eolian Harp (1795). First poem important in substance is written in blank verse beautiful in cadence and easily as fluent as Milton's. His first characteristic[4] poem conceives universal life as automatous; two passages anticipate by three years Wordsworth's climax in *Tintern Abbey*. Coleridge thought it his "most perfect" poem.

Hymn Before Sun-Rise, in the Vale of Chamouni (1802). Poem overworked by exclamatory sentences is an enlargement of German stanzas by Frederike Brun. Conceives of Nature as the mouthpiece of the Deity.

Frost at Midnight (1798). The loving and lovable musing of a father beside the cradle of his child rises to a climax expressing Coleridge's conception of Unity.

---

1 The first version of the *Ancient Mariner*, colored by Chatterton's *Bristowe Tragedie* as shown by E. P. Ellinger, was greatly altered in the second edition (1800). Undoubtedly Coleridge's revisions were of importance in the achievement of artistic unity, in contrast to the "directionless melody" of *Kubla Khan*. McElderry, B. R., Jr., "Coleridge's Revision of 'The Ancient Mariner,'" *Studies in Philology*, XXIX (1932), pp. 68-94.

2 Stork, C. W., "The Influence of the Popular Ballad on Wordsworth and Coleridge," *Publications of the Modern Language Association of America*, XXIX; New Series, XXII (1914), pp. 299-326.

3 For the sources of the *Ancient Mariner* as well as *Kubla Khan*, consult Lowes, J. L., *The Road to Xanadu* (1930), who unfolds the mental processes which lead to creative production with inimitable subtlety, exhaustive learning, and precision. To the sources listed by Lowes, add Robert Paltock's *The Life and Adventures of Peter Wilkins, a Cornishman* (1751): see Moore, J. R., "Coleridge's Indebtedness to Paltock's *Peter Wilkins*," *Modern Philology*, XXXI (1933-1934), pp. 79-83.

4 Coleridge's most substantial Poems of Friendship or Conversation Poems include *The Eolian Harp, Reflections on having left a Place of Retirement, This Lime-Tree Bower, my Prison, Frost at Midnight, Fears in Solitude*, and *The Nightingale*. The qualities common to all are qualities of style and of subject. "These six poems are in blank verse of apparently artless simplicity, very delicate, however, and unsurpassed for flexible grace. Its music is of a kind rarely heard before, except now and then in brief passages in Elizabethan dramas and in Cowper's *Task*. The process of his thought, too, is quiet and natural. The poems all begin serenely, with some notice of the time and place, then generally pass into a mood of self-examination, and end with a 'return' or transposed repetition of the original cheerful tune and mood." See Harper, G. McL., "Gems of Purest Ray," in *Coleridge: Studies by Several Hands on the Hundredth Anniversary of his Death*, edited by Blunden, Edmund, and Griggs, E. L. (1934), p. 134 (pp. 133-147); also his "Coleridge's Conversation Poems," *The Quarterly Review*, CCXLIV (1925), pp. 284-298.

The Nightingale (1795; 1796). Designated by Coleridge himself as a Conversational Poem, it is a memorial to friendship, as is also *The Lime-Tree Bower, my Prison.*

Dejection: An Ode (1802). In no other poem does Coleridge give more complete expression to the transcendental principle mirrored in his soul.[1] Reflects, like *Youth and Age* (1823—1832), his disillusionment.[2] Possibly influenced by Sarah Hutchinson.[3]

Youth and Age (1823—1832). Has the charming "unearthly melody" of *Love* (the "Introduction to the Tale of the Dark Ladie") and of *Kubla Khan.* (Compare with Byron's *Stanzas for Music* and Browning's *Rabbi Ben Ezra.*)

Epitaph (1833; 1834).

> "O, lift one thought in prayer for S.T.C.;
> That he who many a year with toil of breath
> Found death in life, may here find life in death!"

Political Poems[4]

Religious Musings (1794). Desultory poem suffering from a turgid style and somewhat inconsistent thought gains value from the principles of Unity and Hartleian Necessity whereby Coleridge views the poorer features of the French Revolution as stages toward the final good. Eloquence occasionally appears in this poetical alloy of radicalism and faith: Coleridge answers the fiction that the war against the French had to be prosecuted for the sake of Christ and his principles.

Ode on the Departing Year (1796). Review of the year's events, addressed to Liberty, the Revolution, and England, prophesies the downfall of England because of its political sins.

France: An Ode (1798). Evoked by Napoleon's invasion of neutral Switzerland, Coleridge condemns the French as not obedient to the moral law and no longer representing the true spirit of liberty; with Kings, the French "mix . . . . in the low lust of sway." Energetic and eloquent lines, may, according to Harper, express Wordsworth's

---

1 Wordsworth's *Wye*, Coleridge's *Dejection*, and Wordsworth's *Intimations of Immortality* represent three stages in the movement of Hegelian dialectic: thesis, antithesis, synthesis. So contends Edwards, Oliver, *Wordsworth and Coleridge: Three Odes* (1932).

2 His sense of failure and sterility—of "nectar in a sieve"—found expression in several poems, among which are *Dejection, Youth and Age,* and *Work without Hope* (1825; 1828). Consult Moore, J. R., "The Mood of Pessimism in Nature Poetry: Bowles, Coleridge, and Arnold," *The Sewanee Review*, XXX (1922) p. 459 f. (pp. 454-461).

3 Raysor, T. M., "Coleridge and 'Asra,'" *Studies in Philology*, XXVI (1929); pp. 305-324. Whalley, George, *Coleridge and Sara Hutchinson and the Asra Poems* (1955).

4 Patton, Lewis, "Coleridge and Revolutionary France," *The South Atlantic Quarterly*, XXXI (1932), pp. 321-330; Sanders, C. R., "Coleridge as a Champion of Liberty," *Studies in Philology*, XXXII (1935), pp. 618-631.

opinion better than Wordsworth himself has done: Subject-matter and conclusion are similar, for example, to Wordsworth's sonnet called *Thought of a Briton on the Subjugation of Switzerland*. Ode seems to mark the end of Coleridge's impassioned defense of France, and the beginning of his conservative,[1] somewhat Burkite philosophy.

Fears in Solitude (1798). Following *France: An Ode*, it reiterates his abhorrence of French politics. Note the low-keyed blank verse until the moment (line 129) when he relinquishes his pacifism and lashes out at the French. Notwithstanding the dissimilarity in subject and in tone, the general structure is not unlike Wordsworth's later-composed *Tintern Abbey*. After *Fears in Solitude*, Coleridge remained cool to French politics.

Drama

The Fall of Robespierre (1794). Act I by Coleridge; II and III by Southey. Drama, obviously influenced by Shakespeare, not only tends to rhetorical declamation but in portraying the type rather than the individual fails to accomplish the aim of developing the chief characters. (Compare with Southey's *Wat Tyler* and Wordsworth's *The Borderers*.)

Wallenstein (1799—1800). Excellent poetic translation in blank verse of *The Piccolomini* and *Wallenstein's Death*, the last two parts of Schiller's historical trilogy.

Remorse (c. 1798; 1813). Tragedy in blank verse is a dignified endeavor to show the struggle of human volition—a soul's progress towards remorse.[2] Inappropriate diction, loose prosody, improbable plot, action stagnated by protracted dialogue. But redeemed by lack of bombast, by several beautiful passages, and, above all, by an attempt to present a motivated action that is spiritual. Influenced by Shakespeare, Schiller, and the Gothic drama. (In its earlier form, it was called *Osorio*, two scenes of which appeared in the *Lyrical Ballads*.)

Zapolya (1817). Romantic tragedy in imitation of Shakespeare's *Winter's Tale* (note, for example, the twenty-year interval between the first and second acts). Has fewer of the Gothic trappings found in *Remorse*, and its less unbelievable plot is better constructed. Indebted also to Shakespeare's *As You Like It*, *Cymbeline*, and *The Tempest*.

---

1 Hearnshaw, F. J. C., "Coleridge the Conservative," *The Nineteenth Century and After*, CXVI (1934), pp. 104-113.

2 It was through Byron's influence that *Remorse* was acted at the Drury Lane Theatre in 1813. Yet he cruelly satirizes Coleridge in *Don Juan*, I, XCI, 7, 8; CCX, 2-4; III, XCIII, 5-8; while Coleridge himself made several slighting remarks.

Periodicals

Coleridge contributed to several periodicals, including *The Morning Chronicle* (1793—1795), *The Morning Post* (1798—1802), and *The Courier* (1817--1812). More important are—

The Watchman (1796). Failed after ten numbers had been issued from March 1 to May 13, 1796. Alienated both the orthodox and the unorthodox by mocking at their beliefs.

The Friend (1809—1810; book form 1818). Twenty-seven numbers in a period of eight months brought reader-contact with the general results of German philological science and metaphysics. Often said to mark a turning-point in the spiritual and intellectual progress of English letters.

Prose

Biographia Literaria (1817). Rambling literary biography containing some autobiographical material, and much on philosophy, religion, politics, literature, and criticism.[1] He discusses, in the main, such men as Kant, Fichte, and Schelling, but its most important parts are the "Preface" to *Lyrical Ballads* and Chapters IV, XVII, XVIII, XIX, and XX. The last seven chapters of the book abound in ideas and reveal his critical powers. Neither Longinus nor Aristotle, perhaps, has left a more satisfactory treatise on the nature of poetry.

Aids to Reflection (1825). Philosophical treatise in the form of almost fourscore aphorisms or propositions followed by comments, endeavors chiefly to harmonize the tenets of orthodox Christianity with Coleridgean transcendental philosophy. Principal philosophical doctrine advanced is the distinction between Reason (*i.e.,* the Kantian logical faculty) and Understanding (*i.e.,* not the logical faculty, but "illumination" or "the moral sense").[2] His most popular volume, welcomed as a support of traditional doctrines, may represent his most concentrated philosophical, if somewhat formless and dogmatic work.

Anima Poetae (1895). Collection of aphorisms and reflections edited from his unpublished notebooks.[3]

Confessions of an Inquiring Spirit (1840). J. M. Robertson declares this to be Coleridge's "most seminal work."

---

1 Though not of the highest excellence, yet Coleridge's *Biographia Literaria* ranks among the few best books of criticism in English. J. M. Murry is right in his insistence that the valuable part is the critical appreciation of Wordsworth's poetry, not that on poetic diction.

2 Potter, Stephen, *Coleridge and S. T. C.* (1935), p. 175 *ff*.

3 *The Road to Xanadu* by J. L. Lowes "makes clear that the richest field for future students of Coleridge's writings is to be found in the note-books, the unpublished letters, and the marginalia." Coburn, Kathleen, ed., *The Notebooks of Samuel Taylor Coleridge* (I, 1957).

Letters. Illuminate the laughter and sadness of his life. Prolific in suggestion. Style varies from the self-conscious and painstaking to the hastily-written and spontaneous.[1]

Robert Southey, 1774—1843, poet, miscellaneous writer.[2] Son of a Bristol linen-draper. At Westminster School (1788—1792), from which he was expelled for a precocious essay protesting against school-flogging as an inducement to study. Denied admittance at Christ Church College, he finally gained entrance to Balliol College, Oxford. Joined Coleridge in his Pantisocratic Scheme (p. 454). Secretly married Edith Fricker, sister of Coleridge's wife; after 1809 Southey for a short time supported both families. Visited the Iberian peninsula (1795—1796; 1800—1801). Henceforth dedicated himself wholly to literature. Given an annuity of £160 a year by Charles Wynn (1797—*c.* 1807). Returned to England (1801). Settled at Greta Hall, Keswick (1803), where he resided for the remainder of his life. Through Wynn, secured a government pension of some £160 (1807), increased in 1835 to £300. Met Landor (1808), with whom he maintained a life-long friendship. Contributed to the *Quarterly Review* (1808—1839). Poet Laureate (1813—1843). Death of Mrs. Southey (1837), who for two years had been insane. Contracted a second marriage with an old correspondent, Caroline Bowles (1839). Died of softening of the brain. Monument to his memory erected in Crosthwaite churchyard, with an inscription by Wordsworth, who had succeeded him in the laureateship.

Unlike Jane Austen's reputation, Southey's has steadily declined since his death; and for the sake of a fading reputation that should be recorded, the *Outline-History* lists some of the better accomplishments among a voluminous outpouring that in collected form would fill more than a hundred volumes. Even in his own day few would buy his poetry. It possesses eloquence, rhetorical power, skill in versification, and ethical sentiment; but his ability seemed to be only second-rate. In *English Bards and Scotch Reviewers,* Byron declared that "the ballad-monger" Southey and epic-writer of such works as *Thalaba* and *Madoc* would forever reign—"the rival of Tom Thumb!"; and with Byron's other statement one is inclined to agree: Southey's epics "will be read when Homer and Virgil are forgotten—but not until then." Southey's prose, however, is fairly delightful; it is simple, idiomatic, transparent, and unaffected, representative of a kind of nineteenth-century Addisonian style. Finally, concerning his views as a thinker, Southey always adhered to the Godwinian conception of the perfectibility of man and society through joint endeavor; and, although like Wordsworth and

---

1 Griggs, E. L., ed., *Collected Letters of Samuel Taylor Coleridge* (Four vols., 1956-1959).

2 Dowden, E., *Southey* (1902); Lounsbury, T. R., in *Proceedings, Amer. Acad. Arts & Letters,* II (1914); Haller, W., *Early Life of Robert Southey* (1917); Simmons, J., *Southey* (1945); Carnall, G., *Robert Southey and His Age* (1960); Cabral, A., ed., *Journals of a Residence in Portugal 1800-1801 and a Visit to France* (1960).

Coleridge, he began as a Revolutionist and ended as a Tory, he remained a reformer in the midst of his Jacobinism and a radical in the midst of his Toryism.[1]

POETRY

Long Poems

*Thalaba the Destroyer** (1801). First example of his series of epics or cycle of poetic mythologies is a long narrative poem influenced by Gray's odes, Macpherson's *Ossian,* and Landor's *Gebir.* According to Southey, Thalaba is a male Joan of Arc—a hero of single purpose, of complete faith in himself, and of strict adherence to his duty. As a whole, the narrative style is mediocre, and the moral improbable. Its metrical innovations, where Southey manages the pauses with great skill, influenced Shelley's *Queen Mab.*

*Madoc** (1794—1799; 1805). Blank-verse poem of great length (forty-five books) concerning the supposed adventures of a Welsh prince of the twelfth century among the Aztecs of America.[2] It not impossibly influenced the Welsh atmosphere of Tennyson's *Idylls.*

The Curse of Kehama†** (1810). Probably the best of his longer works, sonorous of phrase and complicated of stanza.

*Roderick, the last of the Goths** (1814). Blank-verse poem, suggested by his love of Spanish lore, marks a higher development of Southey's ethical ideal.

Short Poems

Lyrics include *My Days Among the Dead Are Past,* a poem descriptive of his library and the placid love of a bibliolater, and *The Holly-tree.* Among his ballads are *The Inchcape Rock, Bishop Hatto, The Old Woman of Berkeley, The Well of St. Keyne. The Devil's Thoughts,* a humorous satirical poem by Coleridge and Southey, was later imitated by both Shelley and Byron; while *The Old Man's Comforts* was wittily parodied by Lewis Carroll in "Father William" in *Alice in Wonderland.* Other poems include the *Tale of Paraguay,* a narration in Spenserian stanzas; *The Cataract of Lodore,* one of the best sustained purely onomatopoetic poems in the language; *Donica,* which combined two stories found in Thomas Heywood's *Hierarchies of the Blessed Angels;* and *All for Love, or A Sinner well saved,* based on a story in the life of St. Basil.

---

1 Haller, William, "Southey's Later Radicalism," *Publications of the Modern Language Association of America,* xxxvii; New Series, xxx (1922), pp. 281-292; Cobban, Alfred, *Edmund Burke and the Revolt against the Eighteenth Century* (1929), *passim.*

2 *Madoc* reflects in a measure the influence of Coleridge, of Southey's pantiosocratic ideas, and of Southey's stay in the Iberian peninsula in 1795-1796 and 1800-1801, according to Wright, H. G., "Three Aspects of Southey," *The Review of English Studies,* ix (1933), pp. 37-46.

† * **Explanation of symbols immediately precedes Chapter XV.**

Battle Poems

The Battle of Pultowa, an "invective ode"[1]; *The Poet's Pilgrimage,* anticipating the period of disillusionment following the Napoleonic Wars; *The Battle of Blenheim,*† showing not only that soldiers know not for what they fight but also that no good results from war; and *Joan of Arc*† (1793; 1796), an epic purporting to deal with the Europe of the fifteenth century but palpably a tribute to the spirit of freedom and fraternity that had reawakened in France.

Laureate Pieces

Funeral Song, for the Princess Charlotte of Wales, a stately expression of grief in excellent verse; and *A Vision of Judgment* (1821), an impotent apotheosis of George III in hexametric verse, although its exordium is not without beauty; in the preface Southey's homily on "The Satanic School" (a term first used by him, and an unmistakable hit at Byron) provoked Byron's satire (p. 470).

Dramas

The Fall of Robespierre (1794), written with Coleridge (see p. 460); and *Wat Tyler* (1794; 1817), surreptitiously published, was attacked in the House of Commons for its somewhat crude republican enthusiasm.

PROSE

Biographies

Life of Nelson† (1813), an expansion of an article in the *Quarterly Review* of February, 1810. Impressionistic sketch defective in its understanding of naval tactics and bigoted in its discussion of personalities, but a masterpiece because of the beauty and force of Nelson's character; despite its biased judgments, misinterpretation of motives, and false perspective, is the first work on naval history since Hakluyt's *Principal Navigations* (Vol. 1, p. 148) to be accepted without question as a classic.[2] Almost as good a model for the short life is the *Life of John Wesley* (1820).

Historical Works

History of Brazil† (1810—1819), an enormous fragment of facts, part of a contemplated vast project to be entitled the *History of Portugal; History of the Peninsular War*† (1822—1832); and *Lives of the British Admirals* (1833—1840), where his estimate of the Viking character is a notable achievement. As Dowden has said, history as written by Southey is narrative rendered spiritual by moral ardor.

---

1 Wright, H. G., "Southey's Relations with Finland and Scandinavia," *Modern Language Review,* XXVII (1932), p. 161 (pp. 148-167).

2 *Southey's Life of Nelson,* edited by Callender, Geoffrey (1922).

† * Explanation of symbols immediately precedes Chapter XV.

Translations

Southey revised the old translation of *Amadis of Gaul* (1803), preserving the chivalric spirit of the original, and that of *Palmerin of England* (1807). His chief translation is the *Chronicle of the Cid* (1808), which included in its notes a translation of three ballads, *La Mañana de San Juan*, *Paseábase el Rey moro*, and *Moro Alcaide, Moro Alcaide*. He also translated at least two other Spanish ballads, *No con azules tahalíes* and *Abenámar, Abenámar*.

Letters

Letters written during a Short Residence in Spain and Portugal (1797); *Letters from England* (1807), supposedly written by the young Don Manuel Alvarez Espriella, gives light sketches of English landscape, life, and manners of the times; and, finally, Southey's extensive and excellent *Letters* present the truer Southey, on the whole a loyal and tenderhearted man.

Other Prose Writings

Journal of a Tour in Scotland in 1819,[1] which shows an alert observation of social and economic conditions, as do Southey's *Sir Thomas More: or, Colloquies on the Progress and Prospects of Society* (1829), and *Essays, Moral and Political* (1832). *The Doctor, &c.* (1834—1847), an unfinished rambling miscellany, like his *Omniana, or Horae Otiosiores* (1812), in which Dowden finds much of genial spirit and meditative wisdom, and in which Lounsbury finds ghostly facetiousness and bastard wit.

George Gordon Byron, Sixth Baron, Fifth Lord Byron of Newstead, 1788—1824, poet.[2] Son of "Mad Jack Byron," a libertine, and Catherine Gordon of Gight, who alternately caressed and abused her congenitally "lame brat."[3] Became heir-presumptive (1794). Succeeded to the title (1798). Educated at Harrow (1801—1805), where for one year he suffered from a love-affair with Mary Anne Chaworth, probably his only real love. Trinity College, Cambridge (1805—1808). Member of the House of Lords (1809).[4] Grand tour through Spain, Portugal, Italy, and the Balkans (1809—1811), addressing *Maid of Athens, Ere We Part* to Theresa Macri. In England had a notorious

---

1 *Journal of a Tour in Scotland in 1819*, edited by Herford, C. H. (1929). For an excellent example of Southey's understanding of economic problems, read his discussion of Robert Owen's scheme (pp. 263-265).

2 Calvert, W. J., *Byron* (1935).

3 Kemble, James, "Byron: His Lameness and Last Illness," *The Quarterly Review*, CCLVII (1931), pp. 231-243.

4 Byron was a keen critic of contemporary politics. See Raymond, D. N., *The Political Career of Lord Byron* (1924).

intrigue with Lady Caroline Lamb. Married Anne Isabella Milbanke (1815), who bore him a daughter named Ada, and who a year after marriage separated from him on the official ground of incompatibility—but, according to Mrs. Beecher Stowe, actually because of Anne's discovery of an incestuous relationship between Byron and his half-sister, Mrs. Augusta Leigh.[1] Left England, never to return (1816).[2] Passed some time with the Shelleys in Switzerland. Settled at Venice (1817–1819), where, in addition to keeping a virtual harem, he formed a connection with Claire Clairmont, Mary Shelley's stepsister, who bore him Allegra.[3] Began liaison with Teresa, Countess Guiccioli (1819), who until his death was his common-law wife.[4] Moved to Ravenna (1819–1821), to Pisa (1821), and to Genoa (1822). Death of Allegra (1822). Set out to join the Greek revolutionists (1823). Died of fever at Missolonghi (1824).[5]

Byron's weaknesses are many—affectation, insincerity, contempt for propriety, colossal egotism, world-weariness, careless form; no theatrically effective dramas, few genuinely passionate lyrics; tendency to rhetorical oratory and rebellious rhetoric; a veering away from deep character-study and profound intellectuality. Yet his virtues are many; tuneful lyrics, vigorous narrative, dignified dramas; lordly treatment of nature, elemental sweep and grandeur, naturalness of expression, humor, power of scathing satire. Byron the self-assertive, Byron the satirist and observer, Byron the liberator: no modern man except Shakespeare and Goethe, declares Oliver Elton, has affected the spirit of poetry more. One reason for *Le Byronisme* in France, *Der Byronismus* in Germany, and their counterparts in other Continental countries is that the bombastic and spacious rhetoric of Byron lends itself more readily to translation than do Keatsian estheticism and Wordsworthian transcendentalism.

---

1 Hewitt, E. P., (1) "Byron and Astarte," *The National Review*, LXXVI (1920-1921), pp. 551-554; (2) "An Answer to *Astarte*," *The National Review*, LXXVIII (1921), pp. 218-230; and Maurois, Andre, *Byron* (1930), p. VI *f.* (pp. v-x); Knight, G. W., *Lord Byron's Marriage* (1957).

2 For his life from March, 1812, to April, 1816—when he left England—see Du Bos, Charles (translated by Mayne, E. C.), *Byron and the Need of Fatality* (1932).

3 Paston, George, "New Light on Byron's Loves," *The Cornhill Magazine*, CL (1934), pp. 129-144, 2 7-276. George Paston also discusses Byron's other loves—Mary Chaworth Musters, "the Bright Morning Star of Annesley"; Mrs. Spencer Smith, the "Fair Florence" of *Childe Harold;* Lady Frances Wedderburn Webster, the Zuleika of *The Bride of Abydos;* Lady Caroline Lamb; Lady Falkland; Madame de Staël; Miss Mercer Elphinstone; Lady Melbourne; and Anne Isabella Milbanke, "the Princess of Parallelograms." See *The Cornhill Magazine*, CLXIX (1934), pp. 385-400, pp. 513 527, pp. 641-655; CL (1934), pp. 1-16, pp. 129-144, pp. 257-276.

4 E. C. Mayne has endeavored to show that the influence of Teresa Guiccioli upon Byron has been very much exaggerated. See her *Byron* (1924), pp. 322-339, p. 340 *ff.*

5 Sir Philip Sidney died a martyr to Dutch independence; Byron, to Greek. As Henson says, "Zutphen may stand with Missolonghi in the record of Freedom." (See Vol. 1, p. 139.) Consult Pemberton, W. B., "Byron in the Field," *The Fighting Forces*, I (1924), pp. 265-274; Menardos, Simos (translated by A. A. P.), "Byron and Greece," *The Poetry Review*, XV (1924), pp. 211-220; Nicolson, Harold, *Byron: The Last Journey* (1924); Raymond, D. N., *The Political Career of Lord Byron* (1924), pp. 191-315.

Early Period (1807—1812)

Hours of Idleness (1807). Collection of poems on trivial subjects of personal interest. Juvenile verse imitative of such poets as Pope and Burns, and representative of school-exercise translations from Greek and Latin. Banal sentiment, thin expression.

English Bards and Scotch Reviewers (1809). Neoclassical satiric poem in eighteenth-century heroic couplets occasioned by Henry Brougham's sharp criticism in the *Edinburgh Review* on *Hours of Idleness,* over which this work is an improvement. Like *The Dunciad,* after which it is modelled, it is a splenetic satire chiefly pillorying literary people. Of two-fold importance: it is the first to protest against W. L. Bowles's criticism[1] of Pope's morals, and it also reveals the day's antagonism to the so-called Lake School of Poets: Wordsworth is tedious, Coleridge is a half-wit, and Southey—may God help him, and his readers, too.[2] Satiric verse atones for its lack of restraint and its prejudices. Later, Byron recanted his unjust criticisms.

Childe Harold's Pilgrimage† (Cantos I and II, 1812; III, 1816; IV, 1818).[3] Noblest panoramic poem in our literature is a diffuse diaristic travelogue or guide-book lacking in structural unity but effective in splendor of diction, force of Spenserian stanza, rapidity of movement, and sharpness of impact. First two cantos show looseness of phrase and careless choice of words; but also an inexhaustible ingenuity of rime, picturesque descriptions, passionate energy, and spirited sketches tinged with romantic melancholy. The third is a great Nature canto, more varied in its imagery and more sustained in its flow of verse. No finer poem on war has been written than the Waterloo stanzas. The fourth canto, avoiding the "metaphysics" of the preceding ones, is loose in structure, but perfect in its sincerity. The last two cantos are firmer in description and deeper in tone than the first two. The "Byronic hero" emerges as a man sated with the world, who, disappointed and disillusioned, mysteriously moody and pleasantly miserable, defiant and stained with crime, roams from place to place in an endeavor to flee from himself.

Romantic Tales in Verse (1813-1816)

*The Giaour** (1813). Melodramatic tale told episodically by a Turkish fisherman and finally by the Giaour himself. Is not without some narrative power, although its stringiness may have been in-

---

1 Rennes, J. J. Van, *Bowles, Byron and the Pope-Controversy* (1927). What should also be noted is that Hazlitt seems to be the only other romanticist of the age who defended the poetry of Pope.

2 Note the paradox: Byron, a romantic poet, perversely attacks the Romantic school and defends the school of Pope.

3 The second edition of *Childe Harold* included "And thou art dead, as young and fair," a masterpiece of sorrow, the noblest of his Thyrza poems.

† * Explanation of symbols immediately precedes Chapter XV.

fluenced by the careless structure of Samuel Rogers's *The Voyage of Columbus,* conjectured to be fresh in Byron's mind. Apparently influenced by the verse of *Christabel.*

The Bride of Abydos* (1813). Anecdotic tale somewhat more pleasant to read than his other romantic tales in verse, although still containing brazen rhetoric.[1]

The Corsair* (1814). Three cantos elaborate in character-sketching and even more so in declamation. Note the return to the heroic couplet. Like *Lara,* is said to have been based on the career of Jean Laffite (*c.* 1780—*c.* 1825), American buccaneer.

Lara* (1814). Narrative poem in heroic couplets continuing the tale related in *The Corsair.* Not the theatrical falseness of the story should be most observed but the character of Lara, in which one catches glimpses of Byron himself. Reminiscent of the tone of Pope's *Iliad.*

The Siege of Corinth (1816). Poetical version of the siege of 1715, poor in workmanship and splendid in descriptive energy. Versification approaches the irregular *Christabel.*

Parisina† (1816). Best of his early group of tales, simple in plot, precise in development, dialogic in form, sincere if romantic in pathos. Founded on a passage in Gibbon's *Antiquities of the House of Brunswick;* the Azo of the poem corresponds in the main with Nicholas III of Ferrara (1338—1441).

Works Written in Exile (1816—1819)

Childe Harold's Pilgrimage†.   Cantos III and IV. See p. 467.

The Prisoner of Chillon† (1816). Poem is a beautifully written and an artistically finished monologue effective in its character-observation, vivid incident, and elegiac ardor. Note the resonant poem, the "Sonnet on Chillon." Byron seems to have idealized François de Bonnivard, and to have made a somewhat theatrical attack on tyranny—but he avowed that he was not aware of the history of Bonnivard when he composed the poem.

The Dream† (1816). Inspired by his remembrance of a hopeless love for Mary Chaworth, the blank-verse poem tells in clear diction how his thoughts turned away from Miss Milbanke in the very hour of marriage. Note the bold last line. (Mary may have inspired *When We Two Parted* and *Stanzas to a Lady on Leaving England.*)

---

1 Garrod is inclined to believe in the incestuous relations between Byron and Augusta, pointing to *The Bride of Abydos,* a theme of incest wrested by Byron "to a kind of maladroit innocence," and to other works. Garrod, H. W., *Byron* (A lecture, 1924), p. 16.

† * Explanation of symbols immediately precedes Chapter XV.

Manfred (1817). Poem in dramatic form heedless of facts, of plot, and of the unities. Self-searching mood represents Byron's depth of despair, unconquerable pride, and defiance of the orthodox conception of sin. Original in the sense that it has no model, although parallels of his "witch drama" have been noted in *Faust, Mysterious Mother* (p. 404), *Remorse* (p. 460), *Queen Mab* (p. 475), and *Alastor* (p. 476). Note its Gothicism. With *Cain,* another drama of revolt, shocked the British public and earned Byron the fame of being the founder of the Satanic school of poetry.

The Lament of Tasso† (1817). Superb dramatic soliloquy in prison, founded on the legend of Torquato Tasso's passion for Leonora d'Este, and his subsequent imprisonment upon its discovery.

The Prophecy of Dante (1819). Dramatic soliloquy in *terza rima,* nobly prophesying the future liberation of Italy.

THE CLOSING YEARS (1819—1824)

A. Serio-Comic Narratives

Beppo† (1817). *Novella* or *fabliau* (see Vol. 1, p. 32) based on an anecdote is a dramatic, humorous, and arabesque record of his Venetian experiences. Forerunner of *Don Juan,* which, like the brilliant and sustained *Beppo,* found its model in J. H. Frere's *Whistlecraft.* In *Beppo* Byron first used the *ottava rima.*

Mazeppa (1819). Based on a passage in Voltaire's *Charles XII,* the poem tells a tale that is alive with swift action and romantic episodes.

Don Juan† (1819—1823). Humorous-realistic epic satire of sixteen cantos almost completely in *ottava rima.* The most devil-may-care poem in the language is an exhibition of social corruptions, a satire of British hypocrisy and cant, and especially of the European rulers' bungling, cruel business of government and war. Parenthetical divagations, deliberate bad rimes, lack of plan, descents to cheap fun, claptrap fiction, and even dullness are present. Felicitous description of nature; Zola-like scenes of shipwreck and war. Consummate handling of the *ottava rima.* Nimble observation and realistic rendering; flow of mocking wit and impudent vulgarity; spirit of gaiety and irony. Unity of gigantic torso achieved by the crust of rich humor and satire with which it is overlaid. Is the greatest informal satirical epic in its combination of length, variety, and quality.

The Island; or Christian and his Comrades (1823). Romance based partly on Bligh's *Narrative of the Mutiny of the Bounty,* and the

---

† * Explanation of symbols immediately precedes Chapter XV.

life of the mutineers on Tahiti.¹ Some excellent descriptive passages, notably of the waterfall. Masterly management of the decasyllabic couplet.

B. Satire

The Vision of Judgment† (1821). Satirical poem in *ottava rima* is a counterblast to Southey's *A Vision of Judgment* (p. 464). Lashed not only Southey and George III but also such romantic poets as Wordsworth and Coleridge. After *Don Juan*, is his greatest verse satire, joining caricature and burlesque to wit. Has been described as the most effective personal satire in the language, and possibly greater than any work by Dryden or Pope because of its wider range of feeling. Like *English Bards and Scotch Reviewers*, is in the tradition of eighteenth-century satire.

The Age of Bronze (1823). Political satire in heroic couplets directed primarily against the reactionary regulations of the Congress of Verona.

C. Tragic Drama²

Marino Faliero, Doge of Venice (1821). Unsuccessful historical tragedy based on facts and adhering to the unities. Vexatious style, slow motion, stock characters. (Venetian conspiracy is the same theme as that of Otway's *Venice Preserv'd*, p. 300.)

Sardanapalus* (1821). Poetic drama of the Sensualist-Hero pictured with strength and sympathy may be an *apologia* for Byron's life at Venice. Excellent passages on his hatred of war.

The Two Foscari (1821). Tragedy, adhering in the main to the historical facts, is motivated by social forces. According to his letter to the publisher Murray, Byron sought to show "suppressed passion": in *Marino Faliero*, the passion of outraged pride; in *Sardanapalus*, of voluptuousness.

Werner (1822). Best-acting tragedy retold from *Kruitzner, or The German's Tale* in Sophia and Harriet Lee's *Canterbury Tales*. Strong in its borrowed conception, but still an ineffective drama.

The Deformed Transformed (*c.* 1821; 1824). Ineffective fragmentary drama, although some point to the personal bitterness of the first act. Partly influenced by Goethe's *Faust* and Joshua Pickersgill's *The Three Brothers*.

---

1 For documented accounts in the form of fiction concerning the mutiny on the H. M. S. *Bounty* and subsequent events, read Nordhoff, Charles, and Hall, J. N., *Mutiny on the Bounty* (1932), *Men Against the Sea* (1934), and *Pitcairn's Island* (1934).

2 Chew, S. C., *The Dramas of Lord Byron* (1915).

† * Explanation of symbols immediately precedes Chapter XV.

D. Dramatic Mysteries

Cain: A Mystery (1821). Tragedy based largely on the Biblical narrative, except for the first and second acts. Audacious religious scepticism provoked a storm of opprobrium: *Cain* not only challenged the scriptural orthodoxy of Evangelical Christianity but also indicted the doctrine of Calvinistic fatalism and the Augustinian doctrine of original sin.[1] In spite of some vagueness and protraction, and its failure as a character-study, is on the whole Biblical in tone, compact of treatment, and majestic. The verve is not so conspicuous in *Heaven and Earth*.

Heaven and Earth (1821; 1823). Unfinished lyrical drama effective in its setting but with little distinction in its theme, founded on the text of *Genesis* VI,2: "And it came to pass . . . . That the sons of God saw the daughters of men that they *were* fair; and they took them wives of all which they chose." Only play in which no single actor dominates. Sometimes reminiscent of *Cain's* graphic features.

Miscellaneous Works

Epistle to Augusta (*c.* 1816; 1830). Tender, erotic piece. (Read, also, his *Stanzas to Augusta,* 1816.)

Fugitive Pieces (1806). Almost immediately suppressed when the Reverend J. T. Becher objected to an indecent stanza in *To Mary* and to the sensual tone of other parts.

The Waltz (1813). Unimportant satire on the dance imported from Germany. Has some mock-heroic features.

Hebrew Melodies (1815). Collection of short poems, many of them trifling. Includes some love-songs, but most of the pieces deal with scriptural subjects. Well known are (1) *The Destruction of Sennacherib,* which, based on the accounts in *2 Kings,* XVIII—XIX and *2 Chronicles,* XXXII, is quoted frequently for its spirited anapestic speed; and (2) *She Walks in Beauty,* inspired by a meeting with his cousin, Lady Wilmot Horton.

The Blues (1821; 1823). His only satire written in the form of a play and employing the anapestic couplet meter. Skit on literary coteries.

January 22: on this day I complete my thirty-sixth year (1824). Affecting verses ennobled by the spirit within him when assuming the leadership of the Greek expedition.

---

1 Brooke, Stopford, "Byron's 'Cain,'" *The Hibbert Journal,* XVIII (1919-1920), pp. 74-94.

Letters. Though occasionally artificial, are of singular excellence, and they incline one to believe that the traditional "Byronic pose" of Byron may depend more upon the opinions of others than upon Byron's actual character. The letters reveal flashing wit, naturalness, robustness, zest for life, good sense, and open sincerity; perhaps the real Byron may be found more in his letters than in his poetry.

Percy Bysshe Shelley, 1792—1822, poet.[1] Born at Field Place, Warnham, near Horsham, Sussex. At Sion House Academy (1802— 1804). At Eton (1804—1810), where his attitude against the despotism of custom (*e.g.*, against the traditional fagging system) and his secret scientific experiments at unseasonable hours helped earn him the name of "Mad Shelley" and "Shelley the Atheist,"[2] and where he developed a strong hatred of oppression. Went to University College, Oxford, and there met Thomas Jefferson Hogg (1810). Published *Original Poetry by Victor and Cazire* (1810) and *Posthumous Fragments of Margaret Nicholson* (1810). Both Shelley and Hogg expelled from Oxford in consequence of the little pamphlet entitled *The Necessity of Atheism* (1811), and for "contumacy in refusing to answer certain questions put to them." Eloped with sixteen-year-old Harriet Westbrook to save her from parental and scholastic tyranny, and married her at Edinburgh (1811).[3] Went to Ireland in an attempt to convert Catholics to atheism (1812). London (1813). Birth of daughter Ianthe (1813), so-called after the heroine of *Queen Mab*. Doubts having arisen of the validity of their marriage in Scotland, Shelley and Harriet re-married in London (1814), conjecturally so that his father could not declare the offspring of two minors to be illegitimate. Eloped with Mary Wollstonecraft Godwin, daughter of William Godwin (1814). Birth of Harriet's second child, Charles Bysshe Shelley (1814). Death of grandfather, Sir Bysshe Shelley, left him a large income (1815).

Birth of Mary's first child, who died a month later (1815). Birth of Mary's child, William Shelley (1816). Trip to Switzerland (1816), taking with them Claire Clairmont, Mary's half-sister, who wished to keep in close touch with Byron. Returned to London (1816). Suicide of Fanny Godwin (1816), who may have killed herself for love of Shelley. Harriet Shelley, who may have had an affair with another

---

1 Dowden, Edward, *The Life of Percy Bysshe Shelley* (1886), Bailey, Ruth, *Shelley* (1934); Grabo, Carl, *The Magic Plant* (1936); Grylls, R. G., *Mary Shelley* (1938).

2 By "atheist" the schoolmates at Eton probably meant one who memorably opposed the school authorities.

3 In October, 1811, Shelley went to London, leaving Harriet and Hogg in Edinburgh. Hogg's attempted seduction of Harriet is important only because henceforth Elizabeth Westbrook came to live with the Shelleys: it was Harriet's sister who seemed to make reconciliation in 1814 impossible.

man, was discovered drowned in the Serpentine (1861).[1] Legitimized by marriage his relations with Mary Godwin (1816). First meeting with Keats (1817). Deprived of the custody of Harriet's two children by a Chancery suit (1817). Birth of daughter Clara (1817). Left England in March, 1818, never to return. Arrived in Italy in April, where he spent the short remainder of his life. Death of Clara Shelley (1818). Death of William Shelley (1819). Birth of son, Percy Florence (1819). Platonic friendship with Teresa Emilia Viviani, whom he idealized for a time (1820—1821). To the Gisborne's house at Leghorn (1820). Arrival of Edward Williams and his wife Jane, for whom Shelley developed a Platonic attachment (1821), and by whom he was inspired to write "One word is too oft profaned" (1821) and *With a Guitar to Jane* (1822). Visits Byron at Ravenna (1821). Arrival of E. J. Trelawney at Pisa (1822).[2] The Shelleys and the Williamses moved to Casa Magni, near Lerici, on the Bay of Spezzia (1822). Shipwreck of Shelley's boat, the *Ariel*: Shelley and Williams drowned in the Bay of Spezzia (July 8, 1822). Body, originally buried in quicklime, was cremated a month later on the seashore in the presence of Trelawney, Byron, and Leigh Hunt, and the ashes were buried in the Protestant cemetery just outside the wall of Rome.[3]

In the longer works Shelley is strong neither in structural design nor in unity. The construction is loose, the outline is vague, and the purpose is often uncertain. Frequently, the metaphors are inappropriate and the descriptive passages meandering; even his ear fails him, as evidenced particularly by the "rocking-horse" rhythm of his juvenile verse. Not only are there occasional touches of morbidness and frequent patches of argumentative narrative; there are also a vagueness of expression and an obscurity of fancy. Yet through it all flashes the peculiar Shelleyan aspiration for abstract Good and abstract Beauty, and their magnificent embodiment. His lyric gift may be the purest in the whole range of English poetry—spontaneous music, ethereal beauty, unexcelled ideality. All-embracing enthusiasm for humanity, the supremacy of Reason over Passion, the ascription of moral evil to the desolating power of positive institutions, the doctrine of perfectibility,[4] and the conception of Love as the sole productive source of Good and the supreme agency for the regeneration of mankind,—are all reproduced in his revolutionary verse.

1 Read, Herbert, *In Defence of Shelley & Other Essays* (1936), p. 74 *ff.;* Houlden, W. H., "A Vindication of Shelley," *The Poetry Review,* XXIII (1932), pp. 129-138, 213-222.

2 Massingham, H. J., *The Friend of Shelley* (1930).

3 Liveing, Edward, "The Fate of a Great Lyric Poet," *Discovery,* III (1922), Part II, pp. 215-218.

4 Beach, J. W., "Latter-Day Critics of Shelley," *The Yale Review,* XI (1922), p. 730 (pp. 718-731).

ENGLAND (1810—1818)

Prose Romances

Zastrozzi (1810). "Terror" romance with its standard-creaking machinery.[1] Melodramatic approach to "sex." Observe not only Shelley's characteristic subordination of form to his interest in color and movement when giving bits of nature description, but also that in this work is first expressed the story of persecution that runs through all his work.

St. Irvyne; or The Rosicrucian (1811). Like *Zastrozzi,* is a fantastic prose romance in the style of Lewis's *The Monk* and Mrs. Radcliffe's works. Influenced by Godwin's *St. Leon* (p. 408).

Religious Scepticism

The Necessity of Atheism (1811). Two-page prose tract, compact of expression and revolutionary in spirit, argues against the existence of the Deity. Ends with the triumphant Q.E.D. of the geometricians. Led to his expulsion from Oxford University.

A Refutation of Deism (1814). Socratic essay developed in the form of a dialogue between Eusebes, a Christian, and Theosophus, a Deist, leads to the conclusion that there is no golden mean between accepting or rejecting the existence of the Deity. The notes to *Queen Mab* are often repeated verbatim.

Essay on Christianity (c. 1815). Fragmentary essay is an agnostic attack upon historic Christianity, the orthodox form as advocated by the churches. Does not attack the teachings of Jesus himself, whom he venerated.[2]

On the Punishment of Death (c. 1815). Unsuccessful attempt to differentiate between Necessity and Fatalism.[3]

Reform Pamphlets

An Address to the Irish People (1812). Pamphlet distributed in the streets of Dublin by Shelley and Harriet advocated Catholic emancipation and repeal of the Union Act. Like Godwin, is averse to forms of violence, urging that one should resist oppression by constitutional

---

1 The gothic elements in C. B. Brown's novels may have influenced Shelley's prose romances. Solve, M. T., "Shelley and the Novels of Brown," in *The Fred Newton Scott Anniversary Papers* (The University of Chicago Press, 1929), pp. 141-156. The American novelist's influence is also apparent in *The Revolt of Islam*: Sickels, Eleanor, "Shelley and Charles Brockden Brown," *Publications of the Modern Language Association of America*, XLV (1930), p. 1119 f. (pp. 1116-1128).

2 The purpose of the essay seems to be the vindication of Christ and his teaching from perversions imposed by the churches: Brooke, S. A., "Shelley's Interpretation of Christ and His Teaching," *The Hibbert Journal*, XVI (1917-1918), pp. 366-386.

3 Gingerich, S. F., *Essays in the Romantic Poets*, (1924), p. 221.

agitation, by developing a sense of fraternal sympathy, by power of mind and by reliance on truth and justice. Some principles derived from the Sermon on the Mount.

A Proposal for Putting Reform to the Vote Throughout the Kingdom (1817). Written under the pseudonym of "The Hermit of Marlowe," advocated a sensible method whereby it could be ascertained whether or not the majority of English people desired a reform in Parliament.

An Address to the People on the Death of the Princess Charlotte (1817). Inspired by the execution of three weavers on November 7, 1817, Shelley, while regretting the death of the Princess, emphasized the greater tragedy of the death of Liberty in England.

Early Poems

Queen Mab (1813). Immature and rhetorical if eloquent radical production influenced by Godwin,[1] Helvetius, and the French philosophers, by the Bible, and possibly by James Lawrence's *Empire of the Nairs*.[2] Irregular unrimed meter indebted to Southey's *Thalaba* (p. 463). As Grabo has stated, Shelley believes in Necessity,[3] but also in the Spirit of Nature and in the perfectibility of man. Poem, which Shelley later called "villainous trash," assails Christianity for professing love while inciting its zealots to religious intolerance, declaims in juvenile fashion against the corrupting influences of kings as well as priests, indicts the falsity of the world, and forecasts the Golden Age when Reason will be man's sole guide. Shelley's notes to this outspoken attack on Christianity, this plea for atheism and philosophic anarchism, were used in 1817 as evidence against him in the suit for the custody of his children.

The Celandine (1816; published 1925). Poem in which the celandine is a symbol of Wordsworth's failing power and increasing conservatism.

Hymn to Intellectual Beauty (1816). Platonic and transcendental ode. His conception of beauty, while indebted to Plato, yet is opposed to the great philosopher's idea: beauty, according to Shelley, emanates from a "necessitating Reality," which to him is Deity.[4] (Compare with Spenser's *Fowre Hymnes*, Vol. 1, p. 130.)

---

1 Sen, Amiyakumar, "Godwin and Shelley," *Journal of the Department of Letters* (University of Calcutta), xx (1930), Article i, pp. 1-123.

2 Graham, Walter, "Shelley and the *Empire of the Nairs*," *Publications of the Modern Language Association of America*, xl; New Series, xxxiii (1925), pp. 881-891.

3 Gingerich, S. F., *Essays in the Romantic Poets* (1924), "Shelley," pp. 195-239.

4 Gingerich, S. F., "The Conception of Beauty in the Works of Shelley, Keats, and Poe," *Essays and Studies in English and Comparative Literature*, By Members of The English Department of the University of Michigan, viii (1932), p. 170 (pp. 169-194); Zillman, L. J. ed., *Shelley's Prometheus Unbound: A Variorum Edition* (1959).

Alastor, or The Spirit of Solitude (1816). Formless, somewhat incoherent poem in blank verse crowded with a host of delicate and swiftly moving images condemns self-centered idealism, laments our kind of world, and pleads in behalf of human love. Main theme of the restless wandering of an idealist who meets with frustration may have its basis in sexual longing.[1] Its nature-pictures and adventurous wanderings are usually viewed as irrelevant to its stated intention.[2] Furthermore, it is often said to have a vein of unhealthful sentiment. Chief interest is its story of the inner life of a poet; chief glory, the ecstatic delight in wild scenery and the etherealized, sensuous beauty. ("Alastor" is Greek for "avenger.")

The Revolt of Islam, or Laon and Cythna (1817; 1818). Somewhat protracted, rambling, obscure symbolic epic in Spenserian stanzas, his first important poem, contained in its original form violent attacks on theism and Christianity, and also his first treatment of the incest motive. Unlike *Queen Mab,* preaches a bloodless revolution.[3] Shelley's most ambitious work suffers from incoherence, tedious action, moral instruction, and excess sweetness. Valued, however, for its sustained story of man's insurrection against tyranny, and for the glimpse of a golden age; for its autobiographical elements (Laon and Cythna may be Shelley and Mary); for his spirit of intellectual and impassioned energy; and for his conviction that Love, cosmic and uncompromising, alone can regenerate man and deliver humanity from the bondage of Institutions.

IN ITALY (1818—1822)

Dramas

Prometheus Unbound†* (1818—1819; 1820). Drama, featuring a series of soaring lyrics and sustained choruses, is one of the few great subtle philosophical poems in English; neo-Platonism is reconciled with the scientific speculation and the radical social philosophy of the day.[4] While difficult to establish the meaning of the symbolism, critical opinion recognizes Shelley's stately movement and sublime elevation. Has been interpreted not only as an attempt to reconcile science and religion but also as an attempt to unite the theory of good and evil of *The Revolt of Islam* with the necessitarian and naturalistic theories of *Queen*

1 Taylor, E. C., "Shelley as Myth-Maker," *The Journal of Abnormal Pyschology,* XIV (1919-1920), pp. 64-90.

2 For an analysis of an apparent inconsistency between the Preface and the poem, consult Havens, R. D., "Shelley's *Alastor,*" *Publications of the Modern Language Association of America,* XLV (1930), pp. 1098-1115.

3 Sen, Amiya Kumar, "Shelley and the French Revolution," *Journal of the Department of Letters* (University of Calcutta), XXII (1932), Article III, pp. 1-64.

4 Grabo, Carl, *Prometheus Unbound* (1935). See, also, the same author's *A Newton Among Poets* (1930)

† * Explanation of symbols immediately precedes Chapter XV.

Mab.[1] Prometheus is an ideal as well as an allegorical figure of progressive man's desire for intellectual light and spiritual liberty. Denounces the intolerance and tyranny of the Church. (The first three acts are complete in themselves; the fourth act, a hymn of rejoicing, was added as an afterthought.)

The Cenci (1819; first acted 1886). Realistic, brooding tragedy based upon a morbid and sordid Italian tale is primarily a drama of emotion rather than of character. Admixture of classical elements (unity of action, exclusion of comic relief), Gothic accoutrements (dark dungeons, lurid atmosphere), and romantic elements (emotional outpourings, hatred of injustice). Blank verse is wooden, soliloquies are protracted, action is halting, characterizations are warped, style is bleak. Influenced by Calderon's *El Purgatorio de San Patricio*[2] and by Shakespeare's *Macbeth*. Yet frequently accepted as the finest poetic drama since Shakespeare: underneath the austere verse smoulders an intensity of passion.

Hellas (1821; 1822). Lyrical drama in Greek dramatic form, modelled upon the *Persae* of Aeschylus. Inspired by the Greek declaration of independence from the Turkish yoke, Shelley unfolds the story of Salamis in terms of contemporary warfare, and makes a prophecy of Hellenic freedom. Negligible as drama, but widely praised for the beauty of its choruses. The preface recognizes that our laws, our literature, and our arts have their roots in Greece.

Charles the First (1822). Fragment of some eight hundred lines is full of steady power. First scene probably the best. *Cenci*-like use of blank verse. The Fool is fashioned after the fool in Calderon's *Cisma de Inglaterra* as well as in Shakespeare's *King Lear* (Vol. 1, p. 211).[3]

Short Humanitarian Poems

The Masque of Anarchy (1819). Occasioned by the so-called "Peterloo Massacre" on August 16, 1819, the main interest of the poem, which expresses Shelley's revolutionary political views and indicts Castlereagh's administration, lies in the incorporation of the thought into the *Philosophical View of Reform*.[4]

---

1 Both *Prometheus Unbound* and *Queen Mab* have been influenced not, only by Hollbach, Condorcet, and Godwin, but also by P. J. G. Cabanis. Kapstein, I. J., "Shelley and Cabanis," *Publications of the Modern Language Association of America*, LII (1937), pp. 238-243.

2 Madariaga, Salvador de, *Shelley & Calderon* (1920), pp. 3-48; Hespelt, E. H., "Shelley and Spain," *Publications of the Modern Language Association of America*, XXVIII (1923), pp. 890 f., 900 f., 903-905 (pp. 887-905).

3 White, N. I., "Shelley's *Charles the First*," *The Journal of English and Germanic Philology*, XXI (1922), pp. 431-441.

4 Walker, A. S., "Peterloo, Shelley and Reform," *Publication of the Modern Language Association of America*, XL; New Series, XXXIII (1925), pp. 128-164.

Song to the Men of England (1839). The Manchester Massacre on August 16, 1819, renewed Shelley's political enthusiasm.

England in 1819 (1819; published 1839). Sonnet sent by Shelley to Hunt with the statement: "I don't expect you to publish it, but you may show it to whom you please."

Ode to Liberty (1820). Hymned forth the birth of political freedom, occasioned by Colonel Rafael de Riego's revolt in January, 1820, and his proclamation of the liberal constitution of 1812. Note its prophetic ending.

Ode to Naples (1820; 1824). Inspired by the revolt in the kingdom of Naples against the absolute government of the Bourbon King Ferdinand.

Satires

Peter Bell the Third (1819; 1837). Satire on Wordsworth's poem (p. 447) lacks humor.

Oedipus Tyrannus, or Swell-foot the Tyrant (1820). Dramatic satire on George IV's matrimonial affairs. Extravagant speeches, outrageous characters, revolting setting. Note the striking conclusion. Many characters have their originals.[1] Demonstrated again, as did *Peter Bell the Third,* how Shelley watched developments in England.

Occasional Poems

Julian and Maddalo (1818; 1824). Interesting word-paintings of personalities and realistic touches occur in what proves to be much more than a conversation between Julian (Shelley) and Maddalo (Byron).[2] Important delineation of Byron's baffling personality.

A Letter to Maria Gisborne (1820; 1824). Wise and humorous poetical letter written in Maria Gisborne's house at Leghorn while she and her family were visiting England. While not as perfect in its poetical treatment of familiar things as is *Julian and Maddalo,* it is interesting for its recurrence to the theme of liberation. (The "White Snowdonian antelope" is Jane Gryffydh, whom T. J. Peacock married.)

Epipsychidion (1821; 1822). No other poem is more autobiographical than this, addressed to Teresa Emilia Viviani, the story of whose wronged life fired a rapturous outburst in favor of free love, both Platonic and passionate. Nor is any other poem a more natural expression of his genius. This greater hymn to Intellectual Beauty is,

---

1 White, N. I., "Shelley's Swell-Foot the Tyrant In Relation To Contemporary Political Satires," *Publications of the Modern Language Association of America,* XXXVI; New Series, XXIX (1921), pp. 332-346.

2 Clarke, I. C., *Shelley and Byron* (1934).

as Shelley told Gisborne, "an idealized history of my life and feelings, and a kind of *Vita Nuova*": it is another example of his nympholeptic psychology. (The title means "a little soul in addition to a soul" or "a soul within a soul.")

Adonais: An Elegy on the Death of John Keats (1821). Supreme threnody in the Spenserian stanza modelled on the lament of Aphrodite over the body of Adonis by the poet Bion, and on the *Lament for Bion* by Moschus. Is a lament for himself as well as for Keats, and is partly responsible for the false impression that Keats's premature death is ascribable to the bludgeoning criticism of the reviewers of his works—an impression that Byron helped perpetuate by describing Keats as killed by one critique and snuffed out by an article (*Don Juan*, XI). Possibly no person completely understands the end of *Adonais*, although its conclusion is prophetic of Shelley's own doom. Artificial classical atmosphere lost sight of in its unexampled rhythm and emotional warmth, its striking imagery and lofty conceptions. (Compare this pastoral elegy with Spenser's *Astrophel*, Vol. 1, p. 129; with Milton's *Lycidas*, Vol. 1, 179; and with Arnold's *Thyrsis*, p. 571.)

Poems, Chiefly Lyrics

Among his lyrics, in addition to those listed below, are *Mutability* ("We are as clouds that veil the midnight moon,"—1816), *Ozymandias* (1818), *The Cloud* (1820), *To a Skylark* (1820), *Time Long Past* (1820; 1870), *Time* (1821; 1824), *The Indian Serenade* (1822), *Song* ("Rarely, rarely comest thou,"—1824), *To*—("Music, when soft voices die,"—1824), *Remembrance* (1824), *To*— ("One word is too oft profaned,"—1821; 1824), and *A Dirge* (1824).

Lines Written among the Euganeum Hills (1818; 1819). Lyric memorable for its transition from the real to the ideal.[1] Note the prophetic vision of his own fate. Written after a day's wandering among the hills about the villa at Este lent to Shelley by Byron in 1818.

Stanzas Written in Dejection near Naples (1818). Beautiful lyric that in the penultimate stanza contains a prophetic hint.

Rosalind and Helen (1819). Interesting for its autobiographical elements and for the similarity of Lionel's character to Shelley's own.

Ode to the West Wind (1819; 1820). The result of a definite personal experience.[2] Exemplifies his pagan worship of nature, and his myth-making faculty. Concludes with a paean that revolution is still vital. In *terza rima*.

The Sensitive Plant (1820). Lyrical apologue that leans to the belief that Beauty is permanent and Life is unreal, just as Keats's *Ode*

---

1 Campbell, O. W., *Shelley and the Unromantics* (1924), p. 231.
2 Pancoast, H. S., "Shelley's *Ode to the West Wind*," *Modern Language Notes*, xxxv (1920), pp. 97-100.

on a Grecian Urn emphasizes the evanescence of the material life and the perpetuity of the imaginative. Appealing descriptions.[1]

The Cloud (1820). Exquisite lyric exemplifying his myth-making power.[2]

Ode to a Skylark (1820). None of his poems exceeds this ode in popularity.

The Witch of Atlas (1820). Not a lyric. Perhaps his most obscure poem, yet in this poetic fantasy appear glowing expression and exquisite imagery. To Keats, the Witch is Beauty; to E. E. Kellett, she is Creative Imagination; to Grabo, the earthly embodiment of love, or Venus, who is the creative power of the universe.[3] In *ottava rima*.

To Night (1821; 1824). Exquisite in its imagery.

O World! O Life! O Time! (1821). This lament, pitched in a low lyricism, is emotionally and musically perfect. Lafcadio Hearn considered it the most perfect poetry in all English lyrical verse.

When the Lamp Is Shattered (1822; 1824). Stanzas of "piercing desolation," the whole movement of which is "that of a love swaying down, so to speak, toward insensibility. In other poems, such as *To a Skylark*, the same love spirals upward, in swift, ecstatic joyance."[4]

The Triumph of Life (1822). A great fragment based upon a dream. While its immediate suggestion may be found in Petrarch's *Trionfi*, yet its style seems influenced more by Dante.[5] One phrase echoes Milton's description of Death. In *terza rima*.

Prose

A Philosophical View of Reform (*c.* 1819; 1920). Prose essay strikes a rather conservative note concerning Utopia, emphasizing moderation, human sympathy, and peaceful means for the extension of political democracy.

A Defense of Poetry (1821; 1840). Detailed, direct, penetrative, unfinished reply in Peacock's *The Four Ages*.[6] Though hurriedly composed, the polemical fragment is a majestically-languaged and pro-

---

1 Francis Thompson's fine essay on Shelley praises *The Sensitive Plant, The Cloud*, and other poems. Chapman raises two objections: see Chapman, J. A., *Papers on Shelley, Wordsworth, and Others* (1929), pp. 9-12 (pp. 1-18).

2 Kalâpi, another great poet of despondency and sorrow, wrote *Kamalin or The Lotus* in imitation of Shelley's *The Cloud*. Desai, H. M., "Shelley and Kalâpi," *East & West*, xv (1916), pp. 632-646.

3 Grabo, Carl, *The Meaning of "The Witch of Atlas"* (1935).

4 Elliott, G. R., "How Poetic Is Shelley's Poetry?" *Publications of the Modern Language Association of America*, XXXVII; New Series, XXX (1922), p. 319 (pp. 311-323).

5 Kuhns, Oscar, "Dante's Influence on Shelley," *Modern Language Notes*, XIII (1898), pp. 161-165 (cols. 321-329).

6 For a discussion of Peacock's article and Shelley's *Defence*, see *Peacock's Four Ages of Poetry*, edited by Brett-Smith, H. F. B., Introduction, pp. VII-XXV.

foundly-treated thesis on the struggle of Spirit and Matter. Influenced by Plato, and by Sidney's *Defence* or *Apologie* (Vol. 1, p. 139). Not until 1910 was the original draft printed.

Letters.[1] While deficient in Walpole's piquancy, Gray's urbanity, Byron's impulsiveness, and Keats's naturalness, they are, in R. B. Johnson's opinion, among the finest in the language—passionate and logical, wrathful and dignified, argumentative and aesthetic. His letters constitute the most important primary source for any biography of Shelley: the more one reads the letters and journals, the more one believes that the real Shelley is not yet known to the world, and that our picture of Shelley may be the etherealized creation of the biographer.[2]

John Keats, 1795—1821, poet.[3] Son of the Headkeeper of the *Swan and Hoop* livery-stable, Finsbury Pavement, London. At the Clarke School, Enfield (1803—1811), where began his friendship with Charles Cowden Clarke. Father dies of a fall from his horse (1804). Mother marries William Rawlings, stable-keeper at the *Swan and Hoop* (1805), from whom she was soon separated. Mother dies of tuberculosis (1810); from her Keats may have inherited his tendency to consumption. Apprenticed to Thomas Hammond, apothecary-surgeon at Edmonton (1811). Student in Guy's and St. Thomas's Hospitals (1815). Next year meets Hunt (1816), through whom he met Haydon,[4] Shelley, Hazlitt, and Wordsworth, whose *The Excursion* he thought one of the three wonders of the age. Upon passing examinations, received certificate from Guy's and St. Thomas's (1816). Abandoned the medical profession. Publishes *Poems, by John Keats* (1817). Winters at Hempstead (1817—1818). Publishes *Endymion: A Poetic Romance* (1818). Takes walking trip with Charles Brown into northern England, Scotland, and Ireland (1818). Upon his return finds himself attacked as a member of the "Cockney School of Poetry" in an article, probably by J. G. Lockhart, appearing in *Blackwood's Magazine*. Meets and falls in love with Fanny Brawne (1818), and at Christmas the two are betrothed. To her he addressed the *Ode to Fanny,* and two sonnets.

1 *The Complete Works of Percy Bysshe Shelley,* edited by Ingpen, Roger, and Peck, W. E. (1926), Vols. VIII-X; *The Letters of Percy Bysshe Shelley,* selected by Johnson, R. B. (1929); *Shelley's Lost Letters to Harriet,* edited by Hotson, Leslie (1930); White, N. I., "Shelley's Biography: The Primary Sources," *Studies in Philology,* XXXI (1934), pp. 472-486.

2 For example: "One thing is certain, that the traditional likenesses of the mystic Little Lord Fauntleroy popularised by his sentimental family after his death were not accurate. Shelley was as much Demon as he was Angel and looked it." Leslie, Shane, "The Lost Bust of Shelley," *The Landmark,* XI (1929), p. 671 (pp. 671-674); Pottle, F. A., *Shelley and Browning* (1923), p. 7 *f.* (pp. 1-3).

3 Evans, B. I., *Keats* (1934); *Complete Poems and Selected Letters,* edited by Thorpe, C. DeW. (1933); Finney, C. L., *The Evolution of Keats's Poetry* (Two vols., 1936); Rollins, H. E., ed., *Letters of John Keats* (2 vols., 1958); *ibid., The Keats Circle: Letters and Poems* (1948-1955).

4 On the whole, Haydon's influence upon Keats was wholesome. Olney, Clarke, "John Keats and Benjamin Robert Haydon." *Publications of the Modern Language Association of America,* XLIX (1934), pp. 258-275. With Haydon one should always associate Keats's excellent sonnets. *To Haydon* (1817) and *On Seeing the Elgin Marbles* (1817).

Illness and financial difficulties (1818). First attack of consumption (February, 1820). Joins the Hunts at Mortimer Terrace (1820). Publishes *Lamia, Isabella, The Eve of St. Agnes, and Other Poems* (1820). More hemorrhages (1820). Two months later is back in Hempstead, nursed by Mrs. Brawne and Fanny (August, 1820). With Joseph Severn, whose acquaintance he had made in 1815, Keats sets sail for Italy (September 18, 1820). Ten days later, copies out for Severn his *Bright Star* sonnet.[1] Suffers a serious relapse in Italy (December 10, 1820). Dies in Rome of a hemorrhage[2] (February 23, 1821). Is buried in the Protestant Cemetery just outside the city wall (February 26, 1821) under an epitaph that bears among other words those dictated by himself: "Here lies one whose name was writ in water."[3]

Notice his errors in diction, occasional lack of restraint, weakness in dramatic or narrative power, deficiency in character-presentation, and cornucopian sensuousness—then turn at once to his redeeming qualities He is generally recognized as the Apostle of Beauty, and as the incarnation of energetic tranquility and passive romanticism. His odes are not surpassed for dignity, melodic beauty, haunting pathos, the magic of suggestion, and richness of sensuous imagery. Except for Wordsworth, his some threescore sonnets, easy and unpretentious of movement, although uneven in quality, make him the major sonneteer of the Romantic period.[4] As a whole, his poetry is distinguished by picturesque and mimetic words, rich felicity of diction, and opulent perfection of language; by beauty and melody of verse, profusion and concentration of imagery—characteristics of utmost aid to a poet of impassioned stillness. However, it is a grave mistake to regard Keats as a weakling and a decadent; his early poems and letters reveal a real courage and self-reliance, even a pugnacity. In poetry his tradition was carried on by Tennyson and the Pre-Raphaelites,[5] and Keat's influence is still felt. It is a mistake also to view Keats as interested neither in revolution nor reform, as only a pale-lipped votary of Beauty. Numerous

---

1 Severn himself realized that he owed his success not so much to his own talents as a painter, but to the story of his association with Keats. Evans, B. I., "Keats and Joseph Severn," *The London Mercury*, xxx (1934), pp. 337-349.

2 The "exquisite intellectual hyperesthesia" of Keats during his period of incipient and final tuberculosis has often been noted as his *annus mirabilis;* and, furthermore, a study of his methods and development in the period from February, 1818, to September, 1819, is available. See Pitfied, R. L., "John Keats," *The General Magazine and Historical Chronicle*, xxxiv (1931-1932), pp. 543-563; Ridley, M. R., *Keats' Craftsmanship* (1933).

3 Beaumont and Fletcher's *Philaster* (Vol. 1, p. 244): ". . . . all your better deeds shall be in water writ, but this in marble." But Keats also said: "I think I shall be among the English Poets after my death."

4 Garrod, H. W., *Keats* (1926). For the *Odes*, see p. 73 *ff.*; for the *Sonnets*, pp. 138-157.

5 Grendon, Felix, "The Influence of Keats upon the Early Poetry of Tennyson," *The Sewanee Review Quarterly*, xv (1907), pp. 285-296; Shine, Hill, "The Influence of Keats upon Rossetti," *Englische Studien*, LXI (1926-1927), pp. 183-210; and also the *Marginalia* published by George Milner (1883) and reprinted in *Englische Studien*, LXI (1926-1927), pp. 211-219.

references in his early poems establish his radical sympathies; *e.g., Written on the Day that Mr. Leigh Hunt Left Prison* (1815: 1817), a political sonnet; *Anniversary of Charles II's Restoration* (1815; 1925), condemnatory of Charles II as an enemy of freedom; and *To Kosciusko* (1816; 1817), an expression of republican sympathies just as the *Anniversary of Charles II's Restoration* is one of anti-aristocratic attitude. Another case in point is that Keats was pleased by the public demonstrations that followed the "Peterloo Massacre" of 1819. His sympathies were invariably with the oppressed. With quiet conviction he expressed a hatred of the luxury and pomp of European rulers. Contrary to traditional belief, Keats was alert to the social, economic, and political views of the day. Not in water was his name writ.[1]

FIRST PUBLICATION

Poems, by John Keats (1817). Small collection of juvenile verse, wherein Hunt's dominant influence can not muffle the tremulous enthusiasm of Keats. In addition to many notable lines, the volume contains the Chapman sonnet, a full-fledged precursor of Keats's future greatness. Some of the poems are:

(1) *Imitation of Spenser* (*c*. 1813; 1817). His earliest known poem, Spenserian only in form and probably inspired by the description of the Bower of Bliss in *The Faerie Queene* (II, 12—see Vol. 1, p. 133), is crowded with "poetic diction." The description of a swan, possibly the best lines in verse imitative of Spenserians rather than of Spenser himself, is adapted from Milton.

(2) *On Death* (1814; 1817). Serious if conventional poem of eight lines. Like *To Hope* and *To Apollo,* is full of the typical eighteenth-century personified abstractions.

(3) *To Hope* (1815; 1817). Another example of eighteenth-century poetic diction and form.

(4) *I Stood Tip-Toe upon a Little Hill* (1816; 1817). Nature piece captivating in its opening description. Throughout, the Huntian epithets reveal the large extent of indebtedness. In its trance-like experience it may suggest Edna St. Vincent Millay's *Renascence.*

(5) *To One Who Has Been Long in City Pent* (1816; 1817). Beautifully smooth sonnet. The "gentle tale of love and languishment" may have been Hunt's *Rimini.*

---

1 Thorpe, C. DeW., "Keats's interest in Politics and World Affairs," *Publications of the Modern Language Association of America,* XLVI (1931), pp. 1228-1245; Wright, H. G., "Keats and Politics," *Essays and Studies by Members of The English Association,* XVIII (1933), pp. 7-23.

(6) *On First Looking into Chapman's Homer*† (1816). First great poem is one of the greatest sonnets in the language.[1] An emotional and intellectual experience is conveyed by imaginative symbols astonishing in their organic unity: the whole is a single and complex metaphor, yet the octave is one metaphor with its own crescendo, while the sestet, consisting of two similes, has a separate crescendo—all stamped indelibly upon the mind by the consummating poetic image. (For Chapman,[2] see Vol. 1, p. 233.)

(7) *Sleep and Poetry* (1816; 1817). The most ambitious piece in the volume is, possibly, the most interesting; it epitomized Keats's poetical philosophy and foreshadowed (although dimly) his development. One part of the three main divisions surveys the schools of English poetry. Manifesto attacks the neo-classic conventions and champions the new movement as represented by Hunt, who influenced the easy flow of the couplets. Realistic intimations later fully realized in *Isabella*.

SECOND PUBLICATION

Endymion: A Poetic Romance†* (1817; 1818).[3] Main idea is the neo-Platonic quest for ideal beauty; how the poet yearns for full communion with the essential spirit of Beauty, and how "through the exercise of active human sympathies and the toilsome acquisition of knowledge," he achieves his quest. Book I, chiefly retrospective, is famous for the Hymn to Pan; II is the most fantastic part; III,[4] well-known for its passage violently denunciatory of lords and kings, and for the Hymn to Nature; IV, memorable for the roundelay of the Indian maid to Sorrow. Flawed by the remoteness of theme, rambling of episodes, disproportion of structure, and, especially, flaccid sensuousness and lush sentimentality—or "mawkishness," to quote Keats's own epithet. Graced, on the other hand, by fairly competent heroic couplets, prodigality of color, and luxuriance of imagery. The neo-Platonic pursuit of immortal beauty was derived chiefly from Spenser's *Fowre Hymnes* (Vol. 1, p. 130) and *The Faerie Queene* (Vol. 1, p. 131); the theme, probably from the treatment of the myth in Drayton's *Endimion and Phoebe* and the *Man in the Moone*. As usual, too, Keats used

---

1 One of the finest analyses of the sonnet is available in Murry, J. M., "The Birth of a Great Poem," *The Hibbert Journal*, xxvii (1928-1929), pp. 93-99 (pp. 93-110). The essay reappears in Murry, J. M., *Studies in Keats* (1930). Just as J. L. Lowes did in his *Road to Xanadu* for Coleridge's *Ancient Mariner*, so B. I. Evans attempts to penetrate into Keats's mind prior to the composition of his Chapman sonnet: "Keats's Approach to the Chapman Sonnet," *Essays and Studies by Members of The English Association*, xvi (1931), pp. 26-52.

2 His indebtedness to the Elizabethan has often been noted. Probably Keats was less obligated to Chapman than usual'y believed. Landrum, G. W., "More Concerning Chapman's Homer and Keats," *Publications of the Modern Language Association of America*, xlii; New Series, xxxv (1927), pp. 986-1009.

3 *Endymion*, edited by Notcutt, H. C. (1927).

4 What meaning did Keats intend to convey by the story of Glaucus? For an individual interpretation, consult Notcutt, H. C., *The Story of Glaucus in Keats's Endymion* (1921).

† * Explanation of symbols immediately precedes Chapter XV.

Lempriere's *Classical Dictionary*, Spence's *Polymetis*, Tooke's *Pantheon*, and Baldwin's (*i.e.*, William Godwin's) *Pantheon*.[1] Note, finally, that J. W. Croker's attack in the *Quarterly Review* and J. G. Lockhart's description of the poem as "imperturbable drivelling idiocy" in *Blackwood's*, two examples of the tomahawk criticism of the period, partly occasioned Shelley's *Adonais* (p. 479).[2]

THIRD PUBLICATION

Lamia, Isabella, The Eve of St. Agnes, and Other Poems† (1820). Successful volume. Includes:

(1) *Isabella, or The Pot of Basil* (1818; 1820). Stark tragedy, told in Boccaccio's *Decameron*, is metamorphosed into a short metrical tale in *ottava rima* suffused by over-sugared sorrow and sensuous atmosphere. Keats himself, probably recognizing rhetorical phrases and flat triviality, considered it a "weak-sided Poem"; but often the epithets are well-coined, the meter smooth and vigorous, and the realism imaginative. Note especially the Marxian content of the humanitarian stanzas XIV, XV, and XVI.

(2) *Hyperion*† (*c.* 1818—1819; 1820). Fragment in blank verse is Keats's most objective poem. Modelled on Milton's *Paradise Lost,* the heroic theme is wrought of passages eloquent in tone, monumental in scene and character delineation, sustained in passion, sublime in manner and emotional effect. Often Keats departs from the Miltonic influence in *Hyperion* to create passages of dramatic force that are Milton's equal. Garrod sees in it a reflection of the French Revolution. Many possible sources—Hesiod's *Works and Days* and *The Theogony;* Ovid's *Metamorphoses;* Diodorus Siculus' *Historical Library;* Ronsard's ode called *A Michel de l'Hospital;* Spenser's *Faerie Queene;* Shakespeare's plays; Baldwin's (*i.e.,* William Goldwin's) *Pantheon*. Details also drawn from classical dictionaries of Lempriere, Spence, and Tooke.

(3) *Fancy* (1818; 1820). Like "Bards of Passion and of Mirth," this poem, Keats felt, would explain itself—"as all poems should do without comment." With *Lines on the Mermaid Tavern* and *Robin Hood,* is numbered among the examples of his improvisations or his spontaneity.

(4) *The Eve of St. Agnes*† (1819; 1820). Slender narrative, possibly inspired by his love for Fanny Brawne, has a luxurious Spenserian

---

1 For a discussion of the manner in which Keats interpreted primitive Greek myth, and of the extent to which he made "myth a form of self-revelation," consult Sherwood, Margaret, *Undercurrents of Influence in English Romantic Poetry* (1934), pp. 203-264.

2 Until recently it was thought that only three or four reviews of Keats's works were available in the periodicals of his time. Marsh and White not only list further reviews and comments found in publications between 1816 and 1821, but point to the curious fact that Keats's biographers and editors have all failed to appreciate the preponderance of favorable over unfavorable criticisms of Keats. While, however, the criticism was friendly rather than inimical, *Blackwood's* and the *Quarterly* were powerful publications. Marsh, G. L., and White, N. I., "Keats and the Periodicals of His Time," *Modern Philology,* xxxii (1934 1935), pp. 37-53.

† * Explanation of symbols immediately precedes Chapter XV.

sensuousness and Romeo-Juliet passion. Is memorable for delicate beauty and delicate workmanship, haunting cadence and magic atmosphere, richly-wrought detail and all-pervading spirit of medieval romance. Complete control of Spenserian stanza. Ultimate source of theme may be Boccaccio's *Il Filocolo*. Other possible influences are Shakespeare's *Romeo and Juliet*, Mrs. Radcliffe's *Mysteries of Udolpho* (p. 435), and Mary Tighe's *Psyche, with Other Poems*.[1]

(5) *Ode to Psyche* (1819; 1820). Story probably taken from Mary Tighe's *Psyche*. Although not one of his better attempts in strophic form, it is distinguished from the other odes by a greater metrical variety. Despite unevenness and occasional weaknesses, T. S. Eliot thinks it Keats's best ode. According to Keats, it was written in a leisurely fashion.

(6) *Ode on a Grecian Urn*† (1819; 1820). Neither the conception that beauty is truth nor the idea of the worship of beauty for beauty's sake, but the eternality in a thing of beauty is the theme.[2] Colvin has shown how Keats combines into magical unity scenes and figures from the Parthenon frieze, Bacchic vases, and classical paintings by Claude and Poussin. (Read, also, *To Haydon* and *On Seeing the Elgin Marbles*.) More concrete in detail than the other odes. Tense, ethereal beauty. Redolent of the essence of Greek myths, although Keats had no knowledge of Greek. Some weakness in detail, but probably less marked than Robert Bridges would have one believe. Diversity of opinion concerning the concluding lines: poor, say Keats, Quiller-Couch, and T. S. Eliot; redeeming, says Bridges.[3] Possibly it is a mistake to number John Keats solely in the company of those who believe in art for art's sake. (Compare with his *Ode on Melancholy* and, also, with the opening passage in *Endymion*.)

(7) *Ode on Melancholy* (1819; 1820). Imagery and style of all three stanzas are magnificent, the last stanza being not only the best of the three but also among the truest utterances in English poetry. Possibly is a denial of the terminating lines of the *Ode on a Grecian Urn*, although Garrod says that the latter ode is a "strong revulsion from the thesis" of the *Ode on Melancholy*.

(8) *Ode to a Nightingale*† (written 1819; first printed 1819; appeared in 1820 volume). Vital expression of a mood most characteristic of his mind is in part a song to death and in part a song of

---

1 Weller, E. V., "Keats and Mary Tighe," *Publications of the Modern Language Association of America*, XLII; *New Series* XXXV (1927), pp. 963-985; *Keats and Mary Tighe*, edited by Weller, E. V. (1928).

2 Gingerich, S. F., "The Conception of Beauty in the Works of Shelley, Keats, and Poe," *Essays and Studies in English and Comparative Literature*, By Members of The English Department of the University of Michigan, VIII (1932), p. 178 (pp. 169-194).

3 Murry, J. M., *Studies in Keats* (1930), pp. 71-73, p. 116.

† * Explanation of symbols immediately precedes Chapter XV.

despair. In it there seems to be a premonition of his premature death. Influenced by his reading.[1] Not faultless, yet often recognized as his best poem. Opulent imagery, languorous melancholy, restrained emotion; its mood is possibly more intense than the mood of *To Autumn.* Perhaps no other two lines[2] in the language contain more essence of romance than

> "Charmed magic casements, opening on the foam
> Of perilous seas, in faery lands forlorn."

(9) *Lamia†* (1819; 1820). Best narrative poem in heroic couplets, influenced by Dryden, has its source in Burton's *Anatomy of Melancholy* (Vol. 1, p. 272), where Burton transcribes Philostratus's tale *De Vita Apollonii.* While marred occasionally by cheap cynicism and while lacking the complete unity of *The Eve of St. Agnes,* this story of a serpent-woman who loves the young Corinthian Lycius is, except for certain weak passages and some vulgarity, admirably related, firmly constructed, and definitely restrained in its vagaries. Greek manners and customs probably derived from John Potter's *Archaeologia Graeca, or The Antiquities of Greece.* Miltonic style. Unlike *Isabella* and *The Eve of St. Agnes,* it seems to have some symbolic meaning.

(10) *To Autumn†* (1819; 1820). Nature ode drowsily serene in its descriptive personification of the season. Sometimes considered as lacking the organic unity of structure of the other odes; but none is more purely sensuous and imaginative: it is a metaphor of natural beauty. Imagery may have been influenced by Spenser's *Faerie Queene* (VII).

POSTHUMOUS WORKS

Sonnets

To Byron (1814; 1848). Representative of sentimental eighteenth-century melancholy, interesting because of Keats's later change of opinion concerning Byron.

To Chatterton (1814; 1848). Shows Keats's admiration for the poet to whose memory he later inscribed *Endymion.*

On an Engraved Gem of Leander (*c.* 1816; 1829). Notable for the compact, imaginative expression of its close.

On the Sea (written 1817). One of his beautiful sonnets exemplifying his creative inspiration.

---

1 Blunden, Edmund, "Keats and His Predecessors," *The London Mercury,* xx (1929), pp. 282-292.

2 A heretic suggestion has been made that "Charm'd magic casements" reads in manuscript as "Chain'd motile casements." See *A Crossword Puzzle Composed,* by A Brewer (Warner Press Ltd., 1933); title of cover is *Magic Dethroned* by Thompson, L. C.

† * Explanation of symbols immediately precedes Chapter XV.

To— (1818; 1844). Sonnet, addressed "to a Lady seen for some few moments at Vauxhall," is possibly his most Shakespearean.

When I have Fears that I May Cease to Be (1818; 1848). Sonnet, possibly his first use of the Shakespearean form, is usually regarded as a prophecy of his early death. Shakespearean, too, in theme. (Compare it with Milton's "When I Consider How My Life Is Spent," Vol. 1, p. 286.)

Odes

Ode to Apollo (1815; 1848). Another example of eighteenth-century poetic diction, very much in the manner of the rhetoric of Dryden's odes.

Ode on Indolence (1819; 1848). Admirable if uneven ode is a poetic version of a mood and thought Keats had already expressed in prose.

Metrical Romances

La Belle Dame sans Merci† (written 1819; revised version printed 1820; original version published 1888). Ballad-lyric of disillusion is a concentrate of pathetic and phantasmal tragedy freighted with ineffable suggestion. Of further importance because it contains the germ of the Pre-Raphaelite School and because its implications, like those in *Lamia*, find their powerful excess in the works of Swinburne and Baudelaire. Possibly influenced by Spenser's *Faerie Queene* (II, 6) and by *Palmerin of England*. Title probably derived from a ballad of the same name, translated from Alain Chartier, attributed at one time to Chaucer, but now conjectured to be the translation of Sir Richard Ros. (Compare with the same theme treated in the supernatural ballad, *Thomas Rymer*, Vol. 1, p. 101.)

Eve of St. Mark's (1819; 1848). Simple theme, concrete imagery, and pulsing passion of fragmentary poem in the short, or octosyllabic, couplet (four-foot ballad meter) affected the Pre-Raphaelite movement in poetry, painting, and sculpture. Amy Lowell has noted "its swift, although gentle, changes of effect." With *La Belle Dame sans Merci*, it was considered by Rossetti "in manner the choicest and chastest" of Keats's poetry. Like *The Eve of St. Agnes* and *Isabella*, is a short metrical romance.

Poetic Dramas

Otho the Great (1819; 1848). Melodramatic play in blank verse composed piecemeal by Keats as Charles Brown outlined the plot and supplied the characters. The scenes are even less convincing than the weakly realized characters. Some lyrical speeches. Several episodes reminiscent of Shakespeare's *Much Ado About Nothing* and *Cymbeline*.

---

† * Explanation of symbols immediately precedes Chapter XV.

King Stephen (1819; 1848). Fragmentary chronicle play of four scenes totalling less than two hundred lines, not dissimilar in manner to Shakespeare's historical plays. Unlike *Otho the Great,* this fragment of a tragedy is distinguished by dramatic tone, clear characterization, and is a trustworthy picture of the warfare of twelfth-century England.

Miscellaneous Works

Fragment of an Ode to Maia (1818; 1848). Fourteen-line fragment, yet complete in both form and thought. In the expression of a yearning to compose verse in the "old vigour" of Greek poetry, Keats recaptures the Greek qualities of lucidity, quiet beauty, and restrained suggestiveness.

Bright Star, Would I were Steadfast as Thou Art (1819; 1820). The somewhat inferior verses with which his "Last Sonnet" closes are compensated by the opening lofty ones. (Compare with Tennyson's *Crossing the Bar* and Browning's *Epilogue to Asolando.*)

The Cap and Bells (1819; 1848). Unfinished anti-romantic fairy-tale, written in collaboration with Brown, is probably a satire on the marital relations of George Augustus Frederick, Prince of Wales and Prince Regent of England. Not only does Keats parody the style of *Don Juan* but also pokes fun at his own *Eve of St. Agnes.* Criss-cross plot obtained from Shakespeare's *A Midsummer-Night's Dream* (Vol. 1, p. 188). Critics usually repeat Rossetti's verdict that the burlesque poem is unworthy of Keats.

The Fall of Hyperion (1819; 1856). Intention was to express the ideals of humanitarianism.[1] Not only is Dante's influence apparent in the idea of the dream-vision; his influence upon the induction is much greater than usually stated.[2] Miltonic style, neo-Platonic philosophy. Is most likely a revision of *Hyperion.*

Letters. John Keats himself wrote the best biography of John Keats. His letters are a complete record of a poetic mind; through them is re-discovered his sane understanding of real life as well as his prophetic visions of practical problems: he had a more active political conscience than usually thought. Simple, bare, direct, witty, chatty, sensitive, solicitous, charming, straightforward—the epithets describing his letters could be run indefinitely. Finally, despite Matthew Arnold's statement that the letters to Fanny Brawne represent "the abandonment of all reticence and dignity, of the merely sensuous man, of the man 'who is passion's slave,'" and therefore are unworthy of Keats, and despite Coventry Patmore's label of "lust," these love-letters, for all their cloying effusions and feverish passion, are indispensable for an understanding of the complete Keats.[3]

---

1 Finney, C. L., "The Fall of Hyperion," *The Journal of English and Germanic Philology,* XXVI (1927), pp. 304-324.
2 Lowes, J. T., " 'Hyperion' and the 'Purgatoria,' " *The London Times Literary Supplement,* January 11, 1936, p. 35.
3 *Autobiography of John Keats,* edited by Weller, E. V. (1933); *The Letters of John Keats,* edited by Forman, M. B. (1952). See, also, Adami, Marie, "Fanny Keats and Her Letters." *The Cornhill Magazine,* CLII (1935), pp. 385-409; *John Keats and Fanny Brawne,* letters from Fanny Brawne to Fanny Keats, edited by Edgecumbe, Fred (1937).

Chapter XXII

THE TRIUMPH OF ROMANTICISM: THE PROSE WRITERS
(1798—1832)

TWO MAJOR NOVELISTS

Jane Austen, 1775—1817, great novelist of manners.[1] Her life was apparently placid and uneventful. Lived for her first twenty-five years at Steventon Parsonage, Hampshire, where she was born. Attended Mrs. Latournelle's School at Reading (1784). Visited Godmersham Kent, which had become the property of her brother Edward (1798). The Austen family moved from Steventon Vicarage to Bath (1801), where in the following year during a visit to Dawlish and Teignmouth is supposed to have occurred her only love-affair. Offer of marriage from Mr. Bigg-Wither of Manydown Park (1802).[2] Moved to Southampton (*c.* 1806), and to Chawton, near Alton, Hampshire (1809). Jane was persuaded to go to Winchester for better medical advice (1817), where she died two months later. Buried in Winchester Cathedral.

Jane Austen's plots are tame, lacking in romantic reveries or hectic adventures; her atmosphere is serene, seldom touched by real pathos or disturbed by turbulent scenes; her works are oblivious of both the deeper issues of life and of the momentous events shaking the Europe of her day; yet her literary reputation has grown steadily. Indirect revelation of the English character is her forte; her cameo-cut social types reveal themselves naturally in their talk, often exposing themselves by a single phrase. Perhaps the most finished artist among women, her style[3] is crisp and pointed and concrete, and enhanced by a deliberate Fielding-like irony. In outline, her unromantic plots (despite their general description of life as a matrimonial game or man-hunt) show a greater ingenuity of structure than usually attributed to them.

---

1 Austen-Leigh, William, and Austen-Leigh, R. A., *Jane Austen: Her Life and Letters, A Family Record* (1913); Firkins, O. W., *Jane Austen* (1920); Thomson, C. L., *Jane Austen* (1929); Bailey, John, *Introductions to Jane Austen* (1931); Rhydderch, David, *Jane Austen: Her Life and Art* (1932); Rawlence, Guy, *Jane Austen* (1934).

2 Hill, Constance, *Jane Austen: Her Homes & Her Friends* (Third edition, 1923), Chap. XXI, "An Episode in Jane Austen's Life," pp. 232-240.

3 But Herbert Read condemns her lack of expertness, saying that her style is adequate for "quiet" situations. See Read, Herbert, *English Prose Style* (1928), pp. 118-120.

Commend her for subtle wit and abounding humor, for adherence to unity of action and character, for appealing cheerfulness and disinterested sincerity. Towering above every quality is a critical common sense that warred against bombast and affectation and sentimentalism in the novels of her day. Jane Austen, it is true, stayed within the range of her own experiences, never venturing to go beyond the confines of her own world; but within her "small, square, two inches, of ivory," she displayed an unexcelled astringent dramatic power.[1] Her influence upon such novelists as Thackeray and George Eliot is recognized, and her possible superiority over Sterne, Dickens, and Scott.

Novels

Sense and Sensibility (*c*. 1797; 1811). Story first sketched in letters a few years earlier under the title of *Elinor and Marianne*, where one stands for reason and self-control and the other for extreme emotion and sensibility; is a satire on the novel of feeling or of excessive sentimentality. Plot lacks development, character-drawing often weak, didactic purpose too obvious in the long speeches, *dénouement* somewhat inadequate. However, has some pearls of phrasing and of wit; see, for example, John Dashwood's famous discussion with his wife whereby his father's wish is defeated, and Robert Ferrars's excursus on life in a cottage. On the whole, is her poorest and least original novel.

Pride and Prejudice†* (*c*. 1796—1797; 1813). Originally entitled *First Impressions,* her accepted masterpiece exhibits the folly of trusting to such first impressions and describes the clash between the *Pride* of Darcy and the *Prejudice* of Elizabeth. Logical construction, sure portraiture, infectious comedy.[2] Style possibly less finished than that in *Mansfield Park* and *Persuasion,* but in no later work did she surpass the wit and observation in *Pride and Prejudice.* Darcy is not entirely an attractive person; Mr. Collins, a triumph of satiric portraiture, is a toady in whom self-importance has become a passion[3]; and Elizabeth Bennet is her most interesting and possibly greatest creation.

---

1 "There have been two assumptions aways made about Jane Austen—the foundation from which all criticism or appreciation have been established:—
"1. That she was exceptionally modern in her realism; an observer and showman, whose work was based on the study of human nature.
"2. That no writer of equal genius ever owed so little to her predecessors; knew or cared so little about books.
"I believe that both assumptions are fundamentally untrue." See Hopkins, A. B., "Jane Austen the Critic," *Publications of the Modern Language Association of America*, XL (1925), pp. 398-425; Garrod, H. W., "Jane Austen: A Depreciation," *Essays by Divers Hands* (Being the Transactions of the Royal Society of Literature of the United Kingdom), New Series, VIII (1928), pp. 21-24; Chapman, R. W., "Jane Austen: A Reply to Mr. Garrod." *Essays by Divers Hands,* New Series, X (1931), pp. 17-34; Villard, Léonie, *Jane Austen: A French Appreciation* (1924), p. 4.

2 Helen Jerome's dramatized condensation of the novel proved to be one of the best plays of the 1935-1936 season. See *The Best Plays of 1935-1936,* edited by Mantle, Burns (1936), p. 356 *ff*.

3 Priestley, J. B., *The English Comic Characters* (1925), "Mr. Collins," pp. 158-177.

† * Explanation of symbols immediately precedes Chapter XV.

Northanger Abbey* (*c.* 1798; sold 1803; published 1818). Anti-romantic novel originating in and dominated by the desire to burlesque the Radcliffian school of romancers.[1] Lacks firmness in plot and construction, in variety and subtlety, but is of historical significance because of its counterblast to the artificial school of romanticism. Parodies the Gothic tale much in the spirit with which Chaucer parodied the metrical romances (see, for example, the *Rime of Sir Thopas,* Vol. 1, p. 73). Last third of book weakest. Yet *Northanger Abbey,* brief as it is, was a departure in its day.

Mansfield Park†* (*c.* 1812—*c.* 1814; 1814). Her least dramatic novel introduces her most complex plot, one that presents characters in contrasts (worldliness versus unworldliness), that is freer from exaggeration than that found in *Pride and Prejudice,* and that best presents her favorite theme of Repentance. Structure looser than in preceding novels, but nowhere is there a richer display of her artistic resources: character touches, realistic (if somewhat priggish) approach, brilliant parts. Sydney Smith preferred this to her other works.

Emma†* (*c.* 1814—*c.* 1815; 1816). Prose comedy of manners satirizing the self-deceptions of vanity is her only completed novel in which one character receives the main emphasis. Primarily a character-study, *Emma* is more consistently cheerful, humorous, and objective than any other of her works. Plot less convincing than that in *Mansfield Park,* but variety of characters greater; like the latter work, *Emma's* structure lacks the firmness and its style the crisp language of the earlier novels. Here again is a picture of the mixed family and social life of *Pride and Prejudice,* but mellowed by a riper humor and closer approximation to imaginative truth. "In pure ironical humour," says E. V. Lucas, "Miss Austen's only peer among novelists is George Meredith, and indeed *Emma* may be said to be her *Egoist,* or the *Egoist* his *Emma.*"

Persuasion†* (1815—1816; 1818). While not as impeccably constructed as *Emma* and *Pride and Prejudice,* it is a miniature masterpiece slight in plot and unabated in humor. Her last work, in which *Persuasion* is in reality Anne Elliot and where Anne's love-story may reflect Jane Austen's own life, betrays a softening of her prevailing satiric mood. Gains in interest by a subtle interplay of the characters, most memorable of whom is timid, sensitive, pensive, wistful, almost spiritual Anne Elliot. Some critics prefer this, her most sentimental novel, to all the others.

---

1 Sadleir, Michael, "The Northanger Novels," *The Edinburgh Review,* CCXLVI (1927), pp. 91-106.

† * Explanation of symbols immediately precedes Chapter XV.

Posthumous Works

Love and Freindship (c. 1790—1793; 1922).[1] Epistolary novelette that burlesques the romance of sentiment is in reality a rattling little farce revealing Jane Austen's preternatural keenness in detecting absurdities. Sparkling story rich in conventional situations and adventurous in plot. Characters reminiscent of picaresque fiction. All letters (except one) from Laura to Marianne.

Volume the First (*ante* 1793; 1933). Collection of short satirical sketches.[2]

The Watsons (c. 1804; first published 1871; reprinted from MS. 1927). Unfinished fragment of a novel somewhat thin in treatment of incident and riper in that of characterization. Narrative has the lightness of the local ballroom scene in which most of the principal characters are introduced. Like *Sanditon*, the manscript bears no title. (Fragment concluded by L. Oulton in 1923.)

Lady Susan (c. 1805; first published 1871; reprinted from MS. 1925). Unfinished novel in letter-form is a coldly satiric charactersketch of a middle-aged Balzacian adventuress. Its faithful picture of vice or moral depravity is plotted on quiet lines illuminated by flashes of brilliance. Is less a novelette than an epistolary short-story or character-study of a worldling.

Sanditon (1817; 1925). The manuscript has no title, but this *Fragment of a Novel* about the seaside has long been known to members of the family as *Sanditon*. Of her extant fragments none comes nearer to the authentic Austen.[3]

Letters. Jane Austen does not rank among the great letter-writers. She is generally criticized for a devotion to trifling minutiae (an emphasis upon dress, for example); but these trifles reveal her zest and throw light upon the history of the novels. As regards the deeper side of life, her letters are disappointing; the major indictment is that they are almost totally unaware of the French Revolution and the Napoleonic Wars; but, for that matter, so are her other writings. Weak is the defense that Cassandra Austen destroyed references in letters, or entire letters, retaining only those of least interest and minimum revelation.

---

1 *Love & Friendship and Other Early Works*, with a preface by Chesterton, G. K. (1922). *Love & Friendship* is the only completed story in this book of her juvenilia, among which are *Lesley Castle*, an unfinished novel in letters, *The History of England from the Reign of Henry the 4th to The Death of Charles the 1st*, a somewhat dull pseudo-comic series of sketches, *A Collection of Letters*, and *Scraps*. See Hopkins, A. B., "Jane Austen's 'Love and Friendship': A Study in Literary Relations," *The South Atlantic Quarterly*, XXIV (1925), pp. 34-49.

2 For a list of the "Contents of Jane Austen's Juvenilia," see Chapman, R. W., ed., *The Works of Jane Austen*, VI, 1954 (6 vols., 1932-1954).

3 "Jane Austen's Last Work," an excellent anonymous article in *The London Times Literary Supplement*, February 19, 1925, p. 117, col. 3.

Yet, as most letters go, they abound in thumb-nail sketches of persons and accurate pictures of the life of the upper middle class of that time. Occasional cynicism, prominent mockery, and clever if playful malice counterbalanced by vivid presentation, vivacious spirit, matchless sense of the comical, and human interest. But the letters can not stand alone, as do those of Gray and Walpole.[1]

Sir Walter Scott, 1771—1832, novelist, poet, miscellaneous man of letters.[2] Born in College Wynd, Edinburgh. Son of Walter Scott, a writer to the signet. When not yet two years old he was afflicted with a fever (infantile paralysis?) that left him slightly lame. Attended the High School, Edinburgh (1778). Edinburgh University (1783). Was apprenticed to his father (*c.* 1786). Was admitted a member of the faculty of advocates (1792).[3] Rejected by Margaret Belches, said to be the one great love of his life (1796).[4] Active as quarter-master of the Royal Edinburgh Light Dragoons, a volunteer cavalry regiment (1797). Married Mary (or Charlotte Margaret) Carpenter, daughter of Jean Charpentier, a French refugee from Lyons (1797). Appointed sheriff-deputy of Selkirkshire (1799). Secretly becomes a partner in the printing house of James Ballantyne (1805). Was appointed one of the Principal Clerks of Session (1806), but not until 1812 did he begin receiving his salary of £1,300, for the post was still retained by an invalid nominally in charge. Secretary to the Parliamentary Commission for the improvement of the Scottish Jurisprudence (1808). Joined John Ballantyne in a publishing business (1809).[5] Purchased the nucleus of Abbotsford on the Tweed (1812), which he greatly expanded by subsequent purchases and construction. Refused the laureateship (1813), and recommended Southey for the honor. Was created a baronet (1820). Founded the Bannatyne Club, its purpose being the publication of old Scottish documents (1823). Publishing venture collapsed, involving Scott in financial ruin, his own liability being anywhere from

1 *Jane Austen's Letters,* edited by Chapman, R. W. (Two volumes, 1932); Seymour, B. K., *Jane Austen,* (1937), pp. 225-236, 237-251.

2 Lockhart, J. G., *Memoirs of the Life of Sir Walter Scott* (Five volumes, 1901); MacNalty, A. S., "The Great Unknown" (1932); Patten, J. A., *Sir Walter Scott* (1932); Wright, Fowler, *The Life of Sir Walter Scott* (1932); Pope-Hennessy, Una, *The Laird of Abbotsford* (1932); Buchan, John, *Sir Walter Scott* (1932); Falconer, J. A., "Sir Walter Scott: What He Means to Scotland," *English Studies,* XIV (1932), pp. 145-154; McDowall, Arthur, "Scott's Journal And 'Woodstock,'" pp. 162-173; *Scott Centenary Articles,* essays by Seccombe, Thomas; Ker, W. P.; Gordon, George; Hutton, W. H.; McDowall, Arthur; and Rait, R. S. (Oxford University Press, 1932); McKillop, A. D., "Sir Walter Scott in the Twentieth Century," *The Rice Institute Pamphlet,* XX (1933), pp. 196-215; Fox, A. W., "In Praise of Sir Walter Scott," *Papers of the Manchester Literary Club,* LIX (1933), pp. 1-17; Stuart, D. M., *Sir Walter Scott* (The English Association, Pamphlet No. 89, 1934).

3 Chisholm, John, *Sir Walter Scott As A Judge* (1918); Dobie, W. G. M., "Law and Lawyers in the Waverly Novels," *The Juridical Review,* XXXII (1920), pp. 317-333; Dickson, W. K., "Sir Walter Scott and The Parliament House," *The Juridical Review,* XLII (1930), pp. 1-11; Marshall, David, *Sir Walter Scott and Scots Law* (1932).

4 A partial explanation of the note of melancholy in his poetry is the disappointment of an early love affair. MacNalty is not alone in this belief.

5 Gray, W. F., "Scott and the Ballantynes: An Unpublished Correspondence," *The Fortnightly Review,* CXXIX; New Series, CXXIII (1928), pp. 796-807.

£117,000 to £130,000 (1826). Scott refused to take refuge behind the Bankruptcy Act, heroically faced his creditors, and declared he would pay back every pound. In his *Chronicles of the Canongate* (1827) Scott first avowed the authorship of the novels. Despite the grief at the loss of his wife (1826) and the physical suffering caused by his own ill health, he slaved ceaselessly to write off the mountainous debt—spinning gold from his entrails, as Thomas Moore said. Declined a government pension. Engaged in political opposition to parliamentary reform. First stroke of paralysis (1830), and, later in the year, of apoplexy. Second stroke of paralysis (1831); a belated sea-voyage in a Government vessel put at his disposal; after a cruise in the Mediterranean he returned to England, where he died. The proceeds on the sale of his copyrights completed the liquidation of his debts.[1]

Translations

(1) *William and Helen* (1796), imitation rather than close translation of Bürger's *Lenore* is one of Scott's earliest translations from German balladry. Many inaccuracies and faulty rimes. (2) *The Wild Huntsman* (1796), imitative rendering of Bürger's *Der Wilde Jäger* is, like *William and Henry*, "a sort of preliminary canter" for the later ballads and metrical romances. (3) *The Tree of Constancy* (c. 1796), free translation of Bürger's *Das Lied von Treue.*[2] (4) *Erl-King* (1797), translation from Goethe. (5) *Goetz*: see under DRAMATIC WORKS. (6) *The House of Aspen*: see under DRAMATIC WORKS.

Dramatic Works

(1) *Goetz von Berlichingen of the Iron Hand* (1799), fairly excellent translation in racy dialogue of Goethe's storm-and-stress drama.[3] From it Scott borrowed the form of the closing scene in *Marmion;* and also scenes for such novels as *Ivanhoe* (p. 503) and *Anne of Geierstein* (p. 507). (2) *The House of Aspen* (1797), a *rifacimento* rather than a translation of Veit Weber's *Der Heilige Vehme* ("The Secret Tribunal"), is of interest mainly because its lyrics indicate that Scott did not attain perfection of form without much practise. (3) *Halidon Hill* (1822), said to be the work of two rainy mornings. (4) *Macduff's Cross* (1822), of which it is better to say little. (5) *The Doom of Devorgoil* (1830), notable for "Datur Hora Quieti" (Act I, Scene 1) and for "The Ballad of Bonny Dundee," inserted in the second act in 1826. ("Bonny Dundee" is John Graham of Claverhouse, Viscount of

---

1 Hundreds of people wrote to Scott. For evidence of this unprecedented correspondence, refer to (1) *The Private Letter-Books of Sir Walter Scott* (1930), and (2) *Sir Walter's Post-Bag* (1932), both edited by Partington, Wilfred, with a foreword by Walpole, Hugh.

2 Parson, C. O., "Scott's Translation of Bürger's 'Das Lied von Treue,' " *The Journal of English and Germanic Philology*, XXXIII (1934), pp. 240-249.

3 Macintosh, W., *Scott and Goethe*, p. 30 *ff.*, p. 59 *ff.*

Dundee, 1649—1689.)   (6) *Auchindrane, or the Ayrshire Tragedy* (1830), founded on the case of Mure of Auchindrane in Pitcairn's *Ancient Criminal Trials,* this play is, according to Lockhart, his best; but, in John Genest's opinion, "too much is said, and too little done."

Critical and Editorial Works

(1) *The Works of Dryden* (Eighteen volumes, 1808) includes an excellent "Life," while (2) *The Works of Swift* (Nineteen volumes, 1814) includes a "Life" only a little below the competent approach to *Dryden.* (3) *The Minstrelsy of the Scottish Border*† (1802—1803) is a collection of ancient ballads and legends (not all of which are Scottish) that proved to be a great monument of Scottish literature.[1] Delightful are the introduction, the essay on fairies, and the extensive notes. Scott included modern imitations, based on authentic legends, the best of which were written by himself. Familiarity with the songs of the nation led to the writing of *The Lay of the Last Minstrel;* in fact, it is in the *Essay on Imitations of the Ancient Ballads,* prefixed to the 1830 edition of *The Minstrelsy,* and in the introduction to *The Lay,* that Scott reveals how he came to adopt the use of verse. His greatest service to poetry was less through his own verse than through the careful editing of this collection.

Miscellaneous Prose Works

(1) *Paul's Letters to his Kinsfolk* (1816), an autobiographical piece that adds to our understanding of Scott. Like the poem called *The Field of Waterloo,* was the result of a visit to Brussels, Waterloo, and Paris, several weeks after the battle of Waterloo. Shows thoroughness in his investigation into Napoleon's last campaign. (2) *Journal*† (1825 —1832; 1890), neglected masterpiece that is a faithful portrait of the naturalness, depth of feeling, and heroic proportions of Scott. (3) *Letters of Malachi Malagrowther* (1826). Pamphlet, revelatory of Scott's comprehension of the commercial world, is a patriotic plea concerning his "Thoughts on the Proposed Change of Currency." He believes, for example, in the localization of the issue of credit; and, also, he argues against the extreme *laissez-faire* theory. (4) *The Life of Napoleon Buonaparte* (Nine volumes, 1827), written in haste in the shadow of ruin, although a rather tedious and not too colorful study, is clear and proportionate, even if frequently erroneous. (5) *The Tales of a Grandfather* (1827—1831), a rapid view of history as told to Hugh Littlejohn (Scott's grandson, John Hugh Lockhart). Second series of tales dealt with the history of France, whereas the first had dealt with the history

---

1 Scott's mind was essentially creative, not analytical; but, although his lapses from critical soundness are not infrequent, he retains his importance as an unwearied collector and arranger. See *Minstrelsy of the Scottish Border,* edited by Henderson, Thomas (1931).

† *   Explanation of symbols immediately precedes Chapter XV.

of Scotland to the close of the Rebellion of 1745—1746. Easy style, impartial approach, the misrepresentations resulting primarily from the acceptance of traditions and the defects of information.

SCOTT'S POETRY[1]

Tales of Wonder (1801). To "Monk" Lewis's collection of *Tales of Wonder* Scott contributed a group of ballads including (1) *Glenfinlas*, a protracted tale that fails lamentably despite the promise of its beginning; (2) *The Eve of St. John*, a ghostly ballad, placed in the sixteenth century; fitted in skilfully with the story is the central idea of the return of the murdered lover; and (3) *The Gray Brother*, an overlong ballad effective in the opening and the closing stanzas.

The Lay of the Last Minstrel†* (1805). First important original work is a versified romance based on an old border legend of the Goblin Gilpin Horner. Botched workmanship, lapses into Augustan banality, Gothic supernaturalism, and over-sweetness counterbalanced by a well-handled if faulty plot, abounding vitality, and sustained lyric qualities. Although it begins under the influence of Coleridge's *Christabel* and ends with the monotonous eighteenth-century end-stopped line and chiselled rime, yet no other of his longer poems has its freshness and spontaneity. Memorable: "The Ride of William Deloraine," "The Border Raid," "It was an English Ladye Bright," "The Lovely Rosabelle," "Dies Irae."

Marmion†* (1808). Second metrical romance is interesting primarily for its pictorial descriptions (*e.g.,* Edinburgh as seen by Marmion over Blackford Hill; the last stand made by the Scottish Army at Flodden Field, Scotland's most fatal battle on the Border) that often play into the action narrative. Commonplace romantic plot roughly akin to that of *Ivanhoe* (*e.g.,* in an unscrupulous knight, a pilgrim guide who is no pilgrim, a tourney between the rivals). The six introductory epistles make the machinery creak still more. While both are faulty, *Marmion* is better than *The Lay* in architectural design; its meter shows again that Scott's power resided neither in subtlety of phrase nor in richness of imagery, but rather in dashing vigor, spontaneous ease, and decision of movement. Hardy described Scott's most brilliant verse romance as the most Homeric poem in the language. Memorable: "The Poet," "The Judgment of Constance," "Where Shall the Lover Rest," "Marmion and Blackford," "Lochinvar," "The Battle of Flodden."

The Lady of the Lake (1810). Within six months the twenty thousand copies sold had made the Loch Katrine section of the Trossachs a classic country. The *Lay* had revealed a spontaneity, freshness,

---

1 *The Heart of Scott's Poetry*, edited by Holmes, J. H. (1932); Grady, Rose Marie (Sister), *The Sources of Scott's Eight Long Poems* (Thesis, 1934).

† * **Explanation of symbols immediately precedes Chapter XV.**

and vigor; *Marmion,* a sustained narrative and tragic intensity; but *The Lady of the Lake* charmed by an exquisite heroine, a dark villain, a royal hero travelling incognito and gallantly surrendering the woman he loves to a successful rival—and charmed, too, by romantic suggestion, Gothic echoes, and magical glimpses of Highland scenery. Despite slipshod verse (iambic tetrameter, with an occasional trochee), this versified romance in six cantos, each introduced by a short prelude in Spenserian stanza, is on the whole perhaps the production most finished in its fusion of the ballad spirit and the structural forms. Sources include Lindesay of Pitscottie's *History of Scotland,* Thomas Pennant's *Scottish Tour,* Edward Burt's *Letters from the North of Scotland,* Martin's *Description of the Western Islands,* and John Bristed's *Pedestrian Tour.* Memorable: "Harp of the North, Awake!", "Soldier, Rest! Thy Warfare O'er," "Hymn to the Virgin," "Alice Brand," "Lay of the Imprisoned Huntsman."

The Vision of Don Roderick (1811). Hastily completed, yet is a well-constructed tale in dull Spenserian stanzas. Influenced not only by the events of the current Peninsular War (1808—1814) but also by three main sources: John de Mariana's *General History of Spain,* Wordsworth's so-called *Convention of Cintra,* and John Hughes's *Siege of Damascus.* Receives less praise than its due only because it suffers from comparison with Scott's better metrical romances.

Rokeby (1812). Its six cantos tell a complicated, heavy, limping, but clearly-wrought tale of the civil wars in England; generally considered less happy in its choice of a story than the other verse narratives, it is the precursor of the prose novels. Matilda, sketched from "a lady who is now no more,"[1] is more real than any of his verse-heroines; Redmond is the strongest of his verse-heroes; and Bertram, the central figure, praised by Swinburne, is his most superb portrait of a heroic villain. His early wizardry not entirely lacking; see, for example, the beginning of the poem, the opening half of the second canto, and the swift, intense, dramatic climax of the story. Crowning glory is the incomparable songs and lyrics: "Allan-a-Dale," "Brignall Banks," "A Weary Lot is Thine, Fair Maid," "Cavalier Song." Indebted to Clarendon's *History of the Rebellion,* Whitelocke's *Memoirs of the English Affairs,* Baillie's *Letters and Journals,* Holinshed's *Chronicle,* Jonson's *New Inn,* Walpole's *Castle of Otranto.* Yet, none the less, was not a success.

The Bridal of Triermain (1813). Graceful romance of love and magic, enlarged from an earlier venture printed in 1809, is concerned with the breaking of the spell laid by Merlin upon Gyneth, daughter of King Arthur and the fay Guendolen. Indebted to Geoffrey of Monmouth's *Historia* (Vol. 1, p. 43), Spenser's *Faerie Queene* (Vol. 1,

---

1 Sands, Lord, *Sir Walter Scott's Congé* (1929).

p. 131), Shakespeare's *Macbeth* (Vol. 1, p. 213), and Coleridge's *Christabel* (p. 457); main episode reminiscent of *Libeaus Desconus* (Vol. 1, p. 38.)

The Lord of the Isles (1815). The self-sacrifice of Isabel is the central theme of this poem in six cantos founded on the chronicles of the Bruce supplied chiefly by Barbour's *The Brus* (Vol. 1, p. 55) and Dalrymple's *Annals of Scotland.* The spirit of war and adventure is sublimated into a high sense of gallantry and an honorable spirit of patriotism, recreating the past by means of a factual background outfitted with original and historical characters. Frequent long lapses into prosaic verse, yet Scott in this metrical romance exhibits his highest narrative power; in a sense, says Oliver Elton, it is the earliest of the Waverley novels. Memorable: "Robert The Bruce," "The Voyage," "The Battle of Bannockbourn."

Harold the Dauntless (1817). Lifeless attempt to recapture the simple ballad style of *The Lay of the Last Minstrel,* is sprinkled with both allusions from northern mythology and with visions and miracles borrowed mainly from Bartholin's *De Causis Contemptae a Danis adhuc Gentilibus Mortis.* By this time Scott was much more interested in the Waverley novels than in verse narratives. Memorable: "The Castle of the Seven Shields."

COMMENT UPON SCOTT'S POETRY

His great reputation rests much less upon his poetry than upon his novels. As a poet his sense of rhythm is defective and his fluency becomes monotonous. Not only is his verse often careless and diffuse, not only are his moralizings of the tritest, but he is deficient in intellectual and spiritual power. Scott is valued[1] for his sheer energy and unsophisticated style, for the dramatic picturesqueness of his subjects, for a superb power to present heroic action, especially in battle, and for a palpitating narrative swiftly paced by the cross-country gallop of the meter. Like his novels, his verse is often loaded down with description; like them, too, his poetry does not address the soul of man. While not belonging to the order of our greatest poets, Scott achieved two things that were to distinguish his historical novels—a scenic setting steeped in the historic or legendary interest of the past and the suggestion of an epoch. (For the characteristics of his novels, see page 508.)[2]

---

1 We value his poetry because "no one has ever put more of his own nation into his work"—not merely because of Scott's narrative skill, and power in describing scenery. Thus asserts Russell, J. A., "The Poetry of Sir Walter Scott: Its Influence on Van Lennejs, Beets and Hofdijk," *De Nieuwe Gids,* XLVII (1932), pp. 484-491.

2 For a thorough and minute discussion of the early period of Scott's literary life, see Emerson, O. F., "The Early Literary Life of Sir Walter Scott," *The Journal of English and Germanic Philology,* XXIII (1924), pp. 28-62, 241-269, 389-417.

SCOTT'S NOVELS[1]

Waverley (1814). Theme is the failure of the last important Jacobite movement of 1745 to place the Stuart pretenders on the throne, the victory of the Whig ideal in its conflict with the Jacobite Tory, and the establishment of the House of Hanover—all with the implicit purpose of contrasting the world of the Scots Lowland with the medievalism of the Highlands. In fact, the most interesting character-studies are neither those of the hero Edward Waverley, nor of the Highland Chieftain Fergus Mac-Ivor,[2] nor even of the latter's spirited and romantic sister Flora; but rather of the Lowland Scots in Edinburgh. While most famous for the account of the Jacobite rising of '45 and for the portrait of Prince Charles Edward, the tragedy is one in which most of the figures are comedy or "humour" types, such as Davie Gellatley, Bailie Duncan MacWheeble, and Donald Bean Lean. Scott's statement is too harsh when he calls Edward Waverley "a sneaking piece of imbecility." Memorable: Evan Dhu. The love-story is rather tenuous. *Waverley*, laid aside in 1805 and not resumed until 1814,[3] is also interesting in its style variations; *e.g.*, the first six chapters, written about nine years earlier, are not only heavy, prolix, and expository, but so unnecessary that a modern novelist would start the book with Chapter VII or VIII. Elsewhere there are set pieces of description, grandiloquent sentences, loose writing, and, to its glory, spontaneous dialogue. Sources

---

1 Another way of classifying the Waverley novels is by the centuries of which they treat. (1) The Middle Ages: *Ivanhoe, The Betrothed, The Talisman, Count Robert of Paris, Castle Dangerous.* (2) Fifteenth Century: *Quentin Durward, The Fair Maid of Perth, Anne of Geierstein.* (3) Sixteenth Century: *The Monastery, The Abbot, Kenilworth.* (4) Seventeenth Century: *Old Mortality, The Bride of Lammermoor, A Legend of Montrose, The Pirate, The Fortunes of Nigel, Peveril of the Peak, Woodstock.* (5) Eighteenth Century: *Waverley, Guy Mannering, The Antiquary, The Black Dwarf, Rob Roy, The Heart of Midlothian, St. Ronan's Well, Redgauntlet, The Two Drovers, The Highland Widow, The Surgeon's Daughter.* Note that Scott may be neither the medievalist, as some would have it, nor a subjective romanticist. Only five works are concerned with the Middle Ages; while his romanticism is matter-of-fact, not looking toward reform like Byron, Shelley, or even Keats, nor upon life with anxiety and misgiving.

2 In designing the romantic figure of Fergus MacIvor, Scott borrowed, we are told, certain traits from his old acquaintance Glengarry, whose character is discussed by Roughead, William, "Glengarry's Way: A footnote to 'Waverley,'" *Juridical Review,* XXXI (1919), pp. 175-198.

3 One must remember that Scott was forty-two years old when his first novel was published; and before his death some thirty novels appeared, covering a period of eight centuries and the reigns of fifteen English rulers. But several questions have arisen. Was *Waverley* the first novel written by him? Did Scott retain others, written earlier and incorporated later in other novels? The first work of other novelists are not infrequently crude, yet why should *Waverley* be in general as good as his other novels? Is the generally-accepted chronology of Scott's novels detective? Consult Pope-Hennessy, Una, (1) "The Dates of Waverley Novels," *The London Times Literary Supplement,* April 28, 1932, p. 311, col. 1 f.; "Sir Walter Scott in his Works," *Essays By Divers Hands* (The Transactions of the Royal Society of Literature of The United Kingdom), New Series, XII (1933), p. 82 f. (pp. 79-103); Carswell, Donald, "Sir Walter's Secret," *The Scots Magazine,* XX (1933-1934), pp. 192-198; Boatright, M. C., "Scott's Theory and Practice Concerning the Use of the Supernatural in Prose Fiction in Relation to the Chronology of the Waverley Novels," *Publications of the Modern Language Association of America,* L (1935) p. 235-261.

were chiefly tales told to him in boyhood. Memorable: "Waken, Lords and Ladies Gay," "Hie Away, Hie Away," "Davie Gellately's Song," "Flora MacIvor's Song."[1]

Guy Mannering†* (1815). Laid in the period of George III, the world-old theme of the "missing heir" is developed into a delightful novel of character and a comedy of manners that, in the opinion of most critics, places *Guy Mannering* above *Waverley,* even if the hero is more wooden, the love-scenes more perfunctory, and the scenario possibly less vivid. No other Waverley novel is as rich in characters, the most memorable being Hatteraick, Dandie Dinmont,[2] and Dominie Sampson. Famous is Meg's declamatory speech beginning, "Ride your ways, ride your way . . . ." Memorable: "Twist Ye, Twine Ye, Even So," "Gypsy's Dirge."

The Antiquary†* (1816). Colorless are the hero and heroine, artificial and unimportant the scenic description and plot, yet Scott's favorite novel is a brilliant revelation of the ironical humor and pertinacity, the idealism and hard practicality of Scottish character, and of incomparable scenes and vignettes of contemporary Scots manners. Excellent, consistent comedy of Scotch country life in the period of George III is enriched by such characters[3] as Sir Arthur Wardour, Saunders Mucklebaekit, Jonathan Oldbuck "the Antiquary" (a composite picture of George Constable, a boyhood friend, and of Scott himself), and Edie Ochiltree[4] (whose prototype was probably a famous bedesman, Andrew Gemmels). Memorable: "Elspeth's Ballad," "Time."

The Black Dwarf (1816). First of the "Tales of My Landlord," slender in its melodramatic plot, inconsistent in its handling of the supernatural, and Gothic in its story of an eccentric warped in body and mind,[5] is a failure except in its delightful Scots dialogue. The Black Dwarf, his character probably drawn from David Ritchie, is called Elshander the Recluse, or Cannie Elshie the Wise Wight of the Mucklestanes; he is in reality Sir Edward Mauley.

---

1 We wish to hazard a tentative suggestion that the chronology of the novels may in one way or another be connected with the *number* of poems in each of Scott's novels. After graphing the poems in the novels discussed in the *Outline-History,* certain peaks and depths stood out. *The Monastery,* with sixty-seven poems, towered above all, while *The Two Drovers,* with one poem, was at the bottom. The investigation should be pursued further.

2 Until this very day the breed of terriers described as belonging to Dandie is called "Dandie Dinmonts," just as the island on Loch Katrine which Scott made the chief scene of *The Lady of the Lake* is marked on maps as "Ellen's Isle."

3 Scott often uses self-interpreting or tell-tale names, such as Dandie Dinmont in *Guy Mannering* and Dousterswivel in *The Antiquary.* Consu't Parsons, C. O., "Character Names in the Waverley Novels," *Publications of the Modern Language Association of America,* XLIX (1934), pp. 276-294.

4 Harper, G. McL., "Scott's Novels: An American View," *The Quarterly Review,* CCLIX (1932), p. 347 (pp. 344-351).

5 Scott himself, although strong of body and mind, was lame; and it is thought that possibly his personal handicap may have influenced his sympathetic treatment of deformity.

† * Explanation of symbols immediately precedes Chapter XV.

Old Mortality†* (1816). Stirring tale dealing with the later period (1670—1671) of the resistance of the Covenanters against the attempts of Charles II and James II to impose episcopacy, pictures both sides with almost equal fairness, although Scott's sympathies in general were not with John Balfour of Burley and his Covenanters.[1] His reproduction of a departed age four generations back is fitted out with a large number of most admirable characters, of whom none except Henry Morton and Edith Bellenden is weak. The original of "Old Mortality" was Robert Paterson. Construction exceptionally good, except for the beginning and the closing chapters; humor, realism, and narrative power noteworthy. In *Guy Mannering* and in *The Antiquary* he had sketched respectively the Scotland of his early youth and of his early manhood; in *Old Mortality* he reconstructed the past from written records. Memorable: "Major Bellendon's Song."

Rob Roy†* (1817). Taking its title from the historical character, Robert Macgregor (Robert the Red), the story is concerned with the period preceding by two months the Jacobite rising of 1715 and ending soon after the collapse of the insurrection in February, 1716. By common consent Diana Vernon is Scott's most original heroine, sharing only with Catherine Seyton the palm of being his most captivating one, and with none the distinction of being his only complete portrait of a young gentlewoman. Two of his greatest characters are Andrew Fairservice and Bailie Nicol Jarvie. Unlike *Old Mortality*, it is unusually defective in composition and not too lucid in plot; while belonging to the class of *Waverley*, it is superior to it especially in characterization and humor.

The Heart of Midlothian†* (1818). Brilliant canvas of great scenes (the Porteous Riots) is the background of an almost perfect narrative watered down by its protracted conclusion. Only the Byronic Robertson and George Staunton are feebly drawn; memorable minor characters are Bartoline Saddletree and the Laird of Dumbiedikes; among the immortals are Jeanie Deans, Davie Deans, and Madge Wildfire. The final chapters are weak.[2] As in *The Antiquary*, so here is Scott the novelist of character, humor, and manners. Memorable: "Proud Maisie."

The Bride of Lammermoor†* (1819). Probably his most closely-knit and direct story. Important as the characters may be in this his-

---

1 His attitude towards the Catholic Church is still in doubt. In *The Abbot* and *The Monastery*, he seems to be hostile, yet other passages elsewhere are somewhat contradictory of any flat statement concerning his hostility. For his religious, social, and political views, consult Graham, J. E., "Scott's Catholic Tendencies," *The Catholic University Bulletin*, xx (1914), pp. 29-49; Stalker, Archibald, *The Intimate Life of Sir Walter Scott* (1921), pp. 174-191; Crockett, W. S., "The Religion of Sir Walter Scott," *The Hibbert Journal*, xxvii (1928), pp. 483-497; Gray, W. F., "The Religion of Sir Walter Scott," *The Hibbert Journal*, xxxi (1932-1933), pp. 47-60; Patten, J. A., *Sir Walter Scott* (1932), pp. 32-37, 160-163; Muir, Edwin, *Scot and Scotland* (1936), "Scott and Conservatism," pp. 119-175.

2 The climax is Jeanie's success in obtaining a pardon for Effie, but then the story is continued still further, gathering itself steadily into a strong conclusion.

† * Explanation of symbols immediately precedes Chapter XV.

torical novel set in the time of William III, they are secondary to Scott's most dramatic love-story,[1] easily divisible into five dramatic acts progressive in their rapidity and passion until the whirling fall of the unrelieved catastrophe. For the first and last time Scott, in the portrayal of Ravenswood, presents a character who unceasingly dominates a tale.[2] Creation: Caleb Balderstone, who relieves the gloom of the stark tragedy. Note that the characters are strongly contrasted with one another in a story overhung by a shadow that advances steadily and swiftly in the face of all lulls and interludes, and where the landscape, like Hardy's Egdon Heath in *The Return of the Native,* becomes, as Buchan points out, almost a protagonist. Memorable: "Lucy Ashton's Song."

A Legend of Montrose (1819). Slight in action, the last of the "Tales of My Landlord" has for its historical background the 1644 campaign of the Highland clans against the Covenanters of their own country and in favor of Charles I. In portraying Captain Dugald Dalgetty, Scott is said to achieve Shakespearean perfection of character. Is the weakest of the nine novels all Scots in setting. Memorable: "The Orphan Maid," "Pibracht of Donuil-dhu," "Annot Lyle's Song."

Ivanhoe† (1819). First work in which he deals with a subject purely English, the reign of Richard I in the closing years of the twelfth-century. Centers in two chief events, both fictitious—the great tournament at Ashby-de-la-Zouche, and the storming of Front-de-Boeuf's castle of Torquilstone, the latter description borrowed from Goethe's *Goetz von Berlichingen.* The artificialty once condoned, recognize the well-managed stirring episodes and the more than sixscore characters, of whom the most highly individualized and the greatest is Rebecca,[3] who ranks with Jeanie and Catherine Seyton. Not on its historical side is it famous, for its anachronisms and historical errors have been pointed out by E. A. Freeman, the historian; but on its effectively romantic side—paradoxically it is the non-historical features (the melodramatic medieval pictures) that have given *Ivanhoe* its reputation as a great historical novel.[4] Memorable: "Saxon War Song," "Rebecca's Hymn."

---

1 It is the source of Donizetti's opera, *Lucia di Lammermoor.*

2. Walter Bagehot agrees that, except for the characterization of Edgar Ravenswood, Scott's heroes are commonplace and of one type.

3 The original of Rebecca may have been Rebecca Gratz, the beautiful and philanthropic Jewess of Philadelphia. See Jacobs, Joseph, "The Original of Scott's Rebecca," *Publications of the American Jewish Historical Society,* Number 22 (1914), pp. 53-60; Woddis, M. J., "Sir Walter Scott and the Jews," *Views: A Jewish Monthly,* I (1932), pp. 215-223; "Great Americans: Rebecca Gratz," *The Jewish Examiner,* June 2, 1939, page 6, col. 1 *f. Rebecca and Rowena* (p. 539) is an amusing sequel and re-interpretation by Thackeray.

4 *Ivanhoe,* directly or indirectly, has not only helped to build great novels but has influenced the historical writing of Carlyle, Prescott, Macaulay, Froude, Parkman, and others. Maynadier, G. H., "Ivanhoe and Its Literary Consequences," in *Essays in Memory of Barrett Wendell,* by His Assistants (Harvard University Press, 1926), pp. 221-233.

† * **Explanation of symbols immediately precedes Chapter XV.**

The Monastery (1820). The reign of Elizabeth is the period of this historical novel slight yet confused in plot, lamed further by the introduction of supernatural machinery in the form of the White Lady of Avenal, and unredeemed by incidental beauties and authentic historical material. Its prime interest is some excellent pictures of Scottish scenery; its chief importance, that it is the foundation of *The Abbot.* Memorable: "Border Ballad." (See *The Abbot* and *Kenilworth.*)

The Abbot (1820). Sequel to *The Monastery* is concerned with that period in the life of Mary Queen of Scots that she spent in imprisonment at Lochleven Castle, her escape early in May, 1568, and her flight to England after the battle at Langside near Glasgow. Superb theme of the tragic life of the beautiful and sunny-natured Mary brought out Scott's greatest power and pathos in a double plot generally well executed against a background of brilliant pictures. Its plot is merely satisfactory in its conclusion, and rather lacking in the rich comedy of Scott's foremost works. Characters: Mary, Lady Lochleven, Catherine Seyton. (See, also, *The Monastery* and *Kenilworth.*)

Kenilworth†* (1821). Intricate plot knit clearly out of the traditional fate of Amy Robsart, daughter of Sir Hugh Robsart. Most famous episode is the meeting of Queen Elizabeth, Amy, and Leicester in the garden of Kenilworth. This is the third of the three novels of the sixteenth-century group, the other two being *The Monastery* and *The Abbot;* all three suffer from a shallow approach to life.

The Pirate (1821). Although Scott utilized the personal notes of his voyage to the Shetlands and Orkneys, yet the scene laid principally in the Shetland of the seventeenth century never becomes completely alive. Most of the descriptions are of the southern half of the mainland, the only part explored by Scott during his six days in Shetland; description of the landscape often is. as masterly as that in his best work. Melodramatic plot,[1] rhetorical verse. Character: Ulla Troil, known as Norma of the Fitful-Head. Memorable: "Cloud Halcro's Song," "Cleveland's Song," "And You Shall Deal the Funeral Dole."

The Fortunes of Nigel (1822). Glittering narrative, enriched by the unforgettable picture of James I of England and VI of Scotland and by the perfect focus of the historical background, is kept alive by the swift pace of brilliant streetscenes, scenes at Court, and the whole life of Jacobean London and by the impact of various characters. Structure is loose; plot is negligible. King James ranks with Louis XI of *Quentin Durward* in the gallery of Scott's careful historical portraits.

---

1 The prototype of the dashing hero, Cleveland, was John Gow, a native of Caithness. See Fea, Allan, *The Real Captain Cleveland* (1912); Clark, W. F., *The Shetland Sketch Book* (1930), " 'The Pirate' in Real Life," pp. 103-111.

† * Explanation of symbols immediately precedes Chapter XV.

Peveril of the Peak (1823). Not until the fourteenth chapter is the principal theme reached. Longest of all his novels, it is a tedious work concerned in the main with the pretended Popish Plot of 1678; it is as labored as its beginning and as unsatisfying as its huddled ending. Crowded with famous historic characters; *e.g.,* the elaborate portrait of Charles II is just a little below that of Charles II in *Woodstock*. Best-remembered character: Fenella.

Quentin Durward†* (1823). For the first time Scott left his native isles and placed his characters on foreign soil in a brilliant historical novel in which the romance of the fictitious Quentin Durward and the Burgundian countess, Isabelle de Croye, is subordinate to the fifteenth-century intrigues of Louis XI of France, whose character juxtaposed to that of Charles the Bold of Burgundy, is the outstanding artistic achievement of the book.[1] Note that Scott is repeating the Nigel device of a Scot abroad. Of Scott's young heroes, Quentin is one of the best. Memorable: "County Guy."

St. Ronan's Well (1824). The only work in which Scott chose his own generation is differentiated from his other novels in its rejection of the romantic in favor of realistic satire of idle fashionable society found in the Scottish spa of St. Ronan's Well. In no other work, also, do his characters so reveal themselves by their dialogue as in this tragic social comedy relieved by glints of humor. Creations: Meg Dods, Peregrine Touchwood.

Redgauntlet (1824). Somewhat baffling plot, partly told in a series of letters, is as truly Scotch as any of the Waverley novels, and contains parts on a level with his best achievements. Noteworthy for its use of personal memories: the Lady of the Green Mantle is Margaret Belches; Saunders Fairford is modelled on Scott's father, Darsie Latimer on Will Clerk, and Alan in small measure on himself. Leisurely beginning of the narrative, the time of which is approximately the early reign of George II (1763), is swept up in the whirling speed of the final chapters. In this latest Scotch novel of lowland life (the others are *Guy Mannering, The Antiquary, Old Mortality,* and *The Heart of*

---

1 In *Quentin Durward* Scott presents a somewhat one-sided picture of chivalry: the shield is usually bright, seldom tarnished by the misery of the times. While his history is not always accurate and complete, however, he did make readers realize that the earlier centuries had their human beings, not merely (to quote Carlyle) "protocols, state papers, controversies"; although, to keep the record straight, Carlyle also called the protagonists of the Waverley novels "little more than mechanical cases."

† * **Explanation of symbols immediately precedes Chapter XV.**

Midlothian) appears the interpolated short-story of *diablerie*—"Wandering Willie's Tale"—recognized as a miracle of imagination and perfect style, and as one of the greatest presentations of the supernatural in realistic and dramatic form. ("Wandering Willie's Tale," selected as one of the twenty-five best short-stories in the world, should be compared with Burns's *Tam o' Shanter,* p. 433.)

The Betrothed (1825). With its scene provided by the Welsh marches in the time of Henry II (1154—1189), the story, based on a legend told in many parts of Europe, pants audibly with the moral vicissitudes of Eveline Berenger and Damian. Is one of the "Tales of the Crusaders."

The Talisman (1825). Mingling of romance and passion heightened by common human interests reproduces the very atmosphere and life of the Holy Land garnered from G. A. Smith's *Historical Geography of the Holy Land.* Good if histrionic plot is not sustained by its surface portraiture but by its note of gallantry. The principal parts are taken by Richard I (Coeur de Lion) and Saladin. Roswal, the stag greyhound, deserves to rank among the *dramatis personae.*[1] Yet it is such books as *Ivanhoe, Quentin Durward,* and *The Talisman* that have impelled Benedetto Croce to declare Scott merely a minor artist captivating by a superficial picturesqueness.

Woodstock (1826). The period is revealed by the subtitle, *The Cavalier, or A Tale of the Year 1651*: the story centers in the escape of Charles II from England after the battle of Worcester; the scene is the royal park of Woodstock, near Oxford. The trappings are frequently Radcliffian; the character-drawing, which receives the main emphasis of the narrative, is less taut than the compactly-knitted dramatic episodes. From the point of view of Scott's personal history, no other novel is as significant, for *Woodstock* was written in the crisis of his life, in the face of financial ruin, illness of his grandson, and death of his wife.[2] (Plot and characters later used by Thackeray in *Henry Esmond.*)

The Chronicles of the Canongate (1827). Collection of three short-stories (or novels) chiefly notable for the fictitious narrator, Mr.

---

1 Concerning Scott's affection for dogs and the use of dogs in his works, refer to Stevenson, P. R., "Sir Walter Scott and His Dogs," *The Cornhill Magazine,* New Series, XLVII (1919), pp. 585-594.

2 The original of Alice Lee was Scott's daughter Anne.

Chrystal Croftangry (Scott himself) who draws upon the recollections of Mrs. Bethune Balliol (a composite of his own mother, and of his friend Mrs. Keith) who lives in the Canongate, Edinburgh. (a) *The Two Drovers,* by its characterization of Robin Oig M'Combich, illustrates tragically the Highland ethics of not fighting with the fists but of killing with the dirk. (b) *The Highland Widow,* a short tragic tale of the widow Elspeth MacTavish and her son, Hamish Bean MacTavish, after the 'Forty-Five (1745); she is as melodramatic as Helen Mac-Gregor of *Rob Roy.* (c) *The Surgeon's Daughter,* an exotic narrative of the time of George II and George III that jumps from the village of Middlemas to the country of India, is memorable for its sympathetic sketch of Dr. Gideon Gray.

The Fair Maid of Perth; or, St. Valentine's Day(1828). Scene of the second of "The Chronicles of the Canongate" is laid at Perth in the time of Henry IV of England and Robert III of Scotland (close of the fourteenth and opening of the fifteenth centuries). Somewhat lively romance combines stock medieval pictures with real characters, among whom the best are Father Clement, Simon Glover, and Conachar. Is the best novel written after the disaster that befell Scott. Memorable: "Song of the Glee-Maiden."

Anne of Geierstein (1829). The portrait of Charles the Bold, the burlesque court of the troubadour Rene, and the description of the secret brotherhood of the Vehmgericht (the last-named drawn from Goethe's *Goetz von Berlichingen*) are the interesting features of this vigorously-told narrative laid in the reign of Edward IV (1474). Is a kind of sequel to *Quentin Durward.*

Count Robert of Paris (1831). Novel concerned with Constantinople and the First Crusade, and with the plot of Nicephorus Briennius to dethrone his father-in-law, the Emperor Alexius I. Comnenus. Written in failing health, yet first half of book exhibits for the last time Scott's power of recreating the past. Indebted to the *Alexiad* and to Gibbon.

Castle Dangerous (1831). His last novel deals with the defense in 1306 of Douglas Castle by Sir John de Walton against the armies of Robert the Bruce and Sir James Douglas. "The oppression of his spirits," notes Buchan," is curiously reflected in the weather of the tale, for all the events take place under grey skies, in creeping mists and driving rain."

CHARACTERISTICS OF SCOTT'S NOVELS

SUGGESTED MERITS

Romance. Foremost is his romantic sense his characters, descriptions, and dialogue are all picturesque. While showing little interest in the passion of love, he revealed an interesting power of perceptive emotion.

History. His historical knowledge was very extensive; frequently his readjustments are dramatically justifiable. Not the pitter-patter of hearts is involved, but primarily high political interests; yet the main parts in the intrigue are still retained for the conventional hero and heroine.

People. His stage, like that of the world, is crowded with people. Excels in the quiet creation of humble folk; his minor characters are almost always painted with marvelous success. A democratic novelist; whether intentionally or not, the common people, more lifelike than the kings, are the chief source of interest; while the minor figures are often typical, they are just as often class-conscious.[2]

Thought. His works are capable presentations of the drama of a nation's epoch. Customs and costumes are an integral part of his social history. Minor characters, while often class conscious, apparently had no major purpose of crying in the wilderness. (But consult his apologia in Introductory Epistle to **The Fortunes of Nigel**.)

Style and Construction. Highest excellence in the direct style of the Scottish vernacular. Racy characterization, stirring incidents, and dramatic situations compensate the reader for long stretches of description. Innovation of providing exposition and carrying on the action by means of dialogue and soliloquy, was copied by other historical novelists.

SUGGESTED DEFECTS

Romance. Uses melodramatic devices connected with the Gothic tale. Defective love-interest; has little to say about sex. Frequently regarded as a novelist of incident rather than of character.

History. Scott, generally recognized as the creator of the historical novel in its legitimate form,[1] is often charged with historical inaccuracies; e.g., when Leicester in Kenilworth entertained Queen Elizabeth, Amy Robsart had been dead for many years.

People. Pallid delineation of heroes; they have little reality of spiritual worth. Superficial character-painting of heroines; while beautiful, they are ineffectual, lacking in magic of loveliness and mystery of temperament. Abundance of fixed types or stock characters. Like Shakespeare's tragedies, Scott's novels deal primarily with persons of high degree; but his lords and ladies are often watered creatures.

Thought. Weak treatment of two deep human interests, love and religion. In his novels there is the stir of the world but not of the soul. He is a rose-colored chronicler of feudalism, not a prophet of social reform; he is quite blind to the abstract intelligence, and gives no message to the world.

Style and Construction. Loose and diffuse construction, rapid and careless composition. Occasional bad grammar, inept use of words, false rhetoric, stilted and elephantine style of eighteenth-century prose; total lack of subtlety. Lengthy descriptions or dissertations hold up the action, which usually begins slowly and proceeds sluggishly. Preference for the happy ending.

---

1 Scott is generally recognized as the creator of the historical novel in its legitimate form. The Waverley works reveal his profound nationalism; out of some thirty novels, about twenty have their scenes wholly or partly in Scotland, and at least three of the remaining ten also have Scottish heroes (*Quentin Durward, The Fortunes of Nigel, The Talisman*). Consult Canning, A. S. G., *History in Scott's Novels* (1907); Grierson, H. J. C., "Sir Walter Scott," *Columbia University Quarterly*, xxv (1933), pp. 9-25; Dargan, E. P., "Scott and the French Romantics," *Publications of the Modern Language Association of America*, xlix (1934), pp. 599-629.

2 In politics Scott was an unbending Tory. Admittedly, he was actively hostile to the early struggles of trade unionism. Yet, in spite of his aristocratic sympathies, he was a democratic force. Despite his deficient political judgment, the true heroes of his tales are the plain folk. In real life, too, he honored the poor; he arranged in Abbotsford for relief work with full wages; he proposed a scheme of unemployment insurance in factories, the premiums to be paid wholly by the owners. See Dixon, W. M., "Our Debt to Scott To-Day," *Queen's Quarterly*, xxxix (1932), pp. 581-592.

ESSAYISTS

Charles Lamb, 1775—1834, familiar essayist.[1] Born at No. 2 Crown Office Row, Inner Temple, London. Son of a law clerk. At Christ's Hospital School (1782—1789), of which he has left two accounts in *Recollections of Christ's Hospital* and *Christ's Hospital Five and Thirty Years Ago*. His tendency to stammer disqualified him from obtaining a scholarship at a university. Clerk at the South Sea House (1791—1792), the memories of which he later recorded in his first Elian essay, *Recollections of the South Sea House* (1820). Enters the office of the East India House (1792). Close friend of Coleridge (1794). Inchoate love affair with Ann Simmons (*c.* 1794), the "Anna" of his poetry and the "Alice" of his essays. Voluntarily spent six weeks "very agreeably" in a madhouse at Hoxton (1795—1796). Four of his sonnets appeared in *Poems on Various Subjects* (1796), a volume by Coleridge. In a fit of mental aberration, his sister Mary Ann **Lamb** kills her mother, and is temporarily removed to a private asylum (1796). Attachment for Hester Savory (1796—1799), whose death inspired the poem *Hester*. Publication of poems by Lamb and Charles Lloyd in the second edition of Coleridge's poems (1797). Estrangement with Coleridge (1798—1800). Publication of *Blank Verse* by Lamb and Charles Lloyd (1798). Mary Lamb comes to live with him (1799). Publishes *The Works of Charles Lamb* (Two volumes, 1818). Proposes to Fanny Kelly, the actress (1818).[2] Rejected. First meeting with Emma Isola (1820), subsequently adopted by Charles and Mary in about 1823. Visit Paris (1822). Move to Colebrook Cottage, Islington (1823). Retires from the East India House on a pension of £441, representing nearly two-thirds of his salary. Marriage of Emma Isola and Edward Moxon (1833). Charles falls and injures his face (December 22); five days later he dies of erysipelas (1834). Buried in Edmonton churchyard, where he was joined by Mary Lamb in 1847.

As a poet, his place is not high. As a critic, his brief discriminating comments helped revive interest in the dramatists of the Elizabethan period. As a letter-writer, he is entitled to a place beside Cowper and Burns. But it is as a familiar essayist that he holds his unique position. Lamb's intimate essays are artful in their very artlessness. The style, rich with the flavor of the past and redolent of such prose as Burton's *Anatomy* and Browne's *Hydriotaphia* (Vol. 1, pp. 272, 273), is yet almost headlong in the epicurean choice of words. Perfect is the blend

1 Blunden, Edmund, *Charles Lamb and His Contemporaries* (1933); May, J. L., *Charles Lamb* (1934); Ward, A. C., *The Frolic and the Gentle* (1934); Williams, Orlo, *Charles Lamb* (1934); Johnson, E. C., *Lamb Always Elia* (1935).

   Charles Lamb was a warm friend, an engaging host, a gentle humorist, a convivial companion, a devoted and self-sacrificing brother. Later biographers have added details to Lamb's portrait, but fundamentally it seems to remain as T. N. Talfourd painted it. Consult Newdick, R. S., "The First *Life and Letters* of Charles Lamb," *Ohio State University Studies, Contributions in English,* III (1935).

2 Riddell, W. R., "Letters from Charles and Mary Lamb to Fanny Kelly," *Proceedings and Transactions of The Royal Society of Canada,* Third Series, XXIII (Section II, 1929), pp. 95-104.

of the associative qualities of his mind—a blend of restrained pathos and frolicsome humor, of compressed thought and wistful understanding, of grounded sense and winged imagination. Unlike Leigh Hunt and Hazlitt,[1] however, he seems to have cared little or nothing for politics.

Essays

Elia. Essays which Have Appeared under that Signature in the London Magazine† (1823) and *The Last Essays of Elia*† (1833). Typical essays[2] include: (1) *The Two Races of Men* (1820), the germ of which is possibly in a letter to Wordsworth in 1816, are *the men who borrow and the men who lend.* (2) *Mrs. Battle's Opinions on Whist* (1821),[3] glorifying the game and immortalizing a character who in real life was to no small extent Sarah Burney, the wife of Lamb's friend Admiral Burney. (3) *A Chapter on Ears* (1821), resulting from his lack of great enthusiasm for music. "I have no ear"—are the opening words of the essay, which adds, more than sevenscore words later, "for music." The whimsical title is as misleading as the one on *Two Races of Men.* (4) *My First Play* (1821), an expansion of a paragraph in an essay of 1813. (5) *The Old Benchers of the Inner Temple* (1821), a beautiful piece in which the Benchers are not imaginary characters[4]; Lovel is his father. (6) *Imperfect Sympathies* (1821), whose original title was *Jews, Quakers, Scotchmen, and other Imperfect Sympathies.*[5] (7) *Dream Children* (1822), consummately expressive of his reticence and intense feeling. (8) *The Praise of Chimney-Sweepers* (1822), an expansion of a paper published ten years earlier, is almost ablaze with wit. (9) *A Complaint of the Decay of Beggars in the Metropolis* (1822), a criticism of the zealous activity of the Society for the Suppression of Mendicity, founded in 1818. (10) *A Dissertation upon Roast Pig* (1822), delicious in its drollery and rich in literary allusiveness. (11) *Poor Relations* (1823), reminiscent of the Character-Writers (Vol. 1, p. 248). (12) *Old China* (1823), where the portrait of Mary Lamb, begun in *Mackery End in Hertfordshire,* is completed, and where the real theme is the joys of past poverty versus the cares of present affluence. (13) *Barbara S—* (1825), in which Lamb preserves a nice blend of fact, whimsicality, and invention; the heroine is Fanny Kelly. (14) *The Superannuated Man* (1825), an autobiographic record of his life as an

---

1 MacDonald, W. L., "Charles Lamb, the Greatest of the Essayists," *Publications of the Modern Language Association of America,* XXXII; New Series, XXV (1917), pp. 547-572.

2 Jerrould, Walter, *Charles Lamb* (1905), pp. 70-99; *The Essays of Elia,* edited by Woodbridge, H. E. (1929).

3 Manwaring, G. E., " 'Mrs. Battle,' " *The National Review,* CIII (1934), pp. 637-642.

4 *The Old Benchers of the Inner Temple,* annotated by Macinnon, F. D. (1927).

5 Charles Lamb's feeling towards the Jews was not a negative sentiment but an active aversion. Curiously, Lamb himself admits that his facial appearance was somewhat Jewish. See Rich, S. M., "Was Lamb an Anti-Semite?" *The Jewish Guardian,* May 5, 1922; p. 18f.

† * Explanation of symbols immediately precedes Chapter XV.

employee at the India House and of his retirement, but discreet in its omission of the two months of suspense before Lamb knew the verdict upon his request for a pension. (15) *The Wedding* (1825), a description of Louise Burney's marriage in 1821, poised between the light and the pathetic.

Dramatic Works

John Woodvil (1802). Five-act play in blank verse originally called *Pride's Cure*. Labelled a tragedy, yet the death is neither tragic in itself nor in its consequences; slight in story, and, strictly speaking, has no plot. Deficient in the close coupling of incidents and inadequate in character motivation. Whatever merits this Elizabethan drama possesses are in its occasional poetic passages and skilful handling of blank verse: but, ultimately, it falls short even of Southey's declaration that the play is "delightful poetry badly put together. An exquisite picture in a clumsy frame."

Mr. H.: or Beware a Bad Name (1805—1806; 1813). Wire-drawn prose farce: it failed, as Lamb recognized, because the "subject was not substantial enough." Humor, actable dialogue, and good planning could not sustain an inadequate motif. Elizabethan dramatists, especially Beaumont and Fletcher, were his models. Lamb himself hissed it in the second act.

The Pawnbroker's Daughter (c. 1825; 1830). Slight dramatic piece in prose based on his essay called *On the Inconvenience of Being Hanged* is somewhat more substantial in its content than *Mr. H.* Two-act farce strikes a note of whimsicality verging upon romantic drama.

The Wife's Trial; or, The Intruding Widow (1827; 1828). Dialogic piece in blank verse, founded on Crabbe's dramatic poem called *The Confidant,* is fuller in substance and more sustained in suspense than any of his plays. But, nevertheless, a slight, almost preposterous, piece. Wordsworth liked the play "marvellously," objecting only to "a little degradation of character for a more dramatic turn of plot."

Critical Works

Tales from Shakespear. Designed For the use of Young Persons (1807). Purpose of the twenty tales was to outline clearly the main argument of each drama and thereby interest young people in the original. The series of English Histories and the Roman Plays are omitted; Mary wrote the fourteen comedies and Charles the six tragedies: *Romeo and Juliet, Hamlet, Othello, King Lear, Macbeth,* and *Timon of Athens* (Vol 1, pp. 184—186, 204—216). Told with simplicity and pleasant emphasis on the moral of the central situation. Next to his essays, this book is his best-known work; yet its success is attributable more to Mary, whose name did not appear on the title page of the first few editions, than to Charles.

Specimens of English Dramatic Poets, who lived about the time of Shakespeare (1808). Anthology of scenes from ninety Elizabethan plays; pioneering in its appreciative attitude. Admirable selections, enhanced by interesting and critical comment. Value of his opinions occasionally disputed, but never his broad knowledge of Elizabethan plays.

Verse

Lamb, the writer of some one hundred poems, is known for the fancy of *Farewell to Tobacco*, with its famous apostrophe; the pleasant verse-story of an unrequited love told in *Prince Doris;* the virile if morbid verses of *The Gypsy's Malison*, which appeared in *Album Verses* (1830), a thin volume that included the elegy called *On an Infant Dying as Soon as Born* and also *She is Going*, reminiscent of the seventeenth-century lyric. Possibly his best-known two poems are *Old Familiar Faces* (1798), a wistful piece in free verse hinting at the poignant sadness of a suffering soul, and *Hester* (1803), a lyrical ballad sweet in portraiture, controlled in emotion, but pedestrian in gait. But Lamb's verse lacks any outstanding merit, and is a source of distinct pleasure only to those aware of the author's personality and life.

Miscellaneous Writings

A Tale of Rosamund Gray, and old blind Margaret (1798). Prose tale of sentiment, influenced by Mackenzie's *Julia de Roubigné* (p. 401), possesses a beautiful simplicity and crepuscular charm. Its conception may be morbid, its composition incoherent, its catastrophe sentimental—the whole novelette may be feeble and crude in execution; but it has definite traces of the Elian magic. (Southey's poem, *The Ruined Cottage*, is essentially a paraphrase of this moral tale.)

Adventures of Ulysses (1808). Simple, well-told narrative intended by Lamb "to be an introduction to the reading of Telemachus" by Fénelon. Narrative based on Chapman's translation of Homer's *Odyssey* (Vol. 1, p. 235). "Chapman is divine," said Lamb, "and my abridgment has not quite emptied him of his divinity."

Mrs. Leicester's School, or, The History of Several Young Ladies, Related by themselves (1808—1809). In collaboration with Mary Lamb. Of the ten tales in this children's collection, three are by Charles Lamb: *The Witch Aunt, First Going to Church*, and *The Sea Voyage*. (To Landor, *The Father's Wedding Day* was among the most beautiful prose tales in any language.)

Letters.[1] A direct source of any true "life" of Lamb. Records, in addition to his trivial or important activities, shrewd opinions about books and pictures, plays and actors. His letters have not only the inconsequent charm of his better verses and the crisp piquancy of his essays, but also a skylarking audacity of expression and an exuberant fun not to be found elsewhere in his writings. Several of the essays are foreshadowed in the letters.

William Hazlitt, 1778—1830, literary critic, essayist.[2] Born at Maidstone, where his father was a liberal Unitarian minister. Family migrated to New England (1783), but returned to England (1786—1787). Destined for the Unitarian ministry, he entered Hackney Theological College in London as a "divinity student" (1793); but within two years forsook his contemplated profession (1795), later decided to become a portrait painter, and finally gave this up for literature. Had met Coleridge and Wordsworth (1798); for his early relations with them, read *My First Acquaintance with Poets.* Copied portraits in Paris (1802).[3] Married Sarah Stoddart (1808), from whom he was divorced by mutual consent fourteen years later (1822). Rejected by Sarah Walker, he married Mrs. Bridgwater or Bridgewater (1824), from whom he soon separated.

Hazlitt's essays are written in a style that is personal and picturesque, concise and animated, varying from colloquial vigor to weighted aptness; with a lack of subtlety, yet his phrases succeed each other with accelerating brilliance. As he himself claimed in his later years, he had "written no commonplace, and no line that licks the dust." Exuberance, occasionally, and ill-temper, more frequently, may have blurred his acuteness of vision; but as a familiar writer he may not impossibly take a place only a step lower than Lamb[4] and Montaigne; as a literary critic he is a leader of the first rank in the move for a new view of Shakespeare and the Elizabethan drama; and as a critic of books and pictures, of men and manners, he achieves a happy blend of sympathetic penetration, uncompromising love of truth, and imaginative susceptibility. Chief among his characteristics are an abounding memory, an intense enjoyment of books, a contagious gusto, and an independent judgment based less upon reasoned principles than upon

1 *Selected Letters of Charles Lamb,* edited by Clapton, G. T. (1924); *The Letters of Thomas Manning to Charles Lamb,* edited by Anderson, G. A. (1926); *The Letters of Charles Lamb to which are added those of his sister Mary Lamb,* edited by Lucas, E. V. (Three volumes, 1935).

2 Howe, P. P., *The Life of William Hazlitt* (1923); *Essays By William Hazlitt,* edited by Shelley, P. Von D. (1924); Madison, C. A., "William Hazlitt: Man and Critic," *Poet Lore,* XL (1929), pp. 373 390.

3 For a list of the paintings executed by Hazlitt, see Howe, P. P. "William Hazlitt," *Notes and Queries,* Twelfth Series, XI (1929), p. 70 f. (Available, also, in Howe, P. P., *The Life of William Hazlitt,* 1923, p. 435.)

4 Hazlitt and Lamb are seldom compared, but might advantageously be. Such a comparison is given by Reilly, J. T., "The Prince of English Essayists," *The Catholic World,* CXXXI (1930), p. 670 f. (pp. 662-671).

intuitive good taste. However, it may have been both logical reasoning and instinctive taste that made him hew to the line of his republican sympathies: Wordsworth and Coleridge he scorned as turncoats, and Southey as the toadying writer of birthday odes to princesses. Hazlitt, a rationalist in his attitude toward religion and a rebel in his politics, remained steadfastly true to the general libertarian principles of the French Revolution. While not the greatest of thinkers, Hazlitt is primarily important for writing a prose of infectious *discovery*—always he comes upon new enjoyments, and pleasurably shares them with the reader.

His works on art[1] and the drama include *Sketches of the Principal Picture Galleries in England* (1824), *Notes of a Journey through France and Italy* (1826), *The Life of Titian* (1830), and *Boswell Redivivus, or Conversations of James Northcote* (1826—1827; 1830), enlivened by readable gossip and good talk. More important: *The Round Table* (1817), including largely literary essays reprinted from the *Examiner,* marks his emergence as a familiar essayist; *Table Talk; or Original Essays on Men and Manners* (1821—1822), perhaps his best collection of miscellaneous essays, contains some of his most characteristic and mature ones. Like *The Round Table,* there are essays on men and manners as well as upon books: *The Plain Speaker* (1826), a companionable collection chiefly reprinted from the *New Monthly* and the *London* magazines; and the posthumous *Sketches and Essays* (1839) and *Winterslow* (1850), the two containing some of his best efforts. Of a different stamp: *The Characters of Shakespeare's Plays* (1817), attacked by the *Quarterly* and *Blackwood's,* is a popular book abounding in excellent thoughts well expressed, yet, according to Garrod, of his purely literary works is possibly the least satisfactory and certainly the least courageous; *Lectures on the English Poets* (1818), where again Hazlitt's critical outlook is romantic and anti-Augustan; *Lectures on the English Comic Writers* (1819), the third collection of a series of lectures, including praise of Chaucer for pathos and realism; *Lectures on the Dramatic Literature of the Reign of Queen Elizabeth* (1820), another book with a self-explanatory title; and *A View of the English Stage* (1818—1821), a collection of dramatic notices contributed to periodicals, and one revealing his fundamental understanding of the drama and its relation to life.

Essay on the Principles of Human Action (1805). Negligible

attempt in philosophy is "An Argument in favour of the Natural Disinterestedness of the Human Mind," an attack on the doctrines of self-interest and materialism of Hartley and Helvetius. Of interest, first, because of his early style, and, second, because Hazlitt, assuming the exis-

---

1 Chase, S. P., "Hazlitt as a Critic of Art," *Publications of the Modern Language Association of America,* xxxix; New Series, xxxii (1924), pp. 179-202.

tence of abstractions, regards them as the product only of the imagination.[1]

Liber Amoris; or, The New Pygmalion(1823). Sincere account of his nympholeptic love for Sarah Walker was exploited by his political enemies. While his lack of reticence has been deplored, yet his "Book of Love" illumines his intellectual and moral character.[2]

The Spirit of the Age† (1825). Series of masterly, though often one-sided and vitriolic, criticisms of leading contemporaries, where the conversation quality of his writing, especially in the essays on Scott and Coleridge, is best in evidence.

The Life of Napoleon Buonaparte (1828—1830). Occasioned by his worship of Napoleon as the destroyer of kings, especially the Bourbons, as the upsetter of oppressive institutions, and as the main hope of freedom. The four volumes represent his longest work, one possibly superior to Scott's, but by no means Hazlitt's greatest achievement, as he himself rated it.

Chief Essays. Twenty of his most characteristic essays are: (1) *My First Acquaintance with Poets*, (2) *On the Pleasure of Painting*, (3) *On Hogarth's Marriage A-La-Mode*, (4) *On Gusto*, (5) *Of Persons One Would Wish to Have Seen*, (6) *On Going a Journey*, (7) *Macbeth*, (8) *Mr. Kean's Richard* (9) *On Disagreeable People*, (10) *On Taste*, (11) *The Sick Chamber*, (12) *On Reading Old Books*, (13) *On Familiar Style*, (14) *The Fight*, (15) *On the Pleasure of Hating*, (16) *On the Feeling of Immortality in Youth*, (17) *On the Fear of Death*, (18) *On Reading New Books*, (19) *On a Landscape of Nicolas Poussin*, and (20) *On Living to One's-Self.*

James Henry Leigh Hunt, familiarly known as **Leigh Hunt,** 1784—1859, polygraphic writer.[3] Born in London. Educated at Christ's Hospital (1791—1799). Clerk in the War Office (1803—1808). With his brother John, established a liberal weekly called *The Examiner* (1808).[4] Married Marianne Kent (1809). Was fined and imprisoned (1813—1815) for calling the Prince Regent (later George IV) "a fat Adonis of 50" and "a despiser of domestic ties." Was, curiously enough, permitted to edit his periodical while in jail, where he was visited by

---

1 See pages 70-73 in the authoritative *William Hazlitt* by Augustine Birrell (1902) who states that "Neither in 1805, nor in 1836, nor at any time since, did Hazlitt's metaphysical discovery attract attention." Yet Hazlitt had a background of philosophical knowledge, a power of abstract thought, and a strong sense of fact: Consult Schneider, Elisabeth, *The Aesthetics of William Hazlitt* (1933).

2 The *Liber Amoris*, which "has always been accorded recognition, not as a work of art, but as a biographical lapse from virtue," is in reality "not the least of his contributions to our knowledge of the heart of man." Howe, P. P., "Hazlitt and 'Liber Amoris,'" *The Fortnightly Review*, cv; New Series, xcix (1916), pp. 300-310; Pearson, Hasketh, *The Fool of Love* (1934), Part II, "The Lover," pp. 119-239.

3 Blunden, Edmund, *Leigh Hunt* (1930).

4 Blunden, Edmund, *Leigh Hunt's "Examiner" Examined* (1928).

† * Explanation of symbols immediately precedes Chapter XV.

Byron, Moore, and Lamb. Joined Shelley and Byron in Italy (1821—1822). Edited the unsuccessful *Liberal*. Pensioned by the Crown (1847).

Hunt, a liberal in politics and a romantic in literary training, should be remembered notwithstanding his second-rate writings. Lockhart nicknamed Hunt "the Cockney Homer," just as he nicknamed Hazlitt "the Cockney Aristotle"; and Lockhart's christening of the group of writers (that also included Shelley, Keats, and Lamb) as the "Cockney School" is still retained. From Hunt, however, Keats learned Chaucer's way of handling the flowing couplet; from Hunt, Dickens learned a character-sketching utilized in *Sketches by Boz*. His style is undistinguished, yet he gave plasticity to the light miscellaneous essay; his ideas are not profound, yet his compilations and handbooks helped the layman to savor the beauties of literature; his poetry is not of the first rank, yet he recognized and praised the genius of Keats, apothecary, Shelley, atheist, Byron, profligate, and Wordsworth, driveller. Through his periodical writing he labored for such measures as equalization of taxes, education of the poor and amelioration of their sufferings, the reform of prison conditions, the abolition of child labor and the slave trade.

Periodicals

Leigh Hunt contributed frequently to many kinds of periodicals, including *The Morning Chronicle, The Atlas,* and *The New Monthly Magazine*. Moreover, he edited many periodicals—*The Examiner* (1808—1821), a Sunday paper; *The Reflector* (1810—1811), a quarterly; *The Literary Pocket-Book* (1819—1823), an annual; *The Indicator* (1819—1821), a weekly; *The Liberal* (1822—1823); *The Companion* (1828); *The Chat of the Week* (1830); *The Tatler* (1830—1832), concerning itself with literature and the stage; *Leigh Hunt's London Journal* (1834—1835); *The Monthly Repository* (1837—1838); and *Leigh Hunt's Journal Weekly* (1850—1851). As a journalist, he had no equal in his day.

Poetry

Of his poetry, only one long narrative and several short pieces come to mind to-day. These include the eighteen-line poem *Abou Ben Adhem,* his most popular poem, of which the fourteenth line is inscribed on Hunt's tomb: "Write me as one that loves his fellow-men"; *The Nile,* memorable for a superb line describing Cleopatra as "The laughing queen that caught the world's great hands"; "Jenny kissed me when we met," a rondeau written of Jane Welsh, the wife of Thomas Carlyle; "We the Fairies, blithe and antic," translated from the Latin of Thomas Randolph in *Amyntas;* "If you become a nun, dear," as light a love poem as "T'other day, as I was twining," but not as well known as the ironical *The Glove and the Lions; To the Grasshopper and the Cricket,* a poem of nature that should be compared with Keats's *On the Grasshopper and Cricket,* which appeared in the latter's *Poems* (1817), a volume where Hunt's influence is dominant; the apologue,

The Fish, the Man and the Spirit; the delightful *Sneezing* of Hunt's "Pyramid rhinocerostic"; the noble *Jaffar,* who delivered friends "From wants, from shames, from loveless household fears"; and *The Dearest Poets,* where Spenser is chosen as the one "To lay a wounded heart in leafy rest." Finally, there is *The Story of Rimini* (1816), an Italian tale based on the lines concerning Paolo and Francesca in Dante (*Inferno,* V). It is deprecated for its bits of banal dialogue and outright vulgarity but valued, first, as the flowing model for Keats's *Endymion* in not pausing in sense at the close of the rimed ten-syllable couplet (an attempt at the freer iambic pentameter of Chaucer's *Canterbury Tales* in preference to the neo-classical closed couplet), and, second, for a colloquial style that achieved consummate familiarity in Shelley's *Julian and Maddalo* (p. 478) and in Keat's *Lamia* (p. 487). In summary, perhaps the most significant of his contributions to English poetry, was, "first, *the imaginative and novel manner in which he approached his subject matter and with which he handled his style,* and, second, *his extreme sensitiveness to valuable influences from the outside of English literature."*[1]

Other Works

Leigh Hunt is remembered neither for his *Sir Ralph Eshar* (1832), a novel, nor for his *The Legend of Florence* (1840), a play, nor for such prose works as *The Round Table,* to which he contributed about ten of some fifty papers (see Hazlitt, p. 513), *Imagination and Fancy; or Selections from the English Poets* (1844), *Wit and Humour* (1846), *Stories from Italian Poets* (1846), *Men, Women, and Books* (1847), *A Jar of Honey from Mount Hybla* (1848), *The Town* (1848), *Table-Talk* (1851), *The Old Court Suburb* (1855), and *The Wishing-Cap Papers* (1873). The only two prose works now ever mentioned are *Lord Byron and Some of His Contemporaries*† (1828), where he made the error of revenging himself upon Lord Byron, who had withdrawn support from *The Liberal;*[2] and *The Autobiography of Leigh Hunt*† (1850), his best work, a sprightly review of the literary men of his time containing much gossip.

Thomas De Quincey[3] 1785—1859, consummate prose-poet whose polygraphic works nearly all appeared in periodicals.[4] Son of a well-

1 Wheeler. P. M., "The Great Quarterlies of the Early Nineteenth Century and Leigh Hunt." *The South Atlantic Quarterly,* XXIX (1930), p. 300 (pp. 282-303).
2 Hunt's reputation for ingratitude was supposedly crystallized in Dicken's characterization of Skimpole in *Bleak House.* The resemblance is there, but the entire sketch was not impossibly founded upon a cruel misinterpretation of Hunt. Despite Dickens's personal apology, and also his retraction after Hunt's death, the Skimpole tradition persists.
3 Not until after the death of Thomas Quincey, the father, did the Quincey family prefix the particle. It is disputable whether the prefix should be written with a small *d* or a capital *D;* in his later years. Thomas de Quincey seemed to prefer the former, as do his descendants. In the face of custom, which decrees the capital *D,* the *Outline-History* arbitrarily uses the capital letter only when the surname alone is used. (See, also, the spelling of Raleigh, Vol. 1, p. 141; of Shakespeare, Vol. 1, p. 160; and of DeFoe, p. 352.)
4 West. E. S., *A Flame in Sunlight* (1936); Eaton, H. A., *Thomas De Quincey* (1936).
† * **Explanation of symbols immediately precedes Chapter XV.**

to-do Manchester merchant. Educated at Bath School and then at a private school in Wiltshire. At Manchester School (1800—1802), from which he ran away. London (*c.* 1802). Worcester College, Oxford (1803—1808), where he never sat for a degree. Began to take opium (1804).[1] Settled in Wordsworth's vacated cottage at Grasmere (1809—1817), where, especially during the year 1813, he became a slave to the opium habit. Married Margaret Simpson (1816), a dalesman's daughter who had prematurely given birth to his son. Edited *The Westmorland Gazette* (1818 — 1819). Connected with Blackwood's Magazine (1819—1821) and with *The London Magazine* (1821—1823). Death of wife (1837) left him with a family of six children. Except for a few years elsewhere (*e.g.,* at Glasgow, 1841—1843, 1846—1847), De Quincey spent the remainder of his life in Edinburgh.

De Quincey ranks as the first of our imaginative essayists, singing a subtle, sensuous music[2] of romantic revery. He has been condemned as too elaborately rhetorical and too uniformly sonorous; he is long-winded and discursive, fond of long corkscrewing footnotes, inclined to flippant treatment of venerable persons and to vitiating humor. Once accustomed to his passion for Latin words, inverted clauses, vocative passages, and enormous sentences, his gossiping irrelevances become more fascinating than disturbing and his gorgeous rhetoric smells of incense rather than of the candle. Masson has described De Quincey's style as prevailingly intellectual; his dominant trait is, rather, aesthetic intellectuality, for his best work is instinct not merely with thought but with feeling, and his best style resembles poetry in its use of cadences, triads, stately rhythms, and complicated harmonies. It is, to use his own term, "impassioned" prose that he writes; and in him is seen the culmination of romantic prose that aimed at the effects of impassioned verse—an ornate, a rhythmical, and an emotional style that had evolved from that of Berners, Elyot, and Lyly, Ralegh and Jeremy Taylor, and especially Sir Thomas Browne, to whom De Quincey seems to have the closest affinity. (See Vol. 1, pp. 96, 116, 141, 150, 272, 275.) De Quincey, has drawn, also, a critical distinction between the literature of knowledge and the literature of power[3]: the latter at no time is ever

---

1 His addiction to opium was from compulsion rather than from choice: he took his initial dose to quiet a severe attack of rheumatic toothache, and in later years continued the use because of a "slow or intermittent ulceration of the stomach."

2 His style "has a mellowness of tone which suggests the depths of sublimal music," one "consciously or unconsciously modulated, with development and progression strangely similar to musical compositions." There seems to be a vital connection between his love of music and the elaborate prose of this great harmonist. Eaton, H. A., "DeQuincey's Love of Music," *The Journal of English and Germanic Philology,* XIII (1914), pp. 247-258.

3 In a series of papers known as *Letters to a Young Man whose Education has been Neglected* (1823), De Quincey makes keen comments on Latin and German literatures, and defends a classical education. It is, however, most memorable for the contrast between the literature of knowledge and the literature of power, a distinction which he obtained from a suggestion by Wordsworth, and one which he elaborated in his essays on *Style* and *On the Poetry of Pope* (1848).
    For his standing as a literary critic, see Fowler, J. H., *De Quincey as Literary Critic* (The English Association, Pamphlet No. 52, 1922),

superannuated, and to it belongs his best work as a romanticist. However, it is almost by his style alone that he seems to live.[1]

The Confessions of an English Opium Eater† (1821; first edition, 1822; enlarged edition, 1856). *Bizarrerie* of the narrative, partly autobiographical and partly fanciful, caught the attention of the public; the work succeeds as much by the frank self-revelation[2] of the rise and progress of a vice as it does by the poetic prose. Flawed by facetious digressions, irreverent jesting, and chaotic plan; graced by concentrated fluency, passionate ease, and vigorous brilliance. The *Confessions* are not written in the modern tabloid-like manner, but with an irreproachable dignity: he is more a kind of "spiritualized Rousseau" than "a decadent, fin-de-siècle figure." No English autobiography is so classical.

On the Knocking at the Gate in "Macbeth"† (1823). Highly subjective piece of impressionism, appearing in the scrapbook known as *Notes from the Pocket-book of a Late Opium-Eater,* marks a departure in the criticism of Shakespeare. It is an acute, suggestive, and illuminating fragment that endeavors not merely to gauge the seeming triviality of Shakespeare's scene but to plumb its imaginative depths. (See Vol. 1, p. 214 *f.;* also, p. 215, footnote 1.)

Murder Considered as One of the Fine Arts† (First paper, 1827; Second, 1839; Postscript, 1854). Ironical burlesque lecture or disquisition inspired by a series of ingenious murders committed by John Wilkins in 1811. The very title is a cue to De Quincey's humorous conception, one that elaborates with macabre detail and ghastly originality upon an extravagant idea very much in the spirit of Swift's *Modest Proposal* (p. 350), but easily and playfully. It is a type of imaginative criticism not without absorbing narrative and philosophic insight, despite the difference of opinion concerning De Quincey's outbursts ·of extravagant humor and unrestrained bravura.

Klosterheim, or the Masque (1832). Action of this Gothic novel is somewhat dulled by De Quincey's classic tone, yet the sequence of events and the atmosphere of terror are fairly well maintained. The mysteries are explained in a Radcliffian manner.

The Flight of a Tartar Tribe† (1837). Like *The English Mail-Coach,* this prose-poem starts from facts and moves into dreamland.

---

1 In religion and in politics De Quincey always remained a Tory and a conservative Englishman, looking with disfavor upon the removal of Catholic disabilities, the extension of the franchise, the adoption of the secret ballot, the Reform Bill of 1832, the growing trend toward democracy. He disapproved strongly of any move that might militate against the landed interests or disturb the *status quo.* The only work published as a book was his *The Logic of Political Economy* (1842), which was indebted chiefly to principles of David Ricardo, as was *The Dialogues of Three Templars,* a group of papers.

2 To trace the development of De Quincey's introspective habit of mind, read his *Autobiographic Sketches* (1834-1853).

† * Explanation of symbols immediately precedes Chapter XV.

It is an impressive piece of dramatic description, written in a style that is scenic and woven of elaborate magical images. More unity than usual in De Quincey. (Also known as *The Revolt of the Tartars.*)

Suspiria de Profundis: being a Sequel to the Confessions of an English Opium Eater (begun 1845). Only six sections of a planned series of "dreams and noon-day visions" were completed. *Levana and Our Ladies of Sorrow*, the last section, may be an exercise in literary mythology, but is elevated by magnificent prose-poetry into a beautiful dream-legend. The *Suspiria de Profundis* is in reality a philosophical essay, but his "Sighs from the Depths" is most interesting when he is analytically autobiographical. The *Confessions* had drawn upon his experiences from childhood to the year 1818; the *Suspiria* continues with the years from 1819 to 1845.

Joan of Arc (1847). Romantic biography. Elaborate prose lyric, occasionally marred by misapplied humor, achieves in its concluding pages the excellent contrapuntal style of his best works.

The Nautico-Military Nun and Ensign of Spain (1847). Somewhat monotonous tale in a characteristic style of inappropriate humor mingled with earnestness is derived from an article contributed by Alexis de Valon to an issue of the *Revue des Deux Mondes* (1847). Despite some lapses into prolixity and facetiousness, his gossamer filaments are woven and thickened imperceptibly into a strong web. Note the metamorphosis of the vulgar virago of the Spanish original into the charming Kate. (Also known as *The Spanish Military Nun.*)

The English Mail-Coach† (1849). Graphic account of the posthorses galloping along at a speed of thirteen miles an hour depends for effectiveness upon its thrilling evocation of the *sensation* of speed. Memorable for its *Dream Fugue: The Vision of Sudden Death*, where the rolling sentences, as in other paragraphs of this three-sectioned long essay, beat out the rhythmic music of a dream.

Walter Savage Landor, 1775—1864, poet, prose-writer.[1] Born in Warwickshire. Educated at Rugby (*c.* 1783). Entered Trinity College, Oxford (1793), where he showed unrestrained republican sympathies, and which he left without a degree after he had been rusticated for two terms. This incident led to a quarrel with his father, and only by the intervention of a friend was a reconciliation effected. On his father's death in 1805, he inherited the family property and established himself at Bath. Raised and equipped a regiment to support the revolutionaries in Spain against Napoleon (1808); Landor was *Coronel de la*

---

1 The principal source of our knowledge of Landor has been the "Life" by John Forster (1869, 1874), but it is inaccurate and incomplete. Sidney Colvin's, *Landor* (1881) is safer to use. T. E. Welby, who has edited a critical edition of Landor, is preparing a critical biography.

† * **Explanation of symbols immediately precedes Chapter XV.**

Infantería del Ejército real de España.[1] Purchased Llanthony Abbey in Monmouthshire (1809), where he was unsuccessful in his attempts to relieve the wretched lot of his tenants. Married Julia Thuillier (1811), the daughter of a Swiss banker. Lived in Como and Pisa, Italy (1815—1821), and in Florence (1821—1835). Quarreled[2] with his wife and separated from her (1835). Returned to Bath (1838—1858), where a suit for libel growing out of statements in *Dry Sticks* (1858) compelled him to return to Florence, where he spent the remainder of his life.

In point of time, Landor is both a Romantic and a Victorian; in spirit, he is a classicist.[3] His lyrics and epigrams have an icy perfection and extreme condensation; his blank verse has a stately massiveness and statuesque monotony; his dramatic and reflective prose dialogues are noble in sentiment and sane in thought. But both his poetry and prose were affected by his habit of writing in Latin; both reflect the marmoreal sententiousness of his thought. He gives us static, not dynamic, drama. Both, finally, do not communicate ideas of significance today, nor do they often reach the heart of man. Landor himself partly realized this, for he wrote: "I shall dine late, but the dining-room will be well lighted, the guests few and select."

Works include (1) *The Poems of Walter Savage Landor* (1795), in Latin and in English; except for some real feeling in the political pieces, his verses were in the main cold and imitative, as obviously under the influence of eighteenth-century classicism as (2) the prose pamphlet *Moral Epistle, Respectfully Dedicated to Earl Stanhope* (1795). (3) *Citation and Examination of William Shakespeare* (1834), a work of literary criticism, a failure despite its careful writing, solemn humor, and unity. (4) *The Pentameron and Pentalogia* (1837), revelatory of Landor's limitations but also of literary insight, broad toleration, tender humanity, and, of course, his special instinct for style. (5) *Andrea of Hungary, Giovanna of Naples,* and *Fra Rupert,* an historical trilogy (1839—1840) obviously deficient in plot. (6) *Poemata et Inscriptiones* (1847), a collection of Latin poems in the tradition of such masters as Virgil, Catullus, and Juvenal. (Recall that in his *Poems* of 1795 he had in a prose "Defensio" defended and advocated the use of Latin by living writers.) (7) *The Last Fruit off an Old Tree* (1853), which included conversations, essays, epigrams, lyrics, and the superb *Five Scenes* on the martyrdom of Beatrice Cenci; the title of the book was not entirely accurate, for it was followed by (8) *Antony and Cleopatra* (1856),

1 Hawkes, C. P., "The Spanish Adventure of Walter Savage Landor," *The Cornhill Magazine,* New Series, LXXIV (1933), pp. 551-564.

2 The character of Lawrence Boythorn in Dickens's *Bleak House* is generally believed to be drawn from that of Landor. To represent him as an irascible and crotchety gentleman may be unfair. See Wheeler, Stephen, "Landor: The Man and The Poet," *The Nineteenth Century and After,* XCI (1922), p. 237 f. (pp. 236-247).

3 Nitchie, Elizabeth, "The Classicism of Walter Savage Landor," *The Classical Journal,* XIV (1918-1919), pp. 147-166; De Selincourt, E., "Classicism and Romanticism in the Poetry of Walter Savage Landor," *Vorträge Der Bibliothek Warburg Herausgegeben Von Fritz Saxl* (1930-1931), pp. 230-250.

an excellent group of a dozen dramatic dialogues, (9) *Dry Sticks, Fagoted by Walter Savage Landor* (1858), a miscellany, and by (10) *Heroic Idyls, with Additional Poems* (1863), some being translations of his Latin *Idyllia Heroica,* and including several excellent new verse dialogues on classical subjects.

Longer Poems

*Gebir; A Poem, in Seven Books** (1798). Blank-verse epic imitative of Virgil in style and manner, often awkwardly Latinistic in expression, abrupt in transitions, obscure in plot, and unsustained in development. With all its faults, is rich in dignified power and poetic imagination. Oriental tale was found in *The Progress of Romance* by Clara Reeve.

Count Julian (1812). Tragedy in verse is modelled on Greek lines: it is simpler, more unified, and more dramatic than *Gebir,* but is turgid, weak in construction, and unnecessarily complicated in plot. Splendid theme, nobly-conceived hero; but the characters are idealized rather than human, and their motives are obscure. Occasional poetic beauty and grandeur. Influenced by his brief campaign in the Peninsula. (Compare with Southey's treatment of the theme in *Roderick,* and Scott's in *The Vision of Don Roderick.*)

The Hellenics of Walter Savage Landor (1847). Short tales or dialogues on Greek topics are partly verse translations of his Latin *Idyllia* and partly other idyls written originally in English. Later (1859) republished with corrections and additions, and then again (1863). Generally admired. "No modern writer, save André Chénier in France, has equalled the best of these *Hellenics* . . . ."

Shorter Poems

Shorter pieces include (1) *Rose Aylmer* (1806), a compact eight-line elegy on the daughter of the fourth Lord Aylmer, an early love of Landor's who died at Calcutta in 1800 when only twenty years old; (2) *Lyrics to Ianthe* (1831—1863), addressed to Sophia Jane Swift, afterwards Comtesse de Molandé; (3) *Dirce,* a beautiful four-line piece; (4) *I Know Not Whether I am Proud* (1846), frank in its detestation of *hoi polloi;* (5) *On His Seventy-Fifth Birthday* (1850; 1853), possibly his most faultless quatrain, a farewell defiance of man, of the world, and of mortality, and worth comparison with Tennyson's *Crossing the Bar;* (6) *To My Ninth Decade* (1863), where he declares his fearlessness of Death as he did ten years earlier in *Death Stands Above Me.* Read, too, *Mild Is the Parting Year, Past Ruined Illion, On Lucretia Borgia's Hair, The Love of Other Years, Yes, I Write Verses Now and Then, One Year Ago My Path Was Green, Is It Not Better At An Early Hour, A Fiesolan Idyl, The Leaves Are Falling, To Youth, To Age.*

---

† * Explanation of symbols immediately precedes Chapter XV.

Prose

Imaginary Conversations of Literary Men and Statesmen† (1824—1829) and *Imaginary Conversations of Greeks and Romans†* (1853). Consists of nearly one hundred and fifty prose dialogues that reveal wide range of reading and exceptional power to interpret a great variety of character. Dignity and restraint of style can not conceal his mausolean learning, stuffily redolent of the past. Characters include Achilles and Helena, Aesop and Rhodope, Marcellus and Hannibal, Chaucer and Boccaccio, Roger Ascham and Lady Jane Grey, the Empress Catharine and Princess Dashkof, Essex and Spenser, Lord Bacon and Richard Hooker, Louis XIV and Père La Chaise, Henry VIII and Anne Boleyn, Romilly and Wilberforce, Fra Filippo Lippi and Pope Eugenius IV, Bossuet and the Duchess De Fontanges, John of Gaunt and the Duchess of Kent, Queen Elizabeth and Cecil, Dante and Beatrice, Calvin and Melanchthon. Often idyllic or satirical, the dialogues treat of a multitude of matters, political, social, or literary, and frequently of such subjects as love and hate, life and death.

Pericles and Aspasia (1836). Written in the form of imaginary letters passing among Aspasia, her friend Cleone, Pericles, Anaxagoras, and Alcibiades, Landor's longest work is also his maturest. The literary, religious, political, and philosophical discussions vividly reconstruct the intellectual life of the Age of Pericles. Digressive, yet unified by a sympathetic interpretation of antiquity. Scattered throughout are short lyrics and such Landorian jewels as the dramatic fragments written by Aspasia on the story of Agamemnon.

---

† • Explanation of symbols immediately precedes Chapter XV.

CHAPTER XXIII

THE VICTORIAN AGE
(1832—1885)

Historical Background

The Reign of William IV (continued from page 440). (1) Names of Whig Party and Tory Party begin to give way to those of Liberal Party and Conservative Party (1833). (2) Abolition of Slavery (1833); effective 1834. (3) Ashley's Factory Act (1833). (4) Poor Law (1834). (5) Death of William IV (1837); his niece Victoria succeeds.

The Reign of Victoria (1837—1901). (1) Rebellion in Canada (1837). (2) Publication of the "People's Charter," 1838 (See CHARTISM, page 525). (3) Formation of Anti-Corn-Law League (1838). (4) Queen Victoria weds (1840). (5) Penny-Postage Act (1840). (6) Ashburton Treaty (1842). (7) Ashley's Factory Act (1844). (8) Jews obtain eligibility for municipal offices (1845). (9) Famine in Ireland (1845—1846). (10) Repeal of the Corn Laws (1846). (11) Ashley's Act for a ten-hour day (1847). (12) Encumbered Estates Act (1848). (13) Clayton-Bulwer Treaty (1850). (14) Restoration of the Roman Catholic hierarchy in England (1850). (15) Ecclesiastical Titles Act (1851). (16) Crimean War begins (1854). (17) Peace of Paris (1856). (18) Sepoy Mutiny in India (1857—1859). (19) Property Qualification for Parliament abolished (1858). (20) Membership in Parliament opened to Jews (1858). (21) Atlantic Cable (1858). (22) Death of Prince Consort (1861). (23) Insurrection in Jamaica (1865). (24) Second Reform Act (1867), enfranchises the settled working class. (25) Irish Disestablishment Act (1869). (26) Abolition of imprisonment for debt (1869). (27) Irish Land Law (1870). (28) Elementary Education Act (1870). (29) Treaty of Washington (1871). (30) University Test Act (1871). (31) Voting by ballot (1872). (32) Ashanti War (1873). (33) Disraeli obtains control of the Suez Canal (1875). (34) Victoria becomes the Empress of India (1876). (35) Factory Act (1878). (36) Second Afghan War (1878—1881). (37) Zulu War (1879). (38) Irish Land League organized (1879). (39) Employers' Liability Act (1880). (40) Irish Land Act (1881). (41) Irish National League (1882). (42) Corrupt Practices Prevention Act (1883). (43) Third Reform Act (1884). (44) Land Purchase Act (1885).

Social and Economic Background

Chartism. The Reform Act of 1832 had transferred political power from the upper to the middle classes, but failed to benefit the laboring classes. The economic depression that began about four years later, the Poor Law of 1834, and the ruthlessness of the manufacturing classes (*laissez-faire,* iron law of wages, Malthusianism) excited discontent among the working classes, who attributed their hardships to their exclusion from politics. The "People's Charter" of 1838 advocated (1) universal manhood suffrage, (2) voting by secret ballot, (3) annual election of Parliament, (4) abolition of the property qualification for membership in the House of Commons, (5) payment of salary to the members of the House of Commons, and (6) equal electoral districts. After 1840 the movement lost a large part of its parliamentary and took on a more socialistic and revolutionary character. Demonstrations occurred in industrial centers. On several occasions the general strike was measurably effective. As trade improved and economic conditions became more settled, the movement languished and died. By 1918, however, all the objectives of the "People's Charter" had been obtained, excepting that of an annual parliament. The significance of the Chartist movement is that for the first time in England the people were class-conscious in their opposition to the half-way, class-inspired measures of bourgeois reformism: it was the vanguard of the radical working-class movement.

Irish Land Question. Significant factors in the Irish agrarian problem were: (1) Act of 1793. (2) Catholic Emancipation (1829). (3) Failure of the potato crop (1846). (4) Growth of the abuses of absentee landlordism. (5) Lord John Russell's bill (1847). (6) Encumbered Estates Act (1849). (7) The agitation of the Fenian Society (1850—1870) and of the Irish Tenant Right League. (8) Home Rule Movement begins (1870). (9) Reform Act (1867). (10) First Gladstone Land Act (1870). (11) Irish Land League (1879). (12) Second Gladstone Act (1881).

Catholic Emancipation. Not yet has the Act of Settlement been repealed. But, starting with the Catholic Emancipation Act of 1829, most of the civil disabilities of the Roman Catholics in the British Isles have been removed. Catholics, however, are still excluded from a few university places, from offices connected with either of the established churches, and from such high offices as Regent, Lord Chancellor, and Keeper of the Great Seal.

Oxford Movement. Originally known as the Tractarian Movement, the Oxford Movement is the name commonly applied to the revival of the doctrines and practises of an earlier age that took place in the Church of England in the beginning years of the Victorian era. This religious movement, initiated by John Keble's sermon at Oxford

University in 1833 on national apostasy, endeavored to overcome the danger threatening the Church as a result of the political and social trends during the eighteenth and early nineteenth centuries. J. H. Newman, Keble, and E. B. Pusey launched a series of ninety pamphlets called *Tracts for the Times* (1833—1841), which fought against Erastianism and liberalism in behalf of that conservative, patristic, sacramental form of piety and theology represented by such seventeenth-century exponents as William Laud and Lancelot Andrewes. The series was discontinued when disapproval was aroused by Newman's *Tract XC* but not, however, the movement itself, despite the later defection of valuable supporters, including Ward and Newman, and their secession to the Church of Rome. While it was mainly theological, Tractarianism is also associated with the restoration of symbolism and ceremonial known as ritualism and a revival of conventual life. It profoundly affected the Church of England. Extending into many other lands, it enriched education and individual and ecclesiastical experience. Should not be confused with Buchmanism.

Scientific Progress. The century was an age of inventions. In medicine, the figures of Pasteur, Lister, Paget, and Koch stand out; in the field of natural science, those of Charles Darwin, T. H. Huxley, Herbert Spencer, A. R. Wallace, Mill, and Tyndall. In communication and transportation came the greatest advance in material progress: the building of railroads, communication by telephone, telegraph, and the wireless, the beginning of the automobile and of transportation by air. Industry was revolutionized by the application of machinery, steam, and electricity. The art of photography was perfected. Despite all aspects of scientific progress, however, very little was accomplished in ameliorating the sordid industrial slavery of men, women, and children.

Imperialism. The nineteenth century was a century of expansion for many countries, including Great Britain. She appropriated Egypt and the Sudan, acquired control of the Suez Canal, established an empire in India, developed self-governing English colonies in Canada, Australia, and New Zealand, consolidated the British possessions in South Africa, and obtained some African suzerainties from the Turkish Empire. Today the British Empire has colonies, protectorates, and mandated territories in Europe, in Asia, in Africa, in the Americas, and in Oceana. It is recognized as the greatest empire of the modern world.

General View of the Literature

Victorian literature was written in the main for the people, and reflected the pressing social problems and philosophies of a complex era. The age was prevailingly one of social restraints and taboos, reminiscent in this respect of the Puritan period. The writers, whether poets or novelists or essayists, are didactic and moral and purposeful, although that statement is not valid for the members of the Pre-Raphaelite brotherhood. Possibly the dominant literary form was the novel; possibly the least notable form was the drama. Undoubtedly the Victorian age ranks second only to the Elizabethan period.

MAJOR ESSAYISTS

Thomas Babington Macaulay, First Baron Macaulay, 1800—1859, historian, essayist, poet.[1]

Lays of Ancient Rome (1842). His poetry, while not belonging to the highest order, is notable for an unsophisticated directness of expression and a rattling presentation in ballad rime of incidents appealing to the heart rather than to the head. Correct versification, monotonous rhythm, commonplace phrasing, artificial poetry. The lays[2] are: *Horatius,*† *The Battle of Lake Regillus, Virginia,*† and *The Prophecy of Capys.* (The 1848 edition included, also, *The Battle of Ivry* and *The Armada†*).

Critical and Historical Essays contributed to the Edinburgh Review (Three volumes, 1843). These essays[3] may be classified in four groups: (1) ENGLISH HISTORY. *Hallam's Constitutional History*† (1828); *Lord Nugent's Memorials of Hampden†* (1831); *Burleigh and his Times* (1832); *Horace Walpole* (1833); *William Pitt* (1834); *Macintosh's History of the Revolution* (1832); *Sir William Temple†* (1838); *Lord Clive* (1840); *Lord Holland* (1841); *Warren Hastings†* (1841)[4]; The Earl of Chatham (1844). (2) FOREIGN HISTORY. *Machiavelli* (1827)[5]; *Mirabeau* (1832); *War of the Succession in Spain* (1833); *Ranke's History of the Popes* (1840); *Frederic the Great* (1842). (3) LITERARY, CRITICAL, AND MISCELLANEOUS. *Milton†* (1825), possibly his most famous essay, although it is often over-rated[6]; *Essay on John Dryden* (1828) *Moore's Life of*

---

1 Morison, J. C., *Macaulay* (1882); Jones, C. H., *Macaulay* (1902); Canning, A. S. G., *Macaulay* (1913); Hassard, A. R., *A New Light on Lord Macaulay* (1918); Trevelyan, G. O., *The Life and Letters of Lord Macaulay* (Two volumes, 1923); Roberts, S. C., *An Eighteenth-Century Gentleman and Other Essays,* (1930), "Lord Macaulay: The Pre-Eminent Victorian," pp. 105-131; Bryant, Arthur, *Macaulay* (1932); Dobrée, Bonamy, "Macaulay," *The Criterion,* XII (1932-1933), pp. 593-604.

2 Kellett, E. E., *Suggestions* (1923), "Macaulay's Lay Figures," pp. 155-165; Rolfe, J. C., "Macaulay's *Lays of Ancient Rome,*" *The Classical Journal,* XXIX (1933-1934), pp. 567-581.

3 Morison, J. C., *Macaulay* (1882; 1927), Chap. III, pp. 66-106; Canning, A. S. G., *Macaulay* (1913), "Part I: Essayist," pp. 13-148.

4 Skrine, F. H., *India's Hope* (1929), Chap. V, "Some Detractors—Lord Macaulay and Miss May," pp. 48-55.

5 His essay on Machiavelli presents a powerful analysis of "Mandragola" and a revolutionary appraisal of Machiavelli himself; thus asserts Isaac Don Levine in the introduction to *Mandragola,* translated by Young, Stark (1927).

6 Sampson, George, "Macaulay and Milton," a review of three books in *The Edinburgh Review or Critical Journal,* CCXLII (1925), pp. 165-178; Carver, P. L., "The Sources of Macaulay's *Essay on Milton,*" *The Review of English Studies,* VI (1930), pp. 49-62.

† * Explanation of symbols immediately precedes Chapter XV.

Byron (1830); *Robert Montgomery's Poems* (1830); *Southey's edition of the Pilgrim's Progress* (1830); *Moore's Life of Byron* (1831); *Croker's Edition of Boswell's Life of Johnson* (1831); *Lord Bacon* (1837); *Comic Dramatists of the Restoration* (1841); *Leigh Hunt* (1841); *Madame d'Arblay* (1843); *Life and Writings of Addison* (1843). (4) CONTROVERSIAL ARTICLES. *Mill on Government* (1829); *Southey's Colloquies on Society* (1830); *Saddler's Law of Population* (1830); *Civil Disabilities of the Jews* (1831); *Gladstone on Church and State* (1839).

History of England from the Accession of James II† (I, II, 1848; III, IV, 1855; V, edited by Lady Trevelyan, 1861). Masterpiece, originally planned to cover the period from the reign of James II to the time of Sir Robert Walpole, does not go beyond the death of William III.[1] Canvas is crowded, yet limned with admirable clearness and unity of effect; even the minor characters are alive and convincing. Brilliant vignettes, compelling force of imagination, virile clarity, leisurely yet compressed narrative, adroit suspense, mastery of *mise-en-scène*. But his magnificent rhetoric and theatrical pageantry, as well as his obvious tricks and mannerisms, often distort the truth, while his Whig and Protestant point of view frequently colors his judgment.[2] Finally, he is deficient in philosophic insight and in the sense of historical perspective.

Thomas Carlyle, 1795—1881, social pamphleteer, literary critic, historian.[3]

Literary Criticism

German. (1) *The Life of Friedrich Schiller* (1823—1824). (2) *Wilhelm Meister's Apprenticeship and Travels* (1824), a novel from the German of Goethe. (3) *German Romance: Specimens of its Chief Authors* (Four volumes, 1827), translations from Musaeus, La Motte Fouqué, Tieck, Hoffmann, Richter, and Goethe. Critical and miscellaneous essays include: (4) *Jean Paul Friedrich Richter* (1827); (5) *State of German Literature* (1827); (6) *Werner* (1828); (7) *Goethe's "Helena"* (1828); (8) *Goethe* (1828); (9) *German Playwrights* (1829); (10) *Jean Paul Friedrich Richter Again* (1830); (11) *German Literature of the Fourteenth and Fifteenth Century* (1831); (12) *Taylor's "Historic Survey of German Poetry"* (1831); (13) *Goethe's Portrait* (1832); (14) *Death of Goethe* (1832); (15) *Goethe's Works* (1832).

---

1 Most famous is the third chapter. Consult Firth, C. H., "Macaulay's Third Chapter," *History*, New Series, XVII (1932-1933), pp. 201-219.
2 See, for example, Paget, John, *The New "Examen,"* with an introduction by Churchill, Winston (1934).
3 Froude, J. A., *Thomas Carlyle* (Two volumes, 1882); *The Love Letters of Thomas Carlyle and Jane Welsh*, edited by Carlyle, Alexander (Two volumes, 1909); Ralli, Augustus, *Guide to Carlyle,* (Two volumes, 1920); Wilson, D. A., *Carlyle* (Six volumes, 1923-1934); Dunn, W. H., *Froude & Carlyle* (1930); Cazamian, Louis, *Carlyle,* translated by Brown, E. K. (1932); Neff, Emery, *Carlyle* (1932); Lammond, D., *Carlyle* (1934).
† * Explanation of symbols immediately precedes Chapter XV.

English. (1) *Essay on Burns* (1828), a classic that has been attacked by Robertson as an incoherent critical document, "internecine in its theses" and self-contradictory in almost every concrete judgment. (2) *Boswell's Life of Johnson* (1832). (3) *Sir Walter Scott* (1838).

Philosophical and Social Writings

Sartor Resartus: The Life and Opinions of Herr Teufelsdröckh[1] (1833—1834; Boston, 1836; first English edition 1838). Philosophical satire, written under the influence of the German romantic school and especially of Jean Paul Richter, is both a discourse on the "philosophy of clothes" (the title means "the tailor retailored") and, under the thin veil of fiction, a partly autobiographical revelation[2] of Carlyle's own spiritual struggles. Despite its involved constructions, its exclamatory and violent style, and its torrential obscurity of language, the work is notable for a brilliant medley of humor and pathos, moral exaltation and ironical satire. Memorable are the chapters on "The Everlasting No," "Centre of Indifference," and "The Everlasting Yea."

Chartism (1839; dated 1840). Says little about Chartism, but specifies the industrial ills to be remedied and attacks the current theory of *laissez faire*.

On Heroes, Hero-Worship, and The Heroic In History (1841). Series of lectures delivered in 1840, the purpose being to demonstrate that the accomplished work of the world is basically the history of Great Men; *i.e.*, the heroes or natural leaders: the Hero as Divinity (Odin), as Prophet (Mahomet), as Poet (Dante, Shakespeare), as Priest (Luther, Knox,) as Man of Letters (Johnson, Rousseau, Burns), as King (Cromwell, Napoleon). Carlyle did not believe in the theory that the time makes the Great Man. He insisted that divine right on the great scale was identical with divine might.[8]

Past and Present (1843). Contrasts the disorder of his England, dead to spiritual realities, with the order of England in the time of Joselyn de Brakelond (see Vol. 1, p. 35). Again attacks the principle of *laissez faire;* advocates profit-sharing, educational legislation, and the organization of labor, rightly guided by legislative leadership and by a class of "heroes." Not logically arranged, but unites his qualities of historical imagination, social satire, and philosophic insight.

---

1 *Sartor Resartus,* edited by MacMechan, Archibald (1897; 1925); Hagberg, Knut, *Thomas Carlyle: Romantik och puritanism i Sartor Resartus* (1925).

2 Blumine may be Margaret Gordon (Froude), or Catherine Aurora Kirkpatrick (G. Strachey), or Jane Welsh Carlyle (Alexander Carlyle).

3 W. C. Brownell rates Carlyle as a poor historian but a great artist; he calls him also an important moral force, but maintains that his influence has waned because of his opposition to the scientific and the democratic spirit. J. M. Robertson also attacks Carlyle as a moralist and a teacher, even as a man of letters.

The Nigger Question (1849). An attempt to cool the ardor of abolitionists.

Latter-Day Pamphlets (1850). Series of satires that, like *Chartism* and *Past and Present,* attacked the political science of the day, especially liberal cure-alls.

Shooting Niagara: and After (1867). A depreciation of democracy and industrialism, occasioned by the Reform Bill of 1867.

Historical Writings

The French Revolution: A History (1837). Inaccurate, unreflective history, marred by catch-phrases, personal bias, and didactic purpose; but redeemed by swift and vivid narrative, unforgettable scenes, grimly satiric episodes, grand descriptive prose, and arresting imaginative strength. Not a factual history; it is a prose-poem warning England of impending dangers unless social reforms are initiated.

Oliver Cromwell's Letters and Speeches: With Elucidations (1845). Sympathetic portraiture that again illustrates his theory of the Hero.

The Life of John Sterling (1851). Another sympathetic work, written in logical order and impartial in its attitude. It exposed literary fads and educational shams.

History of Frederick II. of Prussia, called Frederick the Great (1858—1865). Monumental survey of a hero-king, hymning the superman. Masterly execution, graphic power, humor.

John Ruskin, 1819—1900, author, critic.[1]

Aesthetics and Art Criticism

Modern Painters (I, 1843; II, 1846; III, IV, 1856; V, 1860). Treatise audacious in its attack upon such painters as Claude, Poussin, and Rosa; sustainedly eloquent in its admiration for Turner and Tintoretto; and acute in its observations upon the principles of true art and in its appreciation of natural landscape, dividing landscape painters into the four orders of Heroic (Titian), Classical (Poussin), Pastoral (Cuyp), and Contemplative (Turner).

---

1 Hobson, J. A., *John Ruskin* (1898); Meynell, Mrs. (Alice), *John Ruskin* (1900); Harrison, Frederic, *John Ruskin* (1902); Benson, A. C., *Ruskin* (1911); Cook, E. T., *The Life of John Ruskin* (Two volumes, 1911); Graham, J. W. *The Harvest of Ruskin* (1920); *Ruskin the Prophet and Other Centenary Studies,* edited by Whitehouse, J. H. (1920); Roe, F. W., *The Social Philosophy of Carlyle and Ruskin* (1921); Williams-Ellis, Amabel, *The Exquisite Tragedy* (1929); Ladd, Henry, *The Victorian Morality of Art* (1932); Wilenski, R. H., *John Ruskin* (1933); Beard, C. A., "Ruskin and the Babble of Tongues," *The New Republic,* August 5, 1936; pp. 370-372; Evans, J. and J. H. Whitehouse, eds., *Diaries* (3 vols., 1956-1959).

The Seven Lamps of Architecture (1849). In this defense of, primarily, Gothic architecture, he applies his principles of painting to architecture, presenting the "Seven Lamps" as those of Sacrifice (of materialistic to spiritual aims), Truth, Power (concerned with shadow and its uses), Beauty, Life (vital energy in organic things), Memory, and Obedience. Of great moral significance.

Stones of Venice (I, 1851; II, III, 1853). Purpose is to glorify Gothic at the expense of Renaissance architecture: the latter is identified with insincerity and corruption, the former with faith and virtue. In other words, its main theme is to affirm that the moral temper of a people reveals itself in the architecture: a theme emphasized in *The Seven Lamps of Architecture*. To Carlyle, it was "a sermon in stones."

Ethical and Social Criticism

Unto this last (1860—1862). Advocated righteousness against self-interest and ideals against materialism in matters dealing with labor: make not more of money but much of it. Many reforms advocated have been adopted.[1] Title taken from the parable of the Laborers in the Vineyard.

---

1 In 1882 Ruskin wrote that *Sesame and Lilies* and *Unto This Last* embodied the chief truths he had endeavored to teach. M. E. Sadler, in the introduction (pp. VII-XII) to *Ruskin's Guild of St. George* by Edith Hope-Scott (1931), states:

"Two seminal books have coloured the economic thought of Europe, including Russia, during the last sixty years. One is *Das Kapital* by Karl Marx, the other *Unto This Last* by John Ruskin. During the same period of years the writers of these two books were living within four miles of one another in London, unknown the one to the other —Marx anchored in the British Museum, Ruskin free to travel. The revolutionary period in Europe culminating in 1848, touched Ruskin's heart and mind, Karl Marx's mind and heart. An appendix to the third volume of *The Stones of Venice* (1853) showed that Ruskin was awake to the revolutionary movement of the age. In the same year Karl Marx was forging in the British Museum library the blade which was to thrust a death wound into the heart of too optimistic *laissez-faire*. *Das Kapital* was published in London in 1873. *Unto This Last* was published in 1862, the four chapters having previously appeared as articles in *The Cornhill Magazine* for August, September, October, November, 1860.

"Ruskin's doctrine is fundamentally Christian: Karl Marx's doctrine is fundamentally deistical. The lever by which Karl Marx has moved the world was logic. Ruskin's call was a cry of compassion. Karl Marx's doctrine is economic determinism: Ruskin's doctrine is that the sinful heart of man may be redeemed by the love of God for man.

"Karl Marx founded the social democratic party of Central Europe: Ruskin's *Unto This Last* was the pocketbook of the founders of the British Labour Party. Both men had a genius for interpreting history. But Karl Marx's history is a tape relentlessly rewinding cause and effect. Ruskin's history is timeless in the sight of God. Both men were pioneers of social revolution. Both had a Pisgah vision of a new age. Neighbours in London, fellow-craftsmen of revolution, they were fundamentally opposed in their reading of human destiny. Ruskin knew nothing of Marx. But Marx knew Ruskin's books and it was Friedrich Engels who said that 'Ruskin has never written anything worthless or unimportant.'

"Who shall say which will be the victor? Ruskin has had no great follower. Marx has had Lenin. England has no Five-Year Plan. England's prodigality on the social services is steeped in Ruskin. There is a deeply sounding assonance between Bolshevism and the United States. Ruskinism seems, at first sight, to have no allies in the modern world. But Marxism through Lenin may on the scene of human affairs be victorious. The issue lies hidden in a menacing future, a future as menacing as Christ foresaw."

Munera Pulveris (1862—1863). Like *Unto this last,* was a treatise directed against the materialism of that day's political economy. Famous for its definition of Wealth. Title borrowed from a line by Horace, meaning "Gifts of the Dust."

Sesame and Lilies (1865). "Sesame: Of King's Treasuries" (first lecture) deals with reading; "Lilies: Of Queen's Gardens" (second lecture), with the sphere, education, and duties of idealistic and heroic womanhood; "The Mystery of Life and its Arts" (lecture delivered in 1868), with man's indifference to religion and life's purpose. (In the title, the lilies possibly represent beauty, and sesame, the nurture of the mind.)

Ethics of the Dust (1865). Imaginary dialogues, on elementary crystallography, between himself and a group of school girls at Winnington.

Crown of Wild Olive (1866). Four lectures on "War," "The Future of England," "Work," and "Traffic" (buying and selling).

Time and Tide (1867). Lectures and letters, addressed to a working man, on such social reconstruction as the elimination of luxury and poverty, greed and suffering.

Fors Clavigera (1871—1884). The redress of poverty and misery is the underlying theme of this series of ninety-six monthly letters to the workmen and laborers of England.[1] As deadly in their earnestness as they are vivacious in their humor and sustained in their charm; but above the understanding of those to whom addressed. (For an explanation of the title, see Letter XIII.)

Autobiographical

Praeterita (1885—1889). Unfinished autobiography, informal in its touches of humor and pathos, its tranquil mood and fragrant retrospect, and its artless style and pellucid atmosphere.

Other Works

(1) Miscellaneous verse, and prose essays (1827—1842). (2) Letters to *The Times* on the Pre-Raphaelites and pamphlet called *Pre-Raphaelitism* (1852), which belongs with the *Modern Painters* group. (3) *Notes*

---

1 It must be emphasized that Ruskin protested against the deification of Mammon and the evils of industrialism, and denounced the gospel of individualism enunciated by Adam Smith and Mill and Ricardo. He believed, not in production for gain, but in production for use; he attacked imperialistic wars; in all cases he directed his energies against the spirit of commercialism or materialism. "It goes without saying, of course, that he was a Communist," says Bernard Shaw in his *Ruskin's Politics* (1921— page 22). But one must also recall his aversion to universal suffrage, his lack of sympathy with radical labor movements, and his determined hostility to revolution as a means of righting social wrongs. In more ways than one he was a reactionary radical, believing in sociological panaceas built upon the theory of re-erecting a new structure upon an ancient one.

on the Construction of Sheepfolds (1851), a pamphlet on the reunion of Protestant sects. (4) *Lectures on Architecture and Painting* (1854). (5) *The Harbours of England* (1856), notes on engravings of marine subjects after Turner. (6) *The Elements of Drawing* (1857). (7) *Political Economy of Art* (1858). (8) *The Elements of Perspective* (1859). (9) *Rede Lecture* (1867). (10) *The Queen of the Air* (1869), nominally a group of lectures on Greek myths. (11) *Lectures on Art* (1870). (12) *Aratra Pentelici* (1872), Oxford lectures on Greek Sculpture. (13) *Lectures on Landscape* (1871; published 1898). (14) *The Eagle's Nest* (1872). (15) *Ariadne Florentina* (1872). (16) *Love's Meinie* (1873). (17) *Val d'Arno* (1874). (18) *Deucalion* (1875). (19) An essay called *Elements of English Prosody* (1880). (20) *The Art of England* (1884). (21) *The Pleasures of England* (1898). (22) *The Storm Cloud of the Nineteenth Century* (1884).

Matthew Arnold.   See page 567.

John Henry Newman, 1801—1890, author, theologian, Catholic divine; a founder of the Oxford Movement.[1]

Chief Prose Works

Tracts for the Times (1833—1841). Series of tracts on religious subjects written by Newman, Keble, Froude, Pusey, and others. Most famous is Newman's *Tract XC* (1841) on the compatibility of the Thirty-Nine Articles with Roman Catholic theology.[2] (These tracts are of great importance in the Oxford or Tractarian Movement.)

The Idea of a University (1852). Volume of lectures written as a full exposition concerning the founding of a Catholic University in Dublin, the purpose of which should be humanistic studies, and not merely the distribution of information; moral training rather than instruction. Wise discourses, lofty passages.

Apologia Pro Vita Sua (1864). In defending himself against Charles Kingsley's charge of insincerity, Newman presents a complete survey of his spiritual life with winning simplicity, limpid clearness, and a "regal" English style. Is often said to rank with St. Augustine's *Confessions* and Pascal's *Thoughts* as a classic of religious autobiography.

---

1 Hutton, R. H., *Cardinal Newman* (1905); Ward, W. P. *Life of Cardinal Newman* (Two volumes, 1912); Cadman, S. P., *The Three Religious Leaders of Oxford and Their Movements* (1916), Book III, "John Henry Newman and The Oxford Movement," pp. 389-789; Reilly, J. J., *Newman as a Man of Letters* (1925); Newman, Bertram, *Cardinal Newman* (1925); Inge, W. R., *Outspoken Essays* (First Series, 1927), "Cardinal Newman," pp. 172-204; May, J. L., *Cardinal Newman* (1929); Atkins, G. G., Life of *Cardinal Newman* (1931); Stockley, W. F. P., *Newman, Education and Ireland* (1933); Kiener, M. A. (*Sister*), *John Henry Newman* (1933); Faber, Geoffrey, *Oxford Apostles* (1933); Ross, J. E., *John Henry Newman* (1933); Harper, G. H., *Cardinal Newman and William Froude*, F. R. S. (1933); Cross, F. L., *John Henry Newman* (1933); Flood, J. M., *Cardinal Newman and Oxford* (1933); Dark, Sidney, *Newman* (1934); Tillotson, Geoffrey, ed., *Prose and Poetry* (1957).

2 *Tract Ninety or Remarks on Certain Passages in the Thirty-Nine Articles*, edited by Evans, A. W. (1933).

The Grammar of Assent (1870). Philosophical or religious treatise that examines the nature of assent or belief.

Chief Poems

Lead, Kindly Light (1833). Hymn written on the return from a trip to the Mediterranean in 1832, when his ship was becalmed off Caprera. Famous despite the obscurity of the last two lines, and the confused imagery.[1] Sung to two familiar tunes: *Lux benigna* by J. B. Dykes, and *Patmos* by Samuel Wesley.

The Dream of Gerontius (1866). Dramatic monologue of a righteous soul leaving the body after death, and passing from earth to purgatory.[2] Has been set to music by Sir Edwin Elgar.

Literary

(1) *Lyra Apostolica* (1863), sacred verses written in collaboration with R. H. Froude. (2) *Verses on Religious Subjects* (1853). (3) *Verses on Various Occasions* (1818—1865; 1867). (4) *Loss and Gain, The Story of a Convert* (1848), his first religious novel. (5) *Callista, A Tale of the Third Century* (1855), another religious novel.

Essays

(1) *Essays on Miracles* (1825—1826, 1842—1843; 1870). (2) *Discussions and Arguments* (1863—1866; 1872). (3) *Essays Critical and Historical* (I, 1828—1840; 1871. II, 1840—1846; 1871).

Sermons and Treatises

(1) *Parochial and Plain Sermons* (1834—1843). (2) *Oxford University Sermons* (preached 1826—1843; published 1843). (3) *Sermons on Subjects of the Day* (1843). (4) *Discourses to Mixed Congregations* (1849). (5) *Sermons Preached on Various Occasions* (1857). (6) *Lectures on Justification* (1838). (7) *An Essay on the Development of Christian Doctrine* (1845).

Historical, Theological, and Devotional

(1) *Historical Sketches* (I, 1824, 1853; II, 1833, 1873; III, 1834, 1872). (2) *The Arians of the Fourth Century* (1833). (3) *Select Treatises of St. Athanasius* (1841—1844). (4) *Tracts Theological and Ecclesiastical* (1835—1871). (5) *Meditations and Devotions* (1893; 1914; 1923.)

---

1 Tristram, Henry, "Lead, Kindly Light—June 16, 1833," *The Dublin Review*, CXCIII (1933), pp. 85-96; Moseley, D. H., "Lead, Kindly Light," *The Catholic World*, CXXXVII (1933), pp. 298-304.

2 Stockley, W. F. P., "'At the Hour of Our Death,'" *The Dublin Review*, CLXII (1918), pp. 87-111.

Polemical

(1) *The Via Media of the Catholic Church* (I, 1837; II, 1841). (2) *Difficulties of Anglicans* (I, 1850; II, 1865—1875). (3) *Present Position of Catholics in England* (1851).

Walter Horatio Pater, 1839—1894, essayist, critic[1]; possibly the inspiration of the *fin-de-siècle*.[2]

Criticism

(1) *Studies in the History of the Renaissance* (1873), which established his reputation. In it appears what is often held to be his best essay, *Leonardo da Vinci,* first published four years earlier in the *Fortnightly Review.* (2) *Appreciations With an Essay on Style* (1889), a collection of essays containing brilliant judgments of Shakespeare, Wordsworth, and others, the most famous being the essay on Style.[3] (3) *Plato and Platonism* (1893), a series of lectures on aesthetic appreciation.

Novels

(1) *Marius the Epicurean†* (1885). Spiritual biography of a Roman youth in the reign of Marcus Aurelius. (2) *The Child in the House* (Macmillan's Magazine, 1878; 1894). Partly autobiographical sketch; yet is "An Imaginary Portrait."

Other Works

(1) *Imaginary Portraits* (1887).[4] (2) *An Imaginary Portrait* (1894); see *The Child in the House.* (3) *Greek Studies* (1895), a series of essays. (4) *Miscellaneous Studies* (1895), another series of essays. (5) *Gaston de Latour* (1896), a fragmentary philosophical or historical romance. (6) *Essays from "The Guardian"* (1896).

MAJOR NOVELISTS

Charles Dickens, 1812—1870, humanitarian novelist, journalist.[5]

---

1 Greenslet, Ferris, *Walter Pater* (1903); Benson, A. C., *Walter Pater* (1906); Thomas, Edward, *Walter Pater* (1913); Welby, T. E., "Walter Pater," in *Revaluations* (Essays by Various Hands, published by Oxford University Press, 1931), pp. 196-215; Symons, Arthur, *A Study of Walter Pater* (1932); Young, H. H., *The Writings of Walter Pater* (Thesis, 1933); Eaker, J. G., "Walter Pater: A Study in Methods and Effects," *University of Iowa Studies,* Humanistic Studies (1933).

2 Pater, who undoubtedly influenced Oscar Wilde and George Moore, is important in any study of the Decadence of the last century.

3 Farmer, A. J., *Walter Pater as a Critic of Literature* (1931).

4 Marshall, D. W., "Walter Pater: Some of His Imaginary Portraits," *Poet Lore,* XXXII (1921), pp. 431-440; Ottley, May (Editor), *"Imaginary Portraits. 2. An English Poet,"* The Fortnightly Review, CXXXV; New Series, CXXIX (1931), pp. 433-448.

5 Chesterton, G. K., *Charles Dickens* (1906); Forster, John, *The Life of Charles Dickens,* edited by Matz, B. W. (Two volumes, 1911); Gissing, George, *Charles Dickens* (1912); Amerongen, J. B. Van, *The Actor in Dickens* (1926); Straus, Ralph, *Charles Dickens* (1928); Forster, John, *The Life of Charles Dickens,* edited by Ley, J. W. T. (1928); Wagenknecht, Edward, *The Man Charles Dickens* (1929); Darwin, Bernard, *Dickens* (1933); Leacock, Stephen, *Charles Dickens* (1933); Kingsmill, Hugh, *The Sentimental Journey* (1934); Maurois, André, *Dickens,* translated by Miles, Hamish (1934); Wright, Thomas, *The Life of Charles Dickens* (1935); *Mr. & Mrs. Charles Dickens,* his letters to her edited by Dexter, Walter (1935).

† * Explanation of symbols immediately precedes Chapter XV.

Experimental Period. (1) *Sketches by Boz* (1834—1836), a series of short papers having descriptive value and appealing primarily because of their humor. (2) *The Posthumous Papers of the Pickwick Club,* a humorous and satirical interpretation of the middle-class, indebted to Washington Irving, Boswell's *Life of Samuel Johnson,* and other sources.[1]

Second Period. (1) *Adventures of Oliver Twist* (1837—1839), with the object of showing "the principle of good surviving through every adverse circumstance," attacked the abuses of the Poor Law and exposed the workhouse system. (2) *Life and Adventures of Nicholas Nickleby* (1838—1839), where Dickens again became a social reformer, one of his principal purposes being to expose the "farming" schools of Yorkshire and their severe mistreatment of children. (3) *The Old Curiosity Shop* (1840—1841), not his best novel but among his most celebrated; not the plot but the central figure of Little Nell has made it popular. (4) *Barnaby Rudge* (1841), frequently called an historical novel, although all the characters, except Lord Gordon, are imaginary.

Mature Period. (1) *Life and Adventures of Martin Chuzzlewit* (1843—1844), a sermonic book melodramatized by a murder and made unequal by trivial burlesque and intricate plot. (2) *Dombey and Son* (1846—1848), memorable for the pictures of Little Paul and the pathos of his death. (3) *David Copperfield* (1849—1850), where, excluding the central figure of David, who narrates his adventures, the chief theme is the betrayal of Little Em'ly by Steerforth and Mr. Peggoty's search for the girl. (4) *Bleak House* (1852—1853), although somewhat deficient in humor, is a great book, its main thread spun from a long-drawn-out Chancery suit.[2] (5) *Hard Times* (1854), a revolutionary problem novel[3] presenting the squalor and misery of a textile town[4]; it denounces trade-union agitators. (6) *Little Dorrit* (1855—1857), intricate in plot but splendid in its indictment of the system of imprisonment for debt and of the dilatoriness of the Circumlocution Office (government departments). (7) *A Tale of Two Cities* (1859), a great historical romance that is among the required reading for high-school students, yet is not typical of Dickens.

Final Period. (1) *Great Expectations* (1860—1861), one of his most artistic novels, restrained both in its melodrama and romantic atmosphere. (2) *Our Mutual Friend* (1864—1865), besides the frequent

---

1 For an interesting introduction to the question of Dickens's literary sources, read Kidd, H. H., "Is Dickens Still a Hero?" *The South Atlantic Quarterly,* XXVI (1927), pp. 280-289.

2 In *Bleak House* the legal atmosphere is pronounced. See Holdsworth, W. S., *Charles Dickens as a Legal Historian* (1928), pp. 79-115.

3 Crotch, W. W., *The Secret of Dickens* (1919), "Dickens as Revolutionist," pp. 135-157.

4 Dickens's *Hymn of the Wiltshire Laborers* (1846) should also be read by all who wish to know Dickens's attitude toward British labor problems.

criticism concerning the dubious grammar of its title, is over complicated in plot. (3) *The Mystery of Edwin Drood* (1870), a fragment of detective fiction that has set up a challenge for completion.[1]

Other Writings. (1) *American Notes* (1842), material collected from a trip to the United States, where he had advocated international copyright and had attacked slavery and piracy. (2) *A Christmas Carol* (1843), a Christmas story followed in each of the following years by (3) *The Chimes* (1844), (4) *The Cricket on the Hearth* (1845), (5) *The Battle of Life* (1846), and (6) *The Haunted Man and the Ghost's Bargain* (1848). (7) *Pictures from Italy* (1846), written in the form of letters describing his visit to that country. (8) *A Child's History of England* (1852—1854). (9) *Household Words,* a weekly periodical which he edited from 1850 to 1859, was succeeded by (10) *All the Year Round* (1859—1870). (11) He wrote a number of stories, including the *Wreck of the "Golden Mary"* (1856), *Message from the Sea* (1860), and *No Thoroughfare* (1867). (12) *The Life of Our Lord* (1934), written for his children.

William Makepeace Thackeray, 1811—1863, novelist, editor.[2]

Experimental Period. (1) *Memoirs of Mr. C. J. Yellowplush* (1837—1838), aimed at novels that gushed about crime and vice. (2) *Catherine* (1839—1840), his first substantial story, was based on facts, and was written as another counterblast to the Newgate school of fiction and its sentimental leaning toward criminals, represented, for example, by Dickens's *Oliver Twist*. (3) *A Shabby Genteel Story* (1840), an unequal work usually serving, in subsequent editions, as a prologue to *The Adventures of Philip*. (4) *History of Mr. Samuel Titmarsh and the Great Hoggarty Diamond* (1841—1842), lacking in seriousness like its predecessor, is possibly autobiographical in the pathetic description of the death of Titmarsh's child. (5) *The Luck of Barry Lyndon, Esq.* (1844), the autobiography of an Irish rogue, following the type-novel of Smollett's *Ferdinand Count Fathom* and Fielding's *Jonathan Wild;* exposure of false and romantic ideas executed with satirical irony,

1 Many attempts have been made to solve the unfinished novel. For an encyclopedic account of the Drood-Jasper controversy, consult Walters, J. C., *The Complete Mystery of Edwin Drood* (1912). See, also, Boyd, Aubrey, "A New Angle on the Drood Mystery," *Washington University Studies*, IX (1921), pp. 35-85; Everett, E. S., "The Cloisterham Murder Case," in *The Fred Newton Scott Anniversary Papers* (1929), pp. 157-174; Duffield, Howard, "John Jasper—Strangler," *The Bookman*, LXX (1929-1930), pp. 581-588; Graeme, Bruce, *Epilogue* (1934).

2 Lord, W. F., "The Apostle of Mediocrity," *The Nineteenth Century and After*, LI (1902), pp. 369-410; Melville, Lewis, *William Makepeace Thackeray* (Two volumes, 1910); *Thackeray and His Daughter*, edited by Ritchie, H. T. (1924); Hirst, W. A., "The Chronology in Thackeray's Novels," *The Cornhill Magazine*, New (3rd) Series, LXVII (1929), pp. 553-563; Melville, Lewis, *William Makepeace Thackeray* (1928); Saintsbury, George, *A Consideration of Thackeray* (1931); Elwin, Malcolm, *Thackeray* (1932); Ellis, G. U., *Thackeray* (1933); Gulliver, H. S., *Thackeray's Literary Apprenticeship* (1934).

historical realism, and swift flow of narrative. (6) *The Book of Snobs* (1846—1847), a series of forty-four lively and ironic miniatures of the principal varieties of snobs[1] in polite society.

Mature Period. (1) *Vanity Fair, A Novel without a Hero* (1847—1848), the epic of a great adventuress, and, through her, of early nineteenth-century British society. Quiet observation of character, excellent dexterity of scene, tone of irony and pathos, great structural scheme. Often compared with *Barry Lyndon,* where the dramatic figures are less firmly conceived and the plot not as skilfully elaborated. (2) *The History of Pendennis* (1848—1850) avowedly written in imitation of Fielding's *Tom Jones,* and like *The Newcomes* a novel without plot; autobiographical elements and ethical aspects in evidence. (3) *The History of Henry Esmond* (1852), an historical romance of a sensitive young man worked out against the brilliant background of the Marlborough war, Jacobite plots, and London life.[2] While romantic, it is a sad tale, a sombre drama. No novel of his is as perfectly shaped, as firm in character-delineation, as sustained in nobility of style, as mature in its gathered strength of literary power. (4) *The Newcomes* (1853—1855), a powerful novel of contemporary society, emphasizing the tragicomedy of worldliness. This middle-class novel has a fairly well-conducted story; but somehow the plot appears as loosely connected as in *Pendennis,* to which it is the true sequel. (5) *The Virginians* (1857—1859), international novel[3] that is a continuation of *Henry Esmond;* while noted for vivacious writing and character-portrayal, falls below its predecessor in excellence of structure. (6) *Lovel the Widower* (1860), a clever portracted sketch; it is a practically unaltered recasting of *The Wolves and the Lamb,* a play he wrote in 1854. (7) *The Adventures of Philip* (1861—1862), an elaborated continuation of the unfinished *Shabby Genteel Story;* it contains some excellent characterizations and vivid scenes, yet is the weakest novel of his mature period. (8) *Denis Duval* (1864), eight chapters of an unfinished historical-domestic novel of great promise.

Miscellaneous Works. (1) *The Paris Sketch Book* (1840), consisting of six stories and thirteen articles by "Mr. Titmarsh." (2) *Cox's Diary* (1840), the story of a barber who found and lost an inheritance. (3) *The Bedford Row Conspiracy* (1840), a story based upon *Le pied d'argile* by Charles de Bernard. (4) *Character Sketches* (1841), including among its three sketches the 1839 "Captain Rook and Mr.

---

1 It is the fashion of the newer biography to denigrate the character of many men, Thackeray among them. But it may be an error to call him both a hypocrite and a snob: see Elwin, Malcolm, *Thackeray* (1933); Ellis, G. U., *Thackeray* (1933).

2 For information concerning Charles Lord Mohun, refer to Forsythe, R. S., *A Noble Rake* (1928). In *Henry Esmond,* Thackeray introduces Dick Steele and his Prue, Swift, and Addison, (pp. 49-61).

3 *The Virginians* was the result of a lecturing tour in America: See Wilson, J. G., *Thackeray in the United States* (1904).

Pigeon," a description of a sharper and his victim. (5) *Fitz-Boodle Papers* (1842—1843), four "confessions." (6) *Bluebeard's Ghost* (1843), where Captain Blackbeard outwits Mr. Sly, the lawyer. (7) *Legend of the Rhine* (1845), a burlesque adventure story based on Dumas's *Othou L'Archer.* (8) *Rebecca and Rowena* (1846), an excellent burlesque continuation of Scott's *Ivanhoe.* (9) *Novels by Eminent Hands* (1847), burlesques and parodies of the style of such authors as Disraeli, Bulwer-Lytton, Charles Lever, J. F. Cooper, and of Thackeray's own *Yellowplush.* (10) *The Kickleburys on the Rhine* (1850), another book by the pseudonymous Mr. M. A. Titmarsh. (11) *The Wolves and the Lamb* (*c.* 1854), a play later recast into *Lovel the Widower.* (12) *The Rose and the Ring* (1855), a fireside pantomime or fairy story giving surface indications of his romanticism, as do his *Ballad of Bouillabaisse* (1849)[1] and his rimes on *The Mahogany Tree.* (13) *The English Humourists of the Eighteenth Century* (1851; 1853), lectures. (14) *The Four Georges* (1855—1860), another series of lectures. (15) *Roundabout Papers* (1863), a group of essays.

George Eliot, pseudonym of **Mary Ann** or **Marian Evans** **(Mrs. J. W. Cross),** 1819—1880, novelist.[2]

Novels

First Period. (1) *Scenes of Clerical Life* (1857), where the tone is pensive and the mood retrospective.[3] It includes: (a) "The Sad Fortunes of the Reverend Amos Barton," a story of a commonplace, middle-aged man, in which there are qualities of humor and tenderness, especially moving in the simple pathos of the death-bed scene; (b) "Mr. Gilfil's Love Story," her first original work, certainly the most finished and artistic of the three sketches; (c) "Janet's Repentance," a novelette known for its excellent sketch of Mr. Tryan, but less attractive than the other two tales. (2) *Adam Bede* (1859), where the story is subordinate to the characters, to the accurate picture of English rural life at the end of the eighteenth century, and to the powerful exposition of an ethical philosophy stressing the irrevocable nature of conduct. Imaginary setting, simple progression of the tale, crowded canvas; climax of book derived from real experience. (3) *The Mill on the Floss*

---

1 Melville, Lewis (pseud. of Benjamin, L. S.), *Some Aspects of Thackeray* (1911), "Thackeray's Ballads," pp. 49-81.

2 *George Eliot's Life as Related in Her Letters and Journals,* edited by Cross, J. W. (Three volumes, 1885); Stephen, Leslie, *George Eliot* (1902); *Early Essays By George Eliot* (Privately printed, 1919), pp. 53-65; Kitchell, A. T., *George Lewes and George Eliot* (1933); Fremantle, Anne, *George Eliot* (1933); Williams, B. C., *George Eliot* (1936).

3 Many of her excellences and permanent tendencies are present, or at least adumbrated, in her first sketches. Consult Deakin, M. H., *The Early Life of George Eliot* (1913), p. 139 *ff.*; Parry, E. A., "George Eliot Centenary," *The Fortnightly Review,* New Series, CVI (1919), pp. 883-895 (pp. 883-903); Tomlinson, May, "The Beginning of George Eliot's Art: A Study of *Scenes of Clerical Life,*" *The Sewanee Review,* XXVII (1919), pp. 320-329.

(1860), a hero-less autobiographical novel, satirizing conventional opinions, often ironic in its humor[1] and intense in detached scenes. Its concluding chapters are disastrously hurried. (4) *Silas Marner: the Weaver of Raveloe* (1861), a benign story of village life, genial in tone, ample in humor, realistic in description of character. According to George Eliot, its theme was "intended to set in a strong light the remedial influences of pure, natural, human relations." Resemblances have been noted in *Jermola the Potter,* a novel by the Polish writer, Kraszewski.

Transitional Period. (1) *Romola* (1862—1863), an historical novel tracing the spiritual history of a noble-minded Florentine who is wedded to a consummate egoist. Aside from the incomparable study of the moral declension of Tito, the artistic purpose is to trace the conflict between Greek culture and Christian faith in Florence during the Italian Renaissance.[2] (2) *Felix Holt, the Radical* (1866), an excellent minor novel psychologically analytical in its study of Radicalism of the time of the Reform Bill; distinguished by the character-creation of Rufus Lyon; marred by improbable elements.

Final Period. (1) *Middlemarch, A Study of Provincial Life* (1871 —1872), her most mature exposition of her own mind and philosophy; while the humor may be quieter than in *Adam Bede* and the *Mill on the Floss,* the two separate stories told in *Middlemarch* are constructed with unfaltering symmetry and are revelatory of George Eliot's sweeping and sad wisdom of life. Without a central character, yet it is saved by rich subsidiary ones. (2) *Daniel Deronda* (1876), composed of two distinct stories: a study of selfishness in the person of Gwendolen Harleth, and a picture of Jewish life and character.[3] Outstanding is the reflective analysis of character and sentiment; also a caustic irony. The work is pro-Semitic in character.

Poetry

Her fourteen shorter poems include: "O may I join the choir invisible"; "Two lovers by a moss-grown spring"; the beautiful and poignant series of eleven sonnets called *Brother and Sister* (1869); *How Lisa Loved the King* (1869), the source of which is the *Decameron* (X, 7); *The Legend of Jubal* (1870); and the Browningesque

---

1 The humorous element in the *Mill on the Floss* and *Daniel Deronda* is of great value: Tomlinson, May, "The Humor of George Eliot," *The Texas Review,* v (1919-1920), pp. 243-248.

2 Parlett, Mathilde, "George Eliot and Humanism," *Studies in Philology,* xxvii (1930), pp. 25-46.

3 It contains the finest picture of Jewish life ever painted by a Christian: thus asserts Hurwitz, Maximilian, " 'Daniel Deronda' Half a Century Ago," *The Jewish Tribune,* July 29, 1927, pp. 2, 6. Consult, also, Slomovitz, Philip, "Daniel Deronda: An Anniversary," *Opinion: A Journal of Jewish Life and Letters,* vii, No. 3 (January, 1937), pp. 11-14.

Stradivarius (1874). Her one long dramatic poem or novel in verse is *The Spanish Gypsy* (1868), a Comtian tragedy of two lovers, one of whom puts duty, and the other, love, ahead of all obligations.

Miscellaneous Writings

(1) *The Life Of Jesus Critically Examined* (1846), a learned translation of Strauss's *Leben Jesu.* (2) *Essence of Christianity* (1854), a translation of Feuerbach's work. (3) *The Lifted Veil* (1859), an eerie tale of clairvoyance, centering upon the thesis that superhuman gifts do not insure happiness. (4) *Brother Jacob* (1860; 1864), another tale. (5) *Impressions of Theophrastus Such* (1879), a series of didactic, satirical essays, autobiographical in the boyhood recollections of Theophrastus Such, a bachelor. (6) *Early Essays* (*c.* 1846; 1919), a small volume containing five essays.

George Meredith, 1828—1909, intellectual novelist, poet.[1]

Novels

(1) *The Shaving of Shagpat* (1865), an entertaining Arabian story composed in a vein of extravagant humor. (2) *The Ordeal of Richard Feverel* (1859), a masterly fusion of intellect and feeling, with effective scenes and tense dramatic situations. (3) *Evan Harrington: or he would be a gentleman* (1861), a partly farcical, partly picaresque tale drawing upon personal experience even more frequently than the preceding novel. (4) *Emilia in England* (1864), subsequently renamed *Sandra Belloni,* his chief treatise on four phases of sentimentality: worldly, patriotic, tragic, amorous. (5) *Rhoda Fleming* (1865), his least analytical or intellectual novel, notable also for an absence of usual irony. (6) *Vittoria, or Emilia in Italy* (1867), a sequel to *Sandra Belloni,* one permeated by the Italian national spirit and crowded with incidents. (7) *The Adventures of Harry Richmond* (1870—1871), another picaresque tale in the style of *Evan Harrington;* it is a poetic romance of his own life. The nominal hero is subsidiary to Roy Richmond; the love of a young man for a girl of superior social rank is the same problem presented in *Evan Harrington.* (8) *Beauchamp's Career* (1876), a political novel suggested by the candidacy of Captain Frederick Maxse of Southampton, and important less for its politics than for its study of character. (9) *The Egoist* (1879), a study of the Comic Idea, and a work more carefully planned than his other novels, superior in strength and brilliance. (10) *The Tragic Comedians* (1880),

---

1 Moffatt, James, *George Meredith: Introduction to his Novels* (1909); Beach, J. W., *The Comic Spirit in George Meredith* (1911); Trevelyan, G. M., *The Poetry and Philosophy of George Meredith* (1912); *Letters of George Meredith,* collected and edited by His Son (Two volumes, 1912); Crees, J. H. E., *George Meredith* (1918); Ellis, S. M., *George Meredith* (1920); Gretton, M. S., *The Writings & Life of George Meredith* (1926); Priestley, J. B., *George Meredith* (1926); Sencourt, R. E., *The Life of George Meredith* (1929); Lindsay, J., *George Meredith: His Life and Work* (1956).

a curious work based on the account given by Helen von Dönniges of her tragic love-affair with the German Socialist, Ferdinand Lassalle. (11) *Diana of the Crossways* (1885), a melodramatic adaptation of the romantic story of Mrs. Caroline Norton dealing with the question of feminism. Story has many improbabilities. (12) *One of Our Conquerors* (1891), a tragi-comedy of love and public opinion baffling almost to obscurity by its riotous metaphors and excessive compressions of thought, but abounding in Meredithian wisdom. (13) *Lord Ormont and His Aminta* (1894), an easy treatment of divorce laws once again. (14) *The Amazing Marriage* (1895), his third and last novel on marriage; simple in plot.

Poetry

His works include *Poems* (1851), *Modern Love, and Poems of the English Roadside* (1862), *Poems and Lyrics of the Joy of Earth* (1883), *Ballads and Poems of Tragic Life* (1887), *Odes in Contribution to the Songs of French History* (1898), *Last Poems* (1909). *A Reading of Life* (1901) contains a very full exposition of Meredith's philosophy. His greatest contribution is *Modern Love,* a novel in verse plotted in fifty sonnet-like stanzas of sixteen lines each, as bold in metaphor as it is obscure in allusion.

Other Works

(1) *Farina: A Legend of Cologne* (1857), a burlesque sketch of superstition and chivalry. (2) *The Sentimentalists,* a conversational comedy produced in 1910. (3) *Celt and Saxon* (1910), a posthumous unfinished story of more than two hundred pages. (4) His lecture in 1877 on *The Idea of Comedy and the Uses of the Comic Spirit* (1897) is an important essay rich in pregnant phrases.[1]

Thomas Hardy, 1840—1928, novelist, poet.[2]

Classification[3] of Novels[4]

Novels of Character and Environment. (1) *Under the Greenwood Tree* (1872), a delicately ironical idyll of the rural courtship of Dick Dewy and Fancy Day; slight of plot, unpretentious of theme,

---

1 Brewer, E. V., "The Influence of Jean Richter on George Meredith's Conception of the Comic," *The Journal of English and Germanic Philology,* XXIX (1930), pp. 243-256.

2 Johnson, Lionel, *The Art of Thomas Hardy* (1894; 1928); Abercrombie, Lascelles, *Thomas Hardy* (1912); Chew, S. C., *Thomas Hardy: Poet and Novelist* (1921; 1928); Brennecke, Ernest, *The Life of Thomas Hardy* (1925); Hardy, F. E., (1) *The Early Life of Thomas Hardy: 1840-1891* (1928) and (2) *Later Years of Thomas Hardy: 1892-1928* (1930); Guerard, A. J., *Thomas Hardy: The Novels and Stories* (1949); Hardy, Evelyn, *Thomas Hardy* (1954).

3 The classification is in the main Hardy's own. He pigeonholed his novels according to the degree of emphasis upon character-analysis or upon unusual event, frowning somewhat upon novels of ingenuity.

4 Fowler, J. H., *The Novels of Thomas Hardy* (The English Association, Pamphlet No. 71, 1928).

light of mood. (2) *Far from the Madding Crowd* (1874), his first important novel, contrasts genuine devotion and love with unscrupulous passion; notable for magic settings, interesting conversations, and searching introspection. (3) *The Return of the Native* (1878), where the true hero is its scene, the sombre Egdon Heath; probably his best novel in its fusion of character and atmosphere, of romantic and realistic elements, and in its plot structure. (4) *The Mayor of Casterbridge* (1886), a powerful novel, memorable for its portrayal of the hay-tresser Michael Henchard, who becomes the Mayor.[1] (5) *The Woodlanders* (1887), where the scene of the wooded country of Blackmoor Vale in Dorset, unlike Egdon Heath, somehow seems to freshen the entire novel. (6) *Tess of the D'Urbervilles* (1891), a masterpiece, beautiful in its rural scenes, sensational in its frankness, ruthless in the bitterness of the final tragedy. (7) *Jude the Obscure* (1895), stark in intention, unrelieved in the *dénouement,* grim in the war between the flesh and the spirit; yet, despite its modernity, rooted in Victorian conventions. (8) *Wessex Tales* (1888) and *Life's Little Ironies* (1894) are two groups of short stories generally classed with the novels of character and environment.

Romances and Fantasies. (1) *A Pair of Blue Eyes* (1873), well-plotted, admirable in its comic relief. (2) *The Trumpet Major* (1880), his most genial novel despite the essentially somber background of the Napoleonic wars; the lapses into melodrama are forgotten because of the simple characters, homely scenes, and sociable humor. (3) *Two on a Tower* (1882), a plot-ridden novel creaking more raspingly because of stilted dialogue and machine-made characters. (4) *A Group of Noble Dames* (1891), a book of leisurely stories including short chronicles of the early part of the seventeenth century, of the late eighteenth century, of the Victorian period. (5) *The Well-Beloved* (1897), published serially in different form five years earlier; it is commonplace in diction, but original in conception and Shelleyan in theme.

Novels of Ingenuity. (1) *Desperate Remedies* (1871), a work of intrigue composed under the influence of Wilkie Collins; it is an immature tale of mystery, entanglement, crime, startling coincidence, and moral obliquity; the only redeeming features are a thoughtful style and the pensive character of Cytherea. (2) *The Hand of Ethelberta* (1876), declared in the preface to be a "somewhat frivolous narrative," yet is in general less stagey and better organized than *Desperate Remedies.* (3) *A Laodicean* (1881), a superficial story of Miss Paula Power, the Laodicean. (4) *A Changed Man, The Waiting Supper and Other Tales, concluding with the Romantic Adventures of a Milkmaid* (1913), a reprint of a dozen minor novels, belonging to the three groups.

---

1 Gardner, W. H., *Some Thoughts on "The Mayor of Casterbridge"* (The English Association, Pamphlet No. 77, 1930).

Poetry[1]

(1) *Wessex Poems* (1898). (2) *Poems of the Past and the Present* (1902). (3) *Time's Laughingstocks and Other Verses* (1909). (4) *Satires of Circumstance* (1914). (5) *Moments of Vision* (1917). (6) *Collected Poems* (1919). (7) *Late Lyrics and Earlier* (1922). (8) *Human Shows* (1925). (9) *Winter Words in Various Moods and Metres* (1928). (10) *The Famous Tragedy of the Queen of Cornwall* (produced 1923), an Arthurian drama. (11) His greatest work is *The Dynasts* (I, 1903, but dated 1904; II, 1906; III, 1908), a colossal epic-drama of the Napoleonic wars, comprised of three parts, nineteen acts, and more than one-hundred and thirty scenes. It is lyric in emotion, dramatic in style, and epic in scale[2].

MINOR NOVELISTS

Edward George Earle Lytton Bulwer-Lytton, First Baron Lytton, 1803—1873, novelist, dramatist; often described as a prose Byron.[3]

Novels

Experimental Period. (1) *Falkland* (1827). (2) *Pelham; or The Adventures of a Gentleman†* (1828). (3) *The Disowned* (1828). (4) *Devereux: A Tale* (1828). (5) *Paul Clifford* (1830).

Parliamentary-Author Period. (1) *Eugene Aram: A Tale* (1832). (2) *Godolphin: A Novel* (1833). (3) *The Pilgrims of the Rhine* (1834). (4) *The Last Days of Pompeii†* (1834). (5) *Rienzi; or, The Last of the Tribunes* (1835). (6) *Ernest Maltravers* (1837). (7) *Leila; or The Siege of Grenada* ʌ1838). (8) *Calderon, The Courtier* (1838).

Third or Mature Period. (1) *Night and Morning* (1841). (2) *Zanoni*[4] (1842). (3) *The Last of the Barons* (1843). (4) *Lucretia; or, Children of Night* (1846). (5) *Harold, The Last of the Saxon Kings* (1848). (6) *Pausanias, The Spartan* (1876).

---

1 King, R. W., "The Lyrical Poems of Thomas Hardy," *The London Mercury,* xv (1926-1927), pp. 157-170; Hsin-Hai, Chang, "A Chinese Estimate of Hardy's Poetry," *The Hibbert Journal,* xxvii (1928), pp. 78-92; Russell, J. A., "The Poetry of Thomas Hardy," *De Nieuwe Gids,* xliii (1928), pp. 611-625; Stanley, Carleton, "The Poetry of Thomas Hardy," *The Nineteenth Century and After,* cviii (1930), pp. 266-280; Strong, Archibald, *Four Studies* (1932), "The Poetry of Thomas Hardy," pp. 81-101.

2 Whitmore, C. E., "Mr. Hardy's *Dynasts* as Tragic Drama," *Modern Language Notes,* xxxix (1924), pp. 455-460; Stewart, Agnes, " 'The Dynasts,' " *The English Review,* xxxviii (1924), pp. 666-680; Russell, J. A., " 'The Dynasts,' " *Die Nieuwe Gids,* xliv (1929), pp. 158-166; McDowall, Arthur, *Thomas Hardy* (1931), pp. 162-173, 174-192.

3 *The Life of Edward Bulwer First Lord Lytton,* by His Grandson The Earl of Lytton (Two volumes, 1913); *Unpublished Letters of Lady Bulwer Lytton To A. E. Chalon, R. A.,* with an introduction and notes by Ellis, S. M. (1914); Van Demark, Henry, "The Amazing Life of the Lyttons," *The Poet and The Critic,* i, No. 2, (1930), pp. 29-34; Sadleir, Michael, *Bulwer: A Panorama* (1931; later reissued as *Bulwer and His Wife,* 1933).

4 *Zanoni,* more than any other book, provided a matrix for the development of modern theosophy in the English language: Stewart, C. N., *Bulwer Lytton As Occultist* (1927).

† * Explanation of symbols immediately precedes Chapter XV.

Legislator-Author Period. (1) *The Caxtons: A Family Picture*† (1849). (2) *My Novel, by Pisistratus Caxton; or, Varieties in English Life*†(1853). (3) *What will he do with it? by Pisistratus Caxton* (1858).

Fifth or Contemporary-Future Period. (1) *A Strange Story* (1862). (2) *The Coming Race* (1871). (3) *The Parisians* (1873). (4) *Kenelm Chillingly: His Adventures and Opinions* (1873).

Plays and Comedies. (1) *The Duchess de la Vallière* (1836). (2) *The Lady of Lyons; or, Love and Pride* (1838). (3) *Richelieu; or The Conspiracy* (1839). (4) *The Sea Captain; or, The Birthright* (1839). (5) *Money* (1840). (6) *Not so Bad as We seem; or, Many Sides to a Character* (1851). (7) *The Rightful Heir* (1868). (8) *Walpole; or, Every Man has his Price* (1869). (9) *Darnley* (1882), unfinished.

Short Horror Stories. (1) *The Haunters and the Haunted.* (2) *A Strange Story* (1862).

Other Works

(1) *Ismael: An Oriental Tale, with Other Poems* (1820). (2) *Delmour; or, A Tale of a Sylphid, and Other Poems* (1832). (3) *The Siamese Twins: A Satirical Tale of the Times, with Other Poems* (1831). (4) *England and the English* (1833). (5) *The Student: A Series of Papers.* (6) *Athens, Its Rise and Fall* (1837). (7) *Alice; or, The Mysteries* (1838), a sequel to *Ernest Maltravers.* (8) *Eva: A True Story of Light and Darkness; The Ill-omened Marriage, and other Tales and Poems* (1842). (9) *The Poems and Ballads of Schiller* (1843). (10) *The New Timon: A Romance of London* (1846). (11) *King Arthur* (1848). (12) *Outlines of the Early History of the East* (1852). (13) *St. Stephens: A Poem* (1860). (14) *The Boatman, by Pisistratus Caxton* (1864). (15) *The Lost Tales of Miletus* (1866). (16) *The Odes and Epodes of Horace* (1869).

Benjamin Disraeli, First Earl of Beaconsfield, 1804—1881, statesman, novelist.[1]

Society Novels. (1) *Vivian Grey* (1826—1827). (2) *The Young Duke* (1831).

---

[1] Howes, R. W., *Disraeli: A Key to the Characters* (1907); Gosse, Edmund, "The Novels of Benjamin Disraeli," *Transactions of the Royal Society of The United Kingdom, Second Series,* xxxvi (1918), pp. 61-90; Whibley, Charles, *Political Portraits* (Second Series, 1923), "Benjamin Disraeli," pp. 215-223 (pp. 108-229); Speare, M. E., *The Political Novel* (1924); Raymond, E. T., *Disraeli: Alien Patriot* (1925); Clark, Sir Edward. *Benjamin Disraeli* (1926); Murray, D. L., *Disraeli* (1927); Maurois, Andre. *Disraeli,* translated by Miles, Hamish (1928); Swinnerton, Frank, "Disraeli as Novelist," *The Yale Review,* New Series, xvii (1928), pp. 283-300; *The Life of Benjamin Disraeli,* new and revised edition in two volumes by Monypenny, W. F., and Buckle, G. E. (1929); *The Letters of Disraeli to Lady Chesterfield and Lady Bradford,* edited by the Marquis of Zetland (Two volumes, 1929); Taylor, G. R. S., *Seven Nineteenth Century Statesmen* (1932), "Benjamin Disraeli, Earl of Beaconsfield," pp. 204-236; Seton-Watson, R. W., *Disraeli, Gladstone, and The Eastern Question* (1935); *Bulwer-Lytton,* by the Earl of Lytton (1948).

† • **Explanation of symbols immediately precedes Chapter XV.**

Political Novels. (1) *Coningsby: Or The New Generation*† (1844). (2) *Sybil: Or The Two Nations*† (1845). (3) *Tancred: Or The New Crusade*† (1847).

Other Novels. (1) *Contarini Fleming: A Psychological Autobiography* (1832). (2) *The Wondrous Tale of Alroy: The Rise of Iskander* (1833). (3) *Henrietta Temple: A Love Story* (1837). (4) *Venetia* (1837). (5) *Lothair* (1870). (6) *Endymion* (1880).

Satires. (1) *The Voyage of Captain Popanilla* (1828). (2) *Ixion In Heaven* (1833). (3) *The Infernal Marriage* (1834).

Polemical Pamphlets. (1) *Vindication Of The English Constitution In A Letter To A Noble and Learned Lord* (1835). (2) *The Letters of Runnymede* (1836).

Miscellaneous Writings. (1) *Lawyers and Legislators: Or Notes on the American Mining Companies* (1825). (2) *The Present State of Mexico* (1825). (3) *England And France: Or A Cure for the Ministerial Gallomania* (1832). (4) *The Crisis Examined* (1834). (5) *Lord George Bentick, A Political Biography*† (1852).

Elizabeth Cleghorn (Stevenson) Gaskell, 1810—1865, humanitarian novelist, biographer, short-story writer.[1]

Novels

Industrial Life. (1) *Mary Barton: A Tale of Manchester Life* (1848). (2) *North and South* (1855).

Idyllic Life. (1) *Moorland Cottage* (1850). (2) *Cranford*† (1853).

Problem Novels. (1) *Ruth* (1853). (2) *Lois the Witch*, in *Lois the Witch, and Other Tales* (1861).

Romance. (1) *Sylvia's Lovers* (1863). (2) *Wives and Daughters: An Everyday Story* (1866), unfinished.

Biography. *The Life of Charlotte Bronte*† (1857).

Other Works

(1) *Libbie Marsh's Three Eras: A Lancashire Tale* (1850). (2) *The Sexton's Hero and Christmas Storms and Sunshine* (1850). (3) *Lizzie Leigh: A Domestic Tale* (1850). (4) *Hand and Heart and Bessie's Troubles at Home* (1855). (5) *Round the Sofa* (1859). (6) *Right at Last: And Other Tales* (1860). (7) *A Dark Night's Work* (1863). (8) *The Grey Woman: And Other Tales* (1865). (9) *Cousin Phyllis: And Other Tales* (1865).

---

1 Whitfeld, A. S., *Mrs. Gaskell: Her Life and Work* (1929); Sanders, G. De W., *Elizabeth Gaskell* (1929): with a bibliography by Northup, C. S.; Haldane, Elizabeth, *Mrs. Gaskell and Her Friends* (1930); *Letters of Mrs. Gaskell and Charles Enot Norton*, edited by Whitehill, Jane (1932).
† * Explanation of symbols immediately precedes Chapter XV.

Charlotte Brontë, 1816—1855, novelist.[1] (1) *Jane Eyre*† (1847). (2) *Shirley* (1849). (3) *Villette* (1853). (4) *The Professor* (1857). (5) *Emma* (1860), a fragment. (6) *The Story of Willie Ellen,* unfinished.

Emily Jane Brontë, 1818—1848, novelist.[2] *Wuthering Heights*† (1847), a novel.

Anne Brontë, 1820—1849, novelist.[3] (1) *Agnes Grey* (1847). (2) *The Tenant of Wildfell Hall* (1848).

Charles Kingsley, 1819—1875, divine, novelist, controversialist, poet.[4]

Novels

Christian-Socialist Works. (1) *Yeast; Or The Thoughts, Sayings, and Doings of Lancelot Smith, Gentleman* (1848). (2) *Alton Locke, Tailor and Poet*[5] (1850).

Historical and Philosophical. (1) *Hypatia: Or, New Foes With An Old Face* (1853). (2) *Westward Ho! Or, The Voyages And Adventures Of Sir Amyas Leigh, Knight* . . . .† (1855).

The Muscular Novel. (1) *Two Years Ago* (1857). (2) *Hereward the Wake,* "*Last of the English*" (1866).

Other Prose Works

(1) *Glaucus; Or, The Wonders Of The Shore* (1855). (2) *Hints to Stammerers* (1859, 1864). (3) *At Last: A Christmas In The West Indies*† (1871). (4) *Prose Idylls, New and Old*† (1873). (5) *The Tutor's Story,* an unpublished novel completed by his daughter, Lucas Malet (1916).

Miscellaneous

Books For Children. (1) *The Heroes; Or Greek Fairy Tales For My Children* (1856). (2) *The Water-Babies: A Fairy tale for a Land-Baby*† (1863). (3) *Madam How and Lady Why* (1869).

Poetry. (1) *The Saint's Tragedy; Or, The True Story of Elizabeth of Hungary, Landgravine Of Thuringia, Saint Of The Romish Calendar* (1848). (2) *Poems* (1856). (3) *Andromeda And Other*

1, 2, 3 Among the best introductions to the work of the Brontë sisters are Bald, M. A., *Women-Writers of the Nineteenth Century* (1923), pp. 28-99; Hale, W. T., "Anne Brontë: Her Life and Writings," *Indiana University Studies,* XVI, No. 83 (1929); Sugden, K. A. R., *A Short History of the Brontës* (1928); Benson, E. F., *Charlotte Brontë* (1932); Cecil, David, *Early Victorian Novelists* (1934), pp. 109-144, 147-193; Delafield, E. M., *The Brontës* (1936).

4 Brown, W. H., *Charles Kingsley and Parson Lot* (1924); Baldwin, S. E., *Charles Kingsley* (1934); Thorp, M. F., *Charles Kingsley* (1937).

5 While Kingsley often pleaded, as in *Yeast,* for economic improvement of the laboring class, he believed that the worker must always stay within his own social caste. His attitude should be compared with that of Dickens's *Hard Times,* Eliot's *Felix Holt,* and Mrs. Gaskell's *Mary Barton.*

† • Explanation of symbols immediately precedes Chapter XV.

Poems (1858). (4) *Ode Performed In The Senate-House, Cambridge, On The Tenth Of June, 1862.* (5) His lyrics and poems include *A Farewell, Young and Old, Sing Heigh-Ho, Song: "Oh! that we two were Maying," Airly Beacon, Margaret to Dolcino, Dolcino to Margaret, The Three Fishers, The Last Buccaneer, The Tide River, The Sands o' Dee, Doll's Song, The Bad Squire.*[1]

Essays, Lectures, and Sermons. (1) *Politics For The People* (1848). (2) *Introductory Lectures* (1849). (3) *Twenty-Five Village Sermons* (1849). (4) *The Application Of Associative Principles And Methods To Agriculture* (1851). (5) *The Message Of The Church To The Labouring Man* (1851). (6) *Tracts By Christian Socialists: II. Cheap Clothes and Nasty. By Parson Lot* (1851). (7) *Phaethon; Or Loose Thoughts For Loose Thinkers* (1852). (8) *Sermons on National Subjects* (1852, 1854). (9) *Who Are The Friends of Order?* (1852). (10) *Alexandria And Her Schools* (1854). (11) *Who Causes Pestilence?* (1854). (12) *Lectures To Ladies On Practical Subjects* (1855). (13) *Sermons For The Times* (1855). (14) *The History and Life Of The Reverend Doctor John Tauler of Strasbourg* (1857). (15) *The Good News Of God* (1859). (16) *Sir Walter Raleigh And His Time* (1859). (17) *The Limits Of Exact Science* (1860). (18) *Why Should We Pray For Fair Weather?* (1860). (19) *Town And Country Sermons* (1861). (20) *A Sermon On The Death Of His Royal Highness The Prince Consort* (1862). (21) *The Gospel Of The Pentateuch* (1863). (22) *Mr. Kingsley And Dr. Newman: A Correspondence On The Question Whether Dr. Newman Teaches That Truth Is No Virtue?* (1864). (23) *The Roman And The Teuton* (1864). (24) *David* (1865). (25) *Plays and Puritans* (1873). (26) *Westminster Sermons* (1874). (27) *Lectures Delivered In America in 1874* (1875). (28) *Village Sermons, And Town And Country Sermons* (1877). (29) *All Saint's Day And Other Sermons* (1878).

Anthony Trollope, 1815—1882, novelist.[2]

Chronicles of Barsetshire. (1) *The Warden*† (1855). (2) *Barchester Towers*† (1857). (3) *Doctor Thorne*† (1858). (4) *Framley Parsonage*† (1861). (5) *The Small House at Allington*† (1864). (6) *The Last Chronicle of Barset*† (1867).

Parliamentary-Political Novels. (1) *Can You Forgive Her?* (1864). (2) *Phineas Finn, The Irish Member*† (1869). (3) *The Eustace Diamonds*† (1873). (4) *Phineas Redux* (1874). (5) *The Prime Minister* (1876). (6) *The Duke's Children*† (1880).

---

1 Some of his most popular poems are found in his novels: "The Sands o' Dee" in *Alton Locke,* "The Bad Squire" in *Yeast,* "Doll's Song" in *Water-Babies.*

2 Escott, T. H. S., *Anthony Trollope* (1913); Nichols, S. Van B., *The Significance of Anthony Trollope* (1925); Sadleir, Michael, *Trollope: A Commentary* (1928); Walpole, Hugh, *Anthony Trollope* (1928).

† * Explanation of symbols immediately precedes Chapter XV.

Social Life and Manners. (1) *The Three Clerks* (1858). (2) *Orley Farm†* (1862). (3) *The Belton Estate†* (1866). (4) *The Claverings†* (1867). (5) *The Vicar of Bullhampton†* (1870). (6) *Ralph the Heir* (1871). (7) *Lady Anna* (1874). (8) *The American Senator†* (1877). (9) *Is He Popenjoy?†* (1878). (10) *Ayala's Angel* (1881). (11) *Marion Fay* (1882).

Social Satires. (1) *The Bertrams* (1859). (2) *Rachel Ray†* (1863). (3) *Miss Mackenzie* (1865). (4) *He Knew He Was Right* (1869). (5) *The Struggles of Brown, Jones and Robinson* (1870). (6) *The Way We Live Now†* (1875). (7) *Mr. Scarborough's Family* (1883).

Historical and Romantic Novels. (1) *La Vendee* (1850). (2) *Nina Balatka†* (1867). (3) *Linda Tressel†* (1868). (4) *The Golden Lion of Granpère* (1872).

Stories of Psychological Analysis and of Single Incident. (1) *Sir Harry Hotspur of Humblethwaite†* (1871). (2) *How the "Mastiffs" Went to Ireland* (1878). (3) *Cousin Henry†* (1879). (4) *Dr. Wortle's School†* (1881). (5) *Kept in the Dark* (1882). (6) *The Fixed Period* (1882). (7) *An Old Man's Love* (1884).

Irish Novels. (1) *The Macdermots of Ballyclorant* (1847). *The Kellys and the O'Kellys* (1848). (3) *Castle Richmond†* (1860). (4) *An Eye for an Eye* (1879). (5) *The Landleaguers* (1883).

Australian Colonial Life. (1) *Harry Heathcote of Gangoil* (1874). (2) *John Caldigate†* (1879).

Short Stories. (1) *Tales of All Countries* (1861). (2) *Tales of All Countries* (Second series, 1863). (3) *Travelling Sketches* (1866). (4) *Lotta Schmidt and Other Stories†* (1867). (5) *An Editor's Tales†* (1870). (6) *Why Frau Frohmann Raised her Prices, and Other Stories* (1882).

Plays. (1) *Did He Steal It?* (1869). (2) *The Noble Jilt* (written 1850; published 1923).

Essays and Monographs. (1) *Hunting Sketches* (1865). (2) *Clergymen of the Church of England* (1866). (3) *British Sports and Pastimes* (1868). (4) *The Commentaries of Caesar* (1870). (5) *Thackeray* (1879). (6) *The Life of Cicero* (1880). (7) *Lord Palmerston* (1882). (8) *An Autobiography* (1883).[1]

Travel Books. (1) *The West Indies and the Spanish Main* (1859). (2) *North America* (1862). (3) *Australia and New Zealand* (1873). (4) *South Africa* (1878).

---

1 Whibley, Charles, "Trollope's Autobiography," *The English Review,* xxxvii (1923), pp. 33-38.

† * Explanation of symbols immediately precedes Chapter XV.

Charles Reade, 1814—1884, documentary novelist, dramatist.[1]

Chief Novels

Romance and Manners. (1) *Peg Woffington* (1853). (2) *Christie Johnstone* (1853).

Historical Novel. *The Cloister and the Hearth: A Tale of the Middle Ages†* (1861), declared by Walter Besant to be the greatest historical novel in the language.

Propagandistic and Didactic Novels. (1) *It Is Never Too Late To Mend: A Matter of Fact Romance* (1856). (2) *Hard Cash: A Matter of Romance†* (1863). (3) *Griffith Gaunt: Or Jealousy* (1867). (4) *Foul Play* (1868). (5) *Put Yourself In His Place* (1870). (6) *A Terrible Temptation: A Story of the Day* (1871).

Other Works

(1) *The Course of True Love Never Did Run Smooth* (1857). (2) *White Lies: A Story* (1857). (3) *The Box-Tunnel* (1853). (4) *Love Me Little Love Me Long* (1859). (5) *The Eighth Commandment* (1860). (6) *A Simpleton: A Story of the Day* (1873). (7) *A Hero and A Martyr: A True and Accurate Account of the Heroic feats and sad Calamity of James Lambert* (1874). (8) *Trade Malice* (1875). (9) *The Wandering Heir* (1875). (10) *A Woman Hater* (1877). (11) *Golden Crowns: Sunday Stories* (1877). (12) *Readiana: Comments on Current Events* (1883). (13) *Single Heart and Double Face: A Matter of Fact Romance* (1884). (14) *Good Stories of Man and Other Animals* (1884). (15) *The Jilt and Other Stories* (1884). (16) *A Perilous Secret* (1884). (17) *Bible Characters* (1888). (18) *A Good Fight* (1910), the original version of *The Cloister and the Hearth.*

Plays. (1) *Peregrine Pickle* (c. 1834). (2) *The Ladies' Battle: Or Un Duel en Amour* (1851). (3) *Angelo: A Tragedy* (1851). (4) *The Lost Husband* (1852). (5) *Gold* (1853). (6) *The Courier of Lyons: Or The Attack upon the Mail* (1854), a translation from the French. (7) *Masks and Faces: Or Before and Behind the Curtain* (in collaboration with Tom Taylor, 1854). (8) *Two Loves and A Life* (with Tom Taylor, 1854). (9) *The King's Rival* (with Tom Taylor, 1854). (10) *Poverty and Pride,* authorized English version of French play (1856). (11) *The Hypochondriac,* an adaptation (1857). (12) *Dora* (c. 1867). (13) *The Double Marriage* (in collaboration with Auguste Maquet, c. 1867). (14) *Kate Peyton: Or Jealousy* (c. 1869). (15) *It's Never Too*

---

1 Sutcliffe, E. G., (1) "The Stage in Reade's Novels," *Studies in Philology,* xxvii (1930), pp. 654-688; and (2) "Charles Reade's Notebooks," *Studies in Philology,* xxvii (1930), pp. 64-109; Elwin, Malcolm, *Charles Reade* (1931); Sutcliffe, E. G., "Plotting in Reade's Novels," *Publications of the Modern Language Association of America,* xlvii (1932), pp. 834-863.

† * **Explanation of symbols immediately precedes Chapter XV.**

Late To Mend (c. 1872). (16) *The Well Born Workman: Or A Man of the Day* (1878). (17) *Foul Play* (1883). (18) *Love and Money* (1883). (19) *The Countess and The Dancer; Or High Life in Vienna* (1883).

Robert Louis Stevenson, 1850—1894, novelist, essayist, poet.[1]

Novels and Romances

(1) *Treasure Island* (1883). (2) *Prince Otto* (1885). (3) *Kidnapped: Being Memoirs of the Adventures of David Balfour* (1886). (4) *The Black Arrow: A Tale of the Two Roses* (1888). (5) *The Master of Ballantrae. A Winter's Tale* (1889). (6) *The Wrong Box* (1889). (7) *The Wrecker* (1892), written in collaboration with Lloyd Osbourne. (8) *Catriona. A Sequel to "Kidnapped"* (1893). (9) *The Ebb-Tide* (1894), in collaboration with Lloyd Osbourne. (10) *St. Ives. Being the Adventures of a French Prisoner in England;* finished by A. T. Quiller-Couch. (11) *Weir of Hermiston. An Unfinished Romance* (1896).

Poetry Volumes

(1) *A Child's Garden of Verses* (1885). (2) *Underwoods* (1887). (3) *Ballads* (1890). (4) *Songs of Travel and other Verses* (1896).

Short-Story Collections

(1) *New Arabian Nights* (1882). (2) *More New Arabian Nights. The Dynamiter* (1885). (3) *Strange Case of Dr. Jekyll und Mr. Hyde* (1886), a short-story that has been dramatized several times. (4) *The Merry Men and Other Tales and Fables* (1887). (5) *Island Night's Entertainment* (1893). (6) *Tales and Fantasies* (1905). (7) *Lay Morals and Other Papers* (1911).

Essays

(1) *Virginibus Puerisque and Other Papers* (1881). (2) *Familiar Studies of Men and Books* (1882). (3) *Memories and Portraits* (1887). (4) *Essays in the Art of Writing* (1905).

Travel Books

(1) *An Inland Voyage* (1878). (2) *Travels with a Donkey in the Cevennes* (1879). (3) *The Silverado Squatters* (1883). (4) *Across the*

---

1 Swinnerton, Frank, *R. L. Stevenson* (1914); Balfour, Graham, *The Life of Robert Louis Stevenson* (1915); Masson, Rosaline, *The Life of Robert Louis Stevenson* (1923); Osbourne, Lloyd, *An Intimate Portrait of R. L. S.* (1924); Steuart, J. A., *Robert Louis Stevenson* (1924); Hellman, G. S., *The True Stevenson* (1925). See, also, Stevenson's *Vailima Letters* (1895), and *The Letters of R. L. S.* edited by Colvin, Sidney (1911).

Plains: with other Memories and Essays (1892). (5) *The South Seas. A Record of Three Cruises* (1890, 1896).

Plays

Four plays written in collaboration with W. E. Henley: (1) *Deacon Brodie, or, The Double Life* (1880). (2) *Admiral Guinea* (1884). (3) *Beau Austin* (1884). (4) *Macaire* (1885).

Samuel Butler,[1] 1835—1902, author.[2]

Novel. *The Way of All Flesh*†[3] (1903).

Satirical Romances. (1) *Erewhon or Over the Range* (1872). (2) *Erewhon Revisited Twenty Years Later* (1901).

Criticism. (1) *A Lecture on The Humour of Homer* (1892). (2) *On the Trapanese Origin of the Odyssey* (1893). (3) *The Life and Letters of Dr. Samuel Butler. Headmaster of Shrewsbury School 1798— 1836 . . . .* (1894). (4) *The Authoress of the Odyssey* (1897).[4] (5) *Shakespeare's Sonnets Reconsidered* (1899). (6) *Essays on Life, Art, and Science* (1904).

Scientific Controversy. (1) *Life and Habit*† (1877). (2) *Evolution, Old and New; or, the Theories of Buffon, Dr. Erasmus Darwin,*

---

1 Paul Elmer More believes that "Erewhon" Butler, so far as he is known to the general reader, owes his fame to Shaw's eulogy of *The Way of All Flesh*. We have observed that almost every edition of Butler's only novel quotes from G. B. Shaw's preface to *Major Barbara* (1907—p. 20):

'The late Samuel Butler, in his own department the greatest English writer of the latter half of the XIX century, steadily inculcated the necessity and morality of a conscientious Laodiceanism in religion and of an earnest and constant sense of the importance of money. It drives one almost to despair of English literature when one sees so extraordinary a study of English life as Butler's posthumous Way of All Flesh making so little impression that when, some years later, I produce plays in which Butler's extraordinarily fresh, free and future-piercing suggestions have an obvious share, I am met with nothing but vague cacklings about Ibsen and Nietzsche, and am only too thankful that they are not about Alfred de Musset and George Sand. Really, the English do not deserve to have great men. They allowed Butler to die practically unknown, whilst I, a comparatively insignificant Irish journalist, was leading them by the nose into an advertisement of me which has made my own life a burden. In Sicily there is a Via Samuele Butler. When an English tourist sees it, he either asks "Who the devil was Samuele Butler?" or wonders why the Sicilians should perpetuate the memory of the author of Hudibras." (For "Hudibras" Butler, see p. 297.)

2 Cannan, Gilbert, *Samuel Butler* (1915); Harris, J. F., *Samuel Butler* (1916); Jones, H. F., *Samuel Butler: A Memoir* (Two volumes, 1919); Stanley, C. W., "The Author of 'Erewhon,'" *Queen's Quarterly*, XXIX (1921-1922), pp. 114-137; Joad, C. E. M., *Samuel Butler* (1924); Lange, P. J. De, *Samuel Butler* (1925); Garnett, R. S. (Mrs.), *Samuel Butler and His Family Relations* (1926); Stillman, C. G., *Samuel Butler* (1932); Rattray, R. F., *Samuel Butler: A Chronicle and An Introduction* (1935); Muggeridge, Malcolm, *The Earnest Atheist* (1936).

3 Butler based the character of Alethea Pontifex on Miss Eliza Mary Ann Savage. For more information about their relationship, consult *Letters between Samuel Butler and Miss E. M. A. Savage*, introduction by Keynes, Geoffrey, and Hill, Brian (Jonathan Cape, 1935).

4 Farrington, B(enjamin), (1) *Samuel Butler and The Odyssey* (1929); (2) "Samuel Butler and The Odyssey," *Revue des Études Homériques*, II (1932), pp. 74-80.

† * Explanation of symbols immediately precedes Chapter XV.

and Lamarck, As Compared with that of Mr. Charles Darwin (1879).
(3) *God the Known and God the Unknown* (1879). (4) *Unconscious Memory* (1880). (5) *Luck or Cunning, As the main means of Organic Modification?* (1887).

Travel Books. (1) *Alps and Sanctuaries of Piedmont and the Canton Ticino* (1882). (2) *Ex Voto: An Account of The Sacro Monte or New Jerusalem at Varallo-Sesia* (1888).

Essays and Miscellanea. (1) *A First Year in Canterbury Settlement* (1863). (2) *Literary Foundlings: Verse and Prose* (1864). (3) *The Fair Haven* (1873). (4) *Gavottes, Minuets, Fugues and other short pieces for the piano* (1885). (5) *Holbein's Dance* (1886). (6) *The Iliad of Homer Rendered into English Prose* (1898). (7) *The Odyssey Rendered into English Prose* (1900). (8) *The Note-Books of Samuel Butler*†[1] (1898; 1912).

Mrs. Humphry Ward (Mary Augusta Arnold), 1851—1920, novelist.[2]

Theological Novels.[3] (1) *Robert Elsmere*† (1888). (2) *The History of David Grieve* (1892). (3) *Helbeck of Bannisdale* (1898). (4) *Eleanor* (1900). (5) *The Case of Richard Meynell* (1911).

Tradition and Progress. (1) *Marcella* (1894). (2) *Sir George Tressady* (1896). (3) *The Coryston Family* (1916).

Feminism. (1) *The Marriage of William Ashe* (1905). (2) *Daphne; or "Marriage à la Mode"* (1909). (3) *Delia Blanchflower* (1915). *Eltham House* (1915).

Other Novels. (1) *Molly and Olly: or a Holiday among the Mountains* (1881). (2) *Miss Bretherton* (1884). (3) *The Story of Bessie Costrell* (1895). (4) *Lady Rose's Daughter* (1903). (5) *Fenwick's Career* (1906). (6) *Canadian Born* (1910). (7) *The War and Elizabeth* (1918).

---

1 *The Note-Books of Samuel Butler,* edited by Jones, H. F. (1912); *Further Extracts from the Note-Books of Samuel Butler,* edited by Bartholomew, A. T. (1934).

2 Phelps, W. L., "The Novels of Mrs. Humphry Ward," *The Forum,* XLI (1909), pp. 323-331; Walters, J. S., *Mrs. Humphry Ward* (1912); Gwynn, Stephen, *Mrs. Humphry Ward* (1917); Trevelyan, J. P., *The Life of Mrs. Humphry Ward* (1923).

3 Stewart, H. L., "Mrs. Humphry Ward and the Theological Novel," *The Hibbert Journal,* XVIII (1919-1920), pp. 675-686; Barnes, E. W., "Robert Elsmere and the Faith of To-day," *The Review of Reviews* (London), LXVIII (1923), pp. 307-316.

† * **Explanation** of symbols immediately precedes Chapter XV.

MAJOR POETS

Alfred Tennyson, First Baron Tennyson, 1809—1892, the most representative poet of the Victorian age.[1]

Chief Publications

(1) *Poems by Two Brothers* (1827), by Alfred and Charles Tennyson; really by three brothers, for Frederick also contributed. The poems are immature and singularly lacking in merit; are faded imitations of Macpherson, Gray, Scott, and Byron. (2) *Poems, Chiefly Lyrical* (1830), a volume containing verses as insignificant as those in the 1827 issue, but also such promise and achievement as found in *Mariana* and *The Poet*. (3) *Poems* (1832; dated 1833), contained thirty new poems including *The Lady of Shalott, The Lotus-Eaters, The Palace of Art, The Miller's Daughter, Clara Vere de Vere, The Two Voices, Oenone*. (4) *The Lover's Tale* (1833, 1879). (5) *Poems* (Two volumes, 1842), including *The Gardener's Daughter, Morte d' Arthur, The Vision of Sin, Ulysses, Locksley Hall, Sir Galahad, Break Break Break*. (6) *The Princess; A Medley* (1847). (7) *In Memoriam* (1850). (8) *Ode on the Death of the Duke of Wellington* (1852). (9) *Maud* (1855). (10) *Idylls of the King* (1859—1885). (11) *Enoch Arden* (1864). (12) *The Holy Grail and Other Poems* (1869). (13) *Gareth and Lynette* (1872). (14) *Ballads and Other Poems* (1880), which includes *The Voyage of Maeldune, Rizpah*, a monologue founded on fact (for the title see 2 Samuel XXI, 8—10), *The Revenge*, a war-ballad. (15) *Tiresias and Other Poems* (1885). (16) *Locksley Hall Sixty Years After* (1886). (17) *Demeter and Other Poems* (1889), including *Merlin and the Gleam, To Virgil*, and *Crossing the Bar*. (18) *The Death of Oenone, Akbar's Dream, and Other Poems* (1892).

Plays[2]

(1) *Queen Mary* (1875), blank-verse drama, first of an historical trilogy, has as its central theme the clash between Rome and Lutheranism. (2) *Harold* (1876), a dramatization not so much of the nominal hero as of the conflict of the rival races (Norman and Saxon). (3)

---

1 Walters, J. C., *Tennyson* (1893); Gwynn, Stephen, *Tennyson* (1899); Griggs, E. H., *The Poetry and Philosophy of Tennyson* (1906); Benson, A. C., *Alfred Tennyson* (1907); Lounsbury, T. R., *The Life and Times of Tennyson* (1915); Bradley, A. C., *The Reaction Against Tennyson* (The English Association, Pamphlet No. 39, 1917); Alden, R. M., *Alfred Tennyson: How to Know Him* (1917); Van Dyke, Henry, *Studies in Tennyson* (1920); *Poems of Tennyson*, edited by Van Dyke, Henry (1920); Abbott, C. C., "A Short View of the Case Against Tennyson," *Humberside*, I (1922-1924), pp. 5-26; Nicolson, Harold, *Tennyson* (1923); Mackail, J. W., *Studies of English Poets* (1926), "Tennyson," pp. 229-251; Perry, H. T. E., "The Tennyson Tragedy," *Southwest Review*, XII (1926-1927), pp. 97-112; Macy, John, "Tennyson, the Perfect Laureate," *The Bookman*, LXIX (1929), pp. 375-386; Brooke, S. A., "Tennyson: His Art and Relation to Life" (1929); Magnus, Laurie, "Tennyson A Hundred Years After," *The Cornhill Magazine*, New Series, LXVI (1929), pp. 660-670; Scaife, C. H. O., *The Poetry of Alfred Tennyson* (1930); Abercrombie, Lascelles, "Tennyson," in *Revaluations* (Oxford University Press, 1931), pp. 60-76; *Alfred, Lord Tennyson*, edited by Lucas, F. E. (1932); Noyes, Alfred, *Tennyson* (1932).

2 Japikse, C. G. H., *The Dramas of Alfred Lord Tennyson* (1926).

Becket† (1884), the last in the trilogy and the greatest of all his plays; best in construction and in dramatic tone, strongest in character and in climax. In depicting the struggle between the Crown and the Church, Tennyson gives a vivid description of the character of Henry II. (4) *The Promise of May* (1882), a dreary exposure of the injurious influence of secularism. (5) *The Cup* (1881, 1884), a dramatization of an impressive incident found in Plutarch's *De Mulieribus Virtutibus*. (6) *The Falcon* (1879, 1884) an idyllic trifle indebted to Boccaccio for the plot. (7) *The Foresters* (1892), a woodland masque founded on the Robin Hood legends.

Important Poems

The Devil and the Lady (1930). An almost incredibly precocious three-act play or poem written at the age of fourteen.

Timbuctoo (1829). Obtained the Chancellor's Medal at the Cambridge Commencement. Simple in theme; academic in purpose; lacking in form, but spiritual in thought. Its departure lies in the fact that it used blank verse, and not the traditional rimed couplet expected of prize poems written for such occasions.

The Poet (1830). Tennyson's hyperbolic conception of a poet's grandeur and destiny; and its sequel *The Poet's Mind* (1830), which shows how the poet's claims upon the outer world can be brought to fulfillment.

The Lotus-Eaters (1832). Spenserian stanzas founded on the Greek legend of the Lotophagi. Extreme in its tendency to aestheticism.[1]

The Palace of Art (1832). Ornate allegory of the mental and moral disaster of an artistic recluse in the pursuit of beauty. Urges people to forswear their ivory towers.

Ulysses (1842). Dramatic monologue in blank verse based on an episode in Dante's *Inferno* (XXVI, 90—129); is compact of expression and masculine in spirit.

Break, Break, Break (1842). Inspired, like *In the valley of Cauteretz,* by Tennyson's sorrow for the loss of Hallam.

Locksley Hall (1842). Important as an expression of embittered personal feeling and grave reflections on civilization; its sequel is *Locksley Hall Sixty Years After* (1886), which, like its predecessor, reveals sentimental tendencies.

---

1 Grendon, Felix, "The Influence of Keats upon the Early Poetry of Tennyson," *The Sewanee Review Quarterly*, xv (1907), pp. 285-296.

† * Explanation of symbols immediately precedes Chapter XV.

The Lady of Shalott (1842). A dream picture with the under-lying allegory on the undesirability and impossibility of seclusion from the world. The story, derived from an Italian source, is fully developed in *Lancelot and Elaine,* one of the *Idylls.*

The Princess, A Medley (1847). Narrative poem in somewhat sterile blank verse centering upon the proper sphere of woman in life, particularly in her relation to education.[1] The verse is now epical, now idyllic, even lyrical; the substance, half-serious, half-farcical. Story and characters weak, diction and epithets over-ornamented; it is as lacking in dramatic interest as it is in unity. Few think it a work of special insight into the main problem of feminism, or a genuine criti-cism of Victorian life; but all praise the lyric interludes and singing lines, found, for example, in *Sweet and Low, The Splendor Falls on Castle Walls, Tears Idle Tears, Home They Brought Her Warrior Dead, Ask Me No More, Now Sleeps the Crimson Petal, Come Down O Maid.*

In Memoriam (1833—1849; 1850). Noble threnody written in memory of A. H. Hallam[2] consists of one hundred and thirty-one short poems, with a prologue and epilogue, all connected loosely by a solemn central theme. Formerly often described as the greatest philosophical poem of the nineteenth century, *In Memoriam* endeavors from first to last to reconcile the world of fact with the world of dreams; it reflects phases of an arresting epoch, its hopes and fears, questions and answers; it gives philosophic embodiment to the great issues of faith and doubt, to the supreme questions of death and im-mortality. It begins with a personal lament for A. H. Hallam, once engaged to Tennyson's sister Emily, and ends with a bridal song for Cecilia Tennyson, who married Edmund Law Lushington. The scope of the poem may be limited, the series of lyrics may lack close con-tinuity, the dramatic sense may be lacking,[3] but on the whole *In Memoriam* shows Tennyson's remarkable felicity of diction, lucid verse, quiet depth of feeling, and rich response to natural beauty.[4] (Compare with Milton's *Lycidas,* Vol. 1, p. 279; Shelley's *Adonais,* and Arnold's *Thyrsis.*)

The Eagle (1851). Vivid, terse.

Ode on the Death of the Duke of Wellington (1852). In dig-nified heroic vein; now soaring, now swooping in the metrical variations of the irregular Pindaric form.

---

1 *The Princess,* edited by Woodberry, G. E. (1898), Introduction, pp. IX-XXIV.

2 For new light on Tennyson's years immediately preceding and following the death of his friend, see Tennyson, Charles, "Tennyson Papers: II. J. M. Heath's Common-place Book,' " *The Cornhill Magazine,* CLIII (1936), pp. 426-449.

3 Taine, who found it possible to praise *Maud,* could not appreciate *In Memoriam:* See Bowden, Marjorie, *Tennyson in France* (1930), p. 27 ff.

4 Its inception, scope, workmanship, meter, and construction are discussed by Johnson, G. C. A., "Tennyson's *In Memoriam,*" *The Poetry Review,* XXII (1931), pp. 181-201.

The Charge of the Light Brigade (1854). Famous piece, based on a news dispatch, may be censured for its low conception of a soldier's duty.

Maud (1855). Long monodrama tells a simple story in an ingenious way; its lyrics are so connected that each represents a scene in the action. Often said to be the poorest of his long narratives, it seems, despite its unevenness of merit and obscurity of expression, rather to be his most moving and strongest flight.[1] Like *The Princess,* it deals with romantic love in a modern way; *Maud,* however, is comparatively as simple and direct as the earlier poem is complicated and diffuse. Both reveal Tennyson as less complacent than usually thought in his acceptance of Victorian standards. Dramatic love-lyrics include "I have led her home," "Come into the garden, Maud," "Oh, let the solid ground," and "O that 'twere Possible," out of which the poem grew.

Idylls of the King (1859—1885). Group of twelve metrical romances loosely bound together by their relation to the Arthurian legend, most of the material being based on Malory's *Morte d'Arthur* (see Vol. 1, p. 92 f.). The key to the moral of the whole poem, which is written in the grand manner and on a grand scale, is "Sense at war with Soul"— the wearing down of virtue by corrosive sin. The *Idylls* are popular; they are written with fine melodic skill and effectiveness of phrase; they have rich pageantry, stirring narrative, imaginative treatment, and lofty thought and imagery. But, it is charged, the knights and ladies lack the robust paganism of Malory; they have Mid-Victorian suavity and moral judgment; they are no longer figures of romance but creatures of the boudoir. Moreover, there is a lack of structural imagination, a want of soul-moving passion, a deficiency of epic and dramatic grasp.[2] The *Idylls,* as ultimately arranged to develop the story, are: *The Coming of Arthur* (1869); *Gareth and Lynette* (1872); *The Marriage of Geraint* (1859); *Geraint and Enid* (1859)[3]; *Balin and Balan* (1885); *Merlin and Vivien* (1859); *Lancelot and Elaine* (1859); *The Holy Grail* (1869); *Pelleas and Ettarre* (1869); *The Last Tournament* (1871); *Guinevere* (1859); *The Passing of Arthur* (1842, 1869).

Enoch Arden (1864). Romantic novelette in verse founded on a Norfolk story told to Tennyson by the sculptor Woolner. Simplicity of narrative, sincerity of feeling, and clearness of outline offset to some extent by ornateness of diction, elaboration of incident, and occasional retardation of movement. (Like *Dora, The Brook,* and *The Miller's Daughter* it is one of the English Idyls, so-called to distinguish them from the *Idylls of the King.*)

---

1 Wolfe, Humbert. *Tennyson* (1930).
2 Boas, F. S., " 'The Idylls of the King,' in 1921," *The Nineteenth Century and After,* xc (1921), pp. 819-830.
3 The only tale in *The Mabinogion* (Vol. 1, p. 41) that Tennyson treated fully was that of Geraint. Consult Wright, H. G., "Tennyson and Wales," *Essays and Studies by Members of The English Association,* xiv (1929), pp. 81-103 (pp. 71-103).

Northern Farmer: Old Style (1864). Suggested by a story told to Tennyson by his grand-uncle, it depicts the farmer with kindly humor and rough vigor; it reflects the ignorance of the agricultural class in the early nineteenth century.

Lucretius (1868). Dramatic monologue, possibly the greatest of Tennyson's poems on classical subjects.

Northern Farmer: New Style (1869). A character-piece in contrast to the earlier one (1864); was suggested by the remark of a rich neighbor. Witty monologue.

The Higher Pantheism (1869). Concrete in form and deep in insight. It provoked Swinburne's parody, *The Higher Pantheism in a Nutshell* (1880).[1]

To Virgil (1889). Called by F. W. H. Meyers his most perfect poem, one touching the high-water mark of English song.

Crossing the Bar (1889). Swan song which has been declared "The Passing of Arthur" in miniature. Platonism expressed in limpid music, utter simplicity, imaginative vividness, moral elevation.

Akbar's Dream (1892). A magnificent prophecy of the ultimate religion of the spirit.

The Church-Warden and the Curate (1892). Dialect poem suggested by a story told by the Reverend H. D. Rawnsley.

Robert Browning, 1812—1889, poet.[2]

---

1 Postma, J., *Tennyson as seen by his Parodists* (Amsterdam, 1926).

2 Santayana, George, *Interpretation of Poetry* (1900), "The Poetry of Barbarism," pp. 188-216 (pp. 166-216); Brooke, Stopford, *The Poetry of Robert Browning* (1903); Chesterton, G. K. *Robert Browning* (1903); Dowden, Edward, *Robert Browning* (1904); Herford, C. H., *Robert Browning* (1905); Symons, Arthur, *An Introduction to the Study of Browning* (1906); Griffin, H. W., and Minchin, H. C., *The Life of Robert Browning* (1910); Whiting, Lilian, *The Brownings: Their Life and Art* (1911); Lounsbury, T. R. *The Early Literary Career of Robert Browning* (1911); Clarke, H. H., *Browning and His Century* (1912); Fletcher, R. H., *Tennyson and Browning* (1913); Phelps, W. L., *Browning: How to Know Him* (1915); Pottle, F. R., *Shelley and Browning* (1923), with a foreword by Phelps, W. L.; Russell, F. T., *One More Word on Browning* (1927); Gleason, K. F., *The Dramatic Art of Robert Browning* (1927); Orr, Mrs. Sutherland, *A Handbook to the Works of Robert Browning* (Revised edition, 1927); Hatcher, H. H., "The Versification of Robert Browning," *Ohio State University Studies* (Graduate School Series), Contributions in Languages and Literatures, No. 5 (1928); Somervell, D. C., "The Reputation of Robert Browning," in *Essays and Studies* by Members of The English Association, collected by Warren, Sir Herbert, XV (1929), pp. 122-138; Macdonald, J. F., "Inhibitions of Browning's Poetry," in *Studies in English by Members of University College, Toronto,* collected by Wallace, M. W. (1931), pp. 203-223; Axson, Stockton, "Browning: His Times, His Art, His Philosophy," *The Rice Institute Pamphlet,* XVIII (1931), pp. 145-199; Duckworth, F. R. G., *Browning: Background and Conflict* (1931); Brockington, A. A., *Browning and the Twentieth Century* (1932); Phelps, W. L., *Robert Browning* (1932); Sherwood, Margaret, *Undercurrents of Influence in English Romantic Poetry* (1934), Chaps. VII and VIII, pp. 265-322, 323-350; Armstrong, A. J., "Browning's Testament of Hope," *The Baylor Bulletin,* XXXVIII (1935). For the letters, consult *The Letters of Robert Browning. 1845-1846* (Two volumes, 1899); *Robert Browning and Alfred Domett,* edited by Kenyon, F. G. (1906); *Letters of Robert Browning to Miss Isa Blagden,* edited by Armstrong, A. J. (1923); and *Letters of Robert Browning, Collected by Thomas J. Wise,* edited by Hood, T. L. (1933). See, also, footnote 1, page 281.

CHIEF VOLUMES

Early Poems

(1) *Pauline* (1833). (2) *Paracelsus* (1835), autobiographical like its predecessor. (3) *Sordello, A Poem in Six Books* (1840), iambic pentameter lines, riming in couplets.

Bells and Pomegranates

The series of eight pamphlets which he called *Bells and Pomegranates* included: (1) *Pippa Passes* (1842); (2) *King Victor and King Charles* (1842); (3) *Dramatic Lyrics* (1842); (4) *The Return of the Druses* (1843); (5) *A Blot in the 'Scutcheon* (1843); (6) *Colombe's Birthday* (1844); (7) *Dramatic Lyrics and Romances* (1845); and (8) *Luria and A Soul's Tragedy* (1846).

The Middle Years

(1) *Christmas-Eve and Easter-Day* (1850), companion poems. (2) *Men and Women* (Two volumes, 1855). (3) *Dramatis Personae* (1864). (4) *The Ring and the Book* (1868).

Later Years

(1) *Balaustion's Adventure, Including a Transcript from Euripides* (1871). (2) *Prince Hohenstiel-Schwangau, Savior of Society* (1871). (3) *Fifine at the Fair* (1872). (4) *Red Cotton Night-Cap Country or Turf and Towers* (1873). (5) *Aristophanes' Apology* (1875). (6) *The Inn Album* (1875). (7) *Pacchiarotto and How He Worked in Distemper: with Other Poems* (1876). (8) *The Agamemnon of Aeschylus* (1877). (9) *La Saisiaz* (1878) and *The Two Poets of Croisic* (1878).

Last Years

(1) *Dramatic Idylls* (First Series, 1879). (2) *Dramatic Idylls* (Second Series, 1880). (3) *Jocoseria* (1883). (4) *Ferishtah's Fancies* (1884). (5) *Parleyings With Certain People of Importance in Their Day* (1887).[1] (6) *Asolando* (1889).

Plays

(1) *Strafford* (1837). (2) *King Victor and King Charles* (1842). (3) *The Return of the Druses* (1843). (4) *A Blot in the 'Scutcheon* (1843). (5) *Colombe's Birthday* (1844). (6) *Luria, A Tragedy* (1846) and *A Soul's Tragedy* (1846).

---

1 De Vane, W. C., Jr., *Browning's Parleyings* (1927).

CHIEF WORKS

Early Poems

Pauline (1833). His first published poem is confessional in nature, revealing much of his adolescent mind. Possibly inspired by Eliza Flower.[1] Important for its light on Browning's struggle with his religious skepticism.

Paracelsus (1835). A lofty soul seeks the unattainable, falls bruised and broken, but is destined for ultimate victory: Paracelsus comprehends the significance of Love.[2] Based upon the actual life of Theophrastus Bombast von Hohenstein (*c.* 1493—1541), who called himself "Paracelsus." Historical facts obtained from Melchior Adam's *Vitae Germanorum Medicorum,* from the *Biographie universelle,* and from the preface to Frederick Bitiskius's edition of the works of Paracelsus.

Strafford (1837). Historical tragedy based upon John Forster's biography of Thomas Wentworth, Lord Strafford. Dialogue halting and intricate, speeches long and abundant, humor entirely lacking. Yet shows unusual promise of Browning's dramatic power. Its political liberalism[3] should be compared with that of *King Victor and King Charles, The Return of the Druses, Colombe's Birthday, A Soul's Tragedy,* and *A Lost Leader.*

Sordello, a Poem in Six Books (1840). Tale of an obscure Mantuan troubadour is a hodge-podge of love and romance, poetry and fiction, psychology, humanitarianism, and philosophy: the details and allusions in "the stress on the incidents in the development of a soul" make interpretation difficult. But many lines and passages will repay study. Indebted to the *Biographie universelle,* to Dante, to Platina's *Historia Urbis Mantuae,* Verci's *Storia degli Ecelini,* Muratori's *Rerum Italicarum Scriptores,* and, possibly, Bartoli's *De' Simboli Trasportati al Morale.*

Pippa Passes (1841). Theme is the power of unconscious influence: the effects are recorded of the songs of Pippa upon Ottima and Sebald, murderers; upon Jules and Phene, an idealistic French sculptor and an ignorant girl; upon Luigi, a revolutionary patriot; and upon a worldly Bishop. The figure of Pippa loosely connects the somewhat fragmentary nature of the four dramatic scenes. Dramatic in spirit, idyllic in song; possibly, however, all the characters should not have been permitted to talk like philosophers; and possibly Pippa's songs are too coincidental. Observe the energetic prose, reminiscent of the Elizabethans.

---

1 Conway, M. D., *Centenary of the South Place Society* (1894).
2 Raymond, W. O., "Browning's Conception of Love as Represented in *Paracelsus,*" *Papers of the Michigan Academy of Science Arts and Letters,* IV (1924), pp. 443-463—edited by Welch, P. S., and McCartney, E. S. (1925).
3 Somervell, D. C., "An Early Victorian Tragedy," *The London Mercury,* XVI (1927), pp. 170-178.

King Victor and King Charles (1842). Blank-verse play thin in incident, obscure in motive, and deficient in clearness. Main source of play, modelled on the lines of Alfieri, is the life of Victor Amédée II as presented in the *Biographie universelle* (1822).

The Return of the Druses (1843). Tragedy in blank verse; is clue to Browning's political thinking. Despite complexity of motives and subtlety of characterization, the play has excellent qualities; the movement is rapid, the scenic effects are striking, the plot is well ordered, the classical unities are preserved. Browning succeeds in his declared theme, the exhibition "of the most wild and passionate love." The idea may have stemmed from the *Biographie universelle*.

A Blot in the 'Scutcheon (1843). A tragedy of the passions—of Nemesis overtaking the innocent. As an acting drama it fails by such handicaps as thin plot, lack of humor, and tendency to minute analysis of moods and motives. In the library it succeeds in its alert passion, human interest, and poetic quality.[1] Influenced by Shakespeare's *Romeo and Juliet*.

Colombe's Birthday (1844). Generally recognized as his most pleasant play, one in which the interest is sustained. Political-historical background, with the emphasis on political liberalism. Story probably adapted from the *Memoires* of the Marquis de Lassay.

Luria (1846). Simple, noble plot; its motive has dramatic potentialities. Possibly too introspective for successful performance. Chief character owes not a little to Shakespeare's *Othello*.[2] Historical background possibly obtained from Amminato's *Florentine History* or from Palmeri's *De Captivitate Pisarum Liber*.

A Soul's Tragedy (1846). Drama in two parts: the first, in blank verse, is strongly dramatic; the second, in prose, is a vivid character-study. J. R. Lowell appreciated its humor; while T. R. Lounsbury has declared that of all Browning's dramatic writings *A Soul's Tragedy* is the one that unites consistency of plot with clearness of expression, and with action that has natural development and is in harmony with the truth of life.

Individual Poems and Works

Cavalier Tunes (1842). Three famous songs: "Marching Along," "Give a Rouse," and "My Wife Gertrude" (later called "Boot and Saddle").

---

1 Clarke, G. H., "Browning's *A Blot in the 'Scutcheon*: A Defense," *The Sewanee Review Quarterly*, xxviii (1928), pp. 213-227.

2 Elliot, G. R., "Shakespeare's Significance for Browning," *Anglia*, xxxii; N. F., xx (1909) pp. 127-134 (pp. 90-162).

My Last Duchess (1842). Concentrated dramatic monologue, the source of which is possibly the life of Vespasiano Gonzaga, by Irenio Affó.[1] Compare this study of the morality of the Italian Renaissance with that presented in *The Bishop Orders His Tomb* and *Andrea del Sarto*.

Incident of the French Camp (1842, 1849). Authentic background, heroic action. Compare with *How They brought the Good News* and *Childe Roland to the Dark Tower Came*.

Soliloquy of the Spanish Cloister (1842). Voices a distrust of asceticism. The soliloquizing ritualistic monk repeats perfunctorily the words of the service while his hating mind damns Brother Lawrence's soul. Tetrameter lines, in trochaic meter. (Compare his treatment of corrupt priests in such poems as *The Bishop Orders His Tomb* and *Fra Lippo Lippi*.)

In a Gondola (1842). Lyric written to illustrate Maclise's picture, which Browning had not seen. Melodramatic close probably influenced by Bulwer-Lytton's plays.

Artemis Prologuizes (1842). Flawless piece that deserves wider recognition.

Porphyria's Lover (1836, 1842). His first study in abnormal psychology.

The Pied Piper of Hamelin; A Child's Story (1842). The ancient legend of the Pied Piper was versified by Browning for William Macready the Younger, a ten-year-old. Richard Verstegen's *Restitution of Decayed Intelligence in Antiquities* (1605)[2] was more likely Browning's main source than Wanley's *The Wonders of the Little World* (1678), Johann Wier's *De Praestigiis Daemonum* (1563), Gaspar Schott's *Physica Curiosa* (1622), or Howell's *Epistolae Ho-Elianae: Familiar Letters* (1650). The legend itself has been variously interpreted: it is most commonly referred to the Children's Crusade of 1212.

How They Brought the Good News from Ghent to Aix (1845). One of his popular poems. Galloping meter.

The Italian in England (1845, 1849). Reveals Browning's sympathy with Italian freedom.

The Lost Leader (1845). Probably refers to Wordsworth—the latter's acceptance of the laureateship and his defection.

---

1 Rea, J. D., " 'My Last Duchess,' " *Studies in Philology*, XXIX (1932), pp. 120-122,
2 Dickson, Arthur, "Browning's Source for *The Pied Piper of Hamelin*," *Studies in Philology*, XXIII (1926), pp. 327-336.

Home-Thoughts, from Abroad (1845). Expresses his home-sickness for the beauties of England in the months of April and May. (Compare it not only with his *De Gustibus* and *Home Thoughts, from the Sea* but also with Rupert Brooke's *The Old Vicarage, Grantchester* and Masefield's *August 1914.*)

Home-Thoughts, from the Sea (1845). A noble expression of patriotism.

The Bishop Orders his Tomb at St. Praxed's Church (1845). Dramatic monologue in blank verse is a summary of a corrupt[1] clergyman's attitude toward his church, his fellow churchman, earthly love, art, and the future: an epitome of the leading characteristics of the Renaissance. Of it Ruskin said: "I know of no other piece of modern English, prose or poetry, in which there is so much told, as in these lines, of the Renaissance spirit,—its worldliness, inconsistency, pride, hypocrisy, ignorance of itself, love of art, of luxury, and of good Latin. It is nearly all I have said of the central Renaissance in thirty pages of the *Stones of Venice,* put into as many lines, Browning's also being the antecedent work." (See Ruskin's *Modern Painters,* IV, Chap. 20, Sections 22 and 24.)

The Laboratory (1844, 1845). Note the concision of statement. Inspired D. G. Rossetti's first water-color.

The Confessional (1845). Indictment of unworthy clerics who prostitute themselves by such methods for so-called spiritual ends. The poem seems to convey the spirit of the Spanish Inquisition.

The Flight of the Duchess (1845). According to Browning, the poem was inspired by the line, "Following the Queen of the Gypsies, O!" in what was probably a Scotch ballad, *The Gypsy Laddie.* It is liked for its vividness, novelty, and romance. Probably indebted to the *Memoires* of the Marquis de Lassay and to the life of Vespasiano Gonzaga by Irenio Affó.

Meeting at Night—Parting at Morning (1845). Two separate poems that are supplementary pictures: in each the speaker is the same; in *Parting at Morning* he turns away from the raptures of love toward the business of life and men.

The Glove (1845). Inspired by Leigh Hunt's *The Glove and the Lions,* Browning's version of the old story adds an original soul-analysis of the lady's character. Partly autobiographical.[2] Influenced by the *Memoires* of the Marquis de Lassay.

---

1 "Robert Browning and the Catholic Church," *The Irish Monthly,* XLI (1913) pp. 117-130. The article is initialed "J. B." See, also Stuntz, H. C., "Browning's Indictment of Roman Catholicism," *The Methodist Review,* XCVIII; Fifth Series, XXXII (1916), pp. 682-696.
2 De Vane, W. C., Jr., *Browning's Parleyings* (1927), pp. 83-86, pp. 86-91.

Love Among the Ruins (1855). The scene may not be Rome, but rather a composite picture of Babylon and Jerusalem, while the phraseology may have been suggested in part by I Chronicles, XVIII.[1] Whole poem might even be a reflection on King David, Israelite.

Evelyn Hope (1855). Weds deep thought and music in its theme, a man's meditation upon his love for a beautiful young girl, who has died before he has declared himself.

Up at a Villa—Down in the City (1855). An "Italian Person of Quality," confined to the boredom of his villa, yearns for the delights of town life. Keen, humorous observation.

Fra Lippo Lippi (1855). Dramatic monologue expressing Browning's belief in art and in the joy of living. Indebted for information to *Vite de' piu eccelenti architetti, pittori, e scultori italiani* (1550) and to Baldinucci's *Delle Notizie de' Professori del Disegno da Cimabue . . .* (1767—1774). Prevailingly in blank verse, except for a half dozen *stornelli*, or flower-songs.

A Toccata of Galuppi's (1855). The main thematic idea is the transiency of life. May be the earliest of his poems devoted entirely to music.[2]

Childe Roland to the Dark Tower Came (1855).[3] An imaginative expression of the philosophy of attainment *via* courageous attempt. Sources are in Edgar's title-line in *King Lear* and in a picture of a blind old horse in a tapestry in Browning's home. The poem is variously interpreted.[4]

Respectability (1855). The antagonism between François Guizot and Charles Montalembert may have been the poet's starting-point; the unconventional lovers may have been George Sand and Jules Sandeau. But the thematic idea is universal rather than local in application.

The Statue and the Bust (1855). The moral seems to be that love must be seized whenever the opportunity offers; the poem may also be a parable.[5]

---

1 Law, R. A., "The Background of Browning's *Love Among the Ruins*," *Modern Language Notes*, XXXVII (1922), p. 312 *f.*

2 De Vane, W. C., Jr., *Browning's Parleyings* (1927), Chap. VII, "The Parleying With Charles Avison," pp. 252-283.

3 Brockington, A. A., *Browning and the Twentieth Century* (1932), pp. 276-278; Golder, Harold, "Browning's *Childe Roland*," *Publications of the Modern Language Association of America*, XXXIX; New Series, XXXII (1924), pp. 963-978; De Vane, W. C., Jr., "The Landscape of Browning's *Childe Roland*," *Publications of the Modern Language Association of America*, XL; New Series, XXXIII (1925), pp. 426-432.

4 Nettleship, J. T., *Robert Browning: Essays and Thoughts* (1890). "Childe Roland," pp. 89-113.

5 Cummings, Prentiss, "Browning's 'The Statue and the Bust'; A Parable," *Poet-Love*, X (1898), pp. 397-416.

The Last Ride Together (1855). Deals, as does *Love among the Ruins* and *Two in the Campagna,* with an unusual aspect of love; and, as in *Evelyn Hope,* with an apparent failure in love. The speaker of the poem, who has declared his love and has been rejected, should be compared with the speaker in Tennyson's *Locksley Hall.*

Memorabilia (1855). Shows again, as in the *Introductory Essay,* his admiration for Shelley.[1] Inspired by an occurrence in the shop of the bookseller Hodgson.

Andrea del Sarto (1855). Possibly his greatest monologue. Facts regarding "The Faultless Painter" obtained from Vasari's *Lives.* Blank verse.

In a Balcony (1855). Closet playlet, while containing long speeches is nevertheless an excellent piece of character-study.

Saul (Sections I—IX, 1845; X—XIX, 1855). Popular religious poem, based upon I Samuel XVI, 14—23, is a dramatic embodiment of an ethical and metaphysical theme, in which the hero is not Saul but David.[2] Partly indebted to the writings of Christopher Smart, and possibly to some tunes in Longus's *Daphnis and Chloe.*

De Gustibus–(1855). Another important poem, the only one in the volume *Men and Women* that gives a glimpse of English landscape.

Cleon (1855). Companion poem or supplement to Arnold's *Empedocles on Etna*[3] and to Browning's own *An Epistle concerning the Strange Medical Experience of Karshish, the Arab Physician* (1855).

Two in the Campagna (1855). Dramatic embodiment of the tragedy of unfulfilled love. Should be read with *Evelyn Hope, Love Among the Ruins, By the Fireside,* and Matthew Arnold's *Isolation.*

A Grammarian's Funeral (1855). Primarily a symbolic representation of the thirst for knowledge, embodying many of Browning's ideas on the truths and problems of human life. Note the quick changes from serious to humorous mood.

One Way of Love (1855). Simple lyric.

One Word More to E. B. B. (1855). Important in any study of the Brownings. See also *By the Fire-Side* (1855).

---

1 Browning's *Introductory Essay to the Letters of Shelley* (1852) pleads for a better interpretation of that poet. Consult *Peacock's Four Ages of Poetry, Shelley's Defence of Poetry, Browning's Essay on Shelley,* edited by Brett-Smith, H. F. B. (1921), pp. 63-83; Sim, F. M., *Robert Browning* (1923), p. 32; and Pottle, F. R., *Shelley and Browning* (1923), with a foreword by Phelps, W. L.

2 For the conclusion to the poem, conult Crawford, A. W., "Browning's 'Saul,' " *Queen's Quarterly,* xxxiv (1926-1927), pp. 448-454.

3 Crawford, A. W., "Browning's 'Cleon,' " *The Journal of English and Germanic Philology,* xxvi (1927), pp. 485-490.

Abt Vogler (1864). In twelve stanzas of eight alexandrine lines each, Browning probably achieves the finest poem on music in the language. The idealistic philosophy of the poem is indebted to Plato, Spinoza, Hegel, and More. Its reverent optimism, spiritual earnestness, and deep seriousness should be compared with other music poems of Browning: *A Toccata of Galuppi's, Master of Hugues of Sax-Gotha,* and *Parleying with Charles Avison,* as well as with passages in *Pauline* and *Paracelsus* and *Fifine at the Fair.*

Rabbi Ben Ezra (1864). Valuable affirmation of Browning's faith is conjecturally an answer to Fitzgerald's *The Rubáiyát of Omar Khayyám;* see especially Browning's stanzas 26—36.[1] The poem is said to give the essence of Jewish faith and hope, "a spiritual strength and wholesomeness, a comforting and rational philosophy, a deeply-rooted verity and sweetness, that touch and vivify the soul."[2]

Caliban upon Setebos; or, Natural Theology in the Island (1864). Probably inspired by Darwin's *Origin of the Species,* Browning's grotesque blank-verse poem is a satire on anthropomorphic theology.

Confessions (1864). Short lyric declared by Augustine Birrell to have a familiar realism that is audacious, a rugged abruptness, and an alert emotion.

Prospice (1864). Written in the autumn following Mrs. Browning's death, the poem seems to be a direct personal affirmation of belief in the immortality of the soul. Compare it with *"Epilogue to Asolando,"* and with Tennyson's *Ulysses* and *Crossing the Bar.*

The Ring and the Book (I, II, 1868; III, IV, 1869). Longest and most characteristic poem tells a tale from the point of view of ten different characters, the primary source of the story being a Roman murder-case related in the Old Yellow Book.[3]

Balaustion's Adventure (1871). Whether it represents or misrepresents the characters of Admetus and Heracles, as given in *Alcestis* by

1 Wayland, H. L., "Remarks on Some Passages in Rabbi Ben Ezra," *Poet-Lore,* I (1889), pp. 57-63; More, P. E., *Shelburne Essays,* Third Series (1905), "Why is Browning Popular?" pp. 143-165; Sargent, F. LeR., *Omar and the Rabbi* (1919).

2 Cohen, M. M., "Browning's Hebraic Sympathies," *Poet-Lore,* III (1891), pp. 250-254; Kelman, John, *Prophets of Yesterday and Their Message for To-Day* (1924), "Robert Browning the Hebrew," pp. 147-162 (pp. 132-162).

3 *The Old Yellow Book: Source of Robert Browning's The Ring & the Book,* edited by Hodell, C. W. (1911); Cook, A. K., *A Commentary Upon Browning's "The Ring and the Book"* (1920); Cassidy, James (Story, E. M.), *A Study of Browning's The Ring and the Book* (1924); Haddow, Alexander, *Browning's Ring and the Book as a Connected Narrative* (1924); Gest, J. M., *The Old Yellow Book* (1925); Raymond, W. O., (1) "New Light on the Genesis of *The Ring and the Book,*" *Modern Language Notes,* XLIII (1928), pp. 357-368, and (2) "Browning's First Mention of the Documentary Sources of *The Ring and the Book,*" *Modern Language Notes,* XLIII (1928), pp. 445-450.

Euripides, it is in many respects an excellent translation of the *Alcestis*. Plutarch's *Life of Nicias* influenced the framework of the poem.[1]

Aristophanes' Apology (1875). Sequel to *Balaustion's Adventure* is not only an imaginative poem but also a significant piece of dramatic discussion on the merits of Euripides and Aristophanes.[2] Loaded with classical references. Indebted to the *Scholia*, or commentary, upon the plays of Euripides and Aristophanes, to Plato's *Symposium*, and to Plutarch's *Life of Lysander*. Memorable: the song *Thamuris Marching*.

La Saisiaz (1878). Central theme is the evidence of personal survival of bodily death, the hope of immortality. Occasioned by the death of Miss Anne Egerton Smith. In the *Locksley Hall* measure.

Ixion (1883). Lyric that shows the poet's revolt against the idea of vindictive eternal punishment.

Why I am a Liberal (1885). Sonnet asserts that political movements must be aggressive and radical. Emphasis upon individualism.

Epilogue to Asolando (1889). These four stanzas of five lines each, which were published in London on the very day of his death in Venice, represent his hope and courage, his character and faith.[3] Compare with Tennyson's *Crossing the Bar*.

Matthew Arnold, 1822—1888, poet, critic; known best as the great apostle of culture.[4]

PROSE

Educational Criticism

(1) *The Popular Education of France* (1861).[5] (2) *A French Eton, or Middle-Class Education and the State* (1863—1864). (3) *Schools and Universities on the Continent* (1868). (4) *Special Report on Elementary Education Abroad* (1886). (5) *Reports on Elementary Schools, 1852—1882* (1889).

---

1 Daniel, M. S., "The Value of Browning's Interpretation of Euripides," *The Methodist Review*, LXXX; Fifth Series, XIV (1898), pp. 55-67; Tisdel, F. M., "*Balaustion's Adventure* as an Interpretation of the *Alcestis* of Euripides," *Publications of the Modern Language Association of America*, XXXII; New Series, XXV (1917), pp. 519-546.

2 Tisdel, F. M., "Browning's *Aristophanes' Apology*," *The University of Missouri*, II, No. 4 (1927), pp. 1-46.

3 Brinton, D. G., "The Epilogues of Browning: Their Artistic Significance," *Poet-Lore*, IV (1892), pp. 57-64.

4 Paul, H. W., *Matthew Arnold* (1902); Sadler, M. E., "Matthew Arnold," *The Nineteenth Century and After*, XCIII (1923), pp. 199-207, 366-377; Woods, Margaret, "Matthew Arnold," *Essays and Studies*, By Members of The English Association, XV (1929), pp. 7-19; Harvey, C. H., *Matthew Arnold: A Critic of the Victorian Period* (1931); Garrod, H. W., *Poetry and the Criticism of Life* (1931); pp. 23-66, 67-84; Chambers, Sir Edmund, "Matthew Arnold," *Proceedings of the British Academy*, XVIII (1932), pp. 23-45; Tinker, C. B., and H. F. Lowry, *The Poetry of Matthew Arnold* (1950).

5 Quotation: " 'Classes of twenty-five or thirty, and an efficient teacher to each class'; that school system is best which inscribes these words on its banner."

Literary Criticism[1]

On Translating Homer (1861); *On Translating Homer: Last Words* (1862). Sweeping statements about the unity of the Homeric poems; in general an important piece of criticism. His lectures on Homer, according to Garrod, are the masterpiece printed in his lifetime.

Essays in Criticism, First Series (1865). The first series, dealing primarily with the nature of criticism, made him famous. The two inferior essays are on Shelley, where Arnold is unappreciative, and on Byron, where he is over-enthusiastic. His three standards of judgment, moral, aesthetic, and sociological, lead him into inconsistencies, while the religious interest is already thrusting itself forward. In the first two essays he develops his principles; the purpose of criticism, in *The Function of Criticism at the Present Time,* and the differences between English and French critical ideals, in *The Literary Influence of Academies.* Possibly his best essays are on Heinrich Heine and on Maurice de Guérin.

On the Study of Celtic Literature (1867). Not without some interesting criticism, but generally considered to lack the heart and soundness of his lectures on Homer. Was influenced by Renan's essay on *La poésie des race celtiques.*[2]

Mixed Essays (1877). Includes "A French Critic on Milton," where Milton is praised both for his style and for his character as a man.

Essays in Criticism, Second Series (1888). The first of the essays is *The Study of Poetry,* which states most completely Arnold's critical method of appraising literature by means of test passages of proved excellence—a touchstone theory that sacrifices the whole for the sake of the part. His three ways of interpreting poetry may possibly anticipate Croce. His essay on Milton has the discursiveness of a lecture; his essay on Wordsworth[3] did much to establish Wordsworth's fame.

---

1 Williams, S. T., "Matthew Arnold as a Critic of Literature," *University of California Chronicle,* xxvi (1924), pp. 183-208.

2 Renan also influenced Arnold in other essays; *e.g.,* the former's *L'Académie française* and *Essais de morale et de critique* influenced, respectively, the latter's *Literary Influence of Academies* and preface to *Essays in Criticism, First Series.* See Angell, J. W., "Matthew Arnold's Indebtedness to Renan's *Essais De Morale Et De Critique,*" *Revue de Littérature Comparée,* xiv (1934), pp. 714-733. Arnold was in several ways influenced by other French writers, including Sainte-Beuve and Senancour: consult Sells, I. E., *Matthew Arnold and France* (1935). See, also, White, H. C., "Matthew Arnold and Goethe," *Publications of the Modern Language Association of America,* xxxvi; New Series, xxix (1921), pp. 436-453.

3 Arnold led many to read Wordsworth, but Arnold's procedure in textual criticism merits censure. Read Cooper, Lane, "Matthew Arnold's Essay on Wordsworth," *The Bookman,* lxix (1929), pp. 479-484,

Social and Religious Criticism

Culture and Anarchy (1869). Central theme is a criticism of Hebraism,[1] and the need in English intellectual life for Hellenism. Of permanent interest is the chapter on the Greek and Hebrew attitude of mind. Divides society into the three classes of Barbarians, Philistines, and Populace. Is "An Essay in Political and Social Criticism" (see title-page) that attacks the false standards of Englishmen, and points a better way.

St. Paul and Protestantism (1870). Plea for true Hebraism is his first piece of pure theology, and possibly the best written. It may, as some assert, fail to grasp the spirit of the real St. Paul, but Arnold's interpretation, which deals chiefly with dissent in regard to the Church of England, endeavors to break down the renderings of St. Paul's theology known as Calvinism and Arminianism and to correct the mistakes of Non-Conformity.

Friendship's Garland (1871). Like *Culture and Anarchy* that preceded it, and *Literature and Dogma* that followed it, fought against weaknesses in society, in politics, and in religion. A few see in it Voltairean qualities of wit and veiled irony; but, if a comparison must be made, he seems closer to Max Beerbohm.

Literature and Dogma (1873). Written "to restore the use and enjoyment of the Bible to plain people who might be in danger of losing it." Even those who deny that it combines Biblical scholarship and polemic directness, accusing Arnold of pseudo-scholarship, choplogic, and refined vituperation, admit that, although the application of principles is on the whole wrong-headed, the principles themselves are dependable as points of approach in the study of literature.[2]

God and the Bible (1875). Sequel to *Literature and Dogma* should be as well-known, for it is not only more cogent in argument but also more scholarly in content. Scholars value Arnold's sustained thesis concerning St. John's Gospel. Both works, and *St. Paul and Protestantism,* were a clarifying influence upon nineteenth-century religious belief.

Last Essays on Church and Religion (1877), *Isaiah of Jerusalem* (1883), and *A Friend of God* (1887).

POETRY

Chief Editions

(1) *The Strayed Reveller and Other Poems* (1849). (2) *Empedocles on Etna and Other Poems* (1852). (3) *Poems* (1853). (4) *Poems, Second Series* (1855). (5) *Merope, A Tragedy* (1858). (6) *New Poems* (1867). (7) *Poems* (First Collected Edition, 1869).

1 Yet Arnold may be far more of a Hebraist than a Hellenist. Quick, J. B., "Hebraism and Hellenism," *The New Adelphi*, New Series, II (1929), pp. 50-56.
2 Brother Leo, "Matthew Arnold," *The Catholic World*, CXVI (1922-1923), pp. 320-337.

Individual Poems

The Strayed Reveller (1849). A faulty experiment in a new blank verse. His Hellenism illustrated by a Greek theme treated in a Greek manner. But fails, as do his other two dramas (*Empedocles* and *Merope*) in plot, in character-portrayal, and in effective action. (Is in part reminiscent of Milton's *Comus*: Vol. 1, p. 279.)

Quiet Work (1849). Sonnet showing Nature toiling on "unsevered from tranquillity" and perfecting "glorious tasks in silence" long after man's "fitful uproar" and discordant life have passed away.

The Forsaken Merman (1849). A romantic Danish theme of other-world love, monologic in structure, lyrical in tone, haunting in its pictures, subtle and plaintive in its half-human, half-unearthly moods. The story is obscure, but subtly-woven; the meters are skilfully manipulated.[1]

Resignation (1849). Urges a quiet mind where passionate hopes no longer vibrate. Characteristic in its grave melancholy.

Tristram and Iseult (1852). Lofty subject treated with human feeling and excelling in Victorian landscape pictures. Arnold's dramatic sense breaks down at the very climax.

Self-Dependence (1852). Frequently criticized for its self-centered point of view, reminds us by its very title—as do the titles of *Morality, Indifference, Resignation, Despondency*, and *The Buried Life*—of his typically Victorian melancholy and intellectual approach.

The Scholar-Gypsy (1853). Drawn from a romantic tale in Joseph Glanvil's *The Vanity of Dogmatising* (1661), reflects on the contrast between the faith of the scholar-gypsy and "this strange disease of modern life, with its sick hurry and divided aims." S. P. Sherman believes that the stanzas betray Arnold's poetical sympathy with the impulse to drift and wander irresponsibly. Note that the last two stanzas, while beautiful, are not altogether relevant. Saintsbury considers this poem nearly faultless.

Requiescat (1853). Its pathos and beauty culminate in an immortal line.

Sohrab and Rustum (1853). Epyllion or epyllic poem retelling an incident in Firdausi's *Shah Namah* or *Book of Kings;* a similar story is found in the great Ulster legend called *Táin Bó Cúalnge* or *The Cattle Raid of Cooley*. Possibly it is justifiably called overwrought in tone, consciously elaborate in decoration, and lacking in true imaginative quality. But many accept the elaborate similes and emphasize the

---

1 Leach, H. G., "The Forsaken Merman," in *Essays in Memory of Barrett Wendell* by His Assistants (Harvard University Press, 1926), pp. 273-282.

Homeric utterance; they do not see the end as an artificial appendage, but as a moving close to a story of deep human interest told with sustained nobility of manner.

"Switzerland" Love-Poems (1853).[1] Arnold wrote a group of love-poems concerned with Marguerite, probably a French girl living at Thun. She influenced not only the "Switzerland" lyrics, but also another group of love-poems published in 1855 under the title of *Faded Leaves*. In the group there is a cheap rhetoric and common-place thought; but unforgettable is "Isolation" and "To Marguerite," where the mood is the same as in Browning's *Two in the Campagna*.

Balder Dead (1855). Avowed by Arnold to possess a natural propriety of rhythm and diction. Has worth and dignity, is somewhat prolix, and its similes, while less intrusive than in *Sohrab and Rustum,* are long-tailed. While it is less mannered than *Sohrab and Rustum,* and leaves a greater totality of impression, yet it is recognized as "faultily faultless, icily regular, splendidly null."

Merope (1858). Closet-drama lacking both native theatrical talent and dramatic genius, and destitute of poetic beauty. Waxen *tour-de-force* is even more uninspired than *Empedocles on Etna*. The action is superior to the characterization.

Empedocles on Etna (1862). Philosophical drama of despair, impossible even as a closet-drama, but memorable for the flawless lyricism of the songs put into the mouth of Callicles.

Dover Beach (1867). Thought and mood, majestic movement and grave cadence blend into meaningless spiritual isolation the feeling that the old religious order is breaking down, that

> ". . . . . we are here as on a darkling plain
> Swept with confused alarms of struggle and flight,
> Where ignorant armies clash by night."

Thyrsis (1867). Monody immortalizes the ideal side of his friend, A. H. Clough,[2] in the tender melancholy of mood and serene beauty of thought, in the cadenced rhythm and apt expression characteristic of *The Scholar-Gypsy*. Both poems are frequently cited as sounding a note of the prevailing *mal de siècle*—Victorian disillusion and despair.

The Last Word (1867). Urges the soul to charge on even in the most desperate circumstances.

---

1 Kingsmill, Hugh (pseudonym of Lunn, H. K.), *Matthew Arnold* (1928), Chap. xv, pp. 69-93; Bonnerot, Louis, "La Jeunesse de Matthew Arnold," *Revue Anglo-Américaine,* VII (1929-1930), pp. 520-537; Walbrook, H. M., "The Novel in Matthew Arnold's Poems," *The Bookman,* LXXVIII (1930), pp. 109-112; Harris, Alan, "Matthew Arnold," *The Nineteenth Century and After,* CXIII (1933), pp. 498-509.

2 *The Letters of Matthew Arnold to Arthur Hugh Clough,* edited by Lowry, H. F. (1932).

Rugby Chapel (1867). Written in memory of his father, Dr. Thomas Arnold, the famous headmaster of Rugby School. Poem, inspired by a review of *Tom Brown's Schooldays* that accused Arnold's father of religious fanaticism, is dignified in diction, solemn in tone, and, possibly, over-didactic. (The review is by Fitzjames Stephen in the *Edinburgh Review*, CVII, 1858, pp. 172—193.)

Calais Sands (1867). One of his best-known poems. Has autobiographical value in its mention of his love for Lucy Wightman, whom he married.

MINOR POETS

Elizabeth Barrett Browning, 1806—1861, poet, wife of Robert Browning.[1]

Essay on Mind; with Other Poems (1826). Title-poem written in undistinguished couplets.

Prometheus Bound (1833). A translation of Aeschylus.

The Seraphim and Other Poems (1838). Influenced by Byron. *The Seraphim* is a dramatic lyric.

Poems (1844). Includes *The Cry of the Children*†, memorable for focusing attention upon child labor; possibly somewhat loose of rime, certainly stirring in rhythm. Social sympathy is also expressed in *The Cry of the Human.*

Sonnets from the Portuguese† (1850). Series of forty-four sonnets giving perfect expression to a pure and passionate love and communicating its emotion in a style as simple as the feeling is sincere. The sonnets, occasionally prolix,[2] record the same romance as do the love-letters.[3]

Casa Guidi Windows (1851). Poem in *terza rima* on Italian political events and aspirations, while containing lines of beauty, fails because of its limited appeal. Second part is even more didactic than the first part is descriptive.

---

1 Burdett, Osbert, *The Brownings* (1928); Willis, I. C., *Elizabeth Barrett Browning* (1928); Clarke, I. C., *Elizabeth Barrett Browning* (1929); Boas, L. S., *Elizabeth Barrett Browning* (1930); Gaylord, Harriet (introduction by Towne, C. H.), *Pompilia and Her Poet* (1931).

2 Robert Browning's influence upon his wife is evident in her *Sonnets from the Portugese*. For an attempt to indicate her influence upon his work, see Cunliffe, J. W., "Elizabeth Barrett's Influence on Browning's Poetry," *Publications of the Modern Language Association of America*, XXIII; New Series, XVI (1908), pp. 169-183.

3 *The Letters of Elizabeth Barrett Browning*, edited by Kenyon, F. G. (Two volumes, 1897); *Elizabeth Barrett Browning: Letters to Her Sister, 1846-1859*, edited by Huxley, Leonard (1929). One should see also *The Letters of Robert Browning and Elizabeth Barrett Browning, 1845-6* (two volumes, 1899).

† * Explanation of symbols immediately precedes Chapter XV.

Aurora Leigh (1856). Romance[1] in nine books of fluid blank verse, the main theme of which is growth through love, was written in order to focus attention upon the state of unfortunate women in large cities and to voice the yearning of Mid-Victorian womanhood for independence and love. Not less daring than *Jane Eyre* in its controversial theme. Undeniably has faults, but also energetic speed, excellent descriptions of Italian scenery, realistic drama, self-confident forthrightness, and high-minded convictions. Influenced by Madame de Staël, George Sand, and Robert Browning.

Poems before Congress (1860). Slim volume of political pieces concerned, like *Casa Guidi Windows,* with Italian affairs. A few of the eight poems are anecdotal; only one is not on an Italian subject: *A Curse for a Nation,* mistakenly thought to be directed against England, but really directed against America because of slavery. Eloquent preface.

Dante Gabriel Rossetti, 1828—1882, Pre-Raphaelite painter and poet.[2]

Chief Volumes

(1) *The Early Italian Poets* (1861), translations from Cuillo d'Almaca to Dante Alighieri. (2) *Poems* (1870). (3) *Dante and His Circle* (1874), translations. (4) *Ballads and Sonnets* (1881).

Chief Poems

The Blessed Damozel (1847; 1850). First version appeared in *The Germ* (1850), a periodical that was the spokesman for the Pre-Raphaelite Brotherhood. Poem, the fundamental idea of which Rossetti ascribed to the influence of Poe's *The Raven,*[3] has a romantic and mystical tone, deepened by longing and pity, passion and sorrow, and nostalgic with echoing music and brooding introspection. None of his later works ever surpassed the technical skill and imaginative power here displayed.

The House of Life (1870 and 1881). Sequence of masterly love-sonnets has for its theme the union of body and soul, a subject that

---

1 Woolf, Virginia, "Aurora Leigh," *The Yale Review,* xx (1931), pp. 677-690.

2 Benson, A. C., *Rossetti* (1904); Trombly, A. E., "Rossetti the Poet," *University of Texas Bulletin,* No. 2060 (1920); Davies, Charles, *Dante Gabriel Rossetti* (1925); Mégroz, R. L., *Dante Gabriel Rossetti* (1928); Waugh, Evelyn, *Rossetti* (1928); Winwar, Frances, *Poor Splendid Wings* (1933).

Various commentators have studied the influences exerted upon Rossetti's poetic development: see, for example, Willoughby, L. A., *Dante Gabriel Rossetti and German Literature* (1912); Shine, Hill, "The Influence of Keats upon Rossetti," *Englische Studien,* LXI (1926-1927), pp. 183-210; Morse, B. J., "Dante Gabriel Rossetti and William Blake," *Englische Studien,* LXVI (1931-1932), pp. 364-372.

3 Is it possible that the source of *The Blessed Damozel* was rather a sonnet by Jacopo da Lentino, translated and entitled "Of his Lady in Heaven" by Rossetti? See Morse, B. J., "Dante Gabriel Rossetti," *Englische Studien,* LXVIII (1933-1934), pp. 236-242 (pp. 227-248).

lends itself to Rossetti's permeating mysticism. Inspired mainly by his love for Elizabeth Siddal, his wife.[1] Not without difficulties and obscurities.[2]

Jenny (1870). Daring poem, intended as a sermon against the evils of prostitution. (Rossetti broke off a twenty-five years' friendship with Robert Browning because he thought that *Fifine at the Fair* was a "running commentary upon *Jenny*."[3])

Sister Helen (1870). Notable for dramatic suspense in its story of a woman who loses her own soul by melting the waxen image of her false lover, Keith of Ewern. Note the characteristic refrain.

The King's Tragedy (1881). Ballad in the form of a monologue by Catherine Douglas ("Kate Barlass"). Swift, concrete. (See Vol. 1, p. 88, under James I.)

Other Poems

Dennis Shand, Stratton Water, Rose Mary, The White Ship, Troy Tower, Eden Bower, The Staff and Scrip, The Bride's Prelude, The Sea-Limits, Cloud Confines, The Card Dealer, The Ballad of Dead Ladies, Autumn Song, My Sister's Sleep.

Christina Georgina Rossetti, 1830—1894, devotional poet; sister of Dante Gabriel Rossetti.[4]

Volumes of Poetry

(1) *Verses* (1847). (2) *Goblin Market and Other Poems* (1862). (3) *The Prince's Progress and Other Poems* (1866). (4) *Sing-Song: A Nursery Rhyme Book* (1872), her most gay and wistful collection, ultimately including more than sixscore couplets, riddles, quatrains, and lyrics: "Mix a Pancake," "If I Were a Queen," "Is the Moon Tired?" "What Are Heavy? Sea-Sand and Sorrow." (5) *A Pageant and Other Poems* (1881). (6) *Verses* (1893). (7) *New Poems* (1896).

---

1 No better analysis of Rossetti's wife has been made than that by Violet Hunt. Bear in mind, however, the latter's own statement that her "sources for this Life are chiefly oral." See Hunt, Violet, *The Wife of Rossetti*. (1932).

2 Each sonnet is analyzed in *The House of Life*, edited by Baum, P. F. (1928).

3 De Vane, W. C., Jr., "The Harlot and the Thoughtful Young Man," *Studies in Philology*, xxix (1932), pp. 463-484; Larg, David, *Trial by Virgins* (1933), p. 323 f.

4 Bell, Mackenzie, *Christina Rossetti* (1898); Mare, Walter de la, "Christina Rossetti," *Essays by Divers Hands* (Being the Transactions of the Royal Society of Literature of the United Kingdom), vi (1925-1926), pp. 79-116; Megroz, R. L., *Dante Gabriel Rossetti* (1928), Chap. v, pp. 81-95; Birkhead, Edith, *Christina Rossetti & Her Poetry* (1930); Stuart, D. M., *Christina Rossetti* (1930); Sandars, M. F., *The Life of Christina Rossetti* (1930); Stuart, D. M., *Christina Rossetti* (The English Association, Pamphlet No. 78, 1931); Shove, Fredegond, *Christina Rossetti* (1931); Thomas, E. W., *Christina Georgina Rossetti* (1931); Winwar, Frances, *Poor Splendid Wings* (1933).

Individual Poems

"When I Am Dead, My Dearest" (1848; 1862). A lilting song expressing a wistfully-intellectual mood; perfect in form, exquisite in its effortless conclusion.

The Three Enemies (1851; 1862). A dialogue of the soul with the world, the flesh, and the devil; it is suffused by the tender love for Christ.

The Heart Knoweth its own Bitterness (1852; 1896). Born of despair, it seems to be an undisguised indictment of human love.

Sleep at Sea (1853; 1862). Delicately-wrought, austere in its realism, yet a blend of the supernatural with moral force. Saintsbury ranks it among the half-dozen greatest devotional poems in English.

Dream Love (1854; 1862). Declared by Walter de la Mare to have "a rhythm and poise, a serpentining of music, so delicate that on clumsy lips it will vanish as rapidly as the bloom from a plum."

My Heart Is Like A Singing Bird (1857; 1862). Lyric poignantly joyous and profuse with imagery.

An Apple Gathering (1857; 1862). Echoing with regret, it blends realistic treatment of nature with allegorical implications that are mystical and symbolic without being moralizing.

Uphill (1858; 1861). A perfect lyric in question and answer form, stern yet tenderly mournful in its embodiment of the idea that life is but a pilgrimage winding uphill to death.

The Convent Threshold (1858; 1862). Energetic and imaginative glorification of feminine ascetic passion: love, renounced on earth, "tarries veiled in paradise," within whose safe door one "shall lift the veil thereof," and "love with old familiar love." (Cf. *The Blessed Damozel.*)

Advent (1858; 1862). Beautiful devotional poem; done with consummate ease. ("This Advent moon shines cold and clear.")

Goblin Market (1859; 1862). Her most original poem,[1] startling in the variety and the visualization of its comparisons, and luxuriating in the faery-fruitful goodness of the market. Mystical, symbolic.

The Prince's Progress (1861—1865; 1866). Long poignant poem that seems to reverse the parable of the foolish virgins; meter effectively varied, implications symbolic, touch sentimental.

A Pageant (1881). Slight theme in which the characters are the twelve months of the year.

---

1 Evans, B. I., "The Sources of Christina Rossetti's 'Goblin Market,'" *The Modern Language Review*, xxviii (1933), pp. 156-165.

Monna Innominata (1881). Series of fourteen dramatic sonnets purporting to be spoken by a "Nameless Lady" telling the story of a love foregone, but probably expressing Christina's own love for Charles Cayley, whose liberal religious views she could not share.

Prose Works

(1) *Commonplace and Other Short Stories* (1852—1870; 1870). (2) *Speaking Likenesses* (1874). (3) *Annus Domini, a Prayer for Each Day of the Year* (1874), each prayer being founded on a text of Holy Scripture. (4) *Seek and Find* (1879), a double series of beautiful short studies as an accompaniment to the *Benedicite*. (5) *Called to be Saints: the Minor Festivals devotionally studied* (1881), a reading diary. (6) *Letter and Spirit: Notes on the Commandments* (1883). (7) *Time Flies: A Reading Diary* (1885), anecdotal and personal. (8) *The Face of the Deep: A Devotional Commentary on the Apocalypse* (1892), gently meditative. (9) *Maud* (1897), a somewhat wistful novel of a girl-poet who dies young.

William Morris, 1834—1896, poet, craftsman, socialist.[1]

Poetry

The Defence of Guenevere and Other Poems (1858). A little book of romantic poems, several of which dealt with the Arthurian legends. In the volume Morris used decorative color with restraint. *The Defence of Guenevere* is written in *terza rima*. Included are *King Arthur's Tomb, The Eve of Crecy, Summer Dawn, Shameful Death,* and, notably, *The Haystack in the Floods,* a medieval murder told with ghastly distinctness of outline and poignant grip.

The Life and Death of Jason (1867). Narrative poem in heroic couplets on a Greek subject, is romantic in treatment and epic in scale; rapid movement, sonorous rhythm, picturesque details, leisurely yet vigorous description, studied simplicity of language. Memorable for the haunting, irreproachable song sung by the water-nymph to Hylas.

1 Spargo, John, *The Socialism of William Morris* (1906); Noyes, Alfred, *William Morris* (1908); Drinkwater, John, *William Morris* (1912); Compton-Rickett, Arthur, (introduction by Cunninghame Graham, R. B.), *William Morris: A Study in Personality* (1913); Clutton-Brock, A., *William Morris: His Work and Influence* (1914); Glasier, J. B., *William Morris and the Early Days of the Socialist Movement* (1921); Mackail, J. W., (1) *The Life of William Morris* (Two volumes in one, 1922) and (2) *Studies of English Poets* (1926), pp. 173-197; Evans, B. I., *William Morris & His Poetry* (1925); Helmholtz-Phelan, A. von, *The Social Philolosophy of William Morris* (1927); Coe, G. D. H., "William Morris" in *Revaluations* (Oxford University Press, 1931), pp. 131-154, Litzenberg, Karl, "The Social Philosophy of William Morris and the Doom of the Gods," *Essays and Studies in English and Comparative Literature,* By Members of The English Department of the University of Michigan (1933), pp. 183-203; Leatham, James, *William Morris* (Fourth edition, 1934); Bloomfield, Paul, *William Morris* (1934); Weekley, Montague, *William Morris* (1934); Arnot, R. P., *William Morris: A Vindication* (1934). For a short autobiography written by William Morris at the request of Andreas Scheu, refer to Kemmis, Beresford, "Unpublished Letters of William Morris to Andreas Scheu," *The Socialist Review,* New Series, No. 26: March, 1928, pp. 26-29 (pp. 24-36). Other letters appear in the April number, pp. 21-24, and in the May, pp. 34-38; Henderson, Philip, ed., *The Letters of William Morris to His Family and Friends* (1950).

The Earthly Paradise† (1868—1870). Consists of a prologue and twenty-four stories in Chaucerian verse, two for each month of the year, of which one is a medieval romance and the other a Greek legend. Fine descriptive passages, interspersed lyrics, and interesting stories atone for a lack of metrical vitality, although the volume represents Morris at his best in intricacy and ingenuity. Two of the best tales are "Pygmalion and the Image" and "The Lovers of Gudrun," a translation of the Icelandic *Laxdaela Saga*.

Love Is Enough (1872). Morality play based on a story in *The Mabinogion* (Vol. 1, p. 41). Its action is involved, but somehow it has a directness of statement and an interesting structure.

Sigurd the Volsung, and the Fall of the Nibelungs† (1876). Epic in four books in an anapaestic couplet with six beats to the line is a superb adaptation of the *Volsunga Saga*, recapturing its terror and pathos.[1]

Socialist Propaganda

Dream of John Ball (1888). Mixed prose and verse represents what may be the culminating point of his whole work, according to Mackail.

News from Nowhere, or an Epoch of Rest† (1891). A reply to Bellamy's *Looking Backward*. Like his *Dream of John Ball*, is a romance of socialist propaganda.[2] No Utopian romance is more humane and idyllic.

Imaginative Romances in Prose and Poetry

(1). *A Tale of the House of the Wolfings* (1888). (2) *The Roots of the Mountains* (1889). (3) *The Story of the Glittering Plain* (1890). (4) *The Wood Beyond the World* (1894). (5) *Child Christopher*

---

1 McDowell, G. T., "The Treatment of the Volsunga Saga by William Morris," *Scandinavian Studies and Notes*, VII (1921-1923), pp. 151-168; Litzenberg, Karl, "William Morris and Scandinavian Literature: A Bibliographical Essay," *Scandinavian Studies and Notes*, XIII (1935), pp. 93-105.

2 Morris often expressed his interest in the welfare of the poorer classes. Famous in his pamphlet called *Chants for Socialists* is "The Day Is Coming"; another chant declares:

"Then all *mine* and all *thine* shall be *ours*, and no more shall any man crave
For riches that serve for nothing but to fetter a friend for a slave."
"A Death Song" was written to aid the family of Alfred Linnell, who died from injuries received when the constabulary attacked marchers in a Socialist parade in London on November 13, 1887; Morris was among the marchers. Furthermore, in a pamphlet entitled *The Why I Ams* (1894), Morris writes on "Why I am A Communist": a communist looks forward to "the development of each man's capacities for the benefit of each and all," and to the abolition of waste "by taking care that one man does not get more than he can use, and another less than he needs." William Morris states: "Communism, therefore, can see no reason for inequality of condition: to each one according to his needs, from each one according to his capacities, must always be its motto." Finally, in the frequently-quoted "The Claim of Socialism," he states bluntly that if Society does not admit such fundamental principles, then "the price to be paid for so making the world happy is Revolution."

† * Explanation of symbols immediately precedes Chapter XV.

(1895). (6) *The Well at the World's End* (1896). (7) *The Water of the Wondrous Isles* (1897). (8) *The Story of the Sundering Flood* (1898).

Translations

(1) *Grettis Saga* (1869). (2) *Volsunga Saga* (1870). (3) *Three Northern Love Stories* (1875). (4) *Aeneids of Virgil* (1875). (5) *Odyssey* (1887). (6) *The Saga Library* (1891—1895). (7) *The Tale of Beowulf* (1895). (8) *Old French Romances* (1896).

Algernon Charles Swinburne, 1837—1909, poet, critic[1]; according to Georg Brandes, "the greatest lyric poet that ever wrote the English tongue, when skill and virtuosity are considered."

Chief Editions of His Poetry

Poems and Ballads (1866)). Included *The Triumph of Time, A Litany, Les Noyades, A Leave-Taking, Itylus, Dolores, Laus Veneris,*[2] and *The Garden of Proserpine,* which was possibly influenced by Delavigne's *Les Limbes.*[3] The volume "raised a storm and founded a school."

Songs before Sunrise (1871). Like the earlier *A Song of Italy* (1867), it is pervaded by enthusiasm for Italian liberty and union. Despite phrasal extravagances, has many exalted thoughts. Included *Hertha,* a blurred personification of the idea of the world-soul. Of all his poems, it contained, according to Swinburne, "the most lyric force and music combined with the most of condensed and clarified thought." The essential thought of the poem, said Swinburne in a letter to W. M. Rossetti, is that Hertha, the principle of growth, "prefers liberty to bondage, Mazzini to Buonoparte." In this volume also appeared *To Walt Whitman in America,* although Whitman is the subject of only two of the twenty-one stanzas.

---

1 Lyall, A. C., *Studies in Literature and History* (1915), "Characteristics of Mr. Swinburne's Poetry," pp. 263-290; Gosse, Edmund, *The Life of Algernon Charles Swinburne* (1917); *The Letters of Algernon Charles Swinburne,* edited by Hake, Thomas, and Compton-Rickett, Arthur (1918); *The Letters of Algernon Charles Swinburne,* edited by Gosse, Edmund, and Wise, T. J. (Two volumes, 1919); Hearn, Lafcadio, *Pre-Raphaelite and Other Poets,* edited by Erskine, John (1922), Chap. III, "Studies in Swinburne," pp. 122-179; Mackail, J. W., *Studies of English Poets* (1926), "Swinburne," pp. 201-225; Welby, T. E., *A Study of Swinburne* (1926); Chew, S. C., *Swinburne* (1929); Rutland, W. R., *Swinburne* (1931); Lafourcade, Georges, *Swinburne: A Literary Biography* (1932); Hyder, C. K., *Swinburne's Literary Career and Fame* (1935) Bragman, L. J., "The Case of Algernon Charles Swinburne," *The Psychoanalystic Review,* XXI (1934), pp. 59-74; Hyder, C. K., "Swinburne and the Popular Ballad," *Publications of the Modern Language Association of America,* XLIX (1934), pp. 295-300; Lang, C. V., ed., *Letters* (four vols, 1960).

2 For possible sources of the poem, see Hyder, C. K., "Swinburne's *Laus Veneris* and the Tannhäuser Legend," *Publications of the Modern Language Association of America,* XLV (1930), pp. 1202-1213.

3 Shackford, M. H., "Swinburne and Delavigne," *Publications of the Modern Language Association of America,* XXIII; New Series, XXVI (1918), pp. 85-95.

Poems and Ballads (Second Series. 1878). Not as outspoken as usual in its repudiation of conventions and in its pagan spirit. Contained *A Forsaken Garden,* beautiful verses that wedded sense and sound with consummate double riming and euphonic strategy, and *Ave Atque Vale,* his greatest short poem, a pure elegy written (prematurely) in memory of Charles Baudelaire, from whose *Les Fleurs du Mal* the imagery is in large measure drawn.[1]

The Heptalogia, or the Seven Against Sense. A Cap With Seven Bells (1880). Not only does he parody Browning and Tennyson: in *Nephelidia* Swinburne parodies his own excessive redundancy and alliteration, but *Nephelidia* is the weakest of all his parodies.

Tristram of Lyonesse† (1882). Romantic poem in agile rimed couplets notable for warmth and color, lyrical richness and variety, and a sustained spiritual sublimity.

The Tale of Balen (1896). Unflagging in its evocation of the spirit of adventure. The work, as Welby states, reveals "Swinburne's recovery of youth and lucid communicativeness."

The Duke of Gandia (begun 1882; completed 1908). Last work is a slight but extraordinary piece.

Early Drama

The Queen Mother (1860). Romantic drama in blank verse influenced by Beddoes and Morris. Marred by obscure motivation and too much attention to subsidiary characters and action. His first book, declares Welby, and his unluckiest.

Atalanta in Calydon (1865). Brilliant drama that reproduced the structure and metrical arrangement of Greek tragedy, yet was removed from the Hellenic spirit by Swinburne's exuberant form and angry fatalism. *The Hymn to Artemis,* the opening chorus, is famous.

Chastelard (1865). The first of his romantic trilogy on Mary Queen of Scots. While *Bothwell* may be his chief work as a dramatic poet, *Chastelard* is his most successful play.

Bothwell† (1874). Long historical drama elaborate in plot, great in scene, spirited in portrait, and sustained in ardor and energy. Second of his three romantic dramas on Mary Queen of Scots.

Erechtheus (1876). Allusive, austere lyrical drama in which he embodied his political ideal. This tragedy of citizenship, exact in organi-

---

1 For a comparison of Shelley's *Adonais* and Swinburne's *Ave Atque Vale,* see Harding, A. T., "Shelley's *Adonais* and Swinburne's *Ave Atque Vale,*" *The Sewanee Review Quarterly,* XXVII (1919), pp. 32-42.
† * Explanation of symbols immediately precedes Chapter XV.

zation and severe in symmetrical unity, surges forward with a spirit more akin to the Greek energy and thought than that found in *Atalanta in Calydon*.

Mary Stuart (1881). Third drama of trilogy, as often suggested, inspires respect rather than enthusiasm. As a whole, however, the trilogy has swiftness of action, acute portrayal of character, and some dramatic power.[1]

Later Drama

Marino Faliero (1885), which focuses sympathy upon Marino (see Byron's treatment, p. 470); *Locrine* (1887), a dramatization confused by the variation of the stanzaic schemes; *The Sisters*, in prose (1892), lively in technique, but his worst failure; and *Rosamund, Queen of the Lombards* (1899), where the besetting fault, as in *The Queen Mother*, is the undue attention to subsidiary issues, but which, unlike *The Queen Mother*, does not end well. (It should not be confused with *Rosamond*, a blank-verse drama that was published in the same volume with *The Queen Mother*, 1860.)

Prose

(1) *Notes on Poems and Reviews* (1866). (2) *William Blake* (1867). (3) *Under the Microscope* (1872). (4) *George Chapman* (1875). (5) *Essays and Studies* (1875). (6) *A Note on Charlotte Brontë* (1877). (7) *A Study of Shakespeare* (1880). (8) *Miscellanies* (1886). (9) *A Study of Victor Hugo* (1886). (10) *A Study of Ben Jonson* (1889). (11) *Studies in Prose and Poetry* (1894). (12) *The Age of Shakespeare* (1908). (13) *Charles Dickens* (1913).

---

1 Pound, Olivia, "On the Application of the Principles of Greek Lyric Tragedy in the Classical Dramas of Swinburne," *University Studies* (University of Nebraska), XIII (1913), pp. 341-360; Strong, Archibald, *Four Studies* (1932), pp. 21-77.

CHAPTER XXIV

YESTERDAY AND TODAY

IMPORTANT NOVELISTS

Joseph Conrad, or **Teodor Jozef Konrad Korzeniowski,** 1857—1924, novelist, teller of tales. NOVELS: *Almayer's Folly* (1895), *An Outcast of the Islands* (1896), *The Nigger of the "Narcissus"* (1897), *Lord Jim* (1900), *Nostromo* (1904), *The Secret Agent* (1907), *Under Western Eyes* (1911), *Chance* (1913), *Victory* (1915), *The Arrow of Gold* (1919), *The Rescue* (1920), *Suspense* (1925). TALES: *Typhoon* (1903), *Youth* (1902), *Within the Tides* (1915). AUTOBIOGRAPHY: *A Personal Record* (1912).

Herbert George Wells, 1866—1946, novelist, sociologist, historian. NOVELS: *Love and Mrs. Lewisham* (1900), *Kipps* (1905), *Ann Veronica* (1909), *Tono-Bungay* (1909), *The History of Mr. Polly* (1910), *The New Machiavelli* (1911), *Marriage* (1912), *The Passionate Friends* (1913), *The Wife of Sir Isaac Harman* (1914), *The Research Magnificent* (1915), *Mr. Britling Sees It Through* (1916), *Joan and Peter* (1918), *Christina Alberta's Father* (1925), *The World of William Clissold* (1926). UTOPIAN WORKS: *The War of the Worlds* (1898), *The War in the Air* (1908). HISTORY: *The Outline of History* (1919). SHORT-STORIES: *The Stolen Bacillus and Other Incidents* (1895), *The Country of the Blind and Other Stories* (1911). PHILOSOPHY: *Experiment in Autobiography* (1934). ESSAYS AND STUDIES: *Mankind in the Making* (1903), *This Misery of Boots* (1907), *The Science of Life,* written in collaboration with Julian Huxley and G. P. Wells (1931).

(Enoch) Arnold Bennett, 1867—1931, novelist, dramatist. *The Old Wives' Tale* (1908), *Buried Alive* (1908), *Clayhanger* (1910), *The Card* (1911), *Hilda Lessways* (1911), *These Twain* (1916), *The Pretty Lady* (1918), *Riceyman Steps* (1923), *Lord Raingo* (1926), *Imperial Palace* (1930). SHORT-STORIES: *The Matador of the Five Towns, and Other Stories* (1912). PLAYS: *Milestones,* with Edward Knoblauch (1912), *The Great Adventure* (1913). ESSAYS: *How to Live on Twenty-Four Hours a Day* (1908), *Literary Taste* (1909), *Mental Efficiency* (1911). AUTO-BIOGRAPHY: *The Truth About an Author* (1903), *The Journal of Arnold Bennett* (1932-1933).

John Galsworthy, 1867—1933, novelist, dramatist, essayist, short-story writer, poet. NOVELS: *The Man of Property* (1906), *The Patrician* (1911), *The Dark Flower* (1913), *The Forsyte Saga:* including *The Man of Property; In Chancery; To Let;* with two connecting interludes: *The Indian Summer of a Forsyte, Awakening* (1922), *A Modern Comedy:* including *The White Monkey; The Silver Spoon; Swan Song* (1929), *End of the Chapter* (1934): including *Maid in Waiting* (1931), *Flowering Wilderness* (1932), *One More River* (1933). PLAYS: *Justice* (1910), *The Pigeon* (1912), *Loyalties* (1922), *Old English* (1924), *Escape* (1926). SHORT-STORIES: *Caravan* (1925), *On Forsyte 'Change* (1930).

David Herbert Lawrence, 1885—1930, novelist, poet. NOVELS: *Sons and Lovers* (1913), *The Rainbow* (1915), *Women in Love* (1921), *Aaron's Rod* (1922),

St. Mawr; together with *The Princess* (1925), *The Plumed Serpent (Quetzalcoatl)* (1926), *Lady Chatterley's Lover* (1928). POETRY: *Look! We Have Come Through!* (1917), *Birds, Beasts and Flowers* (1923). IMPORTANT POEMS: "Snake," "Work," "Service of All Dead," "Kangaroo," "Suspense," "Man and Bat," "A White Blossom," "A Young Wife," "Aware." SHORT-STORIES: *The Prussian Officer, and Other Stories* (1914), *England, My England, and Other Stories* (1922), *Captain's Doll* (1923), *The Woman Who Rode Away, and Other Stories* (1928). STUDIES: *Psychoanalysis and the Unconscious* (1921), *Fantasia of the Unconscious* (1922), *Studies in Classic American Literature* (1923), *Pornography and Obscenity* (1929), *Apocalypse* (1931), *Etruscan Places* (1932). TRAVEL: *Twilight in Italy* (1916), *Sea and Sardinia* (1921), *Mornings in Mexico* (1927).

Aldous Leonard Huxley, 1894— , novelist, poet, essayist. NOVELS: *Crome Yellow* (1921), *Antic Hay* (1923), *Those Barren Leaves* (1925), *Point Counter Point* (1928), *Brave New World* (1932), *Eyeless in Gaza* (1936). POETRY: *Selected Poems* (1925), *The Cicadas, and Other Poems* (1931). IMPORTANT POEMS: "The Cicadas," "Fifth Philosopher's Song." ESSAYS: *On the Margin* (1923), *Do What You Will* (1929), *T. H. Huxley as a Man of Letters* (1932), *Ends and Means* (1937). SHORT-STORIES: *Mortal Coils* (1922), *Young Archimedes* (1924), *Brief Candles* (1930). MISCELLANEOUS: *The World of Light* (1931), a play; *Jesting Pilate* (1926) and *Beyond the Mexique Bay* (1934), travel books,

May Sinclair, 1865—1946, novelist. NOVELS: *The Divine Fire* (1904), *The Combined Maze* (1913), *The Three Sisters* (1914), *The Tree of Heaven* (1917), *Mary Olivier* (1919), *Mr. Waddington of Wyck* (1921), *Anne Severn and the Fieldings* (1922), *Life and Death of Harriett Frean* (1922), *A Cure of Souls* (1924). MISCELLANEOUS: *The Three Brontës* (1912), biography; *A Journal of Impressions in Belgium* (1915), war sketches; *A Defence of Idealism* (1917), a study.

Sheila Kaye-Smith (Mrs. T. P. Fry), c. 1888—1956, novelist. NOVELS: *The Tramping Methodist* (1908), *Sussex Gorse* (1916), *Tamarisk Town* (1919), *Green Apple Harvest* (1920), *Joanna Godden* (1921): see, also, *Joanna Godden Married, and Other Stories* (1926), *Shepherds in Sackcloth* (1930), *The End of the House of Alard* (1923), *The George and the Crown* (1925), *Summer Holiday* (1932). AUTOBIOGRAPHY: *Three Ways Home* (1937).

Dorothy M. Richardson (Mrs. Alan Odle), ? — 1957, novelist. NOVELS: *Pointed Roofs* (Pilgrimage, I, 1915), *Backwater* (Pilgrimage, II, 1916), *Honeycomb* (Pilgrimage, III, 1917), *Oberland* (Pilgrimage, IX, 1927).

Virginia (Stephen) Woolf, 1882—1941, novelist, essayist. NOVELS: *Jacob's Room* (1922), *Mrs. Dalloway* (1925), *To the Lighthouse* (1927), *Orlando* (1928), *The Waves* (1931). ESSAYS: *The Common Reader* (1925), *A Room of One's Own* (1929), *Second Common Reader* (1932).

OTHER IMPORTANT NOVELISTS

Maurice Hewlett, 1861—1923, novelist, poet, essayist. NOVELS: *The Forest Lovers* (1898), *The Life and Death of Richard Yea-and-Nay* (1900), *The Queen's Quair* (1904), *Halfway House* (Volume 1 of trilogy: 1908), *Open Country* (Vol. 2 of trilogy: 1909), *Rest Harrow* (Vol. 3 of trilogy: 1910), *Bendish* (1913). POETRY: *Masque of Dead Florentines* (1895), *Songs and Meditations* (1896), *Singsongs of the War* (1914-1915), *The Song of the Plow* (1916). ESSAYS AND STUDIES: *Earthwork out of Tuscany* (1895), *In a Green Shade* (1920), *Wiltshire Essays* (1922), *Extempory Essays* (1922), *Last Essays* (1924). MISCELLANEOUS: *Pan and the Young Shepherd* (1898), a play; *Quattrocentisteria* (1898) and *Little Novels of Italy* (1899), tales; *Road in Tuscany* (1904), and *Fond Adventures* (1905), travel books.

William Wymark Jacobs, 1863—1943, short-story writer, novelist, playwright. NOVELS AND SHORT-STORIES: *Many Cargoes* (1896), *More Cargoes*

(1898), *Master of Craft* (1900), *Light Freights* (1901), *Night Watches* (1914), *Deep Waters* (1919), *Snug Harbour* (1931). PLAYS: *The Monkey's Paw* (story by Jacobs; dramatised by Louis N. Parker, 1910), *Beauty and the Barge* (in collaboration with Louis N. Parker, 1910).

Arthur Machen, 1863—1947, novelist, essayist. NOVELS: *Great God Pan and The Inmost Light* (1894), *Hill of Dreams* (1907), *The Bowmen, and Other Legends of the War* (1915), *The Great Return* (1915). MISCELLANEOUS: *Hieroglyphics* (1902), and *The London Adventure* (1924), essays and studies; *Things Near and Far* (1923), autobiography.

Eden Phillpotts, 1862—   , novelist, dramatist, poet, essayist. DARTMOOR NOVELS: *Children of the Mist* (1898), *Sons of the Morning* (1900), *The Secret Woman* (1905), *Widecombe Fair* (1913), *The Jury* (1927). PLAYS: *The Farmer's Wife* (1916), *Yellow Sands,* in collaboration with Adelaide Phillpotts (1926). MYSTERY STORIES: *Bred in the Bone* (Book of Avis, I, 1932), *Witch's Cauldron* (Book of Avis, II, 1933), *A Shadow Passes* (Book of Avis, III, 1933).

Sir Arthur Thomas Quiller-Couch, 1863—1944, novelist, critic, poet. NOVELS: *Dead Man's Rock* (1887), *The Astonishing History of Troy Town* (1888), *The Splendid Spur* (1889), *The Ship of Stars* (1899), *Hetty Wesley* (1903). ESSAYS AND STUDIES: *Adventures in Criticism* (1896), *On the Art of Writing* (1916), *Shakespeare's Workmanship* (1918), *Studies in Literature* (1918), *On the Art of Reading* (1920), *Studies in Literature, Second Series* (1922), *Paternity in Shakespeare* (1932), *The Poet as Citizen and Other Papers* (1934).

Henry Handel Richardson, pseudonym of **Henrietta Richardson Robertson,** 1870—1946, (Australian) novelist. NOVELS: *Maurice Guest* (1908), *The Getting of Wisdom* (1910), *The Fortunes of Richard Mahony* (Trilogy: I, 1917; *Way Home,* II, 1925; *Ultima Thule,* III, 1929). SHORT-STORIES: *The End of a Childhood and Other Stories* (1934).

Charles Edward Montague, 1867—1928, novelist. NOVELS: *A Hind Let Loose* (1910), *Rough Justice* (1926), *Right Off the Map* (1927). MISCELLANEOUS: *Fiery Particles* (1923), short-stories; *Dramatic Values* (1911) and *A Writer's Notes on His Trade* (1930), essays.

Norman Douglas, 1868—1952, novelist, essayist. NOVELS AND SHORT-STORIES: *South Wind* (1917), *They Want* (1920), *In the Beginning* (1927). STUDIES: *Good-bye to Western Culture* (1930). AUTOBIOGRAPHY: *Looking Back* (1933). TRAVEL: *Old Calabria* (1915), *Together* (1923).

Algernon Blackwood, 1869—1952, novelist. NOVELS: *John Silence* (1908), *The Centaur* (1911), *A Prisoner in Fairyland* (1913), *The Garden of Survival* (1918). SHORT-STORIES: *The Lost Valley, and Other Stories* (1910).

Ford Madox Ford or **Ford Madox Hueffer,** 1873—1939   , novelist. NOVELS: *The Inheritors* (1901) and *Romance* (1903), both in collaboration with Joseph Conrad; *The Good Soldier* (1915), *Some Do Not* (1924), *No More Parades* (1925), *A Man Could Stand Up* (1926), *Last Post* (1928), *Henry for Hugh* (1934). POEMS: *Collected Poems* (1913), *On Heaven, and Poems Written on Active Service* (1918), *New Poems* (1927). REMINISCENCES: *Thus to Revisit* (1921), *Joseph Conrad,* (1924), *Return to Yesterday* (1931), *It Was the Nightingale* (1933). SKETCHES: *New York is not America* (1927). STUDIES: *Henry James, a Critical Study* (1914), *The English Novel, from the Earliest Days to the Death of Joseph Conrad* (1930).

Henry Major Tomlinson, 1873—1958, journalist, war correspondent, novelist, essayist. NOVELS: *Gallions Reach* (1927), *All Our Yesterdays* (1930). ESSAYS AND STUDIES: *London River* (1921), *Between the Lines* (1930). TRAVEL: *The Sea and the Jungle* (1912), *Tidemarks* (1924), *Out of Soundings* (1931), *South to Cadiz* (1934), *Below London Bridge* (with H. C. Tomlinson, 1934).

William Somerset Maugham, 1874—   , novelist, playwright, short-story writer. NOVELS: *Liza of Lambeth* (1897), *Of Human Bondage* (1915), *The Moon and Sixpence* (1919), *The Painted Veil* (1925), *Cakes and Ale; or, The Skeleton in the Cupboard* (1930), *The Narrow Corner* (1932). PLAYS: *The Circle* (1921), *Our Betters* (1923), *The Letter* (1927), *The Constant Wife* (1927), *The Sacred Flame* (1929), *For Services Rendered* (1932). SHORT-STORIES: *The Trembling of a Leaf* (1921; published as *Sadie Thompson*, 1928; *Rain*, 1932), *Ashenden; or, The British Agent* (1928), *Six Stories Written in the First Person Singular* (1931). *Ah King* (1933), TRAVEL: *On a Chinese Screen* (1922), *The Gentleman in the Parlour* (1930).

Rose Macaulay, 1889—1958, novelist. NOVELS: *Potterism* (1920), *Dangerous Ages* (1921), *Told by an Idiot* (1923), *Orphan Island* (1924), *Crewe Train* (1926), *Staying with Relations* (1930), *The Shadow Flies* (1932).

Theodore Francis Powys, 1875—1953, novelist. NOVELS: *Black Bryony* (1923), *Mr. Tasker's Gods* (1925), *Mr. Weston's Good Wine* (1928), *The White Paternoster* (1930), *Unclay* (1931). SHORT-STORIES: *The Left Leg: The Left Leg, Hester Dominy, Abraham Men* (1923), *The House with the Echo* (1928).

Sir Philip Gibbs, 1877—   , journalist, novelist, short-story writer. STUDIES: *Now It Can Be Told* (1920), *Ten Years After* (1924), *The Day After To-Morrow* (1928), *Since Then* (1930), *European Journey* (1934). NOVELS: *The Street of Adventure* (1909), *The Middle of the Road* (1922), *The Winding Lane* (1931), *The Cross of Peace* (1933).

Edward Morgan Forster, 1879—   , novelist, short-story writer. NOVELS: *Where Angels Fear to Tread* (1905), *The Longest Journey* (1907), *A Room with a View* (1908), *Howards End* (1910), *A Passage to India* (1924). SHORT-STORIES: *The Celestial Omnibus, and Other Stories* (1911), *The Eternal Moment* (1928). CRITICISM: *Aspects of the Novel* (1927).

E. M. Compton Mackenzie, 1883—   , novelist. "SINISTER STREET" NOVELS: *Youth's Encounter* (1913), *Sinister Street* (1914), *The Early Life and Adventures of Sylvia Scarlett* (1918), *Sylvia & Michael* (1919). OTHER NOVELS: *Carnival* (1912), *Plasher Mead* (1915), *The Altar Steps* (1922), *Vestal Fire* (1927), *Extraordinary Women* (1928), *Our Street* (1931), *Water on the Brain* (1933). ESSAYS AND STUDIES: *Literature in My Time* (1933). WAR MEMOIRS: *Gallipoli Memories* (1929), *First Athenian Memories* (1931), *Greek Memories* (1932).

Wyndham Lewis, 1884—1957, painter, novelist. NOVELS: *Tarr* (1918), *The Apes of God* (1930), *Snooty Baronet* (1932). ESSAYS AND STUDIES: *The Art of Being Ruled* (1926), *Time and Western Man* (1927), *Paleface* (1929), *Hitler* (1931). MISCELLANEOUS: *The Wild Body, A Soldier of Humour, and Other Stories* (1927), short-story collections; *Filibusters in Barbary* (1932), travel.

Hugh Seymour Walpole, 1884—1941, novelist. NOVELS: *Maradick at Forty* (1910), *Fortitude* (1913), *The Duchess of Wrexe* (1914), *The Dark Forest* (1916), *The Secret City* (1919), *The Young Enchanted* (1921), *The Cathedral* (1922), *Portrait of a Man With Red Hair* (1925), *Wintersmoon* (1928), *Rogue Herries* (Herries Chronicles, I, 1930), *Judith Paris* (Herries Chronicles, II, 1931), *The Fortress* (Herries Chronicles, III, 1932), *Vanessa* (Herries Chronicles, IV, 1933). CRITICAL STUDIES: *Joseph Conrad* (1916), *Anthony Trollope* (1928). CHILDREN'S BOOKS: *Jeremy* (1919), *Jeremy and Hamlet* (1923), *Jeremy at Crale* (1927).

Frank Arthur Swinnerton, 1884—   , novelist, critic. NOVELS: *Nocturne* (1917), *September* (1919), *Young Felix* (1923), *Harvest Comedy* (1938). CRITICISM: *R. L. Stevenson* (1914), *The Georgian Scene* (1934).

Katherine Mansfield, pseudonym of **Kathleen Beauchamp**, 1888—1923, short-story writer. SHORT-STORIES: *In a German Pension* (1911), *Bliss, and Other Stories* (1920), *The Garden Party and Other Stories* (1922), *The Doves' Nest,* *and Other Stories* (1923). MISCELLANEOUS: *Poems* (1923); *Journal of Katherine Mansfield* (1927) and *The Letters of Katherine Mansfield* (1928), both edited by J. Middleton Murry.

Sarah Gertrude Millin, 1889— , novelist. NOVELS: *The Dark River* (1920), *Adam's Rest* (1922), *God's Step-Children* (1924), *Mary Glenn* (1925), *An Artist in the Family* (1928), *The Coming of the Lord* (1928), *The Sons of Mrs. Aab* (1931). STUDIES: *The South Africans* (1926), *Rhodes* (1933).

Gladys Bronwyn Stern (Mrs. G. L. Holdsworth), 1890— , novelist, dramatist. NOVELS: *Debatable Ground* (1921), *The Matriarch* (1925), *A Deputy Was King* (1926), *Mosaic* (1930). PLAY: *The Man Who Pays the Piper* (1931).

E. M. Delafield, pseudonym of **Edmée Elizabeth Monica De La Pasture (Mrs. A. P. Dashwood)**, 1890—1943, novelist. NOVELS: *Zella Sees Herself* (1917), *The War-Workers* (1918), *Consequences* (1919), *Tension* (1920), *The Chip and the Block* (1925), *Jill* (1926), *The Way Things Are* (1927), *Diary of a Provincial Lady* (1930). SHORT-STORIES: *Messalina of the Suburbs* (1924), *Women Are Like That* (1929). PLAY: *To See Ourselves* (1932).

David Garnett, 1892— , novelist. NOVELS: *Lady Into Fox* (1922), *A Man in the Zoo* (1924), *Go She Must!* (1927), *The Grasshoppers Come* (1931), *Pocahontas, or, The Nonparell of Virginia* (1933).

Stella Benson, 1892—1933, novelist. NOVELS: *I Pose* (1915), *Living Alone* (1919), *The Poor Man* (1922), *Goodbye, Stranger* (1926), *Tobit Transplanted* (1931). TRAVEL SKETCHES: *The Little World* (1925), *Worlds Within Worlds* (1928). SHORT-STORIES: *Hope Against Hope, and Other Stories* (1931), *Christmas Formulas* (1932).

Rebecca West, pseudonym of **Cicily Isabel Fairfield (Mrs. H. M. Andrews)**, 1892— , novelist, essayist. NOVELS: *The Return of the Soldier* (1918), *The Judge* (1922). ESSAYS AND STUDIES: *The Strange Necessity* (1928), *Ending in Earnest* (1931).

Victoria Mary Sackville-West (Mrs. Harold Nicolson), 1892— , poet, novelist. POETRY: *The Land* (1926), *King's Daughter* (1929). IMPORTANT POEMS: "Bitterness," "Sailing Ships," "The Island," "Full Moon," "Making Cider," "Winter Song," "Tuscany." NOVELS: *Heritage* (1919), *Challenge* (1923), *The Edwardians* (1930), *All Passion Spent* (1931), *Family History* (1932), *The Dark Island* (1934).

Sylvia Townsend Warner, 1893— , novelist. NOVELS: *Lolly Willowes, or, the Loving Huntsman* (1926), *Mr. Fortune's Maggot* (1927). IMPORTANT POEMS: "Nelly Trim," "Triumph of Sensibility," "Killing No Murder," "Building in Stone."

John Boynton Priestley, 1894— , novelist, literary critic. NOVELS: *The Good Companions* (1929), *Angel Pavement* (1930), *Wonder Hero* (1933), *I'll Tell You Everything*, written with Gerald Bullett (1933). CRITICAL STUDIES: *Figures in Modern Literature* (1924), *George Meredith* (1926), *The English Novel* (1927). PLAY: *Dangerous Corner* (1932). TRAVEL: *English Journey* (1934), IMPORTANT POEMS: "Overheard," "The Old Man and the Newspaper."

Louis Golding, 1895— , novelist, poet, translator. NOVELS: *Day of Atonement* (1925), *Store of Ladies* (1927), *Magnolia Street* (1932), *Five Silver Daughters* (1934). CRITICISM: *A Letter to Adolph Hitler* (1932), *James Joyce* (1933).

Margaret Kennedy, 1896— , novelist. NOVELS: *The Constant Nymph* (1924), *The Fool of the Family* (1930), *Return I Dare Not* (1931). PLAYS: In collaboration with Basil Dean: *The Constant Nymph* (1926), *Come With Me* (1928).

Archibald Joseph Cronin, 1896—   , novelist. NOVELS: *Hatter's Castle* (1931), *Three Loves* (1932), *Grand Canary* (1933), *Stars Look Down* (1935), *The Citadel* (1937).

IMPORTANT DRAMATISTS

Thomas William Robertson, 1829—1871, dramatist, actor. PLAYS: *A Night's Adventure* (1851), *A Cantab* (1861), *David Garrick* (1864), *Society* (1865), *Ours* (1866), *Caste* (1867), *Play* (1868), *School* (1869), *M.P.* (1870).

Dion Boucicault, 1822—1890, playwright, actor. PLAYS: *London Assurance* (1841), *The Corsican Brothers* (1848), *The Vampire* (1852), *The Colleen Bawn* (1859), *The Octoroon* (1861), *Arrah-na-Pogue* (1864), *Rip Van Winkle* (written with Joseph Jefferson, 1865), *The Shaughraun* (1875).

Oscar (Fingall O'Flahertie Wills) Wilde, 1856—1900, wit, dramatist, poet. PLAYS: *Vera* (1882), *The Duchess of Padua* (1891), *Lady Windemere's Fan* (1892), *A Woman of No Importance* (1893), *Salomé* (in French, 1894), *An Ideal Husband* (1895), *The Importance of Being Earnest* (1895). POETRY: *Poems* (1881), *Collected Poems* (1892), *The Ballad of Reading Gaol* (1898). FAIRY TALES, STORIES, AND NOVELS: *The Happy Prince and Other Tales* (1888), *Lord Arthur Savile's Crime, and Other Stories* (1891), *The Picture of Dorian Gray* (1891), *The House of Pomegranates* (1892). APOLOGIA: *De Profundis* (1895; 1905). CRITICISM: *Intentions* (1891).

William Schwenk Gilbert, 1836—1911, playwright, humorous poet. PLAYS: *Dulcamara* (1866), *The Palace of Truth* (1870), *Pygmalion and Galatea* (1871), *The Wicked World* (1873), *The Happy Land* (written with Gilbert a Beckett, 1873), *Dan'l Druce* (1874), *Tom Cobb* (1875), *Broken Hearts* (1875), *Engaged* (1876), *Sweethearts* (1877), *Gretchen* (1879), *Comedy and Tragedy* (1884), *Foggerty's Fairy* (1891), *Rosenkrantz and Guildenstern* (1891), *The Mountebanks* (written with Alfred Cellier, 1892), *Fallen Fairies* (written with Edward German, 1909). COMIC OPERAS WRITTEN IN COLLABORATION WITH Sir Arthur Seymour Sullivan, 1842—1900: *Thespis; or The Gods Grown Old* (1871), *Trial by Jury* (1875), *The Sorcerer* (1877), *H. M. S. Pinafore* (1878), *The Pirates of Penzance; or The Slave of Duty* (1879), *Patience; or Bunthorne's Bride* (1881), *Iolanthe; or The Peer and the Peri* (1882), *Princess Ida; or Castle Adamant* (1884), *The Mikado; or The Town of Titipu* (1885), *Ruddigore* (1887), *The Yeomen of the Guard* (1888), *The Gondoliers* (1889), *Utopia, Limited* (1893), *The Grand Duke* (1896). POETRY: *Bab Ballads* (1869), *More Bab Ballads* (1873).

Stephen Phillips, 1868—1915, dramatist, poet. PLAYS: *Paolo and Francesca* (1900), *Herod* (1900), *Ulysses* (1902), *The Sin of David* (1904), *Nero* (1906). POETRY: *Primavera* (with others, 1890), *Eremus* (1894), *Poems* (1897).

Henry Arthur Jones, 1851—1929, playwright. PLAYS: *The Silver King*, in collaboration with Henry Herman (1882; 1907), *Saints and Sinners* (1884), *The Middleman* (1889; 1908), *The Dancing Girl* (1891; 1907), *The Crusaders* (1891), *The Case of Rebellious Susan* (1894), *The Masqueraders* (1894), *Michael and his Lost Angel* (1896), *The Triumph of the Philistines* (1895), *The Liars* (1897), *Mrs. Dane's Defence* (1900), *The Hypocrites* (1906), *Dolly Reforming Herself* (1908), *Mary Goes First* (1913). ESSAYS, LECTURES, AND STUDIES: *The Renascence of the English Drama* (1895), *The Foundations of a National Drama* (1913), *My Dear Wells* (1921), *The Shadow of Henry Irving* (1931).

Arthur Wing Pinero, 1855—1934, dramatist. PLAYS: *Sweet Lavender* (1893), *Second Mrs. Tanqueray* (1894), *The Notorious Mrs. Ebbsmith* (1895), *Trelawny of the "Wells"* (1898), *Iris* (1902), *His House in Order* (1906), *The Thunderbolt* (1909), *Mid-Channel* (1910), *A Cold June* (1932).

Sir James Matthew Barrie, 1860—1937, playwright, novelist. PLAYS: *Walker, London* (1892; 1907), *A Professor's Love Story* (1894), *The Wedding Guest* (1900), *Quality Street* (1902; 1913), *The Admirable Crichton* (1902; 1914), *What Every Woman Knows* (1908; 1918), *A Kiss for Cinderella* (1916; 1920), *Dear Brutus* (1917; 1923), *Peter Pan, or, the Boy Who Would Not Grow Up* (1904; 1928). NOVELS: *Better Dead* (1887), *The Little Minister* (1891), *Sentimental Tommy* (1896), *Tommy and Grizel* (1900). STORIES AND SKETCHES: *Auld Licht Idylls* (1888—1889), *A Window in Thrums* (1889), *My Lady Nicotine* (1890). MISCEL-LANEOUS: *The Little White Bird* (1902), for children; *Margaret Ogilvy* (1896), a biography.

Laurence Housman, 1865—   , author, artist. PLAYS: Prunella (in colla-boration with H. Granville-Barker, 1907), *Angels and Ministers* (1921): four plays—*The Queen: God Bless Her, His Favourite Flower, The Comforter, Dethronements* (1922), *Little Plays of St. Francis* (1922), *Followers of St. Francis* (1923), *The Comments of Juniper* (1926), *Palace Plays:* two plays—*The Revolting Daughter, The Wicked Uncles, or Victorious Virtue* (1930), *Little Plays of St. Francis* (Second series, 1931), *The Queen's Progress, Palace Plays* (Second series, 1932), *Nunc Dimit-tis* (1933), *Victoria and Albert* (Palace Plays, Third series, 1933). NOVELS: *Englishwoman's Love Letters* (1900), *Trimblerigg* (1924), *The Life of H. R. H. the Duke of Flamborough, By Benjamin Bunny* (1928). POETRY: *Green Arras* (1896), *Spikenard* (1898). IMPORTANT POEMS: "Love, the Tempter," "Gaffer at the Fair," "The Continuing City," "The Mystery of the Incarnation," "The Settlers."

Harley Granville-Barker, 1877—1946, dramatist, translator, actor. PLAYS: *Three Plays: The Marrying of Ann Leete, The Voysey Inheritance, Waste* (1909), *The Madras House* (1911). CRITICISM: *On Dramatic Method* (1931), *Associating with Shakespeare* (1932), *The Study of Drama* (1934).

John Drinkwater, 1882—1937, poet, dramatist, critic. POETRY: *Selected Poems* (1922), *Summer Harvest, Poems 1924—1933* (1933). IMPORTANT POEMS: "June Dance," "Mystery," "Anthony Crundle," "Birthright," "A Town Widow," "Reciprocity," "Moonlit Apples," "Who Were Before Me," "Prelude." PLAYS: *Abraham Lincoln* (1918), *Bird in Hand* (1927). BIOGRAPHY: *The Pilgrim of Eternity* (1925), *Mr. Charles, King of England* (1926). AUTOBIOGRAPHY: *Inheritance* (1931), *Discovery* (1932). CRITICISM: *William Morris* (1912), *Swin-burne* (1913), *This Troubled World* (1933).

Alan Alexander Milne, 1882—1956, dramatist, humorist, poet. PLAYS: *Second Plays* (1921), *The Dover Road* (1923), *The Truth About Blayds* (1923). CHILDREN'S BOOKS: *When We Were Very Young* (1924), *Now We Are Six* (1927), *The House at Pooh Corner* (1928). MISCELLANEOUS: *Not That It Matters* (1919), *If I May* (1920).

Noel Coward, 1899—   , playwright, actor, musical composer. PLAYS: *The Vortex* (1924), *Hay Fever* (1925), *Easy Virtue* (1926), *Bittersweet* (1929), *Private Lives* (1930), *Cavalcade* (1932), *Design for Living* (1933).

IMPORTANT POETS

Robert (Seymour) Bridges, 1844—1930, poet laureate, essayist, dramatist. POETRY: *The Shorter Poems of Robert Bridges* (1890), *New Verse* (1925), *The Testament of Beauty* (1929). IMPORTANT POEMS: "I Will Not Let Thee Go," "My Delight and Thy Delight," "Winter Nightfall," "A Passer-By," "I Love All Beauteous Things," "London Snow," "The Voice of Nature," "The Windmill," "Como Se Quando," "On a Dead Child," "Absence." ESSAYS AND STUDIES: *On the Elements of Milton's Blank Verse in Paradise Lost* (1887), *Milton's Prosody* (1893), *John Keats* (1895), *The Necessity of Poetry* (1918), *The Influence of the Audience on Shakespeare's Drama* (1927).

Sir Edmund William Gosse, 1849—1928, poet, critic. POETRY: *On Viol and Flute* (1873, 1890), *Firdausi in Exile, and Other Poems* (1885), *Collected Poems*

(1911). IMPORTANT POEMS: "Chloe is False," "The Suppliant," "Revelation," "The Vanishing Boat," "Lying in the Grass," "The Charcoal-Burner," "With a Copy of Herrick," "The Tide of Love." STUDIES: *Eighteenth Century Literature, 1660—1780* (1889), *A Short History of Modern English Literature* (1897), *English Literature,* in collaboration with Richard Garnett (1903). ESSAYS: *French Profiles* (1905), *Books on the Table* (1921), *More Books on the Table* (1923), *Selected Essays* (1928). BIOGRAPHY: *Gray* (1882), *Father and Son* (1909), *The Life of Algernon Charles Swinburne* (1917). PLAY: *King Erik* (1876).

Alice (Christiana Thompson) Meynell, *c.* 1850—1922, poet, essayist, critic. POETRY: *The Shepherdess and Other Poems* (1913), *Poems* (Complete edition, 1923), *Selected Poems* (1930). IMPORTANT POEMS: "The Shepherdess," "Christ in the Universe," "November Blue," "Renouncement," "The Unknown God," "To the Beloved," "The Lady Poverty," "The Two Poets," "A Letter From a Girl to Her Own Old Age." ESSAYS: *Rhythm of Life, and Other Essays* (1893), *The Colour of Life, and Other Essays on Things Seen and Heard* (1896), *Ceres' Runaway & Other Essays* (1909), *The Second Person Singular and Other Essays* (1921).

Sir William Watson, 1858—1935, poet. POETRY: *Lachrymae Musarum* (1892), *The Eloping Angels* (1893), *The Purple East* (1896), *A Hundred Poems* (1922), *Selected Poems* (1928). IMPORTANT POEMS: "Song: 'April, April'," "Ode in May," "Autumn," "Vita Nuova," "World Strangeness," "The Great Misgiving," "Shelley's Centenary."

Alfred Edward Housman 1859—1936, poet, classical scholar. POETRY: *A Shropshire Lad* (1896), *Last Poems* (1922). IMPORTANT POEMS: "Reveille," "Epithalamium," "Loveliest of Trees," "Fancy's Knell," "The Welsh Marches," "Epitaph on an Army of Mercenaries," "The Culprit," "With Rue My Heart Is Laden," "Bredon Hill." CRITICISM: *The Name and Nature of Poetry* (1933).

Sir Henry John Newbolt, 1862—1938, poet, essayist, historian. POETRY: *The Island Race* (1898), *Collected Poems 1897—1907* (1910). IMPORTANT POEMS: "Clift on Chapel," "To a River in the South," "Minora Sidera," "The War Films," "He Fell Among Thieves," "The Final Mystery," "Gillespie," "Drakes Drum," "The Death of Admiral Blake." OTHER WORKS: *A New Study of English Poetry* (1917); *The Idea of an English Association* (1928), an essay; *My World as in My Time: Memoirs, 1862—1932* (1932).

Rudyard Kipling, 1865—1936, poet, novelist, short-story writer. POETRY: *Departmental Ditties and Other Verses* (1886), *Barrack-Room Ballads, and Other Verses* (1892), *The Seven Seas* (1896), *Rudyard Kipling's Verse. Inclusive Edition, 1885—1932* (1933). IMPORTANT POEMS: "The Flowers," "Sussex," "L'Envoi," "The Way Through the Woods," "The Holy War," "A Dedication," "Recessional," "Mandalay," "The Last Chantey," "Gunga Din," "Danny Deever." NOVELS: *The Light That Failed* (1890), *Kim* (1901). SHORT-STORIES: *Plain Tales from the Hills* (1888), *Soldiers Three* (1888), *Under the Deodars* (1888), *Mine Own People* (1891), *The Day's Work* (1898), *Traffics and Discoveries* (1904), *Actions and Reactions* (1909). CHILDREN'S BOOKS: *The Jungle Book* (1894), *The Second Jungle Book* (1895), *Captains Courageous* (1897), *Stalky & Co.* (1899), *Puck of Pook's Hill* (1906).

Arthur Symons, 1865—1945, poet, critic, translator. POETRY: *Poems* (1901), *The Fool of the World, and Other Poems* (1906), *Knave of Hearts, 1894—1908* (1913), *Lesbia and Other Poems* (1920), *Collected Edition* (1921). IMPORTANT POEMS: "Rain on the Down," "Emmy," "The Shadow," "Credo," "The Street-Singer," "Javanese Dancers," "Opals," "Requies," "White Magic," "The Ecstasy," "Indian Meditation." CRITICISM: *An Introduction to the Study of Browning* (1886), *The Symbolist Movement in Literature* (1899), *Studies in Seven Arts* (1906), *William Blake* (1907), *The Romantic Movement in English Poetry* (1909), *A Study of Thomas Hardy* (1928), *A Study of Oscar Wilde* (1930), *A Study of Walter Pater* (1932).

Laurence Binyon, 1869–1943 , poet, authority on Oriental art. POETRY: *Auguries* (1913), *The Winnowing-Fan* (1914), *The Anvil* (1916), *Selected Poems* (1922), *The Sirens* (1924). IMPORTANT POEMS: "Amasis," "O World, Be Nobler," "The Little Dancers," "John Winter," "The Sirens," "The Bacchanal of Alexander," "For the Fallen," "Invocation to Youth," "Hunger," "The Statues." PLAYS: *Attila* (1907), *Arthur* (1923), *Boadicea* (1927).

Thomas Sturge Moore, 1870–1944 , poet. POETRY: *The Poems of T. Sturge Moore* (1931—1933). IMPORTANT POEMS: "A Duet," "Theseus," "To Idleness," "Sent From Egypt With a Fair Robe of Tissue to a Sicilian Vinedresser," "The Panther," "The Dying Swan." ESSAYS AND STUDIES: *Some Soldier Poets* (1919), *Armour for Aphrodite* (1929).

William Henry Davies, 1871–1940 , poet. POETRY: *The Soul's Destroyer* (1905), *Nature Poems, and Others* (1908), *Collected Poems* (1916), *Forty New Poems* (1918), *The Hour of Magic, and Other Poems* (1922), *A Poet's Alphabet* (1925), *The Song of Love* (1926), *Collected Poems* (1928). IMPORTANT POEMS: "The White Cascade," "The Elements," "The Example," "Money," "In Spring-Time," "Songs of Joy," "A Greeting," "Leisure," "One Token," "Truly Great," "The Sleepers," "In May," "Days Too Short," "Sweet Stay-at-Home.". AUTO-BIOGRAPHY: *The Autobiography of a Super-Tramp* (1908).

Ralph Hodgson, 1877—   , poet. POETRY: *The Last Blackbird and Other Lines* (1907), *Poems* (1917). IMPORTANT POEMS: "The Bull," "Time, You Old Gypsy Man," "The Song of Honour," "The Bells of Heaven," "The Bride," "Eve," "Stupidity Street."

Walter (John) De La Mare, 1873—1956, poet, novelist. POETRY: *Poems* (1906), *The Listeners, and Other Poems* (1912), *Poems* (1920), *The Fleeting, and Other Poems* (1933). IMPORTANT POEMS: "The Song of the Mad Prince," "Arabia," "The Listeners," "Nod," "Good-bye," "All That's Past," "Suppose," "The Veil," "The Sleeper," "Mirage," "Farewell," "An Epitaph." NOVELS: *The Return* (1910), *Memoirs of a Midget* (1921). SHORT-STORIES: *The Connoisseur, and Other Stories* (1926), *On the Edge* (1930). CHILDREN'S BOOKS: *Peacock Pie* (1913), *Poems for Children* (1930). CRITICISM: *Desert Islands and Robinson Crusoe* (1930).

Wilfrid Wilson Gibson, 1878—   , poet. POETRY: *Poems, 1904—1917* (1917), *Hill Tracks* (1918), *Neighbours* (1920), *I Heard a Sailor* (1925), *Collected Poems, 1905—1925* (1926), *The Golden Room, and Other Poems* (1928), *Highland Dawn* (1932). IMPORTANT POEMS: "John Pattison Gibson," "The Ice Cart," "Fires," "The White Whippet," "By the Weir," "Solway Ford," "Flannan Isle," "The Voice," "The Stone." PLAYS: *Daily Bread* (1910), *Kestrel Edge, and Other Plays* (1924).

Alfred Edgar Coppard, 1878—   , poet, short-story writer. POETRY: *Hips & Haws* (1922), *Palagea, and Other Poems* (1926), *Yokohama Garland, and Other Poems* (1926), *Collected Poems* (1928). IMPORTANT POEMS: "Winter Field," "The Sluggard," "Stay, O Stay." TALES: *Adam and Eve and Pinch Mc* (1921), *The Black Dog, and Other Stories* (1923), *Fishmonger's Fiddle* (1925), *The Field of Mustard* (1926), *Silver Circus* (1928), *Nixey's Harlequin* (1931).

John Masefield, 1878—   , poet laureate, playwright, novelist. POETRY: *Salt-Water Ballads* (1902), *The Everlasting Mercy* (1911), *The Everlasting Mercy and The Widow in the Bye Street* (1912), *Dauber* (1913), *Lollingdon Downs and Other Poems* (1917), *Reynard the Fox, or, The Ghost Heath Run* (1919), *The Wanderer of Liverpool* (1930). IMPORTANT POEMS: "The Seekers," "Sea Fever," "Cargoes," "What Am I, Life?" "Beauty," "The Rider at the Gate," "The Ballad of Sir Bors," "The Everlasting Mercy," "The Tarry Buccaneer," "Sonnet: 'Go, Spend Your Penny'," "To His Mother, C. L. M." PLAYS: *The Tragedy of Nan* *and Other Plays* (1909), *The Tragedy of Pompey the Great* (1910), *Tristan and Isolt* (1927), *The Coming of Christ* (1928). NOVELS: *Multitude and Solitude* (1909), *Sard Harker* (1924), *The Hawbucks* (1929), *The Bird of Dawning* (1933). MISCELLANEOUS: *William Shakespeare* (1911), a study; *Gallipoli* (1916), essays.

Harold Monro, 1879—1932, poet. POETRY: *Poems* (1906), *Before Dawn* (1911), *Judas* (1911), *Children of Love* (1914), *Trees* (1915), *Strange Meetings* (1917), *Real Property* (1922), *The Earth for Sale* (1928), *Elm Angel* (1930), *Collected Poems* (1933). IMPORTANT POEMS: "Solitude," "The Wind," "The Nightingale Near the House," "A Flower Is Looking Through the Ground," "Milk for the Cat," "God," "Children of Love," "Man Carrying Bale," "Overhead on a Salt-Marsh," "At a Country Dance in Provence." OTHER WORKS: *The Chronicle of a Pilgrimage* (1910), *Some Contemporary Poets* (1920).

Alfred Noyes, 1880—1958, poet. POETRY: *Flower of Old Japan* (1903), *Forest of Wild Thyme* (1905), *Drake* (1906—1908), *Collected Poems* (I, II, 1910; III, 1920; IV, 1927), *Tales of the Mermaid Tavern* (1913), *The Torch Bearers: Watchers of the Sky* (1922), *The Book of Earth* (1925), *The Last Voyage* (1930). IMPORTANT POEMS: "The Paradox," "Sherwood," "The Last of the. Books," "The May-Tree," "The Unconscious," "The World's May-Queen," "The Highway-man," "A Japanese Love-Song," "The Shadow," "On Rembrandt's Portrait of a Rabbi," "The Loom of Years," "Creation," "On the Death of Francis Thompson," "The Barrel-Organ." MISCELLANEOUS: *Sherwood, or Robin Hood and the Three Kings* (1911), a play; *Some Aspects of Modern Poetry* (1924), *Tennyson* (1932), and *The Unknown God* (1934), studies.

Lascelles Abercrombie, 1881—1938, poet, critic, playwright. POETRY: *Interludes and Poems* (1908), *Emblems of Love* (1911), *The Poems of Lascelles Abercrombie* (1930). IMPORTANT POEMS: "Song," "Hymn to Love," "Emblem of Love," "Ceremonial Ode," "Ryton Firs," "The Death of a Friar," "Marriage Song," "Epilogue." STUDIES AND CRITICISM: *Thomas Hardy* (1912), *The Epic* (1914), *An Essay Towards a Theory of Art* (1922), *The Theory of Poetry* (1924), *The Idea of Great Poetry* (1925), *Romanticism* (1926). PLAYS: *Deborah* (1912), *Phoenix* (1923), *The Sale of Saint Thomas* (complete, 1931).

Martin (D.) Armstrong, 1882—   , poet, short-story writer, novelist. POETRY: *Collected Poems* (1931). IMPORTANT POEMS: "Miss Thompson Goes Shopping," "The Buzzards," "Honey Harvest," "The Cage," "In Lamplight," "Autumn," "Green," "Grey." SHORT-STORIES: *Sir Pompey and Madam Juno, and Other Tales* (1927). NOVELS: *The Water Is Wide* (1927), *All In a Day* (1929).

(Herman) James Elroy Flecker, 1884—1915, poet, playwright. POETRY: *The Bridge of Fire* (1907), *Forty-Two Poems* (1911), *The Golden Journey to Samarkand* (1915), *The Old Ships* (1915), *The Collected Poems of James Elroy Flecker* (1916), *Collected Poems* (1923). IMPORTANT POEMS: "Stillness," "The Golden Journey to Samarkand," "The Old Ships," "To a Poet a Thousand Years Hence," "War Song of the Saracens," "Brumana," "Tenebris Interlucentum." PLAYS: *Hassan* (1922), *Don Juan* (1925).

Humbert Wolfe, 1885—1940, poet. POETRY: *Kensington Gardens* (1924), *The Unknown Goddess* (1925), *Humoresque* (1926), *News of the Devil* (1926), *Requiem* (1927), *Silver Cat, and Other Poems* (1928), *This Blind Rose* (1928), *Early Poems* (1930). IMPORTANT POEMS: "Resignation," "Song's Indenture," "Prelude to the Afternoon of a Faun," "Boy in the Dusk," "The High Song," "Iliad," "The Saint," "Not for My Tears." STUDIES: *The Craft of Verse* (1928), *Tennyson* (1930), *George Moore* (1931), *Signpost to Poetry* (1931).

Siegfried Loraine Sassoon, 1886—   , poet. POETRY: *The Old Hunts-man, and Other Poems* (1917), *Counter-Attack, and Other Poems* (1918), *Picture Show* (1919), *War Poems of Siegfried Sassoon* (1919), *Selected Poems* (1925),

Satirical Poems (1926), *The Heart's Journey* (1928). IMPORTANT POEMS: "Aftermath," "Grandeur of Ghosts," "The Kiss," "The Dug-Out," "Sick Leave," "The Death-Bed," "Counter-Attack," "Storm on Fifth Avenue," "Everyone Sang," "Alone." NOVELS: *Memoirs of a Fox-Hunting Man* (1928), *Memoirs of an Infantry Officer* (1930).

Edith Sitwell, 1887—   , poet, critic. POETRY: *The Mother, and Other Poems* (1915), *Clowns' Houses* (1918), *Bucolic Comedies* (1923), *Rustic Elegies* (1927), *Gold Coast Customs* (1929), *Collected Poems* (1930). IMPORTANT POEMS: "The Drum," "Aubade," "Colonel Fantock," "Spinning Song." CRITICISM: *Poetry and Criticism* (1925), *Aspects of Modern Poetry* (1934). STUDIES: *Alexander Pope* (1930), *Bath* (1932), *The English Eccentrics* (1933).

Thomas Stearns Eliot, (of American Birth), 1888—   , poet, critic. POETRY: *Prufrock, and Other Observations* (1917), *The Waste Land* (1923), *Poems, 1909—1925* (1926), *Ash-Wednesday* (Second Edition, 1933), *Sweeney Agonistes* (1932), *Poems, 1909—1925* (1932). IMPORTANT POEMS: "A Song for Simeon," "Marina." CRITICAL ESSAYS: *The Sacred Wood* (1920), *Homage to John Dryden* (1924), *For Lancelot Andrewes* (1928), *John Dryden, the Poet, the Dramatist, the Critic* (1932), *Selected Essays, 1917—1932* (1932). DRAMA: *Murder in the Cathedral* (1935).

Richard Aldington, 1892—   , poet, novelist, translator, critic. POETRY: *Images Old and New* (1916), *War and Love 1915—1918* (1919), *A Fool i' the Forest* (1925), *Collected Poems* (1928), *Love and the Luxembourg* (1930). IMPORTANT POEMS: "To a Greek Marble," "The Faun Sees Snow for the First Time," "Bromius," "Choricos," "At the British Museum." NOVELS: *Death of a Hero* (1929), *The Colonel's Daughter* (1931).

Osbert Sitwell, 1892—   , poet, novelist. POETRY: *Twentieth Century Harlequinade and Other Poems* (written with Edith Sitwell, 1916), *England Reclaimed* (1927), *Argonaut and Juggernaut* (1928), *Collected Satires and Poems* (1931). IMPORTANT POEMS: "The Blind Peddlar," "Mrs. Hague," "Ultimate Judgment," "Fountains." NOVELS: *Before the Bombardment* (1926), *The Man Who Lost Himself* (1929), *Miracle on Sinai* (1933). SHORT-STORIES: *Triple Fugue* (1924), *Dumb Animal, and Other Stories* (1930). TRAVEL: *Winters of Content* (1932).

Robert Ranke Graves, 1895—   , poet. POETRY: *Over the Brazier* (1916), *Fairies and Fusiliers* (1917), *Country Sentiment* (1920), *The Pier-Glass* (1921), *Poems, 1914—1926* (1927), *Poems, 1930—1933* (1933). IMPORTANT POEMS: "Careers," "The Boy Out of Church," "The Rock Below," "Neglectful Edward," "Free Verse," "Children of Darkness," "Star Talk," "Lost Love," "In the Wilderness," "I Wonder What It Feels Like to Be Drowned?" NOVELS: *I, Claudius* (1934), *Claudius the God* (1934). STUDIES: *Lawrence and the Arabs* (1927); *A Survey of Modernist Poetry* (1927) and *A Pamphlet Against Anthologies* (1928), both in collaboration with Laura Riding. AUTOBIOGRAPHY: *Goodbye to All That* (1929).

Edmund (Charles) Blunden, 1896—   , poet. POETRY: *The Waggoner and Other Poems* (1920), *English Poems* (1926), *The Poems of Edmund Blunden 1914—1930* (1930), *Halfway House* (1932). IMPORTANT POEMS: "Almswomen," "The Waggoner," "The Poor Man's Pig," "Gleaning," "The Scythe Struck by Lightning," "Behind the Line," "The Barn," "The Child's Grave," "Old Homes." MISCELLANEOUS: *The Bonadventure* (1922), travel book; *Leigh Hunt* (1930), a biographical study; *Votive Tablets* (1931), essays; *Undertones of War* (1928), reminiscences.

OTHER POETS AND SOME OF THEIR MORE IMPORTANT POEMS

Austin Dobson, 1840—1921. "A Ballad to Queen Elizabeth," "On a Fan That Belonged to the Marquise de Pompadour," "In After Days," "A Dead Letter," "Pot-Pourri," " 'Good-Night, Babette,' " "A Ballad of Antiquaries," "The Ballad of Prose and Rhyme," "A Garden Song."

W. S. Blunt, 1840—1922. "Song: 'O Fly Not, Pleasure, . . .,' " "The Desolate City," "With Esther," "St. Valentine's Day," "Written at Florence," "The Old Squire," "Chanclebury Ring," "On the Shortness of Time."

Thomas Hardy, 1840—1928. "In Time of 'The Breaking of the Nations,' " "Afterwards," "Weathers," "The Absolute Explains," "In the Servants' Quarters," "Ah, Are You Digging on My Grave?" "Great Things." (See page 253.)

Arthur William Edgar O'Shaughnessy, 1844—1881. "Ode: 'We are the music makers,' " "Song: 'I made another garden, yea,' " "The Fountain of Tears," "Doom," "The Lover," "En Soph."

William Ernest Henley, 1849—1903. "I am the Reaper," "College Rosas," "On the Way to Kew," "England, My England," "Margaritae Sorori," "In Hospital," "Romance," "London Voluntaries," "R. T. Hamilton Bruce" ("Invictus"), "Ballade Made in the Hot Weather," "To R. L. S."

Andrew Lang, 1844—1912. "Heliodore," "The Odyssey," "Almae Matres," "Twilight on Tweed," "Of His Lady's Old Age," "Martial in Town," "Scythe Song."

F. W. Bourdillon, 1852—1921. "The Night Has a Thousand Eyes," "The Chantry of the Cherubim."

William Sharp, 1856—1902. "On a Nightingale in April," "Shule, Agrah!" "Desire," "Under the Wattle," "The White Peace," "The Valley of Silence," "The Rose of Flame."

Margaret L. Woods, 1856—1945. "March Thoughts From England," "The Mariners."

John Davidson, 1857—1909. "All Hallows' Eve," "A Loafer," "A Ballad of Heaven," "A Runnable Stag," "Holiday," "The Merchantman," "In Romney Marsh," "The Last Rose."

Sir Ronald Ross, 1857—1932. "Power," "In Exile—Reply," "The Father," "Man," "Petition."

Lord Crewe, The Marquess of Crewe (Robt. O. A. Crewe-Milnes), 1858 —1945. "Seven Years," "Harrow and Flanders."

Francis Thompson, 1859—1907. "Daisy," "The Mistress of Vision," "The Poppy," "The Making of Viola," "Orient Ode," "Dream-Tryst," "Little Jesus," "The Hound of Heaven," "Envoy: 'Go, Songs, . . .' "

Mary Coleridge, 1861—1907. "Night Is Fallen," "Unity," "Gone," "September," "Our Lady."

Sir Walter (Alexander) Raleigh, 1861—1922. "My Last Will."

Michael Field Pen name used jointly by **K. H. Bradley,** 1846—1914, and **E. E. Cooper,** 1862—1913.) "Song: 'I Could Wish to Be Dead,' " "After Soufrière," "Shepherd Apollo," "Mete Me Out My Loneliness."

(Frederick) Herbert Trench, 1865—1923. "A Charge," "She Comes Not When Noon Is on the Roses," "Requiem of Archangels for the World," "Come, Let Us Make Love Deathless," "A Song of Arolilia," "Stanzas to Tolstoi in His Old Age."

A. C. Benson, 1862—1925. "The Phoenix," "The Hawk," "Evensong," "In a College Garden," "Land of Hope and Glory," "Prayer," "Lord Vyet."

Richard Le Gallienne, 1866—1947. "All Sung," "The Second Crucifixion."

Ernest Dowson, 1867—1900. "Non Sum Qualis Eram Bonae Sub Regno Cynarae," "In Tempore Senectutis," "Villanelle of Marguerites," "Dregs," "Extreme Unction," "Impenitentia Ultima."

Lionel Johnson, 1867—1902. "Winchester," "Oxford," "By the Statue of King Charles at Charing Cross," "In Falmouth Harbour," "Westward," "Vinum Daemonum," "Parnell," "The Dark Angel."

John Galsworthy, 1869—1933. "The Downs." (See page 290.)

Charlotte Mew, 1870—1928. "Arracombe Wood," "Song," "Moorland Night," "The Farmer's Bride," "Ken," "The Pedlar."

P. R. Chalmers, 1872—   . "A Dream."

John McCrae, 1872—1918. "In Flanders Field."

H. B. Binns, 1873—1923. "Injunction."

Gordon Bottomley, 1874—1948. "In January," "The End of the World," "Atlantis," "To Iron-Founders and Others," "The Ploughman."

Evelyn Underhill, 1875—1941. "Regnum Caelorum Vim Patitur," "English Easter: 7 A. M.," "Immanence," "Uxbridge Road."

(Philip) Edward Thomas, 1878—1917. "Adlestrop," "Two Pewits," "The New House," "Lights Out," "Tall Nettles," "Swedes," "Words," "Cock-Crow."

Joseph Campbell, 1879—1881. "I Am the Mountainy Singer," "The Nine-penny Fidil," "The Old Woman."

John Freeman, 1880—1929. "Music Comes," "More Than Sweet," "Home for Love," "English Hills," "The Visit," "The Fugitive," "The Evening Sky," "Stone Trees," "Merrill's Garden," "Waking," "Moon-Bathers."

Margaret Sackville, 1881—   . "Epitaphs," "Vale," "The Apple," "Syrinx."

Herbert Asquith, 1881—1947. "The Volunteer."

Robin Flower, 1881—   . "The Pipes," "Saint Ite," "Say Not That Beauty," "Troy."

Alexander Robertson, 1882—1916. "Au Revoir," " 'We Shall Drink to Them That Sleep.' "

Mary Webb, 1883—1927. "The Land Within."

R. H. Mottram, 1883—   . "The Flower of Battle."

J. Redwood Anderson, 1883—   . "Heat," "The Crane," "The Caravan."

F. B. Young, 1884—1954. "Cristo Morto," "Song of the Dark Ages," "The Gift," "The Leaning Elm," "Seascape," "Prothalamion," "Lochanilaun."

Lord Gorell, 1884—   . "London to Paris, by Air."

J. C. Squire, 1884—   . "The Ship," "Winter Nightfall," "Christmas Hymn for Lambeth," "There Was an Indian," "A Fresh Morning," "Rivers."

Anna Wickham, 1884—   . "To Men," "Creatrix," "Divorce," "Sehnsucht," "Meditation at Kew," "Envoi."

A. J. Young, 1885—   . "Good Friday," "Moschatel."

Gerald Gould, 1885—1936. "Portrait," "The Clouds Have Wings," "A Garden Is My Soul," "The Earth Child," "Mortality."

Willoughby Weaving, 1885—   . "August," "Song."

Edward Thompson, 1886—   . "Harbour Music," "The Author Writes His Own Epitaph."

Frances Cornford, 1886—   . "The Old Nurse," "The Hills," "In France," "Out of Doors," "Autumn Morning at Cambridge," "The Unbeseechable," "The Hills," "Susan to Diana," "To a Fat Lady Seen From the Train," "Pre-Existence."

Rupert Brooke, 1887—1915. "Dust," "The One Before the Last," "Second Best," "The Great Lover," "The Hill," "The Chilterns," "The Old Vicarage, Grantchester," "The Soldier," "Mutability," "The Fish," "Heaven," "Clouds," "The Dead," "The Treasure."

Douglas Goldring, 1887—   . "The Spanish Sailor," "West End Lane."

W. M. Letts, 1887—   . "The Spires of Oxford," "Grandeur," "In Service," "A Soft Day."

F. W. Harvey, 1888—   . "The Mole."

Julian Grenfell, 1888—1915. "To a Black Greyhound," "Into Battle."

E. H. W. Meyerstein, 1889—1952. "Ode on Nothing."

Walter J. Turner, 1889—1946. "Death's Men," "Talking with Soldiers," "Romance," "The Caves of Auvergne."

Arthur Waley, 1889—   . "Hot Cake," "The Cranes."

Isaac Rosenberg, 1890—1918. "The Jew," "The One Lost," "The Dead Heroes."

Sherard Vines, 1890—   . "A Song for Grocers."

Iolo Aneurin Williams, 1890—   . "A Monument," "A Dull Day," "Question and Answer," "Spring Sunshine."

Francis Ledwidge, 1891—1917. "Evening in February," "Pan," "The Wife of Llew," "The Wedding Morning," "Had I a Golden Pound," "June," "In September," "The Shadow People," "In France," "The Homecoming of the Sheep."

Edward Buxton Shanks, 1892—1953. "The Rainbow," "Woman's Song," "Memory," "The Glow-Worm," "The Storm," "The Haunting," "The Bitten Grass," "To the Unimplored Beloved," "Fete Galante: The Triumph of Love."

Wilfred Owen, 1893—1918. "The Send-Off," "The Chances," "Strange Meeting," "Anthem for Doomed Youth," "Futility," "Apologia a Pro Poemate Meo," "Greater Love."

Robert M. B. Nichols, 1893—1944. "The Tower," "The Sprig of Lime," "Last Words," "The Pilgrim," "Farewell to Place of Comfort," "Night Rhapsody," "Little Pony."

L. A. G. Strong, 1896—   . "Zeke," "Micky-the-Moon," "The Brewer's Man," "The Mad Woman of Punnet's Town."

F. C. Boden, 1903—   . "The Light," "In Normandy."

Peter Quennell, 1905—   . "Leviathan," "The Divers."

Gwen Clear, 1905—   . "Grief," "The Goodwife Relents," "Fiddle Song."

ESSAYISTS, CRITICS, AND SPECIAL WRITERS

William Henry Hudson, 1841—1922, naturalist, author. NATURE STUDIES: *Naturalist in La Plata* (1892), *British Birds* (1895), *Birds in London* (1898), *Nature in Downland* (1900), *Birds and Man* (1901), *Hampshire Days* (1903), *Afoot in England* (1909), *A Shepherd's Life* (1910), *Adventures Among Birds* (1913), *The Book of a Naturalist* (1919), *A Traveller in Little Things* (1921), *A Hind in Richmond Park* (1922). NOVELS: *Purple Land That England Lost* (1885), *Green Mansions* (1904). SHORT-STORIES: *El Ombú* (1902: also called *Tales of the Pampas* (1916). MISCELLANEOUS: *Little Boy Lost* (1905), stories; *Far Away and Long Ago* (1918), autobiography.

Charles Montagu Doughty, 1843—1926, author-traveller. POETRY: *The Dawn in Britain* (1906), *Adam Cast Forth* (1908), *The Cliffs* (1909), *The Titans* (1916), *Mansoul* (1920). TRAVEL: *Travels in Arabia Desert* (1888).

Edward Carpenter, 1844—1929, poet, social reformer. POETRY: *Towards Democracy* (1883). SOCIAL STUDIES: *England's Ideal and Other Papers on Social Subjects* (1887), *Civilisation: Its Cause and Cure* (1889), *Love's Coming-of-Age* (1896), *The Art of Creation* (1904), *The Intermediate Sex* (1908), *The Drama of Love and Death* (1912), *Towards Industrial Freedom* (1917). MISCELLANEOUS: *Days With Walt Whitman* (1906), criticism; *My Days and Dreams* (1916), autobiography.

R. B. Cunninghame Graham, 1852—1936, author, traveller. SKETCHES AND STORIES: *Thirteen Stories* (1900), *Success* (1902), *Scottish Stories* (1914), *Thirty Tales & Sketches* (1929). HISTORICAL STUDIES: *A Vanished Arcadia* (1901), *Hernando de Soto* (1903), *Bernal Diaz del Castillo* (1915), *A Brazilian Mystic* (1920), *The Conquest of New Granada* (1922), *Inveni Portam, Joseph Conrad* (1924), *The Conquest of the River Plate* (1924), *Doughty Deeds* (1925), *Pedro De Valdivia* (1926), *The Horses of the Conquest* (1930). TRAVEL: *Mogreb-el-Acksa* (1898).

Henry Woodd Nevinson, 1856—1941, essayist, critic. *Farewell to America* (1922), *Changes and Chances* (1923), *More Changes, More Chances* (1923), *Last Changes, Last Chances* (1928), *In the Dark Backward* (1934). OTHER WORKS: *Original Sinners* (1920), sketches; *Lines of Life* (1920), poetry; *Goethe, Man and Poet* (1931), biography.

Vernon Lee, pseudonym of **Violet Paget,** 1856—1935, essayist, novelist. ESSAYS AND STUDIES: *Studies of the Eighteenth Century in Italy* (1880), *Belcaro* (1881), *Euphorion* (1884—1885), *Renaissance Fancies and Studies* (1895), *Spirit of Rome* (1905), *Gospels of Anarchy and Other Contemporary Studies* (1908). *Beauty and Ugliness, and Other Studies in Psychological Aesthetics* (in collaboration with C. Anstruther-Thomson, 1912), *Vital Lies* (1912), *The Handling of Words, and Other Studies in Literary Psychology* (1923). MISCELLANEOUS: *Miss Brown* (1884), a novel; *The Golden Keys, and Other Essays on the Genius Loci* (1925).

(Henry) Havelock Ellis, 1859—1939, scientist, essayist. ESSAYS AND STUDIES: *The Criminal* (1890), *The New Spirit* (1890), *Man and Woman* (1894), *Affirmations* (1897), *The Dance of Life* (1927), *The Art of Life* (1929), *Studies in the Psychology of Sex* (I—VI, 1901—1910; VII, 1928), *Psychology of Sex* (1933). POETRY: *Sonnets With Folk Songs From the Spanish* (1925).

Goldsworthy Lowes Dickinson, 1862—1932, author. STUDIES: *Revolution and Reaction in Modern France* (1892), *The Greek View of Life* (1890), *Letters From John Chinaman* (1901), *War: Its Nature, Cause and Cure* (1923), *The International Anarchy, 1904—1914* (1926). DIALOGUES: *Modern Symposium* (1905), *After Two Thousand Years* (1930).

Roger Elliot Fry, 1866—1934, painter, art critic. ESSAYS AND STUDIES: *Vision and Design* (1920), *Transformations* (1926), *Cézanne* (1927), *Henri Matisse* (1930), *Characteristics of French Art* (1932).

George Gilbert Aimé Murray, 1866— 1957, classical scholar, translator. STUDIES: *Ancient Greek Literature: A History* (1897), *The Rise of the Greek Epic* (1907), *Four Stages of Greek Religion* (1912), *Euripides and His Age* (1913), *Religio Grammatici* (1918), *The Classical Tradition in Poetry* (1927), *Aristophanes* (1933).

Edward Verrall Lucas, 1866—1938, essayist, traveller, critic. ESSAYS: *Old Lamps for New* (1911), *Traveller's Luck* (1930), *Saunterer's Reward* (1933). MISCELLANEOUS: *The Life of Charles Lamb* (1905), biography; *Listener's Lure* (1906), a novel.

Ernest Newman, 1868—   , music critic. STUDIES: *Gluck and the Opera* (1895), *Wagner* (1904), *Elgar* (1906), *Hugo Wolf* (1907), *Richard Strauss* (1908), *A Musical Motley* (1919), *A Musical Critic's Holiday* (1925), *The Unconscious Beethoven* (1927), *Stories of the Great Operas* (1929—1931), *The Life of Richard Wagner* (1933), *The Man Liszt* (1934).

Stephen Butler Leacock, 1869—1944, (Canadian) political economist, humorist. ESSAYS: *Literary Lapses* (1910), *Nonsense Novels* (1911), *Behind the Beyond, and Other Contributions to Human Knowledge* (1913), *Moonbeams From the Larger Lunacy* (1915), *Frenzied Fiction* (1918), *Winsome Winnie, and Other New Nonsense Novels* (1920), *My Discovery of England* (1922), *Over the Footlights, and Other Fancies* (1923), *Afternoons in Utopia* (1932). STUDIES: *Mark Twain* (1932), *Charles Dickens* (1933).

Hilaire Belloc (Joseph Hilaire Pierre Belloc), 1870—1953, extremely versatile writer. TRAVEL: *The Path to Rome* (1902), *The Old Road* (1904), *Hills and the Sea* (1906), *The Four Men* (1912). ESSAYS: *On Nothing & Kindred Subjects* (1908), *On Everything* (1909), *On Anything* (1910), *On Something* (1910). HISTORY: *A History of England* (1925—1928), *Europe and the Faith* (1920), *A Companion to Mr. Wells's "Outline of History"* (1926), *How the Reformation Happened* (1928), *Six British Battles* (1931). BIOGRAPHIES: *Danton* (1899), *Robespierre* (1901), *Marie Antoinette* (1909), *Joan of Arc* (1929), *Richelieu* (1930), *Wolsey* (1930). NOVELS: *Mr. Clutterbuck's Election* (1908), *A Change in the Cabinet* (1909), *The Girondin* (1911), *The Green Overcoat* (1912). CHILDREN'S BOOKS: *The Bad Child's Book of Beasts* (1896), *More Beasts for Worse Children* (1897), *The Modern Traveller* (1898), *Cautionary Tales for Children* (1907). POEMS: "The South Country," "Dawn Shall Over Lethe Break," "The False Heart," "Tarantella," "On a Dead Hostess," "The Night," "To Olive."

Max Beerbohm, 1872—1957, essayist, caricaturist, critic. ESSAYS: *The Works of Max Beerbohm* (1896), *And Even Now* (1920), *Around Theaters* (1924). CARICATURES AND CARTOONS: *Caricatures of Twenty-Five Gentlemen* (1896), *The Poet's Corner* (1904), *A Book of Caricatures* (1907), *Fifty Caricatures* (1913), *A Survey* (1921), *Rossetti and His Circle* (1922), *Observations* (1925). PARODIES:

Zuleika Dobson (1911), *A Christmas Garland* (1912). STORIES: *The Happy Hypocrite* (1897), *Seven Men* (1919).

John Cowper Powys, 1872— , author, lecturer. ESSAYS AND STUD-IES: *One Hundred Best Books* (1916), *Suspended Judgments* (1916), *The Complex Vision* (1920), *Religion of a Skeptic* (1925), *The Meaning of Culture* (1929), *In Defence of Sensuality* (1930), *A Philosophy of Solitude* (1933). NOVELS: *Wood and Stone* (1917), *Wolf Solent* (1929), *A Glastonbury Romance* (1933), *Weymouth Sands* (1934). POETRY: *Wolf's-Bane, Rhymes* (1916), *Mandragora* (1917).

Bertrand (Arthur William) Russell, 1872— , philosopher, mathematician. SCIENTIFIC AND PHILOSOPHICAL STUDIES: *The Principles of Mathematics* (1903), *Principia Mathematica* (in collaboration with Alfred N. Whitehead, 1910—1913), *Why Men Fight* (1917), *Mysticism and Logic, and Other Essays* (1918), *Roads to Freedom: Socialism, Anarchism, and Syndicalism* (1918), *Introduction to Mathematical Philosophy* (1919), *The Prospects of Industrial Civilization* (in collaboration with Dora Russell, 1923), *Icarus; or, the Future of Science* (1924), *What I Believe* (1925), *The Analysis of Matter* (1927), *An Outline of Philosophy* (1927), *Selected Papers of Bertrand Russell* (1927), *Marriage and Morals* (1929), *The Scientific Outlook* (1931), *Education and the Social Order* (1932), *Freedom and Organization, 1814—1914* (1934), *The Meaning of Marx,* a symposium (1934).

Gilbert Keith Chesterton, 1874—1936, essayist, critic, novelist, poet, journalist. ESSAYS AND STUDIES: *Heretics* (1905), *Orthodoxy* (1908), *Tremendous Trifles* (1909), *What's Wrong With the World* (1910), *A Short History of England* (1917), *The New Jerusalem* (1920), *The Superstition of Divorce* (1920), *The Everlasting Man* (1925), *Generally Speaking* (1928), *Come to Think of It* (1930). CRITICAL WORKS: *Twelve Types* (1902), *Robert Browning* (1903), *Charles Dickens* (1906), *George Bernard Shaw* (1909), *William Blake* (1910), *Appreciations and Criticisms of the Works of Charles Dickens* (1911), *The Victorian Age in Literature* (1913), *St. Francis of Assisi* (1923), *William Cobbett* (1926), *Robert Louis Stevenson* (1927), *Chaucer* (1932). NOVELS: *The Napoleon of Notting Hill* (1904), *The Man Who Was Thursday* (1908), *The Ball and the Cross* (1909), *Manalive* (1912), *The Flying Inn* (1914). POETRY: *The Ballad of the White Horse* (1911), *Wine, Water and Song* (1915), *Lepanto* (1929), *New and Collected Poems* (1929). IMPORTANT POEMS: "A Christmas Song for Three Guilds," "Lepanto," "A Cider Song," "The Holy of Holies," "The Donkey," "The Secret People," "The Ballad of the White Horse." SHORT-STORIES: *The Innocence of Father Brown* (1911), *The Wisdom of Father Brown* (1914), *The Man Who Knew Too Much and Other Stories* (1922). MISCELLANEOUS: *What I Saw in America* (1922), travel; *The Judgment of Dr. Johnson* (1927), play.

Maurice Baring, 1874—1945, diplomat, journalist, poet, playwright, novelist, short-story writer, translator. ESSAYS AND STUDIES: *The Russian People* (1911), *The Mainsprings of Russia* (1914), *An Outline of Russian Literature* (1914), *Punch and Judy, and Other Essays* (1924), *Lost Lectures* (1932), *Sarah Bernhardt* (1933). POETRY: *Collected Poems* (1925), *Selected Poems of Maurice Baring* (1930). IMPORTANT POEMS: "In Memoriam: A. H.," "Elegy on the Death of Juliet's Owl," "Julian Grenfell," "Pierre." PLAYS: *Gaston de Foix and Other Plays* (1903), *Diminutive Dramas* (1911). NOVELS: *C* (1924), *Cat's Cradle* (1925), *Daphne Adeane* (1926). SHORT-STORIES: *In My End Is My Beginning* (1931).

Desmond MacCarthy, 1878—1952, STUDIES: *The Court Theatre 1904—1907* (1907), *Portraits* (1931), *Criticism* (1932).

(Giles) Lytton Strachey, 1880—1932, biographer. BIOGRAPHY: *Eminent Victorians: Cardinal Manning, Florence Nightingale, Dr. Arnold, General Gordon* (1918), *Queen Victoria* (1921), *Elizabeth and Essex* (1928), *Portraits in Miniature* (1931). ESSAYS AND STUDIES: *Landmarks in French Literature* (1912), *Books and Characters,* (1922), *Pope* (1925).

Llewelyn Powys, 1884—1939, essayist. ESSAYS: *Thirteen Worthies* (1923), *Impassioned Clay* (1931). AUTOBIOGRAPHY: *Skin for Skin* (1925). SKETCHES: *Black Laughter* (1924).

Julian Sorell Huxley, 1887—   , biologist, writer. STUDIES: *Essays of a Biologist* (1923), *The Stream of Life* (1926), *Religion Without Revelation* (1927), *The Science of Life* (in collaboration with H. G. Wells and G. P. Wells, 1931), *What Dare I Think?* (1931), *A Scientist Among the Soviets* (1932), *If I Were Dictator* (1934). TRAVEL: *Africa View* (1931).

Thomas Edward Lawrence, 1888—1935, adventurer, soldier, scholar. DESCRIPTION AND TRAVEL: *Seven Pillars of Wisdom* (1926), *Revolt in the Desert,* an abridgment of *Seven Pillars of Wisdom* (1927). OTHER WORKS: *The Wilderness of Zin,* in collaboration with C. L. Woolley (1915), an archaeological report; *The Odyssey of Homer,* a translation (1932).

John Middleton Murry, 1889—1957, critic, poet, novelist. ESSAYS AND STUDIES: *Countries of the Mind* (1922), *The Problem of Style* (1922), *To the Unknown God* (1924), *Keats and Shakespeare* (1925), *Son of Woman* (1931), *The Life of Katherine Mansfield,* in collaboration with Ruth E. Mantz (1933), *The Reminiscences of D. H. Lawrence* (1933), *William Blake* (1933). IMPORTANT POEMS: "Serenity," "Train Journey," "Tolstoy."

Ivor Armstrong Richards, 1893—   , critic. STUDIES: *Principles of Literary Criticism* (1924), *Practical Criticism* (1929).

Herbert Edward Read, 1893—   , essayist, poet. ESSAYS AND STUDIES: *Reason and Romanticism* (1926), *The Sense of Glory* (1929). POETRY: *Collected Poems, 1913—1925* (1926).

Sacheverell Sitwell, 1897—   , poet, essayist. POETRY: *Doctor Donne & Gargantua* (1930). IMPORTANT POEMS: "Fountains," "The Red-Gold Rain," "Tulip Tree." STUDIES: *The Gothick North: The Visit of the Gypsies, These Sad Ruins, The Fair-Haired Victory* (1929—1930). OTHER WORKS: *All Summer in a Day* (1926), autobiography; *Far From My Home* (1931), stories; *Liszt* (1934), biography.

THE IRISH LITERARY RENAISSANCE

Important Irish Poets

Douglas Hyde, 1860—   , poet, scholar, first President of Eire (the former Irish Free State). FOLK-STORIES, STUDIES, AND TRANSLATIONS: *Beside the Fire* (1890), *Abhráin Gráidh Chuige Connacht, or, Love Songs of Connacht* (1893), *The Revival of Irish Literature* (in collaboration with Sir Charles G. Duffy and George Sigerson, 1894), *Three Stories of Story-Telling and Ballads of St. Columkill* (1895), *Literary History of Ireland* (1899), *Legends of Saints and Sinners* (1915). IMPORTANT POEMS: "Ringleted Youth of My Love," "My Grief on the Sea," "The Cooleen," "I Shall Not Die for Thee."

William Butler Yeats, 1865—1939, poet, dramatist. POETRY: *The Poetical Works of William B. Yeats* (1906—1907), *The Wild Swans at Coole* (1918), *The Tower* (1928), *Collected Poems* (1933). IMPORTANT POEMS: "The Cap and the Bells," "The Lake Isle of Innisfree," "The Rose of Battle," "The Wild Swans at Coole," "The Rose of Peace," "The Cat and the Moon," "Down by the Salley Gardens," "When You Are Old," "The Fiddler of Dooney," "Where My Books Go," "It Is Time That I Wrote My Will." PLAYS: *Cathleen ni Hoolihan* (1902), *Plays: The Hour-Glass, Cathleen ni Houlihan, The Pot of Broth* (1904), *Plays: The King's Threshold and On Baile's Strand* (1904). REMINISCENCES: *Autobiographies: Reveries Over Childhood and Youth and the Trembling of the Veil* (1926).

George William Russell, known under the pseudonym of **AE,** 1867—1935, poet, painter. POETRY: *Collected Poems* (1913; 1926). IMPORTANT POEMS: "The Man to the Angel," "The Gift," "The City," "By the Margin of the Great Deep," "Babylon," "A Memory of Earth," "Reconciliation," "The Great Breath," "Star Teachers," "Unity," "A Summer Night." BELLES LETTRES: *Imaginations and Reveries* (1915). PLAY: *Deirdre* (1907).

Katherine Tynan (Mrs. Henry Hinkson), 1861—1931, poet, novelist. POETRY: *Ballads and Lyrics* (1892), *Irish Poems* (1913), *Flower of Youth* (1915), *Collected Poems* (1930). IMPORTANT POEMS: "Of an Orchard," "Sheep and Lambs," "A Prayer." AUTOBIOGRAPHY: *Twenty-Five Years* (1913), *The Middle Years* (1916), *The Years of the Shadow* (1919), *The Wandering Years* (1922), *Memories* (1924).

Seumas O'Sullivan (James Starkey), 1878—   , poet. POETRY: *Twilight People* (1905), *The Earth Lover* (1909), *Poems* (1912), *The Poems of Seumas O'Sullivan* (1923). IMPORTANT POEMS: "The Rosses," "Have Thou No Fear," "The Twilight People," "Credo."

Padraic Colum, 1881—   , poet, dramatist. POETRY: *Wild Earth* (1907), *Dramatic Legends and Other Poems* (1922), *Creatures* (1928), *Poems* (1932). IMPORTANT POEMS: "The Plougher," "A Cradle Song," "The Deer of Ireland," "An Old Woman of the Roads," "Wild Ass." PLAYS: *Three Plays: The Fiddler's House, The Land, Thomas Muskerry* (1917). MISCELLANEOUS: *The Bright Island* (1925), *The Road Round Ireland* (1926), *Orpheus: Myths of the World* (1930), all folklore or travel; *The Fountain of Youth* (1927), fairy tales; *Castle Conquer* (1923), novel.

James Stephens, 1882—1950, poet, novelist. POETRY: *Insurrection* (1909), *The Hill of Vision* (1912), *The Adventures of Seumas Beg; The Rocky Road to Dublin* (1915), *Reincarnations* (1918), *Collected Poems* (1926), *Strict Joy* (1931). IMPORTANT POEMS: "The Watcher," "The Snare," "In the Cool of the Evening," "The Seeker," "The Red-Haired Man's Wife," "Deirdre," "The Shell," "The Coolun," "The Fullness of Time," "The Centaurs," "The Devil's Bag," "The Goat-Paths," "The Breath of Life," "What Thomas an Biule Said in a Pub." PROSE FICTION: *Mary, Mary* (1912), *The Crock of Gold* (1912), *The Demi-Gods* (1914), *Deirdre* (1923), *In the Land of Youth* (1924). SHORT-STORIES AND TALES: *Here Are Ladies* (1913), *Irish Fairy Tales* (1920), *Etched in Moonlight* (1928).

Important Irish Dramatists

John Millington Synge, 1871—1909, dramatist, poet. PLAYS: *Shadow of the Glen* (1903), *Riders to the Sea* (1904), *The Well of the Saints* (1905), *The Playboy of the Western World* (1907), *The Tinker's Wedding* (1908), *Deirdre of the Sorrows* (unfinished, 1910).

Lady Augusta Persse Gregory, 1852—1932, dramatist, author, translator. PLAYS: *Spreading the News* (1907), *Seven Short Plays: Spreading the News, Hyacinth Halvey, The Rising of the Moon, The Jackdaw, The Workhouse Ward, The Travelling Man, The Goal Gate* (1909), *New Comedies: The Bogie Men, The Full Moon, Coats, Damer's Gold, McDonough's Wife* (1914). MISCELLANEOUS: *Our Irish Theatre* (1913), autobiography; *Coole* (1931), essays.

George Bernard Shaw, 1856—1950, dramatist, critic, social reformer. PLAYS: *Plays, Pleasant and Unpleasant: Widower's Houses, The Philanderer, Mrs. Warren's Profession, Arms and the Man, Candida, The Man of Destiny, You Never Can Tell* (1898), *Three Plays for Puritans: The Devil's Disciple, Caesar and Cleopatra, Captain Brassbound's Conversion* (1901), *The Doctor's Dilemma, Getting Married, and The Showing-up of Blanco Posnet* (1911), *Heartbreak House* (1919), *Back to*

Methuselah (1921), *Saint Joan* (1924), *The Apple Cart* (1930), *The Complete Plays of Bernard Shaw* (1931). ESSAYS AND STUDIES: *Intelligent Woman's Guide to Socialism and Capitalism* (1928), *Music in London, 1890—1894* (1932), *Our Theatres in the 'Nineties* (1932), *Prefaces* (1934). LETTERS: *Ellen Terry and Bernard Shaw* (1931).

Lord Dunsany (Edward John Moreton Drax Plunkett, 18th Baron), 1878—1958, dramatist. PLAYS: *Five Plays: The Gods of the Mountain, The Golden Doom, King Argimenes and the Unknown Warrior, The Glittering Gate, The Lost Silk Hat* (1914), *Plays of God and Men* (1917), *Alexander; and Three Small Plays* (1925). STORIES: *Gods of Pegana* (1905), *The Sword of Welleran, and Other Stories* (1908), *A Dreamer's Tales* (1910), *Tales of Wonder* (1916), *The Chronicles of Rodriguez* (1922), *The Evil Kettle* (1925), *The Travel Tales of Mr. Joseph Jorkens* (1931), *Mr. Jorkens Remembers Africa* (1934).

Lennox Robinson (Esmé Stuart Lennox), 1886—   , dramatist. PLAYS: *The Cross-Roads* (1909), *Two Plays: Harvest, The Clancy Name* (1910), *Patriots* (1912), *The Dreamers* (1915), *The Lost Leader* (1918), *Whiteheaded Boy* (1920). *The Round Table* (1924), *The Far-Off Hills* (1931), *Is Life Worth Living* (1933). NOVEL: *A Young Man From the South* (1917).

Sean O'Casey, 1890—   , dramatist. PLAYS: *The Shadow of a Gunman* (1923), *Juno and the Paycock* (1924), *The Plough and the Stars* (1926), *The Silver Tassie* (1928), *Within the Gates* (1933).

Irish Novelists

George Moore, 1852—1933, novelist. NOVELS: *Modern Lover* (1883), *Mummer's Wife* (1884—1887), *Esther Waters* (1894), *Evelyn Innes* (1898), *Sister Theresa* (1901 and 1909), *The Lake* (1905), *The Brook Kerith* (1916), *Héloise & Abélard* (1921). SHORT-STORIES: *Untilled Field* (1903), *In Single Strictness* (1922). AUTOBIOGRAPHY: *Confessions of a Young Man* (1888—1889), *Memoirs of My Dead Life* (1906), *"Hail and Farewell!" Ave* (1911—1912), *Conversations in Ebury Street* (1924).

James Joyce, 1882—1941, novelist, poet. NOVELS: *A Portrait of the Artist as a Young Man* (1917), *Ulysses* (1922). POETRY: *Chamber Music* (1907), *Pomes Penyeach* (1927). IMPORTANT POEMS: "O, It Was Out by Donnycarney," "Tutto e Sciolto," "I Hear an Army," "On the Beach at Fontana," "Strings in the Earth." MISCELLANEOUS: *Dubliners* (1914), short-stories; *Exiles* (1918), a play; *Anna Livia Plurabelle* (1930) and *Two Tales of Shem and Shaun* (1932), both from *Work In Progress* (1927—).

St. John Greer Ervine, 1883—   , dramatist, novelist. PLAYS: *Mixed Marriage* (1911), *The Magnanimous Lover* (1912), *Jane Clegg* (1914), *John Ferguson* (1915), *The First Mrs. Fraser* (1929). NOVELS: *Mrs. Martin's Man* (1914), *Alice and a Family* (1915), *Changing Winds* (1917), *The Foolish Lovers* (1920), *The Wayward Man* (1927). MISCELLANEOUS: *The Theatre in My Time* (1933), studies; *Some Impressions of My Elders* (1922), reminiscences.

Liam O'Flaherty, 1896—   , novelist. NOVELS: *Thy Neighbour's Wife* (1923), *The Informer* (1925), *Mr. Gilhooley* (1926), *The Assassin* (1928), *The House of Gold* (1929). SHORT-STORIES: *Spring Sowing* (1924), *Red Barbara; and Other Stories: The Mountain Tavern, Prey, The Oar* (1928). AUTOBIOGRAPHY: *Two Years* (1930).

SUPPLEMENTARY LIST OF WRITERS[1]

A BECKETT, GILBERT ABBOTT, 1811—1856.

ACTON, SIR JOHN EMERICH EDWARD DALBERG, *first Baron Acton,* 1834—1902.

ADAMS, SARAH FLOWER, 1805—1848.

ADAMSON, ROBERT, 1852—1902.

AINGER, ALFRED, 1837—1904.

AINSWORTH, WILLIAM HARRISON, 1805—1882.

AKENSIDE, MARK, 1721—1770.

ALEXANDER, SIR WILLIAM, *Earl of Stirling,* c. 1567—1640.

ALISON, SIR ARCHIBALD, 1792—1867.

ALKEN, HENRY, *fl.* 1816—1831.

ALLEN, GRANT, 1848—1899.

ALLEN, RALPH, 1694—1764.

ALLINGHAM, WILLIAM, 1824—1889.

AMORY, THOMAS, c. 1691—1788.

ANDREWES, LANCELOT, 1555—1626.

ANGELO, HENRY, 1760—c. 1839.

ANSON, GEORGE, *Baron Anson,* 1697—1762.

ANSON, SIR WILLIAM REYNELL, 1843—1914.

ANSTEY, CHRISTOPHER, 1724—1805.

ARBUTHNOT, JOHN, 1667—1735.

ARMSTRONG, JOHN, 1709—1779.

ARNOLD, SIR EDWIN, 1832—1904.

ARNOLD, THOMAS, 1795—1842.

ARNOLD, SIR THOMAS WALKER, 1864—1930.

ASHE, THOMAS, 1836—1889.

ASHMOLE, ELIAS, 1617—1692.

ASTLEY, SIR JACOB, *Baron Astley,* 1579—1652.

ATTERBURY, FRANCIS, 1662—1732.

AUBREY, JOHN, 1626—1697.

AUDEN, W. H., 1907—   .

AUSTIN, ALFRED, 1835—1913.

AUSTIN, JOHN, 1790—1859.

AUSTIN, SARAH, 1793—1867.

AYTOUN or AYTON, SIR ROBERT, 1570—1638.

AYTOUN, WILLIAM EDMONDSTOUNE, 1813—1865.

BAFFIN, WILLIAM, *d.* 1622.

BAGE, ROBERT, 1728—1801.

BAGEHOT, WALTER, 1826—1877.

BAILEY, NATHAN or NATHANIEL, *d.* 1742.

BAILEY, PHILIP JAMES, 1816—1902.

BAILLEE, ROBERT, 1599—1662.

BAILLIE, JOANNA, 1762—1851.

BAKER, SIR SAMUEL WHITE, 1821—1893.

BALFOUR, ARTHUR JAMES, *Earl of,* 1848—1930.

BALLANTYNE, ROBERT MICHAEL, 1825—1894.

BANIM, JOHN, 1796—1874.

BANKS, SIR JOSEPH, 1743—1820.

BARBAULD, MRS. ANNE LETITIA, 1743—1825.

BARCLAY, JOHN, 1582—1621.

BARHAM, RICHARD HARRIS, 1788—1845.

BARING-GOULD, SABINE, 1834—1924.

BARKER, HARLEY GRANVILLE, 1877—1946.

BARNES, BARNABE, c. 1569—1609.

BARNES, WILLIAM, 1801—1886.

BARNFIELD, RICHARD, 1574—1627.

BARROW, ISAAC, 1630—1677.

BARROW, SIR JOHN, 1764—1848.

BATES, HENRY WALTER, 1825—1892.

BAXTER, RICHARD, 1615—1691.

BAYLY, THOMAS HAYNES, 1797—1839.

BEARDSLEY, AUBREY VINCENT, 1872—1898.

BEATTIE, JAMES, 1735—1803.

BEAUMONT, SIR JOHN, 1582—1627.

---

1 To facilitate reference, the arrangement of the authors is alphabetical. It is suggested that some information be compiled about each author in the list, possibly in the manner exemplified by the Charts in the *Outline-History* (pp. 21 33-38, 61, 99).

BECKFORD, PETER, 1740—1811.
BECKFORD, WILLIAM, *c.* 1760—1844.
BEDDOES, THOMAS LOVELL, 1803—1849.
BELLENDEN, JOHN, *c.* 1495—*c.* 1550.
BENSON, EDWARD FREDERIC, 1867—1940.
BENTHAM, JEREMY, 1748—1832.
BENTLEY, PHYLLIS (ELEANOR), 1894— .
BENTLEY, RICHARD, 1662—1742.
BERESFORD, JOHN DAVYS, 1873—1947.
BERKELEY, GEORGE, 1685—1753.
BERTRAM, CHARLES, 1723—1765.
BESANT, SIR WALTER, 1836—1901.
BESIER, RUDOLF, 1818—? .
BICKERSTAFFE, ISAAC, *d. c.* 1812.
BIRRELL, AUGUSTINE, 1850—1933.
BLACK, WILLIAM, 1841—1898.
BLACKMORE, SIR RICHARD, *d.* 1729.
BLACKMORE, RICHARD DODDRIDGE, 1825—1900.
BLACKSTONE, SIR WILLIAM, 1723—1780.
BLAIR, ROBERT, 1699—1746.
BLAKMAN, JOHN, *fl.* 1436—1448.
BLESSINGTON, MARGUERITE POWER, *Countess of,* 1789—1849.
BLOOMFIELD, ROBERT, 1766—1823.
BOHN, HENRY GEORGE, 1796—1884.
BOLINGBROKE, HENRY ST. JOHN, *first Viscount,* 1678—1751.
BORROW, GEORGE, 1803—1881.
BOWDLER, THOMAS, 1754—1825.
BOWEN, ELIZABETH D. C., 1899— .
BOWLES, WILLIAM LISLE, 1762—1850.
BOYER, ABEL, 1667—1729.
BOYLE, ROGER, *first earl of Orrery,* 1621—1679.
BRACTON, HENRY DE, *d.* 1268.
BRADDON, MARY ELIZABETH (MRS. MAXWELL), 1837—1915.
BRADLAUGH, CHARLES, 1833—1891.
BRADLEY, ANDREW CECIL, 1851—1935.
BRADLEY, EDWARD, 1827—1889.
BRADLEY, FRANCIS HERBERT, 1846—1924.
BRADLEY, DR. HENRY, 1845—1923.
BRADSHAW, HENRY, 1831—1886.
BRETON, NICHOLAS, *c.* 1545—*c.* 1626.
BRIGHOUSE, HAROLD, 1882— .
BROOKE, HENRY, 1703—1783.
BROME, RICHARD, *d. c.* 1652.
BROOKE or BROKE, ARTHUR, *d.* 1563.
BROUGHAM, HENRY PETER, (BARON BROUGHAM and VAUX), 1778—1868.
BROUGHTON, RHODA, 1840—1920.
BROWN, G. D., 1869—1902.
BROWN, DR. JOHN, 1810—1882.
BROWN, THOMAS, 1663—1704.

BROWN, THOMAS EDWARD, 1830—1897.
BROWNE, ISAAC HAWKINS, 1705—1760.
BROWNE, THOMAS ALEXANDER, 1826—1915.
BRUCE, JAMES, 1730—1794.
BRYCE, JAMES, 1838—1922.
BRYDGES, SIR SAMUEL EGERTON, 1762—1837.
BUCHAN, JOHN, 1875—1940.
BUCHANAN, GEORGE, 1506—1582.
BUCHANAN, ROBERT WILLIAMS, 1841—1901.
BUCK, SIR GEORGE, *d.* 1623.
BUCKINGHAM, GEORGE VILLIERS, *second duke of,* 1628—1687.
BUCKLAND, FRANCIS TREVELYAN, 1826—1880.
BUCKLE, HENRY THOMAS, 1821—1862.
BUDGELL, EUSTACE, 1686—1737.
BULLETT, GERALD W., 1893— .
BUNBURY, HENRY WILLIAM, 1750—1811.
BURDETT, OSBERT, 1885— .
BURGOYNE, SIR JOHN, 1722—1792.
BURKE, THOMAS, 1886—1945.
BURNABY, FREDERICK GUSTAVUS, 1842—1885.
BURNAND, SIR FRANCIS COWLEY, 1836—1917.
BURNET, GILBERT, 1643—1715.
BURNET, THOMAS, *c.* 1635—1715.
BURTON, JOHN HILL, 1809—1881.
BURTON, SIR RICHARD FRANCIS, 1821—1890.
BUTLER, ALBAN, 1711—1773.
BUTLER, JOSEPH, 1692—1752.
BYROM, JOHN, 1692—1763.
BYRON, HENRY JAMES, 1834—1884.
BYRON, JOHN, 1723—1786.
BYWATER, INGRAM, 1840—1914.

CAINE, SIR THOMAS HENRY HALL, 1853—1931.
CAIRD, EDWARD, 1835—1908.
CAIRD, JOHN, 1820—1898.
CALVERLEY, CHARLES STUART, 1831—1884.
CAMDEN, WILLIAM, 1551—1623.
CAMPBELL, ROY D., 1902—1957.
CAMPBELL, THOMAS, 1777—1844.
CANNAN, GILBERT, 1884— .
CANNING, GEORGE, 1770—1827.
CAREY, HENRY, *d.* 1743.
CARLETON, WILLIAM, 1794—1869.
CARLISLE, FREDERICK HOWARD, *fifth earl of,* 1748—1825.
CARLYLE, ALEXANDER, 1722—1805.
CARPENTER, JOHN, *c.* 1370—*c.* 1441.
CARTER, ELIZABETH, 1717—1806.
CARTON, RICHARD CLAUDE, 1856—1928.

SUPPLEMENTARY LIST OF WRITERS 603

CARY, HENRY FRANCIS, 1772—1844.
CARYLL, JOHN, 1625—1711.
CAVENDISH, GEORGE, 1500—c. 1561.
CECIL, LORD (EDWARD CHRISTIAN)
    DAVID, 1902— .
CENTLIVRE, SUSANNAH, c. 1667—1723.
CHALMERS, THOMAS, 1780—1847.
CHAMBERLAYNE, EDWARD, 1616—1703.
CHAMBERLAYNE, WILLIAM,
    1619—1689.
CHAMBERS, SIR EDMUND KERCHEVER,
    1866—1954.
CHAMBERS, EPHRAIM, d. 1740.
CHAMBERS, ROBERT, 1802—1871.
CHAPONE, HESTER, 1727—1801.
CHEKE, SIR JOHN, 1514—1557.
CHETTLE, HENRY, d. 1607.
CHESNEY, SIR GEORGE TOMKYNS,
    1830—1895.
CHILLINGWORTH, WILLIAM, 1602—1644.
CHRISTOPHER NORTH, a pseudonym
    used by J. Wilson, 1785—1854, q.v.
CHURCH, RICHARD WILLIAM,
    1815—1890.
CHURCHILL, CHARLES, 1731—1764.
CHURCHILL, RT. HON. WINSTON
    (LEONARD SPENCER), 1874— .
CHURCHYARD, THOMAS, c. 1520—1604.
CIBBER, COLLEY, 1671—1757.
CIRCENSTER, RICHARD of, d. c. 1401.
CLARE, JOHN, 1793—1864.
CLARENDON, EDWARD HYDE, First Earl of,
    1609—1674.
CLARK, CHARLES COWDEN,
    1787—1877.
CLARK, JOHN WILLIS, 1833—1910.
CLARKE, MARCUS ANDREW HISLOP,
    1846—1881.
CLARKE, MARY VICTORIA COWDEN,
    1809—1898.
CLARKE, SAMUEL, 1675—1729.
CLARKHILL, JOHN, fl. 1600.
CLERK-MAXWELL, JAMES, 1831—1879.
CLEVELAND, JOHN, 1613—1658.
CLIFFORD, SOPHIA LUCY, d. 1920.
CLIFFORD, WILLIAM KINGDON,
    1845—1879.
CLIVE, MRS. CAROLINE ARCHER,
    1801—1873.
CLOUGH, ARTHUR HUGH, 1819—1861.
COBBE, FRANCES POWER, 1822—1904.
COBBETT, WILLIAM, 1762—1835.
COCKER, EDWARD, 1631—1675.
COKE, SIR EDWARD, 1552—1634.
COLE, G. D. H., 1889— .
COLENSO, JOHN WILLIAM, 1814—1883.
COLERIDGE, HARTLEY, 1796—1849.
COLERIDGE, MARY ELIZABETH,
    1861—1907.
COLERIDGE, SARA, 1802—1852.

COLLINS, ANTHONY, 1676—1729.
COLLINS, JOHN CHURTON, 1848—1908.
COLLINS, WILLIAM WILKIE,
    1824—1889.
COLMAN, GEORGE, the elder,
    1732—1794.
COLMAN, GEORGE, the younger,
    1762—1836.
COLTON, CHARLES CALEB,
    c. 1780—1832.
COLVIN, SIR SIDNEY, 1845—1927.
COMBE, WILLIAM, 1741—1823.
CONINGTON, JOHN, 1825—1869.
CONSTABLE, HENRY, 1562—1613.
COOK, ELIZA, 1818—1889.
COOK, JAMES, 1728—1779.
CORBET, RICHARD, 1582—1635.
CORELLI, MARIE, 1864—1924.
CORY, WILLIAM JOHNSON, 1823—1892.
CORYATE, THOMAS, c. 1577—1617.
COTGRAVE, RANDLE, d. c. 1634.
COTTON, SIR ROBERT BRUCE,
    1571—1631.
COUCH, SIR ARTHUR THOMAS QUILLER,
    1863—1944 .
COURTHOPE, WILLIAM JOHN,
    1842—1917.
COVENTRY, FRANCIS, d.c. 1759.
COWLEY, MRS. HANNAH, 1743—1809.
CRAIK, DINAH MARIA, 1826—1887.
CREEVEY, THOMAS, 1768—1838.
CREIGHTON, MANDELL, 1843—1901.
CRICHTON, JAMES, The Admirable,
    1560—c. 1585.
CROCKETT, S. R., 1860—1914.
CROKER, JOHN WILSON, 1780—1857.
CROKER, THOMAS CROFTON,
    1798—1854.
CROLY, GEORGE, 1780—1860.
CROWNE, JOHN, 1640—c. 1703.
CRUDEN, ALEXANDER, 1701—1770.
CUDWORTH, RALPH, 1617—1688.
CULVERWEL, NATHANAEL, d. 1651.
CUMBERLAND, RICHARD, 1732—1811.
CUNNINGHAM, ALLAN, 1784—1842.
CUNNINGHAM, JOHN, 1729—1773.
CURLL, EDMUND, 1675—1747.
CURZON, ROBERT, fourteenth Baron
    Zouche, 1810—1873.
CURZON OF KEDLESTON, GEORGE
    NATHANIEL, first Marquess,
    1859—1925.
DAMPIER, WILLIAM, 1652—1715.
DANETT, THOMAS, fl. 1566—1601.
DARLEY, GEORGE, 1795—1846.
DARWIN, CHARLES ROBERT,
    1809—1882.
DARWIN, ERASMUS, 1731—1802.
DASENT, SIR GEORGE WEBBE,
    1817—1896.

FITZ STEPHEN, WILLIAM, *d. c.* 1190.
FLATMAN, THOMAS, 1637—1688.
FLECKER, HERMAN JAMES ELROY, 1884—1915.
FLECKNOE, RICHARD, *d.c.* 1678.
FLEMING, MARGARET, 1803—1811.
FLETCHER, GILES (the Elder), *c.* 1549—1611.
FLINT, F. S., 1885—
FLORIO, JOHN, *c.* 1553—1625.
FLUDD, ROBERT, 1574—1637.
FOOTE, SAMUEL, 1720—1777.
FORD, RICHARD, 1796—1858.
FORSTER, JOHN, 1812—1876.
FORTESCUE, HON. SIR JOHN, 1859—1933.
FOX, GEORGE, 1624—1691.
FRANCIS, SIR PHILIP, 1740—1818.
FRANKLIN, SIR JOHN, 1786—1847.
FRASER, ALEXANDER CAMPBELL, 1819—1914.
FRAUNCE, ABRAHAM, *fl.* 1587—1633.
FRAZER, SIR JAMES GEORGE, 1854—1941.
FREEMAN, EDWARD AUGUSTUS, 1823—1892.
FRERE, JOHN HOOKMAN, 1769—1846.
FROUDE, JAMES ANTHONY, 1818—1894.
FROUDE, RICHARD HURRELL, 1803—1836.
FURNIVALL, FREDERICK JAMES, 1825—1910.

GAIRDNER, JAMES, 1828—1912.
GALE, NORMAN ROWLAND, 1862—1942.
GALT, JOHN, 1779—1839.
GARDINER, SAMUEL RAWSON, 1829—1902.
GARNETT, EDWARD WILLIAM, 1868—1937.
GARNETT, RICHARD, 1835—1906.
GARRICK, DAVID, 1717—1779.
GARTH, SIR SAMUEL, 1661—1719.
GARVICE, CHARLES, *d.* 1920.
GAUDEN, JOHN, 1605—1662.
GENEST, JOHN, 1764—1839.
GERARD, JOHN, 1545—1612.
GERHARDI, WILLIAM ALEXANDER, 1895—
GIFFORD, WILLIAM, 1756—1826.
GILBERT, SIR HUMPHREY, *c.* 1539—1583.
GILBERT, WILLIAM, 1540—1603.
GILCHRIST, ALEXANDER, 1828—1861.
GILPIN, WILLIAM, 1724—1804.
GISSING, GEORGE ROBERT, 1857—1903.
GLADSTONE, WILLIAM EWART, 1809—1898.
GLANVILL, JOSEPH, 1636—1680.
GLANVILLE, RANULF DE, 1130—1190.
GLAPTHORNE, HENRY, *fl.* 1635—1643.

GLASSE, HANNAH, *fl.* 1747.
GLOVER, RICHARD, 1712—1785.
GODLEY, ALFRED DENIS, 1856—1925.
GODWIN, MRS. MARY WOLLSTONECRAFT, 1759—1797.
GOLDING, ARTHUR, *c.* 1536—*c.* 1605.
GOOGE, BARNABE, 1540—1594.
GORDON, ADAM LINDSAY, 1833—1870.
GORDON, CHARLES GEORGE, 1833—1885.
GORE, MRS. CATHERINE GRACE FRANCES, 1799—1861.
GORE, CHARLES, 1853—1932.
GOULD, GERALD, 1885—1936.
GOULD, NATHANIEL, 1857—1919.
GRAFTON, RICHARD, *d. c.* 1572.
GRAHAME, KENNETH, 1859—1932.
GRAINGER, JAMES, 1721—1766.
GRAND, SARAH (pseudonym of MRS. DAVID C. M'FALL, *née* FRANCES ELIZABETH CLARKE), 1862—1943
GRANT, JAMES, 1822—1887.
GRAVES, ALFRED PERCEVAL, 1846—1931.
GRAVES, RICHARD, 1715—1804.
GRAY, DAVID, 1838—1861.
GREEN, JOHN RICHARD, 1837—1883.
GREEN, MRS. MARY ANNE EVERETT, 1818—1895.
GREEN, MATTHEW, 1696—1737.
GREEN, THOMAS HILL, 1836—1882.
GREENAWAY, KATE, 1846—1901.
GREG, WALTER WILSON, 1875—
GREVILLE, CHARLES CAVENDISH FULKE, 1794—1865.
GREVILLE, SIR FULKE, *Baron Brooke*, 1554—1628.
GREY OF FALL'ODON, EDWARD GREY, *Viscount*, 1862—1933.
GRIFFIN, GERALD, 1803—1840.
GRIMALD, GRIMALDE, or GRIMVALD, NICHOLAS, 1519—1562.
GROSART, ALEXANDER BALLOCH, 1827—1899.
GROSE, FRANCIS, *c.* 1731—1791.
GROSSETESTE, ROBERT, *d.* 1253.
GROTE, GEORGE, 1794—1871.
GROVE, SIR GEORGE, 1820—1900.
GUEDALLA, PHILIP, 1889—1944.
GUNNING, MRS. SUSANNAH, *c.* 1740—1800.
GURNEY, THOMAS, 1705—1770.

HABINGTON, WILLIAM, 1605—1654.
HAGGARD, SIR HENRY RIDER, 1856—1925.
HAKE, THOMAS GORDON, 1809—1895.
HALDANE, RICHARD BURDON, *Viscount*, 1856—1928.
HALE, SIR MATTHEW, 1609—1676.
HALES, JOHN, 1584—1656.

HALIBURTON, THOMAS CHANDLER, 1796—1865.

HALL, EDWARD, *d.* 1547.

HALL, JOSEPH, 1574—1656.

HALLAM, ARTHUR HENRY, 1811—1833.

HALLAM, HENRY, 1777—1859.

HALLIWELL, afterwards HALLIWELL-PHILLIPPS, JAMES ORCHARD, 1820—1889.

HAMILTON, WILLIAM, of Bangour, 1704—1754.

HAMILTON, SIR WILLIAM, 1788—1856.

HAMILTON, SIR WILLIAM ROWAN, 1805—1865.

HANNAY, J. O., 1865—1950.

HARE, JULIUS CHARLES, 1795—1855.

HARINGTON or HARRINGTON, JAMES, 1611—1677.

HARINGTON, SIR JOHN, 1561—1612.

HARPUR, CHARLES, 1817—1868.

HARRISON, FREDERIC, 1831—1923.

HARRISON, WILLIAM. 1534—1593.

HARTLEY, DAVID, 1705—1757.

HARVEY, GABRIEL, *c.* 1545—1630.

HARVEY, WILLIAM, 1578—1657.

HAWKER, ROBERT STEPHEN, 1803—1875.

HAWKINS, ANTHONY HOPE, 1863—1933.

HAYWARD, SIR JOHN, *c.* 1564—1627.

HAYDON, BENJAMIN ROBERT, 1786—1846.

HAYLEY, WILLIAM, 1745—1820.

HAYWARD, ABRAHAM, 1801—1884.

HAYWOOD, MRS. ELIZA, *c.* 1693—1756.

HEARNE, THOMAS, 1678—1735.

HEBER, REGINALD, 1783—1826.

HEBER, RICHARD, 1773—1833.

HELPS, SIR ARTHUR, 1813—1875.

HEMANS, MRS. FELICIA DOROTHEA, 1793—1835.

HENLEY, JOHN, 1692—1756.

HENSLOWE, PHILIP, *d.* 1616.

HENTY, GEORGE ALFRED, 1832—1902.

HERBERT, A. P., 1890—   .

HERBERT, EDWARD, *first Baron Herbert of Cherbury*, 1553—1648.

HERVEY, JAMES, 1714—1758.

HERVEY, JOHN, *Baron Hervey of Ickworth*, 1696—1743.

HEYLYN, PETER, 1600—1662.

HICHENS, R. S. (ROBERT SMYTHE), 1864—1950.

HIGGINS, MATTHEW JAMES, 1810—1868.

HILL, AARON. 1685—1750.

HILL, GEORGE BIRKBECK NORMAN, 1835—1903.

HOADLY, BENJAMIN, 1676—1761.

HOADLY, DR. BENJAMIN, 1706—1757.

HOBBES, JOHN OLIVER, pseudonym of MRS. P. M. T. CRAIGIE, 1867—1906.

HOBY, SIR THOMAS, 1530—1566.

HODGSON, SHADWORTH HOLLWAY, 1832—1912.

HOGARTH, DAVID GEORGE, 1862—1927.

HOGARTH, WILLIAM, 1697—1764.

HOGG, JAMES, 1770—1835.

HOGG, THOMAS JEFFERSON, 1792—1862.

HOLCROFT, THOMAS, 1745—1809.

HOLE, SAMUEL REYNOLDS, 1819—1904.

HOLLAND, PHILEMON, 1552—1637.

HOME, DANIEL DUNGLAS, 1833—1886.

HOME, HENRY, LORD KAMES, 1696—1782.

HOME, JOHN, 1722—1808.

HONE, WILLIAM, 1780—1842.

HOOD, THOMAS, 1799—1845.

HOOK, THEODORE EDWARD, 1788—1841.

"HOPE, ANTHONY," pseudonym of SIR ANTHONY HOPE HAWKINS, 1863—1933.

HOPE, THOMAS, *c.* 1770—1831.

HOPKINS, GERARD MANLEY, 1844—1889.

HOPKINS, MATTHEW, *d.* 1647.

HORMAN, WILLIAM, *d.* 1535.

HORNE, RICHARD HENRY or HENGIST, 1803—1884.

HORT, FENTON JOHN ANTHONY, 1828—1892.

HOUGHTON, WILLIAM STANLEY, 1881—1913.

HOVEDON or HOWDEN, ROGER of, *d. c.* 1201.

HOWELL, JAMES, *c.* 1594—1666.

HOYLE, EDMOND, 1672—1769.

HUCHOWN or HUCHOUN, *fl.* 14th century.

HUGHES, THOMAS, 1822—1896.

HUME, DAVID, 1711—1776.

HUNTER, JOHN, 1728—1793.

HUNTER, SIR WILLIAM WILSON, 1840—1900.

HURD, RICHARD, 1720—1808.

HUTCHESON, FRANCIS, 1694—1746.

HUTCHINSON, MRS. LUCY, *b.* 1620.

HUTH, HENRY, 1815—1878.

HUTTON, RICHARD HOLT, 1826—1897.

HUXLEY, THOMAS HENRY, 1825—1895.

INCHBALD, MRS. ELIZABETH, 1753—1821.

INGE, WILLIAM RALPH. 1860—1954.

INGELOW, JEAN, 1820—1897.

IRELAND, WILLIAM HENRY, 1777—1835.

JACKSON, HOLBROOK, 1874—1948.

JAGO, RICHARD, 1715—1781.

JAMES I (JAMES VI of Scotland), King of England, 1566—1625 (1603—1625).

JAMES, GEORGE PAYNE RAINSFORD, 1799—1860.

JAMES, HENRY, 1843—1916.

JAMESON, ANNA BROWNELL, 1794—1860.

JAMESON, (MARGARET) STORM, 1897— .

JAMIESON, JOHN, 1759—1838.

JEBB, SIR RICHARD CLAVERHOUSE, 1841—1905.

JEFFERIES, RICHARD, 1848—1887.

JEFFREY, FRANCIS, *Lord Jeffrey,* 1773—1850.

JENNER, EDWARD. 1749—1823.

JENYNS, SOAME, 1704—1787.

JERROLD, DOUGLAS WILLIAM, 1803—1857.

JEWSBURY, GERALDINE ENDSOR, 1812—1880.

JOHNSON, LIONEL PIGOT, 1867—1902.

JOHNSON, RICHARD, 1573—c. 1659.

JOHNSTONE, CHARLES, c. 1719—1800.

JONES, SIR WILLIAM, 1746—1794.

JOWETT, BENJAMIN, 1817—1893.

JOYCE, PATRICK WESTON, 1827—1914.

JULIANA (of Norwich), 1343—1443.

"JUNIUS," (FRANCIS, SIR PHILIP), c. 1740—c. 1818.

KAMES, LORD. *See* Home, Henry.

KAVANAGH, JULIA, 1824—1877.

KEBLE, JOHN, 1792—1866.

KELLY, HUGH, 1739—1777.

KEMBLE, FRANCES ANNE, afterwards MRS. BUTLER, generally known as FANNY KEMBLE, 1809—1893.

KEN, THOMAS, 1637—1711.

KENDALL, HENRY CLARENCE, 1841—1882.

KER, WILLIAM PATON, 1855—1923.

KEYNES, JOHN MAYNARD, 1883—1946.

KILLIGREW, HENRY, 1613—1700.

KILLIGREW, THOMAS, the elder, 1612—1683.

KILLIGREW, THOMAS, the younger, 1657—1719.

KILLIGREW, SIR WILLIAM, 1601—1695.

KING, HENRY, 1592—1669.

KING, WILLIAM, 1650—1729.

KING, WILLIAM, 1663—1712.

KINGLAKE, ALEXANDER WILLIAM, 1809—1891.

KINGSLEY, HENRY, 1830—1876.

KINGSTON, WILLIAM HENRY GILES, 1814—1880.

KNIGHT, CHARLES, 1791—1873.

KIRKE, JOHN, *fl.* 1638.

KNOWLES, JAMES SHERIDAN, 1784—1862.

KNOLLES, RICHARD, c. 1550—1610.

KNOX, JOHN, 1505—1572.

KNYNVETT, THOMAS (of Ashwellthorpe), 1596—1658.

KNYVETT, SIR HENRY, *fl.* 1596.

LAMB, LADY CAROLINE, 1785—1828.

LAMB, MARY ANN, 1764—1874.

LAMPMAN, ARCHIBALD, 1861—1899.

LANCASTER, JOSEPH, 1778—1838.

LANDON, LETITIA ELIZABETH, 1802—1838.

LANDOR, ROBERT EYRES, 1781—1869.

LANE, EDWARD WILLIAM, 1801—1876.

LATHAM, SYMON, *fl.* 1618—1633.

LAUD, WILLIAM, 1573—1645.

LAUDER, WILLIAM, *d.* 1771.

LAW, WILLIAM, 1686—1761.

LAWLESS, EMILY, 1845—1913.

LAWRENCE, GEORGE ALFRED, 1827—1876.

LAYARD, SIR AUSTEN HENRY, 1817—1894.

LEAR, EDWARD, 1812—1888.

LEAVIS, FRANK RAYMOND, 1895—

LECKY, WILLIAM EDWARD HARTPOLE, 1838—1903.

LEE, HARRIET, 1757—1851.

LEE, SIR SIDNEY, 1859—1926.

LEE, SOPHIA, 1750—1824.

LE FANU, JOSEPH SHERIDAN, 1814—1873.

LEFROY, EDWARD CRACROFT, 1855—1891.

LELAND, JOHN, c. 1506—1552.

LEMON, MARK, 1809—1870.

LEMPRIERE, JOHN, c. 1765—1824.

LENNOX, CHARLOTTE, 1720—1804.

LESLIE, JOHN, 1527—1596.

LESLIE, JOHN RANDOLPH SHANE, 1885— .

L'ESTRANGE, SIR ROGER, 1616—1704.

LEVER, CHARLES JAMES, 1806—1872.

LEWES, GEORGE HENRY, 1817—1878.

LEWIS, SIR GEORGE CORNEWALL, 1806—1863.

LEWIS, MATTHEW GREGORY, 1775—1818.

LEYDEN, JOHN, 1775—1811.

LIDDELL, HENRY GEORGE, 1811—1898.

LIDDON, HENRY PARRY, 1829—1890.

LIGHTFOOT, JOSEPH BARBER, 1828—1889.

LILLO, GEORGE, 1693—1739.

LILLY, WILLIAM, 1602—1681.

LILY, WILLIAM, c. 1468—1522.

LINACRE, THOMAS, c. 1460—1524.

LINDSAY, LADY ANNE, 1750—1825.
LINDSAY, ROBERT, *fl.* 1565.
LINGARD, JOHN, 1771—1851.
LITHGOW, WILLIAM, 1582—*c.* 1645.
LITTLETON, SIR THOMAS, 1422—1481.
LIVINGSTONE, DAVID, 1813—1873.
LOCKE, WILLIAM JOHN, 1863—1930.
LOCKER-LAMPON, FREDERICK, 1821—1895.
LOCKHART, JOHN GIBSON, 1794—1854.
LODGE, SIR OLIVER JOSEPH, 1851—1940.
LOGAN, JOHN, 1748—1788.
LOVER, SAMUEL, 1797—1868.
LOWNDES, WILLIAM THOMAS, *d.* 1843.
LUBBOCK, SIR JOHN, *first Baron Avebury,* 1834—1913.
LUBBOCK, PERCY, 1879— .
LUDLOW, EDMUND, *c.* 1617—1692.
LUTTRELL, HENRY, *c.* 1765—1851.
LUTTRELL, NARCISSUS, 1657—1732.
LYALL, SIR ALFRED COMYN, 1835—1911.
LYELL, SIR CHARLES, 1797—1875.
LYND, ROBERT, 1879—1949.
LYTTELTON, GEORGE, *first Baron Lyttelton,* 1709—1773.
MABBE, JAMES, 1572—*c.* 1642.
M'CARTHY, JUSTIN, 1830—1912.
MACDONALD, GEORGE, 1824—1905.
MACHEN, ARTHUR, 1863—1947.
McKERROW, RONALD BRUNLEES, 1872—1940.
MACKINTOSH, SIR JAMES, 1765—1832.
MACKLIN, CHARLES, *c.* 1697—1797.
MADDEN, DODGSON HAMILTON, 1840—1928.
MAGINN, WILLIAM, 1793—1842.
MAHONY, FRANCIS SYLVESTER, 1804—1866.
MAINE, SIR HENRY JAMES SUMNER, 1822—1888.
MAITLAND, FREDERIC WILLIAM, 1850—1906.
MAITLAND, SIR RICHARD, 1496—1586.
MAJOR, JOHN, 1496—1550.
MALLET, (or MALLOCH) DAVID, *c.* 1705—1765.
MALLOCK, WILLIAM HURRELL, 1849—1923.
MALONE, EDMOND, 1741—1812.
MALTHUS, THOMAS ROBERT, 1766—1834.
MANDEVILLE, BERNARD DE, *c.* 1670—1733.
MANGAN, JAMES CLARENCE, 1803—1849.
MANLEY, MRS. MARY DE LA RIVIERE, 1663—1724.
MANNING, HENRY EDWARD, 1808—1892.

MANSEL, HENRY LONGUEVILLE, 1820—1871.
MARKHAM, GERVASE, *c.* 1568—1637.
MARKHAM, MRS., pseudonym of MRS. ELIZABETH PENROSE, 1780—1837.
MARMION, SHACKERLEY, 1603—1639.
MARRYAT, FREDERICK, 1792—1848.
MARSHALL, ARCHIBALD, 1866—1934.
MARSTON, JOHN WESTLAND, 1819—1890.
MARSTON, PHILIP BOURKE, 1850—1887.
MARTINEAU, HARRIET, 1802—1876.
MARTINEAU, JAMES, 1805—1900.
MARTYN, EDWARD, 1859—1924.
MASON, ALFRED EDWARD WOODLEY, 1865—1948.
MASON, WILLIAM, 1724—1797.
MASSON, DAVID, 1822—1907.
MATHIAS, THOMAS JAMES, *c.* 1754—1835.
MATURIN, CHARLES ROBERT, 1782—1824.
MAURICE, JOHN FREDERICK DENISON, 1805—1872.
MAXWELL, WILLIAM BABINGTON, 1866—1938.
MAY, THOMAS, 1595—1650.
MAY, SIR THOMAS ERSKINE, *first Baron Farnborough,* 1815—1886.
MAYNE, JASPER, 1604—1672.
MERES, FRANCIS, 1565—1647.
MERIVALE, CHARLES, 1808—1893.
MERIVALE, HERMAN, 1806—1874.
MERRICK, LEONARD, 1864—1939.
MERRIMAN, HENRY SETON, pseudonym of HUGH STOWELL SCOTT, 1862—1903.
MICKLE, WILLIAM JULIUS, 1735—1788.
MIDDLETON, CONYERS, 1683—1750.
MILL, JAMES, 1773—1836.
MILL, JOHN STUART, 1806—1873.
MILLER, HUGH, 1802—1856.
MILMAN, HENRY HART, 1791—1868.
MILNES, RICHARD MONCKTON, *first Baron Houghton,* 1809—1885.
MILWARD, RICHARD, 1609—1680.
MITCHEL, JOHN, 1818—1875.
MITFORD, MARY RUSSELL, 1878—1855.
MITFORD, WILLIAM, 1744—1827.
MOIR, DAVID MACBETH, 1798—1851.
MONBODDO, JAMES BURNETT, LORD, 1714—1799.
MONTAGU, BASIL, 1770—1851.
MONTAGU, MRS. ELIZABETH, 1720—1800.
MONTAGU, LADY MARY WORTLEY, 1689—1762.
MONTGOMERIE, ALEXANDER, *c.* 1556—*c.* 1610.
MONTGOMERY, JAMES, 1771—1854.

MONTGOMERY, ROBERT, 1807—1855.
MOORE, EDWARD, 1712—1757.
MOORE, DR. JOHN, 1729—1802.
MOORE, THOMAS, 1779—1852.
MORE, HANNAH, 1745—1833.
MORE, HENRY, 1614—1687.
MORGAN, SYDNEY, LADY, *c.* 1783—1859.
MORGANN, MAURICE, 1726—1802.
MORIOR, JAMES JUSTINIAN,
    c. 1780—1849.
MORLEY, JOHN, *first Viscount Morley
    of Blackburn*, 1838—1923.
MORRIS, SIR LEWIS, 1833—1907.
MORRISON, ARTHUR, 1863—1945.
MORTON, JOHN MADDISON, 1811—1891.
MORTON, THOMAS, *c.* 1764—1838.
MOTHERWELL, WILLIAM, 1797—1835.
MOTTEUX, PETER ANTHONY,
    1660—1718.
MOTTLEY, JOHN, 1692—1750.
MOTTRAM, RALPH HALE, 1883—
MOXON, EDWARD, 1801—1858.
MUIR, EDWIN, 1887—
MULCASTER, RICHARD, *c.* 1530—1611.
MUNDAY, ANTHONY, 1553—1633.
MUNRO, CHARLES KILPATRICK,
    1889—   .
MUNRO, HECTOR HUGH, 1870—1916
MUNRO, HUGH ANDREW JOHNSTONE,
    1819—1885.
MURPHY, ARTHUR, 1727—1805.
MURRAY, GEORGE GILBERT AIME,
    1866—1957.
MURRAY, SIR JAMES AUGUSTUS HENRY,
    1837—1915.
MURRAY, LINDLEY, 1745—1826.
MYERS, FREDERIC WILLIAM HENRY,
    1843—1901.

NABBES, THOMAS, *fl.* 1638.
NAIRNE, CAROLINA, BARONESS, *née*
    OLIPHANT, 1766—1845.
NAPIER or NEPER, JOHN, 1550—1617.
NAPIER, SIR WILLIAM FRANCIS
    PATRICK, 1785—1860.
NEALE, JOHN MASON, 1818—1866.
NEWMAN, FRANCIS WILLIAM,
    1805—1897.
NICHOLS, JOHN, 1745—1826.
NICHOLS, ROBERT, M. B., 1893—1944.
NICOLSON, HAROLD G., 1886—   .
NOEL, RODEN BERKELEY WRIOTHESLEY,
    1834—1894.
NORRIS, JOHN, 1657—1711.
NORTH, ROGER, 1653—1734.
NORTHCLIFFE, ALFRED CHARLES
    WILLIAM HARMSWORTH, VISCOUNT,
    1865—1922.
NYREN, JOHN, 1764—1837.

OGILBY, JOHN, 1600—1676.
O'KEEFFE, JOHN, 1747—1833.
OLD MOORE, FRANCIS MOORE,
    1657—*c.* 1715.
OLDHAM, JOHN, 1653—1683.
OLDMIXON, JOHN, 1673—1742.
OLDYS, WILLIAM, 1696—1761.
OLIPHANT, LAURENCE, 1829—1888.
OLIPHANT, MARGARET OLIPHANT,
    1828—1897.
OLIVER, GEORGE, "OLIVER ONIONS,"
    1873—   .
OMAN, CAROLA M. A., 1897—1948.
OPIE, MRS. AMELIA, 1769—1853.
ORAGE, ALFRED RICHARD, 1873—1934.
O'RIORDAN, CONAL, 1874—1948.
ORATOR HUNT, HENRY HUNT,
    1773—1835.
ORME, ROBERT, 1728—1801.
OSBORNE, DOROTHY, 1627—1695.
O'SHAUGHNESSY, ARTHUR WILLIAM
    EDGAR, 1844—1881.
OSLER, SIR WILLIAM, 1849—1919.
OUIDA (MARIE LOUISE DE LA RAMEE),
    1839—1908.
OWEN, JOHN, *c.* 1560—1622.
OWEN, SIR RICHARD, 1804—1892.
OWEN, ROBERT, 1771—1858.

PAGAN, ISOBEL (TIBBY), *d.* 1821.
PAIN, BARRY ERICODELL, 1864—1928.
PAINE, THOMAS, 1737—1809.
PAINTER, WILLIAM, *c.* 1540—1594.
PALEY, WILLIAM, 1743—1805.
PALGRAVE, SIR FRANCIS, 1788—1861.
PALGRAVE, FRANCIS TURNER,
    1824—1897.
PALGRAVE, WILLIAM GIFFORD,
    1826—1888.
PALTOCK, ROBERT, 1697—1767.
PARK, MUNGO, 1771—1806.
PARKER, SIR GILBERT, 1862—1932.
PARKER, MATTHEW, 1504—1575.
PARKINSON, JOHN, 1567—1650.
PARNELL, CHARLES STEWART,
    1846—1891.
PARNELL, THOMAS, 1679—1718.
PARR, SAMUEL, 1747—1825.
PARRY, SIR WILLIAM EDWARD,
    1790—1855.
PATMORE, COVENTRY KERSEY DIGHTON,
    1823—1896.
PATTISON, MARK, 1813—1884.
PAYN, JAMES, 1830—1898.
PEACHAM, HENRY, *c.* 1576—*c.* 1643.
PEACOCK, THOMAS LOVE, 1785—1866.
PEARSON, JOHN, 1613—1686.
PENN, WILLIAM, 1644—1718.
PENNANT, THOMAS, 1726—1798.
PETTY, SIR WILLIAM, 1623—1687.
PHAER, THOMAS, *c.* 1510—1560.

PHILIPS, AMBROSE, c. 1675—1749.

PHILIPS, JOHN, 1676—1709.

PHILIPS, KATHERINE, 1631—1664.

PHILLIPS, JOHN, 1631—1706.

PHILLPOTTS, EDEN, 1862—

PICKTHALL, MARJORIE L. C., 1883—1922.

PICKTHALL, MARMADUKE WILLIAM, 1875—1936.

PIOZZI, HESTER LYNCH, 1741—1821.

PITMAN, SIR ISAAC, 1813—1897.

PLANCHE, JAMES ROBINSON, 1796—1880.

POLLARD, ALFRED WILLIAM, 1859—1944.

POLLOCK, SIR FREDERICK, 1845—1937.

POMFRET, JOHN, 1667—1702.

POOLE, JOHN, c. 1786—1872.

PORDAGE, SAMUEL, 1633—c. 1691.

PORSON, RICHARD, 1759—1808.

PORTER, ANNA MARIA, 1780—1832.

PORTER, JANE, 1776—1850.

PORTER, HENRY, fl. 1599.

PRAED, WINTHROP MACKWORTH, 1802—1839.

PRESTON, THOMAS, 1537—1598.

PRICE, RICHARD, 1723—1791.

PRIESTLEY, JOHN BOYNTON, 1894—

PRIESTLEY, JOSEPH, 1733—1804.

PRINGLE, THOMAS, 1789—1834.

PRIOR, MATTHEW, 1664—1721.

PROCTOR, ADELAIDE ANNE, 1825—1864.

PROCTOR, BRYAN WALLER, 1787—1874.

PRYNNE, WILLIAM, 1600—1669.

PSALMANAZAR, GEORGE, c. 1679—1763.

PURCELL, HENRY, 1658—1695.

PURCHAS, SAMUEL, c. 1575—1626.

PUSEY, EDWARD BOUVERIE, 1800—1882

PYE, HENRY JAMES, 1745—1813.

QUARITCH, BERNARD, 1819—1899.

QUARLES, FRANCIS, 1592—1644.

QUENNELL, PETER COURTNEY, 1905—

RAMSAY, ALLAN, 1686—1758.

RANDOLPH, THOMAS, 1605—1635.

RASHDALL, HASTINGS, 1858—1924.

RASPE, RUDOLF ERICH, 1737—1794.

RAWLINSON, GEORGE, 1812—1902.

RAWLINSON, SIR HENRY CRESWICKE, 1810—1895.

RAWLINSON, THOMAS, 1681—1725.

REEVE, CLARA, 1729—1807.

REID, THOMAS, 1710—1796.

REID, THOMAS MAYNE, 1818—1883.

RERESBY, SIR JOHN, 1634—1689.

REYNOLDS, SIR JOSHUA, 1723—1792.

RICARDO, DAVID, 1772—1823.

RICE, JAMES, 1843—1882.

RICH, BARNABE, c. 1540—1617.

RICH, JOHN, c. 1682—1761.

RIDGE, W. P., c. 1860—1930.

RIDLEY, NICHOLAS, c. 1500—1555.

RITCHIE, ANNE ISABELLA THACKERAY, Lady, c. 1838—1919.

RITSON, JOSEPH, 1752—1803.

ROBERTS, CHARLES GEORGE DOUGLAS, 1860—1943.

ROBERTS, MORLEY, 1857—1942.

ROBERTSON, FREDERICK WILLIAM, 1816—1853.

ROBERTSON, THOMAS WILLIAM, 1829—1871.

ROBERTSON, WILLIAM, 1721—1793.

ROBINSON, HENRY CRABB, 1775—1867.

ROGERS, JAMES EDWIN THOROLD, 1823—1890.

ROGERS, SAMUEL, 1763—1855.

ROGERS, WOODES, d. 1732.

ROPER, WILLIAM, 1496—1578.

ROSCOE, WILLIAM, 1753—1831.

ROSEBERRY, ARCHIBALD PHILIP PRIMROSE, fifth earl of, 1847—1929.

ROSS, ALEXANDER, 1699—1784.

ROSS, SIR JAMES CLARK, 1800—1862.

ROSS, SIR JOHN, 1777—1856.

ROSSETTI, WILLIAM MICHAEL, 1829—1919.

ROUTH, MARTIN JOSEPH, 1755—1854.

ROWLANDS, SAMUEL, c. 1570—c. 1630.

ROWLEY, SAMUEL, d. c. 1633.

ROWLEY, WILLIAM, c. 1585—c. 1642.

RUSSELL, GEORGE WILLIAM, 1867—1935.

RUSSELL, LORD JOHN, first Earl Russell, 1792—1878.

RUSSELL, WILLIAM CLARK, 1844—1911.

RUSSELL, SIR WILLIAM HOWARD, 1820—1907.

SAINT-EVREMOND, CHARLES DE MARGUETEL DE SAINT-DENIS DE, c. 1613—1703.

SANDYS, EDWIN, c. 1516—1588.

SANDYS, SIR EDWIN, 1561—1629.

SANDYS, GEORGE, 1578—1644.

SAVAGE, RICHARD, d. 1743.

SAVILE, SIR HENRY, 1594—1622.

SCHREINER, OLIVE EILIE ALBERTINA, 1855—1920.

SCOTT, ALEXANDER, c. 1525—c. 1584.

SCOTT, MICHAEL, c. 1175—c. 1234.

SCOTT, MICHAEL, 1789—1835.

SCOTT or SCOT, REGINALD, 1538—1599

SCOTT, ROBERT FALCON, 1868—1912.

SCOTT, WILLIAM BELL, 1811—1890.

SEAMAN, OWEN, 1861—1936.

SEELEY, SIR JOHN ROBERT, 1834—1895.

SELDEN, JOHN, 1584—1654.

SENIOR, NASSAU WILLIAM, 1790—1864.

SEMPILL, ROBERT, c. 1530—1595.

SETTLE, ELKANAH, 1648—1724.

SEWARD, ANNA, 1747—1809.

SEWELL, ANNA, 1820—1878.

SHADWELL, THOMAS, c. 1642—1692.

SHAFTESBURY, ANTHONY ASHLEY COOPER, *first Baron Ashley and first earl of Shaftesbury*, 1621—1683.

SHAFTESBURY, ANTHONY ASHLEY COOPER, *third earl of*, 1671—1713.

SHARP, WILLIAM, ("FIONA MACLEOD") 1855—1905.

SHARPHAM, EDWARD, 1576—1608.

SHELLEY, MARY WOLLSTONECRAFT, 1797—1851.

SHENSTONE, WILLIAM, 1714—1763.

SHERATON, THOMAS, 1751—1806.

SHERIDAN, MRS. FRANCES, 1724—1766.

SHERLOCK, THOMAS, 1678—1761.

SHERLOCK, WILLIAM, c. 1641—1707.

SHERWOOD, MRS. MARY MARTHA, 1775—1851.

SHORTHOUSE, JOSEPH HENRY, 1824—1903.

SIDGWICK, HENRY, 1838—1900.

SIDNEY, or SYDNEY, ALGERNON, 1622—1683.

SINCLAIR, CATHERINE, 1800—1864.

SKEAT, WALTER WILLIAM, 1835—1912.

SKEFFINGTON, SIR LUMLEY ST. GEORGE, 1771—1850.

SKINNER, JOHN, 1721—1807.

SLOANE, SIR HANS, 1660—1753.

SMART, CHRISTOPHER, 1722—1771.

SMEDLEY, FRANCIS EDWARD, 1818—1864.

SMILES, SAMUEL, 1812—1904.

SMITH, ADAM, 1723—1790.

SMITH, ALEXANDER, 1830—1867.

SMITH, GEORGE, 1824—1901.

SMITH, SIR GEORGE ADAM, 1856—1942.

SMITH, GOLDWIN, 1823—1910.

SMITH, HORATIO (HORACE), 1779—1849.

SMITH, JAMES, 1775—1839.

SMITH, JOHN (of Cambridge), 1618—1652.

SMITH, JOHN THOMAS, 1766—1833.

SMITH, ROBERT PERCY, 'Bobus Smith,' 1770—1845.

SMITH, SYDNEY, 1771—1845.

SMITH, THOMAS, b. 1790.

SMITH, SIR THOMAS, 1513—1577.

SMITH, SIR WILLIAM, 1813—1893.

SMITH, WILLIAM ROBERTSON, 1846—1894.

SOMERVILLE, WILLIAM, 1675—1742.

SOUTH, ROBERT, 1634—1716.

SOUTHERNE or SATHERN, THOMAS, 1660—1746.

SOUTHWELL, ROBERT, c. 1561—1595.

SPEDDING, JAMES, 1808—1881.

SPEED, JOHN, c. 1552—1629.

SPEKE, JOHN HANNING, 1827—1864.

SPENCER, HERBERT, 1820—1903.

SPURGEON, CHARLES HADDON, 1834—1892.

SQUIRE, SIR JOHN COLLINGS, 1884—

STANHOPE, PHILIP HENRY, *fifth earl*, 1805—1875.

STANLEY, ARTHUR PENRHYN, 1815—1881.

STANLEY, SIR HENRY MORTON, 1841—1904.

STANLEY, THOMAS, 1625—1678.

STANYHURST, RICHARD, 1547—1618.

STEAD, WILLIAM THOMAS, 1849—1912.

STEEL, FLORA ANNIE, 1847—1929.

STEEVENS, GEORGE, 1736—1800.

STEPHEN, SIR JAMES, 1789—1859.

STEPHEN, SIR JAMES FITZJAMES, 1829—1894.

STEPHEN, JAMES KENNETH, 1859—1892.

STEPHENS, JOHN, *fl.* 1615.

STERLING, JOHN, 1806—1844.

STEUART, SIR JAMES, 1712—1780, who assumed the name of DENHAM.

STEVENSON, JOHN HALL, 1718—1785.

STEWART, DUGALD, 1753—1828.

STEWART, JOHN, 1749—1822.

STILL, JOHN, 1543—1608.

STILLINGFLEET, EDWARD, 1635—1699.

STIRLING, JAMES HUTCHISON, 1820—1909.

STOW, JOHN, c. 1525—1605.

STRANGFORD, PERCY CLINTON SYDNEY SMYTH, *sixth visc.*, 1780—1855.

STRICKLAND, AGNES, 1796—1874.

STRONG, L. A. G., 1896—

STRUTT, JOSEPH, 1749—1802.

STRYPE, JOHN, 1643—1737.

STUART, DANIEL, 1766—1846.

STUART, FRANCIS, 1902—

STUBBS or STUBBES, PHILIP, *fl.* 1581—1593.

STUBBS, WILLIAM, 1825—1901.

STUKELEY, WILLIAM, 1687—1765.

SURTEES, ROBERT, 1779—1834.

SURTEES, ROBERT SMITH, 1803—1864.

SUTRO, ALFRED, 1863—1933.

Sylvester, Joshua, 1563—1618.
Symonds, John Addington,
    1840—1893.

Talfourd, Sir Thomas Noon,
    1795—1854.
Tannahill, Robert, 1774—1810.
Tate, Nahum, 1652—1715.
Taylor, Ann, 1782—1866.
Taylor, Sir Henry, 1800—1886.
Taylor, Jane, 1783—1824.
Taylor, John, 1580—1653.
Taylor, John, 1703—1772.
Taylor, Philip Meadows, 1808—1876.
Taylor, Thomas, 1758—1835.
Taylor, Tom, 1817—1880.
Telford, Thomas, 1757—1834.
Tennant, William, 1784—1848.
Tenniel, Sir John, 1820—1914.
Tennyson, Frederick, 1807—1898.
Tennyson Turner, Charles,
    1808—1879.
Theobald, Lewis, 1688—1744.
Thirlwall, Connop, 1797—1875.
Thomas, of Erceldoune, called the
    Rhymer, c. 1220—c. 1297.
Thompson, Sylvia Elizabeth,
    1902—   .
Thoms, William John, 1803—1885.
Thomson, Sir William, first Baron
    Kelvin, 1824—1907.
Thrale, Hester Lynch, Mrs.,
    1741—1821.
Tickell, Thomas, 1686—1740.
Toland, John, 1670—1722.
Tomkis, Thomas, fl. 1604—1615.
Tooke, John Horne, 1736—1812.
Toplady, Augustus Montague,
    1740—1778.
Torrens, William McCullagh,
    1813—1894.
Tourneur, Cyril, c. 1575—1626.
Tradescant, John, 1608—1662.
Traill, Henry Duff, 1842—1900.
Trelawney, Edward John,
    1792—1881.
Trench, Richard Chenevix,
    1807—1886.
Trevelyan, George Macaulay,
    1876—   .
Trevelyan, Sir George Otto,
    1838—1928.
Trimmer, Mrs. Sarah, 1741—1810.
Trollope, Frances, 1780—1863.
Trollope, Thomas Adolphus,
    1810—1892.
Tucker, Abraham, 1705—1774.
Tupper, Martin Farquhar,
    1810—1889.

Turberville, George,
    c. 1540—c. 1610.
Turner, Sharon, 1768—1847.
Turner, W. J. R., 1889—1946.
Tusser, Thomas, c. 1524—1580.
Tyndall, John, 1820—1893.
Tyrrell, George, 1861—1909.
Tyrwhitt, Thomas, 1730—1786.
Tytler, Patrick Fraser, 1791—1849.

Underhill, Evelyn, 1875—1941.
Urquhart, Sir Thomas, 1611—1660.
Ussher, James, 1581—1656.

Vancouver, George, 1758—1798.
Vaughan, Henry, 1622—1695.
Vaughan, Thomas, 1626—1666.
Vaux, Thomas, 1510—1556.
Vergil, Polydore, c. 1470—c. 1555.
Viner, Charles, 1678—1756.
Voynich, E. L. B., 1865—1930.

Wainewright, Thomas Griffiths,
    1794—1852.
Wakefield, Edward Gibbon,
    1796—1862.
Wakefield, Gilbert, 1756—1801.
Walker, Thomas, 1784—1836.
Wallace, Alfred Russel,
    1823—1913.
Wallace, Edgar, 1875—1932.
Wallace, William, 1844—1897.
Wallis, John, 1616—1703.
Walpole, Sir Spencer, 1839—1907.
Wanley, Humfrey, 1672—1726.
Wanley, Nathaniel, 1634—1680.
Warburton, Rowland Eyles
    Egerton, 1804—1891.
Warburton, William, 1698—1779.
Ward, Edward, ("Ned"), 1667—1731.
Ward, William George, 1812—1882.
Warner, William, c. 1558—1609.
Warren, John Byrne Leicester,
    Baron de Tabley, 1835—1895.
Warren, Samuel, 1807—1877.
Warton, Joseph, 1722—1800.
Warton, Thomas, 1728—1790.
Waterton, Charles, 1782—1865.
Watson, Richard, 1737—1816.
Watson, Thomas, c. 1557—1592.
Watt, Robert, 1774—1819.
Watts, Isaac, 1674—1748.
Watts-Dunton, Walter Theodore,
    1832—1914.
Waugh, Alec, 1898—   .
Waugh, Evelyn, 1903—   .
Webb, Mary, 1881—1927.
Webbe, William, c. 1552—c. 1600.

WELLS, CHARLES JEREMIAH,
  c. 1800—1879.
WESLEY, CHARLES, 1707—1788.
WESLEY, JOHN, 1703—1791.
WESTCOTT, BROOKE FOSS, 1825—1901.
WEYMAN, STANLEY J., 1855—1928.
WHATELY, RICHARD, 1787—1863.
WHETSTONE, GEORGE, c. 1554—c. 1587.
WHEWELL, WILLIAM, 1794—1866.
WHITE, GILBERT, 1720—1793.
WHITE, HENRY KIRKE, 1785—1806.
WHITE, JOSEPH BLANCO, 1775—1841.
WHITE, WILLIAM HALE, pseudonym of
  MARK RUTHERFORD, 1831—1913.
WHITEFIELD, GEORGE, 1714—1770.
WHITEHEAD, ALFRED NORTH,
  1861—1947.
WHITEHEAD, CHARLES, 1804—1862.
WHITEHEAD, WILLIAM, 1715—1785.
WHITELOCKE, BULSTRODE, 1605—1675.
WHYMPER, EDWARD, 1840—1911.
WHYTE-MELVILLE, GEORGE JOHN,
  1821—1878.
WILBERFORCE, WILLIAM, 1759—1833.
WILKES, JOHN, 1727—1797.
WILKINS, JOHN, 1614—1672.
WILKINSON, SIR JOHN GARDNER.
  1797—1875.
WILLIAMS, HELEN MARIA, 1762—1827.
WILLIAMS, ISAAC, 1802—1865.
WILLIAMSON. HENRY, 1897—
WILLOUGHBY DE BROKE, RICHARD
  GREVILLE VERNEY, *nineteenth Baron*,
  1869—1923.
WILLS, WILLIAM GORMAN,
  1828—1891.

WILMOT, ROBERT, *fl.* 1568—1608.
WILSON, SIR ARNOLD TALBOT,
  1884—
WILSON, SIR DANIEL, 1816—1892.
WILSON, JOHN, c. 1627—1696.
WILSON, JOHN, 1785—1854.
WILSON, ROMER, pseudonym of
  FLORENCE MUIR WILSON,
  1891—1930.
WINCHILSEA, ANNE FINCH, *Countess
  of*, 1661—1720.
WINZET, NINIAN, 1518—1592.
WODEHOUSE, PELHAM GRENVILLE,
  1881—
WODROW, ROBERT, 1679—1734.
WOLCOT, JOHN, 1738—1819.
WOLFE, CHARLES, 1791—1823.
WOOD, ANTHONY, or as he latterly
  called himself, ANTHONY A WOOD,
  1632—1695.
WOOD, ELLEN, better known as MRS.
  HENRY WOOD, 1814—1887.
WOODFORDE, JAMES, 1740—1803.
WOOLF, LEONARD SIDNEY, 1880—
WOOLNER, THOMAS, 1825—1892.
WORDSWORTH, DOROTHY, 1804—1847.
WOTTON, SIR HENRY, 1568—1639.
WREN, SIR CHRISTOPHER, 1632—1723.
WRIGHT, THOMAS, 1810—1877.

YARRELL, WILLIAM, 1784—1856.
YONGE, CHARLOTTE MARY, 1823—1901
YOUNG, ARTHUR, 1741—1820.
YOUNG, EMILY HILDA, 1880—1949.
YOUNG, FRANCIS ERIC BRETT,
  1884—1954.

ZANGWILL, ISRAEL, 1864—1926.

ALPHABETICAL GUIDE TO MISCELLANEOUS
INFORMATION

Adventures of Roderick Random, The (p. 397). Roderick Random undergoes many experiences on ship and on land, in France and Buenos Aires, and in battles at Cartagena and at Dettingen. Throughout, he is an unscrupulous scapegoat, meeting with rogues of various kinds. In quest of fortune, he makes unsuccessful matrimonial advances to Melinda Goosetrap and Miss Snapper. Finally, he marries Narcissa, whom he loves. Important characters are Lieutenant Tom Bowling, Hugh Strap, and Don Roderigo, who turns out to be Roderick's father.

The Antiquary (p. 501). William Lovel (Major Neville) finally marries Isabella Wardour, daughter of Sir Arthur Wardour, the friend of Jonathan Oldbuck the Antiquary. Of importance are Captain Hector M'Intyre, the German charlatan Herman Dousterswivel, and the bedesman Edie Ochiltree.

Aureng-Zebe (p. 329). Had it not been for the assistance of Arimant, Governor of Agra, and of Empress Nourmahal. Shah Jehan and his son Morat might have succeeded in the attempt to take Indamora, captive queen, from Aureng-Zebe, another son of Shah Jehan.

Beaux Stratagem, The (p. 310). Thomas Archer and his friend Aimwell, two beaux of broken fortunes, achieve the rehabilitation of their estates by respectively marrying Dorinda, daughter of Lady Bountiful, and Mrs. Sullen, the wife of Lady Bountiful's brutal son, Squire Sullen. In this play also appear Boniface the landlord and Scrub the servant.

Beggar's Opera, The (p. 360). Peachum, a despicable "fence," betrays Captain Macheath, leader of a gang of highwaymen, who has dared marry Polly, Peachum's daughter. The Captain is recaptured after Lucy Lockit, daughter of the jailer, has effected his escape. He is tried and condemned to death. After his reprieve, he promises to remain constant to Polly. Famous song: "How happy could I be with either." (See *Polly*, p. 619.)

Bride of Abydos, The (p. 468). Zuleika, daughter of Giaffir, the Pasha of Abydos, dies of a broken heart when her father, who wishes her to marry the rich Bey of Karasman, sabers her sweetheart Selim, a cousin pirate-chief.

Bride of Lammermoor, The (p. 502). Lucy Ashton, daughter of Sir William Ashton, stabs Frank Hayston, the Laird of Bucklaw, whom she has been forced to marry. Edgar, the Master of Ravenswood, who has been secretly betrothed to Lucy, is swallowed up in the quicksands of Kelpies Flow while on his way to avenge the marriage. Meanwhile, Lucy has gone insane and dies.

Caleb Williams, (p. 407). See *Things as They Are.*

Castle of Otranto, The (p. 404). The mysterious death of his son Conrad, who was about to marry Isabella, daughter of the Marquis of Vincenza, makes Manfred, prince of Otranto, decide to divorce his wife and himself to marry the maiden.

While his grandfather's portrait descends from the wall and interviews Manfred, Isabella escapes by the aid of the peasant Theodore, who later is revealed as the true heir of Alfonso, rightful lord of Otranto previously poisoned by his grandson and usurper Manfred.

Cato (p. 341). Marcius Porcius Cato, the republican, betrayed by Sempronius, a senator, and Syphax, a Numidian, falls on his own sword rather than surrender his small republic of Utica to Julius Caesar.

Cecilia, or Memoirs of an Heiress (p. 402). To come into her fortune, Cecilia Beverley must marry a husband willing to take her name. Harrel, Briggs, and Monckton successively fail to exploit her. She finally marries Mortimer Delvile.

Clarissa, or, the History of a Young Lady (p. 390). Clarissa Harlowe, a young lady of gentility, pines to death with grief and shame after Robert Lovelace, a profligate man of fashion, compromises her good name. Lovelace himself is killed in a duel by her cousin, Colonel Morden.

Comical Revenge, The; or, Love in a Tub (p. 303). When Lord Beaufort wins the hand of Graciana, Colonel Bruce, the defeated rival, accepts her sister. Dufoy, the French valet of Sir Frederick Frolic, is tubbed by other servants.

Conscious Lovers, The (p. 344). Bevil is in love with the orphaned Indiana, but has been pledged by his father to Lucinda Sealand, who is worshipped by Bevil's friend Myrtle, and by the greedy Cimberton. The discovery that Indiana is the lost daughter of Mr. Sealand is the beginning of the happy ending.

Conquest of Granada, The, or Almanzor and Almahide (p. 329). Although his love is returned by Almahide, Almanzor does not succeed in winning her until the death of Boabdelin, to whom she is betrothed.

Corsair, The (p. 468). Aided by Gulnare, queen of the harem, Conrad a pirate chief, escapes from the Sultan Seyd. When he reaches the pirate island, he finds that Medora, his beloved, has died from grief during his absence. Conrad disappears. (See under *Lara*, p. 617.)

Country Wife, The (p. 305). Horner, a profligate, brings Mr. Pinchwife to believing in Mrs. Pinchwife's innocence. The relationship of Sparkish and of Alithea, Mr. Pinchwife's sister, illustrates how complacency and credulity on the part of a lover may release a girl into the arms of a new wooer.

Critic, The, or A Tragedy Rehearsed (p. 380). The principal characters are Sir Fretful Plagiary, the poetaster who plagiarized from obscure volumes; Dangle and Sneer, theatrical critics; and Puff, an unscrupulous Professor of the Art of Puffing. The latter's *The Spanish Armada*, an absurd historical tragedy inserted in the play, introduces the moon-struck Tilburina, daughter of the matter-of-fact governor of Tilbury Fort, who is in love with Don Ferolo Whiskerandos, a Spanish prisoner.

Curse of Kehama, The (p. 463). Ladurlad, the father of the beautiful Kailyal, kills Arvalan, the son of Kehama, for attempting to dishonor his daughter. Upon Ladurlad, Kehama pronounces a curse; but this curse eventually turns into a blessing. Kehama himself drinks the "amreeta" or draught of immortality only to find that he has drunk immortal death and punishment.

Don Sebastian, King of Portugal (p. 331). The play is based on legend, for the real Sebastian, King of Portugal, probably fell in the battle of Alcazar. As a captive of Muley Moluch, the Moor, he falls in love with the princess Almeyeda. After many vicissitudes, he comes into control of the Moorish kingdom. When they discover that both have been begotten by the same father, Sebastian becomes a hermit and Almeyeda takes the veil. Important is the character of Dorax, later revealed as Don Alonzo.

Double-Dealer, The (p. 307). Maskwell, the Double-Dealer, aids Lady Touchwood in her scheme to prevent the marriage of Cynthia, daughter of Sir Paul Plyant and Mellefont, prospective heir of Lord Touchwood. Lady Touchwood wants Mellefont for herself, while Maskwell wants Cynthia. Jealousy spoils their treacherous plan.

Elephant in the Moon, The (p. 298). Playful foot-boys discover that a scientist, in making observations, has mistaken a mouse in the telescope for an elephant in the moon.

Emma (p. 492). Almost too late, Emma Woodhouse discovers that unless she marries her brother-in-law, Mr. Knightley, she may lose him to Harriet Smith, whom she is befriending. Harriet marries neither Mr. Elton nor Frank Churchill, but Robert Martin.

Endymion: A Poetic Romance (p. 484). Keats bases his poem on the allegory of Endymion, the beautiful shepherd-king of Mount Latmus, and of Selene (Diana, Cynthia, Phoebe), the moon goddess. (Lyly used the same framework in *Endimion, the Man in The Moone*. See p. 151.)

Evelina, or A Young Lady's Entrance Into the World (p. 402). Evelina is brought up in the country by the kind Mr. Villars. While visiting Mrs. Mirvan in London, she falls in love with Lord Orville, in whose presence she is later exposed to embarrassment and shame by her vulgar grandmother, Madame Duval, by her cousins, the Branghtons, and by an obstinate lover, Sir Clement Willoughby. The heroine is able to marry Lord Orville when she is revealed as the rightful heir of Sir Francis Belmont, who had abandoned his wife and child years before.

Expedition of Humphrey Clinker, The (p. 398). Matthew Bramble, bachelor, his sister Tabitha, old maid, their nephew and niece, Jerry Melford and Lydia Melford, are not the only members of the party travelling through Bath, London, Harrogate, Edinburgh, and the Highlands. With it go Winifred Jenkins, the maid who later marries Humphrey Clinker, the ragged but resourceful ostler's assistant picked up *en route*, who subsequently is revealed as Mr. Bramble's natural son. Tabitha Bramble marries Lieutenant Obadiah Lismahago, and Lydia marries George Dennison.

Fortunes and Misfortunes of the Famous Moll Flanders (p. 357). For a summary, see page 357, footnote 1.

Gentleman Dancing-Master, The (p. 305). Gerrard, in love with Hippolita Formal, is no more a dancing-master than Don Diego, his sweetheart's father, is a Spaniard, and Monsieur de Paris, the cousin to whom she is betrothed, a Frenchman. Only Mrs. Caution, her aunt, sees through the trick of Hippolita in making her father believe Gerrard a dancing-master.

Giaour, The (p. 467). Leila, the concubine of the Caliph Hassan, is killed because she is unfaithful. Her lover, the Giaour, avenges her death by cleaving Hassan's skull.

Good-Natur'd Man, The (p. 376). Sir William Honeywood, by having his good-natured nephew thrown into jail for debt, succeeds in curing the young Honeywood of his credulity and easy disposition. The comedy is heightened by a subordinate love-affair involving Valentine, the son of Croaker, who loves Olivia, and Miss Richland, who loves young Honeywood.

Grace Abounding to the Chief of Sinners (p. 316). Bunyan relates the steps leading to his conversion—his early dread of Hell, his later indifference to religion, and his wicked youth; his marriage to a religious woman, whose two devotional books were read by him; his experiences at Bedford, his oscillations between hope and despair, and his final call to the ministry.

Gulliver's Travels (p. 347). See *Travels Into Several Remote Nations of the World.*

Guy Mannering (p. 501). Dick Hatteraick, the smuggler captain and kidnapper, strangles the rascally lawyer Glossin in prison; Meg Merrilies, the gypsy, recognizes Harry Bertram as the rightful heir of the Laird of Ellangowan, who eventually marries Julia Mannering, the daughter of Colonel Guy Mannering, under whom he had served in India as Brown.

Heart of Midlothian, The (p. 502). Jeanie Deans succeeds in procuring a pardon for her half-sister Effie Deans, who has been sentenced to death on a charge of child-murder and is imprisoned in the Tolbooth or old jail of Edinburgh, known as the "heart of Midlothian." Effie elopes with George Staunton, who had seduced her. Jeanie, now married to the Presbyterian minister Reuben Butler, discovers that the child had been carried off by Meg Wildfire, daughter of Margaret Murdockson.

History of the Adventures of Joseph Andrews, and of his friend Mr. Abraham Adams, The (p. 391). Joseph Andrews, the footman, eventually marries Fanny, the daughter of humble parents. With Parson Adams, he meets many ridiculous adventures. Other characters are Lady Booby, Mrs. Slipslop, young Squire Booby (the husband of Pamela), Peter Pounce, Trulliber, and Mrs. Tow-wouse.

History of Sir Charles Grandison (p. 390). The hero is a paragon. He can not consider the feelings of his own heart for Harriet Byron until released by Clementina Porretta. Meanwhile, Harriet is forcefully and forcibly wooed by Sir Hargrave Pollexfen.

History of Tom Jones, a Foundling, The (p. 392). Tom Jones, a foundling brought up by Mr. Allworthy, has an affair with Molly Seagrim, falls in love with Sophia Western, sets out on his travels accompanied by the lovable Partridge, a schoolmaster, pays amorous attention to Lady Bellaston, but, after many other escapades, turns out to be the son of Allworthy's sister and marries Sophia. Other important sketches are those of Squire Weston, Thwackum, Square, and Blifil.

Holy War, The (p. 317). Emmanuel, the son of King Shaddai, the builder of the city Mansoul (the soul of man), twice defeats Diabolus and recaptures the city, which becomes vulnerable whenever it lapses into ungodly ways.

Hudibras (p. 298). Hudibras, a Presbyterian Justice of the Commonwealth, sets out with his squire Ralpho, an Independent-Anabaptist, to enforce the strict laws enacted by Parliament for the suppression of the amusements of the people. Famous are their encounters with Crowdero, the bear-baiter, Sidrophel, the astrologer, and the widow who plays a large part in the latter two-thirds of this mock-heroic.

Jonathan Wild (p. 392). See *Life of Mr. Jonathan Wild.*

Joseph Andrews (p. 391). See *History of the Adventures of Joseph Andrews.*

Kenilworth (p. 504). Amy Robsart, daughter of Sir Hugh Robsart of Devon, has secretly married the Earl of Leicester, the revelation of which would ruin the latter's political life. To hide the truth, Richard Varney, Leicester's follower, and Tony Foster, her guardian, lure her to death. But truth triumphs.

Lara (p. 468). Continuing the tale related in *The Corsair* (p. 615), Lara is in reality Conrad, the pirate chief, and his page Kaled is Gulnare in disguise, in whose arms he dies.

Lay of the Last Minstrel, The (p. 497). By voluntarily assuming the arms of Sir William Deloraine, and under that guise defeating Sir Richard Musgrave, Lord Cranstoun makes peace with the Lady of Branksome Hall and succeeds in marrying her daughter Margaret.

Life and Strange Surprizing Adventures of Robinson Crusoe, of York, Mariner, The (p. 355). For twenty-eight years the shipwrecked Robinson Crusoe lives on a desert island, relieving the monotony of life by the exercise of great ingenuity. During the last four years preceding the rescue by an English ship, he has "Good Friday" as a companion.

Life of Mr. Jonathan Wild the Great, The (p. 392). Schooled in gambling and pickpocketing by Count La Ruse and Snap, Jonathan outdoes his very teachers. His marriage to the worthless baggage, Letitia Snap, exemplifies the proverb about birds of a feather. Conspiring with Bagshot, another scoundrel, he tricks the jeweller Heartfree, and fools the authorities into the belief that the latter has done away with Mrs. Heartfree, whom Jonathan had induced to leave England. Jonathan Wild, "great" by virtue of his crime and his wickedness, finally ends up on the gallows.

Love for Love (p. 307). Angelica, the ward of the testy Sir Sampson Legend, tricks her guardian out of possession of Valentine Legend's bond, and subsequently reveals that she loves Valentine, whom Sir Sampson has tried to disinherit in favor of his younger brother Benjamin Legend. Other characters include Miss Prue, Jeremy, Tattle, Foresight, and Mrs. Frail.

Madoc (p. 463). Madoc, the youngest son of Owain Gwyneth, king of North Wales, sails to America, founds a settlement, and defeats the Aztecs.

Mansfield Park (p. 492). In love with Edmund, the son of Sir Thomas Bertram of Mansfield Park, who had adopted her, Fannie Price rejects the proposal of Henry Crawford, brother of Maria Bertram, whom Edmund loves. But the ending is happy.

Marmion (p. 497). Constance de Beverley, a perjured nun jilted by Lord Marmion whose suit in turn is rejected by Lady Clare, is betrayed to the convent and buried alive in cell walls. Not until Marmion is slain in the battle of Flodden Field does Lady Clare renounce her convent vows and marry Sir Ralph de Wilton.

Marriage A-la-Mode (p. 330). Rhodophil falls in love with Melantha, not knowing her to be affianced to his friend Palamede; Palamede sets his heart upon Doralia, not knowing her to be Rhodophil's wife. The knot is untangled when the discovery of the true relationship is made.

Mourning Bride, The (p. 307). Almeria, daughter of Manuel, King of Granada, has secretly married Alphonso, son of Anselmo, King of the enemy state of Valencia. Under the name of Osmyn, Alphonso meets his wife; but Zara, a Moorish princess, betrays him. Gonzalez, whose son Garcia is to marry Almeria, discovering that he has by mistake killed Manuel, decapitates the latter in order to avoid detection. Zara, thinking the headless body to be that of Alphonso, poisons herself. Just in time, Alphonso arrives to prevent the suicide of Almeria.

Mysteries of Udolpho, The (p. 405). The Chevalier de Velancourt proves himself a match for the machinations wreaked upon Emily de St. Aubert, an English girl, by her aunt, Madame Cheron, and the latter's robber-husband, Signor Montoni.

Northanger Abbey (p. 492). In love with Henry Tilney, Catherine Moreland accepts his father's, General Tilney's, invitation to Northanger Abbey. Her stay is no longer welcomed when the General is misled into believing that her parents are humble and not well-to-do. But Henry's love brooks no parental interference.

Old Bachelor, The (p. 306). Heartwell, the misogynistic old bachelor, welcomes the discovery that his marriage to Silvia is not genuine. Among the characters are Belmour, Laetitia, Fondlewife, Sir Joseph Wittol, and Captain Bluffe.

Old Mortality (p. 502). The story is told by "Old Mortality," the nickname of the itinerant Robert Paterson. Eventually, Henry Morton of Milnwood, a Presbyterian who joins the Covenanters, marries Edith, grand-daughter of Margaret Bellenden, an antagonistic Royalist. John Balfour of Burley and Lord Evandale, Morton's rival for the hand of Edith, are focal characters.

Oroonoko, or, The Royal Slave (p. 313). With her consent, Oroonoko slays Imoinda, his beloved, so that the slave-drivers will be unable to wreak vengeance upon her after he shall kill Byam, the deceitful deputy-governor of Surinam in the West Indies. Before Oroonoko can carry out the rest of his plan, he is caught and executed.

Orphan, The: or, The Unhappy Marriage (p. 299). Unaware of his twin-brother's marriage to Monimia the orphan, Polydore takes the place of Castalio at night. When Chamont, Monimia's brother, brings the matter to light, the twin-brothers and Monimia commit suicide.

Pamela: or, Virtue Rewarded (p. 389). Pamela Andrews, an unsophisticated maid-servant of Squire B——, astutely repels his attempts at seduction. At length she comes to terms with him, marries him, and even reforms him.

Persuasion (p. 492). Had Louisa Musgrave not become engaged to Captain Benwick, Captain Frederick Wentworth might never have asked again for the hand of Anne Elliot, who this time did not reject his offer. Other characters: Sir Walter Elliot, Admiral and Mrs. Croft, Lady Russell, Henrietta Musgrove, Mrs. Clay, and William Elliot, Anne's cousin.

Pilgrim's Progress, The (p. 316). Christian, with a burden of sins on his back, flees the City of Destruction to find Zion the City of God. His pilgrimage takes him through the House Beautiful, the Slough of Despond, the Valley of Humiliation, the Valley of the Shadow of Death, Vanity Fair, Bypath Meadow, the Delectable Mountains, the Enchanted Ground, the country of Beulah, the River of Death, to the Holy City. He encounters such pilgrims as Mr. Worldly Wiseman, Evangelist, Apollyon, Faithful, Hopeful, and Giant Despair In the second part, Christiana, his wife, and their four sons, Matthew, Samuel, Joseph, and James, and a neighbor, Mercy, set out on the same pilgrimage and are escorted to their destination by Mr. Great-heart.

Plain Dealer, The (p. 305). Manly, a sea-captain, finds that his mistress Olivia is unfaithful. Subsequently, he is not only assisted by Fidelia, a girl in man's clothes, but also saved by her from death at the hands of Vernish, who had married Olivia. The plain-dealing ship-captain marries Fidelia.

Polly (p. 360). Polly, in seeking Macheath in the West Indies, helps the Indians repulse an attack of pirates and capture their leader Morano. The latter, who is Macheath in disguise, is executed, and Polly marries an Indian Prince. (See *The Beggar's Opera*, p. 614.)

Pride and Prejudice (p. 491). While the central characters are Elizabeth Bennet, one of five marriageable daughters, and Fitzwilliam Darcy, nephew of Lady Catherine De Bourgh, the plot is furthered by the relations of Charles Bingley and Jane Bennet, of George Wickham and Lydia Bennet, and of Mr. Collins, Elizabeth, and Charlotte Lucas.

Prince of Abissinia, The (p. 368). With his sister Nekayah and the old philosopher-poet Imlac, Rasselas, prince of Abyssinia, escapes from the paradisaical "Happy Valley." After he has made a study of the conditions or ranks of life for the purpose of discovering which was the most happy, Rasselas decides to return to the "Happy Valley" in Amhara.

Prometheus Unbound (p. 476). Demogorgon, the World-Builder or creator of the material world, overthrows Jupiter. Prometheus, the champion of mankind, is released by Hercules from perpetual torture while chained to a rock.

Provok'd Wife, The (p. 309). The characters are the cowardly Sir John Brute, his faithful wife Lady Brute, who is courted by Constant, and her niece Belinda, who is wooed by Heartfree. Lady Fancyfull does not succeed in stirring up trouble.

Quentin Durward (p. 505). By the destruction of William de la Marck, a notorious brigand whom Louis XI arranges to unite to the Countess Isabelle de Croye, a Burgundian heiress, Quentin Durward wins the lovely Countess for himself.

Rape of the Lock, The (p. 362). While Belinda sips coffee, a lock of her hair is clipped. Great is her wrath. She demands the return of the ringlet, but is told that, like Berenice's hair, it has been wafted to heaven where henceforth, like a new star, it will adorn the sky.

Rasselas (p. 368). See *Prince of Abissinia.*

Recruiting Officer, The (p. 310). Captain Plume and Sergeant Kite, each in his own way, bend every effort to obtain recruits, one of whom is Sylvia Ballance, in love with the Captain and disguised as a man. Captain Brazen, another recruiting officer, is tricked into marrying Melinda's maid, rather than the wealthy Melinda herself.

Relapse, The, or Virtue in Danger (p. 308). Loveless, a reformed profligate now married to Amanda, relapses under the blandishments of the widow Berinthia; but even that does not persuade Amanda to yield herself to the unscrupulous Worthy. The second plot is better known, concerning itself with Sir Novelty Fashion (Lord Foppington), Miss Hoyden, the daughter of Sir Turnbelly Clumsey, and Young Fashion.

Rival Queens, The, or the Death of Alexander the Great (p. 301). Roxana, daughter of Oxyartes, Alexander the Great's first wife, kills Statira, his second wife. Cassander poisons Alexander.

Robinson Crusoe. See *Life and Strange Surprizing Adventures of Robinson Crusoe.*

Rob Roy (p. 502). Rob Roy Macgregor assists Diana Vernon in rescuing Francis Osbaldistone from difficulties. When Scotland's Robin Hood finally removes Rashleigh Osbaldistone, Francis becomes reconciled with his father, inherits Osbaldistone Hall, and marries Diana.

Roderick, the last of the Goths (p. 463). Roderick, the last of the Visigothic kings, dishonors Florinda, the daughter of Count Julian, who in revenge invites the Moors under Muza ibn Nozeir to remove Roderick from the throne. After doing penance for his crime and being forgiven by Count Julian, Roderick saves the day for the Christians at the battle of Covadango. He is never again seen.

Sardanapalus (p. 470). Three times Sardanapalus, the voluptuous and effeminate king of Assyria, defeats Arbaces the Mede and Belesis the Chaldean who have leagued themselves against him. When finally overthrown in the fourth encounter, he burns himself on a funeral pyre with his favorite concubine, Myrra, while the conspirators are besieging the palace.

School for Scandal, The (p. 379). The principal characters are Lord Peter Teazle, Lady Teazle, Joseph Surface, his brother Charles, and his father Sir Oliver Surface, and Maria. Sir Benjamin Backbite, Lady Sneerwell, and Mrs. Candour are the scandalmongers.

She Stoops to Conquer; Or, The Mistakes of a Night (p. 376). Tony Lumpkin cunningly directs young Marlow and his friend Hastings not to an inn, which they seek, but to the private residence of the Hardcastles. Believing Miss Hardcastle to be a barmaid, the bashful young Marlow makes love freely, in marked contrast to his behavior when she is in her real character. The long-winded, hospitable Squire Hardcastle, his "genteel" wife, and the kind-hearted Sir Charles Marlow are other *dramatis personae*.

Spanish Fryar, The, or The Double Discovery (p. 331). The princess Leonora, succeeding her usurping father, becomes Queen of Aragon. She had been betrothed by her dying father to Bertram, but secretly marries Torrismond, who it transpires is the son and heir of Sancho, King of Sargossa, who was mistakenly thought murdered. In the comic plot, the gay officer Lorenzo bribes Friar Domenick to play the part of Pandarus (see p. 67) between him and Elvira, the young wife of old Gomez, a miserly rich banker. The amour is resolved upon the discovery that Elvira is Lorenzo's sister.

Tale of a Tub, The (p. 348). Three sons, Peter, Martin, and Jack, inherit from their father a coat apiece (The Christian faith), and a will (the Scriptures) that prohibits any alterations in the garment. But each of the brothers wishes to adorn his suit with shoulder-knots or gold lace as the fad dictates. Finally, they quarrel among themselves. Pointed references are made to the use of images and ceremonies, the question of papal supremacy, the doctrine of Purgatory, the sale of indulgences, the use of holy water, auricular confession, the issuing of. bulls and dispensations, the celibacy of the clergy, the doctrine of transubstantiation, and bibliolatry.

Thalaba the Destroyer (p. 463). Despite the machinations of Abdaldar, Lobaba, and Mohareb, three magicians who conspire against him, Thalaba, the Moslem whose life is consecrated to warfare on the evil spirits of Domdaniel, finally achieves his goal. By doing so he sacrifices his life, is received into heaven, and is reunited to his beloved Oneiza, who had died on their bridal night.

Things as they Are, or the Adventures of Caleb Williams (p. 407). Caleb Williams, secretary to the aristocratic Falkland, accidently learns that Hawkins and his son have been executed for the murder of the tyrannical Tyrrel, a crime committed by Falkland. The latter persecutes and hounds his secretary, who, driven to desperation, formally accuses Falkland before the Judge of Assizes. Confessing his guilt, the murderer dies of shame.

Travels Into Several Remote Nations of the World. By Lemuel Gulliver (p. 347). Captain Lemuel Gulliver makes four voyages:

1. To Lilliput, where the inhabitants are six inches high, all else being in proportion. It satirizes the political factions and religious dissensions of England under George I, by describing the wearers of high heels and low shoes, and the debate, which involves the whole country in war, over the momentous question as to whether an egg should be broken at the big or little end.

2. To Brobdingnag, where the people are as tall as church steeples, everything else being worked out on the same enormous scale. The giant among the Lilliputians has become a pygmy; what he tells the King about civilization causes the latter to conclude that mankind is "the most pernicious race of little odious vermin that nature ever suffered to crawl upon the face of the earth."

3. To the flying island of Laputa, where the satire is levelled against philosophers who moon over chimerical projects in mathematics and music, astronomy and chemistry. In this part appears the immortal, yet most miserable, race of the Struldbrugs, who are marked off from the rest of the inhabitants in the island of Luggnagg by being born with a circular mark in the forehead; and Lagado, the

capital city of Balnibarbi, a neighboring continent subject to the King of Laputa, with its Grand Academy of Projectors, where professors are engaged in the process of building houses by beginning at the roof, of making fire malleable, of breeding naked sheep, in extracting sunbeams from cucumbers, and in calcining ice into gunpowder.

4. To the country of the Houyhnhnms, peopled by a race of horses endowed with reason and noble qualities, in contrast to the Yahoos, a foul race of brutes, having the shape and all the viciously degrading propensities of man, but lacking the attribute of reason and subject to the Houyhnhnms.

Tyrannick Love, or the Royal Martyr (p. 329). Placidus, an officer who loves Berenice, the Empress, kills Maximin, the Emperor, who has ordered her execution, already carried out upon Catherine, the Christian princess of Alexandria, who has not only rejected Maximin's advances, but also converted Berenice to Christianity.

Venice Preserv'd or A Plot Discover'd (p. 300). When the Venetian senate violates its promise to pardon the conspirators whom Jaffeir has been persuaded to betray by his wife Belvidera, the Venetian youth stabs his friend Pierre to save him from torture, and stabs himself. Belvidera goes mad and dies brokenhearted.

Vicar of Wakefield, The (p. 376). Among the characters are the Reverend Dr. Primrose, the charitable vicar, Job-like in his misfortunes; Mrs. Deborah Primrose, who boasts of her housewifery and aspires to gentility; George Primrose, who later marries the heiress, Miss Wilmot; Olivia Primrose, who is seduced by Squire Thornhill, but is eventually found to be married to him; Moses Primrose, famous for the adventure of the green spectacles; and Sophia Primrose, who is twice saved by Mr. Burchell (Sir William Thornhill), whom she marries.

Way of the World, The (p. 307). The way of the world is love and its intrigues; but Lady Wishfort finally consents to the marriage of Millamant, her niece, and Edward Mirabell. The plot is complicated by the presence of Mrs. Marwood, Waitwell, Foible, the Fainalls, and Sir Wilfull Witwoud.

INDEX

The aim of this *Index* is to cover all *substantial* references to authors, works, events, periods, and the like. No attempt is made to direct the reader to every subject and to every proper name mentioned in the SURVEY-HISTORY. Note, especially, the omission in this *Index* of the hundreds of titles in the final chapter (pages 581-600).

See Vol. I for pp. 1-291. Roman numerals refer to pages at the end of Vol. I.

625

See Vol. I for pp. 1-291. Roman numerals refer to pages at the end of Vol. I.

See Vol. I for pp. 1-291. Roman numerals refer to pages at the end of Vol. I.

See Vol. I for pp. 1-291. Roman numerals refer to pages at the end of Vol. I.

See Vol. I for pp. 1-291. Roman numerals refer to pages at the end of Vol. I.

See Vol. I for pp. 1-291. Roman numerals refer to pages at the end of Vol. I.

See Vol. I for pp. 1-291. Roman numerals refer to pages at the end of Vol. I.

See Vol. I for pp. 1-291. Roman numerals refer to pages at the end of Vol. I.

See Vol. I for pp. 1-291. Roman numerals refer to pages at the end of Vol. I.

See Vol. I for pp. 1-291. Roman numerals refer to pages at the end of Vol. I.

See Vol. I for pp. 1-291. Roman numerals refer to pages at the end of Vol. I.

See Vol. I for pp. 1-291. Roman numerals refer to pages at the end of Vol. I.

See Vol. I for pp. 1-291. Roman numerals refer to pages at the end of Vol. I.